THE SPIRITUAL RECOVERY MANUAL

Vedic Knowledge and
Yogic Techniques to
Accelerate Recovery

Patrick Gresham Williams

Incandescent Press
Palo Alto, California

DISCLAIMER

No book can replace the guidance of a physician, mental health professional, or chemical dependency counselor. Before trying anything in this book, ask your doctor or counselor if it is right for you. The author has vigilantly tried to ensure accuracy and provide all necessary supporting information and precautions; however, the frontiers of human development are still being explored—all facts are not fully known. If you decide to use this knowledge, you must assume sole responsibility. The author and publisher specifically disclaim any and all liability arising directly or indirectly from the use and application of the information in this book.

The views expressed in the text are the author's and not necessarily those of the individuals and organizations mentioned. Readers are urged to deepen their knowledge through the Maharishi Vedic Schools and Medical Centers.

Grateful acknowledgement is made for permission to reprint the following:

The description of the stages of addiction appearing on pages 20–22 is adapted from *The Addictive Personality,* by Craig Nakken, copyright © 1988 and 1996 by the Hazelden Foundation. Reprinted by permission of the publisher.

The list of codependent attributes appearing on pages 32 and 99 and the list of codependency-engendering families on page 31 are excerpted from *Lost in the Shuffle: The Codependent Reality,* by Robert Subby, copyright © 1987 by Health Communications. Reprinted by permission of the publisher.

The case studies of individuals in recovery appearing on pages 238–247 are excerpted from *Self-Recovery: Treating Addictions Using Transcendental Meditation and Maharishi Ayur-Veda,* edited by David F. O'Connell and Charles N. Alexander, copyright © 1994 by The Haworth Press. Reprinted by permission of the publisher.

Library of Congress Control Number: 2002100811
ISBN 0-9709078-1-8

Printed in the United States of America

Transcendental Meditation, TM, TM-Sidhi, Maharishi, Maharishi Vedic Science, Maharishi Ayur-Veda, Consciousness-Based, Maharishi Amrit Kalash, Slumber Time, Worry Free, Maharishi Yoga, Maharishi Jyotish, Maharishi Vedic Vibration Technology, MVVT, Maharishi Vedic Astrology, Maharishi Sthapatya Veda, Maharishi Gandharva Veda, Maharishi Vedic Medical Center, Maharishi University of Management, and Maharishi Open University are registered or common law trademarks licensed to Maharishi Vedic Education Development Corporation.

*This book is dedicated to you, the reader.
It is my deep desire that it save you both time
and suffering, bringing you quickly to a more
fulfilling life, and perhaps even to spiritual
peace and bliss.*

*This book is also dedicated to my family—
my parents, grandparents, and great-
grandparents—with the hope that the
world can benefit from their experience,
which is my legacy.*

CONTENTS

INTRODUCTION

THE YOGA OF RECOVERY

This book offers a yogic approach to recovery. It addresses, from the perspective of consciousness, the specific needs of those who have had any kind of traumatic past or who have been faced with any aspect of addiction. Although this book is written for the individual, it also aims to advance the recovery field itself. It presents a simple framework within which the diverse theories of human development—including the theories of addiction, codependence, and the adult child—can be understood. Such a framework is called a paradigm. Those familiar with the philosophy of science will be aware of the work of Thomas Kuhn, who said that major advances in science require new paradigms.[1]

A complete paradigm for recovery must include consciousness— the most basic awareness of our existence. It is obvious that any discipline is incomplete until it connects to consciousness: if we, the perceiver, are left out of the picture, how real and practical is that science? The consciousness-based recovery paradigm presented in this book allows us to understand why some treatments are effective while others are not, and to compare methods and see what is most useful.

AN OVERVIEW

The goal of this book is to build a bridge from addiction to enlightenment, thus keeping us out of the river of suffering. We start by reviewing the popular literature on addiction; thereby we construct a solid foundation of knowledge on the shore we are familiar with. This is the first chapter. Then we jump to the other side of the river and discuss a theory of the complete personality—introducing, in a straightforward way, the knowledge of enlightenment. This builds a foundation of knowledge on the distant shore. These are the first two chapters. They provide a larger context within which we can go more meaningfully into the details of recovery.

A recovery program that includes consciousness must be a bridge that spans from the darkness of addiction all the way to the furthest shore of enlightenment. We build this bridge in chapter 3.

In chapter 4, we explain that the bridge has firm foundations (is based on ancient wisdom). Two chapters later, in chapter 6, we establish that it is solidly constructed (documented by research). The remaining chapters describe how to walk the bridge. In chapters 5, 7, 8, and 9, we introduce various advanced recovery techniques; we walk our talk right across the bridge. In chapter 10, we consider the possibility of getting everyone—the whole of society, all at once—to the shore of enlightenment. In chapter 11, we cover the remaining points—bliss, behavior, and enlightenment—necessary for total recovery. Finally, in chapter 12, we list resources available to help you master the knowledge. We also review common mental health problems that tend to go along with an addictive background.

To some, the style of this book may seem unusual; this is not your typical self-help book. It is a book of knowledge, almost a textbook, in which I offer you—through a well thought-out systematic teaching—the benefit of my study and experience over the past twenty-five years. I have worked hard to make the concepts straightforward and clear, but haven't held back important information or made explanations simplistic.

Because each chapter builds on the preceding chapters, it is best to read the book sequentially. Take your time; a chapter a day is a good pace. A second reading will pull all the concepts together.

WHERE THE KNOWLEDGE COMES FROM

The premises of this book are simple: our life gets better when we re-establish wholeness of awareness; society's problems decrease when we remove stress from the collective consciousness. These ideas come from Maharishi Mahesh Yogi's *Vedic Science.* Maharishi Mahesh Yogi is perhaps the world's foremost educator of the twentieth and twenty-first centuries. He is well known as the founder of the Transcendental Meditation program. Maharishi's Vedic Science offers complete knowledge. In this book, we focus on several different aspects of vedic science. We will look, for example, at ayurveda—the science of life—which specializes in solutions to physical and behavioral problems. It is important to point out that vedic science—including ayurveda, yoga, and all its other disciplines—is not specific to any group. It applies to all people in all cultures and at all times. The purpose of this book, however, is to make clear how vedic science is relevant to one sector of society—those in recovery. That may not leave out many people.

A WORD OF CAUTION

This book is not a first line of defense against self-destructive behavior. If your addiction is life-threatening (such as alcoholism or any other chemical dependency), or if you are hurting or being hurt by other people (for example, by physical abuse, or gambling away the family's money) then you need individual professional counseling *before* you read any further. Join a self-help group—such as those that use the Twelve Steps—for the knowledge and, especially, the support you will receive. Few people find recovery easy; most need encouragement from understanding friends to keep them going. After you have joined a support group and have started counseling, then pick up this book again and continue reading.

When you finish this book, you will own the deepest essence of knowledge. You will have a more profound and accurate understanding of the mind than most Ph.D.s in psychology; a more useful and powerful understanding of the workings of society than almost any sociologist or politician; a more practical understanding of the body than a medical doctor who went to Harvard; and a clearer understanding of Reality than even the greatest of Western philosophers. You will, in short, be in an excellent position to help yourself to a *very* fulfilling life.

ADDICTION

CHAPTER ONE

In this chapter, we cover the basic concepts found in recovery literature. Among other terms, we explain addiction, codependence, *and* adult child. *If this is familiar territory, skip to chapter 2.*

This chapter gives a glimpse of the contemporary understanding of dysfunction, as expressed in the popular literature. It is possible to recover without any knowledge of addiction or codependence or any other aspect of dysfunction, but it helps to know your path. In a society that glorifies addiction and subtly and incessantly pushes us toward it, almost everyone is going to cross a section of the path that is addictive. Even if *you* are free of addiction, it helps to understand it because you are surrounded by it—we do, indeed, live in an addictive society. Addiction could be greatly reduced if we all had some knowledge of the problem and were aware of practical techniques for human development.

THE ARCHETYPE

Addiction almost never exists by itself. Addicts are usually part of an addictive system.[2] Consider the system in which a smoker is enmeshed. In addition to other smokers, it consists of retailers, cigarette manufacturers, lobbyists, tobacco farmers, the media, educators, the medical profession, and the government. It is a system that perpetuates itself because of the silent collusion of all involved. Research has shown—to take one example—that a large number of patients quit smoking immediately, and permanently, if their doctor intervenes by simply and directly telling them to quit. But doctors, like everyone else, are a part of the system, and it doesn't occur to them to address the issue. Consider another example from the field of medicine: doctors are often too busy to follow up on patients for whom they have prescribed painkillers or tranquilizers. They are too busy because they are churning patients in and out of their offices to maximize profits. They are also too busy to look for the deeper causes of the physical and mental pain. As a result, many patients end up addicts.

Addictive systems can be big or small. Let's go into detail with a smaller system, the family. Right now, the purpose isn't for you to become an expert, but to get a feeling for the dynamics involved. To start with, we will consider the classic example of an addictive system: the alcoholic family. We will conveniently consider an archetypal situation, and then expand on that.

The history of such a system unfolds like a play. One person—we will let it be the husband—is an addict. He is an alcoholic. Being an alcoholic is a difficult job. In fact, it is almost impossible without the help of spouse, boss, co-workers, employees, parents, children, and probably many others. Therefore, for the play that we call *The Addictive Drama,* we need supporting actors and actresses. Let's introduce the wife. She is always nominated for best supporting actress, but never gets the award. Her role is to *enable.* That literally means she enables the alcoholic to continue drinking. She will protest all the time that she is trying to stop him, and that may very well be the case, but she is rarely effective enough to succeed, and she never walks off the stage before the final curtain. The name of her role is *codependent.*

Next, we introduce the children of the alcoholic and the codependent. Children growing up in an alcoholic family don't have a stable and loving environment. They learn to lie to protect the family image. This is the beginning of *denial.* Denial, in addictions theory, refers to an individual or a group of people who unconsciously, yet systematically and consistently, do not allow anyone, *including themselves,* to become consciously aware that there is a problem. (It is said that denial lies at the heart of addiction. Once denial is uncovered and faced, you are on the road to recovery. This is because you cannot solve a problem that you believe doesn't exist.)

The children in an alcoholic family learn to suppress their needs and desires to the point where, as adults, they don't know what their needs are, let alone how to fulfill them. In an alcoholic home, the reality is painful. A child has to hide from this reality to survive. She (or he) cannot face the daily humiliation, shame, anger, uncertainty, and worst of all, the bitter disappointment and abandonment. So she severs the connection between herself and the environment. She learns to withdraw, to not feel, to deny. If she desperately needs something, she learns it is not safe to ask directly. So she acts out her needs. She does something to draw attention to her neediness. Indirectly, somehow, she gets some part of her needs met. *Acting out* is anything we do to try indirectly and inappropriately to get our needs met. Addiction itself can be a form of acting out.

These attributes of adult children—denial, acting out, emotional turmoil, suppression of true desires, a tendency toward addiction—are carried over with full force into adult life. When the children of an alcoholic family grow up, they are called adult children of alcoholics (ACOA or ACA) or just *adult children.* Adult children are emotional children in adult bodies.

Act One ends with the children going off to college or leaving home to get a job. Act Two begins with these young adults trying to find their roles in life. They don't have to enact the addictive drama, but what are the only roles they have seen others play? They are (1) the addict, played by their father; and (2) the caretaker, played by their mother. Almost invariably, an adult child ends up playing one or both of these roles.

Act Three starts when the adult child decides to get married. People seek a familiar environment. Children of alcoholic families unconsciously seek out dysfunctional people to bond with. Adult children are most at home when they are surrounded by addicts, co-dependents, or other adult children. In order to start a new alcoholic family we need a new alcoholic and a new codependent. If experienced addicts and codependents cannot be found, the next best is an understudy. An adult child has all the qualifications. In time, he or she will grow into the role.

In ten or twenty years, we have a new addictive family acting out the same drama, with different props and changed scenery. The script remains the same. Act Three is a rerun of Act One. It repeats generation after generation. Human life gets burned up in the self-perpetuating, all-consuming fire of addiction, fueled by the apathy of society for any real, widespread use of an effective methodology for self-development.

THE TRUE DIVERSITY OF THE ADDICTIVE FAMILY SYSTEM

What we have seen so far is the archetypal version. In reality, the addictive family system takes a thousand different forms. The wife can be the alcoholic. Both parents may be alcoholic. Or neither parent is alcoholic. *There may not be any addiction at all.* The cause may be something completely different from substance abuse. We are not necessarily talking about physical addiction, but about patterns of behaving and ways of feeling. The play of addiction presents an extreme example. Even an apparently normal and happy family can have addictive elements. The situation doesn't have to be extreme for the theory of addictive systems to apply.

So far, we have conveniently separated out the addict, codependent, and adult child. However, it is not that cut and dried; each of us has some of all three. And the process is dynamic over time. We may go through a codependency stage. This may drive us into addiction. We may treat the addiction, then realize that although we are drug free and sober, we have unresolved issues in common with other adult children. Bear in mind that these terms are not the reality; they provide a convenient way to describe a situation.

Now that we have a context for the terms, let's explain each one in more detail.

ADDICTION

Definitions

Craig Nakken, the author of *The Addictive Personality,* defines addiction as "a pathological love and trust relationship with an object or event."[3] John Bradshaw, in *Bradshaw on the Family,* quotes the World Health Organization's definition of addiction as "a pathological relationship to any form of mood alteration that has life-damaging consequences." In *Homecoming: Reclaiming and Championing Your Inner Child,* Bradshaw categorizes addiction as ingestive, activity, cognitive, feeling, or addiction to things.[4] Schaef and Fassel, authors of *The Addictive Organization,* define addiction as "any substance or process that has taken over our lives and over which we are powerless.... If there is something we are not willing to give up in order to make our lives fuller and more healthy it probably can be classified as an addiction."[5] Nakken stresses the importance of understanding "what all addictions and the addictive process have in common: the out-of-control and aimless searching for wholeness, happiness, and peace through a relationship with an object or event."[6]

Doctors and addiction researchers have come up with a more

clinical definition:

> Alcoholism is a primary, chronic disease with genetic, psychosocial, and environmental factors influencing its development and manifestations. The disease is often progressive and fatal. It is characterized by continuous or periodic: impaired control over drinking, preoccupation with the drug alcohol, use of alcohol despite adverse consequences, and distortions in thinking, most notably denial.[7]

You can replace the word *alcoholism* with any other addiction.

Here is my simple seat-of-the-pants definition of addiction:

Definition	**Addiction** is anything we do repeatedly that does not bring us fulfillment. Typically, for society to label an activity as addictive, we have to do it a lot (it becomes an obsession), find it next to impossible to stop, and the results of the addictive process have to be life-damaging.

What are the usual objects of addiction? Addiction can involve substances or actions unusual for a normal person, such as cocaine or prostitution. However, addiction often involves an object more commonplace: something that some use, others abuse, but for the addict it becomes an obsession. The most accepted example is alcohol. But *anything* can become the object of addiction. Here is a far-from-complete list of things we can become addicted to:

alcohol	gambling
illegal drugs	sex
prescription drugs	shopping
cigarettes	stealing
eating (binging, etc.)	coffee, sugar, etc.
not eating	exercise
emotions (fear, anger, etc.)	work
relationships	fantasizing
thinking	danger
violence	TV
religion	lying
being sick or cared for	other people

Why We Do It

Why do we do it? There are a lot of reasons. Addiction has biological, behavioral, psychological, sociological, environmental, and genetic origins. Different addictions have different causes or, more likely, different proportions of multiple causes. Teenage dieting—in a culture that equates thinness with popularity, beauty, and self-esteem—is a risk factor for anorexia and other eating disorders, especially for those with over-controlling parents, or who aspire to sports or careers intolerant of weight gain. Tobacco advertising, specifically targeting youth and reinforced by the popular media, results in higher rates of teenage smoking, the start of a lifetime addiction to nicotine. Some addictions may be psychological: we want to escape emotional conflict, mental pain, or a hopeless, drab-and-dreary world. Some addictions may be purely physical, such as addiction to prescription medication: we didn't start because we wanted psychological escape, but after a long period of use, our body becomes dependent on the drug. Some addictions may be more genetic. There is strong evidence of genetic predispositions to certain addictions.[8] Most researchers believe that some people are genetically vulnerable to alcoholism, and that if these people drink, they have a high risk of ending up drunks. I suspect that, just as there is more than one type of diabetes, alcoholism will turn out to have at least two types: one primarily genetically induced, and the other the result of changed brain chemistry, simply due to years of drinking. There are also theories that chronic stress—originating within the individual and from society—may contribute to addiction by throwing out of balance complex neuro- and biochemical pathways.[9]

Although there seem to be many causes of addiction, in general, addictive actions seem to have something in common: they create a mood change. This is standard addiction theory. Usually, a potential addict, for whatever reason, is unable to appropriately meet his or her emotional needs. The addict discovers addictive behavior as a shortcut, but the addiction doesn't adequately meet emotional needs on a deep level, leaving the individual unfulfilled. Addiction is like shelling peanuts with a hand grenade.

Many consider addiction an "outside-in" approach to fill a gap we feel on the inside. John Bradshaw calls that gap a "hole in your soul." Our most basic drive is for wholeness. We are all involved—some more consciously than others—in a divine quest to be complete. When we feel lack, we try to fill the void. When ordinary activities don't give us wholeness, we look for something out of the ordinary.

I believe the current prevalence of addiction is the inevitable outcome of a society that isn't giving its children (and its adults and its elderly) systematic, reliable, and effective methods for human development. Until a person has found a consistent source for wholeness, they may, in desperation, choose addictive means to meet their needs.

STAGES OF ADDICTION

Dr. Craig Nakken, in his book *The Addictive Personality,* identifies three stages of the addictive process: internal change, lifestyle change, and life breakdown.

Stage One—Internal Change
In stage one we get our first high. In that high, whether it is from alcohol, gambling, shopping, or eating, there is a significant mood change. According to Dr. Nakken, "In the mood change exists the illusion of control, the illusion of comfort, the illusion of perfection.... For the addict this intensity gets mistaken for intimacy, self-esteem, social comfort, or any number of things."[10]

Next, we realize we can use the addictive object or event to avoid feelings or situations that make us uncomfortable. Acting out may then become a habit. Ultimately, we use the addictive behavior to avoid bad feelings from the last addictive action. It becomes a cycle. When the repetitive seeking of fulfillment through an object or event becomes integrated into the personality, we become a stage one addict. Now we start to feel a subtle level of shame. We develop a delusional belief system that allows us to pretend we are in control of our life and of the addictive process. This control is only an illusion, maintained through "addictive logic," which includes denying even the reality of the addiction.

Stage Two—Lifestyle Change

In stage one we are out of control on an internal level. In stage two, we become out of control on a behavioral level. This is when others notice we are addicted. In the later parts of stage two, the addict gets labeled. Even though we may not be called "an addict," our friends and family know we excessively work, eat, shop, or gamble. People around us change their behaviors to accommodate what has become our accepted role.

"In Stage Two a *behavioral dependency* starts to develop," Dr. Nakken writes. As he describes it, a behavioral dependency is when "a person starts to act out the addictive belief system in a ritualistic manner, and the person's behavior becomes more and more out of control."[11] The addictive style of functioning becomes paramount, not the mood change or the objects or events that cause the mood change. Addiction becomes a lifestyle.

We start to see people as objects. We become manipulative, self-righteous, and self-centered. We mistrust others and we manipulate them. The addictive lifestyle has characteristic behaviors: lying, denial, blaming others, ritualizing addictive behavior, withdrawing from others, emotionally isolating oneself, and acting out.

This lifestyle change has concomitant emotional changes. We experience intense internal conflict. Surrendering to the addiction is often the only way of achieving release from inner torment. This inner struggle causes a huge drain of energy. We feel tremendous shame as more and more of our self-control is lost to the addiction. We become "spiritually isolated" and feel empty. The deep connection we normally feel to those around us is severed.

In stage two, the addictive style of functioning has not yet gained complete control. Stage two is characterized by the struggle not to give in to the addiction. If we are unable to overcome the addiction, we try to contain it. We may promise others that we will never do it again. However, our life gets worse and worse as we develop a tolerance to the addictive substance or action, and we must therefore increase the frequency and intensity of our addictive actions. We become more and more out of control.

The delusional belief system, which began in stage one, expands. We believe our problems are other people's fault. Reality becomes fogged, and we cannot see addiction as the cause of our suffering.

Stage Three—Life Breakdown

In stage three, addiction becomes unmistakable. We have lost control to the addiction. We care only about "getting high from acting out." But there is so much pain that even acting out cannot bring release.

Our life literally breaks down under the tremendous stress caused by the ever-increasing pain, anger, and fear that result from continually acting out. Our body starts to deteriorate. We have difficulty keeping a job and have problems with personal and family finances. Our addiction may even cause us to break the law.

We become extremely isolated. We deal only with people who will support our addiction. Paradoxically, even though we isolate ourselves, we are terrified of being alone and will often cling to friends and family. Emotionally, we may cry uncontrollably, go into fits of rage, experience paranoia, or have free-floating anxiety. We may become suicidal.

It is in stage three, according to Dr. Nakken, that even addictive logic breaks down: "The addict's behavior often doesn't even make sense to him or her anymore.... Addictive logic becomes very simple at this stage: 'get high and exist.'"[12]

In most cases, an addict stays stuck at this stage unless there is outside intervention. Addiction is now the whole of life. The addict has tried repeatedly to get out of addiction; they have tried to pull themselves up by their own bootstraps—and have failed. This is why addiction is often described as a progressive disease which, if untreated, is fatal.

IT'S ALL IN THE BRAIN

We have described stages of addiction in terms of mind and behavior —what we feel and what we do. Since what takes place on the inside of the body mirrors what is taking place on the outside, it would be equally valid to describe the stages in terms of brain functioning. And there are researchers who do just that. Neuroscientists and biochemists are actively studying the changes in an addict's brain (and the rest of the endocrine system).

One significant finding is that alcoholism results in (or from) profound, perhaps irreversible, changes in how the body ingests alcohol.[13] It appears that the brain—with its complex, chemistry-mediated neurological communications—is intimately involved in what can become a dysfunctional style of alcohol metabolism. A stage three alcoholic's brain reacts to alcohol in a radically different way than that of a stage one drinker. That is why, for some people—those whose DNA makes them susceptible and those who have a history of alcohol dependence—even a single drink is dangerous.

This is a fascinating field, but it is very, very complicated—and it is foreign to our experience. If you ask someone how they're doing, they don't respond, "My serotonin is low today; my hypothalamic-pituitary-adrenocortical axis is messed up. I think it's all caused by a faulty A1 allele of my D2 dopamine receptor gene." In this book, we will talk about behaviors and feelings, because this is something we can all relate to. This also doesn't make us dependent on researchers, or on multinational pharmaceutical companies, whose stated mission is—above all else—to maximize profit.

If you are interested in the neurochemistry of addiction and recovery, search the Web sites listed on page 212 in chapter 12.

LEVELS OF ADDICTION

Dr. Nakken's stages of addiction go a long way toward describing the addictive process, but they need to be tempered and modified according to the intensity of the specific addiction. So let's try to define degrees of intensity of addictive behavior. I have chosen to divide addictive behavior into three categories. The categories, or levels, of addiction are:

Category One   mental obsession
Category Two   indirect mood-altering
Category Three   strong ingestive addiction

We will go backward through the list, starting with the familiar territory of category three.

Category Three—Strong Ingestive Addiction

Category three is addiction in its most extreme form. In category three, we use a substance that works intensely and directly on the central nervous system, radically changing its state. Here we alter our moods physically, often brutally changing the body's biochemistry. Examples of category three substances are cocaine, heroin, methamphetamine, and alcohol.

Dr. Nakken's stages most clearly describe life-threatening, category three addictions.

This is a good place to point out that there are high-functioning and low-functioning addicts. A high-functioning alcoholic can maintain a job, often for decades, sometimes right up to the start of alcohol-induced dementia. High and low functioning have nothing to do with the degree of dependence on the substance (or the category of addiction). It may, however, affect our ability to hide the addiction and publicly maintain denial.

Category Two—Indirect Mood-Altering

Category two addictions are more prevalent than those in category three. Category two addictions include eating disorders, compulsive shopping, gambling, compulsive sex, codependence, smoking—everything listed on page 18 that is not an extreme, mind-altering drug or a purely mental obsession. These addictions usually involve a level of indirection: an action that leads to a mood change. For example, the bulimic binges and purges. The food itself doesn't directly alter the body's biochemistry. It is the *total process* that alters moods and gives the addict the illusion of control. Furthermore, the activity of addiction distracts us from our needs and problems; if we obsessively shop—as long as we are in our obsessive mode—none of life's fears and insecurities can get to us. But that doesn't mean we are fulfilled. Addiction to gambling, shopping, or food can ruin our life, relationships, and health, leaving us with nothing but despair. Although the deterioration of life is slower than in category three—and less likely to be immediately fatal—category two addictions can cause death.

The addiction that kills the most people is smoking. The World Health Organization realistically predicts that, worldwide, cigarettes will ultimately kill half a billion people.[14] If that were the death toll from a war, I think we would put a stop to it; and death from smoking is more humiliatingly protracted and brutal than being shot by a rifle or blown up by a bomb. Cigarettes are a deceptive addiction. Nicotine creates a dependency as extreme as cocaine; most smokers would like to quit, but can't.

Although smoking is crudely antisocial, in many societies it is still socially accepted. Smoking doesn't seem to impair one's ability to make decisions or contribute to the economy; in fact, it temporarily (until death) helps one endure long hours in a boring job—something prized in industrializing nations. But that is of little comfort to the families of smokers: in Japan, where the majority of the men (but until recently few women) are career chain-smokers, women often live for decades after their husbands have died of lung cancer—not a good retirement for either of them.

In reality, smoking stunts the growth of society. Many smokers die before they have had a chance to give back. They leave us at an age when they would have—by virtue of having gained a sophisticated understanding of the complexity and interconnectedness of society—been able to guide our long-term economic and cultural progress. This is a great loss of leaders and mentors.

Unfortunately, the people of many countries still believe the tobacco industry's propaganda. In some countries (including, until recently, Japan), the tobacco industry is nationalized. Therefore, the government has no interest in reducing smoking: it is itself a cigarette manufacturer—and what government could discipline itself to give up such lucrative profits? In countries where tobacco is not nationalized, most governments levy a cigarette tax: imagine a people addicted to paying taxes!

Category One—Mental Obsession

Category one is characterized by mental addiction. We no longer use anything external as the primary object with which to form an unhealthy relationship. The unhealthy relationship is internal. It is with our self. It is in our head.

Category one is divided into level A and level B. Category one-B borders category two. Category one-B, in its extreme form, is exactly like category two, except there is no obvious addictive object. We still distract ourselves from unresolved emotions, but we do it internally. We mood-alter without a substance or external behavior. Perhaps we lock ourselves into an angry mood and mentally isolate ourselves from those around us. We may incessantly daydream or obsess on our job performance. From the outside, it looks like we are behaving almost normally. On the inside we are unfulfilled and possibly resentful.

The second subcategory, one-A, is particularly important because most of us get stuck there. Category one-A is characterized by a style of brain functioning in which we are alert and rational, but are not having peak experiences. Brain wave activity is not coherent, our blood is filled with stress-induced chemicals, and our response to stimuli is either boredom or fight-or-flight. Category one-A is characterized by conditional happiness—we can be happy, but only if things go our way. Moreover, we do not see our environment in an unbiased way. We experience it filtered through our past impressions. We cannot, in this state, fully enjoy the moment, honestly relate to and enjoy those around us, or significantly contribute to our environment (without damaging it).

In category one-A, we are stuck in a rut of repetitive mental activity—thoughts, moods, and desires—that won't stop. A person who is free of category one-A addictions is free of compulsive thinking. It is no longer: one thought leads to another thought leads to another thought leads to another thought…until we are too exhausted to think, and we go to sleep. This is *not* how our brains were designed to work. Between thoughts there should be silence. The importance of silent consciousness cannot be overemphasized. It is said that everything an enlightened person accomplishes is achieved through the power of silence.

A Point of Clarification

Any addictive substance or activity can be used in any category. That means someone who drinks alcohol could be at any level from category one-A to category three. A category three addict drinks to obliterate emotional pain from the past. A category two addict wants to numb out a little and get to a happier state. A category one-A drinker drinks with friends or associates, not for mood alteration but in deference to custom. So it isn't the substance, it is the person. The person determines the intensity of the process of acting out. But, in general, we don't choose cocaine if all we need is the pick-me-up of coffee. Usually the object of addiction is a good indication of the category of addiction.

STAGES AND CATEGORIES

We can combine stages and categories of addiction. To do this we draw a grid, somewhat like a multiplication table:

	Stage One	Stage Two	Stage Three
Category One-A			
Category One-B			
Category Two			
Category Three			

Figure 1.1 An "addiction grid" that diagrams a spectrum from normalcy (top left) to extreme, life-threatening addiction (bottom right).

To make clear what we are talking about, let's fill in a few of the boxes. The bottom row is the archetypal addict, such as the alcoholic. Often college students are in the early stages of addiction, the left-hand column. Although most students are category one-A or one-B, many are category two (eating disorders are common among college students). Those who turn to drugs or drinking to escape the pressure are category three (many colleges, unfortunately, offer an excellent training ground for future alcoholics). Those students who are self-actualizing are category one-A and pre-stage one.

Business executives who see people as objects—manipulating the public to meet their own short-term goals, such as sales figures —are category one-B and stage two. If the manipulation is deviant (e.g., withholding research on a defective product) or hostile (trying to hurt another company), then they become category two addicts (there is now a specific external focus), perhaps going to stage three, and jail, in their desperation. Many "successful" people are category two, stage two workaholics. It doesn't take much to push such a person to stage three or category three. The media points out how frequently this happens: a mayor becomes a drug addict, a president's wife becomes an alcoholic, a movie star becomes addicted to painkillers.

Filling in the top right of the grid may not be necessary, because these conditions are not what we normally think of as addictions, but we could try. A possibility for stage three of category one-B is obsessive-compulsive disorder (OCD). There is some evidence that OCD shares some of the neurochemical imbalances of eating disorders, thus encouraging us to categorize it along with addictions. Stage two of category one-A could be mild depression: it results in behavioral changes that others notice. Severe depression then fits in stage three: it takes over one's life, it can be fatal, and outside help is often required to overcome it.

As an exercise, consider the stage and category of the government. We will see later that governments simply reflect our collective behaviors and desires.

Adult Children

The addiction grid gives us a simple way to understand the range of intensity of symptoms of adult children. Because the experiences of the parent become those of the child, whatever category and stage of addiction the parents reached typically determine the children's behavior patterns. So the adult child of a stage three, category three alcoholic will have, for example, free-floating anxiety and may even feel suicidal—*but possibly with no apparent cause.* At least the alcoholic can blame his or her problems on the bottle. The adult child may not have obvious addictions, and that can be very confusing. Furthermore, an adult child may quickly become an extreme addict, going rapidly to stage three, because their body has already adapted to an addictive style of behavior. Anyone who grew up in a home characterized by addiction or trauma should have a mental health checkup. For more details, see the mental health section in chapter 12.

Who Should Be Doing the Twelve Steps

From time to time, in the popular media, there is a storm in a teacup about the proliferation of Twelve Step programs. Some question whether they are appropriate for everyone: does every minor problem need one? Some question the spiritual/religious nature of the steps; either they prefer a completely secular program, or they feel court-ordered attendance in Alcoholics Anonymous violates constitutional rights. In some circles, including the courts, the debate continues.[15] These are questions I won't try to answer, but I would like to address whether you should be using the tools in this book, or focusing more on a traditional recovery program. First, a little history.

The original Twelve Step program was Alcoholics Anonymous (AA). It was used by category three, stage three addicts whose "lives had become unmanageable" and who were "powerless over their addiction." Desperation seemed to be the only prerequisite for membership in AA. Initially, AA methods were used by people who had little chance of survival without recovery. Because of its astonishing success, Alcoholics Anonymous quickly became the behavioral equivalent of a miracle drug.

Soon the spouses of alcoholics were involved, and Al-Anon was born. Thus, the Twelve Steps came to be used to treat addicts at stage three of category two—advanced codependents. In the 1980s Twelve Step programs began to be developed for addictions other than alcoholism, spreading from the lower right-hand corner of Figure 1.1 diagonally up across the grid toward the left-hand corner.

So who should be doing the Twelve Steps (or something similar), and who should be using the tools in this book? The answer is, you can do both, but if in doubt, start with a traditional recovery program. If you fit toward the bottom right of the diagram, you need a program, such as those that use the Twelve Steps, that addresses your specific life-threatening situation. Anyone with a parent who at any time was in stage two or stage three of an addiction, no matter which category, should also get some exposure to recovery knowledge and support groups. You can then clearly see your conditioning, heal yourself of your limitations, and prevent addiction from starting. If you place yourself toward the top left of the table (whether you started there or have moved yourself there), other methods for self-development may be more appropriate, such as those described in this book.

CODEPENDENCE

We have already introduced the codependent as an enabler, playing the supporting role to the addict. We need to make our description correspond more to the complexities of reality. Let's start by seeing how experts describe codependence.

Craig Nakken refers to codependents as people who take care of addicts; they "believe in the illusion that they can stop the pain if they can get an addict to stop acting out."[16] This is the traditional way of describing codependents.

Melody Beattie, in her book *Codependent No More,* gives the following definition: "A codependent person is one who has let another person's behavior affect him or her, and who is obsessed with controlling that person's behavior."[17] A codependent, then, is a person who is addicted to another person. (Notice that the other person doesn't have to be an addict.)

John Bradshaw defines codependence "as a dis-ease characterized by *loss of identity*. To be co-dependent is to be out of touch with one's feelings, needs, and desires." Codependents are "dependent on something outside of themselves in order to have an identity."[18]

Robert Subby, author of *Lost in the Shuffle: The Codependent Reality,* says, "In essence co-dependency is the reflection of a delayed identity development."[19] He locates the cause of codependence in "prolonged exposure to and practice of a dysfunctional set of family rules."[20] He states that codependent behavior "reflects a deeply-seated, private and often unconscious belief that the road to love, belonging, acceptance and success is dependent on our ability to do what we *think* others want or expect of us. The practicing codependent looks at 'doing for others' as a means of achieving these goals.... This approval-seeking or people-pleasing behavior becomes a mood-altering drug of choice."[21] Codependents believe that if they solve someone else's problems, their own life will get better.

John Bradshaw identifies the cause of codependence in unmet childhood needs: "When the family environment is filled with violence (chemical, emotional, physical, or sexual), the child must focus solely on the outside. Over time he loses the ability to generate self-esteem from within. Without a healthy inner life, one is exiled to seek fulfillment on the outside."[22]

"Other-directedness" is the primary attribute of codependence. In its broadest sense, codependence is any behavior that avoids looking within ourselves to meet our needs.

In chapter 2 we will give a name to awareness that is predominantly focused on external objects: *object-referral.* Codependence, in the most basic sense, is excessive object-referral awareness.

Here is my definition of codependence:

Definition	**Codependence** is nonstop object-referral awareness, centered especially on other people's needs and opinions. Codependence is usually caused by a desperate need to escape from the pain of the past, which we do using behaviors learned from other codependents.

Most people learn codependence as a child. Robert Subby, in *Lost in the Shuffle,* lists four types of families that engender codependence. According to Subby, it is not so much the categories of families as the unspoken rules practiced in the families that are so damaging. The four types of families are:

1. The alcoholic or addictive family.
2. The family in which one person is psychologically or emotionally unstable. This results in an inconsistent and unpredictable environment.
3. A family that violates an individual's boundaries through sexual, physical, or emotional abuse.
4. The family whose structure is characterized by dogmatism, rigidity, or fundamentalism. "These overly controlled family systems," Subby writes, "tend to operate on a narrow track. They are rigidly constructed and offer their members only a one-dimensional view of the world—a view that stresses order, discipline, regimentation, and above all, sameness."[23]

What It Is Like Being a Codependent

In *Lost in the Shuffle,* Robert Subby lists the problems faced by co-dependents:[24]

1. Difficulty accurately identifying feelings.
2. Difficulty expressing feelings.
3. Difficulty forming or maintaining close or intimate relationships.
4. Perfectionism (including extreme self-criticism).
5. Rigidity in behavior or attitudes.
6. Difficulty adjusting to change.
7. Feeling overly responsible for others' behavior or feelings.
8. Constant need for others' approval in order to feel good about self.
9. Difficulty making decisions.
10. Feeling powerless, as if nothing one does makes any difference.
11. A basic sense of shame and low self-esteem.
12. Avoidance of conflict.

Codependents tend to be reactive. Their poor communication skills, indirectness, and lack of assertiveness make problems worse. However, codependents are not necessarily ineffective in all parts of life. They can have stellar careers and be genuinely giving to their families, yet deep inside something doesn't feel right. In some way or another, codependents abandon themselves.

Codependents often become expert in a one-act play, described by Melody Beattie in *Codependent No More* as the Karpman Drama Triangle.[25] The codependent initially plays the role of *rescuer.* Then, angry that her efforts are not appreciated, she morphs into the *persecutor,* and blames her partner for the problems in their relationship. Finally, giving up on efforts to make lasting changes, she retreats into the safety of being a *victim.* Each role is the corner of a triangle that the codependent goes around and around. A skilled codependent can enact this play many times a day, as a miniseries, or as an epic lasting weeks or even years.

Like addiction, codependence can be fatal. Codependents always seem to be tired. They can die from the wear and tear caused by their constant state of hypervigilance. Codependents also risk developing addiction. And they may pursue their addictions with enough intensity to kill themselves.

Codependence shares with addiction the disease model. Codependence has symptoms, stages, and degrees of intensity. It can get worse if not treated. Similar to the addict, in later stages a codependent may become withdrawn, isolated, suicidal, mentally ill, physically ill, or abusive.[26] Codependents often wonder if they are going crazy. Codependence usually involves denial; codependents are even more reluctant than addicts to admit that there is anything wrong with their lives and behavior.

Codependence is thought by some to underlie *all* addictive behavior.[27] The definition I've suggested for codependence—nonstop object-referral—supports this line of reasoning. Object-referral, we will see in the next chapter, is the root cause of chronic problems. Codependents look everywhere but in themselves to find what they yearn for. Yet what codependents secretly seek is wholeness, completion, and the unconditional love, acceptance, and acknowledgment that can only be gained by going within themselves. Working on the surface to remove codependent behavior, without going deep within and experiencing the bliss of one's own Being, makes recovery a lifelong process.

ADULT CHILDREN

The term *adult child* signifies an adult who carries within him or her the intense pain of growing up in a hostile, invalidating, or unpredictable environment. "Adult child" originally referred to the adult children of alcoholic parents. It was then broadened to include the children of any dysfunctional family.

Dysfunction has many causes besides alcohol. It may be triggered by the early death of one of the parents, inconsistency in child custody following adoption or divorce, religious fanaticism, extreme rule-oriented attitudes, any form of abuse, any form of neglect, any of the other possible addictions (drugs, food, gambling, sex, emotions, etc.)—including socially accepted ones such as dual-parent workaholism. Dysfunction could be caused by a family member be-coming terminally ill, an emotionally unavailable parent, addiction of a sibling or son or daughter, mental illness, a shaming family, or a family history of alcoholism, whether or not either of the parents is an addict. It could even just be insufficient parental nurturing. It is the behavior patterns and feelings that count.[28]

If you are an adult child, when you were growing up, your role models were dysfunctional. Imagine spending fifteen or twenty years having your brain programmed by an addict and a codepend-ent. Not only do you learn to approach everything addictively, you try to rescue everyone. And you don't even know you are doing it. Such a childhood leaves deep stresses in the mind and body. Adult children build up complex Pavlovian responses: certain situations activate childhood stresses that lead to overwhelming and inappropriate reactions.

Adult Child Attributes

Perhaps the best way to characterize adult children is not by their background but in terms of the common problems they share. Adult children tend to have a lot of emotional as well as relationship prob-lems. The following is based on a list in Janet Woititz' book *Adult Children of Alcoholics,* with additions from other experts.[29] Adult children:

1. Don't know what normal, natural behavior is.
2. Don't finish projects they start.
3. Lie unnecessarily and habitually, including about their feelings.
4. Are extremely self-critical and perfectionist.
5. Take themselves too seriously and are unable to have fun.
6. Have relationships marked by problems dealing with inti-macy, trust, and fear of abandonment.
7. Need others' approval, losing heart without continual encouragement and support.
8. Feel uncomfortably different and are often marginalized.
9. Are impulsive and addictive.
10. Are loyal even when they clearly shouldn't be.

11. Get stuck in rigid thinking.
12. Are prone to workaholism.
13. Need to create crises and are unable to enjoy nonchaotic progress.
14. Have problems with teamwork, including difficulty communicating, difficulty giving and receiving criticism, a need to control, a tendency to overreact, and a tendency to be overly responsible or extremely irresponsible.

In addition, adult children are highly stressed. Obvious as it is, this is a major cause of inappropriate behavior because it blocks the mind and body's natural and appropriate response to a situation.

To define adult child, we have to make another forward reference to chapter 2, where we will see that the opposite of object-referral is "self-referral." Self-referral awareness is an extremely healthy and self-actualized style of awareness in which the individual is actively connected to all levels of the mind and personality.

Definition	An **adult child** (of an alcoholic, troubled, or other dysfunctional family) is someone with these three attributes:
	1. They have both addictive and codependent behavior patterns.
	2. The self-referral levels of feeling and ego are impaired (causing emotional and relationship problems).
	3. Some aspects of knowledge—what others might consider to be basic skills of living and interacting—have been left out of their upbringing.

So an adult child is someone who grew up in an addictive-codependent home and thereby took on those qualities, lost the ability for complete self-referral, and did not get all the worldly knowledge they needed to live a fulfilled life. A substantial part of recovery for adult children consists of removing addictive and codependent attributes, and learning skills, especially interpersonal skills, that others might consider obvious and commonplace.

Adult children, like addicts and codependents, need to re-establish self-referral. Adult children have to focus especially on the levels of feeling and ego, because these were the most damaged in their childhood.

ENDING ON A POSITIVE NOTE

So far, our description of the addict and codependent has emphasized the negative, but there is a bright side.

People with an addictive personality are often playful and seek out joy and exhilaration. More often than not, they want to share these experiences with others. With addiction, the completely natural desire to enjoy gets a little off track, and over time addicts end up far from where they can reliably find happiness. In that light, curing addiction involves setting the person back onto the path of genuine fulfillment. Curing addiction doesn't involve suppressing the natural desire to fully enjoy life.

The bright side of codependents is, of course, their unparalleled generosity and kindness. They are natural in the helping professions. They give without limitation. In times of need, who wouldn't want to be helped by someone like that?

ENLIGHTENMENT

CHAPTER TWO

In this chapter, we explore the modern frontier of human development—enlightenment. We focus on the concept of "self-referral," completing the background knowledge needed to understand addiction.

Addiction involves all levels of our individuality—behavior, body, mind, and the deepest aspect of our personality, the Self. A simple, clear, and accurate understanding of how the mind and body work makes recovery much easier. Without it, a huge effort is required. Often we move out of one addiction and into another. If we are hooked strongly enough, we may only teeter on the brink of sobriety. Alcoholics are usually told they will be in recovery for life. This caution serves a vital purpose; but spending your whole life in recovery isn't necessary for everyone. This is the result of ignorance of the laws of nature governing human development. If we can send a man to the moon, we can create programs for complete recovery. Let's see how this is possible.

SELF-REFERRAL

The Body

The body never stops balancing itself. Our physiology has complex systems designed to provide stable frames of reference. Biologists call this homeostasis. For example, when we exercise, the body refers to an internal frame of reference (a kind of built-in thermometer) and senses it is too hot; it then puts into effect various strategies to cool off. This is *self-referral* on a macroscopic level.

On the microscopic level, our DNA has its own feedback loop, whereby it verifies its integrity and repairs itself when necessary. Many factors, such as harmful radiation from sunlight, can distort the sequence of DNA. This is potentially lethal because DNA is the body's blueprint. Therefore, the body has to have a built-in means of checking its structure and repairing itself. This checking and repairing is a self-referral process.

Definition	**Self-referral** describes any process whereby a system dynamically interacts with *itself* to maintain its existence, balance, and progress.

We could describe many levels of self-referral. These are represented by loops A through E in Figure 2.1. Loop A might be the self-repair of DNA, loop D the body's maintenance of stable temperature. The loops represent dynamic connections: some include consciously thinking or deciding, some do not. Addiction involves distortions in the body's self-referral mechanisms.

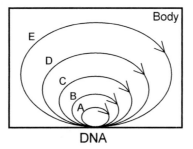

Figure 2.1 A self-referral diagram for the body.

The Environment

Now, let's extend our example of self-referral to include the environment. In the case of someone exercising, at some point they are going to need something to drink. This involves interacting with the environment. When the need is met, the loop gets closed. The new loop, F in Figure 2.2, represents getting and drinking water. Notice that this need involves the deepest level of the diagram, which at this point is DNA.

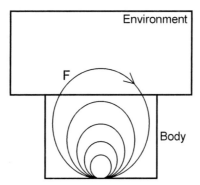

Figure 2.2 Self-referral diagram for the body and behavior.

The Mind

The mind provides an even deeper level of self-referral than the body. DNA has created the body with its tremendously powerful brain. Once the machinery of the body is fully functional, the body becomes the servant of the mind. Thoughts trigger neurotransmitters, the chemical messengers dispatched by the mind. We might think, "I want to pick up the glass of water." The appropriate neurotransmitters are invoked, telling the body to reach out and take the glass. Or, we may feel happiness. Then "happy" biochemicals create euphoria in the body.

Adding the mind to our self-referral diagram (Figure 2.3), we simply draw a smaller box below the body.

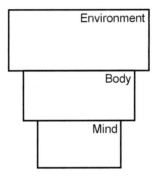

Figure 2.3 Adding the mind to the self-referral diagram.

Levels of the Mind

At this point, we need a more detailed concept of the mind. Just as the body has distinct systems, such as the circulatory system and the respiratory system, so the mind, although an inseparable whole, can, for the purpose of understanding, be broken down into four functional parts: thinking, intellect, feeling, and ego. These are considered to be levels of the mind.

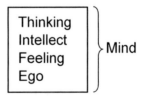

Figure 2.4 The levels of the mind.

Each level has its own task. The first, *thinking,* refers to the ability of the mind to have a coherent thought or stream of thoughts. The next level is the *intellect.* Its role is to discriminate. The intellect says, "Do I go right or left? Is it up or down?" The intellect is dualistic and binary. It divides one into two. And with subsequent divisions it can make remarkably subtle distinctions.

The next level, that of the *feelings,* is more powerful than the intellect. If this were not the case, no one could ever be talked into anything, and most people in sales would be out of a job.

The deepest level is the *ego.* The role of the ego is synthetic. It holds together the levels of the mind above it and synthesizes a personality out of our past impressions. The ego is responsible for identity—the sense of "I." This is our limited sense of "I am," which is always followed by some limitation: I am an engineer; I am a mother. Or, the ego qualifies in terms of "my": my daughter, my new car, my job.

So thinking, intellect, feeling, and ego constitute levels of the mind. They are a hierarchy.

Although not included in these diagrams, note that somewhere in the mind is a storehouse of memories. Most of these are latent, lying hidden and dormant. However, in the process of incomplete self-referral, these past experiences can be activated by sensory input and then acted on, often inappropriately. (This is why advertising is so effective in manipulating our behavior.) For the moment—until chapter 11—we will ignore the storehouse of past impressions.

The Self

The theory of levels of the mind does not seem to stretch our belief system to the breaking point. However, we are not finished yet. How do we account for the experience of simply *being*? Not "I am a lawyer," just "I am." There are no limiting qualifiers; no individual ego is involved. Many, many people have reported sitting in stillness, their mind settling down, becoming quieter and quieter until completely silent, like an ocean with no waves—no thoughts, no intellectual discriminating, no isolated emotions, no ego-based identification.[30] Yet the person remains fully aware. If we say the mind has the quality of awareness, then that is all that is left. In other words, the person is aware of their own awareness. They are conscious of their consciousness. (Awareness and consciousness, as I am using the terms, are the same thing.) Moreover, people say they transcend all individual limitations. They report the experience of *unboundedness:* as if their awareness went out and out forever like the sky, beyond time, beyond words—an unchanging field, transcendental to all that is relative and changing.

What is remarkable is that people who have clear experiences of this state all seem to be describing the same thing—a field of silence and power that lies beneath the superficial aspect of one's personality. This is the *Self.* The Self is a silent center deep within everyone. It is the source of our very thinking. It is, therefore, connected to our creativity, intelligence, and feelings. The Self is responsible for our ability to have a coherent personality. When a person feels centered, they are connected with the Self.

Making great scientific discoveries, having poetic inspiration, effortlessly composing music—all come from the power of the Self. We do not do something great, like composing music, because we think, "I am a great musician." The ego isn't that powerful. The common theme in acts of great creativity is *letting go.* It is not relaxation that gives the insight; it is allowing the mind to go to more powerful levels closer to the Self. Experience of the Self is highly correlated with success in life.[31] *Total recovery is impossible without clear experience of the Self.* The Self constitutes the most profound, complete, and healing level of self-referral. Just as the mind governs the body, so the Self governs the mind. Let's take a moment and define Self.

Definition	The **Self** is the silent, creative, powerful center of intelligence and organizing power deep within each person. Experience of the Self is characterized by: pure awareness, silence, unboundedness, bliss, satisfaction, contentment, complete harmony, unity, being.
Synonyms	**Self**: self-referral awareness, pure consciousness, unbounded awareness, Being, transcendental consciousness, simplest form of awareness, source of thought, Creative Intelligence, the Absolute.

Self is capitalized to differentiate it from the *self* (small "s"), which is the ego-based, limited, and conditioned aspect of our personality.

Our self-referral diagram can now be finished and is shown in Figure 2.5.

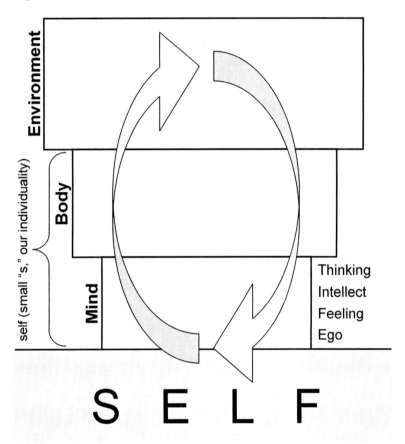

Figure 2.5 A complete self-referral diagram. Desires start from the deepest aspect of the mind, in touch with the Self, and then proceed outward through mind, body, and environment, and then, hopefully, awareness returns to rest in the Self.

Self-Referral Awareness

The Self is revealed when the mind settles down to its least excited state. Then the mind is open to the whole of itself, and has complete self-referral. This is called *self-referral awareness*. This is a natural

and normal experience. It is abnormal to lack self-referral awareness. Its absence is the cause of a host of neuroses and health complaints.

Definition	**Self-referral awareness** is the direct experience of the Self. It is awareness that is aware of itself, instead of projected outward as sensory experience, thoughts, moods, or desires.

By the way, I define all new terms because although they describe
something abstract, each one delineates something very specific. No
meaningful discussion or scientific progress is possible without un-
ambiguously clear and commonly-agreed-upon terminology.

EXAMPLES

Now let's try out this theory. Does it explain what we see in our
lives and in the lives of those around us? If it does, can we use it to
make our lives better? (These are specific examples of the general
goals of science: Does a new theory extend previous theories to explain anomalies? Does it allow us to harness natural law for the
greater good of humanity?)

An Addict

Let's start with an addict. What kind of self-referral does he or she
have? In its most extreme form it looks like Figure 2.6, where the

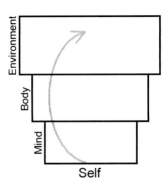

Figure 2.6 An extreme addict.

gray line now represents total, cumulative self-referral—how far awareness goes out and how much it returns. An extreme addict rarely allows her awareness to refer back to the body, let alone to the mind. Certainly, referring to the Self is out of the question.

This diagram (Figure 2.6) explains why it is so hard to cure someone else of their addiction. Any advice we give, and any action we take, is in their box labeled "environment." For them, our advice is object-referral. *They* have to consciously take *their* awareness to a more self-referral level; we cannot do it for them.

A Normal Person

What kind of self-referral does a "normal" person have? Here, when we say *normal,* we really mean usual or average, the kind of ordinary person who walks by us on the street every day. As we will see in a minute, this isn't the most ideal state of the mind and body —the state that really should be considered normal.

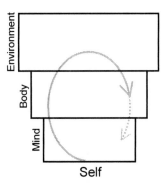

Figure 2.7 A "normal" or non-addictive person

A normal person meets the needs of their body. This is represented, in Figure 2.7, by the solid arrow. However, at deeper levels they are less in touch with their needs. The average person still has suppressed emotions. And their intellect may not be able to discriminate between fine shades of moral values; thus they do not always act in harmony with their feelings and beliefs. In addition, they don't really know who they are, which means lack of self-referral to the ego level. This weak or partial self-referral is represented in the diagram by the arrow with a dotted line.

Perhaps we have given our "normal" person too much credit: just how attuned is he or she even to the body? Maybe the arrow to the body should also be dotted. If people were genuinely in touch with the needs of body and environment, would there be such high rates of heart disease and cancer?

An Above-Normal Person

A modern psychologist, Abraham Maslow, decided to find the most normal people he could. He opted to study exceptionally psychologically healthy individuals, rather than pathological cases. Maslow called these people—who were integrated, progressive, creative, and effective in life—"self-actualizers."[32] They had already met their basic subsistence needs, such as food, shelter, a sense of belonging, and self-worth. Their life was naturally directed toward higher values. According to Maslow, they often had the experience of Being. Maslow estimates that one percent, or less, of the population are self-actualizing.

Their self-referral diagram might look like this:

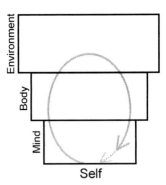

Figure 2.8 A self-actualizer.

Translating the picture into words: self-actualizers are continually in tune with their physical and mental needs, and with their unique sense of self; they interact with the environment in such a way as to get their needs met. These levels all have solid lines. The arrow continues on to the Self, because the attributes of a self-actualizer can be created and maintained only by a connection to the Self.

However, the line is dotted: the connection to the Self is neither complete nor continuous. That would be a distinctly higher level of accomplishment.

A Fully Normal Person

So what about complete self-referral? The diagram is easy enough (Figure 2.9). It is also conceptually simple. The person is in touch with all levels shown in the diagram—environment, body, each level of the mind, and the Self. When complete self-referral becomes spontaneous, automatic, and permanent, we say the person is *enlightened.* Enlightenment is a higher state of consciousness.

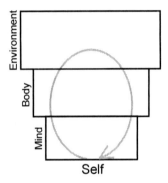

Figure 2.9 Complete self-referral.

If Maslow found only one percent of the population in the process of self-actualizing, the number of fully enlightened people must be extraordinarily small. However, in every generation there must be a few, some perhaps without knowing how they got there, who have stabilized higher states of consciousness.

In fact, we are all inexorably growing toward higher states of consciousness. It is like a three- or four-year-old moving on to a new stage of cognitive development. It is in the natural design of things and results from greater culture of the brain. As with a child's developmental progress, enlightenment brings with it greater joy and power, greater ability to love and enjoy. It is a more integrated state.

Subjectively, people who have had a taste of enlightenment report that life goes more smoothly (it ought to if you are connected to all those levels); that there is much more bliss, happiness, harmony, and love; that they are more powerful and dynamic. Enlightenment has traditionally been described by paradoxes. Inner awareness is silent; outer activity is dynamic. Life seems to go by itself with little intervention by the ego, yet one is completely in command, able to change anything at will. The enlightened know themselves as beyond time, and yet are extremely time-competent. Descriptions such as these are characterized by the balanced coexistence of opposites. What is doing the balancing? Enlightened people share one common experience—the Self.

Like the backdrop in a play, the Self gives meaning and value to what takes place on the stage. Switching to a movie metaphor, imagine that our thoughts and feelings are projected onto the screen of our awareness. Our silent, unbounded consciousness is always there, yet somehow we forget this. We pay inordinate attention to the images of perception. This causes problems if we forget how to get back to unboundedness. Enlightened people are enlightened because they never lose the Self. They don't get inextricably caught up in the movie of life. It is like not forgetting that you are wearing your glasses: you don't go berserk trying to find something you never truly lost.

A while ago we said the average person was "normal." In fact, it is the enlightened who deserve to be called normal. They are deeply in tune with themselves, and are thus capable of honest and genuine interaction with their environment.

Definition	**Enlightenment** is characterized by spontaneous and unbroken experience of the Self. We don't lose complete self-referral no matter how dynamically we act or how deeply we sleep. It is the most natural state of life, free of past conditioning.

BECOMING ENLIGHTENED

What keeps us from enlightenment is the insistence on always focusing outside the Self. Outwardly directed awareness, not supported by the Self, causes problems. We make mistakes, get fatigued, cause our body to rapidly age, and are habitually unhappy. Focusing outwardly and losing the Self is called *object-referral*. Object-referral is the opposite of self-referral. We become preoccupied with objects. These could be external, such as family, friends, or job. Or they could be internal, such as thoughts, moods, and desires. In either case, we gain an object of perception and lose our Self—not a very good trade.

Definition	**Object-referral** is outwardly directed awareness that does not include enough self-referral to support (perfectly) normal functioning of mind and body.

The antidote to any problem is to re-establish self-referral. This means bringing our focus back from the environment to the Self. This going inward is called *transcending*. Transcending is the process of taking the attention from the surface of the mind through the more abstract states of awareness, to the subtlest level, and then going beyond even the faintest thought, leaving awareness open to itself. Without transcending, enlightenment *and recovery* are left up to chance, and may take a very, very long time.

Definition	**Transcending** is the process of taking the attention inward to experience the Self. This re-establishes self-referral awareness.

By repeatedly transcending, we culture the ability to remain fully self-referral even when projecting awareness outward. This is called *self-referral performance*. It may sound a little unusual, but it isn't that far-fetched. After all, a stressed body maintains almost all of its self-referral: DNA repairs itself, the body's temperature stays the same, and so on. Even a fool can do this in his (or her) sleep. Once we release some of our stress, the mind-body system, which is highly sophisticated, is naturally capable of maintaining deeper levels of self-referral.

Self-referral performance means that no matter what happens, no matter how dynamically you act, you remain integrated. No aspect of your individuality gets lost or out of control. You are observant of your environment, you are conscious of your body, you are in touch with your feelings, you are in tune with your individual sense of "I-ness," and, most importantly, you are aware of your Being—of unboundedness that is not overshadowed by thinking, perceiving, or doing.

This description makes it seem like your mind would be filled with a jumble of thoughts and perceptions, or that you would be frantically switching from one level of awareness to another in a mad rush to coordinate everything. That is not the case. The brain is immensely powerful. It can easily stay in touch with all levels simultaneously. In fact, that is how it was designed to work.

Definition	**Self-referral performance** is the spontaneous, non-contrived maintenance—while acting—of all levels of self-referral, including self-referral awareness. It is exactly equivalent to enlightenment. An isolated experience of self-referral performance is a glimpse of enlightenment.

THE FINEST LEVEL OF FEELING

Let's add one last detail, an important one, to the model of the mind. We have introduced four distinct levels of the mind: thinking, intellect, feeling, and ego. Each level rests one on another, and all ultimately rest on the Self. Imagine this as a front view, and then turn the model sideways. A side view reveals that everything merges into a common source.

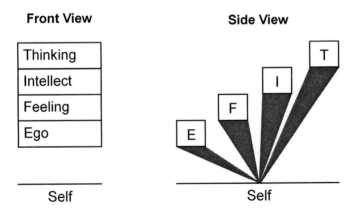

The point where thinking, intellect, feeling, and ego come together is called *the finest level of feeling.* The finest level of feeling is the deepest level of relative self-referral, before the personality merges into the universality of the Self. It is just above Being, and provides us with our most profound sense of who we are. If we lose touch with the finest level of feeling, we become disoriented. Although we may keep acting, and others may praise us for our achievements, we won't be doing what we really want to, and life will lose its luster.

The finest level of feeling is powerful yet delicate. It has to be nurtured, protected, and kept free from rigidity and boundaries. It is at the finest level of feeling that thinking, intellect, emotions, and ego naturally interact in a manner that is joyful, creative, playful, and holistic. Once we learn to act from this level, the different aspects of our mind effortlessly and magnificently perform the intricate and perfectly choreographed dance that is our life.

THE BRIDGE

FROM ADDICTION TO ENLIGHTENMENT

CHAPTER THREE

In the first chapter, we discussed the terms addiction, codependence, *and* adult child. *Now we fit these terms into the framework of self-referral introduced in the previous chapter.*

The true goal of all successful therapies is to restore self-referral on as deep a level as the person is capable of at that time. Better therapies restore self-referral faster and get closer to the Self, but every successful therapy restores self-referral. The Twelve Steps do it. Skills training, journaling, grief work, dream work, breath work, body work, focusing, affirmations, visualization, naming your feelings and feeling your feelings—whatever is useful in recovery—move us in the direction of increasing self-referral. Take something as simple as gratitude. If you feel genuinely and reverently grateful for anything—even something seemingly inconsequential—you take your awareness down to the finest level of feeling. You increase your degree of self-referral.

A FEW EXAMPLES

To make what we have said in the first two chapters more concrete, let's relate it to familiar recovery concepts—traditional approaches that have little (at first glance) to do with the theories of consciousness in this book. We will start with grief work.

Grief Work

This is also called original pain work. It is a therapy tool suggested by Alice Miller[33] and made popular by, among others, John Bradshaw.[34] It typically applies to adult children—those who grew up in an environment, such as an alcoholic family, that caused childhood development to freeze due to extreme stress. Through grief work, adult children get in touch with deep, hidden levels of emotional pain. By experiencing it, they free themselves from the negative emotions frozen inside the mind and body.

Grief work gets its name, by analogy, from the natural process of grieving that occurs after a traumatic event. For example, when someone close to us dies, there is a period in which the loss is mourned. During this time our psychology reorganizes, allowing us to adapt and move on in our life. Those who grew up in a dysfunctional family are blocked from this kind of adjustment. As a result of family rules such as "don't feel" and "don't talk,"[35] they have not been able to mourn the trauma and losses of their childhood. Consequently, the dysfunctional individual's psychology never adjusts to the realities of adult life. Their self-referral diagram is shown in Figure 3.1.

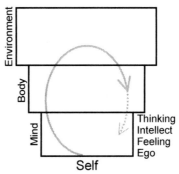

Figure 3.1 An adult child before recovery work. Even partial self-referral doesn't make it beyond the level of the intellect.

Adult children have difficulty feeling their emotions unless they are acting in crisis mode. But that is not a loop. Jumping directly to the level of feelings is not self-referral. The intellect, the body, and the true realities of the environment are ignored.

Grief work is successful because it restores self-referral. It is a limited self-referral, but it is a significant step in the right direction. Acknowledging the pain of the past, and feeling it, activates the feeling level. Because an accepting, come-what-may attitude is adopted, naturalness replaces inner struggle. If a person is more natural, they have more self-referral. After the healing process, the new diagram looks like this:

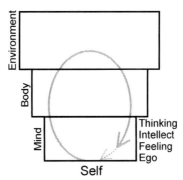

Figure 3.2 Self-referral diagram for an adult child after recovery work.

The solid arrow goes down to the level of the feelings, and a little past, because the ego level is also affected. Hopefully the person slipped a few times into the experience of the Self. So we draw a dotted line down to the Self. We now have the diagram we saw a few pages ago, the one for a self-actualizer. Later we will look at ways to go beyond self-actualization to enlightenment.

The Inner Child

John Bradshaw, in his book *Homecoming,* popularized another concept, that of the inner child or wonder child. People in recovery are drawn to the concept of an inner child. It fascinates them. There is something charming and liberating about it. Why? Because it accurately reflects reality, and it helps us connect with our deep inner nature. What is the "wonder child," and of relevance here, how does it fit in our model of self-referral?

John Bradshaw describes the wonder child as "the core of your spirituality and your most profound connection with the source and creative ground of your being...the part of you that bears a likeness to your creator." John Bradshaw also says, "The natural state of your wonder child is creativity. Getting in touch with your creativity is...a discovering of your essence, your deepest unique self." After uncovering your wonder child, "the urgings and signals from your deepest self can now be heard and responded to."[36]

Getting in touch with your inner child is the same as gaining a deeper level of self-referral. Once you've contacted that level, your behavior moves in the direction of self-referral performance. I believe the wonder child is similar to the finest level of feeling. However, I should point out that grief work and championing one's inner child, as useful as they are, will not result in enlightenment.

Weight Loss and Object-Referral

So far we have talked about programs that work. Let's consider one that often doesn't: dieting. Why do the majority of people who "successfully" lose weight, gain it back within a few years? One reason is that many weight loss programs foster object-referral. If you use a scale to measure your success, you are not learning self-referral; you are structuring the habit of making decisions, not based on how your mind and body feel, but on the advice of springs or electronic circuits in a box. You are systematically structuring object-referral. So what do you do when skillful advertising (often more electronic circuits in a box) tells you that happiness will be yours if you eat their brand of dessert? You take two, because that is your training: to be guided by external prompts. A scale isn't the solution, self-referral is.

Combining Multiple Approaches

Mary Pipher is a clinical psychologist who works with young women. Dr. Pipher wrote the best-selling book *Reviving Ophelia: Saving the Selves of Adolescent Girls.* Over the years, she has seen a steady increase in teenage problems involving addiction—such as eating disorders and alcohol and drug use—and in mental health problems—such as self-mutilation and depression. Dr. Pipher repeatedly points out that our culture, instead of nourishing the population, is *causing* the problems of adolescents. At a time when we should be telling impressionable youth to seek a unique inner experience, we send them instead on an impossible quest for outer conformity. And many of them die trying. (In chapter 10 we talk about changing society.)

In her book, Dr. Pipher gives examples of successful therapy. In the thirteenth chapter, she describes the ingredients of a typical recovery regimen. She has her young clients learn a simple form of meditation, daily spend time getting in touch with their feelings, keep a journal, discover qualities they like about themselves, give service, and uncover how their sense of self-identity has been distorted by the media. According to Dr. Pipher:

> The most important question for every client is "Who are you?" I am not as interested in an answer as I am in teaching a process that the girl can use for the rest of her life. The process involves looking within to find a true core of self, acknowledging unique gifts, accepting all feelings, not just the socially acceptable ones, and making deep and firm decisions about values and meaning. The process includes knowing the difference between thinking and feeling, between immediate gratification and long-term goals, and between her own voice and the voice of others.[37]

Clearly, her clients are learning to use deeper aspects of their mind. They are self-actualizing. Based on what we know so far, it should be clear that all these approaches, put together, move adolescents toward greater self-referral and the possibility of self-referral performance.

ADDICTION

To understand why self-referral is the central plank on the bridge of recovery, it is helpful to look briefly at one model for addiction. I have no intention of throwing my hat into the ring of contention surrounding exactly why people become addicted—whether it is genetic or environmental, whether it is predominantly physical or behavioral or emotional or spiritual. But we have to at least skirt the issue to see, not why it starts, but how it stops. To do this, we will look at the disease model of addiction.

The Disease Model
Disease is a model that we use to understand a certain class of phenomena. What, according to doctors, are the attributes of this class? First, a disease is diagnosable—each disease has a unique set of characteristics that makes it different from other diseases. Second, it has causes. Third, a disease has a life cycle. Fourth, it can be scientifically studied and understood. Fifth, because it can be studied, its causes can be found, and then the disease can, hopefully, be prevented or cured. Treatment usually centers around taking medications, which for some decades have been synthetically produced chemicals.

It turns out there are two traditional disease models: the biomedical and the biopsychosocial. The biomedical model says, You're a body; if you get sick, we are going to pour medicine into your body until we make it better. Basically, the doctor isn't concerned about your mental state—unless it is easily alterable with drugs—and would like very much to ignore any influence from society. You are JUST a body.

The biopsychosocial model was proposed as a response to this unreasonably reductionistic view. The model is usually credited to an American psychiatrist named George Engel. He said, Look around; diseases—diabetes, hypertension, heart disease—are not caused *only* by biological problems, but also by our state of mind and how society tells us to behave. At present, all medical schools talk the talk of the biopsychosocial model. But as a society, we don't walk the talk. We don't insist on mental and behavioral ways to prevent and cure disease. We still treat a disease as if it were purely physical; we wait for it to happen, and then ask for a pill to fix it. With a new theoretical model, yet the same attitude, the rate of diabetes is expected to double. Rates of addiction haven't gone down either.

Addiction as a Disease

Alcoholism was the first addiction the medical community (and insurance companies) universally accepted as a disease. For the most part, alcoholism fits nicely into the disease model, especially the biopsychosocial model. But some things don't quite fit. For example, the causes and cures for alcoholism are not necessarily physical, and the use of drugs to cure addiction is somewhat problematic. Proponents of the biopsychosocial model say, Hey, diabetes is also caused by inappropriate behavior that society "makes" us do, such as eating the wrong food and not exercising; alcoholism is not all that different. But the biopsychosocial model hasn't enabled the widespread prevention of many traditional diseases, including diabetes. And its impact on treatment has also been marginal.

However, if only because it encourages a nonshaming attitude, we should keep the disease model for addiction. It removes the stigma. It opens to addiction the already established feelings of compassion we have toward those recovering from an illness. It allows researchers to think along the same rational lines they would in healing any disease and in fighting an epidemic. And, not least, treatment gets covered under medical insurance.

Addiction as a Spiritual Disease

To say addiction is a disease is extremely useful, but it does not tell the whole story. What kind of disease is it? Some people will tell you it is a *spiritual* disease. In other words, its cause and treatment lie in the realm of the spiritual. I'm not sure what most people mean by *spiritual:* maybe it is religion, minus the dogma, ritual, and political structure; maybe it is one's relationship with oneself or with God; maybe it is everything that is not material or rational. Some people confuse spiritual with mystical. I read with amusement these lines in a pamphlet on the disease model of addiction: "So far, we cannot explain this phenomenon [of the effectiveness of an alcoholic surrendering to a Higher Power] in purely rational terms, and it is not necessary to, as it constitutes the spiritual aspect of the Twelve Step program."[38] Who says we can't use our intellect to understand the laws governing human development? Certainly the process of human growth needs an experience that is beyond the intellect, but that doesn't mean the intellect can't understand the overall process.

One dictionary defines spiritual as "Of, pertaining to, or consisting of the spirit." Spirit is defined as "1. The animating or life-giving principle within a living being; soul. 2. The part of a human being associated with the mind and feelings as distinguished from the physical body. 3. The real sense or significance of something."[39]

The causes and treatments for addiction, if it is a spiritual disease, must have a component that is nonphysical. We must address the "mind and feelings" as well as the essential "life-giving principle." You can't cure addiction with more drugs, as you can a physical disease. You must consider the whole person. Treatment must be holistic.

The spiritual disease model is even more useful than the disease model by itself. Remember, though, that it is still a *model,* and we should check to see if it accurately and most usefully describes the object being modeled. I believe there is a model with an even better fit.

The Biopsychosocial Spiritual Developmental Model

I believe addiction is a *developmental* problem—an *adult* developmental problem. Understanding the developmental component of addiction is the key to total recovery. A disease can be recovered from, and then caught again and again. But you don't usually go back to previous developmental stages. For example, at one point in a toddler's development he or she has no real concept of volume. Show a toddler a cylinder and an obviously much smaller sphere. Ask which holds more water. The answer you get is random. Ask the same question to children two or three years older, and they all know the difference and get it right. They can now effortlessly and spontaneously come to the right conclusion. Children, in their development, rarely go back to an old level of decision-making ability; they don't regress to previous cognitive levels. This kind of development is what we need for addicts (which in its general sense includes all of us). To grow out of our addictions we need a new style of cognitive functioning, one that doesn't include in its repertoire the ability to make the mistakes that keep us unfulfilled.

I don't believe addiction is a *purely* developmental problem. I believe it is a complex problem that has spiritual, biological, psychological (including behavioral), sociological, *and* developmental components. All these have to be addressed, but if society doesn't deal with the practicalities of inner development, people are going to be dissatisfied with their lives and many will turn to drugs and other means of short-term fulfillment. And this is happening on a massive scale.

Here are some of the reasons we should update the disease model:

1. A model that includes adult human development is more accurate. It explains more "data points." For example, why do former addicts make better counselors? The disease model has no answer —a doctor doesn't have to have had a disease to be good at treating it. Unlike medical school or training to be a counselor, recovery from addiction gives you developmental experience. You have what the addict needs to recover.

2. The developmental model explains why treatment for addiction must be on all levels. Recovery from disease can be achieved by taking a pill (or so say some doctors). Recovery from a spiritual disease could be done, I suppose, with a pill and a prayer. Human development requires something more.

3. The developmental model helps us understand that period of transition when a person, on the border between addict and non-addict, is wavering back and forth from brief episodes of drug use to complete abstinence. What is happening is a learning experience. It is similar to our toddler in the previous example: sometimes able to accurately compare volumes, sometimes not. If the child is given sufficient developmental experiences, she will quickly learn to make the right decisions. Similarly, with recovering addicts, this time of transition can be reduced with proper techniques for development of consciousness, resulting in increased awareness and self-referral.

4. The disease model is too no-fault. Addiction doesn't happen like a car accident, with neither party to blame. Addiction has both individual and societal causes that should be looked at. We have been conditioned to accept disease as a normal part of life. By saying addiction is a disease we become apathetic to finding a societal solution. After all, you can't help getting the flu . . . alcoholism must be the same. I believe society *is* at fault. And I believe we *can* do something about the pandemic of addiction.

CODEPENDENCE

Many successful counselors feel that codependence is the deepest cause of both addiction and the problems faced by adult children.[40] Codependents are out of touch with their inner selves—their feelings, priorities, values, and sense of who they are. Codependents focus on the outside, which, as we have said, is object-referral. Let's use the example of overcoming codependence to illustrate how wholeness of awareness can free us from the limitations and conditioning of our past. We will try a new style of diagram (inspired by diagrams in Robert Subby's book *Lost in the Shuffle*).

Figure 3.3 depicts a person's sense of self-identity based on where that person's awareness is centered. The figure shows the inner Self centered within the outer self. The arrow represents outward projected awareness. The boxes around the circle represent roles onto which we project our awareness and which, through

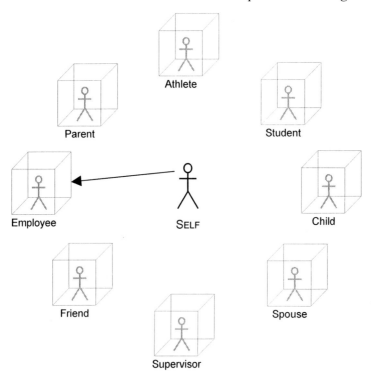

Figure 3.3 This diagram shows how a person's awareness functions. A co-dependent is someone who has trained his awareness to excessively identify with outer values, and has lost the Self. His identity is solely that of an employee, parent, friend, etc.

identification, we become. We think of ourselves as a father or a mother and become that, forgetting our essential nature as unbounded awareness. We think of ourselves as a carpenter or a doctor and become so engrossed in our profession that we are lost to the other aspects of ourselves.

Now, consider a codependent starting recovery. Once someone realizes they are codependent, they try to get in touch with deeper levels of themselves—their feelings, needs, and aspirations. They bring the center of their awareness closer to where it should be—the Self. Figure 3.4 shows this by moving the center of identification (the circled X) toward the center of the diagram.

This is an ideal first step. Recovery is taking place as long as the general direction of progress is to bring the center of attention

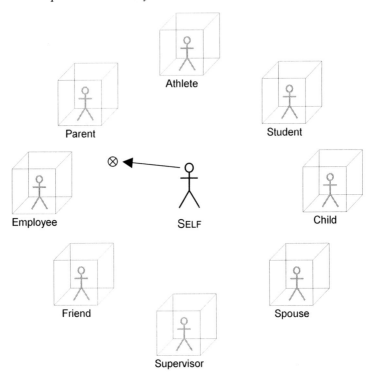

Figure 3.4 A good first step in the recovery of a codependent.

closer to the Self. However, this process may be terminated before attention is fully centered in the Self. If the habit of object-referral is strong, the codependent will soon choose a new "box" and obsess on (excessively identify with) that area of life. It is a different object of focus, but the same pattern of object-referral awareness. This may go unnoticed: the new box was chosen based on getting in touch with deeper feelings—so it feels right, or at least better. And behavior is genuinely less codependent due to increased self-referral resulting from the process of getting in touch with inner needs; some transcending *has* taken place. However, the center of awareness will tend to shift gradually toward the periphery of the diagram. After some time, the codependent behaves in almost exactly the same way toward a new box as he or she did toward the old box. It is a new codependent relationship, with almost the same intensity and degree of dysfunction.

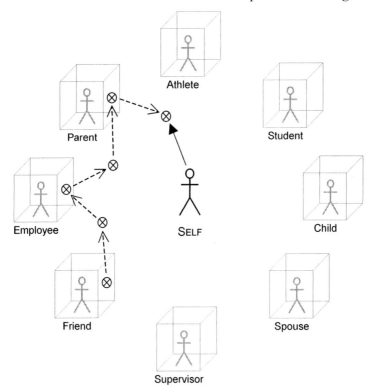

Figure 3.5 An incomplete and perpetual recovery process for a codependent, due to insufficient knowledge and inadequate techniques. This diagram shows how the center of awareness (the circled X) changes with time (the dotted line); the solid line arrow represents where awareness is directed now.

The codependent may keep choosing new boxes (Figure 3.5), and the cycle gets repeated and goes on around the circle until he is back where he started. And then he starts over. This process results in self-knowledge, but not enough to make it the centerpiece of a recovery program.

If we add techniques for activating self-referral awareness, the situation is substantially improved. By regularly and deeply transcending, codependents shift the center of their attention to where it belongs, to themselves. And not just to themselves, but to their source of power and dignity, the Self.

Each time a person transcends, the mind and body are habituated

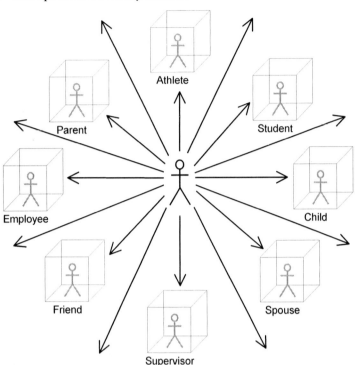

Figure 3.6 The awareness of a fully self-referral person goes out, but remains centered in the Self. This is unbounded awareness.

to remain more self-referral, centered, and normal. Gradually the codependent becomes less obsessed with objects of awareness. Regular transcending, over time, makes full self-referral permanent.

A completely self-referral person keeps the center of attention at its source and yet is able to project awareness out to the objects of attention. This is possible only with unbounded awareness. In this state, all aspects of the personality are integrated. In other words, a woman who works and has a family would be a mother *while* she is a businesswoman, *while* she is a wife, *while* she is everything else —all the time remaining herself because she has not lost her Self. This integration of life is depicted in Figure 3.6, which shows the arrows (of awareness) going out, while the center of awareness remains with the inner Self.

This diagram gives the feeling of unbounded awareness. Totally centered in yourself, you are aware of everything around you. Furthermore, in self-referral performance, you meet whatever needs present themselves from the environment, without sacrificing one iota of your wholeness. You are never lost to yourself. It is very simple, but it is not a mood or an attitude. The experience is on a deeper level. It is the spontaneous, balanced, integrated functioning of all the parts of your individuality with themselves and with the Self. You are not going to learn to do this overnight. But you can learn it, and acting from the stable platform of Being, you'll enjoy your life a lot more.

A COMMON CAUSE (AND SOLUTION)

By now it should be unmistakably clear that I believe addiction, codependence, and the problems of adult children have a common cause—lack of self-referral awareness. We can also put it the other way, that self-referral is the basis of total recovery. This is the central point of this book and cannot be overemphasized:

The rate, quality, and extent of recovery are determined by the frequency, and especially the depth, of self-referral experiences of total integration of mind, body, and consciousness.

In other words, if your mind and body don't know what it feels like to function nonaddictively, there is no way addiction is going to end. You can do a thousand detox programs, and you will still struggle to stay clean and sober. If you move out of one addiction, it will be into another. Only when the mind transcends and feels bliss can it detect a contrast between addictive and nonaddictive behavior. Gaining bliss—the experience of pure consciousness, which results from integration of mind and body—is *the most* effective way of freeing yourself from addiction.

Integrate your brain functioning. Transcend to a holistic, comprehensive state of awareness and learn to act from there. Then not one, but all addictions—from the most extreme to the most mild—will simultaneously fall away.

Why should an addict or codependent work so hard to "recover" and become merely an average person? Sometimes an addict recovers and becomes "normal" and, once the newness wears off, finds it isn't so great after all. Some wonder if it was worth the effort. Doesn't it make sense to continue past normal—with its aches and pains, losses, sorrows, heart attacks, and senility—and go right on to enlightenment? Both traditional recovery and becoming enlightened involve retraining the mind and body. Why not retrain for the highest? It doesn't take that much more effort. Since recovery from intense addiction is often a Herculean task, shouldn't the ultimate goal be worthy of the effort?

PURE
KNOWLEDGE

THE STUFF A GURU
TELLS YOU

CHAPTER FOUR

This chapter answers the question "What is complete knowledge?" It explains and defines Maharishi's Vedic Science and Maharishi Ayurveda, which are the sources of the advanced recovery tools presented in subsequent chapters.

We need a science of complete knowledge. Without it, as a race, we will destroy ourselves. Modern science, with its fragmentary knowledge, has brought many perils. Each frontier of science is a double-edged sword—one that threatens as well as beckons. Nuclear power lights our cities, but creates nearly eternal carcinogenic waste—and the fear of nuclear terrorism. Medicine has worked miracles, but also has created virulent, drug-resistant diseases. Genetic engineering offers the opportunity to improve just about every living thing and, through mistakes or genetic warfare, the possibility of eliminating all life. Vedic science offers a more benign approach, one based on complete knowledge.

WHAT IS COMPLETE KNOWLEDGE?

If we analyze all possible knowledge, we see that it fits neatly into three categories. The first is knowledge of objects. This includes the solar system (astronomy), matter (physics), living objects (biology), a precise language for the description of any system (mathematics), and so on. We call this *objective knowledge,* and it includes all of modern science. Even psychology, with its emphasis on behavior, gets included in the category of objectivity.

Although the objective is most of what we learn in school, it is not all there is. Life is also subjective. Our sense of being, of existing, does not depend on mathematical formalisms. Nor are our feelings much swayed by the equations of physics. The subjective is a totally different domain, which includes the mind and especially the Self. Here we are concerned with ourselves as conscious beings. Thus, the second category is *subjective knowledge.* The subjective is as necessary to study and master as is the objective. It is equally as vast and as useful as all of modern science.

It seems that you could stop there. If you could stand at the junction of objectivity and subjectivity, then all that is subjective would be to one side of you, and all that is objective would be to the other. Everything in the world fits neatly into one of these two categories. Except—how do you know? In Western science we devote relatively little time to practically answering the question, How do you know (what you know)? There is a short tradition of the philosophy of science, and there are some theories of how we learn and how we process information, based on cognitive science. But these disciplines are immature. We need to delve deeply into the *process* of knowing. How does subjectivity come to know the most expressed levels of objectivity? How does subjectivity come to know *itself?* Adequately answering these questions brings power over ourselves and over our environment.

So the *process of knowing* is the third category. To sum up, knowledge is complete only if it covers all three categories: the knower, the known, and the process of knowing. This is the same as subjectivity, objectivity, and the link between the two.

Consider the world as we have set it up. It is object-based. We don't give anywhere near adequate status to inner life. To say that we are materialistic misses the point. Society's knowledge, goals, action, and ideals—our very paradigm, how we model the world on a gut level—completely *exclude* the subjective. You have been left out of your own world.

Trying to exist on one-third of knowledge—only the objective aspect—doesn't work because it is only one-third of life. Incomplete knowledge is ignorance (the opposite of enlightenment). Ignorance causes suffering. If you don't know how to ride a bicycle and keep falling off, you can't say suffering is the inevitable result of riding a bike. It's not. It is due only to lack of skill. In organizing the world, it isn't that we are not skillful enough. We don't know even the basics of how life works. Without basic knowledge, no amount of practice will bring success. Who could learn to ride a bicycle facing backward trying to pedal with their hands? The situation in the world is equally ludicrous.

So we need a science of complete knowledge. Such a science has existed for some time but has fallen into disuse and, until recently, into a state of disrepair. This science of complete knowledge is called *vedic science.* Vedic science includes full knowledge of the knower, the known, and the process of knowing. The purpose of vedic science, and the direct result of studying it, is enlightenment for the individual, and progress and prosperity for society.

KNOWLEDGE THAT IS EXPERIENCE

When we transcend, we experience the subjective aspect of nature —both our nature, and the Nature of the universe. The *process* of transcending familiarizes us with the process of knowing. When we transcend completely, and have self-referral awareness, we gain knowledge of the Self. In vedic science this level of knowledge is sometimes called *pure knowledge.* Pure knowledge occurs when knowledge and experience become one. Knower, known, and the process of knowing unify into one reality that is the simplest form of our awareness—the Self. It is an experience so complete it is also knowledge. Or, conversely, it is an understanding so profound it contains the experience. Experience, knowledge, organizing power, and even inspiration are so intimately woven together in the Self that they form a continuous fabric of Being. We study this level of ourselves in vedic science because it is a level of nature's functioning that has unlimited power. This power is completely benign and progressive, containing no negative elements: because it is universal, holistic, and infinitely correlated, there is no "other" to hurt.

PURE KNOWLEDGE LOST

Vedic science is an ancient science. It consists of many subdisciplines, each of which goes deeply into one area of life. The textbooks of vedic science are at least a few thousand years old. It is logical to ask: If this knowledge has been around so long, why aren't more people enlightened, and why is the world in such a mess? As it turns out, the textbooks are not enough. They assume one vital ingredient that a book cannot supply. *You* must provide the missing ingredient of *consciousness.* Unfortunately, for quite some time, few people have had the experience of pure consciousness. People became caught up in objective existence and forgot they had awareness. (That's like a fish dying of thirst.) If you don't know consciousness, then all the vedic textbooks are useless.

This was the situation for thousands of years. There have been, and still are today, great experts in each area of vedic science, but in general they have not adequately emphasized the basis of their discipline in consciousness. Thus, most are technicians, not real vedic scientists. Knowledge, disconnected from its source in consciousness, is incapable of promoting progress either for the individual or for the world.

This was the situation until the early 1970s, when a scientist (and monk) from India turned his attention from teaching meditation to revitalizing vedic science. Maharishi Mahesh Yogi is best known as the founder of the Transcendental Meditation technique. That, however, is only one accomplishment of a career devoted to unfolding the knowledge of the Self. Maharishi Mahesh Yogi is the world's leading researcher, scholar, and teacher in the field of consciousness. Under his direction, many of the world's top scientists from both East and West are re-establishing vedic science and once again making the knowledge accurate and useful.

PURE KNOWLEDGE FOUND

Because this is a substantial, although back to the original, revision of vedic science, we add Maharishi's name to it. This may seem odd, but it's how things are done in science. In this way the integrity of the knowledge is maintained. It is Einstein's theory of relativity, Newton's laws of motion, and Darwin's theory of evolution. Just so, it is Maharishi's Vedic Science.

Definition	**Maharishi's Vedic Science** is a *practical*, workable vedic science that is integrated with modern science and with our modern lifestyle; it does not leave out the element of consciousness. Maharishi's Vedic Science is a scientific approach to human development based on complete knowledge and systematic techniques. Complete knowledge results in enlightenment and mastery over natural law. In addition to what it offers the individual, Maharishi's Vedic Science provides the knowledge to establish society on any level of fulfillment and with any rate of progress.

Maharishi's Vedic Science is primarily concerned with consciousness, but that doesn't mean surface values are ignored. In fact, almost no area of life is left out. Vedic science contributes to education, mathematics, architecture, defense, astronomy, physics, cosmology, engineering, medicine, psychology, sociology, ecology, music, the performing arts, the visual arts, literature, linguistics, cognitive science, neuroscience, biology, and many other fields.

In vedic science, we study the different aspects of life, but always in relation to our Self (the Veda), and always with an evolutionary purpose. When we study music, we learn how music heals and balances both ourselves and our environment, and how it strengthens the connection between the two; we also learn how sound arises out of Silence. When we study architecture, we try to understand the eternal principles of natural law that structure a harmonious and healthy building, a building that, instead of damaging the environment, enlivens and nourishes it; we also study how form manifests from the Formless. When we study yoga, our goal is to experience the *full* richness and bliss of the Self, resulting in tremendously accelerated growth for the individual and peace for the world; we also study how thought arises from pure consciousness.

Another discipline of Maharishi's Vedic Science is ayurveda. Vedic science, as we have seen, is much bigger than ayurveda, but the knowledge of this specialty is critical for recovery.

WHAT IS MAHARISHI AYURVEDA?

The ultimate goal of ayurveda is to restore balance to all levels of the individual—Self, mind, body, behavior, and the environment—so we can live in enlightenment. It is a science of life. From our object-oriented standpoint, it appears to be only a science of health. That, however, is a misperception. We may then confuse ayurveda with modern medicine, which, although exceptional at treating injuries, is still a poor representative of total health care, often having more to do with business and politics than with healing. If we say ayurveda is a science of health, we have to say it is a science of perfect health.

Ayurveda, in its re-enlivened state, interpreted by Maharishi Mahesh Yogi in the light of consciousness, is referred to as Maharishi Ayurveda or Maharishi Vedic Medicine. This distinguishes it from the ayurveda that existed for thousands of years without doing adequate justice either to knowledge or to human potential.

Definition	**Maharishi Ayurveda** is a science of perfect health. Its knowledge spans the complete range of life, both individual and collective. Its practice emphasizes prevention. It works, not by treating symptoms, but by restoring balance. Maharishi Ayurveda always deals with the whole person.

GIVING CREDIT WHERE CREDIT IS DUE

Most of the ideas in this book come from Maharishi's Vedic Science. It is too cumbersome to attribute each idea and new term to Maharishi. So, assume that if the topic is consciousness, the ideas are Maharishi's; if it is recovery, then the concepts come from the different recovery experts, who are duly cited and referenced. And, if it's in the area joining consciousness and recovery, the ideas are mine (and should, therefore, be questioned even more critically). Also, from here on, the terms *vedic science* and *ayurveda* generally refer to Maharishi's Vedic Science and Maharishi Ayurveda.

I don't want to give the impression that Maharishi Mahesh Yogi is the only source for the knowledge of consciousness. My training and expertise, however, are in Maharishi's Vedic Science, and Maharishi Mahesh Yogi is considered by many of the enlightened to be a guru of gurus. The knowledge from his tradition is especially pure and, although traditional, is unmistakably relevant to our times.

THE REST OF THE BOOK

Based on the knowledge of the first four chapters, you now have a basic, but solid, understanding of consciousness and recovery. I'd like to spend the rest of the book introducing the advanced recovery tools.

When a normal person grows up, they acquire tools—knowledge, attitudes, strategies, and techniques—that allow them to overcome difficulties and create a strong, balanced life. To recover, we need the tools a normal person has, plus a few more. We need to stock our recovery toolbox. The following chapters show you different tools, taken from the tool chest of vedic science, and give you the opportunity to add them to your recovery toolbox. To learn how to use them, like a mechanic, to fix your specific problems, you need guidance more personal than a book can offer. The resources at the end of the book will connect you to people who can help.

Obviously, you will need other tools—ones not in this book—specific to your recovery and your issues. But I believe there are chapters in the story of your life that cannot be written without the knowledge in this book. Although it is possible to recover without it, I don't see how you can get enlightened.

HOW TO
TRANSCEND

CHAPTER FIVE

This chapter discusses meditation as a means for achieving self-referral. The Transcendental Meditation technique is presented as an effective form of meditation. It is Advanced Recovery Tool #1.

The most widespread recovery program, the Twelve Steps, incorporates, among other things, the recommendation for "meditation." However, no specific method is suggested. The word *meditation* has come to mean many things. Common among them is the use of the mind. Apart from that, they are as diverse and different as you can get. The Transcendental Meditation technique is a specific form of meditation. It is a special and distinct way of using the mind.

WHAT IS THE TRANSCENDENTAL MEDITATION TECHNIQUE?

Transcendental Meditation is a technique with one purpose: to transcend and restore self-referral. It enables us to find our Self. In chapter 2 we explained how transcending results in self-referral awareness. Although it wasn't made explicit, what we were really describing was the process of Transcendental Meditation.

Transcendental Meditation (TM) is a simple, natural, effortless, easy-to-learn mental technique. It is practiced for twenty minutes twice a day while sitting comfortably in a chair with one's eyes closed. It does not involve concentration or contemplation (or visualization, or affirmations, or guided imagery, etc.). It is not a philosophy, and it does not require any change in lifestyle. It is certainly not a religion. *TM* refers only to a technique of using and developing the mind.

TM results in profoundly deep rest, which allows the body to release deeply rooted stresses. During this process, the mind becomes highly alert. The combination of deep rest and alertness is responsible for the body adopting a healthier pattern of behavior.

How It Works

Transcendental Meditation allows the conscious mind to identify with its unbounded status. Maharishi Mahesh Yogi, the founder of the TM program, uses something called the "bubble diagram" to explain how this happens.[41]

Figure 5.1 compares the mind to a body of water, such as an ocean. We see a cross-section: waves on the surface and a series of bubbles rising from the depths. The bubbles represent thoughts. A thought starts where you would expect it to, at the source of thought. It proceeds up through all the levels of the mind, becoming less abstract and more concrete, until it reaches the conscious mind, where we consciously recognize it as a thought.

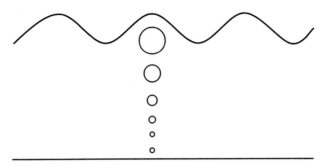

Figure 5.1 The "bubble diagram."

The surface of the ocean represents the active mind. This is the level from where you decide what to watch on TV, where to go for dinner, or, if you work for the Pentagon, how to deploy a nuclear arsenal. In introductory lectures, TM teachers say that, according to psychology, we use only 5 to 10 percent of our mental potential. This is the "conscious capacity" of the mind, which, in terms of the diagram, encompasses only the surface of the waves at the top.

Figure 5.2 adds transcending, where we reverse the direction of attention from outward to inward. Effortlessly, spontaneously, we follow thought back (the gray arrows in the diagram) through finer

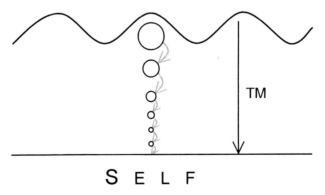

Figure 5.2 The process of transcending to the source of thought.

levels of thinking (smaller bubbles) to its source. The source of thought is an infinite reservoir of creativity, intelligence, and energy. "Source of thought" is synonymous with Self and Being.

In each meditation, we repeatedly dive deep within and then come back up to the surface. This process gives us familiarity with the full range of the mind. That means deeper levels of the mind, which are normally inaccessible, begin to be at our conscious command.

After some time of regular meditation, instead of using 5 to 10 percent of your mental potential, you may use 25 percent (which is what Einstein estimated he was using). After more time, you may use 50 percent; with more time, 75 percent. Once you are using 100 percent, you can go no further, and this is enlightenment.

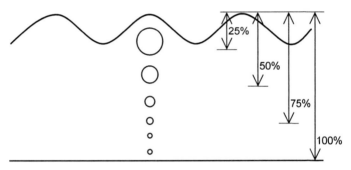

Figure 5.3 The path to enlightenment involves learning to use more and more of one's mind. Over time, we gain increasing familiarity with and command over deeper levels of the mind.

What makes a person great is the ability to act from more abstract and comprehensive levels of the mind. Before the Transcendental Meditation technique, there was no systematic, widely available method to develop this ability.

The surface of the mind—the 5 to 10 percent that most of us use—is the conscious mind. The depths of the mind—the 90 to 95 percent below the conscious mind—is the unconscious or subconscious mind. It is interesting to note that the enlightened have no *un*conscious mind. Enlightenment means consciousness—all of it—fully awakened. For the enlightened, there is no subconscious in which hidden desires can sneak up on them unawares. The enlightened would consider some psychologists' obsession with the unconscious to be somewhat peculiar. Don't examine the unconscious mind, get rid of it; make it conscious. Probing the unconscious here and there, the way some psychologists do it, is like looking for the Loch Ness monster—it is so murky down there that you really don't know what you're finding, and it goes on forever.

It is not normal to have aspects of your personality—levels of your mind—that are not consciously known and fully operable. The mind is the operator of the machinery of the brain. If the mind uses only 5 percent of its capacity, then 95 percent of the brain effectively remains shut down. It is strange that we use such a small fraction of our brain's potential, yet we wouldn't dream of operating any other machine that way. A car with eight cylinders wouldn't even run with only one spark plug firing. And that's working at more than 10 percent of capacity. All the problems of human existence are due to lack of development of our full potential.

THE MYTH THAT ALL
MEDITATIONS ARE THE SAME

Many people will tell you that it doesn't matter which meditation technique you learn. It is simply *not* true that all forms of meditation are equally effective or ineffective (depending on which side of the fence you stand).

If all you want is a sense of relief and a little unwinding, then, of course, any meditation will do. In fact, you don't even need to meditate. A walk in the park, a movie, or a game of racquetball will do the trick. But we all know that these activities have not solved, and cannot permanently solve, our problems. How many movies have we seen, how many pleasant walks and hours of exercise have we done, and still our problems remain?

Any technique that does not facilitate complete self-referral is only *temporarily* useful. It may be temporarily *very* useful; it may provide us with inspiration or propel us out of our current problem. But we will still be left in the field of life's problems. And for the addict, this may be a minefield of suffering.

You should ask three questions of any meditation technique:

1. Does it allow you to transcend the whole field of problems and experience unbounded awareness?
2. Does it release the deep-rooted stresses that keep you stuck in your problems?
3. Is it *systematic*—are you getting maximum benefit each time you do it?

In short, you should be asking: Will this really give me a "spiritual awakening"? If it will, then the knowledge that comes with it should describe the results of the program: higher states of consciousness. This is important to look for.

Moreover, it would seem wise to use something tried and true. Ideally, look for a technique that comes from a tradition of enlightened teachers who have demonstrated, generation after generation, that their knowledge and techniques work. An enlightened tradition provides the surest avenue to the greatest bliss.

WHY LEARN TO MEDITATE?

Everyone should learn to meditate. From the president of the United States to the derelict and homeless, from an addict contemplating suicide to a saint who will be beatified—everyone benefits from transcending and is able to give more to those around them.

For those in recovery, the following points should provide motivation to learn Transcendental Meditation:

1. There is no method more effective for transcending and gaining self-referral awareness.

2. Meditation gives the experience of inner freedom. We get a sample of enlightenment. This motivates the addict (in each of us) to work to make freedom permanent; otherwise, recovery becomes an intellectual game: we don't like how we feel when we act out, but we can't stop ourselves.

3. Once a person learns to meditate they gain the sensitivity to fully feel, sometimes for the first time, the negative effects of addictive

behavior. Then, naturally, there is reluctance to repeat the addictive action. The stronger the addiction, the stronger the painful recoil. The more clearly this is felt, the more intense the desire to give up the addiction. Tens of thousands of Americans have found Transcendental Meditation, by itself, sufficient to release them from addictive behavior.

4. TM doesn't involve the intellect. Therefore, you cannot sabotage your progress. The following may sound a little Zen: if you think about it, you will realize that the intellect is not adequate for guiding life. The intellect's role is bi-discriminatory, capable of choosing between two alternatives. It says left or right, yes or no. When there are a million possible choices—as there are every instant in life—the intellect must be transcended, allowing intuition or feeling to take over. Macroscopic, synthetic, and holistic decision making is necessary. Then the intellect can provide us with a reality check: Is the direction my intuition has chosen correct? That is a twofold decision the intellect can handle.

5. Furthermore, it is impossible to *learn* enough to recover. If your recovery is dependent on learning, you will never fully recover, because you have to *be* the knowledge. TM is a shortcut to Being, which is the "home of all knowledge."

6. TM makes bottoming out unnecessary. Bottoming out—the end of the downward addictive spiral in which life becomes so unbearable that we have to change—is only necessary (self-evidently) if we don't start changing before we hit the bottom. Bottoming out is so prevalent because in all the places where good guidance should be given, few are recommending a practical means for finding one's Self. Instead, businesses, through advertising, push the public toward object-referral. Educators, teachers, health professionals—even friends and family—are often little better. Meditation is a practical method for finding one's Self and is an antidote to the extreme object-referral fostered by society. Because meditation can be learned long before we recognize we are addicts—it has goals that are bigger than just recovery—it can prevent even the beginning of

the addictive spiral.

7. TM offers an approach to self-development that does not involve looking into the past. This way the psychology is saved from reliving trauma. In many situations, we *do* have to come to grips with certain events from the past, especially if we are holding onto feelings from traumatic events, or letting the past push us in unhealthy directions. However, too many people in recovery relentlessly dredge up the past in the vain hope that the more garbage they dig up, the sooner they can get on with their lives. This approach has been taken beyond what is reasonable. The past, the future, and even the present (in the sense of being bound by circumstances) all need to be transcended. It is possible to release stress, even stress caused by the most horrific events, without reliving it.

8. Control is one of the biggest issues for those in recovery. We try to control things that are impossible for anyone to control, and consequently feel frustrated, tired, incompetent, and unworthy. TM shows us how to let go. Throughout Melody Beattie's book *Codependent No More* is the refrain, "Detach." I know of no more powerful, complete, and easy means of accomplishing this than TM. In TM, you transcend everything you possibly can: you detach to the maximum possible extent.

9. We tend to treat the mind like a TV. When we can't handle our emotions, don't like our situation, or just get bored, we "change the channel." We distract ourselves and think about something else. What we should do is turn off the TV. TM is an effective means of "switching off the mind"—of allowing the mind to settle down and just be, resting in its own bliss and silent potential. Then, coming out of meditation, we are free of the programming of our past, free of the annoying static of random thoughts and judgments.

10. Naturalness is probably the most important aspect of TM. Naturalness has two benefits. The first is—and this may seem obvious—that during the process of meditation, we learn to be natural. This has a significant benefit: it resolves the antagonistic relationship

within oneself. The second is that, because TM is natural, you cannot release a stress before you are strong enough to withstand the intensity of the release. With other methods it is possible to "unstress" too soon or too quickly.

11. Transcendental Meditation is an engine that can drive recovery and keep it rapidly moving. You will need a lot more, but without an engine you are not going anywhere. The progress of nonmeditators is not commensurate with the amount of work they put in. They are pushing the car instead of driving it.

12. TM trains the body to maintain high levels of neurotransmitters associated with contentment, a sense of well-being, peace, and inhibition of pain.

13. According to Maharishi Mahesh Yogi, during the process of transcending, the mind traverses all levels of the personality and all levels of creation. Due to the nature of the technique of TM, this means that all aspects of your personality are enlivened and brought into harmony with the universe. If this is true, TM would be an especially effective method for holistic development.

14. Meditators are more alive. They are more attuned to themselves. They are more playful and fun to be with. TM allows inner qualities to blossom. Meditators feel joy inside and grow in inner beauty. People are drawn to that. TM fits well into any strategy for becoming desirable, making friends, and richly enjoying life.

15. When you learn to meditate, you begin the ultimate quest, the quest to find your Self.

DOES IT
REALLY WORK?

CHAPTER SIX

This chapter looks at research showing that transcending (through Transcendental Meditation):

- *promotes recovery from addictive behavior*
- *releases us from the causes of codependence*
- *addresses the problems of the adult child*
- *heals the effects of trauma*
- *restores all levels of self-referral*

ADDICTION

To date, thirty-six studies have looked at how Transcendental Meditation affects substance abuse and how it can be used for the treatment and prevention of addiction.[42] Several researchers—Drs. Gelderloos, Walton, Orme-Johnson, and Alexander—compiled a review of twenty-four studies. They published the results in *The International Journal of Addictions.*[43] I will take you through their findings, which, as you will see, cover a lot of ground.

Let's begin with an overview. In the studies, TM was compared to or used along with relaxation programs, psychotherapy, group therapy, Twelve Step programs such as Alcoholics Anonymous, a number of drug treatment programs (including inpatient treatments), and other programs for self-development. It was routinely found that TM was more effective than other treatments alone, and that adding TM substantially improved an existing program.

TM was found to be effective:

- on an inpatient basis
- on an outpatient basis
- regardless of the addict's age: high school student, college student, or adult
- regardless of the degree of use of the addictive substance— from casual nonaddicted users to skid-row chronic alcoholics
- both short-term and long-term: the effects start immediately, continue over time, do not trail off, and are cumulative
- in prison settings
- regardless of the addict's socioeconomic background
- for a broad range of chemicals: soft drugs, hard drugs, tranquilizers, antidepressants, caffeine, cigarettes, alcohol, and prescription drugs
- in removing the causes of the addictive behavior
- in mitigating addiction's harmful effects on the mind and body
- alongside other treatment methods, where TM increases the effectiveness of the other treatment, makes it work for a larger percentage of the treatment population, and speeds

up the recovery process
- in creating a distaste for the addictive substance
- in assisting in the treatment of mental illness

Studies also indicated that TM meditators are more likely to continue their recovery program than people using other approaches alone.

Now let's look at specific studies, starting with a historical perspective.

TM Used by the General Population

The first step in doing research in a new field is to see whether there is any effect at all. This was accomplished by a retrospective survey: 1,800 TM meditators completed a questionnaire on their drug use.[44] Over 80 percent had misused drugs in the six months prior to starting TM. After an average of twenty months of meditation, approximately 90 percent were drug-free for all classes of drugs—including hard drugs, such as heroin and cocaine, as well as alcohol, cigarettes, and prescription medication.

The next step in research is to determine exactly what causes the change. Researchers started by simply asking. In a 1971 study in Canada, almost all (92 percent) of 400 meditators attributed their reduction in drug use directly to TM.[45]

Then researchers added control groups. A control group, in this case the peers of those learning to meditate, serves as a benchmark for comparison. Studies that included a control group showed nonmeditators experienced no reduction in substance misuse, while those practicing TM had substantial reductions. An example is a study conducted in Australia, funded by the Federal Schools Commission.[46] Forty high school students, average age sixteen, were taught TM. They were compared to carefully matched nonmeditating students. The meditators reduced their drug use, whereas drug use went up for the nonmeditators. This included use of alcohol, hard drugs, and prescription drugs.

Another example is a twenty-month study on cigarette smoking.[47] Over 900 meditators participated. The control group consisted of six thousand people who attended TM introductory lectures but did not start meditation. Eighty-one percent of regular meditators, and 55 percent of irregular meditators, quit or reduced their smoking, whereas only 33 percent of the nonmeditating controls quit or reduced smoking. This study leads us to believe that the effects of TM are long-lasting, not a flash in the pan. Further, as most participants learned TM for reasons other than quitting smoking, healing addiction is likely to be a natural side effect of meditation.

TM Used in Treatment Programs

Next, we'll briefly summarize the results of six studies, each focusing on a different population: young drug users; skid-row alcoholics; mental patients; poor drug addicts; chronic, highly addicted drug users; and kids charged with possession of marijuana. Some of these studies present clinical evaluations of the effects of TM; some are sophisticated experiments using random assignment of participants to matched control groups.

The first study was a clinical observation of five subjects, all juvenile offenders, most of them caught with marijuana. Results: *through TM, drug use went down or stopped, anxiety decreased, self-regard increased, and the results of self-evaluations and parents' reports were more positive.*[48]

The second study evaluated the use of TM in a psychiatric drug treatment program. The subjects were twelve drug users with chronic and strong dependency. Results: *addicts taught TM recovered faster than nonmeditating participants in the same program.*[49]

The third study was on seventy-six young drug users, between ages fifteen and twenty-three, attending a crisis aid program at a drug rehabilitation center in Germany. Results: *usage decreased for all types of drugs, and 75 percent reported no drug use after six months practicing TM.*[50]

The fourth study, done in Sweden, had a rigorous experimental design: random assignment to matched groups. The subjects were twenty poor, hepatitis-infected drug users between the ages of seventeen and twenty-four. One group immediately learned TM. The other group—the control group—waited three months, during which time they attended group therapy. The results: *drug use went down for the TM meditators and up for the control group. Com-*

pared to the therapy group, the meditators grew less anxious, less tense, and more stable. Also, the meditators reported more joy and fulfillment in life.[51]

The fifth study was on forty-two addicts and mental patients at a Veterans Administration Hospital Vocation Rehabilitation Unit. Results: *those in the TM group were better able to get jobs, were less likely to be incarcerated, were more likely to be in outpatient programs than in a hospital or prison, and lived longer.*[52]

The sixth study is the most remarkable. It was funded by the National Institute on Alcohol Abuse and Alcoholism—one of the National Institutes of Health—and focused on chronic alcoholics who were inpatients at the Rehabilitation Center for Alcohol in Occoquan, Virginia. The study is summarized in the *International Journal of Addictions* (the full study is available in the *Alcoholism Treatment Quarterly*[53]):

> One hundred and twenty skid-row alcoholics (70% of whom were black) from Washington, D.C. were randomly assigned to either TM, one of two relaxation programs, or standard treatment. After 3 months of inpatient treatment, the subjects were persistently followed in the field for 18 months using a sophisticated interview procedure, with a total loss of only 5% of the sample. At the end of the 18 months, 65% of the TM subjects were completely abstinent, compared to 25% of the subjects receiving standard treatment. TM subjects also improved more on measures of psychological health than did subjects with the relaxation treatments and had an abstinence rate significantly higher than that of subjects in one of these treatments. During the 3-month inpatient program, attendance at both publicly monitored and covertly monitored daily group meditation sessions was approximately 90%. After 6-months of the outpatient period, even without systematic follow-up to ensure regularity, the majority of TM subjects was still regular in practice. The researchers concluded that severely alcoholic patients with low IQs and moderate brain damage can regularly practice the TM program, obtaining benefits similar to those in more moderate drug offenders.[54]

Of particular note: adding TM increased the long-term effectiveness of the standard treatment—which included attendance at Alcoholics

Anonymous (AA)—by 2.6 times. Simply put, TM makes AA more than twice as effective. If you are trying to stay sober, that is *very* significant.

TM Used by Prisoners with a History of Drug Abuse

The next six studies were done on "prisoners with a history of high drug use who had proven resistant to rehabilitation through other means."[55] Drug use, being against the prisons' strict rules and carrying stiff penalties, was hard to measure. Therefore, other indicators of recovery were needed. The researchers chose to evaluate the prisoners on behavior, self-development, and the return rate to prison.

In different studies, groups of inmates in several prisons were instructed in TM. The prisons included La Tuna Federal Penitentiary, in Texas;[56] Stillwater State Prison, in Minnesota;[57] Milan Federal Correctional Institution, in Michigan;[58] and the Massachusetts Correctional Institution (Walpole).[59] Also included were about 250 men released on parole from three prisons in the California Department of Corrections.[60]

Inmates found physical, mental, and behavioral improvements:

- reduced anxiety
- increased self-esteem
- decreased hostility
- reduced obsessive-compulsive behavior
- decreased rule infraction
- increased emotional stability and maturity
- increased social outgoingness
- increased positive recreational activity
- increased educational activity

Especially noteworthy is the reduction in recidivism (not returning to prison with a new conviction). Two of the studies[61] kept track of the prisoners after release. The meditating inmates had 30 to 40 percent less recidivism than inmates who did other programs— including psychotherapy and drug counseling.

IT IS NOT JUST ADDICTS

Now we take a break from studies that target addicts, and consider the benefits for groups that haven't seemed to warrant direct study: adult children and codependents. Let's start with adult children of dysfunctional families.

It Works for Adult Children

From a researcher's perspective, the ideal would be to gather subjects who identify themselves as adult children, teach half of them TM, let the other half be controls, and then see if, compared to the control group, TM healed adult child attributes and behavior patterns. This would make a nice Ph.D. thesis. To my knowledge, no one has done this. So we have to take an alternative approach and use research on the general population. This is reasonable, as a large percentage of the general population is adult children.

If people who do TM tend to find improvement in each of the areas in which adult children have behavioral deficits, then transcending should facilitate the recovery of adult children. The results are shown in Table 6.1, which lists the primary attributes of the adult child, along with research findings[62] on Transcendental Meditation.

It Works for Codependents

Codependence has been described as a huge rift between our public and private self.[63] What we do on the outside doesn't match what we feel on the inside. This rift starts to close through TM. We gain the ability to express our inner self. We lose the fear of being who we really are.

As with adult children, there is no research on subjects identified as codependents. However, it is evident that transcendence counteracts the primary cause of codependence: outer-directedness. This claim is backed up by research[64] that shows TM meditators have:

- greater inner-directedness
- increased inner locus of control
- growth of inner fulfillment independent of outside stimulation

Table 6.1 The following table matches research on Transcendental Meditation (general population) to the characteristic problems of adult children. The numbers refer to studies in the five volumes of collected papers of research on the TM program[65] (a few of the studies include the TM-Sidhi program). Adult child attributes are adapted from Janet Woititz' *Adult Children of Alcoholics*, with additions from other experts.[66]

Adult Child Attribute	TM Research Finding	Study Number
Don't know what is normal, natural behavior.	Increased naturalness	65, 77, 277, 290, 308
	Increased spontaneity	64, 65, 69, 70, 76, 77, 151, 153, 277, 290, 308, 316
	Increased self-actualization, and increased integration, unity, and wholeness of personality	64, 67, 69, 70, 72, 74, 76, 78, 144, 151, 153, 155, 239
	Growth of higher states of consciousness	19, 99–104, 216, 258, 284, 312
Don't finish projects they start.	Increased time competence: increased ability to think and act efficiently in the present	69, 70, 76, 151, 153, 155
	Increased persistence	153
	Increased effectiveness	65, 77, 161, 272
	Greater organizational ability	164
	Increased practicality and realism	153
Lie unnecessarily and habitually, including about one's feelings.	Increased ability to express one's feelings spontaneously	64, 69, 70, 151, 153, 316
	Greater sense of social responsibility	138, 158
Are extremely self-critical and perfectionist.	Increased self-acceptance	70, 81, 151
	Increased emotional strength: decreased unwelcome thoughts	150
	Greater satisfaction with one's moral worth	156
	Increased ability to see man as essentially good	76, 153, 266
	Decreased sense of physical inadequacy	67
	Less sense of social inadequacy	266

94

Adult Child Attribute	TM Research Finding	Study Number
Take themselves too seriously and are unable to have fun.	Increased happiness	90, 147
	Increased spontaneity	64, 65, 69, 70, 76, 77, 151, 153, 277, 290, 308, 316
	Increased good humor	65, 77, 277, 290, 308
	Increased good-naturedness, friendliness, and loyalty	73
	Increased outgoingness and tendency to participate	73, 150, 153
	Decreased anxiety	33, 35, 61, 62, 68, 71, 72, 74, 75, 78, 81, 84, 88–90, 92, 93, 95, 125, 133, 138, 143, 145, 148, 150, 153, 154, 157, 160, 234, 238, 268, 273, 275, 278, 280, 281, 284, 290, 308, 310, 311, 313, 314, 316
	Decreased depression	65, 67, 74, 78, 95, 143, 147, 150, 158, 238, 239, 268, 273, 277, 290, 308, 313
Have problematic relationships, dealing with issues related to intimacy, trust, and fear of abandonment.	Increased capacity for warm interpersonal relationships	69, 70, 73, 76, 77, 149, 151, 153, 268, 277, 290, 316
	Decreased social introversion	87
	Greater marital satisfaction: greater intimacy	165
	Increased friendliness	65, 77, 277, 290
	Increased self-confidence	65, 77, 150, 261, 277, 290, 304, 308
	Greater selectivity in personal relationships	268
Need others' approval, losing heart without continual encouragement and support.	Less tendency to worry about other people's opinions	164
	Increased inner-directedness: greater independence and self-supportiveness	64, 69, 70, 72, 76, 151, 153, 155, 268
	Less need to belong and be accepted	268

Adult Child Attribute	TM Research Finding	Study Number
Feel uncomfortably different and are often marginalized.	Enhanced self-acceptance	61, 70, 151
	Enhanced self-concept	141, 144, 146, 148, 156, 274
	Increased ego-strength	67, 150, 153
	Greater empathy	149
Are impulsive and addictive.	Decreased impulsive behavior	71, 138, 316
	Improvements in addictive disorders, including alcoholism, drug abuse, and gambling	95, 157, 283
	Decreased behavioral rigidity	83, 103, 250, 300
	Greater self-control	65, 77, 153, 308
	Increased self-discipline	316
Are loyal even when they clearly shouldn't be.	Increased autonomy and independence	62, 71, 151, 153
	Increased self-reliance	65, 77, 153, 277
	Increased self-sufficiency	65, 77, 150, 153, 277, 290, 308
	Greater selectivity in personal relationships	268
Get stuck in rigid thinking.	Greater adaptability of mental orientation	71
	Enhanced creativity	62, 63, 103, 150, 257, 260, 294, 305
	Increased innovation	62
	Increased resourcefulness	150
	Improved problem-solving ability	58, 62
Are prone to workaholism.	Decreased overactive and impulsive behavior	157
	Greater ability to accomplish more with less effort	130, 164
	Greater ability to assign priorities	164
	Greater commitment to personal growth	138
	Increased sensitivity to one's own needs and feelings	69, 70, 72, 151, 153

Adult Child Attribute	TM Research Finding	Study Number
Need to create crises; unable to enjoy nonchaotic progress.	Growth of inner fulfillment independent of outside stimulation	249
	Decreased number of situations in life perceived as problems	142
	Decreased number of serious problems experienced	142
	Increased contentment	65, 67, 77, 150, 277, 290, 308
Have problems with teamwork: difficulty communicating; difficulty giving and receiving criticism; need to control; overreacting; tendency to be overly responsible or extremely irresponsible.	Increased ability to cooperate with others	73, 161, 164
	Less sensitivity to criticism	67
	Greater tolerance of authority	138
	Improved relations with supervisors and co-workers	96
	Greater respect for the views of others	164
	Decreased tendency to dominate	65, 77, 268, 290
	Increased ability to be objective, fair-minded, and reasonable	316
Are stressed out.	Improved resistance to stress	25–28, 123
	Maintenance of a relaxed style of physiological functioning outside of meditation	6, 18, 30, 197
	Biochemical indication of reduced stress	109

97

- increased self-reliance
- less tendency to worry about other people's opinions

TM meditators find they can more richly experience their emotions, and that TM has reduced the chaos they may feel on the inside. As researchers put it, TM meditators have increased sensitivity to their own needs and feelings, and decreased hidden mental turbulence.[67] Furthermore, research shows that self-confidence and self-acceptance grow. This allows meditators to start taking care of their needs and start living their own lives.

Table 6.2 lists the problems of codependents and matches them with research findings.

IT RELEASES US FROM THE PAIN OF THE PAST

Some years ago, as I was reading a paper on TM and treatment for post-Vietnam adjustment, it occurred to me—as it has for many others[68]—that the more extreme symptoms of the adult child are the same as those of combat veterans suffering from post-traumatic stress disorder.

Dr. Charles Whitfield, author of *Healing the Child Within,* holds that post-traumatic stress disorder (PTSD), together with codependence, with which it overlaps and interacts, is quite common in troubled or dysfunctional families. Dr. Whitfield further points out, "PTSD is but an extreme extension of the broad condition that results from stifling the True Self in any form."[69]

If we can show that veterans with PTSD recover through Transcendental Meditation, that would give hope to anyone who has suffered any form of trauma.

In 1981, veterans seeking help at the Denver Vietnam Veterans Outreach (Vet Center) program were randomly assigned to a TM group or a psychotherapy group. The TM group met once a week for three months, which was the duration of the study. They also meditated twenty minutes twice a day. The psychotherapy group had weekly individual psychotherapy sessions with a Vet Center therapist; when appropriate, they could also participate in group or family counseling.

Codependent Attribute	TM Research Finding
Difficulty in accurately identifying feelings	Increased sensitivity to one's own needs and feelings
Difficulty in expressing feelings	Increased ability to express one's feelings spontaneously
Difficulty in forming or maintaining close or intimate relationships	Increased capacity for warm interpersonal relationships
Perfectionism (includes extreme self-criticism)	Increased practicality and realism; increased self-acceptance
Rigidity in behavior or attitudes	Greater adaptability of mental orientation
Difficulty adjusting to change	Decreased behavioral rigidity
Feeling overly responsible for others' behavior or feelings	Less tendency to worry about other people's opinions
Constant need for others' approval in order to feel good about self	Increased inner-directedness: greater independence and self-supportiveness
Difficulty making decisions	Increased ability to think and act efficiently in the present
Feeling powerless, as if nothing I do makes any difference	Decreased number of situations in life perceived as problems
A basic sense of shame and low self-esteem	Greater satisfaction with one's moral worth; enhanced self-concept
Avoidance of conflict	Increased leadership ability, persuasiveness, forcefulness, and influence; growth of a more brave, adventurous, action-oriented nature

Table 6.2 Research on Transcendental Meditation addressing the characteristic problems of codependents. The list of codependent attributes is from Robert Subby's book *Lost in the Shuffle.*

Before starting either TM or therapy, the veterans were tested for degree of symptoms of PTSD and assessed on other stress-related measures. They were tested again after three months.

The results, reported by Brooks and Scarano in the *Journal of Counseling and Development:*

The participants in the TM group reported significant

reductions in depression, anxiety, emotional numbness, alcohol consumption, family problems, difficulty in getting a job, insomnia, and overall symptoms of PTSD....

Veterans in the TM group commonly reported that, "I feel after I meditate that I no longer have the same intensity of tension, rage, and guilt inside—it's as if a huge burden has been lifted."

The therapy group showed little improvement over the 3-month period. It could be that measurable benefits of psychotherapy for PTSD are seen only after an extended period of time. After 3 months of treatment, 7 out of 10 participants in the TM group felt improved enough that they saw no further need for the services of the Vet Center. Three members of the TM group, however, still wanted to work on some issues pertaining to their Vietnam experience. Therefore, these individuals decided to remain in therapy in addition to practicing TM regularly. The TM program may sufficiently relieve the symptoms of many individuals with PTSD. In some cases, however, a combined approach of both TM and psychotherapy (or other approaches) may be the preferred treatment.[70]

It is worth noting the effect on drinking. The veterans rated their alcohol consumption, using a scale of one to four, where four equaled no problem. No one learning TM is told to change their behavior, so there were no strictures against drinking, yet after three months, the TM group's response improved from an average of 2.00 to 3.67. The psychotherapy group remained constant at 2.17.

Because of the well-documented and full range of mental and physical health benefits of Transcendental Meditation, the government will pay for any veteran, with a prescription from a VA doctor, to learn TM.

IS TRANSCENDENTAL MEDITATION *THE* MOST EFFECTIVE?

The point here is not that there is only one path of personal development. All roads do indeed lead to self-discovery and ultimately to enlightenment, but some roads are more direct than others. Let's look at anxiety, self-actualization, and death.

Anxiety

An enormous number of experiments has been done on methods for facilitating relaxation. It occurred to one meditating researcher, Ken Eppley, who at the time was employed by Stanford University, that someone should do a study of studies.[71] This is called a *meta-analysis* or *meta-study*. Dr. Eppley collected all studies indexed under relaxation or meditation. To compare the studies, Dr. Eppley looked for something in common. He chose anxiety because this was the most widely reported finding. He then compared the reduction of anxiety found in each study. This was done by calculating the *effect size,* which is an attempt to create a standard unit of measurement. Dr. Eppley divided the techniques into general categories:

- TM
- progressive relaxation
- other meditation
- all relaxation techniques

He further divided them into subcategories:

- concentration meditation
- Sanskrit mantras used with a permissive attitude (researchers in the original studies trying to mimic TM's general features)
- Benson's technique
- EMG biofeedback
- placebo techniques (in which the subject was told to do something mental or physical that the researchers knew ahead of time had no actual value in producing relaxation)

The results: *TM had a significantly larger effect size than any other relaxation procedure, approximately twice the effect size of the other categories.*

Concentration meditation was the least effective, causing either no change or slightly increasing anxiety. Although concentration techniques (for example, concentrating on a candle flame) were popular twenty years ago, they have all but disappeared. Now we know why: they don't work.

There is another curious finding. Tied for second place is the placebo. In other words, most techniques were no better than, and often not as good as, taking it easy and believing relaxation would occur.

Self-Actualization

Recall that, according to Maslow, self-actualization is associated with Being. Maslow felt that even a single experience of Being could drag a person back from the precipice of self-destructive behavior. He considered the experience of Being pivotal in finding meaning and fulfillment in life.[72]

A second meta-study was done on self-actualization.[73] It might be worthwhile to try to be clearer about what self-actualization is. Self-actualization becomes quite vague when you try to pin it down. However, there are tests for it.[74] Scientists look, in general, for time competence and inner directedness. They look specifically for:

1. The capacity for intimate contact
2. Acceptance of natural aggression
3. Synergy (ability to deal with opposites)
4. Believing that man is basically good
5. Self-regard (you like yourself because of your good qualities)
6. Self-acceptance (you like yourself in spite of your less-good qualities)
7. Spontaneity
8. Being aware of your own needs and feelings
9. An ability to be flexible in applying principles to real-life situations
10. Holding the values of a self-actualizing person

These attributes are, in fact, very similar to the items in the research columns of Tables 6.1 and 6.2, which would lead us to believe that TM is surprisingly effective in facilitating self-actualization. And this, of course, is what the meta-study concluded. TM was found to be more effective in increasing self-actualization than any other meditation procedure or relaxation technique—the TM effect size was about *three times* as large. One of the specific studies found substantial positive gains in every category of self-actualization—in just two months.[75]

Aging and Death

While a post-doctoral fellow at Harvard University, Dr. Charles Alexander embarked on an ambitious study.[76] He chose a very elderly population, average age eighty-one, who were living in retirement homes. He randomly assigned seventy-three of them to learn one of three techniques, or to learn nothing—the control group. The three techniques were TM, "mindfulness," and a pseudomeditation. Mindfulness was a mental procedure designed to make the mind more active and alert, thus attempting to improve quality of life and increase lifespan. Pseudomeditation was a "generic meditation" that many scientists might consider equivalent to TM. It was included to test the hypothesis, held by some researchers (and counselors and therapists), that all meditation procedures yield the same results.

What stands out in this study's design is that no matter which procedure was learned, the participant's expectation for improvement was the same. Each technique was practiced, eyes closed, for twenty minutes twice a day. Each used the same instructional format. And the teacher of each technique touted the same list of benefits.

After three months, changes were measured in several categories of physical and mental health, including cognitive abilities. The TM group improved the most in almost all categories, with mindfulness coming in second.

After three years, the mortality rate was calculated: an average of 62.5 percent of all 478 residents of the retirement homes were still alive. The survival rate for the control group was 77 percent; for pseudomeditation, 65 percent; and for mindfulness, 87 percent. *The TM group had a 100 percent survival rate.* Note that the pseudomeditation had a survival rate about the same as doing nothing. In contrast, the members of the TM group lived longer and had clearer minds and better health.

LEVELS OF SELF-REFERRAL

Let's finish with a whirlwind tour of general (nonaddiction) research on TM, stopping at each level of self-referral, starting with the environment and working our way in to the Self. Once this is done, you will have been acquainted with a fairly good sampling of the six hundred studies done on TM. [77]

Environment

There is a great deal of research which shows that if enough people transcend, or if a much smaller number of expert meditators transcends deeply enough, negative factors in society are positively affected. For example, violence, crime, communicable diseases, accidents, and war have all been shown to be reduced by the collective effects of transcending. This we will discuss in more detail in chapter 10.

Behavior

We have amply discussed the positive changes possible for addicts, codependents, and adult children who practice TM, but there is an even broader range of benefits. Couples and families find greater harmony and satisfaction. Students' grades go up. Workers like their jobs more, have less desire to change jobs, perform better, and improve in relationships with peers and supervisors. They also get fewer headaches and backaches, and are less anxious and tense. Employers find that sick days and absenteeism go down. And, as the number of meditators in a company goes up, so does the company's productivity and profitability.

Body

One of the most impressive studies involves a statistical analysis done during a five-year period on two thousand TM meditators who were part of a health insurance group. They were compared to non-meditating groups matched by age, profession, gender, and health insurance term. Results: *TM cut in half both the number of visits to the doctor and the rate of hospital admissions.* In addition, hospitalization in the TM group went up only gradually with age, whereas with nonmeditating groups, hospitalization started to skyrocket after age forty.

The researchers looked at seventeen categories of health problems requiring hospital admissions. In all categories, the TM meditators were substantially healthier. Examples of the differences between the groups: the TM group "had 87 percent less hospitalization for heart disease, 55 percent less for cancer, 87 percent less for nervous system disorders, 73 percent for nose, throat, and lung problems."[78]

Another study found that meditators not only get healthier, they get younger. Doctors, using purely physiological measures (such as blood pressure, near point of vision, and hearing acuity), can estimate a person's physiological age, which may be older or younger than their chronological age. Using the physiological age, as opposed to the chronological age, meditators (with five or more years of meditation) are an average of twelve years younger than their nonmeditating counterparts. In other words, your passport may say you are fifty, but you look and feel like you are thirty-eight.

Other studies have found that TM meditators:

- sleep better
- have less stress hormones in their bloodstream
- have lower blood pressure and fewer symptoms of hypertension
- have lower cholesterol levels
- are more relaxed and recover quickly from stress

The Thinking Mind
Research shows that TM meditators:

- become more creative
- improve in long-term and short-term memory
- are more focused
- are less distracted by their environment

EEG studies imply that, both during and after meditation, the mind becomes more coherent as a whole, accesses more of the brain, and is simultaneously more calm and alert.

Intellect

It is held by many psychologists that IQ goes up until about age sixteen, and then, in the typical case, gradually declines until death. Surprisingly, college education does nothing for your intelligence. You fill the container of knowledge, but you don't expand that container. *TM actually raises your IQ.* This is the equivalent of putting a bigger engine in your car. You can go from underpowered to high powered.

TM studies have repeatedly documented increased IQ. The most recent study lasted two and a half years. It found that, while non-meditating students kept the same IQ, college students who did TM raised their IQ by five points.[79]

Feelings

Research findings include increased emotional stability, more sensitivity to one's own feelings, ability to express feelings spontaneously, increased good humor, decreased hidden mental turbulence, greater happiness, and decreased depression.

Ego

We have already said TM increases self-actualization. Research shows it also improves ego-strength, self-acceptance, and self-regard.

Meditators change how they see themselves. They also change how they see others. Their sense of self expands to encompass more of their environment. This results in increasingly responsible behavior. Studies done with high school and college students show rapid growth to higher levels of moral reasoning.

One study on self-development found that in six months, TM meditators experienced more personal development than students usually do in four years of college.[80] This is particularly remarkable because most of the meditators in this study didn't graduate from high school, and some didn't finish grade school. They were inmates in a maximum security prison—not a particularly conducive environment for psychological growth. TM was compared to psychological counseling, a drug abuse program, and two personal development programs. TM scored substantially better than each of the others in increased self-development, decreased aggression, and decreased symptoms of mental disorders.

Self

Although some might say that the experience of self-referral awareness is merely a subjective delusion, there is ample scientific evidence verifying its reality. Studies show that when deep in meditation, the body shifts to a dramatically more "relaxed" bio-chemistry, while brain wave (EEG) studies reveal a broad spectrum of intense coherence that is markedly different from mere relaxation. This is a state of consciousness both physiologically and psychologically different from waking, dreaming, or sleeping. It is a fourth major state of consciousness. One study measured the breath rate of long-term meditators. They were told to press a button after they experienced pure consciousness. It was found that, when they transcended, their breath actually *stopped.* Frequently this lasted for 30 seconds, sometimes for up to a minute. Afterward there was little or no compensatory breathing. The mind, resting in the Self, attains an integrated, powerful, and silent state—and the body mirrors this. It is similar to the peak functioning of a well-conditioned athlete.

From a more anecdotal perspective, it has always amazed me how quickly new meditators have clear experiences of the Self— often within the first few instructional meetings.

Transcending—getting closer to the Self—is the source of all the benefits. As we explained earlier, in terms of self-referral diagrams, if you change the deepest level, then, in a domino effect, surface levels spontaneously improve. When we transcend deeply, then mind, body, behavior, and environment are all affected.

AN ETHNOGRAPHIC APPROACH

Science has begun to abandon its idealistic notion that it can attain true objectivity by confining itself to numbers and statistics. There has been a significant shift to a more balanced mix of quantitative and qualitative analysis. The latter pays careful attention to the human side: to context, to culture, to the tiniest details—because that is where we often find the critical knowledge that gives us insight and helps solve the problem. It is said that if you want to know *what* is in a bag-lady's cart, use quantitative analysis; if you want to know *why,* use qualitative analysis. Scientists who eschew numbers in favor of a careful study of context are called *ethnographers.* Their reports read like scholarly novels: they write in narrative, about people and their lives.

Thus, to complete our analysis, we need to look for carefully documented narrative accounts of people who have used meditation, ayurveda, and vedic science in their recovery. An excellent book that takes us a step in that direction is *Self-Recovery: Treating Addictions Using Transcendental Meditation and Maharishi Ayur-Veda,* edited by David O'Connell and Charles Alexander.[81] This book is not formally ethnographic, but it will suit our needs. It has great case studies, and several people give their personal experiences as addicts or counselors. The book is long—over 500 pages—and highly technical. However, five of the chapters (by the authors listed below) complement the knowledge in this book and can be enjoyed even by the lay reader.

Catherine Bleick describes case histories of some of the 250 Alcoholics Anonymous members instructed in TM during a six-year period in Los Angeles. She shows beyond doubt that not only does vedic science not conflict with AA and other Twelve Step programs, but also it enhances the programs' power. In the area of hard-core substance abuse, Pat Corum describes his transformation from a drug addict on death row (for armed robbery and multiple homicides) to a married suburbanite with loving grandchildren; while George Ellis writes, with moving detail, of teaching TM in prisons around the world. Linda Keniston-Dubocq details the application of TM in her medical practice, including a discussion of a female patient who was both an alcoholic and a survivor of childhood abuse. This case is notable in that it includes not only meditation, but also many other tools of Maharishi's Vedic Science. Two chapters are written by individuals who have extensive experience treating addiction and have particularly valuable insights. The first is by Dr. Frank Staggers, medical director of the San Francisco Haight-Ashbury Free Clinic's Drug Detoxification, Rehabilitation, and Aftercare Program. The second is by Dr. David O'Connell, a psychologist with twenty years' experience treating addicts, teaching, and consulting to treatment facilities.

CONCLUSION

In this chapter we looked at what happens to a person's life when they become self-referral. We studied the effects of Transcendental Meditation, because TM is the most widely used, most easily learned, and, according to both theory and research, very likely the most effective method of becoming self-referral.

From what we have seen, it is clear that just about everyone should add a self-referral practice to their recovery program. Consider the points we covered:

1. There is overwhelming evidence that transcending unfreezes adult human development, allowing us to actualize our full potential.
2. The Transcendental Meditation program is tremendously effective for the recovering addict. We have seen that TM works for rich and poor, for young and old, for educated and uneducated. It works at any stage of the addictive process. It works in the streets; it works in inpatient facilities; it works in prisons. It works regardless of the addictive substance. It works alongside any treatment program. TM's effectiveness is immediately felt and keeps working over an extended period of time. It heals the causes as well as the effects of addiction.
3. TM addresses the problems of the adult child.
4. TM heals the causes of codependence.
5. TM, as seen from the study on Vietnam veterans with post-traumatic stress disorder, dissolves the stress of traumatic events.
6. The effects of TM are holistic, enhancing all levels of mind, body, behavior, and environment.
7. TM appears to be *the* most effective.

AYURVEDIC PHYSIOLOGY

HAPPINESS
AND THE BODY

In this chapter, we discover a new way of understanding the body, one that lets us become free—and stay free—of the physical component of addiction. The lifestyle changes suggested by this new understanding constitute our second advanced recovery tool: the ayurvedic art of balancing the body and mind.

The least sophisticated and most outdated understanding of the body . . . is probably the one your doctor has. Certainly it is complicated. It's too complicated to make any sense. And it's practically useless in recovery. Doctors are way out in left field, and addiction is a pinch-hitter that bunts. If current medical theory is so great, why can't doctors—who know this theory best—keep themselves out of addiction? Consider this statistic, reported in the *New York Times:*

> The state Commission of Investigation estimated that up to 16 percent of the 29,000 medical and osteopathic doctors licensed to practice in New Jersey may have drug or alcohol problems. According to the report, the medical society testified that 10 percent of New Jersey's doctors may be alcoholic, 3 percent may be addicted to drugs and 3 percent may be "psychotic, mentally ill" or otherwise impaired.[82]

We need an understanding of the body that lets us deal with the immediate problem of an addictive lifestyle and an addictive environment. We need a new way of looking at the body. The model of the physiology presented in this chapter is simple, accurate, powerful, and useful. It enables us to create vibrant health and free ourselves from craving. In the description that follows, you will get a glimpse of how the body really works. You will be introduced to the basic concepts and vocabulary of ayurveda. This is a primer on perfect health.

This chapter charts a course through the arcane waters of ayurvedic literature. For that you need a certain minimum vocabulary. All new terms are defined in the glossary at the end of the chapter. If you are not going to read other books on ayurveda, or if you don't like jargon, pay attention to the concepts only; that's all you need for now. But I strongly encourage you to study the few books recommended in the resources chapter. Get an owner's manual for your body.

THE BODY

The complex machinery of the body can be reduced to simple functional parts governed by a few basic principles. To illustrate this, we will compare the body to a car's engine. They are remarkably similar in a number of ways. An engine takes in fuel, combusts it, and then eliminates the waste products. Our body does the same thing. We take in fuel—food, water, and air—which goes through various stages of digestion, or metabolism, and the waste products are eliminated.

Ama

Like an engine burning fuel, the body tries to digest everything we eat. If combustion is complete, then no deposits are left. If it is incomplete, then a residue forms that clogs the system and eventually leads to problems. It is the same in the car, where the residue of incompletely burned fuel gums up the spark plugs and other parts of the engine. In the body, the result of incomplete digestion is called *ama* (pronounced AH-muh), which means "poison." Food that the body has not been able to digest becomes a sticky, glue-like substance in the digestive tract. If you don't believe me, look at your tongue first thing in the morning the day after overeating. Your tongue, especially toward the back, will be covered in a sticky white film. That is ama. In your intestines, ama sticks to the walls and prevents absorption of nutrients. Ama goes further afield. It can get into every metabolic process, including that of the cells. PMS, arthritis, allergies—these are examples of health complaints either caused or exacerbated by ama.

Agni and Ojas

The ayurvedic term for digestion is *agni* (AHG-nee), which literally means "fire." Digestion takes place on many levels. One is responsible for assimilation of food into the bloodstream. Other levels of agni progressively transform food to muscle, fat, bone, bone marrow and nerve cells, sperm or ova, and ultimately to *ojas* (OH-juhs). Ojas is a very refined biochemical or collection of biochemicals that constitute the finest product of digestion. Ojas nourishes the entire body. Without it we die. Ojas produces feelings of security and well-being. It enhances self-referral and is the biochemical correlate of the mind's experience of the Self.

Ama and ojas are complete opposites. Obviously, we want to

minimize ama and maximize ojas.

Shrotas and Dhatus

Let's return to the engine analogy. Just as the car's engine has channels—such as air intake, fuel intake, combustion chamber, and exhaust pipe—through which flow different substances, so does our body. Each channel through which digestion takes place is called a *shrota* (SHROH-tuh). The substances flowing through these channels are given the name *dhatu* (DAH-too). If a car's pipes or channels become blocked—or in highly sensitive areas such as the pistons or spark plugs, get even a little rough or corroded—the whole engine may not work. That can hamper the driver's joy.

It is the same with the body. If the shrotas become blocked, it is almost impossible to be happy. Conversely, unblocked shrotas spontaneously give rise to happiness. If the path of the shrotas is clear, the ultimate product of digestion, ojas, will result. Ojas is responsible for our body sending us the signal, "Everything is OK here; go out and have a good time." We feel good. On the other hand, if the shrotas are blocked, something is wrong somewhere, and an inadequate amount of ojas is produced. The body then sends the signal, "Hey, something is not right; you had better drop whatever you are doing and pay attention to me." We lose our sense of well-being. Therefore, to be happy we must keep the shrotas clear.

Dhatu is often translated as "tissue." As an analogy, we say the dhatus flow through the shrotas. Really, it is the energy and intelligence from our food that flows through the shrotas. The food in your stomach is a dhatu. The nutrient fluid in your blood is a dhatu. Fatty tissue, as well as parts of the bones, are also dhatus.

Shrotas are the channels (and microchannels) through which the dhatus flow. For the dhatu of blood plasma, the blood vessels are the shrotas. In this case the analogy is literal. If vital blood vessels to the heart get blocked, we quickly lose our sense of well-being. This is an obvious example of a shrota being blocked. Usually, shrotas refer more abstractly to metabolic pathways, such as the creation and maintenance of muscle tissue. The dhatus are produced in stages, like an assembly line, with ojas as the final product. Normal digestion results in healthy dhatus and an abundance of ojas.

We can summarize the application of what we have covered so far: *minimize ama, maximize ojas, keep the shrotas clear, and keep the dhatus abundant and healthy.* This is critical for maintaining vitality and health.

Nadis and Marmas

Our description of the body is still incomplete. We need to add another component: the electrical system. The body's equivalent is obviously the nervous system. The nervous system, so subtle and intricate, connects the mind and body. The ayurvedic term for nerve is *nadi* (NAH-dee). It is along the nadis that information and intelligence flow within the body, and between the mind and body. The most important nexus of nadis, or vital points, are called *marmas* (MAR-muhs). The three primary *marma points* are in the head, heart, and lower abdomen. These must be protected from physical and emotional damage.

Prana

We started out by saying that a car takes in fuel and combusts it. Even an optimally functioning engine has problems if the quality of the fuel is low. It is the same with the body. We need high-quality fuel. As with a car, we may not notice the problems right away, but sooner or later, we probably will. In ayurveda (which, by the way, is pronounced EYE-your-VAY-duh), there is a name for vitality in food, air, and environment. It is *prana* (PRAH-nuh). Prana is analogous to the octane rating of gasoline; it is not a substance, it is a property or quality. Prana is the nourishing and life-sustaining ability of anything in our environment. It is also the life-energy that animates the body itself. Prana is a measure of the vitality in anything.

The more prana food and air has, the better the body runs. What is high in prana? Topping the list are early-morning air, natural environments such as mountains and ocean, very fresh food, and food cooked with a great deal of love.

Conversely, offices with fluorescent lights and windows that can't be opened are particularly low-prana. Leftovers, packaged food, meat—anything that is dead or stale—is low-prana. Low-prana food is high in what biochemists call "free radicals." Free radicals are highly reactive microchemicals that eat away at the microscopic structure of the body. It is believed that free radicals contribute to rapid aging, cancer and many other health problems.

The Driver Is the Mind

Adding the mind completes the analogy. The mind, of course, is the driver. Just as a well-tuned engine is wrecked by poor driving, so a balanced body is quickly imbalanced by a mind not fully self-referral. The mind, however, has an edge over the driver of a car. While a good driver can minimize wear and tear on the car, a balanced, powerful, and confident mind can *create* health.

Test Drive the Knowledge

Q. How does exercise help keep us healthy?

A. It kindles agni and burns off ama. Exercise unblocks the shrotas; by stimulating metabolism, it removes accumulated toxins throughout the body. It also enlivens the nadis as well as the marma points. One of the most vital nadis is called the *sushumna nadi,* which is at the center of the spine, running from top to bottom. When exercise unblocks the sushumna nadi, we feel exhilaration as the body's intelligence and energy once again flow up to the brain. This, in part, explains runner's high. Since exercise results in so many benefits to the body, it is not surprising that athletes have half the cancer rate of the general population.

Q. When we see someone who is vibrantly healthy, we say they "look radiant" and that their face "glows." What gives a person that look?

A. A person's face reveals a great deal about their health. (Makeup attempts to reproduce the look of vitality and inner health.) There are two prerequisites to having a healthy glow. One is shrotas that are not clogged. This means having good agni (vigorous digestion and metabolism). The second, and even more important, prerequisite is ample flow of the dhatus. That "glow" on the face is the result of ojas, which results in a highly refined oil secreted by the skin.

Q. In terms of the theory of the body introduced in this chapter, which system does acupuncture work on?
A. The marmas. Thus, the effects of acupuncture can be explained by the ayurvedic model of the physiology. However, according to ayurveda, it is not necessary to pierce the skin to stimulate the marmas and heal the body.

YOUR BODY TYPE

We have a model for how the body functions, but we still need a way to explain why different people are different: Why do you like ice cream, but your best friend prefers salty snacks? What makes your boss able to work ten-hour days, whereas you perform best in short, intense bursts of creative energy? To answer these kinds of questions, we return to our car analogy.

Just as there are different types or classes of cars, so there are different types of physiology. Each car is the way it is because it was built according to a set of governing principles. For example, a Porsche is built for speed and handling. A Porsche belongs to a class of cars we call sports cars. Sports cars are designed with one principle in mind: to enable the driver to enjoy a car that handles the road well at any speed, especially fast.

Likewise, each of our bodies was built according to specific principles that govern its style of operation. These principles are called *doshas* (DOH-shuhs). The doshas are for the body what the class, such as sports car, is for the car. The doshas determine the style of functioning of the body. There are three doshas, giving rise to three basic types of physiology.

There is a physiology characterized by motion (like a small sports car). People with this kind of physiology are quick, alert, exhilarating, and always on the move. There is a physiology marked by intensity (like, I suppose, the powerful cars that came out of Detroit in the 1960s, the "muscle" cars). These people are aggressive and articulate. They work hard, play hard, and love to enjoy. There is a physiology marked by substantial physical structure (like a pick-up truck or a plush Cadillac). These people are easygoing, steady, and methodical. They have excellent long-term memories.

Although slow to get going, they can outwork anyone.

The first dosha is called *vata* (VAH-tuh). Vata is characterized by motion. The second dosha is *pitta* (PIT-uh). Pitta is characterized by transformation—that is, by metabolism. The third dosha is *kapha* (KAH-fuh). Kapha is characterized by structure. Each person is a combination of these three characteristics: vata (the Enthusiastic Type), pitta (the Intense Type), and kapha (the Stable Type). Take the Body Type Quiz to find out what you are. The quiz is at the end of this chapter, on page 129.

What Each Type Is Like

Emotionally, people with a lot of vata dosha (we will call them *vatas,* for short) are prone to fear, pittas to anger, and kaphas to depression. In terms of health problems, vata is the main cause of pain—nerves are governed by vata. So nervous disorders and back pain are often caused by vata imbalance. Pittas can have digestive problems, such as ulcers, because metabolic processes are governed by pitta. Kaphas tend to be exceptionally healthy, but they have a propensity to put on weight.

In terms of speech, vatas talk fast, pittas forcefully, and kaphas slowly. In terms of outer appearances, vatas are typically thin, pittas athletic, and kaphas heavy. Vatas have dry hair, often wavy. A pitta's hair is often blond, fair, or red. Pitta men tend to lose their hair earlier in life, or have graying hair. Kaphas have thick, oily hair. In terms of digestion, vatas have variable digestion: sometimes fast, sometimes slow. Pittas can digest large amounts of food quickly; they hate skipping meals. Kaphas have slow but reliable digestion.

There is a reason all this is important. At birth, you had a specific percentage of each dosha in your physiology—for example, 30 percent vata, 60 percent pitta, and 10 percent kapha. That mixture is the equivalent of a car's point of optimal tuning, and it's different for every individual. If your doshas are not in their proper proportions, you will feel uncomfortable. Instinctively, you will try to get your body back in balance. But if you are not in the habit of listening to your body, instinct may not be enough. It helps to understand your body type and know how to systematically get your body back to its natural state of equilibrium.

LIFESTYLE CHANGES:
IF YOU LIKE IT, DRIVE IT HOME

Behavior profoundly affects our health: half of all deaths in the United States are attributed to lifestyle.[83] More importantly, lifestyle affects the quality of your life while you are here. Often a small change can make you a lot happier.

There are two categories of lifestyle changes recommended in ayurveda. One consists of those that increase the vitality of the body and mind. These are general and are the same for everyone. The other consists of those that are designed to pacify your most out-of-balance dosha; obviously there are going to be three sets of these— one each for vata, pitta, and kapha.

Become a High-Energy Person

Everyone should consider these basic lifestyle changes. The parenthetical comments in italics explain *why* we make the changes. This ayurvedic rationale is included to show that even our beginning knowledge of ayurveda is practical, offering useful insights.

1. Meditate regularly *(to experience self-referral awareness)*.

2. Go to bed before ten and get up before six. The quality of the air changes around 4 a.m. As nature wakes up, there is surge of vitality. This is when yogis meditate *(to absorb prana from the environment)*.

3. Give yourself a daily oil massage, followed by a hot shower. This loosens up and moves out accumulated toxins *(thereby eliminating ama)*.

4. Eat *only* fresh *(high-prana)* food. It is important that the building materials for your body be of the highest quality. Unfortunately, most food in conventional grocery stores is definitely not of the highest quality. It may be saturated with pesticides, preservatives, and other synthetic chemicals (including hormones and antibiotics),

contain partially hydrogenated oils, or be genetically modified (as are most soybean products and just about anything containing corn syrup). I would advise you to *completely* avoid all of these. Currently, the only way to do that is to buy organic. It is worth the extra money and effort to ensure your family's long-term health.

Eat varied, delicious, and somewhat rich meals *(allowing an abundance of healthy dhatus and the production of ojas)*. Have your biggest meal at lunchtime *(when pitta—your digestive power—is the strongest)*. Include rejuvenating foods *(those that increase ojas)* in your diet. Examples are milk, ghee (clarified butter), almonds, dates, honey (never cooked or heated), and rice. Avoid alcohol *(it inhibits the production of ojas)*.

Make an effort to give up addictions to caffeine and tobacco. Start this by *enjoying* your habit—consciously, with 100 percent of your attention. *(Attention increases self-referral, naturally reducing self-destructive behavior.)* This has a number of benefits: less use gives the same amount of pleasure; you may notice your "trigger" stresses; you may observe that you don't enjoy these habits as much as you thought; and you may notice *what* you enjoy about the habit. Smokers, for example, get almost as much out of slow, deep breathing as they do from the nicotine. Deep conscious breathing can be done without cigarettes. If you are quitting smoking and would like to explore yogic breathwork, read Donna Farhi's *Breathing Book.* In the back of the book, Farhi lists hatha yoga breathing techniques that provide the same stimulation cigarettes do. For more traditional approaches to quitting, see the resources in chapter 12.

5. Do not deplete your energy. This includes not overexercising, not staying up late, not indulging in too much sex, not excessively worrying, and not being overly ambitious *(all these burn ojas)*.

6. Exercise every day. A good walk is a minimum. *(Exercise burns off ama, enlivens the marmas and nadis, opens the sushumna, and keeps the shrotas clear.)* Yogic exercise and yogic breathing (mentioned in chapter 9) are helpful *(to increase the body's prana and maintain self-referral on the physical level)*.

7. Drink in bliss through each of the senses: enjoy music, hugs, aroma oils, gourmet food, and beautiful scenery *(all these offer self-referral on the level of the senses)*.

8. Do not hurt other people's feelings *(thus protecting yourself from injury to the finest level of feeling)*.

9. Have a life-supporting job in a life-supporting environment. Nurture others and practice charitable acts *(thus maintaining self-referral with the environment)*. Also, take short breaks to revitalize yourself. You don't need to drink coffee to take a coffee break; and you don't need to smoke to go outside and breathe fresh air *(keeps prana high)*.

10. Make happiness a priority *(to maintain contact with deeper, more blissful levels of self-referral)*.

Balancing the Enthusiastic Type

Although each addiction affects the body differently, all addictions primarily involve extreme vata imbalance. This is because addiction is a repetitive motion we cannot stop, and motion is controlled by vata. Treatment of addiction, therefore, should involve, in its earliest phases, pacifying vata.

The following prescriptions should be followed by vata types and anyone experiencing fear or anxiety. In general, pay close attention to your sense of well-being, nourish yourself (both physically and emotionally), and conserve energy. Don't worry if you can't do everything on this list: "take it easy" is the primary injunction for vatas.

1. Get lots of rest: sleep a full night (go to bed early), take naps, and meditate.

2. Maintain a predictable routine: eat meals at the same time, go to bed at the same hour, and so forth. Don't resist natural urges (such as the need to go the bathroom). You are the type that needs those prunes and oat bran; you need regularity in more than just routine.

3. Do not overexercise. Be moderate: go for a brisk, daily, half-hour walk.

4. Keep warm. Stay out of the wind. In changeable weather, carry a sweatshirt or jacket. Even if the weather is warm, the restaurant may not be.

5. Eat regular, hot, fresh, delicious, unctuous (oily or rich) meals. Never skip meals, never eat standing up, never get up—once seated, stay seated—and never, ever, watch TV with fork in hand. Meals are a critical time for balancing, or imbalancing, vata. Don't distract yourself. After eating, rest for a few minutes and then go for a gentle ten-minute walk.

6. Watch out for vata-increasing dishes: avoid spicy, light, dry, and rough food. Favor food that tastes sweet, salty, or sour. Go for rich and heavy dishes (lasagna), carbohydrates (bread, pasta and rice), and warm food. Have nothing cold; consider ice water a cardinal sin. Eat heartily, but because your digestion is variable—sometimes strong, sometimes weak—don't overeat. If you are full after a light meal, stop. Eat again later when you get hungry. Sometimes you need several smaller meals that don't overload your digestive system. Snacking is good. You can buy packages of spices blended to balance vata (or pitta or kapha). These can be sprinkled on top of the meal or used in cooking.

7. Get rid of those stimulants. Switch from coffee or tea to some kind of herbal concoction. Maharishi Ayurveda Products makes a soothing Vata Tea. You can also try plain hot water. Drinking water, especially hot water, helps wash away accumulated ama, which can reduce imbalanced cravings.

8. Give yourself a daily oil massage. Spend about twenty minutes on it. Pay special attention to your head and to the soles of your feet. Use long stroking motions on the limbs, and circular motions on the joints. Use warm sesame oil. The oil should be fresh and organic—after all, your skin "digests" it. If you can't find sesame oil,

you can use olive oil; look for the phrase "extra virgin, first cold pressing" on the bottle. But sesame oil is best. It has special properties; it is anti-inflammatory (also good for the gums if used as a mouthwash) and antibacterial. It nourishes the skin and may help prevent skin cancer. If you can't find it at a grocery or health food store, you can order it from Maharishi Ayurveda Products. This company also has a relaxing massage oil steeped in vata-balancing herbs.

9. Avoid competitive, high-stress environments. Peace around you helps a lot: a forest, the ocean, a park. Avoid harsh noise—turn down the job operating a leaf blower. Soothing music is more your style.

10. Don't-worry-be-happy!

Balancing the Intense Type
Pitta is fire. Anything that reduces heat, soothes digestion, or avoids conflict is going to be good for pitta. These suggestions are for pitta types and those experiencing the "fiery" emotions: hatred, jealousy, envy, criticism, and especially anger.

1. Don't overwork. Keep a good balance of rest and activity, work and play. Remember to meditate. Avoid all overindulgences, including not consuming yourself in the intense fire of your sexual ardor.

2. Although not as crucial as with vatas, you should have a reasonably regular routine. Resist the temptation to consistently stay up late working, playing, or watching TV. Never be late for lunch—that's when the tiger in your tank is most ferocious.

3. Swimming, and any other sport that is cooling, is good for pitta. Don't get involved in aggressive or competitive sports. If you lose, you could be angry for days.

4. Avoid overeating. Pay close attention to your body as you eat. Periodically stop, close your eyes, and put your hand on your stom-

ach. Feel whether you should continue eating. You must catch yourself at the point of optimum fullness: about three-quarters full.

5. Eat regular, fresh, delicious low-fat meals. Avoid: salty, oily, and sour food (that's right, potato chips are out, and so are vinegar and cheese). Try to eat food that tastes sweet, bitter, or astringent. That means: salads, milk, just about all carbohydrates, beans, and vegetables. Eat nothing spicy. Don't eat junk food—you don't store it, you burn it, overheating the digestive organs and making you irritable. Eat moderately (the Intense Type tends to go overboard on everything) but do satisfy yourself. You always have your fun—if you don't get it in one area, you'll sneak it in somewhere else.

6. Unless you enjoy being irritable, eliminate caffeine and cigarettes. Pittas should have, each day, a few large glasses of room-temperature water, taken separately from meals.

7. Give yourself a daily oil massage. As with vatas, you can use warm sesame oil. However, if you are extreme pitta, use coconut oil, which is cooling. Skip the massage if it is really hot out; otherwise, you may feel like a steak in a broiler.

8. Stay out of the sun, especially the midday sun.

9. Don't get into arguments. Be alert for conflict in your life. Hunt for submerged desires that are not being fulfilled. Opposing desires are like two sticks: rub them together long enough and you start a fire.

10. Chill out. Regularly plan fun activities. Being a workaholic, you'll probably have to schedule them.

Balancing the Stable Type
This list is for kaphas as well as those who are feeling dull, lethargic, sad, or depressed.

Kapha and vata are complementary opposites. To balance your kapha, what you need is not rest (you probably already sleep too late), but dynamic exercise. Lift weights. Climb mountains. Join a hundred-mile bicycle trip. You don't need routine, you need vigorous new adventures. Do that scary thing: take the ballroom dancing lessons, buy the house, go to Nepal. And *don't* eat regular heavy meals.

1. People are drawn to your affection and reliability. Try not to go too far and lock yourself up in the structure you build around yourself. Get out of the house. Make an effort to do new activities, or to do old things in new ways. Avoid a predictable routine.

2. Don't be afraid to fast one day a week. If you still feel sluggish and heavy, make a conscious effort to eat lighter and less every day.

3. Exercise, exercise, exercise—every chance you get. Start your day by pumping iron (kapha is strongest in the morning). Intense, competitive, and aggressive sports are for you. Racquetball, swimming, marathons, strenuous yoga routines—these are what you need. Golf and walking aren't going to do it.

4. Avoid heavy, oily, sweet, and cold food, as well as dairy (ice cream, unfortunately, is out). In general, refined foods—such as white rice, white flour, and sugar—have a sweet taste and should be kept to a minimum. Favor spicy dishes, bitter, and astringent tastes (like spinach or kale), raw vegetables, and fruit. Eat more lightly than your natural inclination, but don't go for frequent small meals. Your digestion is strong, yet slow. Infrequent, substantial, but-not-too-large meals are your ticket to health. As with pittas, while you eat, monitor your fuel gauge. As soon as you are three-quarters full, stop. Sit quietly for a couple of minutes, and then get up from the table.

5. It goes without saying, avoid alcohol, which is high in carbohydrates and, not surprisingly, a depressant. Also avoid cold soda—unless you like those love handles. Drink hot ginger tea instead: boil a couple of slices of fresh ginger in a cup or two of water.

6. Kapha types have a special problem when it comes to stimulants: they do decrease kapha. Many kaphas excuse their smoking by saying it keeps their weight under control. It's true, but there are less damaging ways to reduce kapha. Although an early-morning caffeine jolt helps unglue the kapha in your brain, a much healthier approach is to examine your lifestyle and see what is sapping your vitality and why kapha is excessive.

7. Saunas are good for maintaining the body's fluid balance and for eliminating excess salt.

8. Give yourself a daily invigorating massage. Don't use oil. Instead, use a dry hand towel or special silk gloves. This stimulates circulation and gets kapha moving. If you do use oil, which assumes you don't have too much kapha, then use sesame oil, which has a heating quality.

9. You may thrive in high-stress environments, even those with deadlines. Noise is OK for you. Heavy metal may be just the music you need to get going in the morning.

10. Plan big things and do them.

CONCLUSION

Ayurvedic physiology—with its understanding of the doshas—not only explains how lifestyle affects our health, it gives us a way of knowing which changes will be most useful. Having finished this chapter, you will find other books on ayurveda easier reading. These books provide detailed information on daily and seasonal routines, give extensive food recommendations . . . and explain how to do just about everything related to the body, from having babies to living long. Several good books on ayurveda are listed in the resources.

To take a step back and get the bigger picture: recovery involves, on the physical level, increasing the body's vitality and balancing the doshas, and on the mental level, restoring self-referral awareness. When vata, pitta, and kapha are in their natural proportions, pure consciousness shines forth in our awareness.

KEY AYURVEDIC TERMS

agni—specifically: the body's fire of digestion. Generally: the process of metabolism governing all levels of the body's functioning.

ama—the poisonous byproduct that results from incomplete digestion or metabolism of food.

dhatus—the body's tissues. Metaphorically, that which flows through the shrotas. The seven dhatus are: plasma, blood, muscle, fat, bone, bone marrow and nerve cells, and sperm or ova. The dhatus are supported by ojas, and their final product is ojas.

doshas—the three principles (vata, pitta, and kapha) governing the functioning of the body. Through understanding the doshas we get insight into our body, mind, and behavior.

kapha—one of the three doshas. Kapha governs structure. Kapha people are gentle, kind, and capable of hard work, although they take a little longer than most to get going. They have a generous build. Imbalanced kapha results in depression and obesity.

marmas—nerve centers in the body. These are vital points, junctions between consciousness and matter. The three most important are in the head, heart, and lower pelvis.

nadis—nerves or pathways along which intelligence and information flow in the nervous system.

ojas—the most refined product of digestion. Ojas nourishes the entire body.

pitta—one of the three doshas. Pitta governs metabolism (transformation). Pitta people are aggressive, fun-loving, and good at talking. They have an athletic build. Imbalanced pittas tend to be angry and compulsive.

prana—a generic term for energy that is capable of sustaining and nourishing the body. (Analogous to the octane rating in gasoline.) Prana isn't a physical thing; it describes the quality of "freshness" in our food and environment.

shrotas—the channels through which digestion or metabolism takes place. These may be physical, such as blood vessels, or metabolic pathways that are more of a process than a physical conduit.

vata—one of the three doshas. Vata governs motion. Vata people are quick, alert, and lively, and tend to be thin. Imbalanced vata is associated with fear and addictive behavior.

THE BODY TYPE QUIZ

For each of the twenty questions, put a check in the box that best applies to you (only one check per question; if you feel you really must, put a half in two boxes). After you finish, add up the number of checks per column (checks count as one, "halfs" count as a half), and put the number in the total box at the bottom. Then, multiply each total by five to get a percentage. Vata is the Enthusiastic Type, pitta the Intense Type, and kapha the Stable Type.

1. You didn't eat breakfast, and then had to skip lunch. You:	feel OK, but lose energy as the day goes on (perhaps feeling scattered)	feel ferociously hungry (and possibly irritable)	don't notice much change (you'll just eat more at dinner)
2. Your resting pulse rate is:	faster than average (seventy to ninety)	average (sixty to seventy)	below average (fifty to sixty)
3. Your spending habits are characterized by:	quick, impulsive spending	methodical, moderate spending	a tendency to save, and to spend slowly
4. Your body has:	a thin frame with little fat	a medium frame and medium weight	a large frame and a fairly good amount of fat
5. Your speech is:	quick, sometimes skipping over words	clear and sharp (sometimes even biting or sarcastic)	slow and pleasant
6. You get a flat tire on the way to work and will be late for an extremely important meeting. Your first reaction is:	anxiety	anger	disappointment or depression

	six hours or less	between six and eight	more than eight
7. In order to be effective, how many hours of sleep would you need (if you slept that many hours every day):			
8. Your sex drive is best described as:	low; or, easy to excite, but short-lived	moderate, but passionate when aroused	strong (but perhaps slow to get started)
9. When you work (or exercise) you:	have short bursts of energy, but tire quickly	are competitive and aggressive, having medium endurance	get started slowly, but keep going and going
10. Your eyes are:	small and active (with the "whites" tending to be tinted gray or blue)	penetrating or intense (with the "whites" tending to be yellowish or red)	large and attractive (with the "whites" usually clear and bright)
11. Your hair is:	dry, coarse, kinky, or curly (and maybe black)	soft, fine, oily, and possibly thinning or graying (and maybe blond, fair, or red)	thick, plentiful, wavy, oily, or lustrous (and maybe dark)
12. Your skin is:	dry or rough (and maybe dark)	soft, warm, and oily (and maybe reddish)	cool and oily (and maybe pale)
13. The weather you like least is:	cold and dry	hot	humid
14. You approach new ideas with:	enthusiasm (but maybe not practicality)	an aggressive desire to achieve them (possibly preceded initially by skepticism)	caution and methodical practicality

	% VATA	% PITTA	% KAPHA
15. Your digestion is:	variable (sometimes fast, but sometimes it may even stop)	strong and fast	slow but regular
16. Your relationships are:	short and fleeting	tempestuous and fiery (or you tend to be independent)	long and stable
17. You dream about:	flying, running or scary situations	passion, fire or violence	water or romance
18. During trying times in a relationship, your faith in your mate is best described as:	changeable and wavering	tenacious (determined to make the relationship work)	consistently loyal
19. Your thirst level is:	variable	strong	light
20. In terms of memory, you:	are quick to learn, and quick to forget	grasp concepts easily (and express them well)	are slow to learn, and slow to forget
Total			
Percent (total times 5)	% VATA	% PITTA	% KAPHA

131

LISTENING
TO THE BODY

In this chapter, we learn a technique that allows us to tune in to the mind and body's needs. Self-pulse diagnosis is Advanced Recovery Tool #3.

One engine often drives a long train of addictions. Problem drinkers "cure" their drinking and become overeaters, and then cure their overeating and become compulsive gamblers or workaholics. Each addiction has different symptoms, but often a single cause.

LOCATING AND ELIMINATING
THE PATTERN OF ADDICTION

Imagine the mind-body system as a conveyor belt. It starts at the Self and has workers stationed at different points. Each worker (level of the mind-body) fabricates whatever comes along the belt. The product of the assembly line is your behavior. If you find out what is going on at the earliest stages of the process, you will understand why you get the end result. You will understand your behavior. If you change what is happening at the start, what is assembled at each stage will be different, and so will the final product.

On a deep level, the pattern of disruption of the flow of intelligence is similar for all a person's addictions. What is necessary is to locate where the problem first occurs. But how do you look for the cause when your attention is completely caught up by the changing symptoms? You need a technique.

YOUR AYURVEDIC PULSE

When you go to the doctor's office and get a physical exam, the nurse measures your heart rate and takes your blood pressure. Why? Because these tell the doctor a lot about the state of your body and mind. In ayurveda, we also take the pulse. However, ayurveda doesn't count heartbeats; rather, it pays attention to the *quality* of the beats.

Try it yourself, right now. Take your pulse anywhere. You could try on your wrist, or if a pulse there is hard to find, then try the carotid artery, toward the top of your neck, about two inches before the end of your jaw, and about an inch or so down. Use more than one finger, it's easier.

Once you've located a good solid pulse, take a full minute and feel it. Don't count the beats. Pay attention instead to the speed, smoothness, regularity, and intensity—the "shape" of the beats. What you are feeling are the effects of the doshas: the proportions of vata, pitta, and kapha.

Now try to figure out which dosha or doshas are present. Here is a summary of what each one feels like:

> **Vata** pulse is like the pitter-patter of the feet of a small animal, which is startled and running away. Vata pulses are tremulous, quick, erratic—moving here and there, without intense force to each beat.

> **Pitta** pulse is like someone pounding on a door— banging with their fist, demanding to get in. It has power and insistence. Pitta pulses are dramatic and full of energy.

> **Kapha** pulse is majestic. It is like the motion of a large ship gracefully rising and falling on ocean swells. It is closest in form to a pure sine wave. Kapha pulses are like big bellows slowly and rhythmically opening and closing.

If we exaggerate, to make them more characteristic, these pulses might look like this:

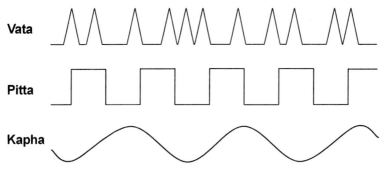

Figure 8.1 An "oscilloscope" picture of the pulse for each dosha.

According to ayurvedic theory, the pulse is a miniature hologram of the body and mind. Because the blood comes from each cell, every part of the body influences the style of the heartbeats and creates a tiny change in the pulse. Hence, anything that has an influence on the body can be felt in the pulse. Like a cork bobbing up and down on the waves of the ocean, your pulse is modulated by everything you do. If you don't believe it, try this experiment. The next time someone cuts you off on the freeway, pay attention to your heartbeat. You should notice a definite increase in vata and pitta. You may even experience the psychological components of these doshas (fear and anger). If stress is a regular part of your lifestyle, then adverse changes to the pulse take on a more permanent quality.

HOW TO DO IT

Let's focus on how to get as much information as possible from the pulse. Ayurveda is quite specific. Self-pulse diagnosis is usually done at the wrist, feeling the pulse as it travels through the radial artery. Three fingers are used.

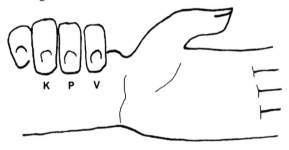

Figure 8.2 How to position the fingers to feel the pulse. This picture is for a woman (right hand taking left pulse—palm facing you). A man uses his left hand to feel his right arm's pulse.

Feel the long bone, the radius, that runs along the thumb side of your forearm. Just inside of that, on the palm-side of your arm, there is a hollow where you can feel a pulse. Your fingers should be together in a line, with the side of your first finger nestled up against the small protruding rounded part of the bone that you can see or feel if you bend your wrist back. To get your fingers in the right position, you will have to wrap your hand around your wrist. Traditionally, a man feels the pulse of his right arm, and a woman her left arm. (The picture in Figure 8.2 is for a woman.) Take your pulse with your wrist and arm relaxed, resting on a table or your lap, or held up against your chest. It may help to close your eyes. Take your time. The process itself—of sitting and feeling the pulse —settles the mind and helps restore self-referral.

The predominant dosha reveals itself in two ways: by the form of the pulse, which we have already discussed, and by which finger feels a stronger beat. If vata is strong, you will feel the most activity under the first finger. The second finger picks up pitta, and the third kapha.

When you press your fingers lightly or bear down hard, you access different pulses. The beats-per-minute is the same, but the quality is different. The pulse on the surface, touching just firmly enough to get a distinct pulse, tells the story of the rapidly changing aspect of the doshas. For example, if you miss a meal, as your hunger increases, so does your pitta, and you will feel this in the superficial pulse.

The deepest pulse—pressing down until the blood stops and then letting up until you feel a pulse again—tends to remain the same. This is the best clue to your natural doshic balance, the one you were born with. If you feel a pitta pulse here, you are probably a pitta type.

THE SUBDOSHAS

An expert can detect seven levels of pulse. One of these is the *subdoshic.* Each dosha—vata, pitta, and kapha—has five subdoshas. Each subdosha is associated with an area of the body, has a specific physiological function, and, when out of balance, gives rise to characteristic pathological symptoms.

Each subdosha is also associated with an emotion. If the pitta in your heart is balanced, you will feel love and compassion; if it is out of balance, you may be prone to excessive jealousy. Too much kapha can give rise to excessive attachment, grief, temptation, possessiveness, or mental rigidity—depending on which subdosha is out of balance. It also works the other way: suppressing an emotion harms the body. We all know that grief hurts our heart. Overwhelming grief (too much to process) eventually creates an imbalance of the second kapha subdosha. If the grief is prolonged, the heart or lungs may be physically damaged.

At the end of the chapter, a chart lists the qualities of the subdoshas.[84] This chart is not meant as a comprehensive medical reference; it is there to give you a sense of the richness of ayurveda.

Learning to Feel the Subdoshic Level

The best way to learn subdoshic pulse diagnosis is from a Maharishi Vedic School or Maharishi Vedic Medical Center. You can take one of three courses. For the general population, there is a sixteen-hour course, which covers the full range of self-pulse reading and explains how to use self-pulse diagnosis to stay in balance. For doctors, there is an intensive, more advanced course, taught over three weekends, which qualifies you as an Maharishi Ayurvedic Physician. You can also learn self-pulse diagnosis as part of a series of general knowledge courses taught through the Maharishi Open University (see resources in chapter 12).

Bear in mind that it does take time to confidently locate the subdoshas. At first, your fingers won't believe what they are being asked to do. The tactile nerves, unless you regularly read Braille, will be surprised to be asked to make such fine distinctions. A calibration process takes place over time. Personal instruction and group practice help a lot.

HOW IT WORKS IN PRACTICE

A few examples—from my own experience—may make things clearer. Note that these involve only lifestyle changes that don't cost anything.

Grumpy

I notice—after it has been pointed out to me—that for some time I have been consistently irritable. The superficial pulse reveals pitta is out of balance. Taking the subdoshic pulse, I feel a spike corresponding to ranjaka pitta, the second subdosha of pitta, connected with removal of toxins. Ranjaka pitta is associated with the functioning of the red blood cells, liver, and spleen. Now I wonder, Why is ranjaka pitta out of balance? Thinking back, I realize I had been eating a lot of rich food. My body is overloaded—and angry about it. So I change my diet: eat less, easing up on the pesto sauce, french fries, and cheesecake—and exercise, to burn off the toxins. Within a few days, the irritability is gone.

Dull

Some months later, I take my superficial pulse and feel an overwhelming abundance of kapha. The subdoshic pulse indicates dullness in the aspect of kapha (third subdosha) responsible for taste. There is also a spike indicating aggravation of ranjaka pitta. I know from experience that if this is the right time of year—late spring or early summer—this combination always means approaching hay fever, which, without pulse diagnosis, is like a train at a crossing: it always seems to come out of nowhere. When the ayurvedic bells start ringing, they get my full attention. Getting stuck on the tracks when the train of allergies comes barreling toward you is not fun.

Both kapha and pitta need balancing. First, I make an effort to vary my food, because eating the same foods repeatedly deadens taste. Dull taste buds don't allow your brain to get or give the signal that you've eaten enough; and even if your brain got the message, you wouldn't stop because you haven't had the enjoyment of tasting your food. So I go way out of my way for diversity, consciously cut down on how much I eat, and follow a strict kapha-balancing diet (much less sugar, and no dairy), modified by the need not to aggravate pitta (nothing too spicy). Bitter and astringent tastes decrease both kapha and pitta, so I eat salads (little or no dressing) and bean dishes, while avoiding sour food.

Next, I exercise a lot. This balances kapha. Upper-body exercise dries up the sinuses by removing excessive kapha in the chest and head. Exercise also soothes ranjaka pitta, as it burns off ama. To further balance kapha, I try not to sleep too much, and I do a daily oil massage in the early morning, concentrating on the face, head, neck, shoulders, and chest. If this doesn't stop the hay fever, at least it slows down the momentum.

Lonely

On another occasion, I feel dull, and I have been sedentary for the past several weeks. The pulse, not surprisingly, shows an overabundance of kapha. I choose to balance this by exercise. This is not the only choice, but it is a logical one based on my current lifestyle. After a few days, I feel good—better than good, I feel great. So I keep exercising every day: if a little is good, a lot is better. Two weeks later, I start to feel some anxiety and tension. My intellect says, "Each day for the past couple of weeks I have exercised, and every time I felt better. So if I exercise today, that will fix things." But when I take my pulse, sadhaka pitta, the subdosha associated with the heart, has a strong spike in it. When I sit and think why the "heart" is not in balance, it dawns on me that what I really want is not exercise, but rest, relaxation, and the company of friends. Exercise would have provided some relief, but it would not have satisfied the real need of the mind and body. Exercise, in this context, would have been addictive: a repetitive action that doesn't bring fulfillment.

To Generalize

These examples are not particularly profound. But go through this process a hundred times and you will have located many of your addictive behavior patterns and have learned to better identify and meet your inner needs. In this way, self-pulse diagnosis frees us from the tyranny of our intellect and breaks the cycle of addictive behavior.

ADVANCED RECOVERY TOOL NUMBER THREE

To use self-pulse diagnosis as a recovery tool, there are three simple steps:

1. Feel the pulse.
2. Assess—and write down—the mind and body's state.
3. Take action, according to ayurvedic principles and common sense, to bring balance.

Become intimate with your pulse. Keep a log. You can photocopy the one at the end of the chapter. Record your observations: Which finger has the strongest pulse? Is the overall pulse vata, pitta, or kapha? Draw what your pulse "looks like." If you notice, for example, that vata is predominant, and over the next few days find fear or anxiety increasing, see if there isn't something in your routine, diet, or exercise that is causing vata to get out of balance.

Since it does take a lot of attention, keep the self-pulse log for short blocks of time, perhaps for two weeks. Take your pulse several times each day; important times are upon waking and before meals. Once a day, write down in detail how your body feels as well as your emotional state. This allows you to connect what you feel in the pulse with the condition of your mind and body. Then list what you need to do to put things right. Writing down the ayurvedic recommendations helps initiate the process of change.

Note that the actions in step three may not be only ayurvedic. You need to deal directly with emotional issues. Once you locate specific emotional imbalances, ask yourself what actions you need to take, or attitudes you need to change, to remove the pressure. Self-pulse diagnosis is motivational. It forces you to get in touch with your body and feelings on a daily basis and *do* something to get back in balance.

Self-pulse diagnosis has a hidden benefit: it lets you uncover repressed emotions without having to recall the past. You deal, instead, with the patterns of imbalance the past has left you with. This way you heal your emotions without being swamped by them.

GET AN EXPERT OPINION

Pulse diagnosis is used by ayurvedic physicians. One of the world's most skilled pulse diagnosticians, Dr. B. D. Triguna, can give a complete medical history as well as a prognosis for any diseases in progress. His diagnostic abilities rival that of a team of specialists using the resources of a billion-dollar hospital. Not only can the state of your health be determined, but also the quality of your relationships, moods, and behavior. Dr. Triguna maintains that everything he concludes is physically detectable in the pulse. Although this is hard to believe, I suspect it is a little like Sherlock Holmes and Dr. Watson: to the truly observant, the facts are obvious; to the rest of us, they are an eternal mystery.

In a personal consultation, the doctor first assesses your body type. Then, he or she diagnoses imbalances—both those that have become frozen into your physiology (and become a part of your life) and those that are just starting and may not have resulted in overt symptoms. Finally, a prescription is given. These suggestions could be very simple or quite sophisticated. You might be told to walk in the early morning, to take herbal remedies, to modify your diet, or to do aroma therapy. Most doctors also recommend a special diet that washes away built-up ama. In the next chapter, we will look at more of the treatments that can be prescribed.

Note: see a regular doctor, an M.D., before you see an ayurvedic doctor. Tell her all your complaints. Once you have exhausted the M.D.'s patience, *then* get an ayurvedic consultation. Even though the ayurvedic doctor will probably be an M.D., he won't be looking for specific complaints. He will search for overall imbalance and plan general strategies to balance the body and prevent future problems. And he probably won't have the skill of Dr. Triguna. It is *very* important you understand that ayurveda doesn't replace regular checkups with your physician, nor is an ayurvedic consultation a substitute for the care or advice of a medical specialist.

CONCLUSION

Self-pulse diagnosis looks deep within, toward the Self. It examines patterns of energy and intelligence that are close to the junction point of consciousness and matter, detecting subtle imbalances before they manifest as disease or addictive behavior. Imbalance is then corrected using the knowledge and therapies of ayurveda.

Pulse diagnosis is a conscious healing process of balancing the mind and body, and thereby breaking the cycle of unconscious addictive behavior. As you seek out and eliminate dysfunctional patterns, you will gradually and gracefully reunite with your body.

SELF-PULSE LOG

Day: _____   Time: _____

Fill in the percentage of each pulse and the active subdosha:

	Vata	Pitta	Kapha
Surface			
Deep			
Subdosha (#)			

Describe (or draw) how the pulse feels:

My body feels:

My mind and heart feel:

What will restore harmony and fulfillment (self-referral) to my mind and body:

What I actually did to restore balance, and the results of those actions:

Vata Subdoshas

#	Name	Location	Function	Pathological Symptoms
1	prana	brain	thinking (and not-thinking, i.e., connecting to the Self), sensory perception, swallowing	insomnia, incessant thinking, ringing in the ears, migraines, anxiety
2	udana	throat	speech, communication of feelings, memory	fatigue, sore throat, difficulty speaking, earaches, memory problems
3	samana	small intestine	peristalsis	digestive problems such as diarrhea and poor assimilation of nutrients
4	apana	lower abdomen (includes colon and sexual function)	elimination, menstruation, sex	low back pain, PMS, sciatica, sexual dysfunction, urinary and prostate problems
5	vyana	heart and the nervous system	circulation, blood pressure, heart rhythm, touch	nervous disorders, heart problems (rhythm, circulation, blood pressure)

Pitta Subdoshas

#	Name	Location	Function	Pathological Symptoms
1	pachaka	stomach and small intestine	digestive fire	pitta-type digestive problems (ulcers, heartburn, etc.) resulting from the digestive fire being either too strong or too weak; a harshly critical or judgmental attitude
2	ranjaka	liver (and red blood cells and spleen)	nourishing and detoxifying through the blood	high cholesterol, anemia, hepatitis, chronic fatigue syndrome
3	alochaka	eyes	vision	eye problems
4	sadhaka	heart (and head)	processing external stimulation into contentment (heart) or understanding (brain); also, governs courage, expression, decisiveness, and concentration	heart disease, confusion, "losing heart," low self-esteem, attention deficit
5	bhrajaka	skin	complexion, sensitivity of the skin	skin disorders (cancer, acne, rashes, etc.)

Kapha Subdoshas

#	Name	Location	Function	Pathological Symptoms
1	kledaka	stomach	assimilation of nutrients	digestion too slow, diabetes
2	avalambaka	chest and heart	supports, strengthens, nourishes, and gives moisture to the entire body (through heart and lungs)	lung problems (congestion, bronchitis, etc.), pain in the mid- to low back, suppressed sadness (grief)
3	bhodhaka	tongue	taste	impaired taste, eating disorders (causing allergies, weight problems, congestion, etc.)
4	tarpaka	head and sinus	sensory perception (storing in the brain), moisture in the nose, mouth, and eyes	sinus congestion, hay fever, impaired smell, dizziness, dullness
5	shleshaka	joints	lubricates the joints	problems with the joints (pain, looseness, stiffness, "cracking," arthritis)

MORE
RECOVERY
TOOLS

CHAPTER NINE

In this chapter, we add nine more tools to our recovery toolbox. These techniques of vedic science not only help remove addiction but also make daily living more reliable and fulfilling.

Think back to something that made you angry—not a little angry, but intensely furious. What happened to your body? Your heart started pounding, muscles stiffened, you clenched your teeth and tensed your shoulders. Now try to picture what happens to the cells of your body. Rage causes anger chemicals to flood into the bloodstream. When these chemicals reach the cells, they cause a hurricane of inner violence.

If this doesn't happen often, once the storm is over, the body can pick up the pieces and get on with it. However, if trauma occurs frequently, the body doesn't recover. It remains agitated. Repeated experience of a strong emotion trains the body to maintain that emotion. We end up with angry cells and a body that is always on the trigger, ready to respond with anger to almost any stimulus.

We could go through a similar scenario for free-floating anxiety, chronic depression, shame—for any emotion. The situation is particularly intense for an adult child, because the negative conditioning lasted for decades and involved suppressed emotions. Suppressing emotions doesn't allow the body to know when the trauma is over, and thus prevents it from returning to normal—even between the storms.

CELLULAR PURIFICATION

We need a physical approach to remove the physical component of emotional trauma. Our past is locked in our bodies. It's not just emotions; it's everything. Wrong eating creates toxins that clog the system. Drugs and alcohol cause biochemical and neurological imbalances. Inappropriate lifestyle dissipates the body's energy. All the physical and emotional garbage stored inside the body has to be cleared out. We have to flush the residual stress-chemicals from the cells. And, we must teach the body, on a cellular and neurological level, to behave more normally and naturally.

Cleaning the Body

There is a powerful and efficient way to restore your body to the state it would have been in if you had never taken drugs, been exposed to anger, or lived with trauma. You can feel what it is like to be fully healthy and emotionally balanced. Part of this restoration process is a physical cleansing regimen called *panchakarma* (punch-uh-CAR-muh). *Pancha* means five; *karma* means action. Panchakarma is a five-fold method of physical purification. Panchakarma loosens up impurities in the body and flushes them out. Once the body is clean, more luxurious aspects of the treatment take over. The body is relaxed and soothed. It is coaxed back into bliss. Although it works only on the body, it has a healing influence on each level of self-referral.

A typical treatment takes one-and-a-half to two hours. You start with a full-body massage, using herbalized oil to balance your doshas. The sequence of motions, done synchronously by two masseuses or masseurs, stimulates the autonomous nervous system to deeply relax. After the massage, which has pushed toxins out of the tissues and into the bloodstream, you are given a steam bath, which moves the toxins from the bloodstream into the digestive tract, where the next step—an oil-based enema—removes them from the body.

Usually a patient receives several sequential days of panchakarma. The basic treatment is modified to suit your needs. One therapy that is often added is called *shirodhara* (she-row-DAR-uh), a stream of warm oil gently poured onto your forehead. By enlivening and relaxing the major marma point (nerve center) in the forehead, shirodhara coaxes the brain to let go and transcend.

Panchakarma opens the floodgates, releasing a lifetime of suppressed emotions. Huge blocks of fatigue, including ones that you had no idea existed, will dissolve. If free-floating anxiety and shame have been your constant companions, they become less all-encompassing, allowing you to deal with them directly. Releasing the emotional patterns locked into your body is the same as balancing the doshas. Put the doshas back into balance, and you heal your emotions.

Panchakarma, in the language of ayurvedic physiology, removes ama, clears the shrotas (thus allowing enhanced ojas production), stimulates the marmas, and balances the doshas.

Panchakarma is Advanced Recovery Tool #4. Further information on panchakarma—and all the other recovery tools described in this chapter—can be found in chapter 12.

GENETIC TUNING FORKS

Once the body is clean, there is an additional approach to fine-tune the body. In chapter 2, we said the mind influences the body: change the mind, change the body; think a thought, activate a neurotransmitter. It turns out we can also work the other way. Chemicals that influence neurotransmitters can be introduced from outside the body. Thus, chemically, we cause the mind to feel, or not to feel, a particular emotion. This phenomenon has long been known to addicts and M.D.s. It is used by the six million Americans who take prescription antidepressants. It is used by everyone who drinks.

If we chemically create the experience of balance, then the mind and body can practice maintaining a nonaddictive state. Restoring the body's balance is, of course, the goal of medicine. (So if your doctor or psychiatrist has prescribed a medication, take it.) But mind-balancing (psychopharmacological) drugs, like all synthetic medications, can have strong and sometimes dangerous side effects —one popular antidepressant causes anxiety, another one causes dizziness, headaches, and fatigue. These drugs work by influencing subtle processes in the body, including brain chemistry and neural interactions. Changes in brain chemistry are natural. What is not natural is how the drugs go about their work. They move in like the police in a raid: smashing down the front door, rushing in, and forcibly subduing and handcuffing the suspects. You don't need that kind of trauma going on inside your body. In the long run, it isn't going to help (although to deal with a more immediate crisis, it may be necessary).

There is a more benign approach, something more akin to a mother calling upstairs to the rest of the family, "Dinner's ready," so that everyone comes down to eat. The body needs to be *gently* encouraged to produce the neurotransmitters associated with normal behavior. Not too surprisingly, since neurochemicals are natural, nature provides its own pharmacopoeia. For each type of imbalance, there is a quality in a plant that can restore harmony by stimulating the body's internal pharmacy. The intelligence embodied in a plant acts like a genetic tuning fork, reminding a part of the body, through resonance, how it is supposed to behave. Ayurveda has cataloged the pharmacological effects of thousands of plants and plant combinations.

Rasayanas

If the primary purpose of an ayurvedic botanical preparation is rejuvenation (as opposed to correction of a disease), the preparation is given a special classification, called *rasayana* (rah-SIGH-yuh-nuh). Rasayanas are sophisticated herbal and mineral preparations—ayurvedic food supplements—used to keep the body and mind balanced. A rasayana may contain anywhere from a single ingredient to more than two dozen. These are combined in traditional sequences, much like a master chef producing a special sauce according to a detailed recipe. Only here, the goal is not to create a specific taste, but to maintain and enhance the intelligence embodied in the plants and minerals. This is the antithesis of the medical approach of "isolating the active ingredient." An "active ingredient" needs a rich biochemical environment—usually the plant in which that chemical is found—to act as a holistic support structure within which to work. Rasayanas are synergistic and natural. Because of this, they have no negative side effects. Just as a mixture of Italian seasonings brings only pleasure and no harm, so it is with rasayanas. Rasayanas are not flashy, like miracle drugs. They are subtle. They coax the body back into balance. They quietly work to enhance the body's feeling of well-being. Rasayanas (Advanced Recovery Tool #5) are the biochemical equivalent of bliss.

Rasayanas can be general or specific. The best known is Amrit Kalash. This, along with panchakarma, helps protect the body from environmental impurities such as pollution and pesticides. Amrit Kalash substantially increases free-radical scavenging, which reduces the likelihood of developing many diseases, including cancer and heart attacks. Other rasayanas—often prescribed by an ayurvedic physician—have specific aims. They may remove ama, restore vitality to the body after excessive sexual activity, or calm chronic anxiety. There are rasayanas designed for men and ones for women. There is even a students' rasayana, which makes the mind more calm, focused, and alert.

Note that there is a big difference between self-balancing and self-medicating. It is up to you—not your doctor—to take care of yourself and figure out how, through proper lifestyle, to keep your body balanced, and how, through proper diet and rasayanas, to keep your body feeling vital. However, for chronic or acute mental or physical problems, you need to get skilled professional help. Do not try, even with natural medicine, to self-medicate. If you are currently taking prescription medication, you must consult your doctor before adding any botanical preparations. In rare cases, there can be unexpected interactions in which one may inhibit the other.

THE FIVE SENSES

Living in an addictive environment is stressful. Over time, we may internalize the trauma, causing the body to lock into rigid patterns of behavior. The more ways we attack this rigidity, the faster we return to balance. Hearing, sight, touch, taste, and smell are all avenues through which we can break old patterns and restore harmony. Through each of the senses, the body can be naturally stimulated to let go of dysfunctional conditioning and return to balance. Gradually we establish new response patterns as we change the body's metabolic norms and neural pathways.

Healing through the five senses, Advanced Recovery Tool #6, includes touch therapy, taste therapy, aroma therapy, color therapy, and music therapy. Let's take one example, music therapy, to see how these programs work. The vedic science of music is called *gandharva-veda* (gun-DAR-vuh VAY-duh).

Gandharva-Veda

In the West, music is used to stir our emotions, to get us moving, or to make us dance. Or, as classical music, it inspires awe, settling us with its beauty. Gandharva-veda goes well beyond this. Gandharva-veda is a physics, mathematics, physiology, psychology, and even cosmology, of sound.

Sound plays a very, very important role in vedic science. It is central to cognition, to cosmology, and to health. Sound is considered in vedic science—as it is in physics—to be a vibration of energy. Every object, as well as every process in nature, has a certain vibratory quality to it. Green light, for instance, is a specific rate of vibration of the electromagnetic field. Green light is the "hum" of a field known to physicists.

Physics, however, does not have a monopoly on things that hum. Gandharva-veda extends the physicist's model of underlying fields. It posits that all objects, including people, are "excitations" of the underlying field of consciousness and that there is a correspondence between the essential, inaudible, vibratory quality of the objective world and the audible sounds we hear. It further maintains that there is a resonance effect: sounds change something subtle in the object. To a certain extent, we already believe this. If we didn't, we wouldn't listen to music: our enjoyment of a piece of music is due to the changes it makes in our neurochemistry. Gandharva rhythms, which are said to have been directly cognized from the patterns of nature rather than humanly composed, are specialized sequences of coherent sounds that resynchronize the individual with the natural rhythms of the environment, setting us back onto the path of evolution. They soothe the mind, wash away stress and fatigue, and restore self-referral.

There are specialized sound therapies that extend beyond the scope of gandharva-veda. For example, the Maharishi Vedic Vibration Technology assists in healing specific diseases and mental disorders, using subtle sounds that resonate with impaired parts of the body.

How to Do the Sense Therapies

Gandharva-veda therapy—sitting, eyes closed, and listening with quiet, relaxed attention to the music—can be done for five or ten minutes any time during the day. It balances vata dosha and brings bliss back to the surface of awareness. All you need is the appropriate tape or CD (available from Maharishi Ayurveda Products). When you buy a CD, you will need to buy it for the time of day you will be listening: each day is divided into eight three-hour segments, and the music is synchronized with a specific period.

You might be tempted to think that any music would work, but this isn't true. For example, I don't recommend CDs of "nature's sounds," such as ocean waves or lightning. These are not truly natural and are out of context. You are not in the same time and place where they were recorded. And they have usually been modified, mixed, and digitally enhanced. If you want to listen to the sounds of nature, go outside.

The more specialized aspects of the sense therapies are prescribed by an ayurvedic doctor. However, you can do a lot on your own. You can experiment with aroma therapy. There are over 250 books dedicated to the subject. Maharishi Ayurveda Products has vata, pitta, and kapha balancing aroma oils, as well as oil mixtures with names like Slumber Time and Worry Free. For touch, you can buy dosha specific massage oils. Taste involves becoming familiar with the effects of common herbs. Coriander, for example, is cooling and good for pitta. Cloves and cardamom cut down kapha. Licorice calms vata and dissipates ama. You can increase these tastes in your diet, or you can suck on the herb throughout the day. *The Yoga of Herbs,* by Dr. Frawley and Dr. Lad, is a complete compendium of the effects of herbs and traditional medicinal plants.

NONADDICTIVE EATING

Dysfunctional Eating

It has been said that over half of Americans have eating disorders.[85] Considering our attitudes toward food and the way we have been taught to eat, this is not surprising. Until ayurveda, there were few, if any, complete sources of information on diet. Most of us couldn't get it from our parents. If they had it, they wouldn't have such high rates of cancer and heart disease. And they wouldn't be on a diet. It certainly doesn't come from advertising. It doesn't come from our schools or from government publications. Even if schools teach a limited aspect of nutrition, they rarely, if ever, walk their talk. Bag lunches and cafeteria food are hardly healthy and enjoyable.

We need to relearn not only what to eat, but *how* to eat. Ayurveda provides principles and guidelines that make eating a healing process, rather than a distraction or a compulsive release of tension. As always, for life-damaging dysfunction, professional counseling is necessary. However, 140 million people (the 50 percent of Americans with potential eating disorders) need knowledge and practical techniques more than they need psychotherapy. They need to transform the process of eating into self-referral performance. Eating is so important that, by itself, it is a recovery tool (number seven, for those that are counting).

Healing Eating: Becoming Blissful, Not Skinny

We cannot regain self-referral by taking pills to suppress hunger. This only blocks the body's signal that it needs something. You may have correctly concluded that the body doesn't need calories. But it may need something else. Let's say your body has taken in carcinogens: stuck in traffic, breathing exhaust fumes; or strolling through a field that minutes before had been sprayed with powerful pesticides. Now your body is going to crave foods, such as green leafy vegetables, that have anti-cancer properties. If you suppress your craving with a pill and eat a protein-powder shake or microwave a frozen low-calorie meal, you may soon look like Miss Universe, but you may also die of cancer.

In the area of diet, ayurveda focuses on nutrition, dosha-balancing, and attention. These three are the keys to freedom from compulsion. Attention is, by far, the most important. Pay attention to your body. Learn how it works. Learn to work with it. Here is a suggested routine—almost a ritual—for eating. Like any ritual, after it is over, you should feel you have had a powerful, balancing, life-affirming experience.

1. Start your meal with a minute of eyes-closed silence. This allows the mind and body to prepare for digestion, which is a non-trivial process.

2. Don't distract yourself. Enjoy pleasant conversation, calming music, or, even better, silence. Never hold animated discussions, have arguments, watch TV, read, or work during meals. Again: DON'T WATCH TV!

3. Take reasonable-sized bites—not too big, not too small. You might try the following: After you take a bite, put your fork down, chew your food well, swallow, and then wait for a slow count to three. Then—and only then—pick up your fork for the next bite. This may seem extreme, but it balances vata and effectively normalizes compulsive eating.

4. Taste your food. *Consciously* enjoy it; experience the exquisiteness of the changing sensations as the taste of each bite fades away. Trust your taste buds: eat only what feels good to you at that moment. When a particular dish is no longer delicious, stop eating it; your body doesn't need any more.

5. Monitor how full you are. Eat only to three-quarters capacity. If you are not sure you are full, put a hand on your stomach and hold it there for a minute. Close your eyes, feel how much food is in the stomach, and then decide whether you want to eat more.

6. Try starting with the heaviest part of the meal first. Starting with cheesecake (the heaviest part of your meal) avoids getting to the end of the main course, being full, but topping off with dessert anyway.

7. Don't count calories. Instead, rely on your body to tell you how much to eat. After a meal, you should never feel dull, tired, or heavy. If this is the case, you have eaten too much, the wrong food, or overly heavy food. After a meal, you should feel great; something wonderful has just taken place. You should be calm but energetic. Your doshas should feel balanced. If you don't feel just right, modify your diet and method of eating.

8. When you are finished, sit for at least five minutes (up to fifteen to balance vata) and then go for a short stroll. Alternatively, you could try lying down on your left side for ten minutes.

Here are a few more tips:

- Eat lightly at breakfast and dinner. Never eat right before bed (unless you are training to be a sumo wrestler).
- Don't eat standing up. Once you sit down, don't get up

until the meal is over. Ayurvedic proverb: a rock eaten sitting down is better than anything eaten standing up.

- Let your previous meal digest before eating again. If you aren't hungry, don't eat. Enjoy being somewhat hungry between meals. Never let yourself get starving; it is counterproductive, especially if you are trying to lose weight.
- Don't eat when you feel upset.
- Don't drink anything cold.
- Don't talk with your mouth full—no matter how exciting dinner conversation is.
- Experience not only the taste, but also the aroma and texture of the food. (Indians traditionally eat with their hands, not because they are poor, but because they want to fully experience and *feel* the food.)
- Appreciate the presentation and the effort that went into the cooking. Find something special about the meal, attentively notice it, and comment on it.
- Experiment with a nonextreme (i.e., almost) vegetarian diet and see how you feel. Try, for example, basmati rice. It is naturally white and whole-grained, with a lot of fiber, nutrition, and protein. It is easily digested and promotes ojas.
- Eat fresh food, as soon as it is cooked; never eat leftovers.
- Cook from the heart. Making meals should be a peaceful, healing time. Don't use a microwave; cook slowly and gracefully. Don't taste (or snack) as you cook; get to know your spices, and then use them confidently. If you do taste, use a fresh spoon each time. While on the subject of cooking: ayurveda insists on stainless steel pots and pans; aluminum shouldn't be used in the kitchen.
- Observe the ayurvedic principles of food selection, food combination, and dosha pacification. These topics are covered in the ayurvedic cookbooks listed in the suggested readings. One of the most important principles is that of taste: all six tastes—sweet, sour, salty, pungent, bitter, and astringent—should be in each meal. Leaving any out results in craving. Lack of bitter and astringent tastes in the American diet is why we incessantly crave coffee and chocolate.

EXERCISE

Exercise is another opportunity for self-referral performance; vedic exercise is our eighth Advanced Recovery Tool. Dr. John Douillard (pronounced DOO-yard), a competitive triathlete, has applied the principles of yoga and ayurveda to exercise. Among other things, he recommends: breathing techniques, the use of attention, and monitoring exertion. These are incorporated into a multiphased workout, tailored to your body type. In his book *Body, Mind and Sport,* Dr. Douillard emphasizes that you can have "runner's high," "peak experiences" and perform "in the zone" whether you are walking around the block or running a marathon. Here is a summary of the principles that will get you in the zone:

- During exercise, start by getting the mind to listen to the body—tuning in to the subtle processes going on. After that, merge your already established state of relaxation into the intensity of your workout. (We will describe this in detail in a minute.)
- Many experts will tell you that systematically entering the zone is impossible. In fact, it *is* possible, but you'll have to exercise a little differently than you are used to. You cannot distract the mind. Take the magazine rack on your exercise bicycle and throw it out. Ignore the row of TVs in front of the gym's step machines. And, most sacrilegious of all, don't listen to music (unless you are so kapha you wouldn't get up off the floor without it).
- Being *in* the zone is always effortless; getting *to* the zone should also be effortless. Discomfort tells you that you are running away from the goal. The purpose of exercise is to rejuvenate—exercise should energize—and the process should be enjoyable. After a workout you should feel exhilarated. If you feel exhausted, you have entered the wrong zone—the danger zone—where risk of injury sky-rockets.
- Start the workout by super-oxygenating your body (and brain). This is done through a deep, slow, rhythmic, dia-phragmatic nasal breathing that Dr. Douillard calls "Darth

Vader breathing." In yoga, it is called *ujjayi pranayama.* Here's how to do it: during the exhale, slightly constrict your throat, so that a quiet, almost snoring noise is made. This should be a continuous sound that doesn't use the vocal cords. This technique has surprising benefits: it activates the lower lobes of the lungs, where, according to Dr. Douillard, most oxygen-carbon dioxide transfer takes place; it uses your abdominal muscles, triggering a relaxation response that counteracts the typical fight-or-flight response initiated by vigorous exercise; and it sends prana to the brain.

- Pay close attention to your breath throughout your workout. Keep it slow, smooth, and deep—and always through the nose. When the level of exertion tempts you to switch to mouth breathing, slow down. Rejuvenation takes place only if the body can eliminate waste products as they are being produced. If exertion is low enough, stress is released rather than incurred.

- Never exercise beyond 50 percent of your capacity. If you are sick, don't exercise (your morning heart rate will be about ten beats per minute higher than usual).

- Choose dosha-appropriate exercise: something gentle for vatas, something cooling for pittas, something vigorous for kaphas. Walking, running, cycling, and other steady exercise are best for learning ayurvedic exercise. These will let you listen, uninterrupted, to your body.

- Exercise at least three times a week. Mornings are the preferred time for all body types.

Here is how to do the Douillard multiphase workout:

1. Warm-up (5–10 minutes). Begin by stretching. Establish inner silence, paying close attention to the body and coordinating breath and motion. Breathe slowly and deeply, always through the nose, and in sync with your stretching. The easiest way to do this is a yoga exercise called *sun salutes,* which consists of a routine that starts from a standing pose, flows through a series of arched and "push-up" positions, and then returns to standing. Sun salutes are described in Dr. Douillard's book and in most books and video tapes on yoga.

2. Resting Phase (5–10 minutes). Start with *very* light exercise. On an exercise bicycle, pedal with no, or almost no, resistance. If jogging, start by walking. Your job is to work out the lungs. Do the Darth Vader breathing, inhaling much deeper than usual. Establish a slow rhythm that you can maintain throughout the whole workout. A typical heart rate for this phase is around 100.

3. Listening Phase (10–20 minutes, according to body type). Increase the level of activity, but not all at once. On the bicycle, add resistance to the pedals. On the track, start slowly jogging. This is the part that requires the most attention. You are looking for the upper limit of comfort (we tend to race right past it), avoiding the fight-or-flight response. You can monitor your heart rate—many exercise bicycles have a built-in pulse detector in the handle, and a digital display. In *Body, Mind, and Sport,* there is a formula—based on age, fitness, and dosha—to calculate the optimum heart rate for the different phases. A typical listening phase rate is 130. As you increase exertion, watch your heart rate. When it goes over 130, ease up for a couple minutes. Then try to push your limit again. Keep repeating this cycle until you reach a steady state. It is even easier if you ignore heart rate and pay attention only to breathing: when your breath rate goes up, lower your level of exertion.

At the same time as you increase your outer activity, sequester yourself in inner silence. You are hunting for the zone.

The length of the listening phase depends on your dosha: 10 minutes for vata, 15 for pitta, and 20 for kapha. Remember, kaphas are slow to get going, but keep going and going.

4. Performance Phase (take as long as you like, but finish still in the zone). Now you are ready to let go. Pay less attention to external signals, such as heart and breath rate, and more to the internal experience of bliss and exhilaration. As you increase the activity around your inner silence, you expand the zone. If breathing becomes labored, or your heart rate shoots up, and especially if your form breaks down, reduce exertion until you return to a comfortable, steady state. Even in the performance phase, your breath rate should still be about the same as it was in the warm-up and resting phases. The efficiency of your breathing is what should go up.

How much to push and how long to maintain the performance phase is determined in the listening phase. If you felt great, go the distance. If you were dragging and felt more tired than usual, then keep the performance phase light, or skip it entirely. Let bliss, not your ego, be your guide.

5. Cool down. Wind down with 5 to 10 minutes of light exertion, similar to the resting phase, breathing deeply. Moving the lactate out of the muscles minimizes the next day's stiffness. Finally, complete your workout with 5 to 10 minutes of stretching or sun salutes. When muscles are warm, stretching is most effective.

Remember to consult a doctor before beginning an exercise program. This is mandatory if you are older, overweight, or have injuries or health problems.

YOGA

What we talked about in the previous section is the type of exercise most of us grew up with: running, swimming, tennis, skiing. In the East, aspirants to enlightenment have traditionally used a different approach. Rather than running around like a horse while panting like a dog, yogis quietly manipulate the body and breath, thereby integrating mind, body, and consciousness.

Yogis use postures, called *asanas* (AH-sah-nuhs), that gently stretch the body. They manipulate the body's prana through breathing exercises, called *pranayama* (PRAH-nuh-YAH-mah). Asanas and pranayama, coupled with the TM technique, are the essence of yoga. If you want a high-powered yoga program, this is it.

Asanas tone the body, balance the doshas, and stimulate marma points. In other words, they keep you fit, looking good, and feeling great. Pranayama increases the body's vitality and is good for balancing the emotions. There are many kinds of pranayama. A common method, called balanced breathing—where you breathe in and out of alternate nostrils, changing after breathing in—is soothing and calming. This pranayama, although good for all doshas, predominantly balances vata. Other more specialized pranayamas release frozen emotional and physiological patterns. Through these techniques, you can douse your anger, release a headache, energize yourself out of depression, soothe away fear, or tone your digestion.

Yoga, including asanas and pranayama, is Advanced Recovery Tool #9. Like meditation, yoga should be learned personally from a qualified instructor. In fact, all the great teachers of vedic science will tell you that you must study under the personal guidance of a skilled teacher. If I were you, I would choose someone enlightened.

Before we go on, a word about *yoga.* Yoga is one of the richest and most significant disciplines of vedic science. Yoga, properly understood, is a comprehensive path to enlightenment. According to Maharishi Mahesh Yogi, "The purpose of Yoga is to gain knowledge by direct perception."[86] The yoga Maharishi teaches is *raja yoga,* or royal yoga. It overlaps with, but is distinct from, hatha yoga, which is famous for its complicated postures. Raja yoga cuts to the quick and doesn't waste time on unnecessary preparation—you don't have to learn to stand on your head before you can learn to transcend. Remember, yoga is a means of getting direct perception of Reality. All the postures and breathing exercises should lead to that goal.

Most people, when they think of yoga, think hatha yoga. And not only hatha yoga, but solely the portion of it that is physical. And, not only that, but the Westernized version. (Even yoga journals are beginning to question if this is really still yoga.) But this is what people think of, so let's discuss physical hatha yoga.

You can try to learn hatha yoga from a videotape or a book. This is not ideal—far from it—and I don't recommend it; but simple things, like sun salutes, can be learned this way. The benefits of sun salutes are tremendous—do them daily.

If you choose to take group classes at your local gym or yoga studio, be advised that the quality of instructors, as well as teaching styles and traditions, vary considerably. Try several different teachers and types of yoga; find something you are comfortable with. Be careful about injuries, both past and those you want to avoid. If the teacher doesn't ask (and she should), go right ahead and tell her at the start of class that you have had problems with your back or your knees or wherever. This is not the time to be shy. There is a saying in body building (which overlaps with yoga in at least this area): "The only thing that can prevent you from getting stronger . . . is an injury." In yoga classes, you may be asked to do intense postures that either last a long time or are pretzel-like. Also, some instructors rigidly focus on form and technical details. This has its place, but remember yoga is about the *experience* of balance and joy, not what you look like on the outside.

Maharishi Vedic Schools offer a course on Maharishi Yoga. This course emphasizes integration and inner experience. And while there are no daily group sessions as a yoga studio might offer, this course will make you self-sufficient in your yoga practice.

DEEPER EXPERIENCES

Once you have learned to meditate, there are a number of ways to deepen your experience. Among these are advanced lectures, advanced meditation techniques, weekend retreats, and the TM-Sidhi program. All these build on your practice of transcending. These we will collectively consider to be Advanced Recovery Tool #10.

Residence Courses (Retreats)

TM residence courses combine knowledge and experience. They offer an opportunity to get deeper rest and to intellectually explore the different facets of vedic science or the path of yoga. Usually they last two or three days, sometimes up to a week. Typically, you arrive after work on a Friday and leave after lunch on Sunday. At a residence course you are taught yoga asanas and pranayama, and you meditate extra.

The TM-Sidhi Program

The TM-Sidhi program, also known as Yogic Flying, is an extension of the TM technique. The difference between TM and the TM-

Sidhi program is that TM opens to your awareness the field of all possibilities (the Self), whereas the TM-Sidhis *activates* the field of all possibilities: you learn to think from a level right next to the Self. This is training for self-referral performance.

Maharishi, the founder of the TM-Sidhi program, describes its effects:

> If we have practiced the TM-Sidhi program, then the conscious mind will always start thinking from that deepest level of the self-referral state of intelligence. And any thought that emerges consciously from there has the support of all the laws of nature. And any thought with the full support of natural law will always be fulfilled quickly without loss of time, without struggle and strife.[87]

LIFE PATTERNS

As we said in chapter 4, vedic science is much bigger than ayurveda; its disciplines cover the full range of life. One particularly intriguing specialty of vedic science is called *jyotish* (JOH-tish). Jyotish is vedic astrology. It deals with time, space, and causality—and the transcending of all that. It comes complete with its own theory, worldview, and techniques. Jyotish is the most way-out of all the recovery tools we present. It is also one of the most useful.

Avert the Danger That Has Not Yet Come

In ayurveda we look for imbalances that are already there. With pulse diagnosis we detect imbalances before they manifest as physical symptoms or emotional states. However, the imbalance is still present on a subtle mental and physical level. Through jyotish, negative influences coming from the environment can be foreseen long before they arise. If we are going to have a rough time in our marriage, or be exposed to an environmental influence that will push us toward addiction or relapse, then jyotish gives suggestions to avoid catastrophe and to make this period more evolutionary.

According to lore, jyotish was "cognized" tens of thousands of years ago by enlightened sages. They wanted a way to help people not only become enlightened but also avoid misfortune and suffering along the way. Jyotish tells us what big events will occur in our lives, and what significant influences will come from the environment. Jyotish also tells us *when* these things will happen. But jyotish does more than that; it fits the pieces of life together. We see why the good things—and the not-so-good things—happen. In Maharishi Jyotish, every event in your life is taken to have an evolutionary purpose. It is exhilarating to know that everything that happens, seen in the big picture, is all-progressive. Confident that evolution is already hard at work, you can let go and let life happen.

Through jyotish, you see the "you" that will unfold in this lifetime—what you can usefully change, what is best left alone, and when is the best time to work out which issues. Jyotish comes as close as you can get to providing a personal curriculum for your Self-unfoldment.

Jyotish is practical: it can help you take advantage of unexpected opportunities; it can help you find a rewarding profession; it can help you understand your relationships. Through jyotish, you can maximize your happiness and prevent misery. Jyotish, because of its ability to reveal life patterns, is Advanced Recovery Tool #11.

Back to Recovery

Let's briefly relate jyotish to an established concept in psychotherapy. Transactional analysis talks of *life scripts*. A life script is the role you unconsciously act out during the course of your lifetime. A life script, because it is a rut, is limiting and deadening. Part of transactional analysis involves analyzing your life to find out which rut you are stuck in, thus motivating you to choose a more fulfilling course of action. Jyotish is a quick and accurate way to determine the life scripts you are acting out. You can see other roles to choose from, ones free from past conditioning but still in consonance with your natural talents and inclinations. Thus, you get closer to your authentic self.

Getting It Done

As in Western astrology, a chart is made using your time and place of birth. This is then interpreted by an expert who explains the influences acting on your life and perhaps gives remedial suggestions. You can get a lifetime overview (natal chart), a detailed picture of one or more years (progression chart), or an analysis of marriage compatibility—which I strongly recommend.

It is important to have an expert do your jyotish. Never consult an amateur! Note that your time of birth *must* be accurate. You should have your birth chart done by three different people. This counteracts any biases in interpretation. At least one of these three sessions should be through Maharishi Jyotish. Maharishi has given a unique angle to jyotish and employs only the world's leading experts. It is best to be at your jyotish session in person, but a telephone call or a taped session also works. Think ahead of the specific questions you want answered.

During the jyotish consultation, you may be advised to buy and wear specific gems and to have *yagyas* (YAHG-yuhs) performed. Yagyas are traditional vedic performances carried out by teams of specially trained vedic pundits—engineers of consciousness. Maharishi has established large groups of these pundits in India; their job is to create world peace through the performance of yagyas, which influence subtle energy fields, thereby reducing the impact of negative past actions and making our life more progressive. Delineating exactly how a yagya works is not easy. Physics is on the verge of being able to explain how the individual and the cosmos are connected, but science still isn't quite there. We do know, at least intuitively, that we *are* connected to our environment, and that the result of our action—our "karma"—does come back to us. Yagyas enliven specific laws of nature, such that our connection to the more universal aspect of nature is restored and any negative influence ("bad karma") is neutralized.

In general, for an addict, I am hesitant to recommend gems. If you want to indulge, fine, but here are the reasons you might want to think twice: first and foremost, addicts and codependents will do anything to get someone else to do their work—gems (and yagyas and anything else) are no substitute for the honest work of recovery; second, gems are expensive; third, I know of no completed and published studies documenting their benefits.

While many of these caveats also apply to yagyas, I encourage you to give them a try and see if you get results. You will be contributing to world peace (by supporting the peace pundits in

India) at the same time as you bring an evolutionary influence to your own life. As always, be a wary consumer: many jyotish consultations don't provide enough information to decide if a yagya is essential or merely a good idea; you are often left with a laundry list of yagyas. If after the jyotish consultation you are still confused, call the national yagya office and ask them to help you figure out what each recommended yagya is for, and how important it is. Yagyas come in different price ranges. You don't necessarily have to get the most expensive; whatever your present level of affluence, nature will support your desire to change.

A final suggestion: don't let yourself become dependent on external guidance. Look within yourself, decide what you want to create, and then create it. There is a story about a guru who wanted to set an example for his students. He announced an especially difficult task for himself, then invited the public to hear a reading of his jyotish chart, which strongly suggested he would fail. Going against all the advice, he still succeeded. Thus, he demonstrated that we are not bound by the past or by circumstances, that it is our actions in the present that create our destiny.

Use your jyotish session as a tool to understand yourself and to see where you should be going and what you need to work on. Don't use jyotish—or any other advanced recovery tool—to limit yourself.

THE ENLIGHTENED INTELLECT

It may seem to you, after reading this far, that becoming enlightened is a complicated business. It's not. Vedic science includes a tool that invokes the intellect to remind us to keep it simple. The approach of the intellect points out that our complicated (addictive-codependent-adult child) behaviors have arisen because we have forgotten the essential unity that underlies the apparent diversity of life. Once this happens, the intellect takes over and we become absorbed in *becoming* instead of *being.* This results in loss of wholeness of awareness. Because the intellect can handle diversity, but cannot grasp unity, memory of the Self becomes overshadowed by the logical-rational part of the mind, and we start doing and doing and doing, without awareness of Being.

This, in Maharishi's Vedic Science, is termed "the mistake of the intellect." It is the fundamental cause of problems and misery. Its removal breaks the cycle of suffering. This is the same concept of restoring self-referral discussed in chapter 2, only here we focus primarily on the intellect getting to know the process of consciousness diversifying itself. Once aware of this process, you can notice when wholeness of awareness starts to become obscured behind the insignificant details of life. Then—before you become unhappy, unhealthy, and resentful—you can bring yourself back to a settled state of mind, such that your awareness includes both the Self and the objects of attention. In other words, you shift back, closer to the Self, the conscious point of origin from which you project your awareness outward.

This is Advanced Recovery Tool #12, and although it may sound trivial (and perhaps a little hard to understand without direct experience of the Self), it is powerful and second only to meditation in its ability to heal and restore balance.

VEDIC ARCHITECTURE

The development of vedic science isn't over. Maharishi is still refining and renovating more of its disciplines. Sthapatya-veda (stah-POT-yuh VAY-duh), the vedic science of architecture, has been a recent focus. Sthapatya-veda shows how to structure our environment so it enhances life—nurturing and supporting us. It gives blueprints for buildings, towns, and even cities. It advises on material, color, shape, orientation, and all the other traditional areas of architecture. The difference lies in strict focus on harmony with the natural environment, and it puts a priority on quality of life—in the direction of enlightenment—of the people living and working in the buildings, towns, and cities.

Of relevance to addiction, sthapatya-veda experts, when they outline the principles of building a family home, recommend that four generations live together. (This means in one estate or compound—not necessarily under one roof.) Now, to someone who grew up in a dysfunctional or addictive family, that sounds like a fate worse than death—four generations of dysfunction compounded in one place! And, of course, if there is active addiction, or extreme dysfunction, such a situation would hinder one's recovery, not to mention be unpleasant for everyone involved. Yet if this ideal were possible, think what it would offer. It would make our lives more rewarding. We would be able to share our fulfillment with our parents, our grandparents, our children, and our grandchildren. We wouldn't feel cut off or isolated. There wouldn't be the burden of working so hard just to buy a home, and hence there would be more time to enjoy and grow to enlightenment. The grandparents, and possibly the great-grandparents, would be there to help in the early, and exhausting, years of raising children. We would live longer and be healthier. Life would be easier, and everyone would benefit.

In a functional multigenerational family, life is more dignified, relaxed, vital, and meaningful. Addiction is less likely to arise because a strongly bonded, integrated multigenerational family doesn't give addiction a chance to take root and grow. Early research on alcoholism revealed that the intergenerational strength of families was inversely proportional to alcoholism rates.[88] The weaker the family bonds, the greater the chances of alcoholism. If you don't like the idea of living near the rest of your family, then imagine restarting the multigenerational family tradition with yourself, after you have solved all your problems. Then you can enjoy the fruits of your labors. Your work doesn't go to waste. Society— at least your family—benefits.

As we said, sthapatya-veda does not limit itself to homes; it has blueprints for villages and cities as well. These emphasize quality of life and sense of community—rather than two-hour commutes, noise, crime, and pollution. Contemporary city planning creates almost no sense of community; ironically, each family is socially isolated but has little privacy. The way our cities and towns are constructed doesn't make sense—it is almost criminally negligent. It shouldn't take much intelligence to design cities well. It needs only proper knowledge.

Sthapatya-veda provides another example of the practicality and usefulness of vedic science. Any grandmother would consider it common sense. Unfortunately, by the time we are grandparents, our life is set in its pattern, and it is too late to create the ideal. With the knowledge of vedic science, someone just starting out in life can move in the direction of perfection.

PUTTING IT ALL TOGETHER

A large part of recovery consists of identifying our needs and learning to meet them. Let's create a simple diagram, using the by-now-familiar self-referral hierarchy, to see how this works. Here we are not concerned with one level being deeper than another; we are interested only in their *separateness*. Each level constitutes a distinct and nonoverlapping category of needs.

Level of Need		Source of Fulfillment
Environment	◄────────	Environment
Senses	◄────────	Senses
Body	◄────────	Body
Mind	◄────────	Mind
Intellect	◄────────	Intellect
Feelings	◄────────	Feelings
Ego	◄────────	Ego
Being	◄────────	Being

Figure 9.1 A need-fulfillment diagram: meeting our needs directly, in a healthy way.

In Figure 9.1, the boxes on the left represent needs, and the boxes on the right represent sources of fulfillment. They are connected with arrows, which indicate *action* taken to fulfill a need.

A fulfilled, balanced, and self-actualized person directly and appropriately meets the needs of all parts of their personality. For example, emotional needs are met by interacting with friends and family—on the level of emotions. Thus, an emotional source meets an emotional need. And so on for each of the other levels.

Contrast this with addictive behavior. In Figure 9.2, an addict tries to fill an emotional void by using the senses (eating), by using the body (taking drugs), and by manipulating the environment (compulsively making money). An addict (or codependent or adult child) uses an inappropriate source for fulfillment. Addicts mismatch their needs and the level from which they try to fulfill their needs. This inevitably means lack of fulfillment.

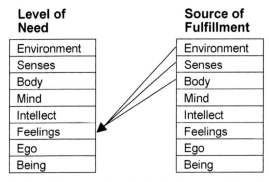

Figure 9.2 An example of addictive (inappropriate and indirect) fulfillment of desires and needs.

Of course, it isn't just the addict who faces this problem. We all do. Consider a few of the levels. For the average person, the level of Being is completely ignored. The senses also are rarely satisfied. Neither is the thinking mind—we do little to strengthen the mind's innocent capacity to have a thought. (And then we wonder why so many people, at the end of their lives, lose the ability to think coherently and become senile—as if it suddenly happened all by itself.)

Consider the somewhat whimsical example of an "ordinary working adult" depicted in Figure 9.3. We can see that a great deal of activity is going on. The person probably thinks they are doing a lot for themselves and for those around them. After all, they know what is going on in the world (they watch TV and read the newspaper); they are working for a better world (well, they do *go* to work, give a few dollars of that hard-earned money to charity, and complain about politicians); and they exercise both their body (sometimes) and their emotions (usually through TV or arguments).

Clearly, in spite of all these efforts, needs are not being met. Is it any wonder that so many Americans are on antidepressants? If you work hard and yet make little progress in fulfilling your needs, of course you are going to be depressed. We don't need more pills. Taking pills to meet emotional needs is an excellent example of an inappropriate source of fulfillment. We need to learn how to meet our needs directly. Until that happens, as long as we deprive ourselves of appropriate stimulation, we are going to have cravings, which is the first step down the slippery slope of addiction.

Don't get me wrong; I do believe mind-balancing medication is sometimes necessary. If you are taking Prozac or lithium, DON'T STOP! Of course, mental disorders, such as severe depression, require medical attention. But it does seem that we (society, as well as the doctors who do the prescribing) often neglect additional approaches.

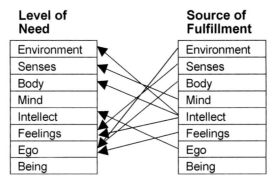

Figure 9.3 Inappropriate and unsuccessful attempts to fulfill basic needs.

I met a young mother who, six months before, had seen her family doctor about panic attacks. Being the mother of a two-year-old and holding down her own job, while her husband both went to school and worked full time, was too much stress for her, and she started having severe panic attacks. Her doctor prescribed an anxiety medication for the fear and heart medication for the heart palpitations. On her own initiative, she enrolled in an adult education class on spirituality, which taught some theory as well asanas, pranayama, and meditation. Within a few weeks, her fear of panic attacks—as well as the attacks themselves—went away. Soon after that, she stopped the medication. She told me she felt she could have died—not from the panic attacks, but from continuing the medication. I asked her carefully about what happened during the visit with the doctor: it was a short consultation during which the doctor made no real attempt to alert her to approaches that didn't involve drugs.

Direct Fulfillment

It may be helpful to create an annotated need-fulfillment diagram for yourself. After a few weeks of careful self-observation, document—with arrows and short explanations—how you attempt to fulfill different needs. This may give you insight into areas where you need to learn new skills.

Figure 9.4 shows how vedic science helps establish the habit of *appropriately and completely* fulfilling our needs—directly from the appropriate level.

Vedic science, as we have said, is surprisingly comprehensive. However, it is good to remind ourselves that there *are* areas of life that get left out. We need more than one approach to healing. Specific dysfunction needs specialized professional attention. Vedic science is meant to complement, not replace, other methods.

SOME WORDS OF CAUTION

A good job and good friends are more important than anything in this chapter. Your basic everyday activity—your job—must be nourishing, and so must your home and leisure activities. A wholesome job that helps others does great things for the ego; friends and family help you learn to enjoy.

Always meet your needs directly. Do not use the programs of vedic science to try to meet the needs of one level from another level. That is just another form of addiction. It is especially important not to try to get your emotional needs or your ego (self-worth) needs met by an organization or a teacher. This includes the TM, vedic science, and ayurveda organizations. Rely instead on yourself, your friends, and your family. If you have an addictive or codependent background—and especially if you have a history of mental disorders—don't hang out at, work, or volunteer for your local TM center or Maharishi Vedic School. Get the knowledge and the tools, and get on with your life. These organizations are set up to effectively *teach* the programs—not to be your long-lost parents or savior or support group. Trying to get your emotional or self-esteem needs met by an organization is like trying to have a fulfilling relationship with a newspaper dispenser. It is foolish and far from fulfilling.

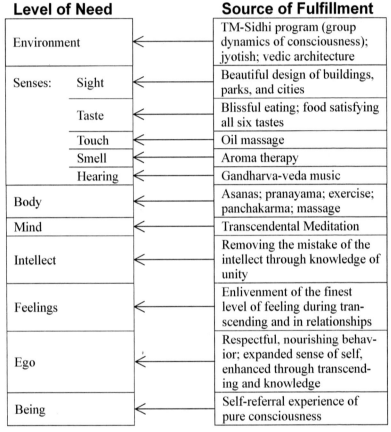

Level of Need		Source of Fulfillment
Environment		TM-Sidhi program (group dynamics of consciousness); jyotish; vedic architecture
Senses:	Sight	Beautiful design of buildings, parks, and cities
	Taste	Blissful eating; food satisfying all six tastes
	Touch	Oil massage
	Smell	Aroma therapy
	Hearing	Gandharva-veda music
Body		Asanas; pranayama; exercise; panchakarma; massage
Mind		Transcendental Meditation
Intellect		Removing the mistake of the intellect through knowledge of unity
Feelings		Enlivenment of the finest level of feeling during transcending and in relationships
Ego		Respectful, nourishing behavior; expanded sense of self, enhanced through transcending and knowledge
Being		Self-referral experience of pure consciousness

Figure 9.4 Summary of vedic knowledge and techniques on each level of need and fulfillment. Notice that levels of need are sometimes naturally met by activity in other levels. For example, behavior meets ego-level needs—but only behavior attentive to the ego and the finest level of feeling can meet needs on the level of the ego.

A few more suggestions:

- Avoid fanaticism.
- Start each program when it is best for you, not before you are ready.

- Have a safety net (friends or a counselor—ideally both—who keep an eye on you).
- Do not expect instant recovery or instant enlightenment. Recovery takes time; enlightenment takes even more time. Enjoy the process.
- If you can, start or join a yogic or vedic recovery group. Share with each other what works and what doesn't work.

CONCLUSION

You now have a good understanding of the kinds of tools vedic science offers. We have introduced some aspects of most of them. We have seen that specific procedures, such as pulse diagnosis or jyotish, determine what needs to be fixed, and that multiple approaches are then used to remove these limitations and restore wholeness. Maharishi's Vedic Science heals through consciousness, the intellect, the emotions, speech, the body, the senses, and behavior. We also heal by eating, exercising, breathing, and properly using our attention.

You have seen a lot of vedic science, but you haven't seen everything. Vedic science is the playground of the enlightened, offering the joy of diving deeply into the Self and exploring the ocean of pure knowledge. Vedic science is too rich and profound for me to cover everything here. This book is a primer, giving you the opportunity to start moving confidently toward the bliss of enlightenment.

HEALING
SOCIETY

CHAPTER TEN

Why is Switzerland prosperous and Bangladesh impoverished? Why do previously peaceful countries destroy themselves with civil wars? We need a model to explain why groups of people behave the way they do. This chapter presents a paradigm for understanding society.

America is a highly addictive nation. We are getting better; we *are* facing the issues. But we still have a long way to go. Almost a quarter of the adults in the United States are addicted to cigarettes. Ten to fifteen percent of Americans, at some point in their lives, deal with alcoholism. Seven percent will abuse, and very likely become addicted to, hard drugs such as cocaine, crack, or methamphetamine. Each year 400,000 smokers and 100,000 drinkers would rather die than quit. Or, in the case of drunk drivers, rather kill than quit. Fifteen million people live in violent families. Six million Americans are on antidepressants, and untold millions more are addicted to prescription drugs. This is most prevalent, and perhaps least noticed, in the elderly, an estimated two million of whom are alcoholics.

But this isn't the whole picture. To say we are addictive misses the point. Our world is incoherent, and *anything* is possible: war, famine, poverty, epidemics, environmental devastation, technological disaster—any one of these could eliminate meaningful life for a region and even, perhaps, for the world.

The current approach to creating a better world—set up institutes and research universities and have our best minds work to solve national and global problems—has failed. Military interventions have also failed—again and again. Individuals, governments, and international organizations, including the United Nations, are unable to radically change the world. Getting out there and "helping" isn't working. If there is chaos in the social structure, you can't get to the people who need help. Consider the Ethiopian famine in the 1980s. The international community offered good intentions, as well as actual food, but people starved because political unrest—incoherence in the region—disrupted food convoys. The 1990s were marked with a dozen similar examples, such as starvation in Somalia and ethnic war in Yugoslavia.

The United States faces the same situation with substance abuse and violence: everyone wants to change the situation, but we can't do it—our good intentions are effectively blocked by incoherence pervading the collective consciousness. If you had any doubts, the terrorist attack on the World Trade Center should have made it unmistakably clear that no one is safe in an incoherent world. And more violence, no matter which side (the "good guys" or the "bad guys") uses bombs to further its agenda, will not solve the problem. It will only make things worse, as a careful study of U.S. foreign policy and post-World War II history will reveal.

We need new knowledge: how to treat society as a whole. We need a new model for societal functioning, and we need practical procedures to change the *overall* behavior of a nation.

A NEW PARADIGM IS EMERGING

In 1983, in the Middle East, an unusual experiment was performed. The results challenge our assumptions about how the world works. They demand a paradigm shift. We have to let go of old and out-dated beliefs—beliefs that haven't worked anyway.

This experiment was designed by a research team working at a world peace institute associated with Harvard University. The researchers wanted to see if a relatively small number of people could make society more coherent. So far, that sounds OK. It doesn't challenge any cherished beliefs. However, the *method* that the researchers proposed for creating the change is, at first, hard to accept. They theorized that, not acting, but transcending, would accomplish the goal. This definitely rocks the scientific boat: can a few people transcending—just meditating—push the collective behavior of a whole nation in a positive direction?

The researchers publicly predicted the results they expected: a more positive society, less crime, fewer accidents, and a reduction in the intensity of the war in Lebanon. During the experiment, these things actually happened.

The experiment consisted of gathering in Jerusalem (next door to Lebanon) experts in the TM-Sidhi program and having them practice the TM-Sidhi program together. The researchers collected data from as many sources as possible to evaluate coherence and progress in the surrounding communities. They also tracked the size of each day's TM-Sidhi group.

Their findings were published in the peer-reviewed *Journal of Conflict Resolution* and are shown in the following graph.[89] Figure 10.1 illustrates the number of participants in the TM-Sidhi program (dashed line) superimposed on an index of society's coherence (solid line). Time progresses to the right, each tick marking one day in the two-month study.

These results are astounding. Look carefully at the two lines and see how closely they follow each other. Remember that this is a *societal* effect. We can't expect a perfect one-to-one correspondence. Now, think of other ways we try to change society, such as attempts to manipulate the economy. If we could find one influence as closely correlated to the economy as TM-Sidhi groups are to society's coherence, and if we could manipulate that factor, poverty would not exist anywhere. We would all be rich. Yet, in spite of all the efforts of the Federal Reserve Board, the World Bank, and all the world's financial experts, we still have virtually no control over the economy. It is particularly rare in the field of social science to find a result like the one from this study; such a close cause-effect relationship is extremely unusual for a large population.

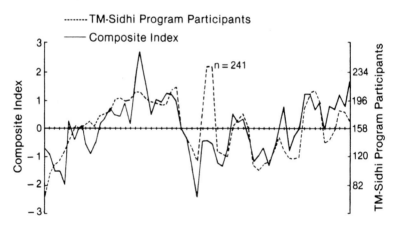

Figure 10.1 Results of the Jerusalem International Peace Project. This graph shows the number of TM-Sidhi program participants and a composite peace index—measuring conflict in Lebanon and quality of life in Israel—during a two-month period.

We need to look at this study from one more angle: causality. To get an idea of how sociologists try to prove "what caused what," think of yourself in front of a TV holding an unfamiliar remote control. You want to "prove" to a friend that you can use the remote to turn on the TV. You experiment by yourself with different buttons, and once you've convinced yourself that a particular button works, you announce to your friend (representing the scientific skeptic) that you will now push that button and the TV will turn on. You do it, and the screen comes to life. There are three important points here: one, you said *ahead of time* what you were going to do and the expected result; two, you pushed the button *and then* the result happened; and three, there wasn't an unknown third factor that was the real cause of the TV turning on. Let's go back to the Jerusalem study. First, the method and the expected results were announced ahead of time. Second, a skeptic might say that improvements in quality of life *influenced* the TM-Sidhi participants—they read good news in the newspapers and then rushed off to meditate. However, statistical analysis shows it was the other way around: more people transcended, *then* society improved. Sometimes the effect was noticed in a day; sometimes it took six days to be reported. Furthermore, a continuous relationship developed such that when more people meditated quality of life got better, and when fewer people meditated quality of life got worse. Thirdly, the researchers looked for anything else, such as weather, that could have been influencing both the numbers meditating and the conflict in Lebanon, but nothing was statistically significant. This analysis, plus the fact that this was not the first study of its kind, goes a long way toward establishing causality.

The TM-Sidhi participants improved the world around them without directly interacting with their environment. How can this be? We can't explain it with our commonsense Newtonian-classical-physics worldview. Using the contemporary model of social inter-action, it's impossible for a few hundred people, sequestered in a room, to radically change the trends of society—certainly not without getting out there and doing something, at least making a phone call or two. We have good, accurate, useful theories that explain the behavior of the physical world, but once we start to deal with the mind, and especially we when try to understand pure consciousness, we are in the dark. There are no socially accepted theories of consciousness. We are in denial, albeit "scientific" denial, that consciousness even exists. We doubt the reality of our own minds. Seems a little psychotic, doesn't it?

It is time to update our model. The theory of *collective consciousness* seems to be a strong contender to explain the collective behavior of society. And, as good scientific theories often do, it offers a technology to harness the power of the natural laws it describes.

MAHARISHI'S THEORY OF COLLECTIVE CONSCIOUSNESS

Picture collective consciousness as an ocean. Each wave represents one person's consciousness. All the waves merge into the ocean of the collective consciousness.

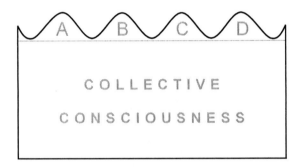

Figure 10.2 Each individual's consciousness (A, B, C, and D) contributes to, and merges into, the collective consciousness.

Every clearly defined group has a distinct collective consciousness. We experience the special characteristics of a nation's collective consciousness when we cross the border to that country. There is something different and unique about the laws of nature that structure each country. That something is the collective consciousness.

Definition	The **collective consciousness** is the sum total of the consciousness of all the individuals in a group. The quality of each person's awareness contributes to the overall quality of the collective consciousness.

The collective consciousness extends beneath the level of the culture, beneath the values and ideals of a society, and beneath what some psychologists call the "collective unconscious." Although these are all aspects of a particular collective consciousness, the collective consciousness is both more macroscopic and more fundamental. The collective consciousness is not the collective conscience; it determines the collective conscience. It is not the culture; it determines the culture. It is not the system of government; it determines the system of government. It is not the collective beliefs; it determines the collective beliefs. Collective consciousness is analogous to individual consciousness, just bigger.

Let's lay out the fundamentals of Maharishi's theory of collective consciousness:[90]

1. There is a hierarchy of collective consciousnesses. For example: family, community, city, state, national, and world. Each level has its own integrity, quality, and attributes.

2. We influence, and are influenced by, each level of the collective consciousness. This is automatic and continuous. It happens whether or not we want it to, believe in it, or are conscious of it. Every action of ours, including thinking, creates a change in our environment. When we are stressed, we pollute the collective consciousness; we make it incoherent. In terms of the ocean analogy: our wave stirs up mud from the bottom of the ocean.

Imagine each wave in Figure 10.2 being muddy. Then the region beneath all the waves is murky. Just as we affect the collective consciousness, so we are affected by the collective consciousness; think how hard it would be for one wave to remain clear if the water below it was muddy.

3. Stress in the collective consciousness is a major confounding factor in the world's problems. Wars, for example, do not start because two heads of state cannot get along. Politicians can create problems, but they are not *that* powerful. Wars result from a buildup of intense stress. Each person may make only a small contribution, but millions or even billions of people harboring strong negative feelings, such as hatred, lodge stresses—millions or billions of them each day—in the collective consciousness. These stresses don't go any-

where, they accumulate. As the stress increases, so does the tension, fear, hostility, and resentment. If nothing is done to ease the tension, violence erupts. What form it takes depends on the situation. It could be anything: ethnic strife, civil war, or urban violence.

A similar line of reasoning could be taken for other societal problems, such as extreme poverty, wide-scale drug abuse, and even imbalance in the natural environment, such as drought or famine.

4. Consciousness is a *field*. Physics uses water and its waves as an analogy for a field and its activity. Water has waves you can see, whereas a field often has waves you cannot see but sometimes can feel. Infrared light is an example of a wave we feel (as heat) but cannot see. A magnetic field, on the other hand, has waves our body cannot detect. It is invisible to us but not to an iron filing. Consciousness is a field we cannot see. That shouldn't surprise us, because most fields can't be seen. Its waves are also invisible to our eyes. Again, not too startling: many other fields, such as the gravitational field, have invisible waves.

Our minds, when we think, generate waves in the ocean of consciousness. When we transcend, a wave of coherent consciousness goes out; like a pebble dropped into a calm pond, the ripples spread out to the surroundings. If you can imagine it, a field is analogous to an invisible, infinite expanse of water in which waves can go in any direction, not just on a flat plane. When we transcend, we influence the whole field of consciousness. The effect is strongest near us, and minute very far away. Nevertheless, to some extent, we influence everything. The influence of transcending is positive, harmonizing, and purifying. When we feel good inside, it radiates out.

These four points summarize the theory of collective consciousness. They show how problems in society are caused, and although they don't outright state a solution to the problems, they do point us in the right direction. You won't be surprised to learn that the solution has to do with transcending. Like rain clearing the air of pollution, transcending washes away the accumulated stress from our environment. Transcendental Meditation, and especially the TM-Sidhi program done in a group, can be considered a technology, just as real and effective as satellites and street lamps. The TM-Sidhi program, when done in a big group, is Advanced Recovery Tool #13. It is a technology used to eliminate stress, restore balance, and maintain an orderly collective consciousness. It is, as far as I know, the only documented method for creating world peace and fostering systemic progress in society.

Large groups that transcend together have a synergistic effect—their influence is much greater than if each person were alone. I will spare you the sociophysics. Suffice it to say that to have a noticeable worldwide effect, with the world's current population, you would need 8,000 people deeply transcending in one place. Fewer people are needed for a regional effect.

WHIRLWIND TOUR OF THE RESEARCH

One experiment is insufficient to substantiate a new theory. So let's quickly review a representative sample of the forty studies done to date. Experiments on collective consciousness vary in scale: city, national, and global. Some are intervention studies, such as the one done in Jerusalem, and some are longitudinal, taking place over many years. We will cover only the highlights. To learn more, read *Creating Heaven on Earth: The Mechanics of the Impossible,* by Robert Oates. The most complete academic summary of the research appears in the journal *Modern Science and Vedic Science,* in an article titled "Maharishi's Program to Create World Peace: Theory and Research." To see how all of this relates to recovery, read Dr. Orme-Johnson's chapter in *Self-Recovery,* "Transcendental Meditation as an Epidemiological Approach to Drug and Alcohol Abuse: Theory, Research and Financial Impact Evaluation."

Creating Coherence for a City

In 1972, a dozen U.S. cities, mostly college towns, reached one percent of the population practicing the Transcendental Meditation program. Quite a few years earlier, Maharishi Mahesh Yogi had suggested that once a minimal percentage practicing TM had been reached, the quality of life should begin to go up for the whole community. Researchers looked for a way to measure changes in society. They decided to use the crime rate, as the FBI had established uniform national standards for reporting and tracking it. The researchers found that crime decreased in a city by about 8 percent when one in every hundred of its residents was practicing TM. Meanwhile, the national crime rate continued to climb at 8 percent per year. Cities demographically identical to those in the study—except with fewer meditators—showed no overall crime reduction.[91]

Subsequently, more cities reached the one percent meditating mark. A second study conducted a few years later and published in the *Journal of Crime and Justice* found a reduction in crime rate in a larger sample of forty-eight cities.[92] Further analysis found reductions in automobile accidents, hospital admissions, and suicide.[93] A study published in *The Journal of Mind and Behavior* concluded—after looking exhaustively at all other possible explanations—that TM caused the crime reduction.[94]

An International Intervention

Several years later, the first experiments were done on what has been called the *Super Radiance Effect.* These involved large groups of TM-Sidhi experts, typically more than a thousand. The first study, conducted in 1979, sent a total of 1,400 experts to the world's three most troubled areas: in southern Africa, to Zimbabwe (known then as Rhodesia) and Zambia; in Central America, to Nicaragua, Honduras, Costa Rica, Guatemala, and El Salvador; and in the Middle East, to Iran, Syria, Cyprus, and Israel (to influence Lebanon). The researchers called this the World Peace Project and described the results as follows:

> The research hypothesis was publicly announced in advance of the experiment in several newspapers, making the experiment public and predictive....
>
> During the World Peace Project the percentage of hostile actions between countries as well as between factions within the trouble spots decreased relative to the baseline period by 16.7 percentage points (from 46.4% to 29.7%). Cooperative events increased by 13.2 percentage points during the World Peace Project relative to the baseline period (from 36.0% to 49.2%, p<.0001). Interestingly, verbal hostilities also increased by 3.5 percentage points,

which may be interpreted as a shift from behaviorally expressed hostilities to verbal hostilities.[95]

There were other results that, while not strictly statistically significant, are still meaningful. For example, according to the researcher, "War deaths in [Zimbabwe] decreased from a baseline of 16.1 per day to 3 per day during the experimental period, and quickly rose again to the baseline level when the group left."[96]

The participants did not try to influence or manipulate their environment. They did not pray or psychically send out "good vibes." Nor did they try to resolve or work out any of the regional conflicts, issues, or problems. Each person was quietly minding his or her own business. They settled down, transcended, and enlivened bliss in their awareness. Whatever changes occurred in society were carried out by the laws of nature, which had been freed from the burden of collective stress.

A Long-Term Study: Creating Coherence for a Nation

Studying trends is an ongoing project at Maharishi University of Management, where the university's staff, faculty, students—and even many residents of the local town of Fairfield, Iowa—take part in the town's Super Radiance program. Since 1979, the university has been attempting to create coherence for the nation. The scientists at Maharishi University of Management claim success. They use this chart to back up their assertion:[97]

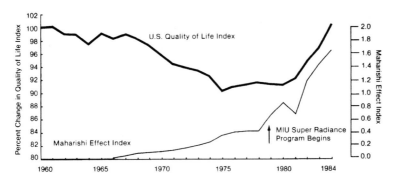

Figure 10.3 Improved quality of life in the United States due to increasing numbers of people transcending.

The bold line is the U.S. Quality of Life Index. It shows quality of life decreasing from 1960 until 1975. The Quality of Life Index consists of:

crime rate	hospital admissions
notifiable diseases	infant mortality
suicide rate	cigarette consumption per capita
traffic fatalities	alcohol consumption per capita
GNP per capita	degrees conferred per capita
divorce rate	patent applications (a measure of creativity)

Interestingly, a number of these categories are addiction related.

The lighter line on the graph is the Maharishi Effect Index. It reflects the combined effect of all meditators and the TM-Sidhi group. When this index reaches one it is equivalent to one percent of a population meditating or the square root of one percent doing the TM-Sidhi program—enough transcending to have an effect.

In 1975 almost a quarter of a million Americans learned the Transcendental Meditation technique. This brought the number of U.S. meditators to 0.4 percent—seemingly enough to stop the decline in quality of life. Then, in 1982, the quality of life index started rising sharply. This coincided with the Maharishi Effect Index reaching one. Although this finding seems a tenuous by itself, it does reinforce the other studies.

Creating Coherence for the World

The final study we will look at was a global test. At the end of 1983, more than 7,000 experts in the TM-Sidhi program came from all parts of the world to the Maharishi University of Management campus. Scientists selected four measures of world coherence: international conflicts, traffic fatalities, notifiable diseases, and the world index of international stock prices (the stock market is often considered a barometer of a nation's optimism and sense of security). These measures were chosen primarily because they are reliable over time and publicly available. As you should by now expect, during the assembly all indicators moved significantly in a life-supporting direction: international conflicts decreased, fewer people died in car and airplane accidents, fewer people got sick, and the world's stock markets rose. For a few weeks the world became safer, healthier, more peaceful, and (at least on paper) more prosperous.[98]

WHAT HASN'T WORKED

In contrast, let's look at what hasn't worked in America. What are the results of well-meaning political efforts that ignore the collective consciousness? We have Superfund toxic dumps, poverty, and epidemics. The United States has one of the world's worst urban homicide rates; it has among the most prevalent and virulent problems of addiction; it has substantial teenage violence and suicide, while high school students feel their education is irrelevant, if not alienating, and consequently drop out in large numbers from inner-city schools; and we, the role model for capitalism, can't even get our financial act together—we are paying almost $500 billion (including indirect costs, such as interest on bonds) to bail out the nation's saving and loans. Think what half a trillion dollars could have done as a humanitarian investment in developing nations.

The problem with trying to solve each problem individually is that the problems' basis—a nonprogressive and incoherent collective consciousness—remains unchanged. We thought the way to solve crime was to get tough. So we built more prisons. In a little over ten years, we doubled the number of inmates. We now have a higher percentage of the population in prison than does any other nation except Russia. Building more prisons hasn't removed the atmosphere of tension.

How about the war on drugs? Did it work? Has the might of the United States stopped the influx of drugs? How about an attitude adjustment—"Just say no." Did that work?

When are we going to wake up and stop throwing money at symptoms, while we wish and hope the problems will go away? They won't go away until the *cause* is treated. The cause is incoherence—lack of a nourishing value in the collective consciousness.

It is said that more than 60 million Americans have high blood pressure and are at risk of developing health-related complications. At one point, the government planned to *pass legislation* to remove hypertension. What were they going to do, work really hard, drink coffee, smoke cigarettes, pull an all-nighter, and get some really tough legislation through? Passing new laws will do nothing to affect the deeper levels of any societal problem. Generating coherence in the collective consciousness is a prerequisite for any kind of long-term progress. We haven't done that, so decade after decade we are mired in the same problems.

It is unmistakably clear: the government is powerless to improve our lives—unless we the people get our act together and support the government with a coherent collective consciousness. If we do not transcend, then our awareness is incoherent. Two hundred eighty million incoherent minds leave the government powerless to enact programs for the well-being of the people.

It Doesn't Have to Be That Way

By the time you read this, the transition to a better world may have already taken place. Using technologies of consciousness, it won't take much to radically transform a country or even the world. It is a matter of priority and commitment; it is not a matter of sacrifice.

Consider the alternative—search the Internet and see for yourself the cost of not putting your weight behind a new approach. Get a pencil and paper and take notes. Find out how many inmates we have in our prisons. Multiply this by the yearly cost of incarceration. (Proponents of tough-on-crime laws say that filling prisons reduces the overall cost to society by deterring crime—and to a certain extent it seems to have worked—but consciousness-based approaches reduce crime *and* prison populations, so you save doubly.) Next, find out how much we, in America, spend every year on the health care costs of tobacco addiction. Then consider alcohol-related accidents. Find out how much the Gulf War and the Kosovo bombing cost. Add up how much was spent to beef up security and defense in the aftermath of the terrorist attacks. Do the math. Even if you look only at dollars spent, I think you will agree there has to be a better way.

Now look up how many children, according to UNESCO (the

United Nations Educational, Scientific, and Cultural Organization), died unnecessarily in the ten years after the Gulf War—because the United States and its allies were unwilling to consider conscious-ness-based methods of removing stress and tension. Look up how many Iraqi citizens our bombs killed and maimed. You will be shocked. That statistic is usually left out of the U.S. media's care-fully crafted stories. And remember, Iraqis join the military for the same reasons our men and women join—they are young, often poor, don't yet have a career, need food and shelter, and are often simply forced to. Shouldn't we—as wealthy, educated, democratic, free people—take *everyone's* best interests to heart? Shouldn't we, who know better, insist on a more humane approach?

What is said in this chapter may seem far-fetched. Yet if an ideal society is possible, shouldn't we at least try? We are overworking anyway, just to maintain the current less-than-ideal state of the world. If we sail on a different tack, we could end up at an alto-gether better destination. Americans are known for coming up with, and implementing, new and unusual ideas. Once there was a time when the world respected Americans for their vision of life in free-dom. Has the dream completely faded?

TOTAL RECOVERY

CHAPTER ELEVEN

There is a general sense, among people in recovery, about what facilitates the beginning and middle stages of recovery. Rarely does anyone understand the final stages. Many think you can't get there.

What completes recovery and fully heals the wounds of dysfunction? How do we recognize total recovery? To answer these questions, we will spend some time on three areas—bliss, behavior, and enlightenment.

> *The experience of pure bliss-consciousness puts an end to all suffering; filling the heart with happiness it brings perfect tranquility to the mind. The principle is that if freedom from suffering, lasting peace, health, and fulfillment are desired, it is necessary to gain bliss-consciousness.* [99]
>
> —*Maharishi Mahesh Yogi*

BLISS

Bliss has been misunderstood. Bliss was thought to be extreme happiness, the positive end of the spectrum of human emotions. Such a spectrum would look like this:

misery   unhappiness   happiness   bliss

This is incorrect. More correct would be to say that bliss is supreme *inner* happiness or joy. Bliss is independent of any outside stimulation. So we could draw bliss as a point lying under the external continuum of misery-unhappiness-happiness.

However, this too, does not go far enough. If each emotion is a wave on the ocean of consciousness, then the ocean itself is bliss.

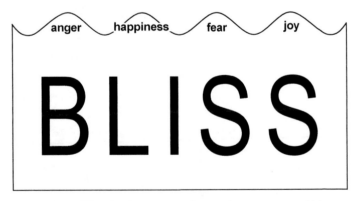

Figure 11.2 Bliss is the ocean of consciousness on which we experience the waves of emotion.

Bliss is enormous; it is an inseparable attribute of consciousness.

Figure 11.2 is much more accurate.

Bliss is not something we create or make; that would be pleasure. Bliss wells up of its own accord once we balance our life. Bliss results from wholeness of awareness. When we stop distracting ourselves, we notice the underlying bliss. If you follow any emotion, even depression, back to Being, you get to bliss, because Being is bliss.

Some recovery authors have dismissed bliss as if it were a transient and inconsequential whim of the mind. Sometimes bliss has been confused with giddiness or even mania. This is the folly of "experts" who have not bothered to personally examine Reality. Bliss is the result of an integrated physiology and a calm mind.

Bliss as Therapy

Bliss is pragmatic. It is healing. *Bliss is the key to total recovery.* Why? Because it breaks the cycle of repetitive action. Let's take a closer look at that cycle.

When we have a strong experience (either good or bad), an impression is made in the mind. The more intense the experience, the deeper the impression. Naturally, we want to re-experience the feeling if it was good or avoid it if it was bad. This is desire. One of the jobs of the mind is to prod us to fulfill desire. What we have just described is the start of a cycle: action causes impression; this becomes a desire; in time, we act to fulfill the desire; this causes a new impression. This is the archetypal wheel of karma, the endless cycle of bondage, kept in motion by ignorance.

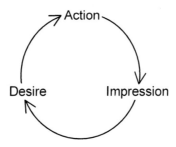

Figure 11.3 The endless cycle of "addictive" behavior.

The addict faces the same situation. When he or she gets "high," a deep impression is created in the mind. This is the seed of craving for the "drug"—whatever situation, action, or chemical that might be. In the right (we should say wrong) environment, the seed of desire sprouts and grows into action: the desire is fulfilled by again taking the drug of choice. Unfortunately, this action leads to more deep impressions in the mind, and the cycle goes on and on.

So, it turns out, recovery and enlightenment have a common goal: breaking the cycle of action-impression-desire. The million-dollar question is: Where do you break it? Traditionally, most of the effort, in the earliest stages of recovery, focuses on not letting desire proceed to action. To say the least, this is difficult.

You can only temporarily suspend addiction if you try to stop the process between desire and action (Figure 11.4).

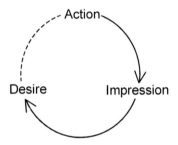

Figure 11.4 Attempts to break the cycle between desire and action are difficult—they require excessive control and effort.

Using control doesn't work in the long run. This is now accepted by most addiction counselors. Control is opposed to the force of evolution, is opposed to life. A caveat: obviously in the case of life-threatening addictions (and if you are in that category, you shouldn't have gotten this far in the book), some control or intervention before action is necessary. However, gaining freedom by controlling the events in our life takes too much energy and wastes time.

Another approach attempts to intercede between impression and desire (Figure 11.5). However, it's hard to stop an impression from growing into a desire. Trying to do that leads to unnaturalness of the mind. On the path to enlightenment, strenuous suppression of desires and culturing ascetic nonattachment are counterproductive.

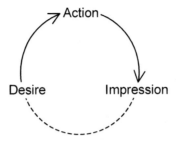

Figure 11.5 Don't try to break the cycle here: too unnatural for the mind.

Neither self-denial nor a mood of nonattachment constitutes a valid path. Fulfilling your desires leads to progress. Suppressing or ignoring them leads to stagnation, which is a fertile ground for addiction. Of course, the other extreme—wild self-indulgence—is also harmful, and has much more immediate consequences.

If our goal is total recovery, then we must work at the point right before impression. We need to stop action from creating an overshadowingly deep impression.

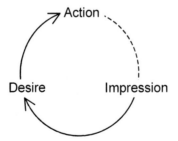

Figure 11.6 Ideal point to work most effectively.

Permanently escaping the addictive cycle involves bliss. Bliss does not allow action to make an impression deep enough to create a new desire. It is said that in enlightenment—when we have non-stop bliss—"the seeds of karma are roasted." Roasted seeds cannot sprout. Roasting the seeds of karma means there is so much inner contentment that past impressions (the seeds of karma or action) can't overshadow our enjoyment of the here and now. We stop recycling our past. We live in the moment. We no longer see the present as an opportunity to fulfill stale past desires. When we have permanent bliss-consciousness, we have lasting contentment and freedom from craving. We live in a dynamic state of peace.

Don't think that when bliss is established in the mind we no longer have desires. We do. It's just that a new mechanics of desiring takes place. We can understand the situation in terms of "identification." In ignorance we are completely involved and identified with our desires. They are a central, if not *the* central, and integral part of our self-identity. Once we start to identify with bliss-consciousness, with its unbounded ocean-like status, we are no longer completely involved with desire. We start to feel less identified with the desires and more identified with bliss or Being (self-referral awareness). From the perspective of the enlightened, being free is easy. How can the ocean be overwhelmed by a wave?

Become the ocean. Identify your awareness with the ocean of consciousness that already is you. Expand your awareness to include the depth as well as the surface of the mind. Fill your heart with bliss and rise above the childish desires that lead to negative emotions such as fear, sorrow, and depression.

Follow Your Bliss

Bliss is starting to lose its stigma, and on occasion a pioneer will boldly proclaim its value. The late Joseph Campbell, the world-famous scholar of mythology (he studied man's innate quest for greater fulfillment in life), is frequently quoted as saying, "Follow your bliss." This way, Campbell maintains, you will do something great with your life. It is wise counsel. However, what if you don't have bliss? How can you follow an experience you don't have? Most people need a technique to have the initial experience. Otherwise, not knowing genuine bliss, a modicum of happiness might be mistaken for true fulfillment. Then, following Campbell's advice, you would avoid a boring life, but not know the deepest joy of intense fulfillment. Not only do you need a way to get your first experience of bliss, you need a way to get rid of deep stress that inhibits the maintenance of bliss. Meditation provides that. Not surprisingly, Joseph Campbell recommended meditation.

Maharishi recommends making bliss the primary motivation for doing anything. Experiencing and enjoying bliss is, in itself, a technique; bliss is Advanced Recovery Tool #14.

BEHAVIOR

For people well into recovery, relationships pose the greatest challenge. So let's turn our attention to behavior.

Again we will use very simple diagrams: two people (stick figures) interacting (arrows). The codependent approach to improving relationships is to focus on other people: it is the other person who needs to be fixed, not us. We recognize this as outdated and ineffective. This is labeled Method A.

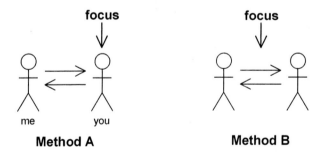

Method A   **Method B**

The next approach focuses on the interaction (Method B). This is popular, and rightly so. Often, the behavior modeled by our parents was abysmal. We need to learn new patterns. So we take seminars on effective communication. While I don't want to undermine their importance and usefulness, communication skills, used by themselves, are limited in how fulfilling a relationship they can structure.

No matter how hard we try to avoid it, whatever we are on the inside will radiate out. The strength, wholeness, and fulfillment within each person primarily determine the strength, wholeness, and fulfillment of the relationship. After the first few days (or years), it is not the words, it is the feeling that counts.

Therefore, each person in a relationship should spend adequate time on Self-development, so that, eventually, behavior becomes self-referral performance, which is bound to make everyone happy. Let's call this Method C. In Method C, the platform on which the relationship is acted out is the combination of each person's inner fulfillment.

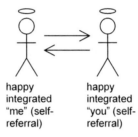

happy integrated "me" (self-referral)   happy integrated "you" (self-referral)

Method C

TM teachers explain this point with an analogy. Imagine bringing two magnets together. The force of the attraction is determined by each magnet's strength. The interaction is not easily influenced by manipulating the magnetic field between them. In other words, the bliss of a relationship is determined by the bliss in each person's heart and by the integration and integrity of awareness.

The Finest Level of Feeling

The purpose of relationships is to enliven bliss. The key to a successful relationship is to uphold, in our interactions, the finest level of feeling (where bliss is the greatest). This level of life must be nourished, strengthened, and protected. We do this not only through meditation, but also, consciously, in our behavior.

The primary behavioral injunction of ayurveda is to avoid hurting others' (and our) feelings. If delicate feelings get crushed, then not only is our relationship jeopardized, but health—both mental and physical—is disrupted and possibly destroyed. Although sometimes overlooked by medicine, this consideration towers above all others for maintaining long-term health. *We should never say anything that hurts another's feelings.* Bliss gives us the strength, even when we feel attacked, to uphold the dignity of the other person. The more inner bliss we have, the easier it gets. And, bliss radiates from us—even when we are not speaking—touching the hearts of others. Bliss and love are closely connected. Bliss is the experience of universal and unconditional love.

Nourishing the feelings—through thoughtful, attentive, and considerate speech and behavior—is so important that it is in its own category as a therapy for balancing and healing our lives. This is the last recovery tool, Advanced Recovery Tool #15. By itself, it is a path to enlightenment. Two people in a relationship, by devotedly paying attention to and nourishing the finest level of feeling, can gain enlightenment faster than the most devout and self-disciplined monk. (Being a couple, as most of us know, is not an easier path, just potentially faster.)

Core Issues

There is a concept in recovery called "core issues." In *Healing the Child Within,* Dr. Charles Whitfield describes an issue as "any conflict, concern, or potential problem, whether conscious or unconscious, that is incomplete for us or needs action or change."[100] *Core issues* are the central issues that drive us in unhealthy directions. They usually don't go away by themselves. And, they are still there whether we are aware of them or not. You can learn a million skills of effective interaction, but if your core issues have not been dealt with, you will never get to use those skills. They will gather dust in the back of your mind while the rest of you is busy creating conflicts that force you to deal with deeper problems. For those in recovery, two of the most painful core issues are self-esteem and shame.

Bliss and Self-Esteem

There may not be a quick fix for low self-esteem. Affirmations help. However, affirmations alone do not go deep enough and are not a permanent solution. Affirmations (as well as visualization) by themselves are not a sufficient engine to propel one's recovery and spiritual progress. They do not, for example, expand the conscious capacity of the mind. You may get what your affirmations aim for, but it is unlikely you are growing as rapidly as possible to enlightenment.

There is an important aspect of affirmations that is usually overlooked: their power is determined predominantly by the depth of the mind from which they are thought. It is not the number of repetitions, it is getting close to the most universal level of the mind (the Self) that determines the results. Transcending, because it allows you to consciously project thought from the most powerful level, is the best preparation you can do for anything, including affirmations.

Furthermore, once one gains enlightenment, every thought has the power of an affirmation; nature then takes it upon herself to fulfill our desires. Enlightenment, it therefore seems, should be one's primary focus.

Life has its up and downs. If your confidence is based on the vagaries of relative existence, there is always the possibility that your self-esteem can be shattered. This is where bliss comes in. Imagine a young child arriving at a friend's birthday party. A lot of people are there. She feels shy and lacks self-confidence—until she starts doing something she enjoys. Once she is happy, she forgets to be self-conscious. This is analogous to bliss replacing our low self-esteem with a high level of confidence.

We need to locate a permanent source of happiness. Bliss puts an end to the problem of low self-esteem. In fact, no substantial problem that is rooted in the deeper aspects of our personality (i.e., the ego level) can be fully solved without knowing the bliss of our Self.

Bliss and Shame

Recovery experts tell us to differentiate "toxic shame" from "healthy shame." In their book *Facing Shame,* Merle Fossum and Marilyn Mason define shame as "the ongoing premise that one is fundamentally bad, inadequate, defective, unworthy, or not fully valid as a human being."[101] This is toxic shame. Healthy shame is the feeling you get when you do something you know you shouldn't.

According to John Bradshaw, toxic shame is one of the central issues, if not *the* central issue, that must be faced in order to recover. Toxic shame is an ego-level issue. Our sense of "I" has been violated or not allowed to develop properly. This means that self-referral on the level of the ego is not possible. Therefore, the self-referral levels above it are crippled. Once we re-establish our connection to the ego, the more superficial levels of self-referral are automatically restored. If you work on removing toxic shame using traditional recovery methods, your emotions will be more balanced, your body will feel better, and your behavior will be more normal. If you go one step further, and work on the level of the Self—by re-establishing self-referral awareness and experiencing bliss—all ego problems, including toxic shame, will diminish, and, if they don't completely disappear, will at least come into sharp focus so you can deal with them using traditional methods.

Toxic shame is a core issue, but shame cannot enter Being. Toxic shame is like mud clouding the water of a shallow pond. If the pond becomes an ocean, then the mud settles to the bottom, and the water is clear. The ocean of your Being is too vast and magnificent to remain polluted by anything relative, including shame.

ENLIGHTENMENT

Now is a unique time in the history of the world—a time when many, many people can quickly gain enlightenment. Enlightenment is the need of our time: our species either self-destructs, or we rise toward enlightenment.

If enough people transcend and stabilize the experience of bliss, a new age will be ushered in. This will be characterized by harmony, health, progress, abundance, peace, and fulfillment. Maharishi calls this heaven on earth, or the Age of Enlightenment. Maharishi holds out hope for a better life for all of us:

> We in this generation are living in the midst of a fundamental transformation in the trend of time. We are on the threshold of a new age in which enlightenment—pure consciousness or the simplest form of awareness—is increasingly guiding the destiny of human life, thought, action and

behavior. The age of ignorance is receding, and the sunshine of the Age of Enlightenment is on its way to bring fulfillment to the noblest aspirations of mankind.

The awakening of the individual's capacity through the Transcendental Meditation and TM-Sidhi program to think, act, and behave from the home of natural law and the field of all possibilities within him, is *enlightenment*. Now, in the Age of Enlightenment, every individual can directly experience and express in everyday life the unbounded and infinite creative potential of intelligence hidden within his awareness.[102]

Why Bother Learning about Enlightenment?

Understanding higher states of consciousness provides a roadmap of human possibilities. It is useful to know about enlightenment, because you are unlikely to get somewhere you don't know about. Would man have gone to the moon if he didn't know it existed? Higher states of consciousness are worth achieving. At each stage, the joy, freedom, and power increases exponentially. In enlightenment one is truly useful to oneself and to society. There is nothing more practical, laudable, or worthwhile than developing your consciousness.

Enlightenment is a developmental process. Just as there are stages of ego, cognitive, and moral development, so there are stages of development of consciousness. Given sufficient time and the right developmental opportunities, anyone can go through them. A consciousness-based model of human development—one that includes higher states of consciousness—is extremely useful. As with all other theories of development, we can ask, and answer, many important questions. For instance: What are the empirically verifiable attributes of each state of consciousness (how do you know you are enlightened)? What activities, environments, and people are developmentally useful at each stage? What remedial efforts may be necessary to overcome problems faced at different stages?

The following sections outline the development and progression of higher states of consciousness. They describe the stages you will ultimately go through. Keep in mind, though, that what is important is not the stage of development you are in, but that you are—right now—in the rapid and unobstructed stream of evolution. Suffering occurs when we get hung up on the rocks of life's problems or circle endlessly in an eddy of nonprogressive activity.

Ignorance

In ignorance, we cycle endlessly from waking to sleeping to dreaming to sleeping to waking—without profound awareness of the Self. In ignorance, we have lost our deepest stable internal frame of reference. The aspect of us that has the capacity of knowing—our consciousness—is underdeveloped. Because we are not anchored to Being, we are at the mercy of the environment. If our surroundings are calm, we are at rest; if the sea of activity around us is tempestuous, we become the victim of that turmoil and lose our peace and sense of security. Because there is no stability to our awareness, we are bounced around by life's ups and downs like a ball in a pinball machine. Instability of awareness means instability of emotions. Life becomes a roller coaster ride that usually isn't fun.

Lack of development of consciousness also damages society. If our awareness is not stable, there is no hope of reliable perception. Without reliable perception, accurate knowledge is impossible. Variable knowledge means poor decisions. Poor decisions . . . you can look around at the world and see what that means. I don't understand why we let ignorant scientists and politicians design our world. Shouldn't we require our leaders to develop a stable basis in consciousness for making good decisions? Ideally, we should require our leaders to be enlightened.

The Seven States of Consciousness

Three major states of consciousness—waking, dreaming, and sleeping—have been accepted by all physiologists. Each of these has individual, unique characteristics that can be identified subjectively as well as measured in a physiology lab. Maharishi suggests adding transcendental consciousness and enlightenment. This would give us five states of consciousness. However, enlightenment, when you dissect it carefully, is found to consist of three stages, each with its own style of functioning of mind and body. Thus, we have seven states of consciousness:

1. waking
2. dreaming
3. sleeping
4. transcendental consciousness (self-referral awareness)
5. cosmic consciousness (self-referral performance)
6. God consciousness
7. unity and Brahman consciousness

Cosmic Consciousness—Enlightenment

The path to enlightenment starts when we learn to transcend. The path from ignorance to cosmic consciousness involves alternating transcending and acting. Transcending is the process of experiencing the fourth state of consciousness (transcendental consciousness or self-referral awareness). Transcending should be as deep and regular as possible. Action should not cause strain; it should be life-supporting.

Eventually the mind and body are cultured such that transcendental consciousness is experienced not only during meditation, but twenty-four hours a day; it is not lost whether we are dynamically active or sound asleep. This is the result of a stress-free nervous system. Enlightenment simply results from the process of release of stress. Release of stress results from the infusion of Being into the nature of the mind. As Being (self-referral awareness) increases, a person starts to have a natural sense of noninvolvement and nonattachment, even while dynamically active. This state is sometimes called "witnessing" or being a "silent witness." When this inner experience of Being has become permanent, we have achieved what is called cosmic consciousness. Cosmic consciousness is the maintenance of transcendental consciousness along with waking, dreaming, and sleeping.

Cosmic consciousness marks the end of the possibility of addiction and the start of the possibilities of enlightenment. *Cosmic consciousness is total recovery.* Total recovery means that you are free from *all* your past conditioning. The symptoms of cosmic consciousness are the hallmarks of a completed recovery.

God Consciousness—More Refined Enlightenment

In cosmic consciousness, we fully know ourselves. What remains is to develop our perception and relationship with everything around us. In cosmic consciousness, only the surface value of an object is seen. God consciousness involves refining the nervous system so that the senses are able to perceive the most refined value of an object. This is called celestial perception. We see the world, for the first time, in its true glory (as God created it, hence the name God consciousness). It is extraordinarily useful to be able to see things as they actually are.

God consciousness develops through the most refined activity of the mind: devotion. Contrary to what we might expect, devotion is not confined to ritual nor bound by beliefs. In God consciousness, devotion becomes the whole of life. What outer form it takes is determined by your inner tendencies and the culture and religion you are familiar with—not by your technique of transcending. Like all stages of human development, God consciousness is natural and spontaneous.

There is one point you should understand: spending a lot of time thinking about God and, especially, talking about God have little developmental value before cosmic consciousness. Moreover, after cosmic consciousness, devotion comes up spontaneously on an *inner* level. Speech has little to do with it.

Unity Consciousness—Ultimate Enlightenment

Once God consciousness is fully established, unity consciousness inevitably develops. It is only a matter of time. Unity consciousness is the result of a cognitive shift precipitated by knowledge and insights. In unity consciousness we see the *total* value of the object of perception, not just the relative aspect. People and objects are seen as expressions of pure consciousness. We appreciate the unity underlying the diversity of life. A slightly more rich value of unity consciousness is sometimes referred to as Brahman consciousness.

Table 11.1 breaks down how we see the world at each level of consciousness.

Level of Consciousness		Quality of Perception
IGNORANCE	Waking	No stable basis for perception, since the knower is not known
	Dreaming	Illusory perception
	Sleeping	Absence of perception
A taste of enlightenment	Transcendental Consciousness	Perception of pure awareness
ENLIGHTENMENT	Stage 1 of enlightenment — Cosmic Consciousness	Knower remains stable; therefore, accurate knowledge is possible for the first time
	Stage 2 of enlightenment — God Consciousness	Full range of relative perception available, even by the senses; perception includes the "finest relative"
	Stage 3A of enlightenment — Unity Consciousness	Perception is now interpreted in the light of consciousness; cognition has changed on an inner level and objects are seen as expressions of unified consciousness
	Stage 3B of enlightenment — Brahman Consciousness	The most complete degree of wholeness of awareness is attained; *everything*— what we see and what we don't see—is intuitively known as consciousness

Table 11.1 The 7 states of consciousness as stages of cognitive development.

Enlightened Guidance

There is a second value—in addition to describing your own experience—to understanding enlightenment: the knowledge of higher states of consciousness will help you understand the lives of enlightened teachers and their message. When a Teacher says unity is all there is, you will know, "Ah, yes. They are speaking from the platform of unity consciousness." And when others describe a period in their life characterized by intense devotion, you will know what they were doing; they were developing God consciousness.

I encourage you to seek out the enlightened. Just being in their presence is purifying. Spend time with them, listen to their teaching —at the very least, read their books.

It makes sense to have, as one of your many sources of inform- ation and guidance, someone who has completed the journey to enlightenment, and therefore knows the whole path. To put this into the context of recovery, if you are lead *solely* by therapists who are telling you only what lies around the next corner (because that is all they know), how can you be sure you are not being lead on the same wild goose chase they are on?

A Final Example: Proactive

An example may make enlightenment seem more real and practical. *Proactive* has become a popular term. It is the goal of many people who wish to be more successful in business.

What is a proactive person like? To be proactive is not to be reactive. Reactive means action based predominantly on external input. Proactive is preferable, as it is a more highly skilled and therefore more effective form of action based on self-direction and values. Action guided by proper values is said to be "principle based." You think for yourself. You have the big picture. You know where you are going and are capable of planning for it. When prob- lems come up, you solve them by looking to a larger context.

Stephen Covey, author of *The 7 Habits of Highly Effective People* and the person who made "proactive" popular, identifies *self-awareness* as an attribute of those who are proactive. The current understanding of proactive overemphasizes principles and undervalues self-awareness. Principles, after all, are only as good as our level of consciousness. Doesn't every tyrant claim he is acting on principle?

The enlightened are the most proactive. Why? Because the enlightened have the most self-awareness: they know the Self. In cosmic consciousness, actions are based on Being, which is automatically aware of our needs *and* the needs of the environment. Like a successful executive, the enlightened make few mistakes and are always progressive. In cosmic consciousness, action is spontaneously right. The Self illumines the path of the enlightened, whereas, in contrast, the guiding light for the ignorant is the past (which is always dim). The past consists of old values and principles (which may or may not be valid), deep stresses, unfulfilled desires, and hidden longings. It is not surprising, then, with perception clouded by so many distorting filters, that the ignorant can't make the best decisions.

Obviously, you cannot be *fully* proactive until cosmic consciousness. What an ignorant person thinks of as proactive is what an enlightened person would call reactive. When the ignorant proactively design their (or others') lives, they do so based on their limitations and unfulfilled needs. Thus, proactive often equals sophisticated neediness-based action; it can be yet another form of object-referral.

In cosmic consciousness, all past impressions deep enough to cause imbalance have been released. The enlightened see clearly. In the moment, every moment, they decide, spontaneously and without stopping life's flow, the best course of action—and decide correctly.

Being truly proactive doesn't mean effectively *organizing* your life; it means enjoying life in a continuous state of complete inner fulfillment and bliss. The enlightened are completely fulfilled on the inside, yet highly sensitive to the needs of the environment; they are nonjudgmental, yet make excellent decisions; they are silent on the inside, yet dynamic on the outside. These are the paradoxes of enlightenment.

RESOURCES

CHAPTER TWELVE

This chapter lists resources—people, organizations, Web sites, and books—that will deepen your knowledge and help you master the advanced recovery tools.

Before you use the tools in this book, there are two prerequisites: you need to address active addictions, and you need to take care of your mental health. So let's start by discussing these two topics.

TREAT YOUR PRIMARY ADDICTIONS

If you are still in an active addiction, get immediate professional help. Do this *first,* before you try anything in this book. Don't go it alone. You need outside help—there is plenty of it available. If you don't know where to go, ask around, or look in the phone book for a counselor, hospital, or professional recovery program.

A federal agency, the Substance Abuse and Mental Health Services Administration (SAMHSA), can help you locate treatment facilities. Call them at 800-662-HELP, or use their interactive Web site. Start from the home page (www.samhsa.gov) or go directly to:

http://findtreatment.samhsa.gov

You can also call your county's department of alcohol and drug services, which offers free counseling and referrals.

Next, find people—for example, the members of a Twelve Step group—who are overcoming, or have already overcome, *your specific* problem. There are Twelve Step programs for:

- addiction—Alcoholics Anonymous, Narcotics Anonymous, Nicotine Anonymous, Overeaters Anonymous, Gamblers Anonymous, Debtors Anonymous, Sex and Love Addicts Anonymous, etc.
- codependence—Co-Dependents Anonymous (CoDA)
- adult children—ACA meetings, which are sometimes a subgroup of Al-Anon
- the families of addicts—Al-Anon, Alateen, Nar-Anon, etc.

Most Twelve Step organizations have their own Web sites. Examples are:

www.alcoholics-anonymous.org
www.adultchildren.org
www.codependents.org

If none of the above works, call the AA central office listed in your phone book and ask how to get in touch with the Twelve Step group you are interested in.

There are also support groups not based on the Twelve Steps. These include groups for addiction (e.g., LifeRing and Women for Sobriety), mental illness, violence, survivors of abuse and rape, the family of people in prison, and many other difficult situations. Your local newspaper may publish times and locations of meetings.

The American Self-Help Clearinghouse maintains a comprehensive list of support groups. Send them a stamped, self-addressed envelope and ask for their lists of state clearinghouses and self-help groups. If you already know what you are looking for, call and ask for that group's national number. Alternatively, go to the clearinghouse Web site. In a few clicks, you can have meeting times, directions, and a map.

> The American Self-Help Clearinghouse
> 100 Hanover Avenue, Second Floor
> Cedar Knolls, NJ 07927
> 973-326-8853 (9–5 EST M–F)
> www.selfhelpgroups.org

Those in need of basic information—perhaps to help a loved one who is addicted—might want to visit a regional office of the National Council on Alcoholism and Drug Dependence (NCADD). They provide information and referrals. NCADD's affiliate offices are well-stocked with addiction literature and videos.

> National Council on Alcoholism and Drug Dependence
> 20 Exchange Place, Suite 2902
> New York, NY 10005
> 800-NCA-CALL (24-hour automated referral to an affiliate)
> www.ncadd.org

There are a number of sources for books on recovery. One is Hazelden (www.hazelden.com or 800-328-9000). Most of their books are aligned with the Twelve Steps. For alcoholism, explore the Betty Ford Center's recommendations. Once you get to their Web site (www.bettyfordcenter.org), click "store" on the banner across the top of the page. I recommend all the recovery books I mentioned in the first few chapters. If you want a second opinion, look at reader reviews on Barnes & Noble or Amazon's Web sites (www.bn.com and www.amazon.com). To get an overview of addiction and treatment read *The Selfish Brain* by Robert DuPont, founding director of the National Institute on Drug Abuse. If your problem is alcohol related, consider Anne Fletcher's *Sober for Good*. She takes the approach of a journalist, interviewing dozens of people who succeeded in recovery, to find out what worked for them. *Sober for Good* has extensive lists of resources, many of them specialized and beyond the scope of this book.

The following Web sites offer research-based information on addiction, including access to large databases of scientific papers:

National Institute on Drug Abuse
www.nida.nih.gov

National Institute on Alcohol Abuse and Alcoholism
www.niaaa.nih.gov

National Clearinghouse for Alcohol and Drug Information
www.health.org

Substance Abuse & Mental Health Services Administration
www.samhsa.gov

National Center on Addiction and
Substance Abuse at Columbia University
www.casacolumbia.org

These sites have a less technical, more popular approach:

www.addictionsearch.com
www2.potsdam.edu/alcohol-info

Smoking Cessation

Obviously, quitting smoking isn't required to use the advanced recovery tools, but there's no time like the present. So stop. Right now. Just quit.

If you relapse, that's okay. The next step is to buy a couple of books—to understand nicotine addiction and your path out of it—

and then design a personal recovery program. Support groups also help. Armed with the weapon of new knowledge, go back into battle. Books to use as a point of departure include *You Can Stop Smoking* by Jacquelyn Rogers and Julie Rubenstein, *The No-Nag, No-Guilt, Do-It-Your-Own-Way Guide to Quitting Smoking* by Tom Ferguson, and *The American Lung Association 7 Steps to a Smoke-Free Life*.

Here are some Web sites to start with:

www.lungusa.org
www.surgeongeneral.gov/tobacco
www.quitnet.com

The World Health Organization, the Centers for Disease Control, and the Surgeon General have all issued reports on the dangers of smoking. You have no excuse not to quit.

SOLVE YOUR MENTAL HEALTH PROBLEMS[103]

There is a very real danger inherent in this book: you may try to skip from addiction to higher consciousness without taking care of your mental health. You would not be alone. Ignorance, denial, stigma—these characterize America's attitude toward mental health. We either don't know about it, don't want to know about it, or, if we have to admit a problem, are ashamed and humiliated. According to statistics endorsed by the government, mental disorders are substantially more common than addiction, costing society almost three times as much. Furthermore, mental illness complicates addiction, making it orders of magnitude more difficult to treat.

Fortunately, there is a growing wave of public interest in mental health and in the disorders that keep us from achieving our full potential. This interest is driven largely by increasing realization of the prevalence of mental health problems. Table 12.1 presents the number of people, per hundred, who have clinically diagnosable disorders. It summarizes the results of two large national studies included in the *U.S. Surgeon General's Report on Mental Health*.[104]

% of population with anxiety disorders:	16.4
simple phobia	8.3
social phobia	2.0
agoraphobia	4.9
generalized anxiety disorder	3.4
panic disorder	1.6
obsessive-compulsive disorder	2.4
PTSD	3.6
% of population with mood disorders:	7.1
major depressive episode.	6.5
unipolar major depression	5.3
dysthymia	1.6
bipolar I	1.1
bipolar II	0.6
schizophrenia	1.3
nonaffective psychosis	0.2
somatization	0.2
antisocial personality disorder	2.1
anorexia nervosa	0.1
severe cognitive impairment	1.2
% of population with any disorder	21.0

Table 12.1 Percentage of the U.S. population, between the ages of eighteen and fifty-four, that experience a clinically diagnosable mental disorder in any given year. (Note: people often have multiple disorders, so the totals are not simple sums.)

According to these figures, this year, one-fifth of us will have a mental disorder. For most people, the mental dysfunction or distress will not last for years, nor will it be devastatingly catastrophic. Only 7 percent of the population has significant functional impairment that lasts longer than a year. A little under 3 percent are the most seriously affected. Their illnesses—such as schizophrenia, bipolar mood disorder, and obsessive-compulsive disorder—are severe, persistent, debilitating, and often lifelong.

The table does not include all the reasons people see a mental health professional. In fact, a little less than half of the 15 percent of Americans who seek help each year from a mental health clinic do so for a reason either not in the table or not clearly defined. A major omission in the table—one that will be included in the next study— is borderline personality disorder, which is thought to apply to between 1 and 2 percent of the general population. Also not in the table is the 6 percent of the population that is addicted but has no mental illness; the 3 percent of Americans who have both mental disorders and addiction is included.

Where to Go for More Information

Before going into the specifics, let's list sources of general information on mental illness. The first places to look are the National Institute of Mental Health (NIMH) and the National Alliance for the Mentally Ill (NAMI). NAMI provides referrals, NIMH doesn't; both provide information. Here are the addresses and Web sites:

> National Institute of Mental Health
> NIMH Public Inquiries
> 6001 Executive Boulevard, Rm. 8184, MSC 9663
> Bethesda, MD 20892
> 301-443-4513 (8:30–5:00 EST M–F)
> nimhinfo@nih.gov
> www.nimh.nih.gov

> National Alliance for the Mentally Ill
> Colonial Place Three
> 2107 Wilson Blvd., Suite 300
> Arlington, VA 22201
> 800-950-6264 (10–5 EST M–F)
> www.nami.org

Particularly useful are NAMI's book reviews (on the Web site, look on the left column of buttons on the home page), and the helpline fact sheets (www.nami.org/helpline/helpfacts.html). I recommend browsing the book reviews, and getting a copy of the best-reviewed, most recent general-interest book on mental health. I also encourage you to carefully go through NAMI's fact sheets on each mental disorder, especially any that might apply to you or your family.

Note that some feel NIMH and NAMI are excessively drug-oriented. To get a (not unbiased) psychiatric perspective that counterbalances that of the pharmaceutical industry, read *Your Drug May Be Your Problem*, by Peter Breggin and David Cohen.

Also worth reading is the *U.S. Surgeon General's Report on Mental Health,* currently available at:

www.surgeongeneral.gov/library/mentalhealth/index.html

This is a research-based yet readable description of the causes and treatments of mental illness. You can request a printed copy by calling 800-789-2647.

A Canadian psychiatrist has built an outstanding site with concise but complete information on all common mental disorders:

www.mentalhealth.com

There is a companion site (www.mytherapy.com) that has an interactive diagnostic feature, and although self-diagnosis can be risky, within the limits of a computer program this seems to be quite accurate. There is currently a ten dollar charge.

If you are looking for a self-help group to help you deal with mental health problems, consider Recovery, Inc. It is respected and well-established—helping people help themselves for over sixty years.

Recovery, Inc
802 North Dearborn Street
Chicago, IL 60610
312-337-5661 (9–5 CST M–F)
www.recovery-inc.com

For further resources, the following clearinghouse, as well as the one listed in the previous section, may be useful:

National Mental Health
Consumers' Self-Help Clearinghouse
800-553-4539 (9–5 EST M–F)
info@mhselfhelp.org

Thirty-Second Primer on Mental Health

Mental health and mental illness exist on a continuum:

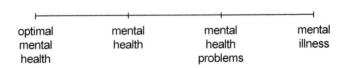

| optimal mental health | mental health | mental health problems | mental illness |

The farther to the right, the more scientists have studied, and therefore, the more we know. According to the Surgeon General, researchers know quite a lot about treating mental illness but little about promoting mental health. The Surgeon General's report doesn't even consider optimal mental health. Obviously, this is a gap that needs to be filled.

The next few sections review the current understanding of common mental disorders. To oversimplify for the sake of clarity, mental disorders can be, somewhat irreverently, categorized as follows: you are either scared, depressed, crazy, or hard to get along with—or a combination of these. There are, of course, dozens of rare disorders that don't fit under these headings, and there are physically induced problems, like sleep apnea and Alzheimer's, but these we won't consider here.

Scared

These are called anxiety disorders. They include:

- Generalized anxiety disorder—constant anxiety with no apparent cause.
- Panic attack—sudden extreme anxiety, often so strong you think you are going to die. It may be cued by the environment, or it may have no external cause.
- Phobia—intense fear of specific objects or events, such as snakes, heights, social situations, and traveling or being in public without a companion (agoraphobia).
- Post-traumatic stress disorder—stress from intensely traumatic past events, such as physical or sexual abuse, a car accident, or war, the terror of which haunts you in the present.
- Obsessive-compulsive disorder—endless intrusive repetitive thoughts that cause overwhelming anxiety (obsession), and/or ritualized compulsive behaviors, such as hand washing or checking the stove, done sometimes for hours a day, to prevent an imagined calamity (compulsion).

One more disorder should be added. Although not traditionally categorized as an anxiety disorder, somatization disorder is common among adult children of alcoholics, especially women with severe, early-onset, alcoholic fathers. It is estimated that 7 to 8 percent of women seeking help from a mental health clinic have somatization disorder. It is characterized by a series of physical complaints for which no medical cause can be found. Somatization disorder is probably due to the body constantly maintaining a state of hypervigilance; like a steam engine running under too much pressure, the body—under intense mental pressure—continually breaks down. Symptoms can include: pain in different parts of the body; gastrointestinal discomfort, such as irritable bowel syndrome or nausea; sexual or menstrual problems; and neurological impairment —in balance, muscles, sight, hearing, touch, or memory.

There is little information on how to treat this. Recovery, Inc., as well as the tools in this book, should prove useful.

To learn more about anxiety disorders, contact:

Anxiety Disorders Association of America
301-231-9350 (9:00–5:30 CST M–Th; 9–3 F)
www.adaa.org

For information on post-traumatic stress disorder, go to the American Psychiatric Association's PTSD Web page:

www.psych.org/public_info/ptsd.cfm

Other PTSD sites to try:

www.thepsych.com/Category/GG.htm
www.sover.net/~schwcof/ptsd.html

For information on obsessive-compulsive disorder try the following site—again, I recommend the book reviews:

Obsessive-Compulsive Foundation
203-315-2190 (9–5 EST M–F)
www.ocfoundation.org

Depressed

Since just about everyone experiences depression, there is no need to explain what it is. It becomes a clinically diagnosable disorder when it is severe (you may be suicidal), is not related to life events, lasts a long time, or is preceded or followed by an extreme and imbalanced high (mania). Here are the different so-called mood disorders:

- Major depressive episode—your depression either has no cause or lasts longer than the cause warrants. Major depressive episodes can be recurrent, but in most cases are not. A single major depressive episode is the most common—and most easily treated—mental disorder.
- Dysthymia—chronic, for some even lifelong, low-grade depression.
- Bipolar (formerly called manic-depressive illness)—this is a cyclic mood disorder. To be diagnosed as bipolar, you must have had at least one manic phase. Typically, your moods go way up—and stay up—and way down—and stay down. However, your moods don't have to alternate consistently and repeatedly, and there are disorders that cycle rapidly with less extreme peaks and troughs. Bipolar mood disorder is of two forms: bipolar I and bipolar II. The difference is in the mania; the high in bipolar II isn't as high, disabling, or uncomfortable as in bipolar I.

To learn more about mood disorders:

National Depressive and Manic Depressive Association
800-826-3632 (8:30–5:00 EST M–F)
questions@ndmda.org
www.ndmda.org

Crazy (Distorted Reality)

Alcohol can make you crazy. Dedicated use can result in delirium on withdrawal—the infamous DTs, which are rare, but can be deadly without medical treatment. Alcohol can cause dementia; 5 to 10 percent of all cases of dementia are alcohol induced. And it can cause psychosis. However, the purpose of this section is not addiction related; it is to make sure everyone is aware of schizophrenia, a common and very debilitating mental illness. Many schizophrenics use addiction to escape their mental discomfort, but addiction is not their primary problem.

To understand schizophrenia, we need to start with psychosis, which is a mental illness in its own right. Psychosis distorts reality. Unlike delirium—which is brief, typically has a known cause, and may include some awareness that things are not right—a psychosis blends the real and the imaginary into a seamless, more permanent reality where the person has no insight into their problem.

Psychosis can include:

- delusions
- hallucinations
- disorganized speech
- disorganized behavior
- no fizz in one's personality, with little or no emotions, speech, or motivation

Hallucinations and delusions are the most common symptoms. A person who is psychotic may, to give a few examples, have a delusional belief, thinking they are Jesus Christ's wife; they may be paranoid—the police are secretly conspiring to kill them; and there are the classic cases of schizophrenics who hear voices convincing them to engage in bizarre behaviors, such as taking off their clothes and wandering the streets.

A psychotic person can, with treatment, usually return to function in the work-a-day world; a schizophrenic frequently cannot. Schizophrenic patients, by definition, have multiple or severe psychoses, with some symptoms present for at least six months. Schizophrenia can begin imperceptibly and grow slowly. Once it starts, it is usually a lifelong illness. In many cases, it can be successfully treated, but not cured, with medication. Remember, those with schizophrenia often cannot recognize their own problem. You have to recognize it and get them help.

The National Alliance for the Mentally Ill is your best resource on schizophrenia. Contact information is on page 215.

Hard to Get Along With

If you have had substantial, lifelong difficulty interacting with others, you may have a *personality disorder.* There are ten of them. The two most likely to go along with addiction are antisocial and borderline.

Antisocial personality disorder is a pattern of behavior that usually starts in childhood. A person with antisocial personality disorder continually violates the rights of others. They may lie, steal, break the law, and, by their aggressiveness and violence, may endanger themselves and others. Typically, these behaviors result in repeated arrests. Substance abuse and drug dealing often go along with this disorder. Most psychiatrists consider antisocial personality disorder untreatable. About three-fourths of the hard-core prison population receive the diagnosis; one of its characteristics is lack of regret for wrongdoing. Antisocial personality disorder is certainly hard to treat, but it isn't impossible. Consider the substantial reduction in recidivism for inmates who learn to meditate.

Borderline personality disorder (BPD) afflicts emotionally highly sensitive children who grew up in emotionally invalidating environments. Seventy-five percent of people with BPD were abused, either sexually or physically, as children. Note that a child can have BPD and *not* have been abused (sometimes it is precipitated by adoption), so not all parents of BPD sufferers can be accused of abuse.

According to *DSM-IV* (*The Diagnostic and Statistical Manual of Mental Disorders,* published by the American Psychiatric Association), people with borderline personality disorder have "a pervasive pattern of instability of interpersonal relationships, self-image, and [emotions], and marked impulsivity beginning in early adulthood and present in a variety of contexts."[105]

People with BPD find it difficult to regulate their emotions. Small bumps on the road of life—things that would briefly annoy someone else—jolt a person with BPD into hours of anger or paranoid fear. Their behavior tends to be compulsive and inappropriate, including eating disorders, overspending, gambling, compulsive sex, and substance abuse. They lack a clearly defined sense of self, tending to change their colors to blend into their environment. They may chronically feel empty or bored, in some cases suicidal; self-inflicted injury is possible. They see everything as either black or white: they deify the people around them, or alternatively, irrationally devalue them. Their partner may be considered ideal one moment and fatally flawed the next—or valued in the beginning of the relationship and seen as worthless in the end. People with BPD are hypersensitive to rejection and will do anything to avoid perceived abandonment. Often they are constantly angry or irritable.

"Borderline personality disorder" is somewhat of a misnomer. At the time the phrase was coined, people with BPD were thought to be on the borderline between psychotic and neurotic disorders. Most researchers would now like the name changed to something indicating emotion dysregulation.

Until recently, the treatment of personality disorders hasn't had much attention. Borderline personality disorder, like antisocial personality disorder, was thought to be untreatable—or at least too difficult to be worth the effort. However, Marsha Linehan, a psychology professor at the University of Washington, pioneered a successful form of therapy she calls Dialectical Behavior Therapy. Dr. Linehan has trained counselors, and her books are considered the most authoritative in the field. Clinical trials demonstrated that Dialectical Behavior Therapy is effective and enables clients to progress substantially. However, recovery from all personality disorders is a slow process. They are, by definition, collections of traits that tend to remain fixed throughout a person's life.

Here are some good sites on BPD. Check their lists of links for further resources. As with all the disorder-specific sites, e-mail lists and chat rooms are especially useful. The last site, BPDCentral, helps nonborderlines deal with family members who have BPD. It is run by Randi Kreger, one of the authors of *Stop Walking on Eggshells: Coping When Someone You Love Has Borderline Personality Disorder.*

> www.soulselfhelp.on.ca/borderpd.html
> www.suite101.com/welcome.cfm/borderline_personality
> www.mhsanctuary.com/borderline
> www.BPDCentral.com

Mental Health and Addiction

It is generally agreed that as much as 50 percent of the mentally ill have a substance abuse problem. For example, 30 percent of bipolar I patients are alcoholic, over 50 percent of those with BPD are substance abusers, and 50 to 60 percent of cocaine or crack addicts have a mood disorder. A diagnosis of both addiction and mental illness is called a *dual diagnosis*. Most addicts—two-thirds—do not have dual diagnoses, but one-third do. *If you've had an addiction, you owe it to yourself to get a mental health checkup.* Do it merely as a precaution. Addiction is often the presenting symptom, and is quite rightfully treated first. Addiction creates its own temporary mood and anxiety disorders, as well as exaggerating existing personality disorders, but addiction itself is not always the deepest underlying cause.

Symptoms that should alert you to the need for assistance are:

- any persistent or severe mental or emotional distress
- consistently being unhappy to the point where you don't look forward to the next day
- disturbances in sleep patterns
- decreased functioning—or greater difficulty than those around you—in job performance, social interaction, or family life
- others complaining about you—that you talk too loud or too fast, are irritable or unreliable, are too introspective, or don't respect other people's boundaries

How to Get Help

Beware: the Surgeon General found a big gap between what researchers know works and what practitioners in the field actually do. Psychiatrists are often out of date. Furthermore, for many therapists, if they don't know how to treat a problem (e.g., psychiatrists and BPD), that problem doesn't exist. Psychiatrists are taught to prefer a diagnosis they know they can successfully work with. All therapists and counselors have a favorite therapeutic approach, but for some it is their inevitable tool; and if all you've got is a hammer . . .

The best way to find a mental health professional is by referral. If you don't know who to ask, here are a few possibilities. SAMHSA can locate mental health treatment facilities, consumer groups, and state resources:

www.mentalhealth.org
800-789-CMHS (8:30–5:00 EST M–F)

The Association for Advancement of Behavior Therapy lists its members by state and specialty:

www.aabt.org
212-647-1890 (9:30–5:00 EST M–F)

You can e-mail or call the American Psychiatric Association:

apa@psych.org
888-357-7924 (8:30–6:00 EST M–F)

Or call the American Psychological Association at 800-964-2000 (8–5 PST M–F). They will connect you to a state association for a local referral.

Experts recommend interviewing at least three potential therapists. Make sure they understand addiction. Find out how many people with your mental disorder they have treated. Ask about credentials, training, specialty, success rates, preferred treatment methods, length of treatment, availability, and, of course, cost. You should feel comfortable with them and they should feel compassionate and empathic toward you.

After you have given yourself a general education and received a professional diagnosis, get in touch with self-help and consumer groups—people who have your specific problem and are looking for the most effective way to deal with it. Then, get another professional diagnosis. Without a second opinion, you risk misdiagnosis and mistreatment, wasting mountains of time and money, while filling your body with needless drugs.

Drugs are a contentious issue, with no end to the debate. Based on how the enlightened guide people (Maharishi says, "Attack suffering from every side"), I wouldn't be afraid to take drugs if your symptoms are severe or your disorder is chronic. If the psychopharmacological approach works, use it. However, don't trust any doctor who, after a brief office visit, gives you drugs and a bill, and thinks his job is over. On the other hand, don't trust someone who never recommends medication to any of her clients, is unaware of therapies targeted to your disorder, and wants you to come chat twice a week, for the rest of your life, at $250 an hour. Get specific treatment for your specific problems.

More and more disorders are being treated without drugs. Two of the most resistant mental disorders are BPD and obsessive-compulsive disorder (OCD). Even these, in many cases, can be healed without medication. Marsha Linehan's approach to BPD is not drug based. Jeffrey Schwartz, a psychiatrist at the UCLA School of Medicine, has developed a nonmedicinal four-step self-treatment method for OCD.[106] However, both Dr. Linehan and Dr. Schwartz are not afraid to have patients take drugs. Dr. Schwartz considers medication necessary—sometimes—to reduce overwhelming symptoms, so the person can focus on changing their behavior. He calls the drugs training wheels.

THE ADVANCED RECOVERY TOOLS

Once you are stable in your recovery and have addressed potential mental disorders, you are ready for the advanced recovery tools described throughout this book. Below, they are listed in the general order I hope you will learn them. Which tools are needed and how you use them is different for each person. However, everyone should start by getting expert advice on balancing their mind, their body, and the influences from their environment—take advantage of meditation, ayurveda, and jyotish. Once you have done that, study how the mind and body work. And keep looking for ways to increase self-referral. This process will increase inner vitality, purity, and coherence—benefiting all aspects of your life.

This book's Web site (www.incandescentpress.com) has additional resources. Please check for updated contact information, especially the ever-changing Web addresses.

LEARN TO MEDITATE

Transcendental Meditation is taught in five ninety-minute sessions. It must be learned personally from a qualified instructor; you can't learn it from a book. My observation is that people who try to learn a meditative technique from a book don't get quality instruction, and hence don't have depth of experience; consequently, they don't stick with it. Plus, with a book, there is no follow-up and no one to ask questions. When you first meditate, you dive deep within the mind. You have subtle experiences of an abstract nature—ones that are completely new. You want someone experienced as a guide. Like a beginning scuba diver, you want an expert, right there next to you, taking you through the steps.

To connect to a nearby meditation center—a Maharishi Vedic School—call 888-532-7686. You can also go to www.tm.org and click on "Where to learn the TM technique." Enter your area code, and you'll get the phone numbers of all teachers and centers near you.

After two or three months of regular meditation, take a weekend residence course.

I should point out that if you have a highly stressful past, you may not have breathtaking experiences in the beginning. You may, but then again you might not. Most likely, you will experience meditation as nice, but not celestial. What happens is the body normalizes neurochemistry—dusting off and putting back into use dormant areas of the brain—and releases stress everywhere. This is a lot of work. Sometimes the mind gets impatient with all this housekeeping. Your job is to patiently put up with it and keep meditating regularly. If you have a lot of tension, there is a threshold effect: you may not notice benefits until a good percentage of the stress is gone. But the bliss will come.

BALANCE YOUR BODY

Get a consultation with an ayurvedic physician, and if you can *comfortably* afford it, schedule a week of panchakarma. For a referral to the nearest Maharishi Ayurvedic physician call 800-811-0550 or contact The Raj (www.theraj.com or 800-248-9050). The Raj, featured in a patient vignette in Andrew Weil's *Eight Weeks to Optimal Health,* is a luxury in-residence facility with just about every ayurvedic therapy you could ask for. If you can (it is pricey), spend a week, or even better two or more weeks, and do everything. Along with the physical purification programs, they can teach you meditation, yoga, and the theory of ayurveda. Their Web site describes the programs.

Here are current locations and contact information for all facilities with full-time Maharishi Ayurvedic doctors. There are plans to build and staff many more Maharishi Vedic Medical Centers. Check www.maharishi-medical.com for up-to-date listings.

Iowa

> The Raj
> Fairfield
> 800-248-9050
> 641-472-9580
> www.theraj.com

Maryland

> Maharishi Vedic Medical Center
> Bethesda
> 301-770-5690
> info@mvc-bethesda.org
> www.mvc-bethesda.org

Massachusetts

> Maharishi Vedic Health Center &
> Center for Chronic Disorders and Prevention
> Lancaster
> 978-365-4549
> info@lancasterhealth.com
> www.lancasterhealth.com

New Mexico

> Maharishi College of Vedic Medicine
> Albuquerque
> 888-895-2614
> 505-830-0415
> mcvmnm@aol.com
> www.mcvm-nm.org

Texas
>Center for Chronic Disorders
>Dallas
>888-259-9915
>214-824-0027
>dallasccd@aol.com

While we're on the subject of ayurvedic doctors, it should be noted that, as with any other specialty, experience and quality vary. Try to find one with some exposure to addiction. On the phone, briefly interview them. Ask questions like: How long have you practiced ayurvedic medicine? How many patients with addictive backgrounds have you seen? What have been the results? In a typical treatment, what ayurvedic therapies would you prescribe? People with addictive backgrounds often respond better to a series of incremental treatments. So ask if the doctor will be available for short, follow-up consultations and how much these will cost.

Finding a Regular Physician with an Addiction Specialty

In chapter 8, I suggested you get a checkup—a routine physical examination—from a regular medical doctor before you go for an ayurvedic evaluation. If you are going to see a doctor, you might as well go to one who knows about addiction and is therefore more likely to understand your medical history. The American Society of Addiction Medicine can make a referral. Call them at 301-656-3920. You will be given the name and number of a regional chapter leader, who will in turn put you in touch with a doctor in your area.

Alternatively, you can try the AMA's online doctor finder. Although difficult to navigate, it has the advantage that you can browse through the list of doctors and see their background and training. Start at www.asam.org and click "AMA Physician Select" on the left banner. Then click on "Search name or medical specialty," then "ACCEPT" (if you agree to the terms), then "Medical Specialty," then "search from expanded list of medical specialties." Next, enter your state *only* (putting in your zip code or city confuses the database—doctors who live three miles away, but in a different zip code or town, won't be listed), select the radio button for addiction medicine, and scroll way down to the bottom and hit search.

And there's the list, although I think you'll agree that a couple of phone calls might be easier. Note that the Web page lists only doctors whose *primary* specialty is addiction medicine; you may not need someone that specialized.

Getting Supplies

Maharishi Ayurveda Products International has a full range of body-balancing goodies including ayurvedic herbs, rasayanas, teas, aroma oils, ghee, massage oil, and gandharva CDs. Their Web site is www.mapi.com and their phone number is 800-255-8332. Call them and they'll send you a catalog.

The Maharishi Vedic Vibration Technology

The Maharishi Vedic Vibration Technology (MVVT) uses vedic sounds to treat chronic disorders. Their Web site has a more detailed description. MVVT may not always live up to the highest expectations set by the Web site, but many people have found it helpful and worth the money. A number of people, including myself, have successfully used it to soften emotional problems associated with addiction. Contact information:

www.VedicVibration.com
relief@mavf.org
800-431-9680

READ SOME MORE

After you start meditation, read one or both of these books by Maharishi Mahesh Yogi: *The Science of Being and Art of Living,* and *The Bhagavad-Gita: A New Translation and Commentary.* For most people, neither of the books make sense until they have learned Transcendental Meditation—experiencing the effortless dive to the bliss within. These books will advance your knowledge of how the mind works. The first was written for the Western mind (logical and a little dry, but filled with profound insights), the second for the Eastern mind (somewhat esoteric). *The Bhagavad-Gita* is a complete, condensed textbook on the philosophy of yoga. Both books expand on the themes of bliss, behavior, and enlightenment

—and remind you of the importance of the experience of Being.

There are four more books I would like you to study. These will advance your understanding of how to take care of your body. These books were chosen because they are the simplest and the best. After you read these, you will be ready for more advanced books and courses.

A Woman's Best Medicine: Health, Happiness, and Long Life through Maharishi Ayurveda. Nancy Lonsdorf, M.D., Veronica Butler, M.D., and Melanie Brown (Putnam, 1994; $15; 380 pages). A thorough guide to ayurveda—readable and spiritually elevating. Although written for women, men should still buy it and read it.

The Book of Ayurveda: A Holistic Approach to Health and Longevity. Judith Morison (Fireside, 1995; $15; 190 pages). A beautiful, full-color book that covers all bases while keeping things simple.

Body, Mind and Sport: The Mind-Body Guide to Lifelong Fitness and Your Personal Best. John Douillard (Crown, second edition, 2001; $14; 250 pages). This offers a practical, step-by-step approach to exercising in the zone, using ayurvedic and yogic techniques. Many professional athletes use Dr. Douillard's methods.

Buy one or both of:

Heaven's Banquet: Vegetarian Cooking for Lifelong Health the Ayurvedic Way. Miriam Hospodar (Dutton Penguin, 1999; $40; 620 pages). Provides all you need to know about ayurveda and food—popular with both novice and experienced cooks.

Ayurvedic Cooking for Westerners. Amanda Morningstar (Lotus Press, 1995; $20; 400 pages). A well-thought-out cookbook that explains how to prepare familiar recipes according to ayurvedic principles.

GET YOUR JYOTISH DONE

Your local Maharishi Vedic School is your best bet for information on vedic astrology. If they can't help, call the national center at 800-888-5797 and ask for an information packet and application. For Maharishi Yagyas, e-mail or call:

MaharishiYagya@Maharishi.net
877-469-2492

STUDY VEDIC SCIENCE

You can study vedic science at home—anywhere in the world, in almost any language—via satellite TV. The Maharishi Open University (www.mou.org) offers a series of courses with the latest knowledge. I strongly encourage you to take advantage of this. For more information, contact the nearest Maharishi Vedic School or sign up on the Maharishi Open University Web site. Local Maharishi Vedic Schools also have classes on ayurvedic theory, self-pulse diagnosis, and Maharishi Yoga. Ask your TM instructor about these.

START A REFERENCE LIBRARY

Here are a few books to consider as resources:

Self-Recovery: Treating Addictions Using Transcendental Meditation and Maharishi Ayur-Veda. Dr. David O'Connell and Dr. Charles Alexander (Haworth, 1994; $25; 525 pages). If you are a therapist or counselor, this is essential reading. Although possibly too academic and technical for the average reader, it is comprehensive, including theory, research, case studies, and the perspectives of clinicians and clergy.

The Yoga of Herbs: An Ayurvedic Guide to Medicine. Dr. David Frawley and Dr. Vasant Lad (Lotus Light Publications, 1986; $13; 150 pages). This is a good way to learn the effects of common, everyday spices, as well as the more unusual, medicinal herbs.

For a Blissful Baby: Healthy and Happy Pregnancy with Maharishi Vedic Medicine. Dr. Kumuda Reddy, M.D., Linda

Egenes, and Margaret Mullins, R.N. (Samhita Productions, 2000; $17; 260 pages). After giving birth, 80 percent of mothers experience mild depression; 10 percent experience severe and prolonged depression. The authors explain how to avoid this—and, of course, how to take care of your baby. Every mother I have talked to who has read this book recommends it.

Vedic Cuisine: A Gourmet Guide for Bliss Consciousness. Scott Peterson (ISBN 0966184955, 1997; $20; 430 pages). This self-published, spiral-bound, no-frills cookbook is packed with straightforward recipes. Although hard to find in stores (Amazon.com now carries it), most ayurvedic households have a copy on their shelf.

Human Physiology: Expression of the Veda and the Vedic Literature. Tony Nader (Maharishi Vedic University, fourth edition, 2000; 600 pages). The textbook used for advanced courses at the Maharishi Open University. It is dense and not for the beginner—Dr. Nader is an M.D. with a Ph.D. from MIT.

Ayurveda is coming into its own. Every year several new books come out, many of them excellent. To see which are good, search an online bookstore and sort by best selling. Maharishi Ayurveda Products has introductory books on Maharishi Ayurveda, many of which you won't find elsewhere. Three of these are ***Freedom from Disease: How to Control Free Radicals*** and ***Forever Healthy,*** both by Hari Sharma, and ***Awakening Nature's Intelligence*** by Kumuda Reddy.

Quite a few books explain the benefits, in different areas of life, of raising consciousness: for business, ***Enlightened Management*** and ***Invincible Leadership***; for schools, ***Growing up Enlightened*** and ***Maharishi Speaks to Educators***; for rehabilitation, ***The Crime Vaccine*** and ***Inside Folsom Prison***; for world peace, ***Creating Heaven on Earth: The Mechanics of the Impossible*** and ***The Maharishi Effect—Creating Coherence in World Consciousness,*** as well as recently published ***Permanent Peace***. Get a catalog from Maharishi University of Management Press, 800-831-6523.

BUILD A HEALTHY HOME

If you plan to build or buy a new home, consider vedic architecture. Maharishi Global Construction—a consortium of architects and builders that promote sthapatya-veda—can help you select a building site, recommend architects, provide model blueprints, or design a custom floor plan with room dimensions and orientation according to proper *vastu* (VAH-stoo). Vastu is a Sanskrit word for the integrity of a house or building; it takes into account the ability of a building, and the site it is on, to nourish its occupants. Good vastu is based on the structure's orientation (in relation to north-south alignment, local geography, and terrain), the placement and size of each room, and the inclusion of a central area, such as a courtyard, that harmoniously pulls together all the components of the house. Vastu is site-specific and, ideally, should be designed specifically for the family moving into the home.

There are a number of ways to learn more. Maharishi Global Construction has a Web site with an online book and particularly informative FAQs. If you are not connected to the Internet, call or write and ask for a basic information packet.

Maharishi Global Construction
500 North Third Street
Fairfield, IA 52556
641-472-9605
www.mgc-vastu.com

In addition, there is a thirty-minute, infomercial-style videotape on Maharishi Sthapatya Veda. See if you can borrow a copy; otherwise, order it ($20) from the Maharishi University of Management Press. The Maharishi Open University offers a beginning course which emphasizes the consciousness component but doesn't include the fine details of design.

HOW TO GET STARTED

I suggest starting with the following: learn Transcendental Meditation, have an initial evaluation from a Maharishi Ayurvedic doctor, get a Maharishi Jyotish consultation—and buy a few of the recommended books. If you can afford it, add panchakarma, yagyas, MVVT, and advanced knowledge and experience courses. Although not cheap, the recovery tools described in this book are worth the money—considering the benefits and that you will have them for the rest of your life. Bear in mind that in the United States, smokers spend an average of $750 a year on cigarettes, while the average drinker spends $950, and each of the 1.7 million American cocaine users spends, on average, over $22,000 per year—which doesn't include the cost of crimes addicts commit to support their habit.[107] In the long run, it is cheaper to develop your consciousness. Invest in yourself; invest in your future. It is never wasted.

I'D LIKE TO DO ALL THIS, BUT I DON'T HAVE THE MONEY

If you genuinely don't have the money, there may be a good, evolutionary reason. Maybe, right now, other areas of your life are a higher priority. For example, you may need to work directly on your mental health before you can profit from meditation or physical purification. Or, you may need to focus on your career.

In the meantime, there is a lot you can do with little money. Read up on ayurveda—lifestyle and dietary changes are free. A couple of gandharva CDs and a bottle of aroma oil are quite cheap. So is a little sesame oil for daily massages. Giving service in your community is free, as is finding work more appropriate to your skills and innate nature. You could also try cutting down on TV and going to bed early. Some say that if you go to bed at 8 o'clock, you don't need ayurveda.

Make learning to meditate a priority. Even if finances are tight, go to an introductory lecture—to find out what it is all about—and then trust that when it is right, things will fall into place. And if things don't happen fast enough for you, open up a bank account and set aside some money every month. Don't put yourself in a position where you depend on charity; make yourself powerful and either rely on support of the universal aspect of nature, or do it yourself, over time.

A FINAL WORD

If you do nothing else recommended in this book, at least try to stay rested. A rested body is better able to reflect inner Being into outer life. It is also important to regularly allow the mind to settle down. A quiet mind has a special quality. It is connected to everything: infinite correlation is the attribute of the settled state of mind. Nature is always gently guiding us in the evolutionary direction. By settling our awareness, we give in to universal intelligence, which then nurtures and supports us.

I offer you my heartfelt encouragement to work toward a permanent state of stability, happiness, and comfort in your life.

May you have peace, may you have understanding.

CASE STUDIES

This chapter consists of four short case studies. These show the knowledge—which we have logically developed throughout the book—working in real-life situations. This chapter is not exhaustively comprehensive. It does, however, provide enough detail to confirm that, using these tools, you will be headed in the right direction.

CASE #1

The first case study is written by Linda Keniston-Dubocq, a medical doctor with a family practice in Waterville, Maine. She describes the recovery of one of her patients over a three-year period, using most of the tools we have introduced. Notice the team approach and the need for repeated consultations and follow-up meetings. It is excerpted from Self-Recovery, *with permission of Haworth Press. The reader is referred to Dr. Keniston-Dubocq's chapter in* Self-Recovery *for a more complete introduction and discussion of the case.*

Introduction

When I was a medical student in New York City, my impression of the alcoholic was quite literally the skid-row drunk who had lost his job, his home, his family, and his health in his pursuit of bottled spirits. My clinical experience with alcoholism did not change much during my Family Practice Residency. My first Christmas as an intern was spent taking care of someone who was drunk, fell down a set of stairs, broke his neck, and almost froze to death. During my first few years of private practice in a middle class suburban neighborhood, the problem of alcoholism seemed to disappear. That changed when a patient who was also a substance abuse counselor suggested on my intake questionnaire that I ask patients about a family history of alcoholism and personal history of substance abuse. A recovered alcoholic and addict, from a prominent New England family, she opened my eyes to a different type of alcoholism, one that is very pervasive and democratic. I have since done much personal and professional work in the area of alcoholism through Twelve Step programs, workshops, and training seminars, and now help to teach Family Practice residents about alcoholism.

To illustrate better how ayurveda and vedic science can mesh with conventional rehabilitation strategies, the following case about a young woman's recovery process is presented. This case was selected because it is representative of many of the common problems faced by alcoholics. These include a history of alcoholism within the family of origin, physical and emotional abuse, low self-esteem, dysthymia (unhappiness), anxiety, anorexia, alienation, and relationship problems. The patient was willing to try both conventional and ayurvedic treatment modalities in her recovery process, with an excellent outcome despite many stressful environmental factors. (This case is presented with the permission of the patient. In order to ensure confidentiality, some details of her social history have been changed.)

Case Presentation

The patient was a 32-year-old female who presented with complaints of insomnia, depression, and anxiety. She was an attorney in private practice with her husband, also an attorney, and had two children less than five years of age. She had been married for six years.

The patient had been generally very well except for an overwhelming sense of fatigue. She had no major surgeries, took no medications, and had never been hospitalized. She admitted that during college her weight dropped to 95 pounds and she had been amenorrheic during that time.

Two months prior to her consultation, her husband announced to her that he was very unhappy in the marriage and was thinking about divorce. Since then she had experienced extreme insomnia and had been drinking two to three glasses of wine almost nightly to help her sleep, and would drink after work two to three times a week to relieve severe headaches. She had intense bowel spasms and chronic constipation. Another doctor had prescribed Xanax as an anxiety reducer but she found that it made her too "groggy and spacey."

The patient expressed a strong desire for a nonpharmacological approach to her symptoms and was very worried about her own use of alcohol. The patient's physical exam was entirely normal except for a moderate kyphoscoliosis. Her weight was 115 pounds, BP 100/70. CBC, SMA-17, and lipid studies were also normal. In terms of Maharishi Ayurveda she had a marked vata imbalance, indicating problems with anxiety, sleep, and constipation; a pitta imbalance that pointed to deeply rooted emotional conflicts; and a kapha imbalance that indicated back pain. The pulse diagnosis also revealed that the patient's overall vitality was very suppressed.

The treatment program was comprehensive, comprising both

conventional and ayurvedic components. She was referred to a psychologist who was sensitive to issues of spirituality to help her cope with some of the severe emotional issues of the divorce. She was also referred to an osteopathic doctor for manipulation therapy for treatment of her headaches and back pain. Multiple modalities of Maharishi Ayurveda were also employed. In addition to her practice of the TM program, herbal supplements, including a supplement to help her sleep (MA-107), one to facilitate digestion (MA-154), and Maharishi Amrit Kalash, were strongly recommended. The patient was strongly advised to go to bed before 10:00 p.m. Aroma therapy and gentle yoga asanas were suggested. The patient was also strongly encouraged to have panchakarma (physiological purification) done as soon as possible.

The issue of the patient's drinking was gently addressed during the first consultation. The patient readily admitted she was drinking and clearly wanted to stop. Both her parents were alcoholic and her father had died when she was 18 years old, of a drug overdose. She had never attended any Twelve Step programs such as Alcoholics Anonymous but was willing to go to Adult Children of Alcoholics. At this point she did not think her drinking impaired her in any way. She thought of herself as a "potential alcoholic," especially given her family history.

The patient followed most of the recommendations. After a few sessions in therapy, the patient realized how abusive, both physically and emotionally, her husband was to her and how that was related to her having been abused as a child. When she realized that there was little hope of her husband changing, she decided to proceed with the divorce. The divorce itself was very complicated and stressful for the patient. She was followed by a private detective, was twice physically assaulted in her office by her husband, and by an unusual court order was forced to live only on alternate weeks in her own home and thus during weeks not at home was unable to see her children.

Despite these significant stressors, the patient's physical symptomatology improved. She had more energy, was sleeping better, had no constipation and far fewer headaches. She started dating again and developed a new circle of friends. She still drank on occasion, largely to help her sleep. Approximately nine months after the patient presented to therapy, she learned that her son had also been abused by her husband. She went on an all-night drinking binge and at times was suicidal. After this, she reluctantly agreed to go to a substance abuse counselor, and after much encouragement started to attend AA meetings on a regular basis. All therapists involved were actively supporting her recovery through ayurvedic techniques and Twelve Step programs.

The next several months were very difficult for the patient. For the first time in her life, through her work in AA and strongly supported by her ayurvedic routine, she became more in touch with her emotions. She had been denying for years how destructive her family had been. Years and years of grief and held-in anger finally began to surface. The patient came to understand how much she had abused alcohol as a drug to medicate feelings of anxiety, anger, depression, and loneliness. After she decided to stop drinking, her subjective experiences during meditation became clearer and more satisfying and, despite some very obvious stressful external forces, she started to experience greater levels of internal well-being, joy, vitality, and a sense of purpose. After nine months of sobriety she underwent a five-day course of panchakarma therapies which consisted of medicated oil massages, herbalized steam treatments, and other gentle purification techniques.

The patient also had a Maharishi Jyotish consultation and a Maharishi Yagya was recommended. Yagyas are vedic procedures designed to restore balance between the individual and the environment. In this particular case, a Maharishi Yagya was done with the intent of settling domestic disputes. Two months later the patient received a favorable settlement in her highly contested divorce.

The patient seemed to be doing extremely well in her recovery process until she started having memories of being badly abused as a child by her father (who incidentally was a physician). The patient was still in regular psychotherapy, attending AA, and was in a group for Adult Children of Alcoholics. She did not resume drinking, but again started having severe bouts of insomnia, headaches, mood swings, and muscular cramps. Because of the intense nature of her backaches, she was referred to a physical therapist who specialized in treating survivors of abuse.

Gandharva-veda music was recommended to help relieve some of the distress caused by her negative memories. The patient played this music at low volume 24 hours a day in her home and over the next few months found her insomnia and mood swings greatly improved.

The patient is currently doing very well. She has been completely sober for two years and occasionally attends AA meetings. She is in a new, committed relationship and has developed a very good support system of friends within her community. Her professional practice is flourishing. Her outlook on life is cheerful and hopeful. Despite significant stresses, both past and present, she lost no time from work, suffered only minor illnesses such as colds and took no medications other than aspirin, during the three years of her recovery process. This is remarkable considering that women admitting abuse have been diagnosed with more long-term chronic illness and more lifetime surgeries than women denying abuse.

CASES #2 AND #3

The rest of the case studies are from Catherine Bleick's work with 250 recovering alcoholics and drug addicts over a six-year period at the CLARE (Community Living for Alcoholics by Rehabilitation and Education) Foundation in Los Angeles. Transcendental Meditation was added to whatever the individuals were already doing— which in all cases included at least one Twelve Step program. These case studies show the power of self-referral awareness as a basis for successful recovery and re-integration into normal life.

These case studies are also from Self-Recovery, *used with permission of the publisher. I have included only three of ten. Find a copy of the book; I think you'll enjoy the other seven.*

Sam

Sam learned TM in our first class, at age 52, after 4 months of sobriety. His sobriety began when he entered a hospital for mental health treatment but was referred to the chemical dependency ward, and attended AA meetings there. Since suffering what he describes as a nervous breakdown associated with domestic violence at age 34, he had been depressed and very frequently in and out of mental hospitals, but was never previously diagnosed as alcoholic and actually recalls ordering wine with hospital meals. He began volunteering at CLARE shortly after his sobriety, attends three or four AA or CA meetings weekly, chairs or assists with AA panels in hospitals, jails, and prisons twice or more a month.

Sam's education stopped after eleventh grade. He learned construction skills from his father, became a partner in a very successful janitorial service, and later a chef. During these days, he had arrests for bad checks, battery in domestic disputes, and DUI (driving under the influence), and was incarcerated for some months. Sam asserts that there has been no time in the last twenty years that he could not put his hands on $1/4 million in drugs; he was a dealer for years before using drugs himself. He also believes he was a social drinker until his mid-thirties.

After the chef job, he worked only briefly. He was first on SSI (Supplemental Security Income, a Social Security benefit available to certain disabled persons) for depression, and then, until several years after learning TM, received disability payments due to back injuries incurred in auto accidents. He was hospitalized on and off for 2-1/2 years, starting when he was 38, for the back problems, and was prescribed major pain killers. Sam began drinking alcoholically due to depression and domestic problems, which the prescribed medicines did not alleviate. He was a round-the-clock drinker. He was never sober for the 16 years prior to his official sobriety, and could not eat until he had a drink. He started using cocaine, heroin, and other drugs after his alcoholism was firmly established. Prior to his sobriety, he suffered from blackouts, and was suffering increasingly from hot and cold sweats.

Because Sam had practiced a Rosicrucian form of concentration in his youth, which he enjoyed but found difficult, he questioned the ease of TM at his first TM lecture. He did find TM much easier, and has meditated extremely regularly and reported very pleasant experiences from the start. He now attends TM center functions occasionally, and regularly helps with coordinating the instruction of new meditators in our program. He says TM has enabled him to find himself and God, inner peace, and joy. He reports that TM helped with his divorce, which was finalized recently, and he is now on friendly terms with his former wife. People say he looks younger. CLARE put him on their part-time payroll as a janitor after he learned TM. He also began doing some construction work at that time, and soon began taking classes in such areas as masonry, electrical, plumbing, roofing, etc. He found his back pain bothered him less. After about three years of TM, he became a supervisor for a small construction firm, and he went completely off his disability payments a couple of years before this publication. He is now self-employed doing construction repairs.

In Sam's own words, "I have a lot less anger and a much clearer mind. This has enabled me to make the right decisions, whether it be on the spur of the moment or whether it requires long-term planning. I believe that TM has been a major factor in my being sober today. I cannot express in words the rewards that I receive daily through meditating."

Tom

Tom learned TM upon the prescription of a physician, five years before the start of our program at CLARE, at age 27, after about a year of sobriety. Tom became drug free and sober without help, on the strength of his own personal decision. Although he had attended AA meetings since his teens (while using drugs), and continued to attend occasionally, he did not become seriously active in AA until 5 years after his sobriety. He presently attends an average of 2 AA or NA meetings per week. He actively recruited for our TM program for alcoholics for several years, and also helped with introductory lectures.

Tom first got drunk at age 13, and always drank to intoxication to gain relief from mental pain. He was prescribed tranquilizers in his early teens and loved them, and used marijuana daily in high school. He studied classics at his state university, and did part-time cleaning jobs, but frequently missed classes due to drinking and hangovers.

His early post-college years were his worst period. During that time, he abused over 20 prescribed and nonprescribed drugs, either by manipulating doctors to prescribe them or by buying illegally or stealing them. During this period he also drank alcohol, in a binge pattern, with binges lasting a few days to several weeks or months. He tried at times to stop using drugs and alcohol, but his longest period of abstinence was about one month. He experienced shakes, blackouts, seizures, and amnesia while sober. He was also hospitalized numerous times for schizophrenia or manic depression rather than for alcoholism or addictions, although his symptoms were likely from the latter cause. He attended a nursing school during this period while on numerous drugs and receiving SSI. He did a little nurse's aide work, but did not graduate.

After his sobriety, he took a depression control class, assertion training with therapy, and self-hypnosis/relaxation. He graduated from a clerical/office technology school while drug free but still on SSI, and he did intermittent house cleaning during this period.

Before Tom subsequently began TM, he was physically sick, shaky, and exhausted from insomnia, all secondary to detoxification, stress, and a profound inability to relax. TM gave him immediate relief from insomnia, and he still uses it to rid himself of the urge to drink or take a pill. He states, "*Nothing,* including prayer, Twelve Step meetings, talking to other alcoholics, or exercise is so effective as TM in controlling my chemical abuse problem and associated feeling of 'insanity.' I believe all my drug and alcohol abuse can be attributed to a desperate search for inner peace, which I find in TM. TM helps me control anger, bitterness, vindictiveness, and other negative emotions; and helps me deal with family and other social problems with strength, courage, compassion, and energy. It has helped to free me of fear of changing myself, and helps me to make amends." TM also decreases his arthritis pain.

Tom's earning power increased radically after he learned TM and took up medical transcription. He presently also practices the TM-Sidhi program twice daily.

CASE #4

The last case study, because it is not an immediate success, is especially important. "Steve" learned TM early in life (long before the

TM program was set up at CLARE), but continued to have sub-stantial problems remaining free of addiction, until he joined AA and started psychotherapy. Steve's case is cautionary and illustrates what has been said many times in this book: specific problems need specific therapies; a general approach to re-establishing self-referral, by itself, may not be enough—you also need traditional recovery knowledge and support.

Steve

Steve learned TM at age 23 when he believed he was dying from habitual use of 20-30 joints of marijuana per day added to injecting morphine and amphetamines. He was unemployable, had weight loss, poor memory, little sleep, and dreams of death. He had thrown away his syringe many times, but could not stop using drugs. His girlfriend, a TM meditator, threatened to leave unless he learned TM. From the first meditation, he was immediately (although temporarily) relieved of compulsive drug use, and his physical crav-ing was (temporarily) lifted. He tried "speed" three weeks later, but had a bad experience, and remained free of drugs with regular TM practice for over two years. During this time he married his girl-friend, became a checker of TM, and succeeded extremely well in business, becoming among other things a partner in ownership of shopping centers and a part-time manager in an investment firm.

However, Steve did not take warning from his past history. Steve began drinking alcoholically at 13, stealing his parents' alcohol and drinking on a job with an alcoholic boss. He was subsequently ar-rested several times for drug-related offences, and was expelled from college for dealing drugs. Thus, when after 2-3 years of drug free, sober, and successful life with regular TM he began drinking wine with dinner, he quickly slipped into heavy drinking, then drug use and trafficking, and within six months had lost his wife and was bankrupt.

For more than ten years he continued to drink and use drugs periodically, initially being drug free and sober for as much as 3-6 months out of the year while practicing TM regularly to regain his health, but meditating irregularly during periods of drinking and using drugs. Once he overdosed on cocaine, but meditated and survived. He worked at various jobs, but by the end of the ten years he was virtually never sober and meditated only occasionally. He experienced shakes, DTs, and blackouts. He had arrests for DUI, public drunkenness, driving a stolen car, and credit card forgery, but escaped all convictions except for a probationary sentence.

When he was 39, after writing a letter to God during a blackout asking for help, Steve entered a 28-day VA hospital residential drug and alcohol abuse program. Hearing an AA panel his first night there gave him hope. He began meditating regularly again about four days into his VA program, and after release began doing both AA service and TM volunteer checking. He worked at restaurant and sales jobs. He started our TM program for alcoholics by setting up the inaugural introductory TM lecture for CLARE staff and by helping give introductory lectures for the next couple of years, before moving away.

Since his lasting sobriety and about eight years of fairly regular TM, Steve has been twice remarried and divorced, and now has half custody of his infant son. During the last marriage he had four severe attacks of pericarditis (a heart ailment), and lost the house he had been buying while working as a chef. During all of these difficulties, Steve has remained drug free and sober. He attends 5-6 AA meetings weekly, and sponsors about twelve newer AA members. He continues to practice TM, although less regularly since the birth of his son, due to the demands of childcare. He also spent 3-4 years in weekly psychotherapy. Recently, he joined a Christian church. He feels he needed AA and psychotherapy as well as TM to remain sober. But he feels he would not have made it without TM, which he believes helps his spiritual and emotional life, and physical and mental health. He feels TM helped him come through his severe pericarditis with no signs of scar tissue. He feels that TM also helps him to be a good father. He quotes a fellow meditating AA member, who calls TM "the crest jewel in the crown of the Twelve Steps," and he continues to refer AA friends to learn TM.

NOTES

Introduction

1. Kuhn, 1962.

Chapter 1

2. Bradshaw, 1988a; Schaef and Fassel, 1988; Woititz, 1983.
3. Nakken, 1996, page 10.
4. Bradshaw, 1990.
5. Schaef and Fassel, 1988, page 57.
6. Nakken, 1996, page 2.
7. www.ncadd.org/defalc.html (cited July 2000).
8. Ketcham and Asbury, 2000.
9. O'Connell and Alexander, 1994.
10. Nakken, 1996, pages 20–21.
11. Nakken, 1996, page 37.
12. Nakken, 1996, pages 56–57.
13. Ketcham and Asbury, 2000.
14. www.who.int/whr/1999/en/pdf/Chapter5.pdf (cited August 2000); Niu et al., 1998; Peto et al., 1994.
15. Peele et al., 2000.
16. Nakken, 1996, page 108.
17. Beattie, 1987, page 31.
18. Bradshaw, 1990, page 8.
19. Subby, 1987, page 84.
20. Subby, 1987, page 84.
21. Subby, 1987, page 22.
22. Bradshaw, 1990, page 8.
23. Subby, 1987, page 11.
24. Subby, 1987, pages 16–17.
25. Beattie, 1987, pages 77–87.
26. Beattie, 1987, page 45.
27. Bradshaw, 1990.
28. Dean, 1988; Subby, 1987.
29. Goldberg, 1986; Bradshaw, 1988a; Ackerman, 1987.

Chapter 2

30. Bucke, 1969.
31. Alexander and Boyer, 1989.
32. Maslow, 1968.

Chapter 3

33. Miller, 1990.
34. Bradshaw, 1990.
35. Subby, 1987.

36. Bradshaw, 1990, pages 250–251.
37. Pipher, 1994, page 254.
38. Miller and Toft, 1990, page 31.
39. American Heritage Dictionary, 1983.
40. Bradshaw, 1990.

Chapter 5

41. Maharishi Mahesh Yogi, 1963, page 48.

Chapter 6

42. O'Connell, 1994.
43. Gelderloos et al., 1991.
44. Benson and Wallace, 1972.
45. Graham, Peterman, and Scarff, 1971.
46. Davies, 1978.
47. Bounouar, 1989.
48. Childs, 1973.
49. Monahan, 1975.
50. Schenkluhn and Geisler, 1977.
51. Brautigam, 1977.
52. Bielefeld, 1981.
53. Taub, 1978.
54. Summary from Gelderloos et al., 1991, page 305.
55. Gelderloos et al., 1991.
56. Orme-Johnson et al., 1977.
57. Ballou, 1977.
58. Ramirez, 1989.
59. Alexander, 1982; Ferguson, 1989.
60. Bleick and Abrams, 1987.
61. Alexander, 1982; Bleick and Abrams, 1987.
62. Maharishi International University, 1984.
63. Orme-Johnson and Farrow, 1976; Chalmers et al., 1989.
64. Goldberg, 1986; Bradshaw, 1988a; Ackerman, 1987.
65. Subby, 1987.
66. Maharishi International University, 1984.
67. Maharishi International University, 1984.
68. Bradshaw, 1990; Whitfield, 1987.
69. Whitfield, 1987, page 58.
70. Brooks and Scarano, 1985, page 214.
71. Eppley et al., 1989.
72. Maslow, 1964.
73. Alexander et al., 1991.
74. Shostroms Personal Orientation Inventory, in Alexander et al., 1991, page 222.
75. Maharishi International University, 1988.
76. Alexander et al., 1989.
77. Maharishi International University, 1984, 1988.

78. Maharishi International University, 1988, page 37.
79. Cranson, 1991.
80. Alexander, 1982.
81. O'Connell, 1994.

Chapter 7
82. Peterson, 1992.
83. Suh, 1996.

Chapter 8
84. Lad, 1996; Chopra, 1990; Frawley et al., 1989.

Chapter 9
85. Bradshaw, 1988b.
86. Maharishi Mahesh Yogi, 1967, page 361.
87. Maharishi Mahesh Yogi, in Gelderloos and van den Berg, 1988, page 380.
88. Siles, 1968.

Chapter 10
89. Orme-Johnson et al., 1988; Orme-Johnson and Dillbeck, 1987, page 240.
90. Maharishi Mahesh Yogi, 1977, 1986a, 1986b; Orme-Johnson and Dillbeck, 1987.
91. Borland and Landrith, 1976.
92. Dillbeck et al., 1981.
93. Landrith and Dillbeck, 1983.
94. Dillbeck et al., 1988.
95. Orme-Johnson and Dillbeck, 1987, page 228.
96. Orme-Johnson and Dillbeck, 1987, page 230.
97. Orme-Johnson and Dillbeck, 1987, page 236.
98. Orme-Johnson et al., 1989.

Chapter 11
99. Maharishi Mahesh Yogi, 1967, pages 118–119.
100. Whitfield, 1987, page 67.
101. Fossum and Mason, 1986, page 5.
102. Maharishi Mahesh Yogi, 1978, page 4.

Chapter 12
103. Adamec, 1996; APA, 1994; Gorman, 1996; Ketcham and Asbury, 2000; Linehan, 1993; Mason and Kreger, 1998; Morrison, 1995; Schwartz, 1996; West, 1997.
104. http://www.surgeongeneral.gov/library/mentalhealth/chapter2/sec2_1. html#table2_6 (cited April 2001).
105. American Psychiatric Association, 1994, page 654.
106. Schwartz, 1996.
107. DuPont, 2000, page 73.

REFERENCES

Ackerman, R.J. 1987. *Let Go and Grow.* Deerfield Beach, FL: Health Communications.

Adamec, C. 1996. *How to Live with a Mentally Ill Person.* New York: John Wiley.

Alexander, C.N. 1982. Ego development, personality, and behavioral change in inmates practicing the Transcendental Meditation technique or participating in other programs: A cross-sectional and longitudinal study. *Dissertation Abstracts International* 43(2):539B.

Alexander, C.N., and Boyer, R.W. 1989. Seven states of consciousness: Unfolding the full potential of the cosmic psyche in individual life through Maharishi's Vedic Psychology. *Modern Science and Vedic Science* 2:324–371.

Alexander, C.N.; Langer, E.; Newman, R.; Chandler, H.; and Davies, J.L. 1989. Transcendental Meditation, mindfulness, and longevity: An experimental study with the elderly. *Journal of Personality and Social Psychology* 57:950–964.

Alexander, C.N.; Rainforth, M.V.; and Gelderloos, P. 1991. Transcendental Meditation, self actualization, and psychological health: A conceptual overview and statistical meta-analysis. *Journal of Social Behavior and Personality* 6(5):189–247.

American Psychiatric Association. 1994. *Diagnostic and Statistical Manual of Mental Disorders,* 4th ed. Washington, DC: American Psychiatric Association.

Ballou, D. 1977. The Transcendental Meditation program at Stillwater Prison. In *Scientific Research on the Transcendental Meditation Program: Collected Papers,* vol. 1, ed. by D.W. Orme-Johnson and J.T. Farrow. Rheinweiler, West Germany: MERU Press.

Beattie, M. 1987. *Codependent No More.* New York: HarperCollins.

Benson, H., and Wallace, R.K. 1972. Decreased drug abuse with Transcendental Meditation: A study of 1,862 subjects. In *Drug Abuse: Proceedings of the International Conference,* ed. by C.J.D. Zarafonetis. Philadelphia, PA: Lea and Febiger.

Bielefeld, M. 1981. Transcendental Meditation: A stress reducing self help support system. Presented at the Annual Convention of the American Psychological Association, Los Angeles.

Bleick, C.R., and Abrams, A.I. 1987. The Transcendental Meditation program and criminal recidivism in California. *Journal of Criminal Justice* 15:211–230.

Borland, C., and Landrith, G.S., III. 1976. Improved quality of life through the Transcendental Meditation program: Decreased crime rate. In *Scientific Research on the Transcendental Meditation Program: Collected Papers*, vol. 1, ed. by D.W. Orme-Johnson and J.T. Farrow. Rheinweiler, West Germany: MERU Press.

Bounouar, A.R. 1989. *The Transcendental Meditation Technique: A New Approach for Smoking Cessation Programs.* Doctoral dissertation, Department of Physiology and Biological Sciences, Maharishi International University, Fairfield, IA.

Bradshaw, J. 1988a. *Bradshaw On: The Family, a Revolutionary Way of Self-Discovery.* Deerfield Beach, FL: Health Communications.

Bradshaw, J. 1988b. *Healing the Shame That Binds You.* Deerfield Beach, FL: Health Communications.

Bradshaw, J. 1990. *Homecoming: Reclaiming and Championing Your Inner Child.* New York: Bantam.

Brautigam, E. 1977. Effects of the Transcendental Meditation program on drug abusers: A prospective study. In *Scientific Research on the Transcendental Meditation Program: Collected Papers*, vol. 1, ed. by D.W. Orme-Johnson and J.T. Farrow. Rheinweiler, West Germany: MERU Press.

Breggin, P., and Cohen, D. 1998. *Your Drug May Be Your Problem.* New York: Perseus Press.

Brooks, J.S., and Scarano, T. 1985. Transcendental Meditation in the treatment of post-Vietnam adjustment. *Journal of Counseling and Development* 64:212–215.

Bucke, R.M. 1969. *Cosmic Consciousness: A Study in the Evolution of the Human Mind.* New York: Dutton.

Chalmers, R.A.; Clements, G.; Schenkluhn, M.; and Weinless, M., eds. 1989. *Scientific Research on the Transcendental Meditation Program: Collected Papers*, vols. 2–4. Vlodrop, The Netherlands: MVU Press.

Childs, J.P. 1973. The use of the Transcendental Meditation program as a therapy with juvenile offenders. Doctoral dissertation, Department of Educational Psychology and Guidance, University of Tennessee.

Chopra, D. 1990. *Perfect Health.* New York: Harmony Books.

Covey, S.R. 1989. *The Seven Habits of Highly Effective People.* New York: Simon and Schuster.

Cranson, R. 1991. Intelligence and the growth of intelligence in Maharishi's Vedic Psychology and twentieth century psychology. *Dissertation Abstracts International* 50.

Davies, J.L. 1978. The Science of Creative Intelligence in high schools: Some psychological effects and evidence for reduced use of drugs. Unpublished manuscript, Maharishi International College, Australia.

Dean, A.E. 1988. *Is This Program for Me?* Center City, MN: Hazelden.

Dillbeck, M.C.; Banus, C.B.; Polanzi, C.; and Landrith, G.S., III. 1988. Test of a field model of consciousness and social change: The Transcendental Meditation and TM-Sidhi program and decreased urban crime. *Journal of Mind and Behavior* 9:457–486.

Dillbeck, M.C.; Landrith, G.S., III; and Orme-Johnson, D.W. 1981. The Transcendental Meditation program and crime rate change in a sample of forty-eight cities. *Journal of Crime and Justice* 4:25–45.

DuPont, R.L. 2000. *The Selfish Brain: Learning from Addiction.* Center City, MN: Hazelden.

Eppley, K.R.; Abrams, A.I.; and Shear, J. 1989. The effects of meditation and relaxation techniques on trait anxiety: A meta-analysis. *Journal of Clinical Psychology* 45:957–974.

Farhi, D. 1996. *The Breathing Book.* New York: Henry Holt.

Ferguson, R.E. 1989. The Transcendental Meditation program at Massachusetts Correctional Institution Walpole: An evaluation report. In *Scientific Research on the Transcendental Meditation and TM-Sidhi Programme: Collected Papers,* vol. 4, ed. by R.A. Chalmers, G. Clements, H. Schenkluhn, and M. Weinless. Vlodrop, Holland: MVU Press.

Fletcher, A.M. 2001. *Sober for Good: New Solutions for Drinking Problems— Advice from Those Who Have Succeeded.* New York: Houghton Mifflin.

Fossum, M.A., and Mason, M.J. 1986. *Facing Shame.* New York: W.W. Norton.

Frawley, D. 1989. *Ayurvedic Healing: A Comprehensive Guide.* Salt Lake City, UT: Passage Press.

Gelderloos, P.; Walton, K.G.; Orme-Johnson, D.W.; and Alexander, C.N. 1991. Effectiveness of the Transcendental Meditation program in preventing and treating substance misuse: A review. *International Journal of the Addictions* 26:293–325.

Goldberg, R.N. 1986. Under the influence. *Savvy,* July, 51–60.

Gorman, J.M. 1996. *The New Psychiatry.* New York: St. Martin's Press.

Graham, R.; Peterman, M.; and Scarff, T. 1971. *Insights into the Richmond Community.* Victoria, BC: SIMS Canada.

Ketcham, K., and Asbury, F.A. 2000. *Beyond the Influence: Understanding and Defeating Alcoholism.* New York: Bantam Books.

Kuhn, T. 1962. The structure of scientific revolutions. In *International Encyclopedia* of *Unified Science*, ed. by O. Neurath. Chicago: University of Chicago Press.

Lad, V.D. 1996. *Secrets of the Pulse: The Ancient Art of Ayurvedic Pulse Diagnosis*. Albuquerque, NM: The Ayurvedic Press.

Landrith, G.S., III, and Dillbeck, M.C. 1983. The growth of coherence in society through the Maharishi Effect: Reduced rates of suicides and auto accidents. In *Scientific Research on the Transcendental Meditation and TM-Sidhi Programme: Collected Papers*, vol. 4, ed. by R.A. Chalmers, G. Clements, H. Schenkluhn, and M. Weinless. Vlodrop, Holland: MVU Press.

Linehan, M.M. 1993. *Skills Training Manual for Treating Borderline Personality Disorder*. New York: Guilford Press.

Maharishi International University. 1984. *Maharishi Technology of the Unified Field: Results of Scientific Research on the Transcendental Meditation and TM-Sidhi Programme*. Fairfield, IA: MIU Press.

Maharishi International University. 1988. *Scientific Research on the Maharishi Technology of the Unified Field: The Transcendental Meditation and TM-Sidhi Programme*. Fairfield, IA: MIU Press.

Maharishi Mahesh Yogi. 1963. *Science of Being and Art of Living, Transcendental Meditation*. New York: Signet.

Maharishi Mahesh Yogi. 1967. *Bhagavad-Gita: A New Translation and Commentary*. London: International SRM Publications.

Maharishi Mahesh Yogi. 1977. *Creating an Ideal Society*. Rheinweiler, West Germany: MERU Press.

Maharishi Mahesh Yogi. 1978. The global Maharishi Effect: New principles of life taking over in the dawning Age of Enlightenment. *World Government News*, vol. 8, August. Rheinweiler, West Germany: MERU Press.

Maharishi Mahesh Yogi. 1986a. *Life Supported by Natural Law*. Washington, DC: Age of Enlightenment Press.

Maharishi Mahesh Yogi. 1986b. *Maharishi's Program to Create World Peace*. Washington, DC: Age of Enlightenment Press.

Maslow, A.H. 1964. *Religions, Values, and Peak Experiences*. Columbus, OH: Ohio State University Press.

Maslow, A.H. 1968. *Toward a Psychology of Being*. New York: Van Nostrand Reinhold.

Mason, P.T., Kreger, R. 1998. *Stop Walking on Eggshells: Taking Your Life Back When Someone You Care About Has Borderline Personality Disorder*. Oakland, CA: New Harbinger Publications.

Miller, A. 1990. *The Drama of the Gifted Child*. New York: HarperCollins.

Miller, N., and Toft, D. 1990. *The Disease Concept of Alcoholism and Other Drug Addiction.* Center City, MN: Hazelden.

Monahan, R.J. 1975. Impressions of the Transcendental Meditation technique in an out-patient drug rehabilitation clinic. Presented at the First International Conference on Psychology and the Science of Creative Intelligence, Fairfield, Iowa.

Morrison, R.R. 1995. *DSM-IV Made Easy.* New York: Guilford Press.

Nakken, C. 1996. *The Addictive Personality: Understanding the Addictive Process and Compulsive Behavior.* New York: Harper/Hazelden.

Niu, S.R., et al. 1998. Emerging tobacco hazards in China: Early mortality results from a prospective study. *British Medical Journal* 317(7170):1423–1424.

O'Connell, D.F., and Alexander, C.N. 1994. *Self-Recovery: Treating Addictions Using Transcendental Meditation and Maharishi Ayur-Veda.* Birmingham, NY: Harrington Park Press.

Orme-Johnson, D.W.; Alexander, C.N.; Davies, J.L.; Chandler, H.M.; and Larimore, W.E. 1988. International Peace Project in the Middle East: The effect of the Maharishi Technology of the Unified Field. *Journal of Conflict Resolution* 32:776–812.

Orme-Johnson, D.W.; Cavanaugh, K.L.; Alexander, C.N.; Gelderloos, P.; Dillbeck, M.C.; Lanford, A.G.; and Abou Nader, T.M. 1989. The influence of the Maharishi Technology of the Unified Field on world events and global social indicators: The effects of the Taste of Utopia Assembly. In *Scientific Research on the Transcendental Meditation and TM-Sidhi Programme: Collected Papers,* vol. 4, ed. by R.A. Chalmers, G. Clements, H. Schenkluhn, and M. Weinless. Vlodrop, Holland: MVU Press.

Orme-Johnson, D.W., and Dillbeck, M.C. 1987. Maharishi's program to create world peace: Theory and research. *Modern Science and Vedic Science* 1:207–259.

Orme-Johnson, D.W., and Farrow, J.T., eds. 1976. *Scientific Research on the Transcendental Meditation Program: Collected Papers,* vol. 1. Rheinweiler, West Germany: MERU Press.

Orme-Johnson, D.W.; Kiehlbauch, J.; Moore, R.; and Bristol, J. 1977. Personality and autonomic changes in prisoners practicing the Transcendental Meditation technique. In *Scientific Research on the Transcendental Meditation Program: Collected Papers,* vol. 1, ed. by D.W. Orme-Johnson and J.T. Farrow. Rheinweiler, West Germany: MERU Press.

Peele, S.; Bufe, C.; and Brodsky, A. 2000. *Resisting 12-Step Coercion: How to Fight Forced Participation in AA, NA, or 12-Step Treatment.* Tucson, AZ: See Sharp Press.

Peterson, I. 1992. New Jersey and New York want to monitor doctors' past problems. *New York Times,* August 27, B1.

Peto, R., et al. 1994. *Mortality from Smoking in Developing Countries: 1950–2000.* New York: Oxford University Press.

Pipher, M. 1994. *Reviving Ophelia: Saving the Selves of Adolescent Girls.* New York: Ballantine.

Ramirez, J. 1989. The Transcendental Meditation program as a possible treatment modality for drug offenders: Evaluation of a pilot program at Milan Federal Correctional Institution. In *Scientific Research on the Transcendental Meditation and TM-Sidhi Programme: Collected Papers,* vol. 2, ed. by R.A. Chalmers, G. Clements, H. Schenkluhn, and M. Weinless. Vlodrop, Holland: MVU Press.

Schaef, A.W., and Fassel, D. 1988. *The Addictive Organization.* San Francisco: Harper and Row.

Schendluhn, I., and Geisler, I. 1977. A longitudinal study of the influence of the Transcendental Meditation program on drug abuse. In *Scientific Research on the Transcendental Meditation Program: Collected Papers,* vol. 1, ed. by D.W. Orme-Johnson and J.T. Farrow. Rheinweiler, West Germany: MERU Press.

Schwartz, J. 1996. *Brain Lock: Free Yourself from Obsessive-Compulsive Behavior.* New York: HarperCollins.

Siles, D.L., ed. 1968. *International Encyclopedia of the Social Sciences,* vol. 4, 268–274.

Subby, R. 1987. *Lost in the Shuffle.* Deerfield Beach, FL: Health Communications.

Suh, O.H. 1996. Lifestyle behavior contributes to health. *The Southern Star,* October 4, 2.

Taub, E.; Steiner, S.S.; Weingarten, E.; and Walton, K.G. 1994. Effectiveness of broad spectrum approaches to relapse prevention in severe alcoholism: A long-term, randomized, controlled trial of Transcendental Meditation, EMG biofeedback and electronic neurotherapy. *Alcoholism Treatment Quarterly* 11(1/2):187–220.

West, J.W. 1997. *The Betty Ford Center Book of Answers.* New York: Simon and Schuster.

Whitfield, C.L. 1987. *Healing the Child Within.* Deerfield Beach, FL: Health Communications.

Woititz, J.G. 1983. *Adult Children of Alcoholics.* Deerfield Beach, FL: Health Communications.

INDEX

This book can be ordered online

www.incandescentpress.com

or by writing

Incandescent Press • P.O. Box 50622 • Palo Alto CA 94303

Enclose a check or money order for $35 (US) per book, plus $4 per order shipping within the US and $10 international. California residents add $3 sales tax.

Hanif Kureishi

NEW BRITISH FICTION

Series editors:
Philip Tew
Rod Mengham

Published
Bradley Buchanan: Hanif Kureishi
Robert Morace: Irvine Welsh

Forthcoming
Sonya Andermahr: **Jeanette Winterson**
Frederick M. Holmes: **Julian Barnes**
Rod Mengham: **Jonathan Coe**
Kaye Mitchell: **A. L. Kennedy**
Stephen Morton: **Salman Rushdie**
Mark Rawlinson: **Pat Barker**
Philip Tew: **Zadie Smith**
Lynn Wells: **Ian McEwan**
Wendy Wheeler: **A. S. Byat**

**New British Fiction Series
Series Standing Order**

ISBN 1–4039–4274-9 hardback
ISBN 1–4039–4275-7 paperback
(*outside North America only*)

You can receive future titles in this series as they are published by placing a standing order. Please contact your bookseller or, in the case of difficulty, write to us at the address below with your name and address, the title of the series and the ISBN quoted above.

Customer Services Department, Palgrave Ltd
Houndmills, Basingstoke, Hampshire RG21 6XS, England

NEW BRITISH FICTION

Hanif Kureishi

Bradley Buchanan

palgrave
macmillan

First published 2007 by
PALGRAVE MACMILLAN
Houndmills, Basingstoke, Hampshire RG21 6XS and
175 Fifth Avenue, New York, N.Y. 10010
Companies and representatives throughout the world

PALGRAVE MACMILLAN is the global academic imprint of the
Palgrave Macmillan division of St. Martin's Press, LLC and of Palgrave
Macmillan Ltd. Macmillan® is a registered trademark in the United
States, United Kingdom and other countries. Palgrave is a registered
trademark in the European Union and other countries.

ISBN-13: 978–1–4039–9049–5   hardback
ISBN-10: 1–4039–9049–2   hardback
ISBN-13: 978–1–4039–9050–1   paperback
ISBN-10: 1–4039–9050–6   paperback

This book is printed on paper suitable for recycling and made
from fully managed and sustained forest sources. Logging, pulping
and manufacturing processes are expected to conform to the
environmental regulations of the country of origin.

A catalogue record for this book is available from the British Library.

A catalog record for this book is available from the Library of
Congress.

10   9   8   7   6   5   4   3   2   1
16   15   14   13   12   11   10   09   08   07

Printed and bound in China

CONTENTS

CONTENTS

GENERAL EDITORS' PREFACE

This series highlights with its very title two crucial elements in the nature of contemporary British fiction, especially as a field for academic research and study. The first term indicates the originality and freshness of such writing expressed in a huge formal diversity. The second evokes the cultural identity of the authors included, who nevertheless represent through their diversity a challenge to any hegemonic or narrow view of Britishness. As regards the fiction, many of the writers featured in this series continue to draw from and adapt long traditions of cultural and aesthetic practice. Such aesthetic continuities contrast starkly with the conditions of knowledge at the end of the twentieth century and the beginning of the twenty-first, a period that has been characterized by an apprehension of radical presentness, a sense of unprecedented forms of experience and an obsession with new modes of self-awareness. This stage of the survival of the novel may perhaps be best remembered as a millennial and post-millennial moment, a time of fluctuating reading practices and of historical events whose impact is largely still unresolved. The new fiction of these times reflects a rapidly changing cultural and ideological reality, as well as a renewal of the commitment of both writers and readers to both the relevance and utility of narrative forms of knowledge.

Each volume in this series will serve as an introductory guide to an individual author chosen from a list of those whose work has proved to be of general interest to reviewers, academics, students and the general reading public. Each volume will offer information concerning the life, work and literary and cultural contexts appropriate to the chosen subject of each book; individual volumes will share the same overall structure with a largely common organization of materials. The result is intended to be suitable for both academic and general readers: putting accessibility at a premium, without compromising an ambitious series of readings of today's most vitally interesting British novelists, interpreting their work, assessing their influences, and exploring their relationship to the times in which they live.

Philip Tew and Rod Mengham

PREFACE

Before concentrating his efforts on fiction, Hanif Kureishi wrote plays, essays, and screenplays; he is perhaps still best known for his Oscar-nominated screenplay *My Beautiful Laundrette*. To write a book about his many works of fiction, therefore, one must account for his decision to concentrate on this genre. In explaining this shift in his work, Kureishi quotes Philip Roth's view (expressed to Kureishi himself) that 'you can give us your world more powerfully in fiction than in films' (*My Ear* 162). With characteristic candour, Kureishi also implies that his decision to focus on fiction was partly motivated by his sense of artistic insecurity: as Kureishi recounted in his interview with Colin MacCabe, 'I remember [Salman] Rushdie saying to me this really cutting thing. "We take you seriously as a writer, Hanif", he said, "but you only write screenplays". And I remember being really hurt by this, and provoked by it. And I thought, well, I'll write a novel then, and then I'll be a proper writer ... in the sense that what you write then goes to the reader unmediated' (MacCabe 42).

This autonomy and lack of mediation, however, has its draw-backs. Kureishi's novels and stories sometimes suffer from a lack of believable or profound characterization, since what film critic Vincent Canby says of *My Beautiful Laundrette* is true of much of Kureishi's work: 'characters behave in a way that has been dictated not by plausibility but [by] the effect it will create' (quoted in Kaleta 228–9). Indeed, Kureishi's indifference to psychological realism in his fiction occasionally smacks of what Ruvani Ranasinha calls a 'performative Brechtian aesthetic' (60). Ranasinha sees a deliber-ately artificial provocativeness as central to Kureishi's plays, as does Kenneth Kaleta, who claims that Kureishi 'draws attention to the artfulness of his creation' (Kaleta 241). This book will suggest that Kureishi's fiction too is concerned with the strategic, constructed nature of our political, sexual or class identities, and with representing the instability these poses create. The difficulty many readers have with Kureishi's fiction is that its theatricality, and that of its characters, sometimes seems contrived or careless. This is a side effect of the unmediated nature of the genre: whereas in films or plays a brilliant performer like Shashi Kapoor or Daniel Day-Lewis can transform slightly stilted dialogue into a believable onscreen or onstage performance, no such assistance is available on the page. Yet once one can understand and accept the fact that Kureishi is not always striving for transparent literary realism, and indeed is systematically debunking the idea of a natural or easily understood self, we can appreciate the complex, sometimes contradictory messages of his novels and stories.

BWB

ACKNOWLEDGEMENTS

I would like to extend my thanks to Philip Tew and Rod Mengham for giving me the opportunity to write this book, and to Kate Wallis and everyone at Palgrave Macmillan for their understanding attitude towards the unpredictable nature of the writing and research process. I am also grateful to my employers at Sacramento State University for giving me the time required to finish this undertaking; I would like to extend a special acknowledgement to Sheree Meyer, the chair of the English Department, who has been exceptionally supportive and helpful throughout. I would also like to express my gratitude to Hanif Kureishi himself, who was gracious enough to grant me the lengthy interview that is included in this volume, and who provided me with an advance copy of his moving and illuminating essay on his father, *My Ear at His Heart*, which speeded up the writing of this book immensely. Lastly, I would like to thank my wife, Kate Washington, for her endless patience and help with this project, as well as my daughter Nora, who was born midway through the composition of the manuscript and who has provided invaluable amusement, affection, and companionship.

The author and publishers wish to thank Hanif Kureishi, Faber and Faber Ltd, and Rogers, Coleridge & White Ltd for permission to reprint excerpts from *The Buddha of Suburbia*, © Hanif Kureishi. Reproduced by permission of the author c/o Rogers, Coleridge & White Ltd, 20 Powis Mews, London W11 1JN and Faber and Faber Ltd.

Every effort has been made to trace the copyright holders but, if any have been inadvertently overlooked, the author and publishers will be pleased to make the necessary arrangements at the first opportunity.

ABBREVIATIONS

Album: Hanif Kureishi's *The Black Album* (New York: Scribner Paperback-Simon & Schuster, 1995).

Buddha: Hanif Kureishi's *The Buddha of Suburbia* (London: Faber and Faber, 1990).

Gift: Hanif Kureishi's *Gabriel's Gift* (New York: Scribner, 2001).

Guide: Nahem Yousaf's *Hanif Kureishi's* The Buddha of Suburbia: *A Reader's Guide* (New York/London: Continuum, 2002).

Intimacy: Hanif Kureishi's *Intimacy* (London: Faber and Faber, 1998).

Hanif: Bart Moore-Gilbert's *Hanif Kureishi* (Manchester: Manchester University Press, 2001).

Laundrette: Hanif Kureishi's *My Beautiful Laundrette and Other Writings* (London: Faber and Faber, 1996).

Love: Hanif Kureishi's *Love in a Blue Time* (New York: Scribner, 1997).

Midnight: Hanif Kureishi's *Midnight All Day* (London: Faber and Faber, 1999).

My Ear: Hanif Kureishi's *My Ear at His Heart: Reading My Father* (London: Faber and Faber, 2004).

Seven: Hanif Kureishi's *The Body and Seven Stories* (London: Faber and Faber, 2002).

PART I

Introduction

TIMELINE

1960   PM Harold Macmillan's 'Winds of Change' speech, Cape
Town, South Africa
John F. Kennedy elected as US President
Aged six, Kazuo Ishiguro arrives in Britain

1961   Adolf Eichmann on trial in Israel for role in Holocaust
Bay of Pigs: attempted invasion of Cuba
Berlin Wall constructed
Yuri Gagarin first person in Space
Silicon chip patented
Private Eye magazine begins publication
Muriel Spark, *The Prime of Miss Jean Brodie*
Jonathan Coe born

1962   Cuban Missile Crisis
Marilyn Monroe dies
Independence for Uganda; followed this decade by Kenya
(1963), Northern Rhodesia (1964), Southern Rhodesia
(1965), Barbados (1966)

1

1963   John F. Kennedy assassinated in Dallas
Martin Luther King Jr delivers 'I Have a Dream' speech
Profumo Affair

1964   Nelson Mandela sentenced to life imprisonment
Commercial pirate radio challenges BBC monopoly

1965   State funeral of Winston Churchill
US sends troops to Vietnam
A. L. Kennedy born in Dundee, Scotland

1966   Ian Brady and Myra Hindley sentenced to life imprisonment for Moors Murders
England beats West Germany 4–2 at Wembley to win Football World Cup
Star Trek series debut on NBC television
Jean Rhys, *The Wide Sargasso Sea*

1967   Six-Day War in the Middle East
World's first heart transplant
Abortion Act legalizes termination of pregnancy in UK
Sergeant Pepper's Lonely Hearts Club Band album released by The Beatles
Flann O'Brien, *The Third Policeman*

1968   Anti-Vietnam War protestors attempt to storm American Embassy in Grosvenor Square
Martin Luther King Jr assassinated
Robert F. Kennedy assassinated
Student protests and riots in France
Lord Chamberlain's role as censor of plays in the UK is abolished
Lindsay Anderson, *If…*

1969 Civil rights march in Northern Ireland attacked by Protestants

Apollo 11 lands on the Moon with Neil Armstrong's famous first steps

Rock concert at Woodstock

Yasser Arafat becomes leader of PLO

Booker Prize first awarded; winner P. H. Newby, *Something to Answer for*

Open University founded in the UK

John Fowles, *The French Lieutenant's Woman*

1970 Popular Front for the Liberation of Palestine (PFLP) hijacks five planes

Students activists and bystanders shot in anti-Vietnam War protest at Kent State University, Ohio, four killed, nine wounded

UK voting age reduced from 21 years to 18

1971 Decimal currency introduced in the UK

Internment without trial of terrorist suspects in Northern Ireland begins

India and Pakistan in conflict after Bangladesh declares independence

1972 Miners' strike

Bloody Sunday in Londonderry, 14 protestors killed outright or fatally wounded by British troops

Aldershot barracks bomb initiates IRA campaign with seven dead

Britain enters Common Market

Massacre of Israeli athletes at Munich Olympics

Watergate scandal

Anthony Burgess, *A Clockwork Orange*

Samuel Beckett, *Not I*

1973 US troops leave Vietnam

Arab–Israeli 15-day Yom Kippur War

PM Edward Heath introduces three-day working week
Martin Amis, *The Rachel Papers*

1974 Miners' strike
IRA bombings in Guildford (five dead) and Birmingham
(21 dead)

1975 Microsoft founded
Sex Discrimination Act
Zadie Smith born in North London
Malcolm Bradbury, *The History Man*

1976 Weak economy forces UK government loan from the
International Monetary Fund (IMF)
Ian McEwan, *First Love, Last Rites*

1977 *Star Wars* released
UK unemployment tops 1,600,000
Nintendo begins to sell computer games
Sex Pistols 'Anarchy In the UK' tour

1978 Soviet troops occupy Afghanistan
First test-tube baby born in Oldham, England

1979 Iranian Revolution establishes Islamic theocracy
Margaret Thatcher becomes PM after Conservative elec-
tion victory
USSR invades Afghanistan
Lord Mountbatten assassinated by the IRA

1980 Iran–Iraq War starts
Iranian Embassy siege in London
CND rally at Greenham Common airbase, England

IRA hunger strike at Belfast Maze Prison over political status for prisoners
Julian Barnes, *Metroland*

1981 Prince Charles and Lady Diana marry in St Paul's Cathedral with 750 million worldwide television audience
Widespread urban riots in UK including in Brixton, Holloway, Toxteth, Handsworth, Moss Side
AIDS identified
First IBM personal computer
Alasdair Gray, *Lanark*
Salman Rushdie, *Midnight's Children*, which wins Booker Prize for Fiction
Hanif Kureishi's play *Outskirts* produced at the Royal Shakespeare Company Warehouse Theatre and wins the George Devine Award

1982 Mark Thatcher, PM's son, disappears for three days in Sahara during the Paris-Dakar rally
Falklands War with Argentina, costing the UK over £1.6 billion
Body of Roberto Calvi, chairman of Vatican-connected Banco Ambrosiano, found hanging beneath Blackfriars Bridge, London

1983 Klaus Barbie, Nazi war criminal, arrested in Bolivia
Beirut: US Embassy and barracks bombing, killing hundreds of members of multinational peacekeeping force, mostly US marines
US troops invade Grenada
Microsoft Word first released
Salman Rushdie, *Shame*, which wins Prix du Meilleur Livre Étranger (France)

1984 Miners' strike
HIV identified as cause of AIDS
IRA bomb at Conservative Party Conference in Brighton kills four

British Telecom privatization shares sale
Thirty-eight deaths during clashes at Liverpool v. Juventus football match at Heysel Stadium, Brussels
Martin Amis, *Money: A Suicide Note*
Julian Barnes, *Flaubert's Parrot*
James Kelman, *Busconductor Hines*
Graham Swift, *Waterland*

1985   Famine in Ethiopia and Live Aid concert
Damage to ozone layer discovered
Mikhail Gorbachev becomes Soviet Premier and introduces *glasnost* (openness with the West) and *perestroika* (economic restructuring)
PC Blakelock murdered during riots on Broadwater Farm estate in Tottenham, London
My Beautiful Laundrette film released (dir. Stephen Frears, screenplay Hanif Kureishi), and wins the Evening Standard Award for Best Film and the New York Critics' Award. Kureishi is nominated for BAFTA Award for best screenplay and for Best Screenplay Oscar
Jeanette Winterson, *Oranges Are Not the Only Fruit*

1986   Abolition of Greater London Council and other metropolitan county councils in England
Violence between police and protestors at Wapping, East London after Rupert Murdoch sacks 5,000 print workers
Challenger shuttle explodes
Chernobyl nuclear accident
US bombs Libya
Peter Ackroyd, *Hawksmoor*

1987   Capsizing of RORO ferry, *Herald of Free Enterprise*, off Zeebrugge kills 193 people
London Stock Exchange and market collapse on 'Black Monday'
Remembrance Sunday: eleven killed by Provisional IRA bomb in Enniskillen

Ian McEwan, *The Child in Time*, which wins Whitbread Novel Award

Jeanette Winterson, *The Passion*

1988 US shoots down Iranian passenger flight

Pan Am flight 103 bombed over Lockerbie, 270 people killed

Soviet troop withdrawals from Afghanistan begin

Salman Rushdie, *The Satanic Verses*

1989 *Fatwa* issued against Rushdie by Iranian leadership (Khomeini)

Fall of Berlin Wall

Exxon Valdez oil disaster

Student protestors massacred in Tiananmen Square, Bejing

Hillsborough Stadium disaster in which 96 football fans die

Kazuo Ishiguro, *The Remains of the Day*, which wins Booker Prize for Fiction

Jeanette Winterson, *Sexing the Cherry*

1990 London poll tax riots

Fall of Thatcher; John Major becomes Conservative PM

Nelson Mandela freed from jail

Jeanette Winterson adapts *Oranges* for BBC television film

A. S. Byatt, *Possession*

Hanif Kureishi, *The Buddha of Suburbia*, which wins Whitbread First Novel Prize

A. L. Kennedy, *Night Geometry and the Garscadden Trains*

1991 Soviet Union collapses

First Iraq War with 12-day Operation Desert Storm

Apartheid ended in South Africa

PM Major negotiates opt-out for Britain from European Monetary Union and rejects Social Chapter of Maastricht Treaty

Hypertext Markup Language (HTML) helps create the World Wide Web

Hanif Kureishi: screenplays for *Sammy and Rosie Get Laid* and *London Kills Me*

Pat Barker, *Regeneration*

1992   'Black Wednesday' stock market crisis when UK forced to exit European Exchange Rate Mechanism
Adam Thorpe, *Ulverton*

1993   Black teenager Stephen Lawrence murdered in Well Hall Road, London
With Downing Street Declaration, PM John Major and Taoiseach Albert Reynolds commit Britain and Ireland to joint Northern Ireland resolution
Film of Ishiguro's *The Remains of the Day*, starring Anthony Hopkins and Emma Thompson
Irvine Welsh, *Trainspotting*

1994   Tony Blair elected leader of Labour Party following death of John Smith
Channel Tunnel opens
Nelson Mandela elected President of South Africa
Provisional IRA and loyalist paramilitary cease-fire
Homosexual age of consent for men in the UK lowered to 18
Mike Newell (dir.), *Four Weddings and a Funeral*
Jonathan Coe, *What a Carve Up!*
James Kelman, *How late it was, how late*, which wins Booker Prize for Fiction
Irvine Welsh, *The Acid House*

1995   Oklahoma City bombing
Srebrenica massacre during Bosnian War
Pat Barker, *The Ghost Road*
Nicholas Hytner (dir.), *The Madness of King George*
Hanif Kureishi, *The Black Album*

1996   Cases of Bovine Spongeiform Encephalitis (Mad Cow Disease) in the UK
Divorce of Charles and Diana
Breaching cease-fire, Provisional IRA bombs London's Canary Wharf and Central Manchester

Film of Irvine Welsh's *Trainspotting* (dir. Danny Boyle), starring Ewan McGregor and Robert Carlyle

Graham Swift, *Last Orders*, which wins Booker Prize

1997 Tony Blair becomes Labour PM after landslide victory

Princess Diana dies in Paris car crash

Hong Kong returned to China by UK

Jim Crace, *Quarantine*

Jonathan Coe, *The House of Sleep*, which wins Prix Médicis Étranger (France)

Ian McEwan, *Enduring Love*

Iain Sinclair and Marc Atkins, *Lights Out for the Territory*

1998 Good Friday Agreement on Northern Ireland and Northern Ireland Assembly established

Twenty-eight people killed by splinter group Real IRA bombing in Omagh

Sonny Bono Act extends copyright to lifetime plus 70 years

BFI/Channel 4 film *Stella Does Tricks*, released (screenplay A. L. Kennedy)

Julian Barnes, *England, England*

Hanif Kureishi, *Intimacy*

1999 Euro currency adopted

Macpherson Inquiry into Stephen Lawrence murder accuses London's Metropolitan Police of institutional racism

NATO bombs Serbia over Kosovo crisis

Welsh Assembly and Scottish Parliament both open

Thirty-one passengers killed in Ladbroke Grove train disaster

2000 Anti-globalization protest and riots in London

Hauliers and farmers blockade oil refineries in fuel price protest in the UK

Kazuo Ishiguro, *When We Were Orphans*

Will Self, *How the Dead Live*

Zadie Smith, *White Teeth*

2001   9/11 Al-Qaeda attacks on World Trade Center and Pentagon

Bombing and invasion of Afghanistan

Riots in Oldham, Leeds, Bradford, and Burnley, Northern England

Labour Party under Blair re-elected to government

Ian McEwan, *Atonement*

Intimacy film released (dir. Patrice Chéreau), wins top prize at Berlin Film Festival

2002   Queen Mother dies aged 101

Rowan Williams named next Archbishop of Canterbury

Bali terrorist bomb kills 202 people and injures a further 209

Inquiry concludes English general practitioner Dr Harold Shipman killed around 215 patients

Zadie Smith's *White Teeth* adapted for Channel 4 television broadcast in autumn

2003   Invasion of Iraq and fall of Saddam Hussein

Death of UK government scientist Dr David Kelly, and Hutton Inquiry

Worldwide threat of Severe Acute Respiratory Syndrome (SARS)

2004   BBC Director General Greg Dyke steps down over Kelly affair

Bombings in Madrid kill 190 people and injure over 1,700

Expansion of NATO to include seven ex-Warsaw Pact countries

European Union expands to 25 countries as eight ex-communist states join

Jonathan Coe, *Like a Fiery Elephant: The Story of B. S. Johnson*

Alan Hollinghurst, *The Line of Beauty*, which wins Booker Prize for Fiction

Andrea Levy, *Small Island*, which wins Orange Prize for Fiction

2005   UK ban on foxhunting with dogs comes into force

7/7 London suicide bombings on transport system kill 52 and injure over 700 commuters in morning rush hour

Hurricane Katrina kills at least 1,836 people and floods devastate New Orleans

After four failed bombings are detected, Brazilian Jean Charles de Menezes is shot and killed by Metropolitan Police officers at Stockwell Underground Station

Ian McEwan, *Saturday*

Zadie Smith, *On Beauty*, which wins 2006 Orange Prize for Fiction

2006   Jeanette Winterson awarded the OBE

Airline terror plot thwarted, causes major UK airline delays

Israel–Hezbollah war in Lebanon

Five prostitutes killed in Ipswich in a six-week period

Saddam Hussein executed by hanging in controversial circumstances

1

INTRODUCTION: KUREISHI IN CONTEXT

When Hanif Kureishi was born in 1954, Britain was still recovering from the devastating economic and social consequences of the Second World War. His childhood and adolescence saw British culture regain confidence and influence in the 1960s, with the emergence of an individualistic counterculture and the worldwide popularity of musicians such as The Beatles. The 1970s, however, were marred – in Britain and elsewhere – by economic stagnation, labour strife and instability, with the result that most of the political promise of the 1960s' ethic of self-fulfilment was discredited. This situation produced three successive Conservative administrations in Britain, run by two Prime Ministers: Margaret Thatcher (who served two terms) and John Major. Thatcher especially fought the unions, privatized the state-owned industries she saw as inefficient, and allowed the British pound to lose value at a rate that alarmed many. Kureishi was one of many Britons who found themselves feeling both threatened and stimulated by the Thatcher-dominated 1980s and early 1990s, and his fiction deals primarily with these periods. The late 1990s and 2000s, when Tony Blair's centrist Labour Party (elected in 1997) has been overwhelmingly dominant, have been less inspiring as fodder for political commentary.

Kureishi's lifetime has seen a number of intense cultural and demographic changes in British society, perhaps the most notable being the arrival of large numbers of immigrants from South Asia and the Caribbean, and the increasing visibility and self-confidence of their communities. Being the son of such an immigrant,

12

Kureishi has to some degree been forced into the role of commentator on the phenomenon of immigration and its long-term effects, and readily admits that his initial willingness to play this role meant that he profited from being a member of a visible minority in Britain. In an interview with Colin MacCabe, Kureishi describes his dealings with the media: '[T]hey were liberal. And they needed an Asian, and I was the Asian' (MacCabe 40). Nevertheless, Kureishi's own experience as the child of a middle-class, white-collar family has been very different from that of many minorities in England (most of whom arrived without his father Rafiushan Kureishi's education and have remained working-class). This singularity means that his work differs substantially from that of postcolonial authors such as Salman Rushdie, Sam Selvon, V. S. Naipaul, and Zadie Smith, with which it is frequently compared. Whereas these writers often critique Western culture (implicitly or explicitly) from a non-Western perspective, Kureishi has largely accepted its traditions (though he frequently satirizes the excesses they can lead to). In Susie Thomas's words, 'Unlike Salman Rushdie ... or V.S. Naipaul ... [Kureishi] is not a displaced postcolonial writing *back* to the centre; he writes *from* the centre' (Thomas 1). Thus Kureishi adopts some classically Western theories as narratives that have informed his own life, among them the Freudian idea of the Oedipus complex (often mocked as a specifically Western obsession), which will be discussed in depth in later chapters.

Because of the increasingly obvious uniqueness of Kureishi's cultural and political position as a fully Westernized child of an immigrant father, recent critics have turned away from viewing Kureishi in terms of postcolonialism. For instance, Bruce King argues persuasively that 'it is difficult to understand why postcolonialism should be applied to ... someone writing about ... life in England and the difficulties of accepting life's limitations' ('Abdulrazak Gurnah and Hanif Kureishi: Failed Revolutions' 93). In relation to his previously assumed allegiance to Rushdie's globalizing viewpoint, as Peter Hitchcock writes in his article 'Decolonizing (the) English', 'The work of Hanif Kureishi, while indebted to Rushdie's in important ways, complicates the tokenist assumptions of cosmopolitanism by foregrounding hybridity yet questioning its role as the nirvana of subjectivity' (755). In a similar vein Hitchcock remarks on the potential for isolation in Kureishi's stance, noting that while Kureishi displays no nostalgia for life in his family's ancestral homeland, his life in England is plagued by an 'apparent rootlessness' which implies that 'he is effectively rejected by both sides' (756). Such rhetoric can seem hyperbolic, but it has a certain truth. Similarly, although King's assertion that 'Kureishi was not concerned with matters of decolonization, migration, exile and cultural conflict' ('Abdulrazak Gurnah' 89) is contestable (and in some instances demonstrably untrue), King makes the valid point that on the whole Kureishi's work is more concerned with other, less typically postcolonial problems.

Thus the central features of Kureishi's depiction of English life are arguably not based on stable racial or ethnic identities but instead on the blurring of class boundaries, the rise of feminism, the emergence of gay and lesbian movements, and the institutionalization and commercialization of youth culture and popular music, as well as an increased postmodern awareness of the arbitrariness and contingency of identity (be it racial, religious, or cultural). Thus Kureishi sees identity both as 'performative' and as subject to 'active negotiation' (Hitchcock 757), and his work chronicles not a straightforward clash of fixed identities but a complex interplay of many cultural movements. Such a project precludes simple political allegiances or old-fashioned displays of commitment or sincerity, as for Kureishi 'earnestness is a pathetically unimaginative mode of responding to ideological opposition' ('Abdulrazak Gurnah' 85). Irony is Kureishi's most reliable trope, and he evinces scepticism about the capacity of any group or ideology to effect lasting or meaningful change. Bruce King notes that 'there is a tension in Kureishi's work between the enterprising individual's desires and the comforts and security of family and the communal' ('Abdulrazak Gurnah' 91). In his early work, Kureishi's sympathy seems to lie with the individual in such situations, though this orientation can be seen to change as his fiction develops, and as he loses his initial faith in the power of youth to gratify all desires.

Indeed, the mature Kureishi becomes ambivalent about the emergence of self-consciously marginal identities that seem to threaten any universalizing, humanistic worldview. As the narrator of *The Black Album* observes, 'These days everyone was insisting on their identity, coming out as a man, woman, gay, black, Jew ... as if without a tag they wouldn't be human' (*Album* 102). Such pronouncements have prompted Bruce King to exclaim that '*The*

Black Album is a plea for real literature … and, yes, even England, in contrast to those who regard them with scorn as the products of elitism, liberal decadence, and racist imperialism' ('Abdulrazak Gurnah' 92). To some extent, King's argument is sound: Kureishi's fiction does suggest that because of the unnecessarily isolationist, antagonistic stances of identity theorists, humanity has become fragmented into artificially oppositional categories. For Kureishi, our differences — be they due to gender, psychological makeup, geography, religion or age — are less significant than they might seem. (Hence his acceptance, in the interview chapter of this book, of the unfashionable label 'humanist'.) In Kureishi's fiction, this stance increasingly takes the form of a critique of the leftist, supposedly progressive movements of the late twentieth century, and a nostalgia for a more stable, unified culture. While it is true that, as Bruce King notes, 'Kureishi's plays and screenplays of the 1980s were part of an angry response to Thatcher's government and its dismantling of the Welfare State', King's observation that 'Kureishi felt the excesses of the Left … were partly responsible for England's problems' ('Abdulrazak Gurnah' 89) is perhaps more germane to his fiction.

It is therefore possible to portray Kureishi as both a victim of and a participant in the postwar backlash against immigrant and civil rights movements. In 'The Rainbow Sign', Kureishi reveals: 'In the mid-1960s, Pakistanis were a risible subject in England … . I tried to deny my Pakistani self … I read with understanding a story in a newspaper about a black boy who, when he noticed that burnt skin turned white, jumped into a bath of boiling water' (*Laundrette* 73). In a similar passage from *The Black Album*, the protagonist Shahid confesses that he too has internalized the racism he had encountered in his youth: 'My mind was invaded by killing-nigger fantasies … going around abusing Pakis, niggers, Chinks, Irish, any foreign scum … The thought of sleeping with Asian girls made me sick' (*Album* 18–19). Such racism is not confined to the characters, however; the novel's impersonal narrator jokes that Shahid's college, whose racial makeup is 'sixty percent black and Asian', has a reputation for 'gang rivalries, drugs, thieving, and political violence' and holds its reunions in Wandsworth Prison (32).

Although Kureishi suggests that his own encounters with racism (being beaten by white classmates and called 'Pakistani Pete' by a teacher, for example) were responsible for most of the internalized racism that occasionally comes out in his work, he seems less interested in exploring this aspect of his own character or in placing blame on English people in general than in exploring the class issues raised by racial divisions. Few critics have taken the cue and tackled the connections between race and class in Kureishi's work, but those who have done so seem to agree that the issues are intertwined. Nahem Yousaf argues that Kureishi's 'hybridised citizens' and their 'cultural identities' are 'inextricably linked with class politics' ('Hanif Kureishi and "The Brown Man's Burden"' 17). Others, such as Bart Moore-Gilbert, note Kureishi's 'perception that … the most immediate and violent expressions of racism have tended to emerge from working-class formations' (*Hanif Kureishi* 10). Most critics, however, have steered clear of such questions, in part because of the complex issues they raise.

Perhaps the most obviously disconcerting feature of Kureishi's class-consciousness is his view that racial solidarity between immigrants is made problematic by persistent class antagonisms; for instance, Kureishi attempts to contextualize some of his South Asian characters' contempt for their fellow immigrants when he notes: 'The Pakistani middle class shared the disdain of the British for the émigré working class and peasantry of Pakistan' (*Laundrette* 92). Yet Kureishi implicitly concedes that his own upbringing in a lower-middle-class household, under the eyes of an educated father with a white-collar job, may have produced some of the dismissive attitudes his characters evince. Kureishi speaks for the lower middle classes when, in 'Some Time with Stephen', he asserts: 'There is great lower-middle-class snobbery, contempt for the working class and envy of the middle class' (*Dreaming* 170). Kureishi himself is not, however, totally unsympathetic to those who share his class origins, as we see when he depicts the unfairly narrow social and intellectual expectations placed upon lower-middle-class children. In his view: 'This is partly what it means to be lower middle-class … the notion of who you can be, is severely limited. It is the Other who are qualified to receive the good things. Being articulate wasn't a virtue; it was regarded with suspicion' (*My Ear* 130). Yet Kureishi's right to speak for (or about) any given class has been controversial; Bart Moore-Gilbert notes that Kureishi has been denounced as a 'middle-class exploiter' of working-class struggles (*Hanif Kureishi* 16).

Notwithstanding such critiques, Rita Felski has made a persuasive case that in Kureishi's *The Buddha of Suburbia*, the Amir family
belongs squarely to the lower middle class, and her depictions of
the unappealing characteristics of this class are readily applicable
to many of Kureishi's families: 'Lower-middle-classness is … a
"cage of umbrellas and steely regularity" [26], marked by
respectability, rigidity and gray routine … guilt about money,
anxiety about status, and fear of the neighbors' disapproval'
('Nothing to Declare: Identity, Shame, and the Lower Middle Class'
37). Felski also notes that 'the social life of the lower middle class is
almost nonexistent, since the ubiquitous English pub is considered
vulgar, working class' (37). Felski has argued that in the mid and late
twentieth century, the lower middle class, as portrayed by authors
such as George Orwell, 'inhabits a world that is almost completely
lacking in spontaneity, sensuality or pleasure' (36) and is often
associated with racism (42). The lower middle class is also a largely
feminized social group, according to Felski, in that its 'peculiar
joylessness' is 'most vividly embodied' in 'female characters' (36)
and because 'many of the values and attitudes traditionally associated with the lower middle-class are also identified with women:
domesticity, prudery, aspirations towards refinement' (42). Thus
we may well understand the wanderlust of Kureishi's protagonists
as a response to the fact that, as Felski remarks, 'the lower middle
class is … associated with the triumph of suburban values and the
symbolic castration of men' (43). No doubt defending his decision
to escape this castrating class straightjacket, Kureishi himself has
asserted that 'there should be a fluid, non-hierarchical society with
free movement between classes' and predicts that 'these classes
will eventually be dissolved' (*Dreaming* 145).

To say the least, the class politics of Kureishi's texts (like those of
Kureishi's own life) are complex. For instance, in *The Buddha of
Suburbia* Karim's family represents an ambiguous mixture of class
identities. His mother Margaret was 'a pretty working-class girl
from the suburbs' when Karim's father Haroon met her (*Buddha*
25), but by virtue of her marriage, she becomes a pillar of the lower
middle class. For his part, Haroon is a displaced Indian aristocrat
who has taken up a marginal position in the British civil service.
Karim sketches his father's (and his uncle Anwar's) privileged
upbringing with an envious air: 'They went to school in a horse-
drawn rickshaw. At weekends they played cricket … . The servants

would be ballboys ... . Dad had had an idyllic childhood, and ... I often wondered why he'd condemned his own son to a dreary suburb of London' (*Buddha* 23). Haroon's exalted ancestry not only torments the downtrodden Karim, but also seems to cement the family's isolation and immobility. As Karim recounts, 'If Mum was irritated by Dad's aristocratic uselessness, she was also proud of his family. "They're higher than the Churchills", she said to people ... . This would ensure that there would be no confusion between Dad and the swarms of Indian peasants who came to Britain in the 1950s and 1960s' (*Buddha* 24). In this respect, Margaret's own race- and class-consciousness seems to be to blame for Karim's sense of being an outcast. It also arguably reflects a wider social phenome- non that Kureishi himself encountered: snobbish scorn for the mass of non-white immigrants in Britain.

Karim is never made to feel at home in the lower-middle-class milieu either. Part of the problem lies in the social limitations placed on such groups; Kureishi paints a bitter picture of the educa- tion Karim is afforded as a lower-middle-class youth: 'all my Dad thought about was me becoming a doctor. What world was he living in? Every day I considered myself lucky to get home from school without serious injury' (63). Yet Karim also denounces lower-middle-class youth culture itself for its complicity in this culture of reduced expectations, and portrays it as a ghettoizing obstacle to his improvement: 'We were proud of never learning anything except the names of footballers, the personnel of rock groups and the lyrics of "I Am the Walrus". What idiots we were!' (*Buddha* 178). In this depressing environment, the winds of political change seem rather bracing, and they come in the shape of Haroon's lover (and eventual second wife) Eva Kay. Eva is Kureishi's embodiment of Thatcherite ideals and capitalist energies, and she provides a stark contrast to the self-pitying inertia of Margaret.

The respective symbolic positions of these two women seem to be Kureishi's clearest commentary on the surprising virtues of Thatcherite ruthlessness. Eva is a 'glorious middle-aged woman, clever and graceful' (*Buddha* 261) who has finally completely tran- scended her earlier middle-class status: 'There was nothing subur- ban about her; she'd risen above herself ... ' (*Buddha* 261). During one interview, Eva embarks on a curious political speech in which she parrots Thatcherite ideas about individual initiative and self- reliance: 'We have to empower ourselves. Look at those people who live on sordid housing estates. They expect others – the Government – to do everything for them. They are only half human, because only half active. We have to find a way to enable them to grow' (*Buddha* 263). Furthermore, when Eva and Haroon announce their engagement, the news of 'who was going to be the next Prime Minister' (i.e., Margaret Thatcher) makes everyone at the family party 'ecstatic' (*Buddha* 282). Plainly, both Eva's desires and her political values have triumphed, to Karim's satisfaction; he gloats at his newfound 'money-power' (*Buddha* 283) and rejoices at the fact that (despite their difficulties) Eva and Haroon are to be married.

For her part, Margaret seems to be symbolic of the generally downtrodden tenor of working-class British life in the late seventies and early eighties. After Haroon leaves her, however, she loses weight and embarks on a campaign of intellectual self-improvement. Her transformation reinforces Karim's own ethic of self-centredness; tasks that were once a 'chore' for her when she and Haroon were together (*Buddha* 144) cease to be so now, since she's doing them for herself. One could also see a justification of Thatcherite 'tough love' behind Haroon's abandonment of Margaret; she is portrayed as an inefficient organism who responds favourably to a challenge. The novel thus conveys a major message of the 1980s milieu in which Kureishi was writing; when *The Buddha of Suburbia* was published in 1990, the Conservative Party was still in power, and their ideology of self-improvement and individual responsibility still seemed dominant.

Kureishi also offers us a comic version of British history in Karim's career, which arguably begins with an echo of the long, bitter labour disputes of the 1970s and 1980s. In a brief negotiation with Eva, Karim demands equal wages for himself and Eleanor, and Eva agrees, but only on the condition that both of their wages be 'reduced by twenty-five percent' (*Buddha* 206). This faint echo of a major social crisis is extremely ironic, in that Karim soon becomes a happy worker, soothed by music and fast food, despite the fact that Eva is plainly exploiting him and Eleanor. As if to show that British society rewards such unquestioning industriousness, Karim soon converts his pop-culture savvy into rapid fame as an actor and exults: 'I enjoyed being recognized in the pub afterwards, and made myself conspicuous in case anyone wanted my autograph' (*Buddha* 158). Karim still faces two obstacles to his quest to overcome his class limitations and social conscience: his friend Terry and his cousin Jamila. Karim confesses his liking for the Marxist Terry, but in terms that reveal his contempt: 'we talked every day. But he did believe the working class – which he referred to as if it were a single-willed person – would do some unlikely things. "The working class will take care of those bastards very easily," he said, referring to racist organizations' (*Buddha* 149). Terry's naïveté where race is concerned annoys Karim, in part because of Jamila's struggles against working-class racism as a woman of colour. Terry's profession as an actor also leads him to betray his basic political values and become a hypocrite: his major professional success comes in the role of a policeman, an authority figure who props up the political structure Terry professes to despise. Jamila is less easily exposed as a fake, but Kureishi does suggest that Jamila's originally class-based anti-racist politics have become socially irrelevant when she retreats from the real world of her working-class neighbourhood into a commune. Against the backdrop of Jamila's principled retreat from society, Karim's own success looks suspiciously like a bargain with the devil. Nevertheless, although both Terry and Jamila display some admirable traits, they are decisively marginalized by the end of the book, suggesting that they are excluded from the main narrative of recent British history, unlike Karim, who witnesses the unlikely engagement of the immigrant guru Haroon to the Thatcherite Eva (a prospective marriage that echoes the pro-business message of Kureishi's film *My Beautiful Laundrette*).

There are some important links between the cultural and social commentaries of *The Buddha of Suburbia* and those in *The Black Album*. Though less admirable than Eva, Shahid's older brother Chili is also a typical product of the excesses of the 1980s. As the narrator notes: 'money had come too easily to Chili in the 1980s. He didn't respect where it came from' (*Album* 63). Moreover, like Thatcherites gaining inspiration from Ronald Reagan's conservatism, Chili looks to America for models of how to succeed as a member of a minority culture. His heroes, however, are the gangsters glorified in *The Godfather* and other movies about the Italian-American mafia. Kureishi's juxtaposition of Shahid with such hyper-masculine figures makes Shahid seem especially effeminate; even Shahid's father sees his son as a 'bloody eunuch fool' (*Album* 61) for failing to live up to their example. Through Chili, the narrator articulates a philosophy that sounds very much like Eva's (and Thatcher's): 'people were weak and lazy … people resisted change, even if it would improve their lives; they were afraid, complacent, lacking courage. This gave the advantage to someone of initiative and will' (*Album* 60). Chili's sexual aggression sets him apart from these two feminine figures, however: 'Chili called himself a predator. When a woman offered herself – it was the most satisfying moment. Often, it wasn't even necessary to sleep with her. A look in her eyes, of eagerness, gladness, acquiescence, was sufficient' (*Album* 60). Like a rapist, Chili does not covet sex as much as he covets control and mastery over women. This tendency, however, is checked by his wife Zulma, who, like Chili, is both 'arch-Thatcherite' in her politics and aggressive in her emotional relationships (*Album* 97).

Kureishi comments on the essential futility of the Left in modern Britain through *The Black Album*'s Andrew Brownlow, a stuttering upper-middle-class twit turned academic class warrior. Despite (or perhaps because of) this pedigree, Brownlow cannot even utter a word in his initial appearance, though he is shown being 'collectively willed' to speak and 'working his mouth, and thumping himself on the side of the head as if to repair a connection' (*Album* 39). Flustered by his stammer, Brownlow merely shakes hands with everyone and leaves, as if to underscore the Left's inability to articulate anything of relevance to young Britons. His stutter, we learn, is linked to the fact that leftist ideology has apparently been discredited by history, since, as Shahid's friend 'Hat' remarks: 'He been developing this s-s-s-stutter … it come on since the Communist states of Eastern Europe began collapsing. As each one goes over he gets another syllable on his impediment' (*Album* 40). Brownlow's upper-middle-class identity seems to disqualify him from cultural relevance, although he is given some redeeming features, such as his anti-racism.

The inheritor of Brownlow's academic and social mantle is his wife, Deedee Osgood, who seduces Shahid and leads him on a whirlwind tour of London's intellectual and sexual demimonde. As a former sex worker and lower-class student, Deedee's working-class credentials are impeccable, and yet she dismisses Brownlow's preoccupation with 'politics' on the grounds that 'It all makes you feel guilty' (*Album* 66), and she turns to drugs such as Ecstasy, which she asks Shahid to share with her. In a telling moment, Deedee celebrates her discovery of a 'perfect venue for a house party' by quoting Coleridge: 'A savage place! as holy and enchanted / As e'er beneath a waning moon was haunted / By woman wailing for her demon lover' (72). The juxtaposition of Deedee's educated delight and the joy of the 'runty' working-class youth who is seen proclaiming 'E for the people. Up the working class!' (72) makes the point that drugs are a way to bring aesthetic bliss and Dionysian excitement to the masses, who cannot attain Deedee's level of literary sophistication. This democratization of a once-aristocratic privilege is not as harmless as it might seem, however, as we infer from the fact that Shahid sees drugged-out 'kids ... lying on the floor not moving ... as if they'd been massacred' (73).

Perhaps attuned to this destructive undertone, Shahid soon rejects the pretence of academic curiosity that authorizes Deedee's interest in the drug and rave subculture, and turns to a more down-to-earth working-class drug dealer nicknamed Strapper. At first, Strapper's life in the drug subculture affords Shahid a glimpse of the absolute solidarity that class-based political awareness once promised falsely. Yet, paradoxically, Strapper covets the more legit-imate, above-board brand names of the consumer culture whose core values he embodies: 'Strapper saw lads his age in Armani, Boss, Woodhouse; he glanced into the road and saw broad BMWs, gold-colored Mercs, and turquoise turbo-charged Saab convert-ibles ... . None of this would be his – ever. It just wouldn't be. It didn't make sense' (*Album* 209). Indeed, in Kureishi's eyes, as in Strapper's, there is no distinction between the acceptable signs of material wealth under capitalism and illegal drugs.

Given these equivalent and extreme choices, Islamic funda-mentalism seems a reasonable alternative, at least as it is initially represented in *The Black Album*, where Kureishi puts a number of strong indictments of Western culture into the mouths of his Muslim characters. For instance, Shahid's friend Chad warns Shahid about becoming involved in this seductive secular culture, claiming that he had once been like Shahid, controlled 'by the music and fashion industries' (*Album* 89). Chad goes on to link music and clothes to drugs, and testifies to his own addictions to cocaine, LSD and heroin. Kureishi portrays the rise of Islamic fundamentalism among young Pakistanis as a youthful move-ment of rebellion against a decadent, thrill-seeking, and

Westernized older generation: 'While their parents would drink bootleg whiskey and watch videos sent from England, Shahid's young relatives and their friends gathered in the house on Fridays before going to pray' (*Album* 101). Kureishi understands the motives behind this religious rebellion and sympathizes with the Muslim impulse to reject the excesses of the West, but his underlying hostility to Islam's sacred text comes across clearly in his non-fictional writings, as when he observes: 'Open the Koran on almost any page and there is a threat' (*Dreaming* 218). Muslim fanaticism is also corrupted by racial antipathy; as he writes, 'I saw the taking up of Islam as an aberration, a desperate fantasy of world-wide black brotherhood' (*Laundrette* 79).

Kureishi does not, however, ignore the racial prejudices that motivate much Muslim extremism in Britain. For instance, the intransigence of working-class racism is underscored when Shahid confronts an angry woman, a denizen of the miserable 'mildewed flats' (as he unwisely reminds her [*Album* 149]) who hurls racist epithets at him: 'Paki! Paki! Paki! ... You stolen our jobs! Taken our housing! Paki got everything! Give it back and go back home!' (*Album* 149). Thus, in the eyes of some of Kureishi's non-white characters, racial solidarity is called for, even if it must take place under the dubious umbrella of religious fanaticism. Indeed, Kureishi seems to posit that religion can sometimes provide a needed defence for British Asians; as we see in *Buddha*, the only thing that saves Jamila's husband Changez when he is attacked by racists is 'his Muslim warrior's call' (*Buddha* 224). In fact, we see an important shift in Kureishi's picture of racial resistance when Jamila's secular, class-based anti-racist militancy in *Buddha* is reborn in *The Black Album* as Riaz's fundamentalist combativeness: 'We're not blasted Christians ... . We don't turn the other cheek. We will fight for our people' (*Album* 92). Shahid, still smarting from the racism he has endured, identifies with Riaz (at least for a time), and feels 'a physical pride in their cause' (*Album* 93).

Shahid ends up in conflict with his Islamic friends, partly because of the controversy provoked by the reaction of many Muslims to the appearance of an unnamed controversial novel (presumably *The Satanic Verses*, which was published in 1988). Rushdie's depiction of the prophet Muhammad as a fallible and inconsistent leader provoked outrage and book-burning protests in Britain as well as in many parts of the Muslim world, and in 1990 the Iranian Ayatollah Ruhollah Khomeini issued a *fatwa* calling for Rushdie's death. Kureishi evidently deplores such extreme reactions to a literary text, and Shahid does not participate wholeheartedly in the demonstrations against the embattled author. Shahid also differs from his fellow Muslims depicted in *Album* precisely because he is inclined to view the debate over the disputed novel in a racial context rather than in a purely religious one. Shahid tries to minimize the writer's alleged guilt as a slanderer of Islam, reminding Chad and Farhat that 'this man ... hasn't spat on us or refused us a job. He never called you Paki scum, did he?' (*Album* 229). Thus through Shahid, Kureishi tries to remind his fellow non-white Britons of the need for racial solidarity, which (in his view) ought to overcome religious intolerance.

As the complexity of these texts suggests, Kureishi's overall political orientation is somewhat ambiguous. On one level, he is a card-carrying liberal who professes a moral mistrust of capitalism ('I still think of businessmen as semi-criminals' [*Dreaming* 145]) and deplores what he sees as the Conservative Party's racist and misanthropic agenda; Kureishi recalls hearing Margaret Thatcher say that 'To pursue pleasure for its own sake was wrong' (*My Beautiful Laundrette* 116). Yet Kureishi also complains that 'The Left, in its puritanical way, has frequently dismissed pop as capitalist pap' (*Laundrette* 118), suggesting that his allegiance to popular culture is more important to him than any stable ideological position. Moreover, as we have seen, he has created characters who embody some of what he sees as the positive aspects of Thatcher's influence on an otherwise moribund British culture. Indeed, if we look at the rest of Kureishi's fiction, we can see that Thatcherism is the single most important political ideology in his characters' lives, having outlived Marxism, racial solidarity and feminism.

For instance, the narrator of 'In a Blue Time', the first story of the volume *Love in a Blue Time*, describes the 'mid-eighties' as a time when 'everything had been forced forward with a remorseless velocity' and makes it clear that Roy, the story's protagonist, participated fully in the decade's unapologetic materialism: 'Roy had cancelled his debts to anyone whose affection failed to yield interest' (*Love* 3). Roy's excesses as a consumer in the 1980s seem to rival Chili's:

... at the height of the decade money had gushed through his account ... he drank champagne rather than beer ... he used cocaine and took taxis from one end of Soho to the other five times a day .... The manic entrepreneurialism, prancing individualism, self-indulgence and cynicism appealed to him as nothing had for ten years. (*Love* 15)

This description seems negative enough to sour us on Roy, but it is followed by a more attractive picture of the new and invigorating honesty of eighties culture:

Pretence was discarded. Punk disorder and nihilism ruled. Knowledge, tradition, decency and the lip service paid to equality; socialist holiness, talk of 'principle', student clothes, feminist absurdities, and arguments defending regimes – 'flawed experiments' – that his friends wouldn't have been able to live under for five minutes: such pieties were trampled with a Nietzschean pitilessness. It was galvanizing. (*Love* 15)

In Kureishi's depiction here, all the big ideas that once stood in the way of the Thatcherite vision of unrestrained capitalist exploitation have been cleared away: Marxism has been disproven by history, feminism has apparently been shown to be a collection of 'absurdities', and 'knowledge' has been deemed worthless.

Thatcherite ideals are also triumphant in 'Lately' from *Love in a Blue Time*. The initially detestable Vance stands for Thatcherite moralism and self-reliance, saying, 'These days people don't want to make moral judgements. They blame their parents, or society' (*Love* 156). Vance defends psychological repression and frustration, claiming that 'suppose we all did what we wanted the whole time. Nothing would get done' (*Love* 156). Vance is verbally abusive to his wife Karen and feels that Rocco, the story's protagonist, and Rocco's wife Lisa, are 'Typical of the sentimental unemployed' who 'think people are suffering because I've taken their money ... There's more and more of them about. People don't contribute. What we'll do with them is the problem of our time' (*Love* 165). Vance's credo is that 'Selfishness, wanting something for oneself, is the law of reality', though he tries to moderate his position by couching it in terms of trickle-down economics: 'But if I benefit, others will benefit' (*Love* 181). Plainly, Kureishi distrusts such self-serving rhetoric, but the only character who seems likely to oppose it is the contemptible Rocco, a disaffected bohemian whose ethos is equally suspect. Rocco rationalizes his selfishness by blaming others for setting up arbitrary and vindictive rules: 'Other people wanted you to live lives as miserable as theirs. This they considered moral behaviour' (*Love* 176).

When the inevitable fight between the two antagonists happens, Rocco quickly collapses and urges Vance to 'Kick my head in' (*Love* 185). Initially, Vance tries to fight according to more gentlemanly rules, helping Rocco back to his feet and punching him squarely in the face. Rocco and Lisa decide to leave for London together, leaving Lisa's would-be lover Moon and Rocco's friend Bodger behind them. Vance takes all the credit for Rocco's change of heart where his marriage is concerned, telling Bodger that 'they've been wanting to get out for weeks. And I'm paying for it … It's amazing, he's actually doing something' (*Love* 187). Given Vance's crucial intervention, he seems to be the most important and active character in the story, and ultimately the most admirable. We are told that Feather 'liked him in spite of his personality' (*Love* 157) and his reactions to Feather's broken finger, as well as to Rocco's recovery, show him to be capable of compassion. The story suggests that Kureishi, rather than hoping for some champion of the Left who might oppose Thatcherism with an effective alternative, merely hopes that the Right will evince some human compassion despite itself.

At first glance, Kureishi's novella *Intimacy* appears to be a rejection of Thatcherism; the protagonist Jay may be taken as a representative of mainstream British public opinion in the 1990s, which has finally abandoned the Thatcherite values of the 1980s and turned back to a nostalgic leftism that attempts to justify itself with a rhetoric of emancipation and self-fulfilment. Such a reading has a strong basis in the text; after all, Jay professes to despise capitalism as a social and psychological phenomenon: 'I never understood the elevation of greed as a political credo' (*Intimacy* 70). Yet Jay's analysis of his generation's leftist ideology seems more like a condemnation from Kureishi's own mouth: 'We were dismissive and contemptuous of Thatcherism, but so captivated by our own ideological obsessions that we couldn't see its appeal … Some remained on the left; other retreated into sexual politics; some became Thatcherites. We were the kind of people who held the Labour Party back' (*Intimacy* 70). Indeed, leftist politics are seen as a mere prelude to the true vocation of Jay's age-group: 'we went on the dole for five years in order to pursue our self-righteous politics, before starting work in the media and making a lot of money' (*Intimacy* 69). This portrait of a generation is really Jay's self-portrait, and we infer that he is the one who is the target of his puritanical wife's indictment:

> Susan ... thinks we live in a selfish age. She talks of a Thatcherism of the soul that imagines that people are not dependent on one another. In love, these days, it is a free market; browse and buy, pick and choose, rent and reject, as you like. There's no sexual and social security; everyone has to take care of themselves, or not. Fulfilment, self-expression and 'creativity' are the only values. Susan would say that we require other social forms. What are they? Probably the unpleasant ones: duty, sacrifice, obligation to others, self-discipline. (*Intimacy* 68–9)

By rejecting these dour virtues, Jay allies himself with 'Thatcherism of the soul', quite clearly. He does his best to justify his decision, though, which suggests that Kureishi is still chastising himself for his earlier naïve affection for leftist causes.

Gabriel's Gift is perhaps Kureishi's least overtly political novel, yet it too contains some familiar, if oblique, commentaries on politics and culture. For instance, we are informed that Gabriel's mother had tried to 'become entrepreneurial' in the frenetic 1980s to keep up with the rest of the country, but her business, making party clothes for musicians and others, had failed to expand and she had fallen into debt (*Gift* 12). This failure seems at first to vindicate the shiftlessness of Gabriel's father Rex, a part-time musician and idealist whose lack of financial responsibility causes a rift in his marriage. Rex still idealizes the sixties, and pays lip service to the 'revolutionary struggle of making the world a better place, with free food and marijuana all round' (*Gift* 41), and he rationalizes the squalor in which he lives by critiquing the English obsession with property: 'They'd trade their souls for a sofa' (*Gift* 42). However, in an effort to win back his straying wife, Rex changes political and economic credos as the book progresses. Like many other Kureishi characters who once professed leftist radicalism, Rex has joined the Thatcherite movement, despite himself, as Gabriel notes: 'Along with ... other dependants and pseudo-servants, Dad had found a place at the table of the rich ... . If wealth was to "drip down", as people had been told it inevitably did, it would find its level through Rex' (*Gift* 168). In becoming 'a businessman' (*Gift* 176), Rex has, in essence, grown up, telling Gabriel that 'I have to do my job, now that I have one' (*Gift* 170–1). Rex and his estranged wife Christine are reconciled, just as Eva and Haroon are engaged at the end of *Buddha*, and it is difficult to avoid the conclusion that Thatcherism has proved to be extremely salutary to Kureishi's characters in both the financial realm and the familial one.

Yet even Kureishi's leftist critics would concede that he is capable of pointing out the ironies of all economic and social doctrines. For instance, Kureishi defends the young drug dealers portrayed in his work as 'incredibly enterprising' and wonders why they have been demonized by Tory politicians; after all, they are 'living out the Thatcherite dream' ('Requiem for a Rave' 12). Of course, Kureishi also condemns what he calls 'the old Left' for what he sees as its 'contempt for pop culture' which was based on the assumption that pop was 'capitalism in disguise' ('Requiem for a Rave' 11). In other words, leftists too have been guilty of insufficient love for the hedonistic youth culture they have been portrayed by the right as condoning and even encouraging.

Indeed, when we examine Kureishi's cultural politics carefully, we can see that Kureishi's real allegiances lie with a dynamic youth culture that he believes to be capable of cutting across political and class lines. He frequently depicts this phenomenon as the sole antidote to class imprisonment: 'For a lot of kids, Pop was the only hope for a creative, unpredictable life … . Otherwise we were locked into the post-war vision of a controlled – married, of course – and secure life, the life my parents wanted to live' (*My Ear* 130). His work is a celebration of the creative energy of young people, and a suggestion of their power to inspire cultural (and, by extension, political and social) change:

> These kids called themselves 'freaks', which was how I saw myself. They didn't, though, only want to watch Disney's *Fantasia* on acid … but were thinking about what they would do in music, fashion, photography. They made me feel competitive, so that before getting into my velvet trousers, I'd do a couple of hours at the typewriter, trying to see what sort of stories I could make out of our lives, stories I hadn't seen in other people's books: teenage sex, overdoses, sadistic teachers, the weird lives of parents when perceived by children … there is always something shocking and exhilarating about seeing the contemporary world in fiction. (*My Ear* 125)

Kureishi's own literary enterprise seems, in this passage, to be explained in terms of adolescent rivalry and imitative reflexes. Thus, if there is a source of hope for cultural progress in his work, it seems as if it is to be found in the young, whose relatively unsullied perceptions and openness to new sensations, chemicals and ideas make them infinitely more interesting than older people.

Kureishi's latest novel, *The Body* (2002), in which a middle-aged man trades his body in for the gorgeous corpse of a younger man, is another eloquent testament to his abiding obsession with the power of youth, and another recognition of how central this power is to his conception of contemporary culture. The trouble is that Kureishi is beginning to recognize mortality (as he notes in the interview included in this book) and thus can't fully enjoy the heedlessness of youth. *The Body*'s protagonist, initially (and fittingly) named Adam, suspects that 'to participate in the world with curiosity and pleasure, to see the point of what is going on, you have to be young and informed' (*Body* 4); however, although Adam (or Leo, as he is known after his transformation) becomes younger in appearance, he never quite manages to become 'informed' enough to enjoy popular culture. As if to rationalize his detachment, he summarizes the fallen state of contemporary life: 'there was culture, now there is shopping' (*Body* 35). Although Adam/Leo is dissatisfied with what he calls 'book knowledge', he feels even more threatened by visual media: 'if I watch TV for too long I begin to feel hollow .... I am no longer familiar with the pop stars, actors, or serials on TV. I'm never certain who the pornographic boy and girl bodies belong to' (*Body* 4). It is tempting to see Kureishi declaring his own ultimate allegiance to the printed word here, and disavowing his ventures into other media (films and plays especially) as inferior imitations; as Jay's friend Asif says in *Intimacy*, making fiction into films is akin to 'Turning gold into dross' (*Intimacy* 46).

In the end, though, Adam/Leo is content to use popular media such as television and films to justify the timeliness of his own decision to shed his old body in favour of a newer one; as he notes, the surgical procedure enabling 'old ... men and women' to live vicariously in 'the bodies of the young' is merely a logical extension of the voyeuristic impulses behind popular culture (*Body* 12). Such self-serving hypocrisy where popular culture is concerned is a familiar trait in Kureishi's protagonists; they appropriate and exploit in practice what they condemn in theory. This attitude is also visible in their political and racial attitudes; it is perhaps part of what Nahem Yousaf terms Kureishi's own 'apparently cynical hardiness' (*Body* 20), though perhaps we might more charitably conclude that it is more often a trait he consciously deploys and exposes in his characters in order to undermine its self-destructive consequences.

Kureishi's cultural politics (as exposed in *The Body* and elsewhere) may make him seem vulnerable to A. Sivanandan's indictment of post-New Left British intellectuals: 'The self that New Timers make so much play about is a small, selfish, inward-looking self that finds pride in lifestyle, exuberance in consumption and commitment in pleasure – and then elevates them all into a politics' (*Communities of Resistance* 5). Many of Kureishi's characters seem to fall into this category, as their creator seems increasingly to realize to his own amusement, annoyance and occasional sadness. Yet for Kureishi, our political lives – which concern our racial, religious, class and gender identities – matter much less than does the fact of being (or having once been) teenagers. Kureishi comes close to making youth into its own cultural ideology, albeit a provisional and self-consciously superficial one. Whether this is a satisfactory position for a writer whose work has been invested with such social and political significance is an open question, as the many critics with differing views cited in Chapter 8 of this book attest.

2

A BIOGRAPHICAL READING

Hanif Kureishi was born in Bromley, a South London suburb, on 5 December 1954. He attended the University of London, where he studied Philosophy, and after leaving school rose from the rank of usher to become the writer in residence at the Royal Theatre. His early plays were produced by London's Theatre Upstairs, the Royal Court Theatre, and the Royal Shakespeare Company, and he enjoyed international success with the 1985 screenplay *My Beautiful Laundrette*, for which he was nominated for an Academy Award. In 1990, his novel, *The Buddha of Suburbia*, won the Whitbread Book of the Year Award for first novels. His fiction has since appeared regularly in prestigious periodicals such as the *New Yorker, Granta*, the *London Review of Books* and the *Atlantic Monthly*. Kureishi was married to Tracey Scoffield, his former editor at Faber & Faber, with whom he had twin boys (born in 1993) named Sachin and Carlo (he and Scoffield are now divorced). He began a relationship in 1995 with Monique Proudlove, and 1998 the couple had a son, named Kier.

Kureishi's successful literary career is in strong contrast to the vexed ambitions of his father, Rafiushan (Shanoo) Kureishi, who arrived in England to study law in 1947, having fled the cultural and political instability that led to the partition of India and Pakistan. Rafiushan abandoned his legal studies, became a civil servant with frustrated literary ambitions, and married Kureishi's mother, Audrey (née Buss), who is of English origin, all the while nursing frustrated literary urges. Kureishi's rapid success as a writer may have bred some guilt in him, given his father's struggles, and this feeling resulted in Kureishi's recent memoir, *My Ear at His Heart*, in which he deals with the painful themes of paternal expectations and filial hostility, anxiety or inadequacy. This memoir is a very complex one, and it sheds a great deal of light on Kureishi's upbringing. For instance, Kureishi makes it plain that he finds his father's attitudes towards bodily pleasure hypocritical and self-serving:

> … he did consider … white girls to be slutty, though he'd married a white girl himself … . Father disliked Muslim conservatism, but didn't like my sister looking 'tarty'. If the immigrant always lives in a world he cannot quite grasp, he might seek to petrify it by controlling his children and … their sexuality. (*My Ear* 115)

As we see, Kureishi attempts to contextualize his father's selective puritanism as the reflex of an immigrant. Kureishi also adduces an example from *The Buddha of Suburbia* to make his point: 'part of the plot concerns … Jamila, whose father goes on hunger strike to compel her to marry. Even if she does comply, as Jamila does, the child inevitably turns into someone the parent cannot quite recognise, someone who can never be enough like him, because she was born later and in another place' (*My Ear* 116).

Notwithstanding Kureishi's emphasis on the cultural aspects of this generation gap, the idea that he has had recourse most often to in explaining this generation gap is not recent theories of hybridity articulated by writers such as Homi Bhabha or Robert Young, but rather the Freudian theory of the Oedipus complex. Kureishi describes the formative encounter in which his uncle Achoo first expounded Freud's idea:

> … my uncle … told me that I wanted to have sex with my mother and kill my father. Anticipating my protest, he said all men, including him, had felt like this; surely I'd noticed that literature was full of such desires? … He could remember, he continued, wanting to have sex with his mother … .This shocked me in the best way: I was intrigued, fascinated. That family life was Oedipal seemed a wild thing for an educated adult to say, more improbable than anything I'd heard from my friends or in pop music … if the sane were also mad, how did we live with this? (*My Ear* 87)

In *My Ear* this passage serves to explain many facets of Kureishi's complex relationship to his father, who is the central focus of Kureishi's autobiographical musings. Kureishi's personal sense of

Oedipal guilt where Rafiushan was concerned may be seen from his observation that 'It is as if your robustness, vigorous curiosity and sexual enthusiasm is an insult to the parent's suffering, to their loss of power and potency. How can you live your life when your father is failing to live his?' (*My Ear* 12). These Oedipal dynamics no doubt contributed to Kureishi's own decision to leave home as a young man, a move which greatly distressed Kureishi's father. As Kureishi recounts: 'I think my father was shocked by my leaving, by how sudden and definitive it was, that such a passionate involvement can just end. It seemed to make dad iller and more bitter, as though he wanted me to fail in London and be forced to return home where the two of us would continue as before' (*My Ear* 141). Kureishi did not cease to look for paternal figures after his departure, however, as he concedes: 'After leaving home, my propensity to find fathers and brothers who had better lives than me ... seemed to increase' (*My Ear* 142).

In *My Ear*, Kureishi explicitly compares this father-seeking side of himself to Karim Amir of *Buddha* (*My Ear* 116), and there is some truth to this, since *Buddha* seems to revolve around the search for male role models: Charlie, Shadwell, Pyke, Anwar and Changez successively occupy Haroon's deserted place at the centre of Karim's Oedipus complex. However, as if to reverse the truth about Kureishi's departure from his father and mother (and to displace Kureishi's own guilt), *Buddha* begins with a formative act of paternal desertion: Haroon's abandonment of Margaret is the first event in a chain reaction that will force Karim to achieve some sort of maturity. In theory, Haroon's infidelity offers Karim license to return to a pre-Oedipal intimacy with his mother, but in practice it means that Karim's aggressive Oedipal urges are initially frustrated by Haroon's refusal to occupy his traditional fatherly role. With the knowledge of Haroon's persistently infantile craving for domestic bliss in mind, Karim uses the news about Margaret's new boyfriend and reinvigorated attitude to life to hurt his father in the classic Oedipal manner; when Karim tells Haroon that Jimmy has 'injected [Margaret] with new life' we are told that the information 'practically assassinated [Haroon] there and then' (*Buddha* 281). The challenge of making Haroon suffer only has a sporadic appeal, however; when Karim sees a pitifully weak, overweight Haroon at the end of the book, he contemplates the wreckage of his first Oedipal conflict: 'I'd become the powerful one; I couldn't fight him

– and I wanted to fight him – without destroying him in one blow. It was a saddening disappointment' (*Buddha* 261).

Aside from these vexed parricidal themes, there are incestuous overtones in the novel as well. In the tones of an Oedipal son, Karim complains that Margaret – a 'plump and unphysical woman' (*Buddha* 4) much like Kureishi's own mother (Kureishi says of her: 'mother hid her body – it was private' [*My Ear* 62]) – cannot provide him with the necessary maternal comforts. His quest for a substitute mother figure thus justified, Karim eagerly accompanies his father Haroon to a party, where he encounters Eva Kay, Haroon's lover, and her son Charlie (soon to be Karim's lover). Eva is a maternal figure who is also a much more suitable 'transitional object' (to use a phrase Kureishi himself employs in *Intimacy* [19]), whose physical characteristics are much more clearly defined and sexualized than his own mother's are. This contrast between Eva and his own mother accounts for Eva's attractiveness, as Karim confesses: 'Plain prurience was one of the reasons I was so keen to go to her place, and embarrassment one of the reasons why Mum refused. Eva Kay was forward; she was brazen; she was wicked' (*Buddha* 8). Margaret represents the lower-middle-class libidinal restrictions that Kureishi himself chafed against as a child, and Karim has already begun to identify with his father's quest for freedom from her influence. Hence Karim's realization that 'I was reluctant to kiss my mother, afraid that somehow her weakness and unhappiness would infect me' (*Buddha* 104). Despite his growing independence from his mother, however, the spectre of incest follows him around, as we see when he reminds himself that he has slept with Jamila, 'the woman I'd always characterized … as "sister"' (*Buddha* 134).

We may compare Karim to *The Black Album*'s Shahid Hasan, another of Kureishi's autobiographical heroes, who fantasizes about a woman who is as 'warm as mother' and dreams about having 'dissolved' in her arms in an unmistakably sexual way (*Album* 76). Shahid becomes romantically involved with Deedee Osgood, an older woman who teaches at his college. Deedee admits that 'she was too often tempted to mother' her students, 'especially the Asian girls' (*Album* 37), and this maternal feeling spills over into her passionate relationship with Shahid. A young drug dealer named Strapper alludes to the Oedipal subtext of this liaison when he asks her: 'Feeding the little student boyfriend, eh?', and muses in an aside, 'Mummy's cooking [is] always tastiest' (*Album* 275). Although Shahid evinces the same incestuous traits as Karim, the latter's reconciliation with his father is not a possibility for *Album*'s protagonist, whose father has recently died. The first and most obvious candidate to replace Shahid's dead father is his overbearing and violent brother Chili. However, Chili's life quickly falls apart due to his own drug use, and he seeks refuge with Shahid, whose displaced Oedipal feelings about his father have refocused to some extent on his older brother: 'Shahid couldn't help being glad that Chili was in trouble … . If there was such a thing as natural justice, Chili deserved punishment. When younger, Shahid had, himself, continually attempted revenge' (*Album* 156). With his father gone and Chili reduced to addled help-lessness, Shahid needs to fill an emotional void in his life, and turns to drugs and religion in an attempt to do so.

Once again, these fictional troubles have an apparent biograph-ical origin. Kureishi, as he wrote *Album* (after his own father's death), embarked on a similar course of self-destruction. He confesses that his drug use spiralled out of control:

> Looking at my diary for that period, it is mostly accounts of my drug and alcohol consumption: cocaine, amyl nitrate, ecstasy, alcohol, grass, as though I were trying to kill something, or bring something in myself to life … . In the morning I'd lie there thinking what I'd score that day, and from whom, as well as considering, once I was stoned, how I would get down again, get to sleep … . Released from the harsh command of father, from writing as solution, drugs enabled me to talk to others, in some broken form. (*My Ear* 165)

Kureishi was torn between a feeling of relief at being free of his father's judgmental presence and a sense of needing to punish himself for having wanted his father to die. As he confesses: 'After father's death I find in my journal such things as, "violent fantasies; thoughts of suicide"; "I have never loathed myself like this before"; "On the edge mentally, thinking people have been sent in cars to kill me"' (*My Ear* 166).

Some critics have remarked on the Oedipal themes in Kureishi's first two novels. Minna Proctor sees an unusual 'Oedipal crisis' in *The Buddha* and *The Black Album*, in which 'society rather than the father' is 'the specter to be reckoned with' (Proctor 38), but does not explore the issue further. Mark Stein posits a more personal

'Oedipal need' in Shahid to 'distinguish himself' from what Stein (rather opaquely) calls 'his prior other' (Stein 130) but notes that this need is an ironic one, given Shahid's use of his father's notepaper to write his stories. Such critical insights have not forced Kureishi to turn away from or minimize the Oedipal tropes in his later fiction. These tropes, however, become more complex in their manifestation, perhaps in part because Kureishi himself had become a father and was starting to write about paternity. An important shift in Kureishi's work occurs when his protagonists cease to be young men and become paternal figures themselves. Unwilling to admit their desire to retain the authority they once resented in others, they absent themselves from the familial circle by infidelity or some other form of mid-life crisis. When their youthful air of innocence is gone, they are forced to realize that the power of the father is not a purely artificial construction that has been forced on them, but rather an important aspect of their own identities.

The tension between Kureishi's impulse to identify with children and his need to act out the role of a father is perhaps most painfully clear in his infamous novella *Intimacy*, which many have read as an account of the acrimonious breakup of Kureishi's relationship with his ex-wife Tracey Scoffield, though Kureishi has denied this. Kureishi was widely portrayed as a heartless and irresponsible philanderer for having chosen to leave Scoffield, and to many, *Intimacy* seems a defensive manoeuvre designed to win public sympathy by casting Scoffield as Susan, a castrating shrew who refuses to allow Jay, her fed-up husband, the slightest bit of respect or affection. There is little doubt that the portrayal of domestic disputes in the book is monotonously one-sided. For instance, Kureishi shows us a scene in which Susan's banal tyranny forces Jay to interrupt his writing:

> Susan is speaking – asking me to get my diary.
> 'Why?' I say.
> 'Why? Just do it, if you don't mind. Just do it!'
> 'Don't speak to me like that. You are so harsh'.
> 'I'm too tired for a negotiation about diaries'. (*Intimacy* 32)

Susan's 'harsh' demands make her seem like an implacable virago that few men could tolerate for one night, let alone ten years. It is, however, difficult to know how much of *Intimacy* is in fact a personal attack on Scoffield, or how many of the charges against her have their basis in reality.

There are certainly parallels between Kureishi and Jay: Jay recalls the guilty feelings he experienced when first leaving his parents to live with Nina, emotions which Kureishi himself evidently felt. Jay also realizes that his father would disapprove of his decision to leave Susan, but decides that both his parents were 'frustrated' because they were 'loyal and faithful to one another' but 'Disloyal and unfaithful to themselves' (*Intimacy* 57–8). His parents' fidelity (which mirrors that of Kureishi's parents) is a necessary but fatal by-product of their class and their historical milieu, in Jay's eyes: 'Separation wouldn't have occurred to a lower-middle-class couple in the fifties' (*Intimacy* 59). As an upwardly mobile man, Jay feels luckier than his parents, though he still seems haunted by the family he outgrew as a youth; in this respect, he seems to be remarkably similar to his creator. Like Kureishi after his father's death, Jay is frequently disoriented and depressed, though he admits to enjoying some aspects of his psychological disturbances: 'I don't always know where I am, which can be a pleasurably demanding experience' (*Intimacy* 5).

Intimacy continues the theme of familial tensions and aggression: Jay violently rejects his own children: 'once I threw him backwards into his cot, hitting his head. I booted him hard up the nappy before he was even walking' (*Intimacy* 113). This aggression is linked to Jay's excrementally tinged anger at his own father; as he muses: 'At times I hated Father … I'd put laxative in his cereal so he'd shit himself on the train. I hate my children, at times, as they must hate me. You don't stop loving someone just because you hate them' (*Intimacy* 108). We also see related Oedipal motifs of maternal lovers and male infantilization that have marked Kureishi's often autobiographical work: for instance, when Susan brings Jay to a therapist, he feels 'like a child being taken to the doctor by an impatient mother' (*Intimacy* 92). Although Jay chafes at Susan's demands, he still requires a maternal figure to protect him; he confesses that, even as an adult, 'I used women to protect me from other people. Wherever I might be, if I were huddled up with a whispering woman who wanted me, I could keep the world outside my skin' (*Intimacy* 19).

Jay conflates a husband's wish to stray sexually from a pregnant or nursing woman with the son's need to break from his mother to achieve sexual maturity, symbolically equating marital fidelity with incest, when he asks, 'Is it when their women become mothers that they [fathers] flee? What is it about mothers that makes it so essential that they be left?' (*Intimacy* 140). Jay's departure can be read as a delayed rejection of the smothering figure who has retarded his development, and can seem to be a necessary step towards sexual maturity and emotional independence, and thus as a vindication of Kureishi's own departure from his first marriage. Such a conclusion seems inevitable when we consider the correlation between Jay's difficulties with women and similar problems Kureishi has experienced. Once the desired level of emotional intimacy has been achieved with a woman, for instance, Jay views the woman herself as a mother-figure, and thus as being out of bounds where sex is concerned: 'Unsurprisingly, Susan is the one woman, apart from Mother, with whom I can do practically nothing' (*Intimacy* 20). It is little wonder that Jay has to leave this relationship, and Kureishi himself seems to feel that a similar need to escape has shaped his life as a writer and husband; as he concedes in *My Ear*, 'I liked women ... but there was always a moment when I had to flee them. The things I've wanted the most, I've fled' (*My Ear* 156).

It is intriguing, from a biographical point of view, to note that Oedipal tropes are still present in *Gabriel's Gift* and *The Body*, Kureishi's two most important later full-length works. In *Gabriel's Gift*, Gabriel's mother Christine gets exceedingly drunk, giving the eager Gabriel a chance to 'put his arms around her' and drag 'her heavy body further onto the bed' to put on her pyjamas (*Gift* 91–2). She responds to this by kissing him and calling him 'darling' then falls asleep (*Gift* 92). Later in the novel, Gabriel induces Rex and Christine to go to dinner together, but not before Gabriel and Christine have 'cuddled' in her bed, and Gabriel has helped Christine dress with 'his quivering hands' (*Gift* 184–5). *The Body* has fewer explicitly Oedipal moments, although there are some hints of Kureishi's abiding obsession. For instance, when Adam's brain is removed from his body, he meditates on his relationship with his mother, who (like so many mothers in Kureishi's work) refused to offer him the bodily comforts he wanted: 'Mother never let me see her body or sleep beside her; she didn't like to touch me' (*Body* 36). In search of another maternal figure, Adam travels to a spa where he is comforted by the older women, and enjoys 'just hanging around them, as I had my mother as a child' (*Body* 79). Not surprisingly, Adam is determined to act 'the obdurate adolescent' in this environment, and thus he casts Patricia, the leader of the group of women, in the role of his mother (*Body* 80).

'Goodbye Mother', one of the stories included in the 2003 edition of *The Body and Seven Stories*, also engages with the problem of Oedipal desire, and dramatizes some of Kureishi's own intellectual struggles. The Oedipal subtext of this story is underlined by the protagonist's dismay that his elderly mother's body, especially her 'formidable bosom' (*Seven* 168), is 'inaccessible to him' (*Seven* 194). As if to aggravate this deprivation, she crows: 'I might meet a nice young chap! ... I'm a game old bird in me old age' (*Seven* 200). Yet as they sit in an empty restaurant, she seems to encourage her son's incestuous passions, and exclaims, 'It's so lovely, the two of us', and reminisces with surprising pleasure: 'You were such an affectionate little boy, following me around everywhere' (*Seven* 201). Somewhat perversely, Harry (the protagonist) refuses to endorse his wife's desire to enlighten him about the sources of his fixation on his mother, claiming that 'clarity ... kept the world away. A person needed confusion and muddle ... . Someone could roll up their sleeves and work, then' (*Seven* 199). In this revealing story, the irrational Harry and his would-be therapist wife arguably represent two conflicting aspects of Kureishi's writing and personality. The desire to understand and diagnose the problems of a person (or indeed of an entire generation) is a central aspect of Kureishi's work and life, but in both of these contexts it is often contradicted by a dogmatic insistence on the need for chaos, unpredictability, violence, irrationality and freedom.

Given the many obvious connections that appear between Kureishi's work and the broad movements of his life, it is difficult to avoid the hypothesis that Kureishi's work is primarily autobiographical rather than social, or confessional rather than political. His own upbringing, family life and early education seem to have produced the Freud-inflected pessimism about love and sex that his characters express so frequently, and his later struggles with substance abuse, marital problems and paternal responsibility colour his vision of the world considerably. Furthermore, this personal aspect of Kureishi's work is weighted towards childhood and adolescence; although Kureishi is now middle-aged and enjoys the lifestyle of a successful author and celebrity, his work continues to be marked by the tragic sexual and racial conflicts that marked his early life. His oft-professed interest in popular culture's portrayal of young people, therefore, is perhaps as much a symptom of his preoccupation with his own youth as it is a systematic engagement with the overall political and social trends of his era.

PART II
Major Works

3

THE BUDDHA OF SUBURBIA
AND *THE BLACK ALBUM*

Kureishi's first two novels, *The Buddha of Suburbia* (1990) and *The Black Album* (1995), are undoubtedly his best known. They also have a great deal in common: in both, a young protagonist of Asian descent undergoes various picaresque adventures as a way of exploring his relationship to issues of race and class, the two major social forces that in Kureishi's view shape identity in contemporary Britain. As Susie Thomas has argued, 'In all Kureishi's work there is an emphasis on how race can affect class and vice versa' (Thomas 74), and nowhere is this more obvious than in Kureishi's first two books. Nevertheless, the social milieus of the two novels are quite different; *Buddha* focuses on the middle class (both upper and lower) and on the culture industry, whereas *Album* centres on more marginal groups: radical university professors, Muslim students, former prostitutes, and drug dealers. Yet both novels come to the same conclusion: there is no possibility of establishing any meaningful class-based or racial solidarity that can protect one from the commodification, exploitation, inequality and inauthenticity of contemporary British life. The best Kureishi's young British-Asian heroes can do is accept their lot in a world driven by hypocrisy, selfishness, racism and class confusion, and, by immersing themselves in the pleasures of consumption, salvage what personal enjoyment they can. Fortunately for them, they manage to enjoy themselves a good deal, even amid the ruins of their former naïve idealism.

Buddha follows Karim Amir, a British-born child of a mixed-race marriage, as he navigates the complex social currents of the 1970s. Karim's world is full of class and racial tension, as his encounter with a white girlfriend's racist father (a.k.a. 'Hairy Back') makes clear. 'Hairy Back' forbids Karim to see his daughter, and professes his solidarity with the views of Enoch Powell: 'We're with Enoch. If you put one of your black 'ands near my daughter I'll smash it with a 'ammer' (*Buddha* 40). 'Hairy Back's' dropped 'h', as well as his choice of weapon, mark him as a likely member of the working classes. The persistence of such racist views on the part of those who ought, by their class status, to identify most with the largely lower-class immigrant community, partly explains Karim's wish to climb the social ladder, though it also seems to have produced what Susie Thomas sees as 'Karim's unacknowledged loathing of his Pakistani self' (Thomas 79).

Working-class racism is also the cause of Karim's friend Jamila's extreme militancy. Much more politicized and aggressive than Karim, Jamila confronts racists head on: 'She was preparing for the guerrilla war she knew would be necessary when the whites finally turned on the blacks … . The area in which Jamila lived was closer to London than our suburbs, and much poorer. It was full of neo-fascist groups' (*Buddha* 56). Jamila's geographic and socio-economic closeness to the working classes makes her both unwilling and unable simply to avoid their racism, as Karim attempts to do. Jamila, who claims to represent the 'real world' of 'unemployment, bad housing, boredom' (*Buddha* 195), embodies the possibility of establishing a solidarity between immigrants and the English working classes, but her gradual marginalization over the course of the novel (as well as Karim's estrangement from her) is a measure of Kureishi's unwillingness to put much faith in that solidarity. There is some irony in Karim's salute to Jamila near the end of the novel; he lauds her 'feminism' and admires the 'sense of self and fight which it engendered' and imagines her as a sort of secular angel: 'the things she had made herself know ... seemed to illuminate her tonight as she went forward, an Indian woman, to live a useful life in white England' (*Buddha* 216). The admiration in Karim's tone here is undercut by the facts that he has just called Jamila a 'supercilious bitch' (*Buddha* 216) and that she herself has retired from her more 'useful' public role to live in sheltered domesticity.

One of the many subtle strategies Kureishi uses to discredit Jamila's apparently noble commitment to social justice is to portray her as a hypocrite and potential oppressor in her own right. He includes a telling scene in which Karim and Jamila make love against a background of noises, including 'The uproar of the unemployed arguing in the street' (*Buddha* 107). Karim, who is also out of work, has found a sort of job (we may infer by this juxtaposition) in servicing Jamila, though his heart isn't really in it: 'Jamila asked me to touch her and I rubbed her between the legs with Vaseline according to instructions, like "Harder" and "More effort, please" and "Yes, but you're making love not cleaning your teeth"' (*Buddha* 107). Like a demanding boss, she urges him on, but she refuses to let the workmanlike activity stand on its own; she wants to see some sign of enthusiasm or love. In the end, Karim distances himself from Jamila because she, not he, is the dominant partner: 'I was beginning to see how scared I was of her, of her "sexuality" ... of the power of her feelings and the strength of her opinions' (*Buddha* 195). The footloose Karim resents Jamila's intellectual and physical hold over him, and Kureishi suggests that he has reason to do so. In any case, the threat or promise Jamila offers to the social status quo is largely defused by the fact that her father, Anwar, coerces her into marrying Changez, a harmless buffoon recently arrived from India. This imposition of male power compromises Jamila's integrity, as Nahem Yousaf has argued: 'In Jamila and her mother we have two very strong women who are conscious of the roles assigned to them within a traditional working-class family unit ... they choose to uphold a patriarchal structure that they know to be crumbling' (*Guide* 42).

Changez's presence makes the novel's treatment of racial and class issues even more complicated. On the one hand, he is attacked by racist thugs who attempt to carve letters into his chest, and defends himself with a Muslim warrior's call; on the other, he spouts politically incorrect platitudes: 'Changez talked of how much he liked English people, how polite and considerate they were. "They're gentlemen .... They don't try to do you down all the time like the Indians do"' (*Buddha* 223). Changez shows snobbish disdain for the majority of Asians and Africans in Britain; as he tells Karim, 'I'm the intellectual type, not one of those uneducated immigrant types who come here to slave all day and night and look dirty' (*Buddha* 107). Changez is also the catalyst for Karim's onstage exploitation of his own racial identity; having joined a theatrical group, and prompted by the unprincipled director, Matthew Pyke, Karim invents a character named Tariq who shares many of Changez's own cartoonish qualities, and who affords Karim the chance to contemplate the process of constructing an identity – which is Karim's main task in the novel.

Karim relishes the 'invention' of Tariq because the process of creating an identity makes him feel 'more solid myself' (*Buddha* 217). Karim is tempted to conflate his successful dramatic stage personalities with his true identity, as we see when he describes what he calls the 'paradox' of acting as Pyke articulates it: 'To make your not-self real you have to steal from your authentic self ... to be someone else successfully you must be yourself' (220). The paradox Kureishi asks us to consider here is one that recurs in much of his fiction: in pursuing or representing an inauthentic self, one discovers a more pleasurable, profitable or useful way of being. In Susie Thomas's words, 'Kureishi suggests that posing can be a rehearsal for the real thing' (Thomas 66). As if to further this theme of inauthenticity as a tool of progress, Karim discovers that his father, Haroon, has been moonlighting, pretending to be a Buddhist guru to the suburban middle classes as well as having an affair with Eva Kay. After learning what ought to be somewhat troubling facts, Karim seems to gain a new respect for his father. He facetiously calls Haroon 'God', but beneath the smirk there is a serious point: Haroon has shown Karim the God-like power to reinvent oneself in another's image. Thus Karim finds it merely peculiar, and by no means objectionable, that Haroon has suddenly embraced Buddhism and is 'exaggerating his Indian accent' in order to appear more genuinely guru-like (*Buddha* 21).

Karim follows Haroon on his fraudulent adventures, and learns to employ similar strategies to make himself marketable to an English populace eager for exotic stimuli. For instance, Karim's

nickname, 'Creamy', not only describes his relatively fair complex-
ion, which occasionally enables him to pass for something other
than a Pakistani, but also functions as a sort of slogan advertising
his desirability for men and women. Jamila even calls him 'Creamy
Jeans' (*Buddha* 55), which implies sexual arousal and thus further
brands Karim as the universal object of desire. However, this nickname becomes uncomfortably literal when he is forced to smear
himself with 'shit-brown cream' to play the part of Mowgli (146).
This humiliation symbolizes the many false attitudes Karim feels
compelled to adopt to please what he terms 'those whites who
wanted Indians to be like them', the very 'enemies' with whom he
feels he has been 'colluding' (*Buddha* 212). However, he feels no
organic or essential connection to his racial and cultural ancestry;
as Karim tells us, 'if I wanted the additional personality bonus of an
Indian past, I would have to create it' (*Buddha* 213). Fortunately,
Western culture is eager to consume images of exotic others, and
Karim finds plenty of buyers for what he is inventing and selling.
For instance, his flamboyant taste in clothing gains encouragement from Eva, who shows her eagerness to objectify Karim's
contrived otherness: 'holding me at arm's length as if I were a coat
she was about to try on, she looked me all over and said, "Karim
Amir, you are so exotic, so original!"' (*Buddha* 9).

Eva's son Charlie is another pivotal influence on Karim; Charlie
steers Karim away from the more aggressively proletarian,
African-American blues-influenced Rolling Stones and towards
Pink Floyd, a more sedately middle-class band. Charlie's supercilious attitude authorizes Karim's assumption that the Kays are
from a higher class than his own family; at any rate, they behave
with a certain aristocratic abandon foreign to his household.
Karim treasures Charlie's guidance, though Karim cannot hope to
match Charlie's capacity to impersonate whomever he wishes. For
instance, Charlie reinvents himself as a Ziggy Stardust-like 'space-
man' with 'short, spiky hair dyed white' as well as 'silver shoes and
a shiny silver jacket' (*Buddha* 35). Charlie's new look, which he
explains as an attempt 'to have more fun', convinces Karim that 'a
new hair era' is at hand (37).

One of the implicit questions of the first parts of the novel is to
what degree Charlie's rebellious stance poses a serious threat to the
established political order. When Charlie substitutes The Beatles'
'Come Together' for a piece of classical music in school, he is caned.

The episode, as well as Charlie's later identification with Nazism as a punk (he wears a swastika), suggests pop's power metaphorically to explode the comfortable certainties of British culture. Yet as the novel proceeds we realize that Charlie's motives for his outlandish behaviour are plainly more Machiavellian than political, as Karim suggests by his analysis of Charlie's mastery of what he calls 'the friendship trade' (*Buddha* 92). Karim also admires the 'false and manipulative' way Charlie deals with girls (119), citing his advice: 'Keep 'em keen, treat 'em mean' (*Buddha* 71). Karim soon discovers that there is a tragic side to this ruthless hipness, however; 'if you're too eager others tend to get less eager. And if you're less eager it tends to make others more eager' (*Buddha* 6). Taking these rules to heart, Karim laments: 'Whenever I did find someone attractive it was guaranteed by the corrupt laws which govern the universe that the person would find me repellent' (31). Thus, although there is plenty of sex going on, love in the novel is perpetually vexed, as Karim observes: 'Helen loved me futilely, and I loved Charlie futilely, and he loved Miss Patchouli futilely, and no doubt she loved some other fucker futilely' (*Buddha* 38).

When Karim and Charlie arrive in London, Charlie is enthralled by the punks they encounter, whereas Karim feels that an insuperable class barrier still exists between him and them. As Karim says to Charlie: 'We're not like them … We're not from the estates' (*Buddha* 132). Charlie has no such qualms about appropriating punk's political energy for his own purposes, however, and when Charlie's band makes it big, Karim is effusive in his praise of Charlie's performance: 'Charlie was magnificent in his venom, his manufactured rage, his anger, his defiance' (*Buddha* 154). The logic of Charlie's ascendancy is consistent with Karim's worldview; if showing true feelings puts one at a disadvantage, no wonder the entirely synthetic Charlie gets ahead. It is precisely the Bowie-esque artificiality of Charlie's poses that makes them so successful; such insincerity spells the end of punk's authenticity, of course, but in Kureishi's novel it merely makes punk an appropriate tool for Charlie's advancement. As Berthold Schoene puts it, 'Charlie turns into a pop commodity … [he] appropriates working-class youth culture as his mother appropriates Indianness, and for the same reason, which is to become culturally visible at any cost' (Schoene 116).

Charlie's tutelage is a useful preparation for Karim's entry into the theatrical world, where he meets an assortment of fakes and would-be exploiters. The first of these is the unctuous Shadwell, who discovers Karim and forces him to act the part of Mowgli in a production of Kipling's *The Jungle Book*. Karim condemns Shadwell's inauthenticity ('He was being totally homosexual ... except that even that was a pose, a ruse, a way of self-presentation' [*Buddha* 133]) although Karim's own sexual strategies, like Charlie's, are equally self-serving, at least in theory. In Shadwell Karim sees an embarrassing, unflatteringly dull early version of himself, a self he is eager to leave behind. If so, the muscular communist Terry offers a more promising alter ego, and as Karim's star rises, he maintains strong emotional ties to Terry: 'I helped him sell his newspapers outside factories, on picket lines and outside East End tube stations' (158). Whereas Shadwell's clumsy efforts to get Karim to discuss the racism he has faced are ridiculed, Terry's attempts to broach the topic of race are treated more respectfully: 'As an active Trotskyite he encouraged me to speak of the prejudice and abuse I'd faced being the son of an Indian' (*Buddha* 148). Still, Terry's inability to dissuade Shadwell from presenting Karim as a brown-skinned Mowgli casts doubt on the sincerity of Terry's anti-racism. Furthermore, Terry's careerist ambitions lead him into a conflict with his own political ideology: 'he'd always claimed the police were the fascist instrument of class rule. But now, as [an actor playing] a policeman, he was pulling a ton of money' (*Buddha* 197).

Another would-be revolutionary of the theatre is Matthew Pyke, who represents the world of radical chic; Pyke's plays are attended by a very 'fashionable audience' who come 'dressed in such style they resembled Chinese peasants, industrial workers (boiler suits) or South American insurgents (berets)' (*Buddha* 160). Such make-believe does not go down well with Terry, who denounces Pyke's ideas: 'It's plump actors pretending to be working class, when their fathers are neuro-surgeons. It's voluptuous actresses ... hand-picked and caressed by Pyke' (*Buddha* 160). As if sensing this hostility, Pyke snubs Terry and offers Karim a part in a play he has imagined which will 'revolve around the only subject there is in England ... . Class' (*Buddha* 164). This proposal seems more like an attempt to console Karim for abandoning the working-class Terry than a serious promise; as it turns out Pyke is (predictably) more interested in Karim's racial identity than in his lower-middle-class roots. By portraying both Terry and Pyke in an ironic light, Kureishi suggests that in leaving one for the other, Karim merely abandons one hypocritical would-be-revolutionary for a more prosperous and prestigious one; in a world where no one's politics are authentic or consistent, Karim is free to adopt whatever position suits him; he admits that his own protests against society's injustices are self-serving and strategic: 'although I hated inequality, it didn't mean I wanted to be treated like everyone else. I recognized that what I liked in Dad and Charlie was their insistence on standing apart' (*Buddha* 149).

Still, there are new indignities in store for Karim. Pyke offers his wife Marlene to Karim as a 'very special present' (*Buddha* 191), but it soon becomes clear that Marlene and Pyke both desire Karim as a bedmate more than he wants either of them. Karim believes that his rough-and-ready upbringing has inoculated him against some of the abuse to which he is subjected; when Pyke inserts 'his cock between my speaking lips' Karim resents this 'imposition' and gives Pyke's penis 'a South London swipe' (*Buddha* 203). Surprisingly, however, Pyke seems to relish this treatment, as Karim notes: 'When I looked up for his reaction it was to see him murmuring his approval' (*Buddha* 203). This little exchange speaks volumes about the complexities of Pyke's class position and political attitudes; although Pyke has essentially joined the elite, he still approves of the antagonism shown by those lower down. Trying to come to terms with Pyke's ambiguous influence, Karim wonders: 'Hadn't [Pyke] betrayed me? Or perhaps he was helping to educate me in the way the world worked' (*Buddha* 227). Karim understands Pyke and Marlene's rapacity all too well, sensing that it is merely a middle-aged caricature of his own. Indeed, Karim's assessment of Pyke and Marlene's sexual adventures might also apply to his own: '[They] seemed to me to be more like intrepid journalists than swimmers in the sensual. Their desire to snuggle up to real life betrayed a basic separation from it. And their obsession with how the world worked just seemed another form of self-obsession' (*Buddha* 191). Despite Karim's insight into Pyke and Marlene, he fails to get the better of them; in a telling scene, Pyke gloats over his accurate prediction about the one-sided relationship between Karim and the aloof and self-centred Eleanor.

Although Eleanor appears to be a bland, relatively innocuous character (especially next to the poisonous Pyke), her complex class identity fascinates Karim. She comes from a wealthy family, and Karim initially reads her as essentially upper class, though he soon decides that she is more 'middle class' than he had once thought she was (*Buddha* 173). Nevertheless, Eleanor's intermittent access to privileged circles allows Karim a glimpse of the English upper classes, whom he sees in vivid if caricatured terms:

> The voices and language of those people reminded me of Enid Blyton, and Bunter and Jennings ... a world of total security that I'd thought existed only in books. They lacked all understanding of how much more than anyone else they had. I was frightened of their confidence, education, status, money, and I was beginning to see how important they were. (*Buddha* 174)

In a more critical mood, Karim confesses: 'after a couple of hours with [Eleanor's] crowd I felt heavy and listless. Life had offered these people its lips, but ... it was the kiss of death', although he concludes, with typically apolitical irony, that 'the ruling class weren't worth hating' (*Buddha* 225). Karim registers the essential divide that separates him, with his lower-middle-class roots, from those who have effortlessly attained the social polish and educational achievements he finds so desirable: 'For Eleanor's crowd hard words and sophisticated ideas were in the air they breathed from birth, and this language was the currency that bought you the best of what the world could offer. But for us it could only ever be a second language, consciously acquired' (*Buddha* 178). Karim relishes the task of acquiring things not naturally his own, and enjoys the sexual and social conquest Eleanor herself represents, at least for him.

In addition to her class markers, Eleanor takes over from Jamila as the central spokesperson for feminism in the novel, which tends to damage its credibility. In explaining her own capricious and neurotic behaviour, Eleanor self-servingly casts herself as a victim of her gender training, telling Karim that 'Women are brought up to think of others ... When I start to think of myself I feel sick' (*Buddha* 176). Eleanor's feminism is sadly incoherent, as we deduce from her convoluted defence of her affair with Pyke to Karim: 'I want you to be with me, Karim, and I've done a lot for you. But I can't have people – men – telling me what to do. If Pyke wants me to be with him, then I must follow my desire. There's so much for him to teach me' (*Buddha* 226). For Eleanor, feminism is a blanket justification for her selfish whims, even if they involve subordinating herself to a tyrannical and exploitative man such as Pyke. Fittingly, Jamila writes off Eleanor's self-hatred as a peculiar reverse narcissism: 'that's exactly what they're like, these actresses ... The world burns and they comb their eyebrows' (*Buddha* 176). Not surprisingly, Karim allows his obsession with Eleanor to damage his friendship with Jamila and compromise his own already dubious political integrity: he promises to attend an anti-fascist rally with Jamila, but ends up spying jealously on Eleanor instead.

Eleanor also embodies the idea of liberal white guilt in *Buddha*: she is haunted by her dead boyfriend Gene, a black actor who committed suicide out of despair at the racism of the theatre community. Gene's professional complaints overlapped with the real-life slights he incurred as a black Briton, as Marlene suggests: 'The police were always picking him up and giving him a going over. Taxis drove straight past him. People said there were no free tables in empty restaurants. He lived in a bad world in nice old England' (*Buddha* 201). Marlene suggests that Gene's entire identity was tied up in his status as an actor; without a designated role to play in 'one of the bigger theatre companies' (*Buddha* 201) he simply ceased to exist, in his own mind, and chose to kill himself. The implication of Gene's death for Karim is clear: if Karim cannot find his own role to play in British society, whether onstage or off, he too is doomed. No amount of self-confidence or determination can resist society's indifference, and thus it is better to inhabit racial or class-based stereotypes for the sake of being accepted (as Karim does) than to challenge the culture's assumptions about race or class (as Gene does).

Still, when Eleanor jilts Karim, he casts himself in the (Gene-inspired) role of the racial martyr, and tries to analyse his (and thus Gene's) motives in pursuing her in the first place:

> Sweet Gene, her black lover ... killed himself because every day, by a look, a remark, an attitude, the English told him they hated him; they never let him forget they thought him a nigger, a slave, a lower being. And we pursued English roses as we pursued England; by possessing these prizes, this kindness and beauty, we stared defiantly into the eye of Empire and all its self-regard ... We became part of England and yet

proudly stood outside it. But to be truly free we had to free ourselves of all bitterness and resentment, too. How was this possible when bitterness and resentment were generated afresh every day? (*Buddha* 227)

Karim himself has shown little sign of the 'bitterness and resentment' that animated Gene, and his racially ambiguous features are clearly unlike Gene's unmistakable blackness. Nevertheless, Karim is ready to appropriate Gene's experiences.

Despite Gene's unambiguous tragedy, *Buddha* reminds us that no racial or class category is without contradictions, and that any dogmatic position taken in relation to these issues is bound to be riddled with hypocrisy. Two marginal characters in the theatre world illustrate this principle with almost painful clarity: Heater and Tracey. Like Karim himself, Heater (who is 'the local roadsweeper, a grossly fat and ugly sixteen-stone Scot in a donkey jacket whom Eleanor had taken up three years ago as a cause' [*Buddha* 175]), is a token presence in the middle-class world of the theatre:

> Heater was the only working-class person most of [the actors] had met. So he became a sort of symbol of the masses … . If you didn't adore Heater – and I hated every repulsive inch of him – and listen to him as the authentic voice of the proletariat, it was easy … to be seen by the comrades and their sympathizers as a snob … a proto-Goebbels. (*Buddha* 175)

Karim compares Heater's performance in the role of working-class hero to that of mainstreamed rock stars: 'Heater gave these satisfactions, as he knew he had to, like Clapton having to play "Layla" every time' (*Buddha* 176). This parallel implies that political experiences are every bit as corrupted by a need to pander to an audience as pop music is. The irony of Heater's persona is that he is determined to rise above his class expertise and discuss highbrow culture; though he is asked to repeat stories about 'knife fights' in Glasgow, he prefers to discuss 'Beethoven's late quartets' and 'Huysmans' (*Buddha* 176).

Their similarly marginal and inauthentic status makes Heater and Karim natural rivals, as Karim admits: 'I found myself competing with Heater for Eleanor's love' (*Buddha* 175). The ever class-conscious Karim shouts at Heater: 'Go and clean dog turds from the street with your tongue, you working-class cunt!' (*Buddha* 185). This rhetorical feminization of working-class masculinity appears to be an effective gesture; Karim shoves Heater out of Eleanor's apartment and becomes her lover. This sexual victory is underscored later in the novel during Karim's decisive fight with Heater, when Karim uses the phrase 'I mounted him' to describe his manner of attacking his foe (*Buddha* 234). In their final showdown, each displays the aggressive traits that their social class and educational background have afforded them. Karim runs at Heater, grabs his lapels and gives him a head butt, 'using the velocity to bounce my forehead against his nose in the way I'd been taught at school. Thank God for education' (*Buddha* 234). As he runs away, Karim realizes that Heater has gained a measure of revenge: 'blood was everywhere … Heater had learned at school never to go anywhere without razor blades sewn into the back of his lapels' (*Buddha* 234). The episode serves to underline the basic similarity between the two characters, despite their class- and race-based antagonism.

Whereas Heater offers an overt and hostile alter-ego to challenge Karim, Tracey poses a more subtle problem. Although she is the daughter of an irreproachably working-class single mother, Tracey has become an actress and is afflicted with the same lower-middle-class disorders Karim has tried to transcend; she is 'respectable in the best suburban way, honest and kind and unpretentious, and she dressed like a secretary' (*Buddha* 179). She is also black, which complicates Karim's attitude towards her even more; he is forced to see that she is like him in many ways, and thus her disapproval of his stereotypical portrayal of Anwar is compelling. In her outspoken manner, Tracey is an extension of Jamila, whose disapproval of Karim's career as an actor induces him to steer clear of her for most of the last half of the novel. Tracey too has her hypocrisies and blind spots, however; Karim notices that she is 'completely different' when there are 'only black people present': free from her internalized deference and submissiveness, Tracey becomes an 'extrovert' and displays the 'passionate' side she has been repressing in order to succeed in white England (*Buddha* 180). Furthermore, like Terry, Tracey also puts her career above her principles; having become a valued member of Pyke's theatrical group, and thus asserted herself, she raises no objections to Tariq, Karim's satirical portrait of Changez, which is just as mocking as was his version of Anwar.

As we see, Karim's acting career brings the latent racial issues in his life to the forefront, though his own attitude to such issues is far from straightforward. Sangeeta Ray argues that when Karim joins Pyke's troupe 'we see [him] actively trying to resist the clutches of a paternalistic and tyrannical racist discourse' (Ray 235), though Seema Jena disagrees, contending that Karim is 'miserable' at the end of the novel 'because he realizes he has become a non-person, a coward who couldn't face the hard facts of life' (Jena 6). Trying to justify both positions, Thomas sums up the ambiguity of Kureishi's text: 'one could interpret it either way; it is both selling out and "changing the script of what it means to be English"' (Thomas 69). Indeed, Thomas captures the tone of many reactions to *Buddha*'s sometimes dizzying play of political and national identities, suggesting that the novel 'shows Englishness as changing and unstable, varying according to class and gender as well as over time. National identities ... are inevitably presented as a matter of cultural performances' (Thomas 64). In a similar vein, A. Robert Lee claims that *Buddha* 'proceed[s] from, and inscribe[s] a quite ineradicable and historical multicultural Englishness' (Lee 75), implying that national identity is always a combination of heterogeneous, constructed and contingent identities. Thus to call Karim a 'non-person' for abandoning some 'other' non-English self, as Jena does, is naïve.

The character who most obviously represents the factitious, chameleon-like nature of English (or indeed any) identity is Charlie, whom Karim encounters after he falls out with his theatrical friends. Now known as 'Charlie Hero' (an allusion to his real-life model Billy Broad's stage name: Billy Idol), Charlie has moved to New York. Karim marvels at the ease with which Charlie has made it big in America: 'He was selling Englishness, and getting a lot of money for it' (*Buddha* 247). Karim realizes that Charlie's 'rock-star' image is not 'his essence' but merely 'a temporary, borrowed persona' (*Buddha* 246), and admires the degree to which Charlie admits his inadequacy to the role in which he has been cast: 'The ferocity was already a travesty, and the music ... had lost its drama and attack when transported from England with its unemployment, strikes and class antagonism. What impressed me was Charlie knew this. "The music's feeble, OK? I'm no Bowie"' (*Buddha* 247). Undeterred by Charlie's admitted spuriousness, Karim muses on their shared felicity: 'We were two English boys in America ....'.

This was the dream come true' (*Buddha* 249). Karim decides that 'fame, success and wealth really agreed with [Charlie] .... He could set aside ambition and become human' (*Buddha* 248). Despite Karim's starry-eyed adulation, we soon see that Charlie's 'humanity' seems uncannily like simple greed; Charlie recounts an epiphanic moment in which he realized that 'I loved money. Money and everything it could buy' (*Buddha* 248).

Trapped in Charlie's self-indulgent world, Karim understands that Charlie has become a drug and sex addict in quest of ever greater enjoyments. Intent on his pursuit of the 'ultimate experience' (*Buddha* 252), Charlie criticizes Karim for not joining in, for being 'so English ... . So shocked, so self-righteous and moral' (*Buddha* 254). Indeed, Karim has not entirely lost his moral compass; when Charlie beats up a persistent journalist, Karim feels a certain affinity with this unfortunate character, upon whose hand Charlie has stamped savagely: 'The man lived nearby. I had to see him at least once a week on the street, carrying his groceries with his good hand' (*Buddha* 252). As if to show that he is capable of moralization, if not morality, Karim watches Charlie suffering under a dominatrix's cruel ministrations and muses: 'That would teach him not to stamp on people's hands' (*Buddha* 254). Seeing Charlie trussed up with a sack on his head, Karim decides that 'half' of his friend's 'humanity' was 'gone' (*Buddha* 254) and, more importantly, that he has ceased to love Charlie. When Karim finally asks Charlie for money to go back to England, his friend protests against his departure in vaguely political terms: 'England's decrepit. No one believes in anything ... it's a fucking swamp of prejudice, class confusion ... . Nothing works over there. And no one works' (*Buddha* 256). Fortunately, by this point, Karim has learned to discount such self-serving political rhetoric or at least to prefer his own.

Having rejected Charlie and the destructive options he presents, Karim returns to London. There, however, he finds his personal situation is no clearer, mainly because the city seems to have changed dramatically in his absence. Karim's brother Allie guides Karim through London's new club scene:

> No hippies or punks: instead, everyone was smartly dressed, and the men had short hair, white shirts and baggy trousers help up by braces. It was like being in a room full of George Orwell lookalikes, except that

Orwell would have eschewed earrings. Allie told me they were fashion designers, photographers, graphic artists, shop designers and so on, young and talented. (*Buddha* 270)

Karim does not fit into this world, and realizes that his loneliness makes him vulnerable: 'I looked around for someone to pick up, but was so lonely I knew they'd smell it on me. I wasn't indifferent enough for seduction' (*Buddha* 271). In this state, Karim decides that he wants to 'make up' with his family, and that he 'did love them' after all (*Buddha* 271). As if to suggest the difficulties of completing such a reconciliation, Allie informs Karim about their mother Margaret's new suitor, a 'respectable' lower-middle-class white man named Jimmy (*Buddha* 268). When Karim hears of Jimmy's existence, he assumes, quite equably, that Margaret 'must have had enough of Indians' (*Buddha* 270), and thus Karim and Allie decide to hide from Jimmy, on the pretext that they are concealing the truth about their mother's age from him. Of course, they are also protecting her from what they assume to be Jimmy's potential for racism; in any case, they tacitly assume that Margaret's mixed-race children would hardly be an asset for her in the marriage market (*Buddha* 268).

This development is balanced by another bit of family news: Haroon and Eva are to be married. Although Haroon is not happy with Eva's 'new woman business' as he calls it, he manages to overcome his feelings of 'hate' towards her by contemplating 'Moments when the universe of opposites is reconciled' (*Buddha* 266). Through this implied marriage of 'opposites', Kureishi seems to be gesturing towards a vision that might reconcile the mutually exclusive political movements of the 1970s and 1980s in Britain. Unfortunately, this reconciliation seems nowhere in evidence in the real world: the political and economic conditions that meet Karim upon his return to London are complex and conflict-ridden. Great and disturbing changes seem to be afoot: 'the rotten was being replaced by the new, and the new was ugly. The gift of creating beauty had been lost somewhere. The ugliness was in the people, too. Londoners seemed to hate each other too' (*Buddha* 258). This ugliness and hatred are implicit causes of the election that will bring Thatcher to power at the end of the book, though how her right-wing political agenda could represent a synthesis of the opposing forces in English culture is unclear.

The reactions of *Buddha*'s characters to the crisis tell us more about them than about the realities of the situation: Terry reads the signs of this social crisis accurately enough, though he misdiagnoses their causes and effects: 'England's had it. It's coming apart. Resistance has brought it to a standstill. The Government were defeated in the vote last night. There'll be an election. The chickens are coming home to die. It's either us or the rise of the Right' (*Buddha* 258). Karim agrees, noting that 'the bitter, fractured country was in turmoil: there were strikes, marches, wage-claims' (*Buddha* 259). The last word on the subject, however, is given to Karim's brother Allie, who despises what he terms 'whingeing lefties' and deprecates 'people who go on all the time about being black, and how persecuted they were at school, and how someone spat at them once' (*Buddha* 267). Karim is intrigued by his brother's opinions (and flattered by Allie's enthusiasm for the soap opera in which Karim will be starring), and muses: 'I liked him now; I wanted to know him; but the things he was saying were strange', comparing him to a Thatcher-like 'Sunday school teacher telling you not to let yourself down' (*Buddha* 268).

Paradoxically, Karim's career flourishes in these uncertain conditions; indeed, his success seems to be both a symptom of and a self-conscious commentary on the social problems that afflict Britain. He is initially contemptuous of the producers of the soap opera that offers him a part: 'these were trashy, jumped-up people in fluffy sweaters' (*Buddha* 259). The social relevance of the role, however, appeals to him, as does the promise of fame and fortune: 'I was being given a part in a new soap opera which would tangle with the latest contemporary issues: they meant abortions and racist attacks, the stuff that people lived through but that never got on TV .... I'd play the rebellious son of an Indian shopkeeper .... I would have a lot of money. I would be recognized all over the world' (*Buddha* 259). Thus Karim's decision to take the role seems personally admirable, as well as socially responsible, and the book ends on a guardedly confident note: 'what a mess everything had been, but ... it wouldn't always be that way' (*Buddha* 284).

Tracing the literary lineage of Kureishi's first novel is a complex and often contradictory task. Susie Thomas claims that '*Buddha* extends a [British] tradition that stretches back through the 1950s novels of social mobility by John Braine ... Kingsley Amis ... and Alan Sillitoe ... through Dickens, to the eighteenth century picaresque' (Thomas 62). Bart Moore-Gilbert has compared *Buddha* to Rudyard Kipling's *Kim*, seeing both novels as examples of the *Bildungsroman*, a genre in which, as he puts it, identity is 'a developmental, unstable and shifting process, rather than a given and stable product' (*Hanif Kureishi* 127). Moore-Gilbert also juxtaposes *Buddha* to other books focused on British youth culture, among them Colin MacInnes's *Absolute Beginners*, and places them in the 'condition of England' genre of novels, arguing that J. B. Priestley and George Orwell are implicitly criticized by Kureishi through Eva, who sees the 'self-myth of tolerant, decent England' as obsolete (*Hanif Kureishi* 110). Others have suspected different influences on Kureishi's work: Alamgir Hashmi points to the similarities between Kureishi's novel and the works of H. G. Wells: 'both Wells ... and Kureishi are easily seen to evince an interest in the study of suburban drolls [strange people], social mores, and people on the make' (Hashmi 91). Susheila Nasta argues that, 'in a way similar to [Sam] Selvon's "boys" in *The Lonely Londoners*', *Buddha* celebrates an 'anti-hero who navigates the city, reterritorializing and renaming its spaces' and claims that Kureishi also uses Selvon's 'iconoclasm, polyphony and parodic inversion' (Nasta 197). For his part, Donald Weber claims that Kureishi is to be 'situated as a striking variation on American "ethnic" writers, especially Philip Roth', rather than as 'an example of "Black British" expression' (Weber 130).

Critics have been less eager to establish the provenance of Kureishi's second novel, *The Black Album*, perhaps because the novel has generally been less well-received than *Buddha*. For one thing, the attractively insouciant tone of *Buddha* is lacking in *The Black Album*; whereas Karim's story is told through the ironic eyes of an unreliable first-person narrator (Karim himself, grown slightly older), *Album* is presented as if observed by an infallible narrator with privileged access to the protagonist Shahid's mind. This change has itself been the subject of some critical commentary: Ruvani Ranasinha argues that whereas *Buddha* is '"dialogic", making the reader provide closure', *Album* is '"monologic", less complex and nuanced' (Ranasinha 85). On a similar note, Frederick Holmes comments on the incongruity of the fact that, as he puts it, 'In a context in which Kureishi confounds existing definitions and categories of all kinds, the capacity of an undramatized narrator to convey an authoritative, objectively accurate, seamless representation of this turbulent, multiform new reality is never called into question' ('The Postcolonial Subject' 297). Holmes is disappointed to realize that, 'despite the fact that Kureishi's protagonist [in *Album*] is a budding author, his novel lacks the metafictional dimension' of a novel such as *The Satanic Verses*, and concludes that '[t]he absence ... of such fictional self-scrutiny ... is a curious blind spot in an otherwise postmodernist novel' ('The Postcolonial Subject' 297).

Such complaints may seem a bit tendentious, since Kureishi has rarely shown any interest in being 'dialogic' or 'postmodernist', but it is plain to any reader that Karim's frank sensuality and quirky amiability in *Buddha* are in sharp contrast to the much more objective, journalistic tone of *Album*'s unnamed narrator. Kureishi took a much more journalistic approach to writing *Album* than he did with *Buddha*, and he even encodes links between the investigator's curiosity and literary ambitions in the text itself; we are told that Shahid 'knew that he wanted to be a journalist of some sort, in the arts area, either on a paper or in television. In his spare time he would write stories and, eventually, a novel' (*Album* 42). Moreover, whereas *Buddha* makes a virtue of its episodic, collage-like structure (its cover features a collage of cut-out portraits and images that alludes to the cover of The Beatles' *Sergeant Pepper's Lonely Hearts Club Band* album), *The Black Album* seems to aim for a smoother, more linear, almost logical development. Indeed, *Album* shows us the major influences on Shahid's life (the family business, religion, academia, and popular culture) being introduced and forced to fight it out, as it were, until a clear winner emerges.

The same interpenetration of reality and theatrical performance that is so salient in *Buddha* can be seen in *Album*; for example, when Shahid is under the influence of Ecstasy he sees a 'resplendent street' that seems to be 'lit like a stage set for a musical' (*Album* 71). Yet whereas Karim uses this blurring of the borders between reality and fiction to his advantage, playfully and purposefully appropriating others' experiences and turning them to his professional advantage as an actor, Shahid is stuck in a naïve realism, endlessly searching for his true nature, or for the object of his real desires. Hence Shahid's frustration at his feeling like he is lost in 'a room of broken mirrors, with jagged reflections backing into eternity' (*Album* 157); he can't accept that the world is anything other than a faithful reflection of his own identity. The narrative seems designed to teach him that he must complicate this picture of himself, and *Album* spends even more time undermining its characters' integrity, as well as the possibilities of solidarity between them, than does *Buddha*. Witness Shahid's musings, as reported by the narrator: 'His own self increasingly confounded him. One day he could passionately feel one thing, the next day the opposite … . How many warring selves were there within him? Which was his real, natural self? Was there such a thing? How would he know it when he saw it? Would it have a guarantee attached to it?' (*Album* 157). The irony of the final question is obvious: Shahid has grown so used to consuming drugs, music and experiences to stimulate his self-awareness that he views his 'self' as just another product (one without a guarantee attached to it).

Not surprisingly, *Album* presents a fragmented, conflict-ridden world in which there are no reliable voices of moral integrity. In a telling touch, Jamila's place as an outspoken Asian woman in *Buddha* is taken by Shahid's much less likeable sister-in-law, Zulma. The pampered, intimidating Zulma is aggressively materialistic and attempts to assimilate Shahid into her Thatcherite money-mindedness by asking him to 'take charge' of the family travel agency that her husband, Shahid's drug-crazed brother Chili, has abandoned (*Album* 202). Shahid refuses, in part because Zulma's ostentatious lifestyle seems like a prison; he 'needed to escape Zulma's part of town, with its embassies, hair salons, couturiers, and sleek traffic' preferring the 'seedy variety' of his own neighbourhood (*Album* 204). This gesture marks a departure from the enterprising attitudes of Kureishi's earlier protagonists: for example, whereas in Kureishi's early film *My Beautiful Laundrette* (discussed in Chapter 7) the young Omar jumps at the chance to emulate his uncle Nasser's material success, Shahid balks. This new pattern of rejecting the straightjacket of the well-to-do will become a familiar one in Kureishi's later fiction.

Zulma's offer is also made less attractive because of Zulma's association with the gauche, upper-class Charles Jump. This incongruous friendship becomes problematic, given Jump's racial and religious prejudices. For instance, displaying a 'mixture of commiseration and disapproval' to Shahid, Jump joins Zulma in her interrogation of her brother-in-law, at first echoing her words and then adding his own paranoid (and tacitly racist) details: 'isn't it a fact that you have joined the militant Muhammadans? … we know they are entering France and Italy through the south. Soon they will be seeping through the weakened Communist regions into the heart of civilized Europe, often posing as jewellery salesmen while accusing us of prejudice and bigotry' (*Album* 201). Jump happily conflates Muslims with 'terrorists' (*Album* 202), claiming that mosques are 'where the disorder is fomented' (*Album* 201) and accusing Shahid of plotting mass murder: 'You will slit the throats of us infidels as we sleep' (*Album* 202). Given these attitudes, it is evident that Zulma's world, and the prosperity it affords, is corrupted. To join Zulma would be to revert to the self-disgust from which Shahid has tried to escape.

Shahid therefore throws in his lot with the Islamic students whose anti-racist rhetoric helps him to accept his difference from mainstream British culture and shows him the error of his Westernized ways. The first and most important of these Muslim characters is Riaz Al-Hussain, a 'sallow, balding man' (*Album* 10) who has many virtues: he is an effective activist who conducts what one of his followers calls 'his weekly advice surgery' (*Album* 45), to heal the victims of British racism and anti-Islamic sentiment. He organizes groups to defend minorities against violent attacks, stands up for young Muslim men who have been arrested by the police, and even saves Shahid from choking to death on his own vomit (*Album* 80). Nevertheless, like many of Kureishi's characters, Riaz is a complex and often contradictory figure. He has all the obvious trappings of hybridity: he is 'originally' from Lahore, but has lived in Leeds since he was fourteen; hence his accent, which 'sounded like a cross between J. B. Priestley and Zia Al Haq' (*Album* 14). However, Riaz emphasizes origins at the expense of environment; he sees his birthplace as the 'biggest thing of all' about himself (*Album* 14) and speaks of people from Pakistan who 'lose themselves' in coming to England (*Album* 15). Furthermore, in a frame of mind that, in a non-Asian, might seem patronizing and simplistic, Riaz assumes that Shahid will 'really feel at home' in the Indian restaurant he leads him to (*Album* 12). Kureishi gradually exposes the hypocrisy and misanthropy that underlie Riaz's postures: 'Shahid had taken it for granted that [Riaz's] smile indicated humour, a love of humanity, patience. Yet if you looked closely, it was disdain' (*Album* 108).

Yet Riaz's rivals in the struggle for Shahid's allegiance are not initially very promising either. Andrew Brownlow is a stuttering, self-contradictory left-wing academic and apologist for the Soviet

Union. At first depicted as a pop-culture-hating elitist, Brownlow asks Shahid to play The Beatles' 'Hey Jude' (*Album* 256). Shahid resents Brownlow's uncharacteristic appropriation of pop culture and the rhetoric of 'Love, freedom, peace, unity' as he puts it, and gives Brownlow a 'ferocious kick in the arse' as a farewell gesture (*Album* 256). Brownlow is also divided in his views about a religious controversy (presumed to be the Rushdie affair, discussed more fully in Chapter 1), which forms the narrative centre of the last half of the book. Despite his liberal convictions about the need for freedom of expression, Brownlow ends up taking part in the public burning of a book (which is presumed to be Salman Rushdie's *The Satanic Verses*) out of misguided political correctness. Hs discomfort with the situation is implied when Shahid notices, 'his stutter had returned' (*Album* 234), and Brownlow himself later admits that 'the c-c-c-onflagration did stick in my throat' (*Album* 253).

Deedee Osgood, Brownlow's estranged wife and lover to Shahid, seems to have no such conflicting attitudes. 'Fiercely resolute' in her opposition to the Islamic students' attempts to suppress Rushdie's novel, she is 'angry enough to clout' and berate Brownlow, who responds only by 'making futile spastic gestures' with his inarticulate lips (*Album* 234). Deedee's strong convictions, as well as her willingness to use violence when necessary, link her to Jamila in *Buddha*. We soon see, however, that Deedee's politics are dilettantish; her mistrust of her own maternal and feminine instincts has gradually driven her away from activism: 'she feared that her politics had merely been an extension of nurturing, taking care of the oppressed instead of a husband' (*Album* 125). Deedee does espouse a form of feminism, but expresses mixed feelings about what she sees as its puritanism:

> She said that women in the 1980s, even the lefties, had aimed to get into powerful positions, be independent, achieve. But it had cost them ... .Too many had forfeited the possibility of children. For what? In the end a career was merely a job, not a whole life. How little enjoyment there had been! In those days of commitment while the world remained unchanged ... pleasure could only be provisional and guilty. (*Album* 126)

Happily for Shahid, Deedee has chosen pleasure over politics, and is willing to 'prospect for sensation' with her erstwhile pupil (*Album* 223). What she cannot offer him, however, is a way of integrating the various aspects of his identity: intellectual, racial and religious. Her interest in popular culture and her dependence on drugs make any alliance between the major influences on Shahid's life impossible.

Worse, Deedee is also subtly portrayed as an exploitative lover who is using Shahid to gain a measure of revenge for her own humiliations as a sex worker. We get a hint about the reasons for this tactic when she recalls her experiences in the underworld of prostitution: 'Those days London was full of Arabs ... We sat in their apartments all night, taking coke and waiting to be pointed at' (*Album* 124). The narrative implies that Deedee has selected Shahid in part because he reminds her of these Arabs, as if she wished to even the score with these men through her enjoyment of Shahid's exotic body. Indeed, Deedee seems determined to enjoy Shahid's body as Pyke and Marlene exploit Karim in *Buddha*: 'She had said she liked him naked while she was dressed ... she sat up and licked her lips. He shrank back. "You're looking at me as if I were a piece of cake. What are you thinking?" "I deserve you. I'm going to like eating you. Here. Here, I said." On his knees he went to her' (*Album* 127). Shahid's posture suggests fear and abjection; he has been objectified by Deedee's desire.

As a number of critics have pointed out, Shahid and Deedee also play gender-role-switching games in bed. Deedee's take-charge demeanour is evidently intended as a sign that she wishes to take the role of the masculine aggressor: 'she had really screwed him, getting on top, not sitting up, but lying on him, legs straddling his, shoving down on his cock. He had thrown his arms out, saying, "I want you to fuck me." "Don't worry," she had panted. "Leave it to me"' (*Album* 122). Such role-playing extends well beyond the physical act of intercourse and involves broader issues of identity and representation; Deedee persuades Shahid to make up his face to look like a woman. At first this disorients and disturbs him ('It troubled him; he felt as if he were losing himself' [*Album* 127]) but soon enough the easygoing Shahid has reconciled himself to his new passivity: 'he let her take over; it was a relief ... he liked the feel of his new female face. He could be demure, flirtatious, teasing, a star ... a certain responsibility had been removed' (*Album* 127). Deedee has him walk 'like a model' and he enters into the spirit of the thing: 'he swung his hips and arms, throwing his head back, pouting, kicking his legs out, showing her his arse and cock' (*Album*

128). While some critics have suggested that this scene is liberating in its play with gender roles, the reversal of the usual trajectory of the objectifying gaze hardly seems a positive development. In adopting the mindless posture of a 'model' Shahid has essentially been turned into a commodity for Deedee to consume and identify with, and he has lost his autonomy in precisely the same way that feminism argues that women have lost theirs when their bodies are objectified by men. This scene also carries unpleasant overtones of Edward Said's theory of Orientalism, which describes the process whereby Asian male bodies are seen as feminine, perverse and abjectly animalistic.

Even when Deedee decides to put her own vengeful agenda aside and pleasure Shahid, the sinister language of sexual commodification seems inescapable. For instance, when they make love, she treats Shahid as a sex-seeking client, which makes Shahid feel mildly guilty: 'He felt a little bad about taking. She said it was OK, she liked pleasing him in that way, she'd had plenty of practice' (*Album* 130). Shahid's infantile vagueness about his own pleasure is licensed by Deedee's businesslike attitude towards sexual activity: 'When she wanted something she would put in a request' (*Album* 130). Furthermore, Deedee's most reliable aphrodisiacs turn out to be commodities, including pornography. She fantasizes about becoming a sex slave, citing a literary heroine who says 'I'll be whatever you want me to be' (*Album* 128). She also indulges Shahid's own voyeuristic desires; the drugs she feeds him allow him to watch her 'in magazine soft-focus' as she displays herself (*Album* 129). This utopian picture of the confusion of commodity-desire and sexual-desire is dangerously seductive for Shahid, who is 'pleased' to see that 'she was turning herself into pornography' (*Album* 129). Deedee creates the conditions whereby the commodified simulacra of sexuality overrun its physical reality, at least in Shahid's mind. He wonders 'who was actually doing it, unless they were getting paid?' (*Album* 160), thus equating all sex with exploitation.

Despite Deedee and Shahid's desire for mutual objectification, their liaison is threatened by controversy, when he sides (temporarily, at least) with the Muslim students who want to burn a supposedly offensive book (presumably Rushdie's *The Satanic Verses*). The dispute brings out the worst in everyone: Shahid's friend Farhat describes a classroom confrontation in which Deedee stalks around 'like some dictator' insisting on discussing the controversial book (again, indubitably the unnamed *Satanic Verses*) while some Muslim students object and make enough noise to silence her (*Album* 227–8). In a bizarre scene towards the end of the novel, a group of Muslim students gather in Shahid's unlocked apartment, and even when Shahid comes home and addresses them, they go on with a disapproving discussion of Deedee as if he were not present. Shahid tries to defend Deedee against their accusations, but fails to win them over. He tries to warn her, but the students pay no heed and even begin to chant, 'Osgood – no good! Osgood – no good!' (*Album* 242). Given such an extreme and obtuse response to her attempted intervention, it is perhaps no wonder that Deedee looks uncharacteristically 'fragile' after the book-burning episode: 'the flat was cold, the heating broken. Her coat was around her shoulders' (*Album* 268). Her life seems to have gotten dramatically worse, and Shahid's tendency to reject the downtrodden works against her for a time.

Deedee's limitations lead Shahid to form a brief alliance with a blond working-class drug dealer named Strapper who has 'some Jamaican attitude' in him (*Album* 150). Strapper is similar to Johnny from *My Beautiful Laundrette* in many ways; as he confesses to Shahid, he used to be a racist skinhead. Like Johnny, Strapper also seeks economic advancement by alliances with Asians; in Strapper's case, it is Shahid's brother Chili who has 'promised Strapper a way up … injecting him with that misleading substance, hope' (*Album* 209). Strapper is cast in the role of the working-class individual seduced and exploited by the ruling classes; the drugs he peddles and takes are metaphorical equivalents of the opiates fed to him by those higher up the social scale. At first, Strapper seems to be an entirely attractive figure in Shahid's eyes; able to go where Deedee cannot, he entertains Shahid by offering him a 'guided tour of his life and work in drugs' (*Album* 207). Shahid is clearly captivated by 'the intensity and intimacy' drugs create, and he feels that he 'wanted Strapper's life of no responsibilities, no tomorrows, taking pleasure and money as they came and went, moving on' (*Album* 208). Moreover, Strapper seems initially to be devoid of the racism Shahid has experienced, and testifies to Shahid that 'it's the white people who've treated me like shit. None of them believe in love outside the family. Blacks and Pakis, the Muslims, the people put down, and outside, they generous and lovin'' (*Album* 151). Yet when Shahid snaps out of his dreamy indifference and becomes assertive, Strapper becomes abusive, saying, 'You just wanna be white and forget your own ... . You and your bro just wanna shag the white bitches' (*Album* 275).

Strapper's overt hostility marks another difference between *Buddha* and *Album*: in the latter novel, the issue of race is decoupled from the problem of class, and is treated more directly. This treatment, however, is also laced with heavy-handed irony, much of which suggests that the racial dynamics of British culture as a whole are reversed in the communities portrayed in *Album*. For instance, the college residence Shahid inhabits at the start of the book is a marginal community within 'white England'; we are told that its 'rooms were filled with Africans, Irish people, Pakistanis, and even a group of English students' (*Album* 9). This sentence suggests that here the English are the exotic outsiders, and that the racial dynamics of this world are radically inverted from those that dominated *Buddha*. Hence Chili's complaint about his share of what he terms 'The brown man's burden': 'That Strapper's becoming a bloody responsibility. But I can't just throw him over ... . Everyone's done that to him' (*Album* 259). As the play on the familiar phrase 'the white man's burden' suggests, the complex dynamics of the last throes of colonialism are reversed in Chili's relationship with Strapper. Such unexpected reversals achieve a certain comic effect in the novel, but they do little to assuage Shahid's still vivid sense of racial alienation.

The racial themes of the book seem to be closely related to its depiction of religion; for instance, in explaining the fanatical Chad's background, Deedee blames white society for being 'too racist' (*Album* 177) in much the same way that Kureishi himself has blamed British racism for the rise of Muslim fanaticism in British Asians. When Deedee forgets her own sympathetic anti-racism and attacks the authenticity of religion and its value as 'culture', Shahid explodes angrily, invoking the spectre of racism once more: 'We're third-class citizens, even lower than the white working class. Racist violence is getting worse! ... We're not equal! It's gonna be like America. However far we go, we'll always be underneath' (*Album* 220). This link between race and religion, however, is not unchallenged; for instance, Zulma offers a much less flattering, class-conscious explanation for the presence of religion in the lives of his Asian friends, telling Shahid that 'religion is for the benefit of the masses, not for the brainbox types. The peasants and all – they need superstition, otherwise they would be living like animals' (*Album* 197). Thus she treats Shahid's flirtation with religion as a sort of class treachery, exclaiming, 'But you had a decent upbringing!' (*Album* 198). This snobbery, however, is less than convincing in the context of the novel; it drives Chili to defend Riaz and company to Zulma: 'they've got something to believe in, to lean on! It gets them through the night. If we believed in something, we would be happier! It is us who have the lack!' (*Album* 262).

Like Chili, Shahid seems unconvinced by Zulma's snobbish anti-clericalism, and he experiments with the trappings of faith as a gesture of racial and cultural solidarity, and dons a white cotton *salwar kamiz*, which he terms 'national dress' (*Album* 141). In this dress he feels 'empty of passion and somewhat delivered and cleansed' (*Album* 141), and pays a visit to a mosque. Here he finds that a mellow atmosphere of human fellowship seems to reign: 'race and class barriers had been suspended .... There were dozens of languages. Strangers spoke to one another' (*Album* 142). Nevertheless, as soon as he steps out of the mosque into the street he realizes that 'he found it difficult to reconcile what went on in the mosque with the bustling diversity of the city' (*Album* 143). This 'diversity' no longer has to do with race or class, since the mosque was diverse in these ways, but with market forces. For Shahid, the secular world is essentially a marketplace, and its diversity, as he sees it, involves commodities, not people: 'shouting men tried to peddle machines for threading needles, gadgets for crushing oranges, and plastic geegaws for ruched curtains' (*Album* 143). For Shahid, these objects create a world 'more subtle and inexplicable' than religion can account for, because they are desirable without being either moral or immoral (*Album* 143).

The problem of the novel lies in articulating the nature of this 'subtle and inexplicable' world that lies outside religious narrowness; Shahid finds it difficult to accept any stable ideology that reconciles secular and spiritual realities. Disappointed by Brownlow's defeatism and hypocrisy, but equally disgusted with Riaz, Shahid nevertheless tries to synthesize their positions to understand his own situation better. Thus he applies a partly religious, partly economic critique to his life with Deedee: 'without a fixed morality ... love was impossible ... people merely rented each other ... they hoped to obtain pleasure and distraction; they even hoped to discover something which would complete them ... .

Surely [his and Deedee's] lovemaking was merely an exchange of performances? ... They had been tourists in one another's lives' (*Album* 251). The language of ownership and possession that Shahid had used earlier in relation to Deedee's body has finally been exposed as illusory; the trouble is that, as in *Buddha*, illusion is more substantial than reality. Hence the determined shallowness of Shahid and Deedee's final pledge that that their relationship will go on 'Until it stops being fun' (*Album* 287). Nothing more lasting or meaningful than 'fun' can exist in the world they inhabit, we may conclude, though the novel affords us ample cause to be dissatisfied with such a superficial view of life's complexities. Frederick M. Holmes points out that 'Shahid chooses Deedee over Riaz, but the ephemerality and indefiniteness of what she stands for ... seems to undercut the value of his choice' and argues that 'what is sacrificed in [the] fluid world' they inhabit 'is stability and enduring purpose' ('The Postcolonial Subject' 308).

Other critics have objected to the novel's denouement, though from a more politically engaged, racially aware and culturally defensive viewpoint. For instance, Ranasinha claims that *The Black Album* 'uncritically reflects and embodies rather than questions [the white mainstream's] predominant fears, prejudices and perceptions of devout Muslims as "fundamentalists", constructed as particularly threatening in the West. His caricatures further objectify this already objectified group, whilst reinscribing dominant liberalism as the norm' (82). Bart Moore-Gilbert contests what he terms these claims of Kureishi's 'Islamophobia', arguing that Riaz's group shows a laudable 'desire for social justice ... [and] hostility to the unrestrained capitalism of the Thatcher era' as well as providing a 'second chance in life' to marginalized people (*Hanif Kureishi* 135). Moreover, Moore-Gilbert suggests that 'the degree of real threat posed by Riaz's group is put into perspective by the novel's references to the violence of the extreme Right and the campaign of urban terror waged by the IRA ... The arson attack on the bookshop is, by comparison, a relatively minor incident, which ... is primarily self-destructive' (*Hanif* 135–6). Moore-Gilbert also comments on the novel's critical portrait of Deedee, and adduces Kureishi's apparent belief that 'Certain kinds of feminism ... may be no less absolutist – and no less unwilling to resort to force and censorship ... than ... fundamentalism' (*Hanif Kureishi* 143).

Kureishi's first two novels are distinct from the rest of his fiction in that they show two young men attempting to mediate between their individualistic, knowledge-and-pleasure-seeking urges, and the traditional morality and emotional support offered by the nuclear family and religion. While Karim seems more successful than Shahid at balancing these forces, both novels assume that such a balance is desirable and, in a better world, possible. Kureishi's later fiction will suggest otherwise, but these two early novels hold out a tantalizing promise: that we can have the cake of our desires and eat it in good conscience too. If others see a conflict between Karim's family and his career, or between Shahid's love of sex and drugs and his religious inclinations, there is no special reason to worry. Contradictions are in the eye of the beholder, in Kureishi's early fiction, and his ingenuous heroes happily pursue apparently incompatible courses with equal ardour. They escape serious consequences, primarily because of their youth. Kureishi's later, older characters, who have become fathers and husbands, will not be so fortunate.

4

LOVE IN A BLUE TIME, INTIMACY AND *MIDNIGHT ALL DAY*

After *The Buddha of Suburbia* and *The Black Album*, Kureishi's fiction seems to lose some of its public, political character. Instead, it centres on the trials and tribulations of private life (especially marriage and parenthood), probes the depths of disturbed psychological states and mental illness, and becomes increasingly self-conscious about the act of writing itself. As Bruce King writes, Kureishi's 'later books are about self-doubt, the onset of middle age, and the breakdown of long-term relations and moral rule' ('Abdulrazak Gurnah and Hanif Kureishi: Failed Revolutions' 92). This new focus has led many readers to suppose that Kureishi moved into a more autobiographical phase in *Love in a Blue Time* (1997), *Midnight All Day* (1999), and the novella *Intimacy* (1998). This supposition gains some credence from Kureishi's own admission that in writing his middle works, he followed the model of the 'confessional monologue', which as Susie Thomas reminds us, 'achieved its contemporary prominence first in America with works by J. D. Salinger, Sylvia Plath ... Philip Roth and Saul Bellow' (Thomas 136). Thomas does acknowledge that 'the blurring of autobiography and fiction emerges as a preoccupation' in Kureishi's 'middle' period (Thomas 137), but she argues that 'it is not the case that there was a sudden break from the social themes to the self: Kureishi has always experimented with autobiographical fiction' (Thomas 164). Thomas concedes that 'at times [Kureishi's] focus has been on ethnicity and racism, at other times less so' but argues that 'from the very beginning, Kureishi has highlighted the ways in which the personal is always political' (Thomas 164–5).

Thomas credits feminism for Kureishi's habit of connecting the personal with politics, and even claims that 'his concentration on unhappy love, the frustrations of domesticity and the politics of personal relationships might be seen as traditionally female' (Thomas 165). Nevertheless, Thomas observes that 'critics tend to view this work in the context of the "male testimonial", and litera-ture which explores new forms of masculinity in a post-feminist era' (Thomas 133). One such critic, Ruvani Ranasinha, far from linking Kureishi with feminism, asks rhetorically whether Kureishi's work is 'a justification of "older" forms of male selfish-ness ... repackaged as "a new restlessness" and "new" masculinity' (111). In one of many withering assessments of the men in these three books, Ranasinha summarizes the characteristics of Kureishi's 'derailed generation': 'they are intimidated by female strength and resentful of women's refusal to fulfil all their sexual demands. Nurtured on therapy ... they are in touch with their feel-ings to the point of self-obsession ... wayward and immature' (111–12). Such a verdict is indeed severe, and perhaps excessively hostile; still, to say the least, the three books dealt with in this chap-ter certainly reflect Kureishi's loss of faith in the power of sexuality and youthful 'fun', as he terms it in the carefree conclusion to *The Black Album* (*Album* 287). From being a chronicler of the delights of popular culture, Kureishi becomes a fatalistic apologist for a vanishing humanistic tradition. Moreover, while Kureishi employs new, sometimes disorienting fictional tricks, such as the grotesque surrealism of 'The Tale of the Turd' and 'The Penis', to try to disguise or reverse this discouraging trend, the message of his later fiction is clear: family and sexual problems erode life's pleasures.

Kureishi's decision to write shorter pieces (most of the works in *Love* and *Midnight* are short stories and *Intimacy* is more of a novella than a full-length novel) is worth some discussion, though he has not commented on it himself. Some critics have praised the effect this change of fictional forms has had on Kureishi's writing: for instance, Bruce King notes the 'conciseness' of the stories in *Love in a Blue Time*, remarking that 'Everything appears to happen at once ... with no time for reflection' ('Love in a Blue Time' 371). To King, Kureishi's predilection for 'the sudden ... shift into the mind of someone on drugs or having sex' is both an 'effective' equivalent to the cinematic 'jump-cut', and a fitting mode of capturing the 'amusing but self-destructive drug-taking' that characterized the

1980s, which are Kureishi's topic in this volume ('Love in a Blue Time' 371). Others see the turn to briefer works as a mistake; for instance, Sukhdev Sandhu deplores what he sees as Kureishi's 'inability to exploit [the short story]', arguing that while short stories 'require a metonymic imagination, a desire to distil experience', Kureishi's writing 'thrives on aggregation and accumulation ... pile-ups of disparate characters and social worlds' ('Paradise Syndrome' 33–4) which work better in longer pieces. In a similar vein, Sean O'Brien is dissatisfied with 'Lately' (a story from *Love in a Blue Time* which he feels 'has the legs to become a novella') because it 'tidies itself away too soon and rather mechanically' (O'Brien 20). For his part, Sandhu suspects that this change of genre may have a stylistic cause, and he diagnoses an increasing austerity and flatness in Kureishi's middle period: 'The idiomatic ... dialogue of his early work has disappeared. Prim ... stiff-backed, shorn of excess, his prose – as well as his characterization – lacks warmth ... . His work is sapped and weary' ('Paradise Syndrome' 35).

While there may be some justice in this harsh critique, Sandhu is certainly overstating the case when he sums up *Midnight All Day* as follows: 'It hasn't even the passion or swagger to merit the accusations of misanthropy and misogyny that have recently been hurled at him' ('Paradise Syndrome' 35). This is demonstrably untrue (as we shall see, especially in Chapter 8), though Kureishi does tend to steer clear of some of the more controversial issues he tackles in his earlier fiction. For instance, the issue of race becomes less visible in his writing after *Album*. Nevertheless, a few stories from *Love in a Blue Time* still foreground racial problems; among these is 'We're Not Jews', a fictionalized account of some of Kureishi's own experiences growing up in a mixed-race family. In this story, Azhar's Indian father is embarrassingly eccentric, from his son's point of view, and his command of English is unreliable: 'Bombay variety, mish and mash' as the narrator calls it (*Love* 47). As an unsuccessful author frustrated with English society, like Rafiushan Kureishi, Azhar's father declares that his family is in the 'front line' of the racial problems in England, and repeatedly threatens to go 'home' (*Love* 45–6). Azhar's English mother is more aware of Azhar's sufferings, but she cannot prevent the race-based torments he must endure.

The pain of the cultural distance Azhar feels between himself and his father is exacerbated by his relationship with a boy he calls 'Little Billy', a bully whose father is known as 'Big Billy'. Together, 'the Billys' tease Azhar about being a 'Cry baby' (*Love* 41) and make racist jokes about Azhar's Asian background. Even Azhar's mother is not free of racism herself: 'she refused to allow the word "immigrant" to be used about Father, since in her eyes it applied only to illiterate tiny men with downcast eyes and mismatched clothes' (*Love* 44–5). Moreover, when she tries to come up with a reply to the Billys' abuse of Asians, she falls back on her own prejudices about other minorities: 'We're not Jews' (*Love* 45).

The examination of mixed-race families continues in 'With Your Tongue Down My Throat', a story from *Love in a Blue Time* in which we meet Nina, who, abandoned by her Pakistani father and patronized by her English mother, fights back by trying to assert her Asian identity. Her new 'Paki gear' earns her the unwanted attentions of 'communists and worthies' who see her as an archetypal Asian woman and thus necessarily 'oppressed ... beaten up, pig-ignorant with an arranged marriage and certain suttee ahead' (*Love* 69). She is also suddenly a target for 'racial abuse' from local teenagers, 'one of them black', as she notes (*Love* 69). Nina travels to Pakistan, where she falls in love with yet another character named Billy, who, with his mixed parentage and Canadian accent, is a male version of Nina. However, she fails to win the approval of her father, who terms Billy (and, by extension, Nina herself) 'A half-caste wastrel, a belong-nowhere, a problem to everyone, wandering around the face of the earth with no home like a stupid-mistake-mongrel dog that no one wants and everyone kicks in the backside' (*Love* 100). In Pakistan, Nina finds herself in the dehumanized status of the racial 'hybrid' in nineteenth-century ethnography (as recently described by Robert Young in *Colonial Desire*), thus showing that England is not the only country that makes mixed-race families feel unwelcome.

These tense family dynamics are given a slightly different twist in 'My Son the Fanatic' (*Love*) which centres on the conflict between Parvez, a Westernized taxi driver in London, and Ali, his newly fundamentalist Muslim son. Having decided that 'this is England. We have to fit in', Parvez embraces English culture and eats foods forbidden by the Koran: 'Parvez couldn't deny that he loved crispy bacon ... In fact he ate this for breakfast every morning' (*Love* 125). Predictably, Ali accuses his father of being 'too implicated in

Western civilisation' and justifies his own position by citing English racism, claiming that '[t]he Western materialists hate us' and promising 'jihad' unless the unspecified 'persecution' facing Muslims stops (*Love* 126). The story ends with the father getting drunk and then kicking and beating Ali as he tries to pray. The final passage demonstrates Ali's sense of moral superiority to his father: 'The boy neither covered himself nor retaliated; there was no fear in his eyes. He only said, through his split lip: ' "So who's the fanatic now?" ' (*Love* 131). Ali's remark seems to be addressed to the reader rather than to his father, since at no point in the buildup to this violence has Parvez actually called his son a 'fanatic'. Clearly, Kureishi wants to draw our attention to the violence that underlies the West's supposedly tolerant attitudes towards non-whites and their religious practices.

Kureishi's depiction of race turns bizarre in 'The Tale of the Turd', a surreal first-person account of a middle-aged man's visit to his teenaged girlfriend's parents' house for dinner. The narrator complains that in the eyes of this 'severe' family he has many 'disadvantages' (*Love* 132), though he admits 'injecting' his 'little girl' with drugs, while disavowing any real responsibility for this activity: 'she's a determined little blonde thing and for her friends it's fashionably exciting … she's made up her mind to become an addict' (*Love* 134). Perhaps not surprisingly, the narrator's encounter with 'what they call a happy family' produces discomfort of a visceral sort: 'I've got to have a crap. In all things I'm irregular. It's been two days now and not a dry pellet. And the moment I sit down … with the family I've got to go' (*Love* 132). When the anticipated 'turd' emerges, it is termed 'the corpse of days past' as it 'slides into its watery grave' (*Love* 133). The turd, however, will not be dismissed so easily and refuses to be flushed down, prompting the narrator to re-examine it and find new significance in its 'exquisite' shape, comparing it to 'a mosaic depicting, perhaps, a historical scene' (*Love* 133). This description suggests that the purely personal and digestive history the turd once represented has changed, and become a public historical record of sorts, an impression confirmed by the hallucinatory details that follow: 'I can make out large figures going at one another in argument. The faces I'm sure I've seen before' (*Love* 133).

The narrator becomes desperate to be rid of this fascinating yet disgusting object, the 'eternal recurrence' that haunts him; he grabs it and feels it 'come alive' in his hand (*Love* 135). He contemplates trying to 'bash it' (*Love* 135) as if it were a member of a hated minority and he a violent racist. This impulse seems to transform the turd into a little person: 'I ... notice little teeth in its velvet head, and a little mouth opening. It's smiling at me ... I think it wants to sing' (*Love* 136). Meanwhile, his hosts have begun to kick at the bathroom door, prompting the narrator to imagine escaping with the turd out the window: 'I am about to fall. But I hang on and instead throw the turd, like a warm pigeon, out out into the air, turd-bird awayaway' (*Love* 137). The Rushdie-esque repetitions of 'out out' and 'awayaway' seem to underline the narrator's identification of his own fecal matter with Asian characteristics and speech patterns. Furthermore, as if to associate the turd to other non-white people, the narrator calls it 'the brown bomber' (*Love* 135), inviting comparisons with Joe Louis, the African-American boxer who shared this nickname. Thus the 'turd' seems to represent the stigma attached to non-white identity, which the narrator wishes to jettison in order to placate the hostile British population represented by the young girlfriend's family. Some readers might decide that such a gesture seems symbolic of Kureishi's own strategies as a writer; his fiction has been increasingly empty of racial signifiers, as if he had attempted to evacuate the Asian characters and themes from his body of work, with mixed success.

The novella *Intimacy* offers an example of the attenuated, though still visible, presence of race in Kureishi's later fiction. For much of the book, we are unaware of the protagonist Jay's Asian ancestry, perhaps because of his cynicism about the naïve assumptions underlying identity politics (he notes that 'the more subordinate you are, the more "genuine" they imagine you to be' [*Intimacy* 51]). When his racial identity does emerge, though, we see some possible motives behind Jay's emotional difficulties. He explains his current 'agitated' state by referring to the 'fear' that has haunted him since childhood, citing his still-vivid recollection of being afraid of 'being kicked, abused and insulted by other children' (*Intimacy* 35). Kureishi's own traumatic childhood, which was marked by racist bullying, here forms an inevitable subtext of Jay's emotional disorders. Jay's personal torments are made all the more disagreeable by his belief that that 'British kids are innate meritocrats' (*Intimacy* 145), since by this logic he deserved the bullying he received. Kureishi's feeling of being an unwelcome outsider in a racist environment may also explain Jay's split psyche. Jay muses: 'It isn't surprising that you become accustomed to doing what you are told while making a safe place inside yourself, and living a secret life. Perhaps that is why stories of spies and double lives are so compelling' (*Intimacy* 36). Jay identifies strongly with spies (who maintain allegiances to groups opposed to the dominant ideologies they seem to accept), perhaps because for him racial otherness, even of a very well-camouflaged sort, functions as a marker of inner difference and produces paranoia and alienation.

Jay's confession of his racial identity invites us to see his resistance to (and eventual departure from) his wife Susan as the story of a put-upon, downtrodden man of colour finally standing up to white bullying, if only belatedly or indirectly. After all, Jay often seems to be intent on playing the role of passive, feminized native servant to Susan's white, excessively masculine authority figure: 'Sometimes I go along with what Susan wants, but in an absurd, parodic way, hoping she will see how foolish I find her' (*Intimacy* 33). Jay's imitation of servile collaboration is perhaps a sign that minorities in England must behave as if still under colonial rule; as Susie Thomas puts it in her analysis of *Buddha*, 'The creation of compliant mimic Englishmen in the Empire was a strategy that was repeated when the immigrant was expected to assimilate (although he would never be accepted as a "real" Englishman)' (Thomas 66). Nevertheless, some have seen the book's racial politics in less than sympathetic terms; in his scathing review of *Intimacy*, Frederick Luis Aldama denounces Jay as 'a pathetic middle-class heterosexist black Brit deep in racial denial' who has 'internalized the fantasies of the black self as a degenerate other' ('Review of *Intimacy*' 1098). For Aldama, Jay's decision to leave Susan is hardly liberating; it is instead a symptom of 'the accumulation of years of self-hatred' ('Review of *Intimacy*' 1098).

'Girl', a less provocative story (from *Midnight All Day*), could be seen as a sort of sequel to *Intimacy*. Majid, Nicole's older boyfriend, who has 'relinquished his home, wife and children for her' (*Midnight* 97), is more obviously 'other' than Jay: Nicole has anticipated racial tension between Majid and her mother, worrying that the fact that he is 'dark' will be a problem (*Midnight* 93). Majid is also more domineering and judgmental than Jay: he forces Nicole to cover her 'spots' with makeup 'In case we run into anyone I know', as he says (*Midnight* 94). Majid is also fond of reminding Nicole that she is ill-educated and socially inferior to him. These traits are not primarily racial ones, however; they seem like a product of his adaptation to English life. When Nicole's mother meets Majid she is disappointed to find him so assimilated: 'I thought you'd be more Indian' (*Midnight* 104). This remark, impolite though it is, defuses the racial tension in the story, and the conflict shifts to familial issues: Nicole and her mother argue about Nicole's lack of a job, and we come to see the arrogant, psychologically frail Majid not in racial terms but as a necessary evil who will keep Nicole from falling back into her mother's clutches.

As *Intimacy* and 'Girl' demonstrate, once race has been relegated to the background, the disintegration of the family becomes the major theme of Kureishi's fiction. The causes of this familial breakdown are simple enough: middle-aged men who desert their joyless relationships in pursuit of keener sensations, whether sexual, chemical or emotional. The symptoms of the problem, however, can become rather complicated and contradictory. For instance, 'In a Blue Time' (from *Love in a Blue Time*) introduces Roy, a confused fugitive from domesticity in the throes of an acute mid-life crisis. While conventional heterosexual longing is certainly part of Roy's urge to flee his pregnant girlfriend Clara, unfulfilled homosexual desire also seems to be part of his sense of lost opportunity, as we may deduce from Roy's highly charged reunion with Jimmy, a dissolute friend of his youth. The homo-erotic tensions between Roy and Jimmy seem obvious enough; during one bout of excessive drinking and smoking drugs, Jimmy tells Roy not to get 'queenie' (*Love* 14). In the same scene we see some suggestive physical interactions: 'After smashing into a tin of baked beans with a hammer and spraying the walls, Roy climbed on Jimmy's shoulders to buff the mottled ceiling with a cushion cover then stuffed it in Jimmy's mouth to calm him down … the two of them stripped in order to demonstrate the Skinhead Moonstomp' (*Love* 14)· The images here are suggestive of ejacula-tion ('spraying'), anal eroticism (the opened tin of baked beans), oral sex (climbing on one another's shoulders), sado-masochism (stuffing the cushion cover in a mouth) and exhibitionism (strip-ping). As if to certify that such images have their roots in the men's own unconscious fears, we are told that Jimmy (mistakenly) believes that he and Roy are about to be beaten up for being 'poofs' (*Love* 34).

Roy cannot bring himself to acknowledge or fulfil these homosexual leanings, however, and he is left to try to negotiate a compromise between his wish for erotic adventure and his curiosity about his unborn child. Thus Roy's last gestures in the story are ambiguous; he asks a strange woman named Candy for her phone number, no doubt planning an affair with her, then returns home and accompanies Clara to a prenatal class. He even tries to muster some enthusiasm for his foundering relationship with Clara: 'He wanted to get back, to see what was between them and learn what it might give him. Some people you couldn't erase from your life' (*Love* 40). Although Roy cannot 'erase' Clara from his life, Kureishi suggests that he probably should. The story offers vivid impressions of Clara's frigidity: during their foreplay Clara either watches television or else scolds him 'for minor offences' (*Love* 12). Clara's poisonous attitude becomes all the more incomprehensible when juxtaposed with her earlier aggressive wooing of Roy: 'Never had a woman pursued him as passionately as Clara over the past five years' (*Love* 13). The narrator suggests that Clara was playing a masculine role in seducing Roy, and that Roy, despite his boasting of having 'kept other women', is 'overrun' (as a woman might be in traditional depictions of a siege-like courtship) by Clara's 'onslaught' (*Love* 13). Indeed, Kureishi's fiction is replete with examples of couples reversing traditional sexual roles, often showing women falling into the stereotypically male pattern of intense courtship, satisfaction and indifference.

Kureishi's sombre picture of heterosexual relationships continues in 'D'accord, Baby' (*Love*) in which a character named Bill gets revenge on the man who has cuckolded him by sleeping with the man's daughter. Curiously, Bill professes to understand his wife Nicola's impulse to infidelity, and even muses: 'These days every man and woman was a cuckold. And why not, when marriage was insufficient to satisfy most human need?' (*Love* 54). Bill is plainly very angry with Nicola as well, despite his laissez-faire principles, and as usual in Kureishi's work, his hostile impulse towards infidelity is couched in socio-political terms. Nicola's affair is portrayed as a side effect of her professional ambitions; she met Vincent through her job with a 'late-night TV discussion programme' (*Love* 52), which suggests that her media career has disrupted the marriage. Bill cannot bring himself to punish Nicola, but Vincent's daughter Celestine becomes an easy vehicle for indirect revenge; she even offers Bill a chance to act out his anger, asking Bill to hit her and saying 'I deserve to be hurt' (*Love* 59). Bill agrees, with a typical rationalization: 'He liked to think he was willing to try anything. A black eye would certainly send a convincing message to her father' (*Love* 59).

Such avoidances and concealments, however, are unsatisfying to Kureishi, who in his middle period has seemed determined to strip away the conventions and distractions that have obscured the physical joys of heterosexuality. The most obvious example of this is the story 'Nightlight' (from *Love*), which depicts a nameless couple who meet every Wednesday 'only for sex' (*Love* 138). The liaison seems uncannily like a straightforward pornographic fantasy, and indeed its events are quickly transformed into the raw material of solitary enjoyments by the nameless male protagonist: 'When she's gone he masturbates, contemplating what they did, imprinting it on his mind for ready reference …. Fancy could provide them with more satisfaction than reality' (*Love* 140–1). This habit of objectification stems from the protagonist's unexamined fear of women; as the narrator puts it, 'when [women] come close he can only move backwards, without comprehending why' (*Love* 139). The fact that he 'can't recall' his lover's name (*Love* 139) suggests his urge to blot out women's individual identities and focus entirely on their bodies, which exist to be penetrated and fantasized about. Thus he seeks solace in anonymous women, who offer him the illusion of endless quotidian pleasure; he envies them as they 'sit in cafés drinking good coffee' or as they 'eat peaches on the patio' (*Love* 144). In these women's lives, 'Everyday sensations are raised to the sublime' (*Love* 144). Armed with this idealizing and objectifying reflex, he imagines his nameless lover to be a symbol of all he cannot be or possess.

Not surprisingly, the male protagonist's estranged wife is an unsympathetic figure, although it is he who has abandoned her. Described as a formerly 'successful woman' who recently 'found she could not leave her bed at all' and who now forces her family to 'minister to her' (*Love* 139), she has forbidden him to enter their home or see their children. Their marriage is caricatured as a failed feminist experiment: 'For a while he did try to be the sort of man she might countenance. He wept at every opportunity …. He tried not to raise his voice, though for her it was "liberating" to be wild' (*Love* 141). Apparently still traumatized by his wife's self-serving hypocrisy, the protagonist fears that 'his romantic self has been crushed' (*Love* 143), and his aim in pursuing the anonymous affair is to reconstruct his self-image and conjure up fantasies for it to desire. His 'unfulfilled' feelings about the relationship centre on 'the puzzle of his own mind' and he suspects that the trysts are part of 'a web of illusion' that he is 'fool' enough to believe (*Love* 140).

Kureishi implicitly critiques his nameless protagonist's solipsism through the narrative itself: the onanistic attraction he feels for his lover is jeopardized when she doesn't show up for one week's tryst. As he waits for her he feels 'like a child awaiting its mother' and then 'like an old man' (*Love* 140), and soon realizes that 'he has never loved anything so much – if love is loss of self in the other' (*Love* 142). Laura Miller has summed up the protagonist's delusions with acuity: 'When [he] brushes aside the impulse to talk to his lover, he tells himself that "clarity" will wreck their understanding, meaning that the reality of another human being only interferes with the illusion of romantic salvation' (Miller 11). If there is any growth or progress in the story, it lies in the (temporary) demise of this idea of 'romantic salvation' and in Kureishi's indirect endorsement of the need to find the 'reality of another human being' in order to attain one's own desires.

No such encouraging message about relationships is perceptible in 'Lately' (from *Love*). 'Lately' is based on Anton Chekhov's long story 'The Duel' which centres on a moral crisis: Layevsky, a discontented and indolent intellectual, wishes to be rid of his lover, Nadezhda. Layevsky's counterpart in 'Lately' is Rocco, a 'thin dark-haired man of about thirty', who confesses to his friend Bodger that he has lost interest in his girlfriend Lisa, whom he has seduced away from her husband, feeling that his 'curiosity' about her has been exhausted (*Love* 146). Rocco is humiliated by the right-wing Vance, but Lisa's own feminist ethos of free love and individualism must also be critiqued for the story to attain closure. Karen, Vance's embittered but well-matched wife, recommends matrimony to Lisa: 'marriage will make you secure. I know I'm all right with Vance and he'll take care of me. If I ask for something he writes a cheque … however much a woman wants a career, for most of us it's a load of day-dreams. We aren't going to make enough to have a top-class life. The only way to get that is to marry the right guy' (*Love* 169–71). Well-versed in the hypocrisy of conventional marriages, Karen also recommends going to bed with other men: 'Just to try another body' (*Love* 171). The story seems to support Karen's pessimistic assessment that 'Men only think about work … they never think about love, only sex' (*Love* 170). Anyone who believes or behaves differently, be they male or female, is in for a nasty shock, it would seem.

'The Flies', the final story in *Love*, is a surrealist tale that features a couple whose stale relationship is symbolized by an infestation of flies. The male protagonist, named Baxter, has recently had a child with his wife; he is the first to notice the presence of flies in the apartment, and tries to conceal the signs from his wife, as if they were his own guilty secret. When Baxter finally tells his wife about them over a rare dinner out, she implies that 'it is his fault' (*Love* 191). As a result of these recriminations, the flies start emanating directly from his wife's body: 'he notices a black fly emerge from her cornea and hop onto her eyelash' (*Love* 191). Yet when Baxter calls his mistress up and visits her, he soon sees 'a fly emerging from his lover's ear' as well (*Love* 201). Baxter realizes, to his horror, that he is 'carrying the contagion with him, giving it to everyone' (*Love* 201). He flees back to his wife in a panic, resolving not to 'let' her 'down', and decides that he can cope with his dissatisfaction, but 'The Flies' concludes in typically open-ended fashion, with Baxter waking up at night, going to observe and touch his son, and then walking out into the street with the boy's rattle in his pocket.

The surrealism of 'The Flies' recurs in 'The Penis' (from *Midnight All Day*), which centres on Doug, a porn star whose penis has gone missing and been taken home by Alfie, a married male hairdresser. Alfie and Doug meet up briefly, with both of them having a sense that they were 'together' the previous night, but neither one being able to remember what they had done (*Midnight* 213). The implication is clear: Doug and Alfie have had a homosexual encounter that neither one of them can acknowledge or even remember fully. Alfie, as a hairdresser, is unlikely to suffer professional setbacks from this episode, but for Doug it is a major career and identity crisis. Alfie offers Doug a free haircut, clearly eager to continue their relationship, but Doug is too preoccupied to respond. The story implies that Doug's one-night stand with Alfie (or even the gap in which such an encounter might have occurred) jeopardizes Doug's sense of his own masculinity so severely that he loses the body part that signifies it. Still, when Doug recaptures his organ, he is forced to sign a contract 'pledging to make [pornographic] films for what seemed like the rest of his life' (*Midnight* 217). Doug feels 'weary' at the thought of the 'numerous exertions ahead' (*Midnight* 217), and we sense that, paradoxically, endless promiscuity (heterosexual or otherwise) is as burdensome to Doug, in the long term, as marriage seems to be for other Kureishi protagonists.

The novella *Intimacy* offers the most comprehensive account of a man's decision to abandon his family to be found in Kureishi's work. The novella is written in the first person, and offers charitable explanations of Jay's behaviour:

> I have been trying to convince myself that leaving someone isn't the worst thing you can do to them .... Perhaps every day should contain at least one essential infidelity or necessary betrayal. It would be an optimistic, hopeful act, guaranteeing belief in the future – a declaration that things can be not only different but better. (*Intimacy* 5–6)

Such pronouncements sound like desperate slogans behind which Jay can hide his real emotions and motives, but as they proliferate in the narrative, they seem as if they are serious calls for a new conception of familial and romantic relationships. As Ruvani Ranasinha puts it, 'while he is undermined as self-obsessed, selfish and weak, there is a simultaneous construction of Jay as courageous enough to leave' (Ranasinha 111).

Nevertheless, this positive self-presentation is undermined by Jay's bias against women, especially his wife Susan. Jay's summary of Susan's defects is too abrupt and dismissive to be taken at face value: 'She finds even interesting self-awareness self-indulgent. The range of her feeling is narrow; she would consider it shameful to give way to her moods .... Because she has never been disillusioned or disappointed ... she hasn't changed' (*Intimacy* 30–1). Here Jay sounds bitter and defensive, as he does when he analyses Susan's professional success: 'Like many girls ... she likes to please. Perhaps that is why young women are so suitable for the contemporary working world. They are welcome to it' (*Intimacy* 30). Such descriptions are much more effective as suggestions of Jay's bitter anti-feminism than they are as characterizations of Susan; at one point Jay says, 'She thinks she's a feminist but she's just bad-tempered' (*Intimacy* 103). In a move reminiscent of misogynistic patriarchal authority at its most hypocritical, Jay also displaces the immoral element in his promiscuous sexual appetites onto women: 'there are some fucks for which a person would have their partner and children drown in a freezing sea … Women, I've noticed, are particularly tenacious in this respect. When they want someone there's no stopping them' (*Intimacy* 120). In other words, Jay defends himself by claiming that women are acting as he is doing. Apparently taking his cue from such assertions, Bart Moore-Gilbert argues that '*Intimacy* draws heavily on the conventions of feminist testimonial', but soon concedes that this strategy is a hostile one, and merely displays *Intimacy*'s anti-feminist agenda, as well as its wish for 'a reassertion of traditional forms of patriarchal masculinity' (*Hanif Kureishi* 173–4).

Jay's defensiveness plainly stems from his sense of his own vulnerability to Susan's domineering yet demanding nature. Although Jay was initially attracted to Susan because of her 'dexterity and ability to cope' and he liked the fact that 'She wasn't helpless before the world, as I felt myself to be' (*Intimacy* 29), this asset is in Jay's spiteful mood quickly turned into a defect: 'She is as deliberate in her friendships as she is in everything else' (*Intimacy* 28). Jay is even tempted to become violent in order to make it 'absolutely clear' that he doesn't want to be with Susan any more: 'I should have given her a backhander or a finger in the eye' (*Intimacy* 99). In a similarly bloody-minded mood, he secretly gives Susan one more chance to submit to him: 'if she lets me fuck her here, now, on the floor, I won't leave. I will put my straight shoulder to the wheel and accept my responsibilities for another year' (*Intimacy* 135). Not surprisingly, Susan fails to meet this unspoken ultimatum, which is really a covert attack on her autonomy.

Jay is naturally unwilling to attribute his departure solely to this misogynistic animus, and thus he decides that leaving the pampered middle-class existence he has enjoyed with Susan is an act of heroic resistance, a gesture of solidarity with the lower orders he has temporarily abandoned. However spurious this gesture may be, class dynamics have clearly been very important in Jay's marriage; after describing the lavish lifestyle his upper-middle-class wife has created for the family, Jay distances himself from it, citing his own humbler origins: 'Being lower-middle class and from the suburbs, where poverty and pretension go together, I can see how good the middle class have it, and what a separate, sealed world they inhabit. They keep quiet about it, with reason' (*Intimacy* 29). By claiming this class difference, Jay implies that his refusal to marry Susan is an anti-establishment gesture, though his cruelty comes through clearly: 'I enjoyed making her the only unmarried woman in her group of friends .... She learned that her love involved sacrifice .... I still took it for granted that not marrying was a necessary rebellion. The family seemed no more than a machine for the suppression and distortion of the free individual' (*Intimacy* 72). For her part, Susan unwisely plays into Jay's fantasy of class difference when she insults his appearance by comparing him to working-class men: 'You look like a builder' (*Intimacy* 36). Nonetheless, Jay never commits to a full rupture from his relatively privileged position and its proprietary responsibilities; surveying a ceiling in need of repair in his soon-to-be-erstwhile home, he muses: 'Someone has to be here to sort it out. Without me looking authoritative, the workmen could take advantage' (*Intimacy* 77). In other words, Jay mistrusts the working classes far too much to dream of joining forces with them against Susan.

Part of Jay's pathos as a character stems from the fact that, despite all the gender and class antagonism between him and Susan, he has great difficulty severing his ties with his sons. Jay professes to have 'fallen in love' with one of his sons, though this bit of news is made unsettling by the fact that he claims this process 'happened as it did with [his former girlfriend] Nina' (*Intimacy* 113). The line between sexual and familial love has been blurred, in Jay's eyes, and he decides he must choose one or the other. Jay realizes that his departure will scar his children forever, because it teaches them the necessary lesson that familial love has limits and can simply disappear, but he is so convinced of the doomed nature of such love that he remains obdurate. Indeed, he seems to go out of his way to remind himself of the unpleasant responsibilities of fatherhood as the story wears on; we learn that, not surprisingly, the smell of the 'soggy nappy' is 'sharp and familiar' to Jay, who identifies it as the very essence of his son's identity: 'it is him' (*Intimacy* 112). Thus on a certain intellectual and aesthetic level, his children are essentially excrement, to Jay, a disgusting by-product of bodily life, a leftover of sexual pleasure.

Nina, the woman who gradually emerges as the motivation for Jay's escape from his family, is a 'shadowy figure of male fantasy' as Ranasinha has termed her (Ranasinha 109). Jay's first mention of

Nina comes eight pages into the story, and seems to be a mere aside, a detail that adumbrates Jay's own emotional neediness (which seems every bit as all-consuming as Susan's): 'If I feel a bit low, I fear a year-long depression. If my once-girlfriend Nina became distant or sharp, I was convinced she was permanently detaching herself from me' (*Intimacy* 14). Later, Jay addresses parts of his story to Nina, ostensibly reminding her of their affair, but mostly conjuring her up as an ideal fantasy figure who once said things like: 'If you want me, here I am. You can have me' (*Intimacy* 45). Jay describes Nina as 'a woman as sad as me, if not sadder' (*Intimacy* 23), and she seems to mirror Jay's own ambivalence about desire itself; as Jay says of Nina, 'I've never known a woman who wanted so much to be wanted, or a woman who was so afraid of it' (*Intimacy* 86). The self-reflexive nature of their affair is suggested by the presence of mirrors in the bedroom where they make love, and by the fact that Jay contemplates his own image in the mirror when she enters the room: 'I waved at myself in the mirror! How happy I looked' (*Intimacy* 90). Nina seems to justify Minna Proctor's comment that 'Jay's is an embarrassing admission of creative and physiological onanism' (Proctor 38); she is an idealized creature who has few characteristics of her own beyond Jay's imagination. Indeed, on a more literal level, she is quite happy to be a passive prop for Jay's 'solo efforts': in sharp contrast to Susan, who is 'offended' by Jay's onanistic impulses, Nina 'encouraged me to masturbate on her back, stomach or feet while she slept' (*Intimacy* 103–4). The novel seems to have a happy ending, sexually speaking, in that Jay is reunited with the more accepting, compliant Nina, but as Moore-Gilbert argues, 'His desire for intimacy is … called into question by the fact that he has chosen for his soul-mate someone who is so evidently not his equal' (*Hanif Kureishi* 177).

Midnight All Day features variations on *Intimacy*'s themes of infidelity and unhappy marriages. 'Strangers When We Meet' recounts the end of an affair between Rob, the protagonist (a rare former working-class Kureishi hero), and Florence, a married woman. As his interest in Florence wanes, Rob forms an unlikely attachment to her husband Archie. This foreshadows the homo-erotic dynamics of 'A Meeting At Last', a more intriguing story which begins with a meeting between Morgan, the protagonist, and Eric, the man whose wife (named Caroline) he is sleeping with. Eric compliments Morgan on his appearance, saying 'You look good in your white shorts and white socks, when you go out running' (*Midnight* 152) and confides that he 'might be better off without my wife and kids', implying that as a single man he would be free to take Caroline's place in Morgan's life (*Midnight* 153). For his part, Morgan is entranced by Eric's 'energy' and his 'spirited' demeanour (*Midnight* 152). When Eric prolongs the interview by getting into Morgan's car uninvited, saying 'I haven't finished with you' (*Midnight* 272), Morgan is nonplussed, but the expected violent confrontation never happens. Instead, Eric induces Morgan to choose between him and Caroline, and Morgan ends up affirming his heterosexuality, despite his apparent distaste for long-term committed relationships with women. Having prompted this reluctant decision, Eric obediently gets out and is left standing in the road, as if heartbroken, while Morgan drives away. This image of an unexplored, barely acknowledged homosexual affinity is among Kureishi's more poignant endings.

Many of the stories in *Midnight* seem like speculative, incomplete attempts to make some sense of unpromising relationships. For instance, 'Four Blue Chairs' is a brief parable about a couple, John and Dina, who endure a self-imposed ordeal when they decide to bring home four new chairs in time for a dinner guest's arrival, suggesting that the small satisfactions of love and domesticity come at too high a price. The enigmatic 'That Was Then' features Nick (a 'pop journalist' and 'arts correspondent' turned novelist), his former lover Natasha (an ex-pop star), and his wife Lolly, in a love triangle. Natasha tells Nick that she doesn't want to be 'cancelled, wiped out' from his life (*Midnight* 70), though she also takes him to task for using her 'sexual stuff' (*Midnight* 71) in one of his novels and for failing to make the character who represents her 'strong' (*Midnight* 72).

Natasha diagnoses some of Nick's neuroses and habits in terms that feminist readers of Kureishi's work might find appropriate: 'You were always retreating to that womb or hiding place … you placed the madness outside yourself – in me … . Isn't that misogyny?' (*Midnight* 75). These complaints, however, which might have been legitimately voiced by many of the women in Kureishi's fiction, are trivialized and undermined by Natasha's selfishness and insecurities: Natasha presses some cocaine on Nick, and when he comes back for more, she demands that he kiss her for it. Pinned down on Natasha's bed and tied up while they have sex and fall asleep, Nick becomes upset when he realizes that their bondage has left him 'marked' (*Midnight* 89). She retaliates by expressing a wish that she might become pregnant: 'It's the right time of the month … It would be a good memento. A decent souvenir' (*Midnight* 89). After objecting that having a child with Natasha would be a 'nuisance' to him, Nick leaves in a huff. He goes home to Lolly and his son, musing that, despite the traces of bondage on his arms, 'pleasures erase themselves as they occur' (*Midnight* 90). This final phrase is perhaps a commentary on the ephemeral quality these titillating but slight stories seem to cultivate. Nick's sexual adventures with Natasha have taught him the rather vague lesson that 'there was little that was straightforward about humanity' (*Midnight* 81), but he seems more interested in moving closer to the nexus of drugs, sado-masochism, infidelity and consumerism that is the goal for so many Kureishi characters.

The title story, 'Midnight All Day', is centred on Ian, who has left Jane, his now-suicidal wife, and is staying with Marina, his mistress, in a Paris flat belonging to Anthony, his 'closest friend and business partner' (*Midnight* 158). Anthony, another male friend of ambiguous sexual preferences, ruthlessly writes Jane off as a 'bloody blackmailing nuisance' (*Midnight* 174), and congratulates Ian for having achieved freedom. Yet Ian's departure from Jane was the trigger for a spell of self-destructive behaviour; he has not been to work for three months, preferring to walk drunkenly around London 'talking only to the mad and derelict' (*Midnight* 161). Jane's attempted suicide, which lands her in a hospital, looms like a 'shadow' in Ian's guilty mind, but he knows Marina doesn't want him to speak about it, the more so because Marina is now pregnant (*Midnight* 158). Ian tells Marina anyway, adding the painful detail that 'she did it after I told her about the baby. Our baby' (*Midnight* 172), and thus tempts Marina to leave him and bring up their child alone. Kureishi attempts to broaden the significance of this dilemma, as we see when Ian ponders the reality of how badly he has 'damaged' his wife and realizes his kinship with the 'marauding men of the twentieth century', deciding in the end that he would rather be 'a beast' than 'a castrated angel' (*Midnight* 171). Ian's precarious moral position is summed up by the narrator: 'Without guilt we lose our humanity, but if there is too much of it, nothing can be redeemed!' (*Midnight* 171).

'The Umbrella' deals with a separated couple who end up in a grotesque scuffle because Roger, the protagonist, is caught in a rainstorm and asks his (unnamed) wife for an umbrella, which she peevishly refuses to give him. The violence Roger initiates is disturbing, not least because the narrator minimizes it as it is described: 'He placed his hand on his wife's chest and forced her against the wall … . She did bang her head, but it was, in football jargon, a "dive"' (*Midnight* 191). Nevertheless, this aggression prompts him to remember an experience of violence in childhood, which had provoked a 'shattering' of his infantile 'feeling that the world was a safe place' (*Midnight* 192).

'Morning in the Bowl of Night' describes a similarly fractured family; this time Alan comes from a fight with his current girl-friend, Melanie, to visit his son Mikey at his wife Anne's house. Melanie is pregnant, though we later learn that she has made an appointment for an abortion. Notwithstanding his troubles with Melanie, Alan begins to doubt the wisdom of the planned abortion, musing that 'a child wasn't a fridge that you could order when you wanted. … The child in her belly already had a face' (*Midnight* 200). As if to display his change of heart, he even announces to Anne that he and Melanie are 'having a baby' (*Midnight* 202).

As Kureishi's work progresses, he seems increasingly eager to use family troubles not merely to examine the plight of his tormented fathers, boyfriends and husbands, but also to explore the escape and fulfilment offered to them by the process of artistic and creative achievement. A representative example is Roy of 'In a Blue Time', an aspiring writer whose 'work had gone stale … . He felt increasingly ashamed of his still active hope of being some sort of artist' (*Love* 16). The way out of these artistic doldrums is unclear; we are told that 'What he wanted was to extend himself. He tormented himself with his own mediocrity' (*Love* 17). Roy's artistic desires (like his sexual ones) are ambiguous, since the project of 'extending himself' might take two rather different forms: the first sense in which one might 'extend' oneself is to enlarge the self by appropriating more and more from other people by keeping up 'with the latest thing', as Roy has stopped doing (*Love* 17). The other possibility is of making an unexpectedly serious effort to do some-thing alone; to 'extend oneself' in this sense means to force oneself to do something unusual or almost impossible. Roy arguably fails to distinguish between these two possibilities, and thus he remains frozen between them, mistaking appropriation for originality and escape for exertion.

Although Roy's predicament is typical, the story 'With Your Tongue Down My Throat' is perhaps Kureishi's most complex statement about originality and creativity. It appears to be narrated by Nina, a young woman of Pakistani descent, but in the end turns out to be told by an Englishman named Howard Coleman, who has imagined the workings of Nina's mind and embedded himself in the narrative (the title of the story is plainly a reference to this act of speaking on behalf of another person). This fiction-within-a-fiction is very difficult to interpret, all the more so because Kureishi has admitted that his decision to make Howard into the hidden narrator was a belated one. This change of approach, which is unusual in Kureishi's fiction, may have been born of a fundamental insecurity about the authenticity of the ostensible narrator's voice in the first place. Indeed, to Ron Page, writing in the *Spectator*, the story illustrates 'the ultimate failure of [Kureishi's] writing, the solipsism of the single voice' (Page 37), and perhaps Howard's intervention at the very end is an attempt to overcome that solipsism, albeit at the price of believability. In the story itself, Howard defends his narration as 'doing what I have to do'; as he says, 'it's my job to write down the things that happen around here' (*Love* 104). Howard's conception of authorship is initially tied up with his revolutionary political urges, though it is debatable whether such a link is tenable by the end of the story, when a melancholy Howard sums up his loneliness and fantasizes about coercing Nina to stay: 'I can't let her go ... "Don't go", I keep saying inside my head ... she won't look at me because she is think-ing of Billy ... I write down the things she said but the place still smells of her' (*Love* 106). Writing has been poor substitute for the sexual relationship Howard still longs for, and seems unconnected to any sort of positive political vision; instead, it reads as an attempt to force Howard's tongue down Nina's throat, as it were, by speaking for her.

Another parable about the artistic process, 'Blue, Blue Pictures of You' (from *Love*) tells the story of Eshan, a photographer who is asked by one of his friends (Brian) to photograph him and his lover, Laura, as they have sex. Like many Kureishi heroes, Eshan consid-ers himself to be 'some sort of an artist' (*Love* 108), though it is not quite clear what sort. He agrees to Brian's proposals, partly out of artistic ambition, but mainly because he is overcome by his own voyeuristic impulses; as he puts it, 'Laura was … a woman anyone would want to look at' (*Love* 114). Laura herself decides that the pictures say 'too much' and burns them in front of Eshan (*Love* 118). The story seems to represent Kureishi's own authorial struggles with his conscience and to foreshadow the conflict between humanistic values and his increasing preoccupation with hidden, transgressive aspects of sexuality in his fiction. After the pictures have been taken, Eshan tells himself that 'He had omitted nothing human' (*Love* 116), and thus has kept faith with his own aesthetic and moral standards, suggesting that Kureishi is reassuring himself that he too may keep his humanistic outlook even as he delves into depravity.

It seems to have been in the same spirit that Kureishi wrote *Intimacy*, whose protagonist, Jay, is a writer who admits to 'putting more of myself' into his work, and making it 'more difficult' than it used to be (*Intimacy* 46). Both of these phrases suggest that Kureishi is referring to his own writing career, and perhaps encoding a reference to the process of creating *Intimacy* itself. Such self-referentiality has also been noted in the book's title: Ranasinha claims that 'The title [of *Intimacy*] … refers to the experience of reading the text: none of his previous works expose a character in this way' (Ranasinha 106). The text hints that Jay is seeking aesthetic distance from his family: on Jay's last evening at home, he tries to 'develop a mental picture' of the life he is about to leave forever, so that he can 'carry around and refer to' it when he departs (*Intimacy* 12). Jay's otherwise bizarre need to 'refer to' his memories of his soon-to-be-abandoned home seems like a version of the artist's dependence on everyday events for inspiration. The novella can therefore be seen as a metaphorical account of the artist's necessary withdrawal from daily life, which enables him or her to describe and transform the 'mental picture' into something that, paradoxically, the reader can experience as 'intimacy'.

'That Was Then', a story from *Midnight All Day*, also suggests that the artistic drive is of greater importance than the need for sexual or emotional satisfaction. As soon as Nick (a novelist) gets home from an extramarital sexual encounter, he goes to his desk, begins to write, and resolves to continue writing later, after his wife has gone to bed. This urge to work is also clearly an urge to erase the reality of what has just happened, to alter the past and to begin transforming it back into the fantasy Nick needs. As Nick writes, he ponders not what actually happened, but what he wishes he had said to his lover, and the story seems to revolve around a few of the insights and memories Nick has recaptured thanks to her; for instance, he remembers 'his parents urging him to be polite' and wishes 'for the time when good manners protected you from the excesses of intimacy, when honesty was not romanticized' (*Midnight* 67), as if longing to become a part of that innocent family propriety again. Unfortunately for Nick, it seems to be too late to recapture that primal loving state, although he has written 'an uninhibited memoir of his father' (*Midnight* 68) that seems to resemble Kureishi's own *My Ear at His Heart*. Such productivity, for Nick, has become a substitute for the lost delights of the bedroom.

The fifth story in *Midnight All Day*, 'Sucking Stones', is entirely focused on the difficulties of writing meaningful and satisfying work. It examines the depressing life of Marcia, a schoolteacher and aspiring writer who makes contact with a very successful author named Aurelia Broughton in the hope of advancing her own career. Broughton humours Marcia, but only because she is interested in exploiting Marcia's experiences in the lower social strata for her own advantage. Marcia is a self-absorbed, deluded and pathetic person, but Kureishi seems to identify with her to some extent; like him, she has had to evolve survival mechanisms to deal with both her father's 'enthusiasm' and her mother's 'helplessness' (*Midnight* 118). Marcia shares some traits with Kureishi's male protagonists, among them a wish to 'harm herself' (*Midnight* 111), immaturity and directionlessness. Aurelia too shares some of Kureishi's traits: for instance, she informs Marcia that 'the Americans want me to make a film about my London', which seems to be a project similar to his film *London Kills Me* (*Midnight* 136). As though she were Marcia's exact opposite, Aurelia exults in her own work and lifestyle, saying things like 'Creativity is like sexual desire. It renews itself day by day … I never stop having ideas' (*Midnight* 115) or 'Writing is my drug. I go to it easily' (*Midnight* 129). Such mottoes seem unconvincingly shallow and self-congratulatory, compared to the angst of Marcia's life as a writer.

Still, Aurelia wins the verbal battle over what the ideology of an artist should be: when Marcia tries to blame 'blasted men' for keeping her 'down', Aurelia will have none of that: 'We've kept ourselves down ... . Self-contempt, masochism, laziness, stupidity' (*Midnight* 130). Despite Aurelia's stern advice, Marcia cannot rid herself of her flaws, and the story ends on a pessimistic note, as Marcia fears that '[s]he might ... turn into her mother, sucking stones at the TV night after night, terrified by excitement' (*Midnight* 143). The figure of the semi-comatose mother is among the most terrifying in Kureishi's repertoire of negative images, and it suggests that the negative aspects of creativity (symbolized by Marcia's fear of failure) have begun to outweigh the positive ones. If Marcia is partly a surrogate for Kureishi, and if writing truly is 'a contact sport', as Marcia calls it (*Midnight* 113), then it would appear that the rough-and-tumble of Kureishi's transformation of his life into art has resulted in more than a few bruises. Nevertheless, art is one of the few consolations available to the characters in Kureishi's mid-career fiction, and the mere existence of the stories themselves may be taken as a victory, however pyrrhic.

In the three books discussed in this chapter, Kureishi's outlook on life has become much more tragic and conflicted. His once-carefree characters have been dragged into the mud of maturity, where they become husbands, fathers, divorcé(e)s, men and women with stagnant careers, and self-hating failures. The battle between pleasure and morality has become a bloody one, and most of his heroes have chosen the former. This hasn't brought them much happiness, however, and they frequently make a virtue of their dissatisfactions; if pleasure is supposed by many to be immoral, then surely to be disillusioned by the reckless pursuit of pleasure is a way of being moral. Kureishi is plainly dismayed by the traditional bonds that keep difficult relationships together: marriage, shared responsibility, social propriety and duty. Yet his heroes' rejection of these shackles is never more than a partial escape from the torments of adulthood, which only become more painful when the innocence of childhood is recalled. These books are sad, angry, despairing testaments to the difficulties that attend one's adult obligations, whether one accepts them fully or not.

5

GABRIEL'S GIFT AND *THE BODY*

In *Gabriel's Gift* (2001) and *The Body* (2002), Kureishi is striving to break free from the cynicism, gloom and uncertainty that pervade *Love in a Blue Time*, *Intimacy*, and *Midnight All Day*. This effort, however, is more rigidly confined to the realm of the personal than any of the previous three books had been; Susie Thomas remarks that in his latest books Kureishi seems finally 'to have lost faith, or lost interest, in the 1970s agenda which saw literature as an agent for political change' (Thomas 151). The compensating factor that attends this public disillusionment is that 'there is optimism about the possibilities for change and renewal ... on a personal level' though Thomas senses that 'there is an element of willed optimism' in this positive stance (Thomas 151–2). Moreover, there is a contradiction implicit in the books' depiction of youthful innocence: both books are heavily freighted with an awareness of mortality, loss and loneliness.

Kureishi also chooses some relatively uncharacteristic fictional strategies in these two volumes, employing a somewhat inconsistent version of magical realism in *Gabriel's Gift* and a science fiction-like premise in *The Body*. Aside from the more morbid surrealism of 'The Tale of the Turd', 'The Flies' and 'The Penis', there is little in Kureishi's previous books that foreshadows such devices, and their sudden prominence is perhaps a signal of just how 'willed' his new outlook truly is. Critics have been somewhat at a loss to explain or justify Kureishi's alteration in fictional voice and genre; for instance, Nick Laird points out that 'the mode of narration' in *Gabriel's Gift* is 'problematic': 'It is almost exclusively from Gabriel's point of view, with occasional intrusions from the narrator ... Kureishi is unwilling to let the novel be told by an average teenager and tries to load his point of view with intellectual gravitas, which can mean a hasty justification among the casual cultural references' (Laird 22). There have been similar complaints about *The Body*, whose introspective, typically Kureishian first-person narrative is at odds with its superficial air of futuristic speculation. Thomas argues that given Kureishi's lack of 'interest in the medical or mechanical aspects of brains being implanted into recently deceased bodies', *The Body* 'does not read like science fiction but rather allegory or fable' (Thomas 154). John Updike, who notes Kureishi's background in philosophy, complains that in *The Body* he merely 'glances at the ontology shivering in his ectoplasmic subject matter, but then turns away' (Updike 95). Such a lack of apparent interest in the real social impact of the technology he imagines in *The Body* suggests that, as Thomas puts its, he 'does not feel the same urgency about contemporaneity as he once did' (Thomas 163). Nevertheless, this latest phase of Kureishi's career is of a piece with his middle three books, at least insofar as it minimizes concerns such as race and class, instead concentrating on family, personal identity (especially in terms of gender and masculinity), sexual experimentation and artistic achievement.

Race is not an important factor in *Gabriel's Gift*, though issues of national identity and immigration are raised by the presence of Hannah, the repulsive family *au pair*, 'a refugee from a former Communist country ... from a town called Bronchitis, with a winding river called Influenza running through it' (*Gabriel's Gift* 16–17). In her selfishness, treacherous secrecy, repressive stupidity and greed, Hannah seems to embody the invasive totalitarian governments who ruled Eastern Europe for most of her life: 'to Hannah, being a kid in the first place was to be automatically in the wrong ... . Perhaps her experience of Communism had given her this idea. Wherever she had obtained it, she would prefer it if Gabriel didn't move at all, ever again' (*Gift* 20). Hannah's grotesque appearance, outsized appetite for food, mangled English, oafish endearments and talent for spying make her an ideal vehicle for demonizing Eastern European newcomers to Britain. In a particularly ugly moment that resonates unpleasantly with earlier depictions of xenophobia and anti-immigrant sentiment in Kureishi's fiction, Gabriel threatens to have Hannah deported back to Bronchitis unless she stops spying on him (*Gift* 163). This crude and cruel depiction of Hannah is all the more surprising given the fact that Kureishi himself has had two close friends with roots in Eastern Europe, one of Czech ancestry and one from Bulgaria.

Hannah is not the text's only unprepossessing immigrant, however, as we see in the narrator's portrait of London:

> The city was no longer home to immigrants only from the former colonies, plus a few others: every race was present … .There was … little chance of being understood in any shop. Dad once said, 'The last time I visited the barber's I came out with a bowl of couscous, half a gram of Charlie and a number two crop. I only went in for a shave'. (*Gift* 15)

The humour here veils anti-immigrant stereotypes: Gabriel's otherwise sympathetic and open-minded father, Rex (whom the third-person narrator inexplicably calls 'Dad'), seems inclined to blame his own appetite for drugs ('Charlie') on foreign pushers, and calls them 'madmen', predicting that '[t]hey're not going to last into the next century' (*Gift* 49). Furthermore, the narrator notes, 'In the latest restaurants there was nothing pronounceable on the menu and, it was said, people were taking dictionaries with them to dinner' (*Gift* 16). The ethnic diversity that Kureishi once celebrated in his portraits of London has suddenly become grounds for curmudgeonly and xenophobic asides.

Neither race nor nationality is foregrounded in *The Body*, although after the protagonist Adam takes on a more youthful physique he refers to himself as one of 'us dark-skinners' and feels that others regard him 'with fear and contempt' because of his exotic appearance (*Body* 61). We get no further analysis of this situation, however, and the short stories included in *The Body and Seven Stories* also treat such issues rather casually. 'Hullabaloo in the Tree' describes the mixed feelings of an Asian man (called only 'the father') who worries that his children are displaying 'disrespect and indiscipline' because of his own permissive attitudes (*Seven* 131). The father has decided that the best strategy for assimilating into British society is to be an indulgent parent rather than to live according to the stricter laws of an alien Indian culture. Not surprisingly, the children reject their Indian heritage: one of the father's Indian friends expresses shock at the children's erratic behaviour, and the child responds by later referring to the friend as 'a brown face' (*Seven* 131).

The fourth story in *The Body and Seven Stories*, 'Straight', follows

Brett, a divorced and dissipated Londoner, on his failed quest to remain sober as he attends a series of parties. Brett has recently been rescued from drowning by a North African taxi driver, a brush with death which has produced in Brett a desire to get 'straight'. Brett also feels an urge to contact the taxi driver, a man described as 'tall and dark-skinned, a North African of some sort, wearing worn-out shoes' who has told Brett that he is 'a law student with two children' (*Seven* 213). Brett speculates that 'Probably the man was religious' although he decides that 'you didn't need religion to save someone' (*Seven* 213). As Brett flirts half-heartedly with a drunken woman named Francine, meets a former business partner, and visits a nightclub with the all-too-fitting name of 'Gaga', he begins to think more and more about the taxi driver, and even to identify with him: 'Like the taxi driver, Brett seemed to be in a world where everyone ... spoke in a foreign language' (*Seven* 217). The story ends with Brett declining Francine's sexual invitation in order to try to find his saviour / alter ego, which he now thinks of the cabbie as being. 'Straight' offers an allegory (albeit a rather slight one) of a rejection of the mainstream hedonistic culture Kureishi has generally embraced, in favour of a return to a non-Western, more religious perspective that might afford greater stability and safety.

'Touched' (from *The Body and Seven Stories*) centres on the sexual adventures of Ali, a thirteen-year-old boy who is seduced twice: first by Zahida (his older cousin from Bombay who is visiting London with her family) and then by Miss Blake, a blind neighbour in her late thirties or early forties. Ali's family is of mixed race (his mother, Joan, is English while his father is Indian) so these two seductions may be taken to represent the conflicting sides of Ali's identity. Zahida informs Ali that he is 'invited to stay with us' in Bombay, and for a time he is excited at the prospect of returning to his roots (*Seven* 257). To Miss Blake, however, Ali is 'Alan', an English boy who bears no racial or cultural markers whatsoever. Ali enjoys this deracialization: 'it was a relief. Sometimes he went all day being Alan' (*Seven* 261). The conflict between India and England in Ali's life and psyche is complex. On the one hand, Indian influences seem to promise Ali the public rewards of masculinity and adulthood: his father's relatives 'had begun to speak to him as another man. One even called him "the next head of the family"' (*Seven* 256). On the other hand, England seems to trap him in perverse and illicit Oedipal entanglements with older, maternal figures who prevent him from growing up.

Miss Blake is a defenceless and sexually accessible version of Ali's mother, as well as of Margaret Amir from *Buddha*; she is the realization of many fantasies cherished by Kureishi's characters, but her attainability is contingent on the loss of Ali's Indian identity. Although she learns that Ali's family is from India, she never asks his real name or sees his origin as a sign of racial difference, noting that her own father was in India for twenty years as well (*Seven* 262). Thus she effaces the racial and cultural difference of Indians as completely as any of Kureishi's more openly racist English characters. Miss Blake gives Ali money in exchange for furtive caresses, and the story ends with Ali accepting sixpence and abandoning his friend Mike to follow Miss Blake back into her house for another sexual encounter, clearly having chosen to remain in England and continue his fictional life as 'Alan' rather than follow the dream of returning to India. Readers might see the final tableau of the story as an indirect confession from Kureishi himself of his decision to play the lucrative and in some ways gratifying role that English people have projected onto him. 'Touched' can thus be seen as a manifesto for the erasure of racial themes that marks Kureishi's later fiction.

Just as *Gabriel's Gift* and *The Body* assume or aspire towards a colour-blind world where racial difference no longer plays a role, they also take the fragmentation of family life for granted. Gabriel's parents are estranged, and in any case the teenaged Gabriel seems to regard families as retarding influences. As Gabriel muses, 'children understood tyrannies ... living with those vicious moody bosses called parents, under a regime in which their thoughts and activities were severely constrained' (*Gift* 96). Especially stifling is Gabriel's censorious mother Christine, who treats her son with resentful disdain. Nevertheless, Gabriel demonstrates a strong attachment to Christine, and wishes to reunite her with his father, Rex, an indolent but talented musician. Indeed, *Gabriel's Gift* is perhaps unique in Kureishi's oeuvre to this point, since it suggests that the nuclear family is worth preserving, despite its flaws. As Thomas points out, 'for the first time in Kureishi, it is no longer assumed that marriage is bourgeois idiocy' (Thomas 150). Nevertheless, there is also a strong homosexual undercurrent in the novel that makes nostalgia for conventional family life seem problematic. For instance, Gabriel connects his father's departure with unfulfilled homosexual desires; as he tells Rex, 'I thought you'd gone gay' (*Gift* 44). Gabriel says, accusingly, 'You used to wear glitter and makeup', to which Rex responds: 'Of course I did! I was a pop boy. Heterosexual Englishmen love getting into a dress. It's called pantomime' (46). Although apparently unfounded, Gabriel's suspicion reminds them both of Gabriel's friend Zak, whose father turns out to be gay. Despite his concerns about Rex's sexuality, Gabriel himself seems keen to follow the example of the David Bowie-like character Lester Jones, and overcome the taboos against homosexual behaviour that he has internalized, urging himself not to 'be held up by inhibitions, terror and self-loathing' (*Gift* 190).

Kureishi is not merely content to show straight men flirting with gay identity, however; we meet a restaurant owner named Speedy, an openly gay man who admires Gabriel's looks (*Gift* 115–16). Speedy's prurient interest in Gabriel is evident; he says 'I want you to come and see me ... I know what it's like ... [t]he turbulence that young guys are prone to' (*Gift* 124). Like Karim letting Pyke have his way with him, Gabriel tacitly offers Speedy sex in exchange for a picture Speedy owns. Speedy gives him the picture, but only after stipulating that 'a part of you has to belong to me' (*Gift* 157). This sounds uncomfortably like a bargain with the devil, and indeed a few pages later we see that Gabriel, walking near the 'Underground grills', wonders 'if he weren't in hell' (*Gift* 159). Nevertheless, Speedy has his sympathetic side; he asks Gabriel to paint him in the nude, but noticing Gabriel's lack of enthusiasm, he sensibly puts his clothes back on (188). Moreover, despite his earlier sexual overtures, Speedy assures Gabriel that 'I won't hustle you' (*Gift* 189) and keeps his promise. Speedy is also generous; he offers Christine a job, and ends up hiring Hannah, which removes the last remaining obstacle to Rex and Christine's reunion. Most importantly in Gabriel's eyes, Speedy also represents the fast-moving world of show business, specifically film-making. In his capacity as cultural impresario, Speedy introduces Gabriel to celebrities such as Karim Amir (in a self-conscious reference to *Buddha*), calling Gabriel a 'film-maker' and showing himself eager to advance Gabriel's career as an artist (*Gift* 191). These traits may not make Speedy into a completely positive figure, but as a portrayal of a gay man, he is nevertheless an advance on the closeted and remorselessly exploitative Pyke of *Buddha*.

The sexual and familial dynamics of *The Body* are no less complex than those of *Gabriel's Gift*; the protagonist, Adam, loves his wife Margot, but complains about her judgements on his original body (which he soon trades in for a younger one): 'She liked to accuse me of not being "toned", of being, in fact, "mush", but threatened murder and suicide if I mentioned any of her body parts without reverence' (*Body* 17). Still, when Adam asks for a 'six month sabbatical' from their relationship to inhabit his new body, Margot is hurt (*Body* 20). Adam's wish for a new body is not merely born of a desire to escape ageing, however; it is based on his conviction that there is something deeply wrong with who he is. As he says, 'Nothing has cured me of myself, of the self I cling to' (*Body* 3). Still, this reinvention of the self comes at a high price; Adam pays for his operation with 'money that would otherwise have gone to my children' (*Body* 22). Partly due to this decision to cheat his family of their rightful inheritance, Adam has some unexpected second thoughts after the operation, especially when he catches a glimpse of his wife on the street, and this is the first clue that life as a 'Newbody', as Adam calls himself, is not as delightful as it might seem.

Indeed, the name Newbody sounds perilously close to 'nobody', a word which Adam (or Leo, as he calls himself after he has been rejuvenated), finally accepts as a self-description: 'I was a nobody' (*Body* 74). Adam/Leo's loss of identity takes many forms; for instance, he realizes that, despite all his sexual adventures, 'I was like a spy, concealed and wary' (*Body* 69). The impossibility of fully disclosing his emotions to his casual sexual partners means that he, like the rest of his 'generation', is 'fascinated by' double agents and pays 'the emotional price of a double life, of hiding in your mind' (*Body* 70). The mind-body dualism that drives *The Body* inevitably makes these feelings of alienation seem universal; either one's mind is younger than one's body and thus feels betrayed by physical decay, or else the mind is older than the body and wears unseen and unspeakable scars of emotion. In a scene that underscores this truth, Adam/Leo tries to recover the feelings he once experienced on Ecstasy by participating in what he calls 'the pornographic circus of rough sex' where he derives a 'sexual high' by begging 'to be turned into meat' (*Body* 67). Even these scenes of abandon, however, have moments when 'the other, or "bit of the other", as we used to say, would turn human … would indicate a bruised history or ailing mind. The bubble of fantasy was pricked ... I saw another kind of opening then ... into the real. I fled ... I was interested only in my own feeling' (69). No wonder Adam/Leo calls such encounters 'awful fun' (*Body* 38), an oxymoronic phrase that underlines the contradictory and often terrifying or transgressive nature of sexuality.

Some of Adam/Leo's sexual adventures involve ambivalent encounters with gay culture. Ralph informs Adam/Leo that his new body's first owner was homosexual, adding with apparently unconscious irony: 'Most hets, apart from actors, have the bodies of corpses' (*Body* 52). In any case, Adam/Leo's interest in gay life has its roots much earlier: 'As a young man ... I liked being an admired boy ... surrounded by older men' (*Body* 62). He also envies what he sees as the spontaneity of gay life: 'Like many straights, I'd been intrigued by some of my gay friends' promiscuity ... They were reinventing love, keeping it close to instinct' (*Body* 65). Here Adam/Leo immediately distances himself from his evident homoerotic feelings by aligning himself with the 'many straights' who supposedly share his views. In one scene, Adam/Leo is accosted by two gay men who once knew his new body; they call him 'Mark' and inform him that the former owner of his body was a professional model who played in 'a boy band' and also did what they call 'the other thing' for money (*Body* 49–50). There is a strong implication that his body's former owner was a prostitute, a hint that gains strength when Adam/Leo begins calling himself a 'tart' (*Body* 62).

Such language raises problems of gender identity that go well beyond homoeroticism, however; there is a larger crisis in sexual identity in the novel. Adam/Leo hints at this crisis at a party when he marvels at 'how well groomed' the young men are: 'Apart from the gym, these boys must have kept fit twisting and untwisting numerous jars, tubs, and bottles' (*Body* 8). In other words, men have begun using the same strategies to care for and present their bodies as women have. Men too are beginning to blur the distinction between 'inside' and 'outside' (*Body* 8). Adam/Leo is rather troubled by this, though his own transformation is plainly a symptom of this encroachment onto traditionally female territory. The chief irony of the book in this respect is that Adam/Leo loses much of his masculine power and authority even as he gains sexual potency and desirability when he assumes his new body. Unwilling to continue his writing career, he decides to trade on his body exclusively, and models for some fashion shows where, in one of the reversals of expectations that Kureishi delights in creating, he is the victim of gender discrimination: 'The models didn't earn anything like as much as the girls' (*Body* 60).

Adam/Leo suffers further gender-based indignities when he gets a job doing menial labour at a spa run by and for women. Patricia, the woman in charge of this 'spa', presents Adam/Leo with a more virulent sort of female authoritarianism than he had bargained for, as he says: 'I could recall her variety of feminism … its mad ugliness, the forced ecstasy of sisterhood, the whole revolutionary puritanism' (*Body* 74). The spa is a satire on an all-female utopian ideal, and Kureishi's suggestion that women in power are a recipe for simple reverse gender discrimination is heavy-handed. For instance, there is a scene in which Adam/Leo and Patricia make love, at her instigation: 'Patricia howled, "Adore me … you little shit!"; she dug her fingers into me, scratched and kicked me, and, when she came, thrust her tongue into my mouth until I almost gagged' (*Body* 93). Adam/Leo is feminized by this reverse penetration, and is 'furious' about 'what Patricia had done to me' (*Body* 98). Nevertheless, he is induced to remain quiet by his sense of Patricia's greater authenticity: 'I began … examining the folds and creases of her old neck … there was something in her I didn't want to let go of. Her body and soul were one, she was "real"' (*Body* 122).

Soon enough, however, a young aspiring writer named Alicia appears and falls in love with Adam/Leo (76). Alicia speaks for the women at the spa and Adam/Leo himself when she confesses that 'we masochists are drawn to Patricia' (*Body* 83). Nevertheless, Alicia is plainly attracted to Adam/Leo when he begins to assert himself in a more traditional fashion: 'Alicia seemed to like the authority I was able to muster' (*Body* 85). In the end, playing the role of a gender liberator finally taking power, Adam/Leo complains to Patricia: 'What you do to me is a description of what you say men do to women' and she reacts 'as if something had exploded inside her body' (*Body* 123). This description suggests that she is every bit as divided and false as Adam/Leo or other men. Most tellingly of all, Alicia informs Adam/Leo that Patricia was gratifyingly devastated by his departure, as if to show that all feminists simply want 'some intensity of feeling with a man' (*Body* 129).

In the end, however, what Adam/Leo really longs for is not a gay lifestyle, nor life as a boy toy, nor a career as a spokesperson for

authority, but sex of a certain kind, sex that is stylized, commodified and depersonalized – what he calls 'sex without a hurting
human face' (*Body* 65). Indeed, *The Body* offers Kureishi's most
telling analysis of the economic and power-based dynamics of
desire since *The Buddha of Suburbia*. This is foregrounded in the basic
conceit of the book: living in a beautiful corpse's body is perhaps
the most striking image of amoral consumerism one could wish
for. The process of selecting a new body also underlines the casual-
ness with which people commodify others' flesh; in viewing the
bodies he is to choose from, Adam/Leo is reminded of 'the rows of
suits in the tailor's I'd visit as a boy with my father' (*Body* 26). The
conflation of clothes and bodies is a familiar one; bodies in
Kureishi's world have long been as mutable and socially
constructed as clothes. Untroubled by the dehumanizing implications of his attitude, Adam/Leo describes his rejuvenated love life,
for instance, as narcissistic and voyeuristic: 'We could imagine
around each other, playing with our bodies, living in our minds.
We became machines for making pornography of ourselves' (*Body*
55). Adam/Leo delights in treating his new body like a commercial
product, realizing that if he doesn't like something, he can alter it
to his specifications: 'I would customize myself' (*Body* 46).
Adam/Leo hints at the deeper implications of the process he has
undergone, noting that such a 'transformation … worked better
for people who didn't have theories of authenticity or the
"natural"' (*Body* 59), evidently congratulating himself on never
having believed there was anything 'natural' about humans in the
first place.

However, there are more sombre signs that Adam/Leo has
betrayed his humanity entirely by assuming another's body; he
calls himself and those like him 'mutants, freaks, human unhu-
mans' (*Body* 120). He feels as if he belongs to a new, dehumanized
world in which 'all the meanings, the values of Western civilization
since the Greeks, have changed' and laments the fact that 'We seem
to have replaced ethics with aesthetics' (*Body* 114). For a younger
Kureishi, such a replacement might seem perfectly acceptable, but
now he seems to endorse this moralistic condemnation of a purely
youth- and beauty-centred worldview. The character who embodies this condemnation in the text is Matte, a Newbody who ends up
hounding Adam/Leo, seeking a new body for his dying brother.
Matte's place in the novel is an intriguing one; he is clearly an

unscrupulous and violent man, but his motives for wanting Adam/Leo's body are selfless, and he comes to seem an unwitting agent of morality who punishes Adam/Leo for his hubristic transgression of natural, familial and human laws. Adam/Leo's final words are full of foreboding: 'I was a stranger on the earth, a nobody with nothing, belonging nowhere, a body alone, condemned to begin again, in the nightmare of eternal life' (*Body* 149). Adam/Leo's sense of simultaneous renewal and loss is believable, as well as familiar; Kureishi's protagonists often feel as if they have begun life all over again when they leave their wives and children, and *The Body* takes this idea of a new beginning to a nightmarish extreme.

Most of the stories in *The Body and Seven Stories* deal with troubled families, and distribute the blame for them haphazardly, sometime faulting women, sometimes men. The story that scapegoats women most clearly is 'Goodbye, Mother', which revolves around Harry, a middle-aged married man who takes his emotionally manipulative mother to visit his father's grave. Harry also meditates on his embattled marriage to Alexandra, who evinces a feminist misanthropy reminiscent of Patricia's in *The Body*; she plans to attend a 'workshop' where she hopes 'there aren't … any men' (*Seven* 178). As part of her feminist consciousness-raising enterprise, Alexandra has begun to write a 'life journal' which poses a slapstick threat to his well-being: 'She would write furiously … picking out different coloured children's markers … and flinging them on the floor where they could easily upend him' (163). As this passage suggests, for Harry (as for other Kureishi men), women's writing is both a betrayal of what have traditionally been their domestic duties and an indirect act of aggression against men. Harry demands to read his wife's journal, but she refuses, perhaps because she has begun a lesbian affair with 'Amazing Olga', an Eastern European hypnotherapist.

Harry is caught between his mother's passive, voyeuristic acceptance of the public world and Alexandra's feminist conviction that the world of business and news is just 'a cover story' on the 'surface' of things (*Seven* 183). Although Harry finds Alexandra's claim that women are 'closer to the heart of things' absurd (*Seven* 183), he nevertheless sides with her against his mother. Partly prompted by Alexandra, Harry decides not to withdraw from life as his parents have done, but instead to immerse himself in family life and its enjoyments. There is little to suggest that Alexandra will find life with Harry any better than before, but Harry shows no special concern on this score, assuming that once his own interest in Alexandra is revived, her lesbian affairs will end. There is even an implication that Alexandra will serve as a sort of therapist for Harry, as if to make his farewell to his mother permanent. Not surprisingly, however, Harry refuses to give credit to feminism for changing his priorities; the narrator says that 'It had taken him a while to see – the screechings of the feminists had made him resistant – that the fathers had been separated from their children by work' (*Seven* 189). In other words, the story suggests that feminism harms families more than it helps them.

'Remember This Moment, Remember Us' concentrates on men's overt self-destructiveness rather than on women's subtler flaws. The forty-five-year-old protagonist, Rick, is a heavy drinker whose father's suicide, the narrator implies, has left him feeling 'unloved' and therefore 'dangerous' (*Seven* 229). As if determined to continue this unhappy cycle, Rick passes out in front of his young son Dan, who has wet himself and is 'running around with a glass of wine in his hand' when Rick's partner Anna gets home. Undeterred, she suggests that they make a video for Dan to play on his own forty-fifth birthday, reminding Rick of how much it would mean 'if your father was [sic] to speak to you right now' (*Seven* 228). The story ends with a somewhat sentimental tableau: Daniel kissing both his parents, climbing into his mother's arms for the camera, waving 'to himself', and closing his eyes. Yet this scene is shown to be fragile and temporary, given Rick's reckless behaviour, which shows no signs of abating, and the valetudinarian tone of the message itself: '"Goodbye, goodbye", they say together' (*Seven* 231). The interdependence of tragedy and sentimentality has seldom been so efficiently and movingly suggested in Kureishi's fiction, and 'Remember This Moment, Remember Us' offers a microcosm of the bittersweet tone of Kureishi's two most recent books of fiction, which celebrate family life while demonstrating its embattled place in contemporary culture.

'The Real Father', a significantly less affecting story, also concentrates on relationships, and brings to a crisis the many father/son antagonisms that have figured in Kureishi's fiction. We are immediately told that, although Mal is Wallace's biological father, he never wanted Wallace to be born, and 'couldn't bear his son … and dreaded seeing him' (*Seven* 335). Mal's distaste is amply justified by the narrator's descriptions of Wallace, who, although around ten years old, still requires a 'comforter' in his mouth to fall asleep (*Seven* 249) and proclaims his stupidity by spilling his food everywhere. In trying to explain his son's disgusting habits and demeanour, Mal rehearses the platitudes of therapy, saying 'Underneath Wallace's whimpering, moaning and abuse, a child was screaming for help' (*Seven* 240), and 'You couldn't pathologize him for hating his father' (*Seven* 242), but despite these realizations he finds himself employing his own distancing strategies when his son visits: drinking and using drugs.

Mal's feelings about the cartoonishly awful Wallace become more complex as the story proceeds, however; although he has been in the habit of 'admitting how little there was of him in the boy – and semi-forgetting him', he is happy to spend more time with Wallace: 'Mal was relieved to have … his son back before it was too late' (*Seven* 238). Mal realizes that Wallace's anti-social behaviour is a product of feeling unwanted, and tries to express a love he doesn't feel towards Wallace, stroking him and comment-ing (albeit with a menacing undertone): 'No one's going to love you if you behave like this' (*Seven* 237). In an absurd attempt at estab-lishing intimacy between father and son, Mal parades naked in front of Wallace, 'showing him the stomach flopping above the thin legs, the weak grey pubic hair, the absurd boyish buttocks. Wallace needed to take him in … as Mal believed people in complete families did daily' (*Seven* 242). Mal also begs Wallace to 'cuddle' him, and, rather surprisingly, Wallace begins to warm up to Mal, despite himself, calling him 'Dad' (*Seven* 250). Mal finally pledges his version of unconditional love to Wallace, saying 'I will think of you' at all hours of the day (*Seven* 251).

Mal finally decides to open up and tell Wallace about his own chequered past as a runaway and squatter, which induces Wallace to behave better during an important business meeting between Mal and Andrea, a film director. Andrea, who wants to employ Mal, tells father and son that they look 'exactly the same' (*Seven* 247). Andrea is strangely charmed by Wallace, and offers him a small part in her film as an actor. Mal is pleased by this develop-ment, since it will mean more time for him to work on improving Wallace and showing his love for his son. At the end of the story a self-satisfied Mal toasts himself: 'To Mal … And everyone who knows him', a benediction that no doubt includes Wallace, albeit only indirectly (*Seven* 251). This rather backhanded blessing, as well as the fact that the 'real father' and his son can only be brought together by a new female acquaintance, lends a final tinge of irony to a story already teetering on the brink of the ridiculous.

In a similar comic vein, 'Face to Face With You' depicts Ed and Ann, a couple who notice that another couple, nearly identical to them and also named Ed and Ann, have moved in upstairs. Ed tries to sum up the situation to a friend: 'It's as if they're the originals and you're only acting out their lives' (*Seven* 150). Neither Ed nor Ann is blamed for the situation, however; indeed, they are both rejuvenated (albeit initially troubled) by its absurdity. The element of the supernatural hovers at the edges of the story, but the point lies not in the duplication itself but in its psychological effect on the couple. Ed and Ann begin arguing over the other couple's habits, but are really arguing about themselves:

> He's going to read! … You're like that. He only opens books.
> He doesn't know anything except there's a hole in the centre of him. He's hungry for information.
> Doesn't he want information about her?
> That's not enough. (*Seven* 146)

Spurred on by this challenge to their sense of themselves (both as individuals and as a pair), Ed and Ann try to change their lives. They buy new clothes and shoes, exercise, and contemplate getting tattoos, but find that the other Ed and Ann have done exactly the same things. Far from dismaying them, this duplication seems to galvanize Ed and Ann's relationship, as if they can only begin to see the results of their self-improvements when these are reflected back to them in the mirror provided by the other couple. The other Ed and Ann move away, but they have served their purpose: restoring the first Ed and Ann to a precarious sense of well-being. The story suggests that imitation is the only path to happiness, because no originality is possible in modern relationships. In any case, for couples chafing against the bonds of marriage, absorption in others' similar lives is preferable to direct self-scrutiny. Such a carefree conclusion, like the comical grotesqueness of 'The Real Father', may provide welcome relief from the otherwise unrelenting misery of family life as it is presented in these two books, but it also suggests a certain trivialization of a theme that has exercised Kureishi a great deal.

The newly dominant theme (which arguably replaces issues of race and family) in *Gabriel's Gift* and *The Body* is artistic creativity, the same one that plays a secondary role in much of the previous three books. In the former novel, Gabriel's artistic life takes on a magical quality when he copies a picture of a pair of old work boots and finds that the boots actually materialize in front of him, complete with a smell of 'dung, mud, the countryside and grass' (*Gift* 28). This little miracle does not last long, since the real boots leave a 'boot-shaped hole' on the page where they were drawn, and are eventually 'sucked back' onto the page so that 'everything returned to normal' (*Gift* 28). The fact that the reality produced by such secondhand copying is itself evanescent, and likely to be returned into a text, is perhaps a warning about the temporary nature of such postmodern creativity. Still, it is clear that for Kureishi, as for Lester Jones, the pop star who takes Gabriel under his wing, art can replace identity for much of the time. As Jones says, 'When I'm doing this I disappear. There's no me there. I don't know who I am' (*Gift* 67).

Lester Jones, as a pop star turned all-round artist, closely resembles David Bowie, one of Kureishi's idols and a recurrent inspiration for many of Kureishi's most glamorous characters. Kureishi has described his experience of interviewing Bowie in 1993, gushing that Bowie 'had movie-star glamour, that unbuyable, untouchable sheen … he appeared creative all day, drawing, writing on cards' (*Dreaming and Scheming* 212). Jones strives to live up to this high standard, doodling joyfully as he expounds his theory of creativity as a mixture of the conscious and unconscious minds: 'You can't will a dream or an erection. But you can get into bed … in dreams the maddest connections are made' (*Gift* 67). Despite all this self-congratulatory rhetoric about creativity, Jones confesses that he constantly fights 'the rising tide of boredom' (67), as if the 'expanse of nullity' (*Gift* 64) that he inhabits were always threatening to engulf him. Lester's main difficulty is that he is dogged by imitators. The paradox in Jones's teachings – and perhaps indeed in the entire creative ethos of the 1970s, for Kureishi – is summed up in Gabriel's unconsciously self-contradictory decision to 'follow Lester's example and go his own way' (*Gift* 83), as if one could be both imitative and original at the same time. The fact is that Lester is an imitative creature with no original core of selfhood whatsoever: 'Like most pop heroes, Lester ... was neither completely boy nor girl, changing continuously as he expressed and lost himself in various disguises' (*Gift* 52). In this respect, Lester is like Bowie himself, who testifies to having 'always felt like a vehicle for something else' and to having never 'sorted out ... who Bowie is' (quoted in Sandford 103).

Despite the debatable origins of Jones's talent, he helps Gabriel to connect with the elusive imitator/creator in himself; he gives Gabriel a signed drawing he has done, and later looks at Gabriel's pictures and recognizes the boy's ability. Inspired by Lester, Gabriel speculates about the factitious, even plagiaristic nature of art: 'Lester might have said that most art is theft; William Burroughs might have written that 'all pictures are fakes' (*Gift* 118). Jones's influence seems dangerous as well as encouraging, however, as we see in a scene in which, on his way out of Jones's hotel, Gabriel takes an apple from Jones's fruit bowl and leaves it on the floor of the lobby, thinking that the 'little patch of colour would cheer people up' (*Gift* 70). This artistic gesture sets off a minor stampede as 'several colourless figures' can be seen 'scampering towards the anarchic apple' (*Gift* 71). Gabriel's gratuitous, Jones-inspired aesthetic impulse becomes mischievously divine, as he sets down a version of the apple of knowledge for the celebrity-hunters to covet. The public overreaction to his imaginative impulse dampens Gabriel's spirits when he thinks of the anarchic fun he and his father once had, musing sadly that 'There was no opportunity for amusement now' (*Gift* 71). Here Kureishi seems to be echoing Gabriel's sentiments from his own experience as a much-maligned celebrity, albeit of a lesser calibre than Bowie. As Rex puts it, 'fame is a handful of foam' (*Gift* 75), but Kureishi has learned that this 'foam' can suffocate and constrain.

The story's allusions to creativity itself are occasionally negative: once Rex has moved back in, Gabriel destroys the copies he had made of Jones's picture, leaving the original to hang above the family fireplace in his newly reconstituted home, suggesting that artistic creativity is a mere side effect of domestic discontent. Moreover, when Kureishi shows Gabriel in the process of directing his much-anticipated movie, with the full support of his friends and parents, the exploitative dimension of this initial project seems problematic. Gabriel's friend Jake advises him that becoming a film director will enable him to 'get girls' because 'a lot of women like cameras' (*Gift* 210), suggesting that women have either a fetishistic attitude to the camera as a phallic substitute or a narcissistic fascination with their own appearance. In any case, they can be manipulated because of this attraction to art. The immediate object of Gabriel's aesthetic and sexual desires, a girl named Ramona, responds to his offer of a part in his movie with a mixture of defensiveness and professional ambition that seems to confirm Jake's assessment: 'How do you know I want to be an actress? Do I look like an exhibitionist?' (*Gift* 211). We soon see that the once-sharp-tongued, supercilious Ramona has been reduced to 'weeping with fear' in anticipation of her appearance in Gabriel's film (*Gift* 220). Gabriel has not merely regained control over his own psyche and ceased 'to be alone' (*Gift* 221), he has used art to reduce others to the emotional vulnerability that he once felt.

Kureishi's vision of creativity becomes even more pessimistic in *The Body*. Once Adam/Leo has assumed his new body, he decides that 'writing … was a habit I needed to break' (*Body* 99). Adam/Leo's physical transformation seems like a replacement for (and the logical conclusion to) his earlier forms of artistic self-expression; his new body is a sort of canvas. However, Kureishi makes it plain that having reattained youthful vigour, Adam/Leo no longer has any need to be creative or even intellectually active; as he notes with some satisfaction, 'I was almost free of the desire to understand' (*Body* 79). Such an attitude suggests that for Adam/Leo, creativity is not necessarily an end in itself; rather (like acting for Karim in *The Buddha of Suburbia* or drugs for Shahid in *The Black Album*) it is a means to an enlarged sphere of enjoyment. Once the enjoyment is attained, the creativity is dispensable. As Kureishi makes plain in the interview included in Chapter 6, his own view of the creative process has gone in exactly the opposite direction; the closer he gets to his own mortality, the more he values his imagination and the act of writing that expresses it. Indeed, if there is one central message that emerges from Kureishi's most recent works of fiction, it is his dedication to the task of analysing and valorizing the habit of creation. His latest works' covert pessimism about once-promising artists and their ambitions, however, gives readers cause to wonder how successful Kureishi believes that his own struggle to reinvent himself as a mature writer has been.

Kureishi's two most recent books of fiction bring his work full circle: having shown us the seemingly infinite power of youth to wear different masks and pursue opposing ideals in his first two books, and then watched that power dwindle with the onset of adulthood in his next three, Kureishi tries to recapture either innocence itself, in the shape of the youthful artist Gabriel, or its desperate, guilty facsimile, in the form of Adam, the middle-aged inhabitant of a younger body. The transformative potential of the adolescent body and mind has been a leitmotif (not to say obsession) in his writing, and in these later books it is juxtaposed to its opposite: the clutching, covetous adult self (Speedy in *Gift*, Adam and Matte in *Body*). In these books, however, there is a distinct suggestion that the innocence of Gabriel and his fellow youngsters is inextricably linked to those who wish to exploit and enjoy it. The metaphor of young women murdered for their beautiful corpses in *The Body* seems apt; in Kureishi's fallen but nostalgic world, the perfect beauty of novelty is under remorseless and constant threat from a corrupt world that gives it its only meaning. Indeed, Gabriel's 'gift' is merely to imitate a pre-existing object and bring it temporarily to life; perhaps this is the only power the young finally have, in Kureishi's view.

The false promise of Kureishi's recent return to youthful themes (invoking the potential of innocence and rejuvenating beauty only to suggest their fraudulence and limitations) has caused some critics to give up hope in his future as a writer. Brian Budzynski terms *Gabriel's Gift* 'incomplete' by comparison with his earlier, more ambitious work, and senses 'a distinct lack of attention' in Kureishi's approach to his characters and material (Budzynski 235). Thomas concedes that 'These books are ... more disciplined and compressed', but contends that 'these qualities do not altogether compensate for the loss of ebullience and bravado. Craft cannot substitute for conviction, energy and creative engagement with others' (Thomas 163). Some of Kureishi's disapproving reviewers, however, seem to react to his worldview rather than to the quality of his work on its own terms; for instance, Jessica Mann (reviewing *The Body* in the *Daily Telegraph*) finds Kureishi's obsession with 'disappointment' and 'decline', themes which some readers might be prepared to grant Kureishi as his *donnée* (and thus not subject to criticism *per se*), to be ultimately 'dispiriting' (quoted in Thomas 158). Happily for Kureishi and his remaining admirers, some reviewers have felt very differently; for instance, Alexander Linklater of the *Guardian* praises Kureishi's 'continentally inspired, disciplined' style, and savours Kureishi's habit of playing with the 'confessional illusion' (quoted in Thomas 159). As long as some readers remain captivated by Kureishi's curious and seductive charisma as both an author and personality, his work will no doubt continue to be published around the world.

PART III
Criticism and Contexts

6

AUTHOR INTERVIEW

One of the things you talk a lot about is coming from a lower-middle-class family. What political views do you associated with lower-middle-class life? Is 'lower middle class' a stable category of people with a certain political viewpoint, or is it ambiguous?

Well, my story's really more complicated that that. My father came from a very wealthy Indian upper-class family, and moved to England and married a woman, my mother, who was lower middle class. But to answer your question, from my point of view, it's a sense of where you are in relation to other people. As a teenager, it's a sense of what you can and can't achieve, where you can and can't go. So the expectations of us, as lower-middle-class kids, were that we would be clerks, like my dad, or work in banks or insurance agencies, and so on. One of the things that happened in the sixties was that you were slightly liberated from your sense of class, because the pop stars that we knew, who were mostly lower middle class, like John Lennon or The Who, had liberated themselves from the straightjacket of class. We identified with them, and felt that we could then make our way in London, in culture, in pop, fashion, and in my case writing. So I think of class in terms of constraint, and also in terms of the intellectual deprivation, you might call it, of people who didn't take culture seriously.

Can class remain a straightjacket, even once you have escaped from the lower-middle-class setting? I'm thinking of the acts of marital infidelity in your fiction, which frequently seem to involve escaping from a bourgeois or middle-class domestic space into a lower-class or working-class space. Is this deliberate? Are your unfaithful, extramarital lovers really subverting class boundaries as well as monogamy?

I think all my characters are trying to enlarge their sense of self, struggling against constraint, and that may have to do with struggling against an original sense of class that they're trying to throw off. They're trying to find out who else they may be, or who else might be inside them, or what identifications with other groups are possible to enlarge the sense of self. Most of my characters, most of the men, are pretty restless, but even the women. *The Mother* is about a lower-middle-class woman who is restless. So what I'm interested in, what a lot of my characters are interested in, is 'Who can I become?', 'What are the possibilities of life for me?'. And that really isn't a lower-middle-class idea. The lower middle class have a much more fixed sense of identity, I think. They know who they are.

How would you characterize that identity?

In terms of respectability.

Or prudery?

Yes. They're employed. They own property. You get a lot of this in Orwell. They don't really like the working class; they think the working class are less cultured.

Does that antagonism sometimes go the other way? You've written about how you were harassed as a schoolboy, and I'm wondering if that had to do with a class antagonism as well as racial prejudice.

Yes. The kids that beat you up were the working-class kids, and the kids that sneered at you were the middle-class kids.

I'm wondering about whether Marxism has been an important intellectual presence in your life. In Intimacy, *Jay says he was once 'some sort of Marxist' way back when; would you ever have identified yourself as a Marxist?*

I would say that for a writer these identifications are only ever temporary. I've never joined a party. Well, I was in fact in the Labour Party, but I don't consider that a party of any seriousness, really.

Why not?

Because everybody was in the Labour Party. It was not like joining the Communist Party. As a writer, I would say that the two biggest influences on my generation and my time were Freud and Marx, sexuality and class, to put it simply. And I guess I've always been on the Left, but I'm not really a joiner, and I don't think writers are on the whole joiners. I've certainly never thought of myself as espousing any political cause in my writing, though I've written about people who are leftists and are involved in politics.

I'm wondering about some of those characters, for instance Brownlow in The Black Album. *Is he purely a buffoon, or does he represent anything you admire?*

He's a caricature, because this book was written in the early nineties, and the Left of that time was really fucked. It was the end of the Berlin Wall, the collapse of Eastern Europe and Russia. That kind of Left had nothing left. You can see in *The Black Album* what filled that ideological hole: radical Islam and pop culture. Over the last ten years these things have gradually emerged, and the old Left has more or less died. So he is a buffoon, because he's really at the end of the Orwellian, good English puritanical, Fabian-influenced leftism. It's a terrible loss in a sense.

How do you see the working class in Britain as having changed in the past thirty years or so? Is it still a meaningful political presence in British life?

Well, the working class under Thatcher really divided into the respectable working class, the *working* working class, the guys who became builders and car salesmen, the entrepreneurial hustlers that Thatcher so worshipped, and the underclass, who were on the dole, who were involved in drugs and alcohol, and couldn't get involved in the so-called Thatcher revolution. There was a big split in terms of the working class around the time of the miners' strike. So it's much more fragmented. The other thing in terms of class in Britain was the huge influence of Asians and Afro-Caribbean people, of course, who joined the working class, and then transformed it in the last twenty years in other ways as well.

And they were not always welcomed by the English working classes they attempted to join, were they?

No, absolutely. Some of these conflicts I've written about.

You associate punk with Thatcherism in your story 'In a Blue Time', but it also seems to be a way for the members of the working class who have not been assimilated into Thatcherite economics. What is the legacy of punk in British culture, do you think, and has it had any impact on your writing?

I don't know if it's had any impact on my writing. Certainly, what I loved about punk was the energy and fury and hatred, because all of that had been dissipated into soft middle-class hippiedom. But it's also a kind of individualism as well; they hated all that hippie unity. Culturally it was very important, because it was about art as shock, art as outrage. Out of that came pretty interesting music as well, such as Elvis Costello, Vivian Westwood in fashion, and a lot of American bands as well, like Nirvana. They sounds like a cross between a heavy metal band and a punk band. But also the angst, the sense of misery that is punk has been a great influence on rock and roll. But to be honest, it's pretty much gone from my work.

But there still seems to be a desire to shock and provoke sometimes, to express anger and outrage; that doesn't seem to have faded.

That's true, I mean, go and see *The Mother*. But there's a romantic streak in my work, which Johnny Rotten probably lacked. There's a softness, a tenderness in parts of my work, which I like to think gives it more variety.

It would be hard to sustain a literary career on purely punk themes, I imagine.

(*laughs*) Yeah. I guess if you're a punk, you have only one voice as a writer, you'd be like someone like Bukowski, for instance. I guess

I'm far more interested in character, in speaking from different points of view, particularly now.

Why do you think that is the case?

I think you develop as a writer in different ways, and you become less interested in yourself, and more interested in other people, in entering the minds of other people. I began to write because I wanted to speak for myself, as an Asian kid who didn't have a voice, as an Asian kid who'd never been represented, as part of a community, the Asians, who'd never been represented, and so on. It seemed important to me then to speak of myself, of my experience, you know, in that particular Joycean way. *A Portrait of the Artist as a Young Man* is also the portrait of the community and the time as well. I don't feel anymore that I'm saying things that nobody else is saying, or that I'm in that position, therefore exploring myself is less interesting.

In writing about the Muslim community in Britain in The Black Album, *you went out and did some research. It was almost a journalistic process. Are there any other works of fiction for which you've done similar things? For instance, the lives of drug dealers in London are very convincingly portrayed in your work.*

Yeah, but I knew those guys anyway. I didn't go out of my way to research them as I did with *The Black Album* and *My Son the Fanatic*. I don't like doing research because I'm rather lazy, and I don't normally do it. I did it partly because of the book, and the film, but I mostly did it out of curiosity, after having been in Pakistan in the eighties and then knowing Rushdie as he'd been involved in the *fatwa*, and during that period. I really wanted to go and have a look and see what was happening with these guys. But that was really the only time. I mean, a lot of research goes on all the time; it's just what happens between you and your wife in the kitchen, or you and your parents.

What do you think about drugs? Have drugs done young people more good than harm, in your view? Is there any distinction to be drawn between different kinds of drugs?

I don't think dropping acid is the same thing as having a joint. Taking Ecstasy is also a different kind of experience, so I'd make a big distinction between all those things. I would probably put them in a different category as well, which has to do with pleasure. Pleasure is always an issue for human beings: how much of it should we have? Where does it stand in relation to morality, and to all kinds of other things? If you look at it like that, it's much more interesting than talking about whether dropping acid is bad for a twenty-year-old or not. I would look at it in relation to pleasure, and terror, and inhibition, and our relation to pleasure in the end is our relation to our own sexuality, and our bodies.

Is taking drugs just another form of consumption, in the same way that we consume other things that give us pleasure?

Yes. Pleasure in its purest sense, but also pleasure as an anaesthetic. In my mind, and in my life as well, there's a difference between using drugs as an anaesthetic, a cure for depression, and using drugs recreationally. Often that distinction is blurred and you get muddled up. For me, drugs have been dangerous when I've been depressed and I tried to cure myself through taking drugs. But what I'm much more interested in are our relations to our pleasures.

It seems that youth is itself a source of pleasure in your writings. Does finding this pleasure become more difficult as you age?

Well, you find new pleasures. You can see this in *The Mother*. You need to dig them out. The pleasures for me, in my life, have mostly to do with the pleasures of my children, and their well-being. The pleasures for me in writing a new book are not the same as the pleasure of writing, like, *The Buddha of Suburbia*. One feels less guilty about that too, as one gets older, and less simplistic.

There are some interesting passages in Gabriel's Gift *in which pop culture is associated with paedophilia and with what one character calls 'the gay underground'. I'm wondering if, in your mind, pop has always been about trying to win social acceptance for sexual behaviour of one form or another, and is it possible for that to go too far?*

There's no doubt that pop and children have gone together, and the commodification of their bodies, you see that. Pop is owned and manipulated by older people, who have sort of owned and used the bodies of young people to a lesser or greater extent, so it's a teaching relationship with a greater or lesser erotic edge to it. I've always liked pop, but I have to say that pop's not enough, it's never been enough. Only last night I was looking at *A Hard Day's Night*, which is a great film, a really great film, a masterpiece, really, a minor masterpiece of the cinema. On the other hand, to have a complete culture, you need other things as well, not just The Beatles. You need Mozart and you need Freud, and so on. Pop culture has never entirely satisfied me, because it's surface, which *A Hard Day's Night* is, a beautiful surface. Though it's not entirely surface-like, because there's a bit of Truffaut in that film, actually, there's a lot of French new wave in that film, so it does point to deeper cultural aspects. So, as I would say, pop has never been enough for me.

You've mentioned Freud, and he comes up quite a bit in your recent essays from Dreaming and Scheming. *There are also some interesting Oedipal and incestuous motifs in your fiction; I'm thinking of* Gabriel's Gift, *for instance. How consciously have you used Freud to structure your storylines?*

I wouldn't say that I used him consciously or unconsciously, by which I mean that Freud is just part of our landscape. For writers of my generation and our time, really, the whole postwar world, you can't think seriously about emotional relationships, sexual relationships, without Freud. But I wouldn't sit down and write an Oedipal story, you see what I mean? I'd write a story about a boy and his father that turned out, oddly enough, to be Oedipal, and not the other way around. I try and write, like most writers, as instinctively as possible. If I write about an old woman having sex with a young man, I wouldn't think about my mother. I'd think about these two characters, you know, and then later on, I'd look at it from a Freudian point of view, and see there was all this stuff in it, but I couldn't think about that when I was writing.

A lot of writers go out of their way to attack Freud. They seem to feel threatened by Freud; D. H. Lawrence, for instance, writes about very Oedipal themes, but is angry at Freud for…

… for having got there first. It's very annoying. Freud and creative writers had a very conflicted relationship. Freud was very jealous of what he called creative writers, and very envious of them, and artists on the other side have often been envious and threatened by Freud as well. It's quite an interesting relationship, both ways, actually. They are working on the same thing, which is getting inside the human mind, and inside the family, inside sexuality. Freud always said, rather patronizingly, that writers had got there before him.

Do you think of Freud's conception of the death drive as something that your characters might embody as well, not necessarily consciously? Someone like Jay [from Intimacy], for instance, may be searching for something beyond the pleasure principle.

I think every single writer would be fascinated by what is self-destructive in human life, by what you might call self-sabotage, and who that is on behalf of, let's say. So I would absolutely agree with that, because what's amazing about human life is how self-destructive people are. Their pleasures are not simple, and their sexuality is not simple. You might say: Why can't people just be happy sexually? Why are their lives so difficult? And a lot of the difficulty with their lives is not only economic or social, it's really coming from another part of themselves. It's not identified as a split, and as conflict. I think we're the centre of the human project, and I think every writer would be interested in that too.

Do you think there is a desire, related to the death drive, that has to do with sexuality and commodification? Your narrator in The Body talks about wanting to be turned into meat, or turned into pornography; is there maybe a narcissistic or masochistic desire to be objectified and commodified?

I think there's something very difficult about our pleasures, and we were talking about this earlier, in regard to drugs, that our pleasures are too much for us, and we have terrible complexes about being overwhelmed by our pleasures and locked in our pleasures, of losing our selves in our pleasures and so on. Therefore to convert them into difficulties is often more convenient than to consume them as pleasures. Think of turning alcohol into alcoholism, and so on.

Unlike a lot of writers who are labelled 'postcolonial' writers, you don't seem to see the word 'human' as a senseless generalization. Would you call yourself a humanist? A lot of people from non-Western backgrounds view humanism as a disguise for Western ideals that need to be interrogated, so they're reluctant to commit themselves to it. It has been Western thinkers, such as Marx and Freud, who have defined what humanism is.

I'm interested in the same stuff, broadly, as the men and women you would describe as humanists are interested in, the same stuff as say, Ibsen or Freud, Chekhov or Oscar Wilde, or whatever, in my own way. I'm still thinking in their terms, too, I'm in on their projects, even though it's much later. I certainly wouldn't compare myself to any of these writers, I'm saying this is where I consider myself to be coming from.

You're comfortable being viewed as a humanist, then?

Well, we're still working on the same problems: What are men and women doing?

Does the conception of hybridity disturb that idea of humanism for you? A lot of people have used that word to analyse your work, and it's very much part of the postcolonial vocabulary to be seen as creating something new that may push the boundaries of the human by crossing ethnic or racial lines.

Yeah, but it's a vague idea, because there's hybridity everywhere, there always has been. Look at a child with a mother and a father, and is composed, therefore, as Freud wrote, of at least two genders, and the pulling together of these genders into a sexuality and so on. And in fact these parents have come from different places psychologically, so there's a lot of hybridity going on all the time, if you think of hybridity as meaning the putting together of disparate things. People, when they talk about hybridity, are really talking about someone with an Indian mother and an English father, aren't they?

So it's everywhere we look?

It's so vague, isn't it? Somebody from West Germany and somebody from East Germany; at certain times, that would have been very different to negotiate for a child, for instance. But it's usually used in terms of black and white.

You seem to be saying that there's a limit to the utility of that term where your work is concerned, that your work is not necessarily privileged in its access to hybridity.

I don't mind if people use that term, but it's not something that I think much about myself, because it goes on all the time, in so many other places and ways. But I've no objections to what people say about my work.

Some of your stories such as 'The Penis', 'The Tale of the Turd' and 'The Flies' seem to use non-realistic imagery to suggest that people can be dehumanized or robbed of their individual identities by their bodies, or by the natural world. Is that a reasonable interpretation of those stories?

Yeah, well, I particularly enjoy writing those kinds of stories. Mostly I suppose I write a kind of realism. Did you mention *The Body*? *The Body* is a weird one as well, isn't it? I've always loved writers like Kafka, and other Eastern European writers, who use the fantastic. There's obviously a tradition in British writing like that, with writers like Robert Louis Stevenson, with Jekyll and Hyde, and Dorian Gray and so on, that certainly influenced me while I was doing *The Body*.

Do you think there's any conflict between a humanistic urge to understand ourselves through rational, realistic discourse and the fantastic surrealism of people like Kafka?

I don't really. I believe that both of them are symbol systems. So there may be, say, your waking life and your dreaming life, and both of these are parts of the self to be understood, and there may be many different methods of understanding them. So you might write a straight Oedipal drama or play, or you might do 'The Metamorphosis' etcetera. They're both ways of symbolizing human experience, so I don't see any conflict between them. The work is to find some accommodation for both these things.

So fiction is a genre that is big enough to span both sides, both realism and surrealism. There doesn't seem to be a sense in your work that one has to choose between them.

Well, because the two greatest British writers, Shakespeare and Dickens, it would be impossible to put them in either bag. Clearly, they both use the fantastic, and both use realism too. If you're a writer at full stretch, you use the fullest range of possible symbol systems to make any sense of what's going on.

I'm curious about this question in relation to Gabriel's Gift. *He [Gabriel] has this magical possibility of creating objects out of his imagination, out of art, but he doesn't seem to exploit that as fully as we might like to see him do so.*

He's going crazy. What I'm interested in is the difference between living in your mind or fantasy and the ability to create real objects that other people can use, the difference between dreaming and making a story or film, a work of art. What I'm interested in as a writer is how people convert fantasies, impulses, ideas, dreams, whatever, their internal world, into objects or culture for other people, and I think that is what's valuable about human life, and Gabriel is trying to move from one to the other, but it involves a lot of fantasy. There's a real connection there. It's the difference between pornography and being with a real other person.

Is there maybe an ethical message here?

It's not ethical, it's to do with narcissism, I guess it's to do with seeing outside of yourself into a common world, making shared objects, cultural objects.

One of the personages who presides over Gabriel's development in Gabriel's Gift *is Lester Jones, a fictionalized version of David Bowie. Bowie is somebody whose narcissism seems to have borne fruit, in the sense that he has created new personalities and new cultural objects for people to identify with. Do you see that sort of constant reinvention of the self as something that is part of your writing life?*

I guess I'm interested in identification, which is what Bowie both does and is capable of inspiring in other people. Freud talks a lot about this, in how we grow up identifying first with our fathers, then with our uncles, then with the wider family, and then with the wider world. Human development is really a sort of plagiarism. Influence is identification and plagiarism. Bowie is a good example of someone in the postwar period, when it seemed very dramatic and radical to steal a number of styles from somebody else.

Is there something about that which strikes you as typically postmodern? Is the postmodern a category you're interested in applying to your own work?

Well, I was interested in it as a child, as a young lad, because one day someone would come to school looking completely different, as does Charlie Hero in *The Buddha of Suburbia*. Karim is amazed by this; not only does he look totally different, but he's joined another sort of world. He's not just dyed his hair, he's somehow joined another time, identified with another group of people, become somebody else. It's not only a question of style; he's left one self behind, and Karim is very confused. The idea of becoming someone else, someone better, someone more sexualized, someone who has more pleasure, is very appealing to him.

You talk a little bit about Lacan in The Body; your narrator jokes that he can only understand Lacan when he's drunk, but it does seem like the Lacanian concept of the mirror phase is relevant to your work.

Well, our mirror was television. We were really the first generation to see images from all over the world all the time, and therefore images that you could identify with, and that you could use. Clearly there is a Lacanian aspect to it, but we had a multiplicity of images, a constant stream of images, running right into your house, hour after hour, and it had an effect on all of us, showing who was around you. If you grew up in the suburbs, you saw the same people every day, the same people wearing the same clothes over and over; it was a very narrow world. I mean, you might as well have been in an eighteenth-century village. And then suddenly, you saw the Vietnam war, you saw Jimi Hendrix, you saw the students, the whole thing. In my early work I was trying to write about the ones living in the small, narrow world of this kind of suburban village being confronted by this multiplicity, this incredible range of possible identifications.

Is there a way in which some of your writing is an attempt to recreate the conditions whereby we form our identities out of infancy? There are some mentions of Winnicott's 'transitional objects' in Intimacy (I think Jay is talking about skirts, at that point). A lot of fiction tends to dramatize early identity formation much later in life than it would normally occur. Did the profusion of images to which your generation was exposed delay the process of identity formation?

There aren't any formed identities, any finally formed identities. There isn't a day when you're there, when you're made. It keeps on going, you keep on engaging with your past in new ways all the time, over and over. Think of the way you think about your parents; I used to think there would be a day when I would have figured out my parents and could stop thinking about them, but it goes on and on and on. So I don't believe that there is a final resting place in terms of identity; it's a continuous process. I mean here I am, a man nearly fifty, and I'm thinking about how in the next twenty years I'm going to die, and who I'm going to identify with as an older man. I'm going to read and think and look at other old guys, and find an identity out of all these bits and pieces.

I'm wondering who you're looking towards now? What writers offer formative conceptions of what that last phase of life might look like?

It's very hard for me to say, now. Certainly I'm a big admirer of Roth. His last novel, *The Human Stain*, is certainly decent and extended and very fine indeed, his last four or five books are fantastic. That's one who comes to mind. There are numerous others. I mean, mostly, we have a picture of ageing from our parents, and how they age. Certainly, I'm not like my father, I'm not enough like him to be able to draw much on that for inspiration.

Do you think that your life as a writer will change over the next few years? Are you going to be able to choose what you work on, for your own personal development and curiosity, or is there a balance that has to be drawn between continuing to pay the bills as a writer and exploring what is of deepest interest to you?

Yes, I have to bear in mind both those things. I've got three children I've got to send to school and to college, and I want to do stuff, particularly as time runs out for me, that interests me. I like to do drama, and novels and fiction, and all the other stuff as well. And there is also the struggle of writing, which is important, when I am working on something that is difficult for me to do, and interesting and challenging and hard, and which I don't feel I've done before. I'm always looking for that.

7

OTHER WRITINGS

Although Kureishi has produced a considerable body of fiction, he is perhaps best known to the general public for his films, which have garnered a good deal of critical attention. Kureishi's work in these different genres is often deemed to be homogeneous; in her article 'The Politics of Intimacy in Hanif Kureishi's Films and Fiction', Annabel Cone writes: 'His writing … has a visual quality that transcends the separation between the written word and the filmed frame' (Cone 261). However, many of his screenplays, and many of the films made out of his work, tend to share some traits not necessarily equally prominent in his fiction. The first of these traits concerns an obvious visual contrast between public and private spaces; as Cone puts it: 'From his first film, *My Beautiful Laundrette*, to the novella *Intimacy* (1998), the need for love and intimacy plays out in an "indoors" completely turned away from … public spaces' (261). The juxtaposition Cone describes of desiring bodies with Kureishi's public London, a city that has become both 'austere' and 'bland', an 'alienating urban environment that has become completely devoid of romance' (Cone 261–2), is indeed a consistent, though not universal, feature of Kureishi's films. Two less obvious but occasionally related features of many of Kureishi's cinematic ventures are, as we shall see, a clear attribution of moral and psychological significance to the contrast between light and darkness, and a willingness to stretch the boundaries of realism in strategic ways.

Kureishi's first (and possibly still most famous) screenplay is *My Beautiful Laundrette* (released in 1985), for which he was nominated for an Academy Award. *Laundrette* centres on Omar, a young man of mixed Pakistani and English descent whose sick father and dead mother have left him feeling alone in the world. Omar's Westernized uncle Nasser takes him under his wing and offers him the chance to manage a laundrette; with some help from his formerly racist skinhead friend (now gay lover) Johnny and some drug money from his unscrupulous uncle Salim, Omar makes a success of it. *Laundrette* also features working-class racist thugs named Genghis and Moose; Nasser's mistress, a sexy Englishwoman named Rachel; Nasser's rebellious and sexually aggressive daughter Tania; and Nasser's much-put-upon and vengeful wife Bilquis. The film's politics are ambiguous: the capitalistic Nasser's tactics (evicting unprofitable tenants from his properties) are shown to be callous, though his overall view that immigrants must 'squeeze the tits of the system' – in other words, do whatever it takes, to make it in England – is plainly endorsed (*My Beautiful Laundrette* 17). Nasser's gambling addiction (a subtle extension of his economic ideas) ends up ruining him; still, his successful business ventures lay the groundwork for Omar's stylish laundrette and the much-needed racial harmony it promotes.

The film opens with a scene of eviction in which the chaos and mess of derelict public spaces intrudes on the precarious domestic peace of the squatters' rooms. Omar's own suburban home, where trams pass much too close for comfort and his drunken, damaged father lies about untidily in bed, is merely an extension of this urban disorder. The sanctity of private space is re-established in Nasser's luxurious home, though that too is symbolically destroyed by Nasser's profligacy and Bilquis's recriminations after his affair with Rachel becomes known. The only consistent respite from the glare and grime of public life is sexual love: the warm, intimate, nearly pink lighting in Nasser's office where he and Rachel first make love suggests that erotic enjoyment is the only real escape from a gloomy, crowded world. In a scene which underlines the precarious nature of this amorous escapism, Johnny and Omar kiss in a dim, rose-coloured alleyway before being interrupted by violent skinheads. After the two friends transform Churchill's, a dilapidated laundrette, into a shiny and inviting place, they also make love inside it, to underline its status as a special respite from the impersonal public world.

The film has a mild surrealistic tinge which centres on the magical space of the laundrette: mysterious bubbling sounds (the movie's theme music) suggest the irrepressible nature of Omar's ambitions, and sure enough we soon see a washer overflowing with impossible amounts of frothy foam. The laundrette's uncanny aura is enhanced by a man who continually chatters into the pay phone, apparently trying to salvage an endangered relationship. The strangeness of this leitmotif is enhanced by the bizarre things the man says; speaking about a child he hopes to have, he tells its reluctant mother, 'Of course I'll look after it. I'll come round every other night'. The supernatural quality of the laundrette is also linked to the effects of drugs; the place's new name is 'Powders', a reference to the cocaine stolen and sold by Omar to pay for renovations. The laundrette, as a respectable business, effectively 'launders' the ill-gotten money, a tribute to the power of capitalism to make crime respectable. Far from using anti-realism to indict capitalism, as some have claimed Kureishi does in his later films, *My Beautiful Laundrette* seems to be romanticizing the magical properties of money.

The magic of commerce is rivalled by another apparently supernatural force, however: the potions concocted by Bilquis to torment Rachel. These give Rachel a nasty rash, and apparently even begin to rearrange the furniture in Rachel's apartment. These effects suggest the persistent power of family life in British Asian culture, and discourage Rachel from continuing her liaison with Nasser. The final surrealist or quasi-magical scene in the film is perhaps a refutation of this suggestion of the family's persistence. In it, Nasser sees his daughter Tania waiting for a train on a platform (she is plainly running away from home). We see her standing still when two trains cross in front of her at top speed, cutting her off from view. When the trains have passed and the platform is visible again, Tania is gone. She has only been hidden for a matter of seconds, so she hasn't walked away, and since the trains did not stop, there is no way she could have boarded one. Her disappearance is thus a mysterious vanishing act which disturbs the already confused Nasser even more and is no doubt intended to show the unpredictable, fugitive nature of family relationships.

Kureishi's second film, *Sammy and Rosie Get Laid* (1987), was much less well-received than *Laundrette*, although it focuses on many of the same themes: interracial love affairs, politics, drugs and the economic troubles afflicting Britain in the 1980s. It depicts a London seething with racial tensions (brought on by police shootings of innocent minorities) and subversive sexual desires. The titular characters, married to each other, are both carrying on extramarital affairs as they watch London collapse into violence. The couple's mutual tolerance is strained, however, by the arrival of Sammy's father Rafi. Rafi's sinister past soon comes to light: as a powerful politician in his homeland, he repressed public protests and countenanced the torture of his opponents. As if to show that he no longer supports tyranny, Rafi storms out and joins a group of young squatters fighting for their rights against a property developer who plans to evict them from their shantytown. However, haunted by the ghost of a man he has had tortured and killed, Rafi ends up hanging himself in his son's flat, leaving Sammy and Rosie united in grief and shock.

The contrast in *Sammy and Rosie* between chaotic, near-apocalyptic public spaces and the fragile peace of hedonistic privacy is almost impossibly extreme. For instance, when the police invade the home of a black family, we hear a dog barking loudly outside the building, while inside the only sounds are chips frying quietly and a mournful trumpet playing. Rafi comments on the 'world war' going on in London's streets, and it is difficult not to conclude that the public world is indeed in a constant state of war. This conclusion, however, would be premature, since there are idyllic moments of public tranquillity and goodwill that emerge in the unlikeliest places, in part thanks to a group of buskers who create a carnivalesque spectacle wherever they go. Moreover, there are hints that the violence itself is a kind of performance: for instance, two men pose for photographs in front of some burning wreckage. Sammy's indifference to the mounting disorder around his home also contributes to this impression that the fires and protests are all for show: he continues to munch his hamburger as he watches the riot police and rock-throwing protestors confronting each other, and even enters the fray without so much as ruffling his hair.

Such moments have inspired some critics to group *Sammy and Rosie* with more obviously magicorealism films such as Oscar 'Zeta' Acosta's *Autobiography of a Brown Buffalo*, or Julie Dash's *Daughters of the Dust*. Frederick Luis Aldama argues that *Sammy and Rosie Get Laid* is a cinematic example of what he terms a 'magicorealist narrative' that depicts 'late-capitalist society … as being more and more unreal' (Aldama, *Postethnic Narrative Criticism* 42). In such a work, according to Aldama, 'the world … is a grand theatrical performance that covers over the estranging effect of exploitation and oppression by capitalism' (42). What Aldama calls 'magi-coreels' employ defamiliarizing, anti-realist strategies to 'expose and critique a globalizing late capitalism that turns real violence and oppression of the underclass worldwide into a spectacle' (42). In Aldama's view, Kureishi's films undermine the older 'visual narratives that systematically represent dark characters as primitive and white characters as civilized' (51). Thus Aldama remarks on the use of 'sepia-hued light' in Alice's flat, which signifies Alice's 'nostalgia ... for an idealized, colonial past' (59).

Aldama also notes that through 'subjective filtering shots ... hued lighting that paints him as radically innocent, close-ups, and camera angles that magnify physical presence', the film makes Danny (a Londoner of mixed racial background who befriends Rafi) its catalyst (58). In Aldama's view, Danny is a 'trickster/pícaro' who wanders through the world, and 'creates zones of cultural and racial contact as he collapses hierarchies of ... difference' (58). Aldama writes:

> As a trickster/pícaro, Danny ... inhabits the story-world both to disrupt the lives of the other characters controlled by monologic ideologies, and also as a reminder of the film's mixing of genres ... to open audience eyes to its own fictional representation of such characters and their own internalizing of ... restricting ideologies. ... Danny ... also functions like the trickster in traditional Sanskrit drama who is a self-reflexive device to exaggerate an 'emotional flavor' ... and thereby call attention to the story as a fictional construct. (Aldama, *Postethnic Narrative Criticism* 57)

Aldama's analysis of Danny is persuasive, though (like many of his insights) not clearly grounded in specifics. Still, viewers of the film will see an example of Danny's trickster/pícaro's border-crossing habits when he cuts the ribbon around the scene of a racialized police shooting, prompting the crowd to surge forward. Danny is also the film's conscience, wrestling with his conviction that non-violence is preferable to angry confrontations, but joining the fight to save a fellow Londoner from a policeman's clutches. Danny lives in a vacant lot under the freeway, where transients have created an autonomous society of sorts, complete with agriculture and printing equipment. This alternative urban space is preternaturally peaceful and harmonious; it is also the place where Rafi is finally confronted by the ghost. Unfortunately, this authentic-city-within-a-false-city is bulldozed by developers eager to cash in on the Thatcherite plan to gentrify London, and to make it more like the 'respectable' suburbs where Alice dwells in neo-colonial stagnation. Danny is forced to vanish along with the little urban utopia he embodies, and leaves Rafi to face his demons alone.

Aldama notes the film's 'parodic blend of the West's 'other forms' with Indian film genres' and claims that it works to 'denaturalize ... political forces that ... distract people from the harsh reality of ... oppression' (43). Aldama claims that *Sammy and Rosie*'s 'self-reflexivity' turns it into a positive, critical 'denaturalization' instead of being mere fantastic escapism or exploitation. After all, for Aldama, it is because magicoreels 'foreground their own artificiality' that they can function outside the norms of conventional mainstream films. *Sammy and Rosie* seems to fulfil Aldama's criteria for subversive self-reflexivity; he even argues that the inclusion of the 'Unreal City' passage from T. S. Eliot's 'The Waste Land' is another 'self-reflexive moment' that locates its own 'heteroglossic resistance within the realm of fiction and not ontological fact' (60). Nevertheless, Aldama's claim that 'the audience is never allowed to confuse its fiction with ontological fact' is undermined by his contention that the film is intended to 'open eyes to an Other London, populated with characters who daily struggle against a homophobic, racial – even a politically correct liberalist – apartheid' (52). How a pure 'fiction' can simultaneously be a trenchant critique of reality is hard to fathom, though plainly the film strives to seem to be both things at once.

Moreover, the one aspect of the film that in most people's minds would be its primary claim to 'magical realism' is not a straightforward critique of capitalism or Hollywood at all. Indeed, the scenes where Rafi is haunted are arguably less an attempt to defamiliarize or denature the physical world than they are a visual representation of an invisible, psychological phenomenon: guilt. As Aldama puts it, Rafi seems to be 'consumed by images of a magically appearing Hindu figure' who 'interacts with Rafi, placing his torture-headgear on Rafi's head ... then interrogating him' (61). Aldama notes that '[t]here is nothing to suggest that this is not real' within the discourse of the film's visual imagery itself: the formerly "spectral, unreal presence' is now 'tangible and real' (61). While it is possible to see the appearance of Rafi's ghost victim-turned-tormentor as an instance of magical realism, as Aldama suggests, it is presented as an outgrowth of Rafi's growing disenchantment with his once-beloved London and his withdrawal into solipsistic self-doubt. Although this ghost's appearance does superficially violate the laws of nature, superficially, it hardly enacts the broader critique of conventional Hollywood movies that Aldama claims as central to the film's anti-realist project. Indeed, in its reinscription of conventional ideas of moral retribution and supernatural justice (repressed memories of evils done will literally haunt an evil-doer, as in Dickens's *A Christmas Carol*) the film's ending seems to comfort its viewers with a familiar picture of psychological justice within a capitalist society.

London Kills Me (1991) was a critical and popular failure, despite its sympathetic portrayal of Clint, a charming and quixotic drug addict who embarks on a tortuous quest for a pair of shoes that will enable him to start a new life as a waiter. Clint's troubled past, which includes childhood sexual abuse and a murdered father, has plainly derailed his natural skills as a salesman and entrepreneur (talents he uses as a drug dealer and con man), and he has fallen in with a much less attractive figure, the businesslike Muffdiver. Clint devotedly pursues a junkie named Sylvie (who ends up with Muffdiver); steals shoes from various people, including his prospective employer; is beaten and stripped naked by sinister creditors; takes Muffdiver's drug money and gives it back; finds shelter in a luxurious squat; and brings his fellow drifters back to visit his mother's home in the countryside. Clint is obsessed with the need to kick drugs and escape his homeless limbo into respectable employment, a task he finally accomplishes thanks to a pair of stolen cowboy boots. Ironically, Kureishi's free-spirited men long for stable, monogamous relationships: Clint and Muffdiver vie for the fragile Sylvie's drug-addled affections. As with Rosie, Sylvie is unwilling to forgo any male attention, it would seem, though in the end she decides to jilt Muffdiver in order to stay in London with the newly employed Clint.

Despite the film's title, London is portrayed as a much friendlier, more harmonious place than in *Sammy and Rosie*. Moreover, the contrast between public and private spaces is minimized, since the story follows a group of homeless characters as they seek out places to squat, make love, and use or sell drugs. This has the effect of making London's streets seem more colourful and friendly than is usual in Kureishi's films, but it also diminishes the safety provided in supposedly private spaces: for instance, Clint is grabbed and beaten up at a party inside an apartment building. In a less disturbing vein, Bike is known for bringing his bicycle wherever he goes, including inside people's homes (Lily, Clint's mother, wishes Bike would 'wipe his tyres' the next time he visits). Some of the squatters evince a wish for a real home, but this goal is elusive and daunting. Moreover, home ownership seems to entail certain unpleasant emotional limitations: Lily admits that in order to restore her formerly 'derelict' house she has had to give it 'all [her] love and affection' to the apparent exclusion of Clint himself (who doesn't get along with his stepfather). It is thus unclear whether Clint's desire for a job is a rejection of the nomadic but emotionally generous squatter ethos celebrated by the film (as by *Sammy and Rosie*), or merely a wish to get out of the violent and unsavoury drug business.

The main characters of *London Kills Me* are compulsive, erratic and volatile, as in many of Kureishi's works, and these traits seem realistic, given their drug-oriented lives. Nonetheless, the film eschews realism in many respects: in one scene, Clint appears to ascend on white angelic wings past a window (he crashes through another window moments later). This oddly symbolic moment, however, is presented as the hallucination of a follower of Eastern mysticism whose guru holds chanting and dancing sessions in the flat beneath Clint's squat. Another pseudo-magical moment occurs when Clint's stepfather appears out of nowhere in an Elvis costume and is mistaken for 'Elvis Aaron Presley' himself by Tom-Tom, a strung-out white Rasta. The implication of these surreal moments seems merely to be that people's perceptions can be clouded or warped (for better or worse) by drugs or religion. The fact that the pill-peddling Muffdiver is also an amateur magician of sorts (his magic act lends an air of the carnivalesque to confrontations with the police as well as with big-league drug dealers) implies that drug-taking is as trivial as watching a magic show. Thus *London Kills Me* does not use magicorealism to make the political statements that Aldama reads into Kureishi's *Sammy and Rosie*; since the marginal characters are every bit as deluded, or 'boring' and 'stupid' (as Tom-Tom terms his fellow 'druggies') as those in mainstream society, they can offer no serious critiques of its injustices, unlike in *Sammy and Rosie*.

The Mother (released in 2003) follows May, an older woman who travels to London with her ailing husband to visit her two adult children, Robbie and Paula. May's husband soon dies, leaving her to ponder her fate. Invited to stay in London by Robbie (despite his wife's resentment), May babysits for Paula, a single mother and failed writer. May sleeps in the same bed as her grandson, Jack (played alternately by Kureishi's twin sons Sachin and Carlo), and hears Paula first making love and then fighting with her married handyman, Darren. When May tries to comfort Paula, her daughter blames May for not praising her enough as a child and asks her to talk to Darren on her behalf. May and Darren hit it off, and begin a tender liaison which rejuvenates May, whose feelings for Darren are a mixture of erotic and maternal ones; she repeatedly prepares meals for him and then propositions him sexually (he underlines these incestuous overtones by calling her 'Mother').

The self-absorbed Paula remains oblivious to this affair until she discovers some of May's lewd sketches of Darren. After May is finally cornered and bedded by the repulsive Bruce, whom Paula has selected as a more age-appropriate would-be boyfriend, Paula announces that Darren has at last agreed to leave his wife and move in with her. To make matters worse, Robbie takes his career and marital frustrations out on May and Darren, leading a cocaine-fuelled Darren to explode at May. Paula stops May from committing suicide, but hits her mother, who meekly accepts the blow as her signal that she must leave London. In a final life-affirming gesture, however, May decides to take a solitary version of the trip abroad that she and Darren had discussed taking together.

The film seems like a tribute to a vanishing traditional vision of femininity and family life: the patient and soft-spoken May seems more admirable than the distracted, fickle and insecure Paula. Furthermore, May's liaison with Darren is initiated through her domestic virtues: she ceremoniously prepares tea for him, and serves it to him while asking him indirect but personal questions, and scrubs the floor after having sex with him. Nevertheless, Kureishi encodes some characteristic transgressive or subversive touches into *The Mother* which make the central story line (the love affair between Darren and the much older May) seem less implausible. For instance, there is a strong homoerotic camaraderie between Darren and May's son, Robbie; they murmur with mock hostility, whisper, laugh and drink together. Darren is very upset when he learns that Robbie plans to sell the house when he's done fixing it up; he evidently takes this as a personal betrayal of sorts, and breaks some of the windows he has carefully installed. In another telling moment, Darren admits that he's just 'making [his life] up' as he goes along, thus identifying himself with an authorial figure whose improvisational skills are a bit like Kureishi's own talent for the unexpected. Darren's impulsiveness, fear of commitment, pathological drug-taking and insouciant air also brand him as the film's closest representative of Kureishi himself.

Images of light and dark dominate *The Mother*'s visual effects; May's home in the suburbs, which is darkened, and full of shadows, and the creepy Bruce's flat is sombre and full of dark furniture; when he and May have sex, their faces and bodies are full of shadows. May's fruitless conversations with the neurotic Paula also take place in dark rooms. There is a stark contrast between these places and Robbie's London home, which is painted white, well-lit and full of large windows. Indeed, when May first enters Robbie's domicile, she exclaims, 'It's like Buckingham Palace'. Robbie's urban home also features an amazingly spacious back yard, where (incongruously enough) no city sounds are audible. This soothing green space is closely associated with Darren, a workman who is constructing a new sunroom in the back area of the house. Darren's respectful, attentive manner represents a sharp contrast to the callousness of the harried Robbie, his preoccupied wife, and their obnoxious children, whose loud conversations dominate the central domestic spaces when they're home.

Windows are central to the film's symbolic imagery as well; for instance, May's room in her son's house has a single window with a white drape over it that she stares at obsessively, as if awaiting some mystical awakening. This eventually comes, symbolically at least: when Darren strokes her genitalia, we see that the window has been opened and the curtain blows in a faint breeze. In one scene May sits in the dim light cast by a window, whose faint vertical lines seem to trap her like bars in a cage. May also sees Paula and Darren kissing through a window, and sees her own distorted image in a darkened window that suggests her inability to see or present herself as she truly is. Moreover, May sits in front of a (now bar-less) window as she contemplates killing herself with a kitchen knife (she is interrupted by the peevish Paula). Finally, we watch May from inside her own living room window as she walks off into bright daylight on her way out of the country for the long-anticipated trip.

Such details tend to remove the hard edge of realism from *The Mother*'s presentation of unconventional romance. The film also skirts the edges of realism in more subtle ways; despite much play with mobile phones (which constantly interrupt personal exchanges), Robbie fails to phone ahead to inform his wife of May's arrival back at their home. There is also an intriguing scene where we see Robbie's family from May's point of view as she leaves their home for the last time; we observe their false friendliness and embarrassed, apologetic expressions through her eyes, a somewhat heavy-handed trick that vindicates her decision to sever relations with them, even if that means giving up on her love for Darren. There are also self-reflexive hints of Kureishi's own disruptive presence at the edges of the narrative: for instance, when Robbie sees the revealing erotic drawings May has made of Darren, he complains 'I feel as if I've just had a very hot curry', an apparent reference to Kureishi's own South Asian heritage which links English encounters with cultural otherness to shock, pain or nausea which may in fact be rather salutary, for arrogant urbanites like Robbie (Robbie is played by Steven Mackintosh, the same actor who was Charlie Kay in the BBC's *Buddha* and Muffdiver in *London Kills Me*, and who invests Robbie with a brittle arrogance familiar to viewers of Kureishi's films.

An occasional deliberate mismatching of picture and sound undermines the conventions of realism as well; in a scene where May's resentful coldness towards her increasingly incapacitated husband is clearly supposed to be emphasized, she tells him that he'll have to go to the bathroom by himself: it is 'one thing [she] can't do for [him]'. When he collapses on his solitary errand, Robbie's cry of 'Mother!' rings out as May is pictured sitting impassively, later on, contemplating her dying husband. This overlap of one scene's sounds onto a later scene's image suggests May's fundamental lack of responsiveness to the urgency of the present moment, and implies that she lives largely in the past. Another similar overlapping moment occurs later in the film, albeit to very different effect. When Robbie brings May back home to live with them, Robbie's wife asks him, 'What the fuck are you playing at?' as he and his mother are pictured silently staring at her illuminated window. This rude intrusion on their private (albeit awkward) moment implies that May has become a passive victim of the battles between Robbie and his wife.

Because of their success, Kureishi's fictional narratives have been used as the basis for a number of films, many of them controversial. The BBC adaptation of *The Buddha of Suburbia*, though critically acclaimed, was seen as more provocative than the novel itself. In addition to the numerous sex scenes (which caused a stir in the press, as well as some predictable outrage from conservative viewers) the filmed scenes between Eva and Karim are erotically charged; the one in which Eva reads to Karim in his bath is a far cry from the innocent baths of childhood suggested in the novel, and becomes literally steamy. Kureishi himself lauded the faithfulness, realism and attention to detail of the adaptation, and reacted angrily to possible cuts in the series. Nevertheless, many of the minor characters in the film lose some of their glamour and humour onscreen without Karim's ironic and affectionate narration to frame them. For instance, Jamila is shown as a bookishly intense girl with large, unattractive glasses, Charlie is first a cynical, one-dimensional David Bowie clone, then a Johnny Rotten imitator, and Terry loses all his Welsh charm and intellectual power to become a pale, balding whippet-like man with little to say. Shadwell is a purely ridiculous figure, while Pyke is severe and sinister. For his part, Haroon spends a good deal of time slapping or patting his stomach, while Changez is frequently shown eating with his mouth open, talking with food in his mouth, and otherwise drawing attention to his wet lips and bulging cheeks: both become symbols of the grotesquely greedy, pleasure-seeking self that Karim seeks to indulge.

In his review of the BBC's *Buddha*, James Wolcott sees hints that 'AIDS waits in the wings' after all the 'swinging' is finished, and notes that '[t]he filmmakers know that the party will soon be over, even if the characters don't. They've factored in their own sense of futility' (Wolcott 75). Wolcott's perception is apt; the background images, music and sounds in the filmed version tell us a good deal that the novel leaves unsaid. The series begins with daytime views of a grimy, rain-soaked suburb seen from the train. The Amirs' house is very much of a piece with this unpromising setting: it is cluttered, drab and full of earth-toned seventies decorations. The

Kays' home is first seen by night, and its spacious, light interiors look glamorous and elegant by comparison. This contrast sets up the basic opposition between the Amirs' status as lower-middle-class and the Kays as aristocratic and socially at ease. Eleanor's clean, white-painted flat is very much the sort of upper-class place Eva Kay has striven to create, and we see why Karim is so attracted to her.

If private spaces in the BBC's *Buddha* reek of class awareness and fixed identities, public spaces in the film seem at first to offer only limited possibilities of connection or social awareness: when Karim and Haroon have an emotional argument on the pavement, passers-by studiously ignore them and scarcely turn a hair. The punk movement, however, changes all this: punk rockers parade around the streets with open defiance and a lack of inhibition. The dichotomy between public and private spaces is also dispelled to some degree when Karim and Helen make love in an open shelter, saying, 'This is our park too'. This scene suggests that sexuality could open up new spaces for mass consciousness to change, but punk is portrayed as a more immediate and compelling social force than sexual liberation.

The series presents an unresolved conflict between the racial tensions present everywhere in public spaces (as in *Sammy and Rosie*) and Karim's refusal to participate in the usual form of identity politics. Even though posters from the National Front scream 'White Unite' right next to signs for Rock Against Racism in a colourful local market, Karim sidesteps the issue. As he tells Pyke, 'I'm not sure I know anyone who's black' and he refuses to put himself in that category, exclaiming 'I'm beige'. Pink Floyd's 'Us and Them' (with its undertones of racial tension) plays just after Karim witnesses Haroon's transgressive sexual encounter with Eva in the garden, and a racist poster provides the backdrop for Changez's descriptions of life on the Commune. The complex relationship between right-wing politics (which are often tinged with racism, in Kureishi's view) and Karim's own struggle for personal freedom is suggested by the fact that Eva (a liberating influence on Karim) is portrayed as more explicitly right-wing throughout the film; for instance, after Karim calls Thatcher 'suburban', Eva claims that 'we live in a suburban country', as if the upcoming Tory triumph in the election were a natural consequence of Britain's essential identity.

The rise of Thatcherism is, however, counterbalanced by the punk movement, and indeed the series suggests that the way punk's violent, democratic form of theatricality spills offstage and into everyday life appeals strongly to Kureishi. Punk's deliberate artificiality also seems to corroborate his view that all identity is a construction of sorts. Charlie's appropriation of punk as a purely public identity (he jumps into a moving car and vanishes from Karim's sight) leads him to New York, where we see him walking with Karim though streets lined with fashionable shops as well as uncollected garbage. Kureishi's point about the double nature of the public world could scarcely be more obvious: today's trends are the garbage of tomorrow, and Charlie's fame has made him toxic and self-destructive. There are more playful social commentaries as well; for instance, Bowie's 'Changes' punningly plays just prior to the distinctly non-rebellious Changez's arrival on the scene.

The film version of *My Son the Fanatic* also departs from its story in a number of significant ways: Parvez and Bettina are encouraged to become romantically involved by a German tourist, who opines that 'respect is no substitute for pleasure', and goads Parvez, whom he calls 'little man', to follow his hedonistic urges. In one scene, Parvez is taunted by a foul-mouthed racist comedian, who pretends to mistake him for Salman Rushdie and offers to shoot him on the spot. Parvez and his friend Fizzy have a falling-out in Fizzy's successful restaurant, as if to suggest that Parvez is unable to stomach his friend's assimilation by Western commercialism. The climax of the film occurs when Islamic protestors (with Parvez's son Farid among them) firebomb prostitutes' houses and beat some of them up, including Bettina. Parvez eventually takes action, rescues Bettina, kicks the German out of his cab to make room for his son, and carts Farid off. This flurry of positive-seeming action is only slightly offset by Farid's cutting question, voiced after Parvez has struck him: 'Who's a fanatic now?'. In the film's denouement, we are tempted to side much more squarely with Parvez than in the story, and to see his act of violence as relatively benign, compared to the firebombings. In that respect, the irony that governs the story's last line is largely lost, and the film seems to be more of an exposé of Muslim intransigence than an indictment of Parvez's hypocrisy.

Still, the film version of Parvez is not wholly admirable; indeed, at first he seems a grotesque caricature of an obsequious immigrant: he drops articles left and right, assures Mr. and Mrs

Fingerhut (the parents of his son's fiancée) that the photographs he takes of them are 'for private use exclusively', and makes a show of his son's professional ambitions. Aside from this opening scene, however, the mood and tone of *My Son the Fanatic* are sombre. Most of the action takes place at night, when Parvez drives prostitutes from one customer to another, and we become accustomed to seeing urban England as a sort of underworld filled with shadows and lurid neon lights. The theme of light and darkness is emphasized when a crude comedian tells Parvez that 'if you fuckers all left town on the same day, we'd have two hours extra bleeding daylight'. This racist remark suggests once more how marginal Parvez's status in England really is: not only is he still made fun of because of his darker skin, but he is also symbolically scapegoated for the depraved goings-on of English night life (ironically, Farid echoes this criticism of his father as well). The film reinscribes this binary opposition between light and darkness in a number of ways; for instance, Parvez tries to fix the light on top of his taxi, a clear signal of his attempt to maintain his own moral awareness in an immoral world, but the bulb explodes and dies, as if to show that any attempt at moral clarity is doomed.

The final scene of the film offers some hope, however, if we keep this contrast between light and darkness in mind. Having slept with Bettina and rescued her from Farid, Parvez returns to his darkened house, from which his wife and son have both departed, and systematically turns all the lights on. He drinks whisky and listens to jazz, defiantly asserting his Westernized tastes, and lies down in contented, well-lit exhaustion. The implication is clear: having finally dispensed with the hypocrisy of his loveless family life, forged a lasting emotional tie to a younger woman, and alienated his hostile son, Parvez can relax, be himself and make his world a brighter, better place. The presence of his wife and son have forced him to live in the dark, we may infer, and their exit allows him to begin to live a more enlightened, authentic life. Whether this compensates for what he has lost is difficult to say, but given the film's thematic similarity with other Kureishian tales of doomed marriages, we must be tempted to see Parvez's escape from his family (or its escape from him) as liberating and overdue. Such complexities of characterization are absent from Kureishi's original story.

Patrice Chéreau's filmed version of *Intimacy* departs so greatly from the plot of Kureishi's novella as to seem like a collage of various Kureishi tales. In describing his collaboration with Patrice Chéreau on the film, Kureishi remembers that they decided that the novella was 'too internal, and, probably, too dark, to make a film' and notes that 'Some of the material from ... "Strangers When We Meet" went into the film; parts of "In a Blue Time" were utilized, and, possibly, ideas from other stories' (*Dreaming* 228). The main character is still called Jay, but like the nameless protagonist from 'Nightlight' he meets a woman for sex once a week, and, as in 'Strangers When We Meet', his lover turns out to be a married actress performing in a pub.

The film gained notoriety for its unglamorous sex scenes between actors Mark Rylance and Kerry Fox, both of whom have earned critical acclaim for their performances. Kureishi reports that he and Chéreau agreed that the sex scenes in the film would not be 'sanitized' since '[t]he point is to look at how difficult sex is, how terrifying' (*Dreaming* 230). The writhings on the floor of Jay's squalid apartment seem more awkward than explicit, however, and suggest the workings of a morbid fantasy. Indeed, at one point Jay leaves Claire lying on the floor naked and sits watching her, very much in the pensive attitude of a patient voyeur. The lack of realism in their relationship makes his quest to understand her seem like an attempt to bridge the gap between fantasy and reality; however, after he glimpses Claire's career as an actress, Jay begins to question the truth of his own experiences. His doubt seems justified: he waits for her beyond their usual time at their next assignation, lying on the floor and clutching himself.

Claire's abandonment of Jay underscores the fact that their situation is in many ways a reversal of a more usual extramarital affair, in which a married man has a 'kept woman' as his mistress. Although Claire does not pay Jay, she appears to be using him, rather than the other way around. At any rate, Jay takes no responsibility for his part in instigating their trysts, claiming that he has never 'asked anything' of Claire, and lamenting that 'it really fucks me up'. Jay seems to resent his position and admits to her that the idea of her being intimate with her husband Andy 'tears him apart'. He asks her to 'stay' with him, but she refuses, tearfully, telling Jay that she has not left Andy. When Jay criticizes her (he clearly envies her marriage and acting ambitions) she tells him bitterly, 'I didn't picture you like this'. We suspect that she too has been in thrall to an imaginary lover who bears little resemblance to the real Jay.

The focus of the film eventually shifts from Jay to Claire, and we see that her apparent motives are as humdrum as his (she has a dull husband and is frustrated in her career). No deeper feelings emerge until Claire breaks down and weeps with remorse after insulting her acting students and telling them that their love scene isn't working. Her overreaction suggests that she is facing her private doubts about her own affair and is recognizing that the part she has been playing with Jay is false. In trying to explain what she wants from her students, she uses her own situation (perhaps unconsciously) as a measure of sexual passion: 'what you're supposed to be doing is to make Betty gather up all her things, find an excuse to go out, and cross the whole of London to come and see you'. She is obviously using her students (unsuccessfully) to try to understand her own sordid affair, and doesn't much like what she sees.

The film is full of incidental touches that signal Kureishi and Chéreau's wish to convey anger and sadness; some menacing strains from The Clash's 'London Calling' play as Claire enters Jay's apartment at the start of the movie. As if endorsing this punk-inspired pugnacious spirit, Jay shouts angrily at a bus on his way to work, calling the driver a 'cunt' and when he arrives he immediately berates his bosses and insults his co-workers, calling them 'assholes'. His anger, however, is mawkishly dissolved by the memory of his cherubic children in the bath at home, and this rapid mood swing sets the tone for the film's nearly schizoid oscillation between urgent, manic energy and depressed torpor. Kureishi himself sees the film's music-video-like quick cutting and loud soundtrack as emblematic both of 'the force, speed and impersonality of London today' and of 'the wild fury of Jay's mind' (*Dreaming* 232). In that respect, the film is plainly a faithful reflection of Kureishi's wish to capture a private emotional truth rather than striving for superficial visual or social realism.

The visual appearance of the film supports this idea; *Intimacy* begins with lingering shots of naked, sleeping bodies, as if to suggest that the film itself is about (or even set in) the unconscious, or the Freudian id. Nothing in the film is ever completely dark or light, which also suggests a kind of in-between, semi-conscious state. Jay's angry, restless demeanour (as well as the scar on his forehead) imply that he symbolizes a wounded, vulnerable aspect of the self, but perhaps the most obvious human representative of the id is Jay's friend Victor. A divorced drug addict who speaks with uniformly feverish and irritable passion, Victor claims that he and Jay have always been 'in thrall to our desires', though his pinched, balding, middle-aged demeanour makes him slightly ridiculous as a representative of unrestrained libidinal urges. Victor's scenes with Jay are filled with resentful, bitter passion, and he is predictably jealous of Jay's trysts with Claire; indeed, it is difficult to say whether he resents his friend's greater sexual success or his loss of Jay as a potential lover. The friends seem oddly symbiotic in many ways; during one scene, they speak the same words simultaneously. In one particularly grey and dismal scene in a drug den, Jay kicks Victor and shouts, 'Take a look at yourself!', though their interdependent relationship suggests that Jay is really seeing himself portrayed in Victor's plight as well as in the grim, selfish, mistrustful faces around him.

Like many of Kureishi's films, *Intimacy* highlights the difference between public spaces, where Jay and Claire chase each other through traffic with hopeless anxiety and try unsuccessfully to hold normal conversations, and private spaces, where their hidden, unspeakable desires are unleashed. Their final encounter makes this contrast especially poignant: the sounds of dogs and cars intrude on their lovemaking, and when Claire leaves, she gets on a bus which merges into traffic that gets louder and louder, as if to suggest that the city which had miraculously permitted Jay to enjoy such anonymous intimacy to take place has repossessed her at last. Perhaps because of the ever-present threat or promise of the intrusive city around them, the sex scenes have a surreal quality about them, with the actors groping each other in a tense, wordless desperation relieved only by non-stop heavy breathing, a sexual cliché which seems so overt as to suggest a kind of deliberately inarticulate speech. The lovers' bodies are also illuminated against a largely dark, grey, ill-defined background, as if the film were acknowledging that their sexual acts are a spectacle, even for the participants.

Nevertheless, Jay and Claire seem incapable of seeing the squalor of their own behaviour; as Jay concedes, 'when you're caught in the middle, you can't see anything.' Tellingly, Jay's visual memories of his children are shown unfolding in slow motion, suggesting a traumatic or obsessive flashback. The haunting quality of these images is perhaps explained by his wife Susan's accusatory question to him: 'You do love [the children], don't you?'. Jay's angst implies that his answer is not exactly the resounding or unambiguous affirmative we might expect. The film's psychologically tinged surrealism also spills over into Claire's friendship with her student and confidante Betty, a bond which mirrors Jay's co-dependent relationship with Victor. Betty describes her feeling of having already died, and suggests that Claire too is emotionally dead (a description which might fit many of Kureishi's latter-day characters). Claire also introduces a self-consciousness into her conversations with her husband, which suggests her alienation from her situation: 'Claire's telling Andy she's going to stay with him'. Andy himself, a jowly, bucktoothed grotesque reminiscent of Changez in *The Buddha*, seems so jovial and naïve as to evoke incredulity.

In addition to his films, Kureishi has also written a number of plays, and was voted Most Promising Playwright of the Year by the London Theatre Critics in 1981. His early plays have not met with broad popular success, however, and remain relatively obscure. His first important play, *The King and Me* (performed in 1980), paints a bleak picture of a married couple obsessed with Elvis Presley. Bill, the husband, enters Elvis look-alike contests, where he is tripped up by banal trivia questions, while Marie, his wife, waits anxiously at home, hoping he can win a trip to Memphis so they can temporarily escape their dreary lives. The play ends with a sense of melancholy and despair; Bill wants a 'fresh start' but feels 'like an old man' (*Plays One* 27–8) after giving up his pop-culture-inspired dreams.

Outskirts (performed in 1981) centres on two male friends, Bob and Del, whose relationship is shown developing over a period of twelve years. They seem merely mischievous at first, but we soon see that together they have engaged in racist beatings. Over the years, however, they have reacted very differently to their crimes, with Bob remaining stuck in adolescent disaffection and indolence (despite his marriage to Maureen), and Del moving on to become a successful teacher. We learn that Bob has even joined a xenophobic group, as if to justify his youthful hate crimes. The play paints a surprisingly intimate and understanding picture of the reasons for Bob's deviant behaviour. Much of the play is taken up with

Beckettian dialogue that suggests the hopeless tedium of Bob's life with his domineering, capricious but affectionate mother, who is ultimately blamed for Bob's inability to grow up.

Borderline (performed in 1981) deals with two secret lovers, Haroon and Amina, who are caught up in the racial tensions of their working-class neighbourhood. Haroon, an aspiring writer, plans to leave to pursue his education, though he is pressured by Anwar, a local activist, to join in various political protests before he goes. Haroon throws a chair through the window of his father's restaurant (on the grounds that his father disapproves of anti-racist agitation), but in the end, he decides his personal quest for racial justice and revenge requires education. In the meantime, Amina's father Amjad has decided that she must marry Farouk, but Amjad's eventual death from heart disease spares her. The climax of the play occurs when a fascist meeting is scheduled in a nearby church and Amina, her friend Yasmin, and Anwar prepare grimly for a violent protest. Haroon, having made his self-consciously 'Oedipal' statement against his father (*Plays One* 143), leaves his friends to their struggles, much like Karim in *Buddha*.

Birds of Passage (performed in 1983), features a representation of suburban life that also prefigures *Buddha* in many respects: a man named Ted (a former working-class racist turned owner of a central heating firm), teams up with a recently wealthy immigrant student named Asif to renovate a vacant house. The play also contains a married middle-aged woman named Eva, but here she is Ted's estranged wife and does not emerge as an independent figure. Most of the play concerns the family's decline, which symbolizes the death of the dream of a classless suburban lifestyle. The father, David, accepts a voluntary redundancy package, while the daughter, Stella, works as a prostitute, and the disaffected, unemployed son Paul engages in rancorous and ineffectual leftist political activity on the local estates. The play's conclusion, with its unexpected convergence of capitalist xenophobia and immigrant money, suggests that the liberal middle class no longer has any real role to play in resolving Britain's social and economic difficulties.

A much more recent play, *Sleep With Me* (performed in 1999), features one of Kureishi's most disagreeable adulterous authors: the rich and successful Stephen, husband to Julia, who produces such hedonistic would-be profundities as 'There are some fucks for which a man would watch his wife and children drown in a freezing sea' (*Sleep With Me* 31). Stephen decides to leave his wife Julia for Anna, but his self-indulgence in romantic affairs is portrayed as only a more extreme and honest version of an apparently universal need for extramarital dalliances; most of the other characters in the play are also either involved in adultery or recovering from it. For instance, the recently divorced Charles touts the virtues of rebelling against all that is 'dead' in one's life, meaning primarily marriage (*Sleep With Me* 17). Another couple, Barry and Sophie, are on equally thin marital ice: Barry is interested in Lorraine (as is Charles), while Sophie is mulling over an offer to go to America and work with Russell, a prominent filmmaker and womanizer. Stephen gradually loses his witty poise as his hopes of winning Anna recede, but he decides to leave Julia anyway. She hits him, and he must find solace in his mildly homoerotic professional relationship with Charles, whose pledge to work closely with him on his film partly compensates for Julia's refusal to allow Stephen to see his children. The play ends on a note of irony: the abandoned Julia croons to her youngest child about how much she and Stephen love him, as if all the vicissitudes of adult relationships in the play have been irrelevant distractions from what really matters: parental love.

Kureishi is also a prolific writer of essays and journalistic articles, many of which have been collected into books. His most famous early essay, 'The Rainbow Sign' (1986), traces his personal history as a child of a mixed-race family against the contrasting backgrounds of racial tension and social unrest in Britain during the 1960s and of the lives of his Westernized Pakistani relatives. It ends with an examination of the current state of race relations in Britain in the 1980s and a critique of the Labour Party's failure to address racism among its constituents. The rest of the essays collected in *My Beautiful Laundrette and Other Writings* (1996) are slighter and more impressionistic: 'Eight Arms to Hold You' describes Kureishi's fascination with The Beatles as a symbol of personal fulfilment through unfettered creativity; 'Bradford' analyses the racial and religious tensions in Bradford between Muslims of Asian origin and increasingly xenophobic Caucasians (represented by Ray Honeyford, a working-class educator who published racially charged criticisms of the influence of Asians in the community); 'Wild Women, Wild Men' follows the real-life adventures of two Asian strippers who entertain Asian men, many of them practising Muslims; 'Finishing the Job' recounts Kureishi's experiences as a visitor to the Conservative Party's annual conference in Brighton, where he encounters overtly racist and homophobic attitudes among the Thatcher-worshipping participants.

A more recent collection, *Dreaming and Scheming* (2002), includes introductions to the films *My Beautiful Laundrette, London Kills Me* and *My Son the Fanatic* (discussed earlier in this chapter), and three other accounts of his experiences in the film industry. The longest of these three essays, 'Some Time with Stephen: A Diary', is a journal of his involvement with Stephen Frears during the planning and production of *Sammy and Rosie Get Laid*. The journal records many disputes and changes of direction in the process of making the film (for instance, Rafi's suicide was not part of the first draft sent to Frears), as well as various personal episodes, including abusive phone calls from Kureishi's aunt complaining about *Laundrette*'s portrayal of Asians. Kureishi also divulges how important the 'Oedipal relationship' between Rafi and Sammy is to the film's emotional impact (155). Additionally, it recounts Kureishi's meetings with celebrities including Philip Roth, Shashi Kapoor, Claire Bloom, David Byrne and Roland Gift. Kureishi also mentions the resentment of a former girlfriend who feels that Kureishi has betrayed her by representing their relationship. The piece ends with a juxtaposition of the final stages of filmmaking with the Tory victory in the 1987 election; Kureishi claims that the 'anger and despair' over the results have 'gone straight into the film, giving it a hard political edge' (*Dreaming* 197).

The next noteworthy piece in *Dreaming and Scheming*, entitled 'The Boy in the Bedroom', is a brief narrative about the production of the BBC's version of *Buddha*, explaining Kureishi's decision to write the screen adaptation of the novel. It also tells of Kureishi's medical troubles, his excessive use of painkilling drugs, and his collaboration with David Bowie, a highlight of Kureishi's career. 'Filming *Intimacy*' explores Kureishi's contentious partnership with the filmmaker Patrice Chéreau and ends with a statement of Kureishi's acceptance of Chéreau's creative control over the film. The final important essay in the book, 'Dreaming and Scheming', is a frank exposition of Kureishi's own confessed shortcomings as a writer and teacher of writing. Here he opines that 'originality' often occurs when a writer 'distorts or uses someone else's work' (*Dreaming* 247) and also strikes some remarkably conservative poses, lamenting his students' lack of interest in reading canonical texts, advocating Freudian ideas about the virtue of self-knowledge and decrying the corrupting influence of the contemporary literary marketplace.

Kureishi's most recent book, *My Ear at His Heart*, is a partial biography of his father, Rafiushan Kureishi, and an account of his father's obsessive literary strivings and endless setbacks. Kureishi's own later successes as a writer did not sit well with his father, as the book makes plain, and there was tension between the two men until Rafiushan's death. *My Ear* begins with Kureishi's discovery of his father's semi-autobiographical novel *An Indian Adolescence*, and traces Kureishi's feelings as he reads his father's uneven but often flamboyant and humorous tales of growing up in India. The book includes descriptions of and passages from Rafiushan's other unpublished writings, as well as a refreshingly tender look at Rafiushan's central role in Kureishi's childhood. It also follows Kureishi's own early career as a voracious reader, music lover, aspiring writer, drug user, and, finally, successful author. The book discusses Kureishi's discovery of Freudian ideas (the Oedipus complex being the most prominent one) and ends with a moving meditation on Kureishi's intellectual and emotional debt to his father. There is a strong sense that the book is an attempt to displace the burden of guilt Kureishi has carried for many years, by virtue of having succeeded where his father had failed.

8

CRITICAL RECEPTION

Although Kureishi remains a consistently provocative and controversial writer, Susie Thomas's recent book *Hanif Kureishi: A Reader's Guide to Essential Criticism* (Palgrave Macmillan 2005), which offers a comprehensive account of the criticism of Kureishi's plays, films and fiction, makes it plain that academic criticism of Kureishi's fiction has concentrated primarily on his first two novels. Thomas's book also shows clearly that reactions to Kureishi's work have grown increasingly evaluative (and largely hostile) as he has moved decisively away from the racially specific, international issues that are a central feature in postcolonial writing.

In an influential essay entitled 'Herald of Hybridity', Berthold Schoene has lauded *The Buddha of Suburbia* (and *The Black Album*, to a lesser extent) for its destabilization of rigid conceptions of personal and racial identity, and has grouped Kureishi with the 'hybrid' school of British or Britain-based writers whose work has become part of the postcolonial canon, including Salman Rushdie, Caryl Phillips, Zadie Smith, and others. Schoene argues that Kureishi's 'hybrid' characters are 'a radically deconstructive presence in a world obsessed with clear cut definitions of ... identity' (Schoene 117). Schoene's argument sometimes seems contradictory, as when he first claims that 'what Kureishi exposes ... is the contrived nature of concepts of ethnicity which accentuate difference while eradicating all traces of potential sameness' (Schoene 121) and then later cites Kureishi's 'unequivocal' conviction that 'Everybody is entitled to their own singular cultural identity' (Schoene 123). Schoene's own celebration of the novel's liberating comedy is heavily inflected with an awareness of what he deems the peculiar position of the English middle classes, who, according to him, 'find themselves demoted from the cultural centrality of colonial civil stations to the politically inconsequential realm of post-imperial suburbia, are presented as especially suffering from severe cultural dislocation' (Schoene 112). In Schoene's eyes, 'The exoticism of Indianness [seems] to be able to fill the gaping void at the disheartened core of middle-class suburban Englishness' (Schoene 113–14). Bart Moore-Gilbert disputes Schoene's optimistic reading of this cultural exchange, noting the ' "centre's" selective appropriation of alien cultures ... not as a symptom of "lack" but of a confidently enduring neo-colonial mentality' (*Hanif Kureishi* 206).

Many have reacted in the same way as Schoene, reading Kureishi through 'hybridity' and other key terms of postcolonial theory, yet there are some dissenting voices in this chorus. For instance, Judith Misrahi-Barak claims: 'Kureishi is not quite part of the post-colonial crowd: he was not born in a former British colony, he did not exile himself like many first-generation writers, he does not speak the mother tongue of his family' (Misrahi-Barak 37). Furthermore, in an interview with Colin MacCabe, Kureishi himself questions the very idea of 'postcolonialism' and muses, 'it seems to me that colonialism hasn't come to an end .... Colonialism has entered our heads' (MacCabe 45). As this remark attests, Kureishi himself resists his automatic inclusion in the category of postcolonial writing, and a closer look at critical reactions to his work (both friendly and unfriendly) confirms this self-characterization.

Many critics sympathetic to postcolonialism have noted with disfavour Kureishi's tendency to portray characters in full flight from their marginal ethnic status; for instance, Kenneth Kaleta (the title of whose study of Kureishi dubs him a 'postcolonial storyteller') points out that in *Buddha* Karim's goal is 'assimilation into the white London scene' and argues that 'Karim is in love with power' (Kaleta 179). Ruvani Ranasinha echoes this critique of the book's racial politics, depicting Changez as 'a Peter Sellers stereotype' (Ranasinha 65), which is evidence for her view that Kureishi's attitude to Asian culture is 'rather West-centric' (Ranasinha 4). Not everyone is so certain of Kureishi's biases, though Frederick M. Holmes argues that 'the political critique' of racism and snobbery in *Buddha* is 'compromised' by [Karim's] self-seeking actions' ('Comedy' 645–6). For his part, Bart Moore-Gilbert notes that 'the ' "Other" is represented in *Buddha* as an object of consumption by the centre' (Moore-Gilbert, 'Hanif Kureishi's *The Buddha of Suburbia*' 201), but he does mention some problematic passages depicting racism and otherness: 'Karim is … complicit … in the abuse suffered by the Indian at Penge station … [and] he has nothing but contempt for the "stinking gypsy children" who assail Charlie' ('Hanif Kureishi's *The Buddha of Suburbia*' 205). Others have accused Kureishi's portrayal of Asians of 'conforming … to the very racist clichés he opposes' (Dasenbrock 724). Kureishi has also felt the scorn of critics who scoff at his marketability as a writer of colour: in the *New Republic*, Ian Buruma writes accusingly: 'Kureishi's combination of talent, charm, exotic ancestry, and subversive posturing is just what people who are chic, liberal and a trifle bored like' (Buruma 34).

Kureishi has not been without defenders, however. Moore-Gilbert notes that British Asian writers have accused Kureishi of being 'sexist, politically conservative, an insufficiently good stylist and opportunistic in his uses of British Asian experience' (*Hanif Kureishi* 193), but he is careful to point out the irony of these responses: 'the strong criticisms of Kureishi from minoritarian critics like Dhillon-Kashyap and hooks are hard to sustain given the response to Kureishi from New Right sympathisers like Norman Stone – particularly when it is exactly the same texts which they are all objecting to' (*Hanif Kureishi* 215). In another defence of Kureishi's racial attitudes, Nahem Yousaf quotes Kureishi's own awareness that 'the Asian community in Britain think that I'm perpetually throwing shit at them' (*Guide* 54) and attempts to deflect such issues by celebrating Kureishi's creations as 'complex and contradictory hybridized citizens whose cultural identities are inextricably linked with class politics' (*Guide* 55). Yousaf reiterates the familiar view that 'Kureishi can be read as refuting any vestigial belief in transcendental racial or cultural categories' and that his work undermines those who 'espouse an uncritical orthodoxy' whether they be of English or Asian descent (*Guide* 44). In a more confrontational tone, Kaleta defends Kureishi's contrarian attacks on political correctness with the claim that 'it is … racist to depict all minority persons as well educated, high income, law abiding and family oriented' (220).

Given the war of words over Kureishi's own identity and his representations of it, we might do well to follow Ranasinha as she invokes the notion of the 'specular', as depicted in the work of

Abdul JanMohamed and others, and claims that 'certain border intellectuals act as mirrors in "reflecting" their context' (Ranasinha 13). In her mind, Kureishi clearly falls into 'the traps of specularity' (Ranasinha 13), which are fatal to a sense of identity: Ranasinha argues that Kureishi's 'caricatures' of Muslims are examples of these traps, in that they 'further objectify this already objectified group' by reflecting Western stereotypes rather than the complex reality of Islam (Ranasinha 82). Ranasinha also argues that this absence of essential self applies even to Kureishi's more secular male protagonists, who 'tend to reflect the opposing factions that surround them ... at the core, there is a nullity; they remain spectral and specular figures with no strong sense of self' (Ranasinha 18). Ranasinha links Kureishi's portraits of these ciphers, whose gender and racial performances are essentially empty constructions, with Judith Butler's notion of 'gender "masquerade" ', but she decides that 'Butler's concept contrasts with Kureishi's representations of the conscious performance of ethnicity, wherein a notion of a residual sense of self behind the performance, however elusive, remains' (Ranasinha 69). This idea seems to contradict her accusations about 'specularity', but is perhaps the more convincing because of it: after all, this stubborn 'residual' self is precisely the locus of the shame and self-hatred that Karim and Shahid both evince. Without some sense of this elusive reality behind the performance of identity, there would be very little point to any of Kureishi's narratives.

The importance of the theme of identity as a performance has been underlined by many critics, especially with regard to *Buddha*. Moore-Gilbert notes that '*The Buddha* argues persistently that identity is constructed, multiply-determined, mixed, provisional and relational ... identity emerges from a process of negotiation with the characters who surround one ... .This [is] emphasized in ... the time [Karim] spends in front of reflecting surfaces, whether mirrors or shop-windows' ('Hanif Kureishi's *The Buddha of Suburbia*' 202). Schoene goes still further towards redeeming Karim through the rhetoric of destabilized identities, declaring that 'Karim would make a perfect citizen of [Marxist critic Terry] Eagleton's ideal socialist democracy involving "at once self-determination and self-decentring" ' (Schoene 118). Moore-Gilbert is less utopian, choosing a rather unpleasant moment – 'The literal "browning" of Karim' (when Karim is smeared with brown cream to make him appear more Indian) as an illustration of 'Kureishi's point that ethnicity is … constructed' ('Hanif Kureishi's *The Buddha of Suburbia*' 201). Others have been less impressed with Kureishi's treatment of race as a secondary trait to be acquired or jettisoned: John Clement Ball invokes the irony behind 'Karim's idea of the suburbs as "in the blood and not on the skin"' and claims that it is 'a deliberately outrageous appropriation of race-politics language to describe a bored suburbanite's makeover' (Ball 22).

Nevertheless, some critics have observed that there are exceptions to Kureishi's rules against stable identities, as Moore-Gilbert notes in Jamila's case, for example: 'Jamila's politics can be understood as exemplifying what Gayatri Chakravorty Spivak has termed "strategic essentialism" in the pursuit of "a scrupulously visible political interest". Thus, for Jamila ethnicity … constitutes the basis of mobilisation towards determinate ends' (*Hanif Kureishi* 133). In other words, as Ranasinha writes, Jamila's 'sustained commitment' to both anti-racist politics and class consciousness is shown 'contributing to a more stable sense of self' (Ranasinha 75). In a book full of inauthentic poseurs, those characters who, like Jamila, are committed enough to project an image of an authentic self onto the world are rewarded. Whereas (in Moore-Gilbert's words) 'Karim and Charlie often act as a "mirror" to each other … which suggests their individual ontological incompleteness' (*Hanif Kureishi* 128), Jamila requires no such alter ego to complete herself. Unfortunately, this capacity to project an authentic self is also open to racists such as 'Hairy Back', Helen's father, though his nickname suggests that he has not managed to transform himself as fully as he would like. Jamila's often-mentioned wisps of moustache may function in a similar way.

More sympathetic critics have shown themselves willing to endorse Kureishi's occasionally utopian vision of pop culture's capacity to promote racial harmony; for instance, in Bart Moore-Gilbert's words, Kureishi 'consistently corroborates [cultural critic] Dick Hebdige's argument that pop music has led the way in cross-racial cultural syntheses and transfers' (*Hanif Kureishi* 8). Moore-Gilbert also suggests that 'Kureishi's interest in popular music derives from his perception that it is in this context that a process of cross-cultural exchange first emerged … This is symbolized by the fact that Haroon and Margaret meet at a music venue' ('Hanif Kureishi's *The Buddha of Suburbia*' 197). Moore-Gilbert gives Kureishi credit for disrupting what he call the post-World War II 'consensus ... that "mass" or industrialised forms of popular culture ... were a damaging development' ('Hanif Kureishi's *The Buddha of Suburbia*' 197). For most critics, Kureishi's work has convincingly shown that such a dismissal of pop culture was premature and simplistic, even if he himself has later made deprecatory remarks such as 'we have to have a serious culture that isn't just ... rubbish television' (Moore-Gilbert, *Hanif Kureishi* 53), and 'The cinema cannot replace the novel or autobiography as the precise and serious medium of the age while it is still too intent on charming its audience' (*Hanif Kureishi* 163).

Despite Kureishi's appearance of being well-versed in contemporary cosmopolitan culture, some scholars, Moore-Gilbert foremost among them, have attempted to place him in the British literary tradition, where Kureishi himself – a native of England and lifelong monoglot – plainly believes he belongs. Moore-Gilbert claims that 'Kureishi's primary generic affiliations are to traditional social realism' (*Hanif Kureishi* 109) and notes that his first two novels are clearly intended as a kind of 'reportage', given their inclusion of historical personages (*Hanif Kureishi* 110). Thus Moore-Gilbert compares Kureishi's work with that of Alan Sillitoe, David Storey, and Keith Waterhouse, who chronicle the struggles of working-class men to rise in British society, and minimizes its links to Salman Rushdie's cross-continental and experimental fiction. Moore-Gilbert also notes the similarity between Karim's 'social rise' in *Buddha* and the ambitions of Joe Lampton, the hero of John Braine's *Room at the Top*: 'Both ... rely ... on the mentoring of older women in achieving their "social translation"' (*Hanif Kureishi* 111).

Perhaps the most insightful critic to have offered the English aspects of Kureishi's work serious attention in a high-profile forum is Rita Felski. In her article 'Nothing to Declare: Identity, Shame, and the Lower Middle Class', Felski cites Orwell's portraits of lower-middle-class life as models for Kureishi's; in both writers' works, 'the lower middle class is strongly feminized ... . Whereas the working class is represented through images of a virile proletariat' (Felski 43). She points out that 'intellectuals and artists ... have their own fantasy, of an authentic working-class existence. But the lower middle class is no one's fantasy and no one's desire' (Felski 38). Furthermore, Felski argues that lower-middle-class people 'think of themselves as middle class' (41), and that 'scholarly writing about lower-middle-class life is almost invariably produced by individuals who are distanced from that life' (Felski 42). Thus Felski claims that, although the lower middle class is 'resistant to the romance of marginality' (Felski 42), it is in fact the most marginal of all classes, in part because of 'the intense, often visceral sense of alienation that intellectuals from the lower middle class often feel towards their origins' (Felski 44).

Felski makes a cogent case that *Buddha*, being 'a novel about the shifting meanings of class in the 1960s and 1970s' (Felski 37), expresses the lower-middle-class mindset in all its mistrustful self-hatred. She also notes that 'the novel ... traces the tenacity and continuing power of class distinctions, as Kureishi's hero is constantly confronted with the differences between his back-ground and that of his new friends' (Felski 38). To Felski, Karim is a 'kind of class detective' who is 'hypersensitive' to the 'profound divisions between those who aspire upward and those whose status and cultural capital allow them to go slumming' (Felski 38). Felski's article considers other works as well, but many of her general insights may be applied directly to Kureishi's text; for instance, Karim's hostility to Marxist intellectuals may be explained by Felski's claim that 'the Marxist grand narrative ... perceives the lower middle class as an unfortunate anachronism on the path to socialism' even though in reality it 'is not disappear-ing but expanding' (Felski 44). Moreover, Karim's critiques of his socialist friends' hypocrisy (especially towards working-class characters such as Heater) anticipate Felski's polemical assertion that 'It is the ultimate act of bad faith among left intellectuals to want the working class to remain poor but pure, untainted by consumer culture and social aspirations' (Felski 44). The book's turn towards a Thatcherite economic stance fits what Felski terms 'the growth of self-employment and small businessness' among lower-middle-class people who have become 'artists, designers, computer experts and the like' (Felski 44), once the demise of the trade unions had made socialism seem impractical. These people remain 'progressive' in their 'social attitudes' (Felski 44), but they are eager to move with the economic times, just like Karim, Allie and Eva.

Two other important readings of *Buddha* attempt to see it in rela-tion to previous British writers. Frederick M. Holmes quotes

Kureishi's own remark that 'I was influenced more by [British] books like [Kingsley Amis's] *Lucky Jim* and early Evelyn Waugh than I was by *On the Road*', and goes on to argue that *Buddha* is an example of 'carnivalesque comedy' very much like *Lucky Jim*, in that 'Karim's language inverts social norms of decorum in the process of exposing and reviling the abuses of power that he encounters' (Holmes, 'Comedy' 645). Holmes reads Karim's flatulence as a subversive gesture, an example of what he terms 'grotesque realism', noting what Bakhtin says of this genre: 'To degrade, is to bury, to sow, and to kill simultaneously, in order to bring forth something better' (Bakhtin 21). The question is whether Kureishi's version of 'grotesque realism' really offers such an alternative. Holmes reads the final scene of the book as an 'appropriate' one for 'a thoroughly carnivalesque novel' since it acts out what Bakhtin calls a 'merry triumphant encounter with the world in the act of eating' ('Comedy' 656). Holmes's analysis is undermined somewhat by the Thatcherian triumph that is the meal's political background, as well as by his own admission that Terry Eagleton (in *Walter Benjamin: Towards a Revolutionary Criticism*) has argued that 'carnival is always inherently conservative in ... constituting no more than a licensed release valve for potentially revolutionary energies' ('Comedy' 646).

For his part, Nahem Yousaf claims that 'Kureishi follows Orwell for whom class was the hole waiting to be filled' (*Guide* 33) but his own analysis concentrates almost exclusively on the novel's engagement with myths of Englishness and racial otherness, as well as its analysis of Karim's suburban plight. Yousaf astutely observes that although 'the suburbs have to be sufficiently banal for the protagonist to wish to escape them', some of the 'most surreal' episodes in the book occur in Karim's neighborhood (*Guide* 40). Yousaf implies that Karim's journey from the suburbs to the city is intended as a search for an authenticity not found in Bromley, but notes that we soon see that there is no greater reality to be reached. Yousaf briefly mentions 'the fantasy of self-renewal' that 'underpins' the novel (*Guide* 40), but does not define its ideological or cultural basis at any great length. He does, however, argue (no doubt inspired by Homi Bhabha's writings on the subject of 'mimicry') that imitation can be 'a form of subtle and potentially subversive power' (*Guide* 47), and he notes the degree to which Haroon's and Karim's successes involve imitating stereotypical

Indian behaviour that will make them acceptable to the English world around them. Yousaf ends his own analysis of the novel rather disappointingly, however; he simply restates the indisputable fact that *Buddha* 'was and still is a huge critical, commercial, and popular success' (*Guide* 57). This laudatory tone glosses over unresolved issues and contradictions, reproducing Karim's own insouciance about everything except success.

The Black Album has received fewer positive critical or scholarly reviews than *The Buddha of Suburbia*. Some of this negative reaction may be due to the perception that, as Schoene puts it, 'Kureishi's utopian vision of *The Buddha of Suburbia* clashes markedly with the grim realism of his second novel' (Schoene 123–4); in Anthony Appiah's eyes, the humour which might have leavened the book's more pessimistic air 'largely fails' in part because the characters are 'schematic and ... unloved' (Appiah 42). Some critics have also complained about the novel on stylistic grounds: Tom Shone terms the book's prose 'adolescent mulch' in which 'descriptions' are 'so flamboyantly imprecise that, groping their way through a fug of instant amnesia, they end up bumping into themselves' (Shone 20), and claims that the novel's 'feverish attempts to date-stamp itself' end up 'flattening' the recent cultural past 'into a cardboard backdrop' (Shone 20). Even some of Kureishi's more sympathetic readers have implicitly acknowledged the partial accuracy of Shone's remarks. For instance, Kenneth Kaleta has noted the 'disorganization and confusion of language and structure' in many crucial passages in the novel (Kaleta 71).

Such disappointed reactions are perhaps based on the fact that, despite his reference to Prince (and, secondarily, to The Beatles) in the title of his novel, the Kureishi of *The Black Album* has lost faith in the revolutionary capacity of pop culture. As Moore-Gilbert has remarked, '*The Black Album* barely refers to British pop' (*Hanif Kureishi* 120), which, according to him, Kureishi represents 'as fragmenting along the fault-lines of ethnicity' (*Hanif Kureishi* 117). Holmes diagnoses another problem, namely that culture has become mere consumption: 'Although Shahid sees the moral vacuity of his brother Chili's brand-name consumerism ... the supposedly more progressive, alternative way of life he adopts with Deedee nevertheless involves a good deal of rather aimless shopping' ('Comedy' 309). Holmes implies that Antonio Gramsci's celebration of youth culture's capacity to appropriate mainstream discourse for subversive purposes is invoked and ironized in *The Black Album*, as Holmes notes: 'Liberatory slogans such as the one displayed in Deedee's office at the college ("All limitations are prisons") are easily appropriated by corporations' ('Comedy' 309).

James Saynor adumbrates a common political critique of *Album*'s message when he claims that 'Kureishi's solution to Shahid's dilemmas smacks, inevitably, of evasion and conservatism. Shahid ends up longing for "order and proportion"' (Saynor 41). Bruce King is more explicit about what he sees as the reactionary subtext of the book: '*The Black Album* is a plea for the superiority of real literature' as opposed to popular culture, and thus amounts to a defence of England against those who regard both 'real literature' and Englishness 'as the products of elitism, the Enlightenment, and racist imperialism' (King, '*The Black Album*' 406). Moore-Gilbert argues that '*The Black Album* ... lends itself in certain respects to being interpreted as an example of the "Orientalist" thinking which it is ostensibly so keen to challenge', citing the stereotypes of ' "eastern" despotism' and superstition that the novel's portrayal of the fanatical Riaz and the absurd sacred aubergine seems to endorse (*Hanif Kureishi* 147). In dealing with the question of religion more fully, Moore-Gilbert argues that *Album* 'counters many stereotypes about "fundamentalism"' with its depiction of 'the hybrid nature of Islam's adherents', and represents 'positively' Islam's 'hostility to the unrestrained capitalism of the Thatcher era' and the 'second chance' it offers to those whom Western secularism has corrupted or confused (*Hanif Kureishi* 135). In supporting this claim, he notes (rightly) that the incidents of violence instigated by Riaz's group are 'relatively minor' and 'primarily self-destructive' (*Hanif Kureishi* 136). Still, Moore-Gilbert observes 'the absence of any other kind of Muslim than those associated with Riaz' and claims that '[t]he inference might be drawn than there is no such thing as a moderate Muslim' (*Hanif Kureishi* 148). Moore-Gilbert concludes that the novel's condemnation of Riaz's fundamentalism suggests that 'Kureishi's liberalism proves ... absolutist' (*Hanif Kureishi* 148).

Nevertheless, Moore-Gilbert also notes that Kureishi also gives Brownlow's 'more self-aware and sophisticated radical-Left anti-racist politics' short shrift: '[Brownlow's] attitude of "unmistakeable lewdness" towards Tahira aligns him with the male Orientalist gaze anatomized by Edward Said and his consistent misrecognition of

Shahid … implies that even to Brownlow all British Asians "look the same"' (*Hanif Kureishi* 139). Moore-Gilbert goes on: 'Brownlow sees racism … as an expression of economic disadvantage … implicitly reducing race to a secondary category in the more important dialectic of class struggle' (*Hanif Kureishi* 140). Thus Brownlow's attitude matches Jamila's, but what in her is portrayed as heroic utopian activism becomes in him grotesque and insensitive. Thus, according to Moore-Gilbert, we can see how much Kureishi's view of leftist politics has already changed between *Buddha* and *The Black Album*. Still, Moore-Gilbert sees many connections between these two novels: he claims that in neither one does Kureishi take any single political position. Rather, Kureishi equivocates with those positions that seem most attractive; Moore-Gilbert argues that while ' "liberal" anti-racism' is never 'dismissed out of hand' by Kureishi it is 'consistently linked to an unhealthy veneration of cultures of non-western origin' (*Hanif Kureishi* 137). Moore-Gilbert disapproves of the 'adolescent desire to be part of the dominant cultural formation' that he sees in both Karim and Shahid, but he concedes that they are forced into 'disavowing important parts of themselves while they are growing up' (*Hanif Kureishi* 210). Moore-Gilbert also notes the double bind in which Karim and Shahid find themselves; they are criticized by some for being too Westernized, but become targets for racism unless they do their best to assimilate.

The criticism devoted to Kureishi's work since *Album* has been overwhelmingly evaluative and usually negative; reviewers have debated the merits of his books while academic critics have largely steered clear of them. In a review essay published in the *London Review of Books*, Sukhdev Sandhu sees *Love in a Blue Time, Intimacy* and *Midnight All Day* as instalments in 'the ongoing decline of a once vital writer' (Sandhu, 'Paradise Syndrome' 35). *Love* and *Midnight All Day* have come in for some especially curt dismissals; Ranasinha notes, with justice, that 'some stories are closer to dramatic monologues than fiction' (Ranasinha 106), and complains that 'It is hard to care about his self-absorbed, angst-ridden and indulgent characters', who seem 'interchangeable' (Ranasinha 108). In a similar vein, Phil Baker characterizes the style of *Midnight All Day* as 'flat, jerky, over-full, unhelpfully explanatory' (Baker 24). Even a more positive reviewer, Laura Miller, writes off *Love*'s 'paeans to the redemptive power of eros' as 'not very convincing' (Miller 11). For Moore-Gilbert, 'the sheer unloveliness of … Kureishi's characters' gives these stories a disappointingly 'downbeat tone' (*Hanif Kureishi* 158), yet he notes the presence of 'hilarious passages' in many stories, and even sees elements of successful 'farce' in 'D'Accord, Baby', 'Lately' and 'Four Blue Chairs' (*Hanif Kureishi* 159). The apparent incongruity between the stories' testimony to serious depression and their farcical components is hard to accept, however. One of the few who have troubled to place these stories in any kind of literary context, Moore-Gilbert notes that *Love* emphasizes 'suspense and dramatic revelation' as well as 'surprising reversals' in the vein of 'Maupassant, the early Kipling and Saki' (*Hanif Kureishi* 151).

Still fewer have tried to put Kureishi's novella *Intimacy* into perspective, either as part of Kureishi's ongoing oeuvre or as an addition to a British fictional tradition. Kathryn Harrison's essay 'Connubial Abyss' derides *Intimacy*'s 'cynical, worldly pose, its ennui' as a poor disguise for 'a desperate faith in old-fashioned biblical *knowing*, in which physical intercourse implies a thorough penetration of mind and soul' (Harrison 86). Mark Stein theorizes about the book's agenda: 'Historicizing [Kureishi's] extended flirtation with the postcolonial, *Intimacy* attempts to leave behind the colonial cultural and oedipal anxiety' (Stein 124). If this is the case, the book is a bitter failure; as I have argued in the biographical chapter of this book, Kureishi shows himself to be very much caught up in Oedipal anxieties, at least if Jay is any indication of his creator's frame of mind. Clearly, Stein is right to suggest that 'In *Intimacy* there is a notion of a common "we" which comprises … a shared middle-class background and political leanings, and a shared sense of ageing and mortality' (Stein 138). This erasure of the racial difference in Jay's identity may not be altogether positive, however, especially if one adduces (as Ranasinha does) Coco Fusco's claim that 'to ignore white ethnicity is to redouble its hegemony by naturalizing it. Without specifically addressing white ethnicity, there can be no critical evaluation of the construction of the other' (Fusco 91). Most critics seem to agree with Fusco's views, and few have applauded Kureishi's decision to bracket the issue of race in his later work.

Given the critical consensus that has emerged about Kureishi's apparent decline from relevance to obscurity, it is no surprise that Kureishi's two most recent books of fiction have been greeted with little enthusiasm. In reviewing *Gabriel's Gift*, Pankaj Mishra laments 'the flatness that becomes inevitable when the novelist surrenders his task of description and explanation' (Mishra 52). Brian Budzynski deplores the absence of both 'gritty detail' and 'grander social themes' in the book (Budzynski 235). More recently, John Updike calls *The Body* 'less a novel than a parable' and suggests that it 'might make a good movie' (Updike 94). Updike regrets that 'the fascinating idea of a haunted body, whose previous tenant makes himself felt throughout its nervous system and utmost cells, fades away as *la dolce vita* ... takes over the narrative' (Updike 95). As usual, British readers have been even less charitable than American ones; the *Sunday Times*'s Tom Deveson notes the 'well-intentioned but unconvincing fuzziness' of the stories in *The Body*, finding them 'ingratiatingly sentimental', 'obstinately sententious' and 'intellectually complacent' (Deveson 48). Writing in the *Spectator*, D. J. Taylor diagnoses a 'gimmicky air' in *The Body* and senses that Kureishi has become 'detached from the things that are worth writing about' (Taylor 71).

Kureishi's fiction has also produced increasingly negative reactions from critics who have found it difficult to pinpoint Kureishi's political views. Many have noted Kureishi's dissatisfaction with the way in which, as Moore-Gilbert puts it, 'Old Left' politics subsumes 'racial, gender and sexual differences ... under the rubric of class' and 'reorganises them in a new hierarchy in which (the working) class is the privileged term' (*Hanif Kureishi* 202). Moore-Gilbert also observes Kureishi's condemnation of leftists who 'claim an "objective" understanding of the migrant's predicament, often based on crudely deterministic adaptations of Marxist class analysis' ('Hanif Kureishi's *The Buddha of Suburbia*' 201). Yet this critique seems blunted by the fact that, as Moore-Gilbert himself notes, 'middle-class members of minorities often take advantage of their own people as well as of the white working class' and that 'there is as much class snobbery within Asian Britain as in mainstream society' (*Hanif Kureishi* 203). Still, the hypocrisy and racial insensitivity of many of what Kaleta calls Kureishi's 'limousine liberals' (Kaleta 234) have created a climate in which, in Moore-Gilbert's words, 'many of Kureishi's more recent characters endorse the Thatcherite counter-revolution' (*Hanif Kureishi* 11). The confusing mixture of obnoxious Thatcherites and risible, decaying leftists in Kureishi's oeuvre has led some to posit that 'Kureishi is more interested in social satire than political analysis' (Weber 129), since those of his characters who indulge in 'a revolt', of whatever political stripe, only do so as a means of 'self-assertion' (O'Brien 20).

This emphasis on individuality is another familiar theme in Kureishi criticism; as Ranasinha states, 'his work appears to privilege individualism and disengagement, although the extent to which he is thematizing this as failure or naturalizing it remains open to question' (Ranasinha 18–19). Tariq Rahman is less patient with the individualist strain in Kureishi's work, objecting that 'only the consequences of anarchic individualism are condemned; the philosophy itself is endorsed' (Rahman 370). Some have seen this condemnation as too simplistic, however, given Kureishi's frequent scepticism about individual autonomy. For instance, Ranasinha cites the erosion of any 'sense of self' in Kureishi's characters once they grow up and assume responsibilities (Ranasinha 103), and Stella Tillyard notes that Kureishi 'celebrates the liberation and loss of self that he discovers in the maelstrom of a decayed physical and moral universe' (Tillyard 39). The 'self' is a masquerade, in Kureishi's work, a confection of arbitrary or fungible gender, race and class traits, to the point that, as Schoene puts it, 'it seems as if make-believe triumphs over truth and authenticity, but then being and acting … interpermeate each other' (Schoene 115). Such a contingent notion of the individual self means that some critics have claimed that Kureishi is in tune with many postmodern conceptions of the self; as John Clement Ball has argued, Kureishi's work is completely compatible with both 'Baudrillard's "simulacrum" as the replica of the vanishing real' and with 'Jameson's "depthlessness" as an aesthetic consequence of late capitalist commodification' (Ball 22).

This notion of the 'depthless' self has, however, brought Kureishi into sharp conflict with more identity-based strains of queer theory and feminism. Kureishi's men often assume the mask of gay identity, although sometimes they seem to be in denial of their own desire to do so. Discussing *Intimacy*, Frederick Luis Aldama argues that 'Jay's intimations of a transgressive same-sex desire are cut short' (Review of '*Intimacy*' 1099), and thus leave him in a condition of unenlightened heterosexist denial. According to Aldama's perceptive critique, Jay's attitudes are at one with the commodifying cultural trends that 'contain queers and lesbians by hyping same-sex sexuality as a fashionable look – and not a perma-nent reality with very real consequences' (Review of 'Intimacy' 1100). As Aldama points out, Kureishi stops short of allowing his protagonists to embrace the gay lifestyle in a meaningful manner.

Still, Kureishi cannot resist making casual homosexual behav-iour a leitmotif of his work in such a way that, as Ian Buruma muses: 'One is reminded of Auden and Isherwood's camp prole-tarianism … Isherwood remarked that if homosexuality had not existed, he would have invented it' (Buruma 36). Whether this parallel is apt or not, it is plain that Kureishi's adoption of homo-sexual themes is a strategic one and may strike readers as being irresponsible or dilettantish. Less hostile readers have pointed out that for leftists of the 1980s, representing homosexuality as accept-able and accepted behaviour as well as attacking homophobic atti-tudes was a priority. For instance, Sukhdev Sandhu notes that in 1988 the Conservatives introduced the Local Government Act, legislation that, among other things, 'forbade local authorities … from promoting homosexuality' ('Pop Goes the Centre' 149). Thus Sandhu argues that 'for Kureishi, a preoccupation with sex neither entails individualism, nor a neglect of the social realm' ('Pop Goes the Centre' 150).

If Kureishi has proven an elusive target for queer theorists, he would seem much easier for feminist critics to attack, although few female critics have troubled to take him to task. Ruvani Ranasinha, one of the few women to comment on Kureishi's subversions of feminism in Buddha, terms them 'witty' rather than problematic (Ranasinha 76). Male critics such as Moore-Gilbert have argued that Kureishi's work contains an increasingly 'angry vein of … misogyny', since, as Moore-Gilbert himself notes, 'Avowed femi-nists … are generally represented as … inadequate and foolish' (Hanif Kureishi 156). Sean O'Brien notes that in Love in a Blue Time 'the female characters … are male shorthand for menacing female strength and irritating female weakness, there to make up the numbers in what are always boys' games' (O'Brien 20). Moore-Gilbert also observes that Kureishi's 'antipathy towards strong women' is coupled with 'the recurrence of "girl-women" as objects of desire' (Hanif Kureishi 156).

Still, critics who term Kureishi an anti-feminist have been forced to account for Kureishi's occasionally flattering portraits of feminist characters such as Jamila, who not only 'embodies to a considerable degree the "conscience" of *The Buddha*' (Moore-Gilbert, 'Hanif Kureishi's *The Buddha of Suburbia*' 200), but also 'rebuts the Orientalist stereotypes of silent, passive Oriental women' ('Hanif Kureishi's *The Buddha of Suburbia*' 198). There is in such characters a superficial justification for Kureishi's suggestion that, in Moore-Gilbert's words, 'men should respond [to feminism] ... by aspiring to some of the freedoms achieved by the Women's Movement' (*Hanif Kureishi* 157). Yet the reasons behind this aspiration are more complicated than Moore-Gilbert would have us believe when he claims that 'the stories [of *Love*] reflect Kureishi's continuing sympathy for feminist ideas' and exhibit many 'satiric examples of ... appalling sexism' as well as exposing men's lack of a 'sense of responsibility' (*Hanif Kureishi* 155). After all, the men in Kureishi's fiction who appropriate the rhetoric of gender liberation from the women's movement, as Jay does in *Intimacy*, generally do so in a hostile and defensive mood.

While we have seen that Kureishi's critics often have cogent reasons for their disapproval, they also commonly underestimate his self-awareness as a writer, and lose track of the degree to which he is deliberately presenting unsympathetic, cynical or deluded characters for his readers to judge. For instance, writing of *Gabriel's Gift*, James Campbell notes 'the obligatory presence of glamorous people, whose glamor stubbornly refuses to shine' (Campbell 7). The possibility that Kureishi is undertaking a critique of 'glamor' (albeit a lighthearted one) in the novel is left unexplored here, though Campbell notes that 'few' of those in the 'glamorous zone' are 'contented' (Campbell 7). Similarly, it is inaccurate to say, with Ranasinha, that Kureishi 'does not engage with the possibility of a rethinking of liberal ideology' (Ranasinha 83); indeed, Kureishi's critiques of consumerism, if occasionally glib, are at least indications of a 'possibility' of 'rethinking' the cycles of exploitation encouraged by liberalism. Kureishi has amply demonstrated what Moore-Gilbert calls his 'Adornian cynicism about the narcotic effect of pop as a mass cultural commodity' (*Hanif Kureishi* 10–11); as Moore-Gilbert goes on to say, the 'great tradition' of liberalism proves 'useless' to most of his characters, since 'culture has ... been entirely subsumed into the market' (*Hanif Kureishi* 160–1).

Critics who have tired of Kureishi's world-weary poses and pessimistic rhetoric, however, have failed to embrace the more positive side of Kureishi's agenda. Indeed, many of them are troubled by Kureishi's apparent belief that, in Simon Gikandi's words, he can 'valorize the logic of a secular and enlightened English culture and use it against the unreason of the racists' (Gikandi 204). Kureishi makes it clear that he sees the humanistic tradition as the main defence against racism, arguing persuasively that 'The evil of racism is that it is ... a failure to understand or feel what it is one's humanity consists in' (*My Beautiful Laundrette* 95). Kureishi is quite explicit about this broader, trans-racial agenda as an escape from both racism and racial self-consciousness; Ranasinha quotes him as saying that his subject after *Love* is 'what it is like to be a human being' (Ranasinha 102). Thus in *Intimacy*, Jay believes that he is finally 'coming to [his] senses as a human being' and he feels 'ready to study' the classics (*Intimacy* 51). The wish for what Jay terms a humanistic 'general culture' comes with its own discontents: 'a general culture isn't getting me anywhere tonight', though 'without a general culture nothing can be understood' (*Intimacy* 48). Jay elaborates his humanist creed in a manner that does not minimize its contradictions and dangers: 'I like the human imagination: its delicacy, its brutal aggressive energy' (*Intimacy* 132). The difficult coexistence of 'delicacy' and 'brutal aggressive energy' is perhaps Kureishi's central theme, and it is what differentiates his work from the 'serene' liberalism that he criticizes (*Dreaming* 220).

Kureishi broadens the focus of his fiction to encompass what he plainly sees as universal human themes that transcend racial, cultural or class barriers. For instance, in his introduction to *Plays One*, Kureishi explains his urge to write plays and fiction, claiming that 'there is something necessarily human, both prurient and objective, in our desire to become familiar through complex stories with the lives of others' (*Plays One* xiii). Critics have noted this self-confessedly humanistic tendency with varying degrees of dismay or approval. Some, like James Saynor, say dismissively that 'Kureishi is ultimately ... just a liberal humanist' (Saynor 41), using a phrase that has become equally pejorative with left-wing postmodern academics and right-wing ideologues. Perhaps the best compliment one can pay Kureishi (given the weaknesses and contradictions critics have observed in his work) is that he has done his part to demonstrate that his own unfashionable acceptance of human nature is both necessary and necessarily unconditional. His characters are frequently immoral, cruel, selfish, short-sighted, sexist, homophobic, racist, self-hating, or self-destructive; they are also human, however, and for Kureishi that remains their defining (and ultimately perhaps even redemptive) characteristic. Kureishi's fiction attempts to show us that seeing human beings at their worst does not mean that we are seeing humanism at its weakest; on the contrary, where complex people such as Kureishi's are displayed at their least attractive, we are forced to recognize the many traits we share with them and consider the degree to which we share in their degradation. It is not a pleasant prospect, but to refuse to face it is, in Kureishi's view, a failure of the mind, heart and imagination.

ANNOTATED FURTHER READING AND BIBLIOGRAPHY

PRIMARY SOURCES

Kureishi, Hanif. *The Black Album*. New York: Scribner Paperback / Simon & Schuster, 1995.

———. *The Body*. London: Faber and Faber, 2002.

———. *The Body and Seven Stories*. London: Faber and Faber, 2002.

———. *Borderline*. London: Methuen, 1981.

———. *The Buddha of Suburbia*. London: Faber and Faber, 1990.

———. *Collected Screenplays 1*. London: Faber and Faber, 2002.

———. *Dreaming and Scheming: Reflections on Writing and Politics*. London: Faber and Faber, 2002.

———. *Gabriel's Gift*. New York: Scribner, 2001.

———. *Intimacy*. London: Faber and Faber, 1998.

———. *London Kills Me*. London: Faber and Faber, 1991.

———. *Love in a Blue Time*. New York: Scribner, 1997.

———. *Midnight All Day*. London: Faber and Faber, 1999.

———. *My Beautiful Laundrette and Other Writings*. London: Faber and Faber, 1996.

———. *My Ear at His Heart: Reading My Father*. London: Faber and Faber, 2004.

———. *Outskirts and Other Plays*. London: Faber and Faber, 1992.

———. *Plays One*. London: Faber and Faber, 1992.

———. 'The Rainbow Sign.' *My Beautiful Laundrette and the Rainbow Sign*. London: Faber and Faber, 1986.

———. 'Requiem for a Rave.' *Sight & Sound*. 1(5) (August 1991): 8–13.

———. *Sammy and Rosie Get Laid: The Script and the Diary*. London: Faber and Faber, 1988.

———. *Sleep With Me*. London: Faber and Faber, 1999.

———. 'Some Time with Stephen: A Diary.' *London Kills Me: Three Screenplays and Four Essays*. Harmondsworth: Penguin, 1992. 115–94.

ANNOTATED FURTHER READING

Acheson, James, and Sara C. E. Ross, eds. *The Contemporary British Novel Since 1980*. Basingstoke and New York: Palgrave Macmillan, 2005.
This collection of essays offers a survey of various important recent British writers, grouping them under broad categories such as Realism,

Postcolonialism, Feminism and Postmodernism. Authors discussed include Salman Rushdie, Ian McEwan, Kazuo Ishiguro, James Kelman, Pat Barker, A. S. Byatt, and Peter Ackroyd. Readers of Kureishi will be struck by Bruce King's essay 'Abdurazak Gurnah and Hanif Kureishi: Failed Revolutions', in which King claims that the book's determination to group Kureishi and Gurnah under the 'Postcolonial' banner is misleading.

Kaleta, Kenneth C. *Hanif Kureishi: Postcolonial Storyteller*. Austin, TX: University of Texas Press, 1998.
Kaleta's eclectic book is billed as a 'critical biography' of Kureishi, and its organization is unconventional. It includes an interview with its subject, an examination of some important revisions to *Buddha*'s opening paragraph, and essays on Kureishi's various plays, films, and fictions. It also features four essays on general topics in Kureishi's work: 'Lovers and Love', 'Immigrant Dreams', 'Redefined Nationalism', and 'Storytelling'.

Kureishi Hanif. *My Ear at His Heart: Reading My Father* (London: Faber and Faber, 2004).
Kureishi's book-length essay on his father Rafiushan's unsuccessful career as a writer offers an invaluable glimpse of Kureishi's upbringing and obsession with family life. The book dwells unsentimentally on the clash between father and son, as well as on the guilt and anger their conflict produced, though it also attempts to enter imaginatively into the colourful fictional world created by Rafiushan Kureishi.

Kureishi Hanif. *Dreaming and Scheming: Reflections on Writing and Politics*. London: Faber and Faber, 2002.
This book collects Kureishi's many essays on his own work, his observations about British culture and politics, and his reflections on the experience of seeing his writings turned into films. It also includes two recent meditations on the creative process itself, 'Something Given' and 'Dreaming and Scheming'.

Moore-Gilbert, Bart. *Hanif Kureishi*. Manchester: Manchester University Press, 2001.
Moore-Gilbert's book focuses primarily on placing Kureishi within a global context, and deals with issues of postcolonial discourse, identity politics and national culture. Moore-Gilbert also engages extensively with Kureishi's plays and films, somewhat at the expense of his more recent fiction, though his readings of *Buddha*, *Album*, and *Intimacy* draw usefully on biographical, critical and historical contexts.

Ranasinha, Ruvani. *Hanif Kureishi*. London: Northcote House, 2002.
Ranasinha's book concentrates mainly on issues of race and religion in Kureishi's writing, and is perhaps the most openly ambivalent of all full-length studies of his work. Her book explores the many apparent ideological contradictions within Kureishi's fiction, and exposes his sometimes cynical persona to rigorous scrutiny. Though Ranasinha is intensely critical of Kureishi's apparent misogyny, 'Muslimophobia', and insensitivity, she affirms his importance as what she terms a 'crossover' writer who articulates many of the complex problems faced by British Asians.

Reichl, Susanne, and Mark Stein, eds. *Cheeky Fictions: Laughter and the Postcolonial*. Amsterdam: Rodopi, 2005.
This collection's premise is that there is a crucial link between the political agenda of postcolonial writers and their satirical or parodic stances. Authors examined include V. S. Naipaul, Shyam Selvadurai, Timothy Mo, and Zakes Mda. Readers of Kureishi will note Helga Ramsey-Kurz's essay, 'Humouring the Terrorists or the Terrorised? Militant Muslims in Salman Rushdie, Zadie Smith and Hanif Kureishi', which juxtaposes Kureishi with two comparable (albeit very different) writers who also deal with Islamic extremists in a humorous fashion.

Tew, Philip, Rod Mengham, and Richard Lane, eds. *Contemporary British Fiction*. Cambridge: Polity, 1996.
This book features a range of critical essays on contemporary British novelists, among them Salman Rushdie, Martin Amis, Zadie Smith and Will Self. Readers interested in Kureishi will find Anthony Ilona's essay entitled 'Hanif Kureishi's *The Buddha of Suburbia*: "A New Way of Being British"' to be a compelling examination of Kureishi's focus on London and its relationship to larger questions of identity.

Thomas, Susie, ed. *Hanif Kureishi: A Reader's Guide to Essential Criticism*. Basingstoke: Palgrave Macmillan, 2005.
This book offers a comprehensive survey of the critical reaction to Kureishi's plays, screenplays, and fiction. It catalogues the many responses, both positive and negative, to Kureishi's writing, and briefly juxtaposes them to current theoretical ideas such as hybridity, metrophilia, post-feminism, 'diaspora identity', and postcolonialism. Thomas also quotes at length from the critics themselves, allowing their arguments (and potential biases) to emerge in their original contexts.

Yousaf, Nahem. *Hanif Kureishi's* The Buddha of Suburbia: *A Reader's Guide*. New York and London: Continuum, 2002.
Yousaf's brief book explores the themes of *The Buddha of Suburbia*, concentrating on its picture of London, the Asian family and the politics

of representation. It also contains an interview with Kureishi which deals briefly with his other, more recent fiction. Furthermore, it examines the novel's largely positive critical reception, and also deals with the acclaimed but controversial BBC adaptation of the book into a lavish four-part mini-series.

SUGGESTED SECONDARY READING

Abell, Stephen. 'Just Touching.' *Times Literary Supplement.* 5197 (11 August 2002): 25.

Aldama, Frederick Luis. 'Review of *Intimacy.' Callalloo.* 22(4) (Fall 1999): 1097–1100.

——. *Postethnic Narrative Criticism: Magicorealism in Oscar 'Zeta' Acosta, Ana Castillo, Julie Dash, Hanif Kureishi, and Salman Rushdie.* Austin, TX: University of Texas Press, 2003.

——. 'The Pound and the Fury: A Postcolonial Interview with Hanif Kureishi.' *Poets & Writers.* 29(5) (Fall 2001): 34–9.

Allison, Terry L. and Renée R. Curry. ' "All Anger and Understanding": Kureishi, Culture, and Contemporary Constructions of Rage.' Eds. Terry L. Allison and Renée R. Curry. *States of Rage: Emotional Eruption, Violence, and Social Change.* New York: New York University Press, 1996.

Anthias, Floyd and Nira Yuval-Davis. *Racialized Boundaries: Race, Nation, Gender, Colour and Class and the Anti-Racist Struggle.* London: Routledge, 1992.

Appiah, K. Anthony. 'Identity Crisis' [Review of *The Black Album*]. *New York Times Book Review.* 42(2) (17 September 1995): 42.

Ashcroft, Bill, Helen Tiffin, and Gareth Griffiths. *The Empire Writes Back: Theory and Practice in Post-Colonial Literatures.* London: Methuen, 1989.

Baker, Phil. 'Umbrella Rage.' *Times Literary Supplement.* 5041 (12 November 1999): 24.

Bakhtin, Mikhail. *Rabelais and His World.* Trans. Hélène Iswolsky. Bloomington, IN: Indiana UP, 1984.

Ball, John Clement. 'The Semi-Detached Metropolis: Hanif Kureishi's London.' *ARIEL.* 27(4) (1996): 7–26.

Bhabha, Homi K. *The Location of Culture.* London: Routledge, 1994.

——. *Nation and Narration.* London: Routledge, 1990.

Budzynski, Brian. 'Review of Hanif Kureishi, *Gabriel's Gift.' Review of Contemporary Fiction.* 22(2) (Summer 2002): 235.

Buruma, Ian. 'The Buddha of Suburbia.' *New Republic.* 203(8–9) (20 August 1990): 34–6.

Campbell, James. '*Intimacy* and *Midnight All Day.' New York Times Book Review.* (30 September 2001): 7.

Carey, Cynthia. 'Hanif Kureishi's *The Buddha of Suburbia* as a Post-Colonial Novel.' *Commonwealth: Essays and Studies*. Special Issue no. SP 4 (1997): 119–25.

Chappell, Helen. 'Below the Scampi Belt.' *New Society*. (8 October 1981): 51–4.

Chekhov, Anton. *Stories 1889–1891. The Oxford Chekhov, Vol. V*. Trans. Ronald Hingley. London: Oxford University Press, 1970.

Cone, Annabelle. 'The Politics of Intimacy in Hanif Kureishi's Films And Fiction.' *Literature/Film Quarterly*. 32(4) (2004): 261–4.

Connor, Steven. *The English Novel in History: 1950 to the Present*. London: Routledge, 1996.

Dasenbrock, Reed Way. 'World Literature in Review: English.' *World Literature Today*. 66(4) (Autumn 1992): 724.

Deveson, Tom. 'Pleasures on the Dark Side.' *Sunday Times*. (15 December 2002): 48.

Eberstadt, Fernanda. 'Rebel, Rebel: For Allah and England.' *New Yorker*. (21 & 28 August 1995): 118–20.

Felski, Rita. 'Nothing to Declare: Identity, Shame, and the Lower Middle Class.' *PMLA*. 115(1) (January 2000): 33–45.

Fusco, Coco. 'Fantasies of Oppositionality – Reflections on Recent Conferences in Boston and New York.' *Screen*. 29(4) (1988): 80–93.

Gallix, Andrew. 'Et in Suburbia Ego: Hanif Kureishi's Semi-Detached Storeys.' Ed. François Gallix. *The Buddha of Suburbia*. Paris: Ellipses, 1997. 148–64.

Gallix, François, ed. *The Buddha of Suburbia*. Paris: Ellipses, 1997.

Gikandi, Simon. *Maps of Englishness*. New York: Columbia University Press, 1996.

Gilroy, Paul. *There Ain't No Black in the Union Jack*. London: Routledge, 1992.
———. *The Black Atlantic*. London: Verso, 1993.

Greenberg, Kevin. [Review of *Gabriel's Gift*]. *Book*. (November–December 2001): 68–9.

Hall, Stuart, and Martin Jacques, eds. *New Times: The Changing Face of Politics in the 1990s*. London: Verso, 1993.

Harrison, Kathryn, 'Connubial Abyss.' *Harper's Magazine*. 300(1797) (February 2000): 83–8.

Hashmi, Alamgir. 'Hanif Kureishi and the Tradition of the Novel.' *International Fiction Review*. 19(2) (1992): 88–95.

Hitchcock, Peter. 'Decolonizing (the) English.' *South Atlantic Quarterly*. 100(3) (2001): 749–71.

Holmes, Frederick M. 'Comedy, the Carnivalesque, and the Depiction of English Society in Hanif Kureishi's *The Buddha of Suburbia* and Kingsley Amis's *Lucky Jim*.' *English Studies in Canada*. 28(4) (December 2002): 645–66.

Holmes, Frederick M. 'The Postcolonial Subject Divided between East and West: Kureishi's *The Black Album* as an Intertext of Rushdie's *The Satanic Verses*.' *Papers on Language & Literature*. 37(3) (Summer 2001): 296–313.

Hopkins, James. 'The Horror of Being Hanif' [Review of *Midnight All Day*]. *Guardian*. (30 October 1999): 10.

Ilona, Anthony. 'Hanif Kureishi's *The Buddha of Suburbia*: "A New Way of Being British".' Eds. Richard Lane, Rod Mengham, and Philip Tew. *Contemporary British Fiction*. Cambridge: Polity, 1996. 87–105.

Jena, Seema. 'From Victims to Survivors: The Anti-hero as a Narrative in Asian Immigrant Writing with Special Reference to *The Buddha of Suburbia*.' *Wasafiri*. 17 (Spring 1993): 3–6.

Kaleta, Kenneth C. *Hanif Kureishi: Postcolonial Storyteller*. Austin, TX: University of Texas Press, 1998.

King, Bruce. 'Abdurazak Gurnah and Hanif Kureishi: Failed Revolutions.' Eds. James Acheson, and Sara C. E. Ross. *The Contemporary British Novel Since 1980*. Basingstoke and New York: Palgrave Macmillan, 2005. 85–94.

——. '*The Black Album*.' *World Literature Today*. 70(2) (Spring 1996): 405–6.

——. 'Love in a Blue Time.' *World Literature Today*. 72(2) (Spring 1998): 371–2.

Kumar, Amitava. *Bombay London New York*. London and New York: Routledge, 2002.

Laird, Nick. 'Delinquent Dreamers in the Smog.' *Times Literary Supplement*. 5109 (2 March 2001): 22.

Lee, A. Robert, ed. *Other Britain, Other British: Contemporary Multicultural Fiction*. London and East Haven, CT: Pluto, 1995.

Linklater, Alexander. 'Death of the Ego' [Review of *The Body*]. *Guardian*. (16 November 2002).

MacCabe, Colin. 'An Interview: Hanif Kureishi on London.' *Critical Quarterly*. 41(3) (1999): 37–56.

Mann, Jessica. 'Peter Pan's Midlife Crisis' [Review of *The Body*]. *Daily Telegraph*. (16 November 2002).

Mendelsohn, Jane. 'Review of *Intimacy*.' *New York Times Book Review*. 104(13) (28 March 1999): 13.

Miller, Laura. 'Sammy and Rosie Get Old.' *New York Times Book Review*. (9 November 1997): 10–11.

Mishra, Pankaj. 'Bring on the Babes.' *New Statesman*. 130(4527) (5 March 2001): 52.

Misrahi-Barak, Judith. 'The Scope of Fiction in Hanif Kureishi's *The Buddha of Suburbia*: From Margin to Margin and Back to the Centre.' *Études Britanniques Contemporaines: Revue de la Société d'Études Anglaises Contemporaines*. 13 (January 1998): 31–9.

Moore-Gilbert, Bart. *Hanif Kureishi*. Manchester: Manchester University Press, 2001.

——. 'Hanif Kureishi's *The Buddha of Suburbia*.' *Q/W/E/R/T/Y: Arts, littératures et civilisations du monde anglophone*. 7 (October 1997): 191–207.

——. 'Justice and Morality in the Plays of Hanif Kureishi.' *European Studies: A Journal of European Culture, History, and Politics*. 17 (2001): 241–53.

Nasta, Susheila. *Home Truths: Fictions of the South Asian Diaspora in Britain*. Basingstoke: Palgrave Macmillan, 2002.

O'Brien, Sean. 'Eighties Vanities.' *Times Literary Supplement*. 4904 (28 March 1997): 20.

Page, Ron. 'Review of *Love in a Blue Time*.' *Spectator*. 278(8806) (10 May 1997): 36–7.

Proctor, Minna. 'Buddha Leaves Suburbia.' *The Nation*. 268(14) (19 April 1999): 38.

Rahman, Tariq. 'World Literature in Review: Pakistan.' *World Literature Today*. 65(2) (Spring 1991): 370.

Ramsey-Kurz, Helga. 'Humouring the Terrorists or the Terrorised? Militant Muslims in Salman Rushdie, Zadie Smith and Hanif Kureishi.' Eds. Susanne Reichl, and Mark Stein. *Cheeky Fictions: Laughter and the Postcolonial*. Amsterdam: Rodopi, 2005. 73–86.

Ranasinha, Ruvani. *Hanif Kureishi*. London: Northcote House, 2002.

Rance, Polly. [Untitled review of *Intimacy*]. *Richmond Review*. 1999. N. pag. <www.richmondreview.com>

Ray, Sangeeta. 'The Nation in Performance: Bhabha, Mukherjee and Kureishi.' Ed. Monika Fludernik. *Hybridity and Postcolonialism: Twentieth Century Indian Literature*. Tübingen: Stauffenburg, 1998. 219–38.

Said, Edward. *Orientalism*. Harmondsworth: Penguin, 1991.

Sandford, Christopher. *Bowie: Loving the Alien*. New York: Da Capo, 1998.

Sandhu, Sukhdev. 'Paradise Syndrome' [Review of *Midnight All Day*]. *London Review of Books*. (18 May 2000): 32–5.

——. 'Pop Goes the Centre: Hanif Kureishi's London.' Ed. Benita Parry. *Postcolonial Theory and Criticism*. Cambridge: Brewer, 1999.

Saynor, James. 'Mirror Shades' [Review of *The Black Album*, by Hanif Kureishi]. *New Statesman & Society*. 3 (March 1995): 40–1.

Schoene, Berthold. 'Herald of Hybridity: The Emancipation of Difference in Hanif Kureishi's *The Buddha of Suburbia*.' *International Journal of Cultural Studies*. 1(1) (1998): 109–27.

Sethi, Robbie Clipper. [Untitled review]. *IndiaStar: A Literary-Art Magazine*. 1999. N. pag. <www.indiastar.com>

Shone, Tom. 'I'm All Shook Up' [Review of *The Black Album*, by Hanif Kureishi]. *Times Literary Supplement*. (3 March 1995): 20.

Silverstone, Roger, ed. *Visions of Suburbia*. London: Routledge, 1996.

Sivanandan, A. *Communities of Resistance: Writings on Black Struggles for Socialism*. London: Verso, 1990.

Stein, Mark. 'Posed Ethnicity and the Postethnic.' *English Literature in International Contexts*. Heidelberg: Carl Winter Universitätsverlag, 2002.

Taylor, D. J. 'More Debit Than Credit.' *Spectator*. 290(9091) (2 November 2002): 71.

Thomas, Susie, ed.. *Hanif Kureishi: A Reader's Guide to Essential Criticism*. Basingstoke: Palgrave Macmillan, 2005.

Tillyard, Stella. 'A Vision of the Prophet Hanif.' *The Times*. (2 March 1995): 39.

Tremlett, George. *David Bowie: Living on the Brink*. New York: Carroll & Graf, 1996.

Updike, John. 'Mind/Body Problems: New Novels by Andrew Sean Greer and Hanif Kureishi.' *New Yorker*. (26 January 2004): 90–5.

Vega-Ritter, Max. 'La crise d'identité dans *The Buddha of Suburbia*.' Ed. François Gallix. *The Buddha of Suburbia*. Paris: Ellipses, 1997. 26–36.

Weber, Donald. ' "No Secrets Were Safe from Me": Situating Hanif Kureishi.' *Massachusetts Review*. 38(1) (Spring 1997): 119–36.

Werbner, Pnina, and Tariq Modood, eds. *Debating Cultural Hybridity: Multi-Cultural Identities and the Politics of Anti-Racism*. London: Zed, 1997.

Wolcott, James. 'A Time to Boogie.' *New Yorker*. (10 January 1994): 74–5.

Young, Robert J. C. *Colonial Desire: Hybridity in Theory, Culture and Race*. London: Routledge, 1995.

Yousaf, Nahem. 'Hanif Kureishi and "The Brown Man's Burden".' *Critical Survey*. 8(1) (1996): 14–25.

——. *Hanif Kureishi's The Buddha of Suburbia: A Reader's Guide*. New York and London: Continuum, 2002.

INDEX

SUSAN NATHAN was born in En... ... ... doctor. An AIDS Counsellor in London, she ...... fifties, recently divorced and with grown-up children, to move to Israel. She now lives in Tamra in the Galilee, but regularly visits Britain. This is her first book.

Visit www.AuthorTracker.co.uk for exclusive information on your favourite HarperCollins authors.

From the reviews of *The Other Side of Israel*:

'Nathan traverses a country deprived of inter-ethnic friendship with extraordinary observation, sensitivity, and insight'
JON SNOW, *Guardian*

'*The Other Side of Israel* is a deeply troubling book. It should be read by anyone who wants to understand the reality of life for the Arab citizens of Israel ... Her experience transforms her from an ardent Zionist into an eloquent but sorrowful critic of the state she had previously revered. Her account is the more telling because she writes with just as much warmth about her Jewish friends as she displays towards the Palestinians who befriend her. This important book not only has the ring of truth about it but an aura of hope as well'
JONATHAN DIMBLEBY

'*The Other Side of Israel* could not be more timely ... It deserves wide attention as a profoundly human story, thoughtful and funny and unafraid'
TLS

'An eye-opening account' *Sunday Times*

'A powerful, readable and courageous book' *Tablet*

SUSAN NATHAN

The Other Side of Israel

MY JOURNEY ACROSS
THE JEWISH–ARAB DIVIDE

HARPER PERENNIAL

London, New York, Toronto and Sydney

Harper Perennial
An imprint of HarperCollins*Publishers*
77–85 Fulham Palace Road
Hammersmith
London W6 8JB

www.harperperennial.co.uk

This edition published by Harper Perennial 2006

First published in Great Britain by HarperCollins*Publishers* 2005

A catalogue record for this book is available from the British Library

ISBN-13 978-0-00-719511-4

Set in PostScript Linotype Minion by
Rowland Phototypesetting Ltd, Bury St Edmunds, Suffolk

Printed and bound in Great Britain by Clays Ltd, St Ives plc

In memory of my parents,
Sam and Maisie Levy.

And for my children,
Daniel and Tanya.

Contents

Illustrations

Unless otherwise stated, all photographs are from the author's collection.

Me aged about eighteen months, with my father.

My parents on the beach at Blouberg Strand near Cape Town, April 1976.

A view of the street from my terrace in Tamra.

View of Tamra from my apartment.

My street in Tamra.

Election poster for the Hadash party in Tamra, 2004.

An Arab home with a farmyard of sheep, goats and chickens in the garden. *(Jonathan Cook)*

My neighbours in Tamra during an engagement party.

A Tamra neighbour making traditional pitta.

Engagement party in Tamra.

Street scene in Tamra during the festival of Eid al-Adha.

A Palestinian family stand on the site of their former home, demolished by the Israeli authorities in February 2004, in the Galilean village of Beaneh. *(Jonathan Cook)*

The Dona Rosa restaurant in the Ein Hod artists' colony, which before Israel's creation in 1948 was a mosque in the Palestinian village of Ayn Hawd. *(Jonathan Cook)*

At an event held to mark the Palestinian 'nakba' (catastrophe) on

27 April 2004 – Israel's Independence Day – an Israeli Arab boy distributes signs naming some of the four hundred Palestinian villages destroyed by the Israeli army in the 1948 war that founded the Jewish state. *(Jonathan Cook)*

Eitan Bronstein of the Israeli Jewish lobby group Zochrot helps erect a signpost alerting local residents in Haifa to the fact that Arab neighbourhoods existed there before they were cleared during the war to found Israel. *(Jonathan Cook)*

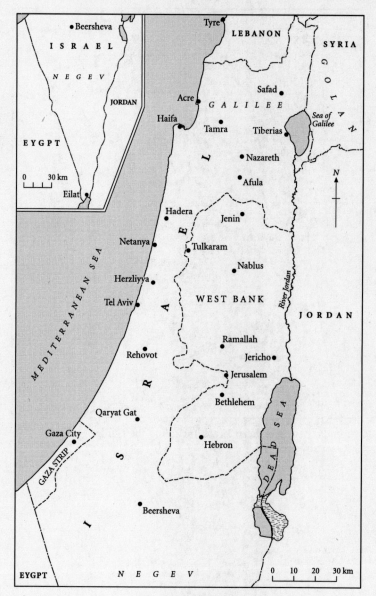

The state of Israel

Northern Israel, including the Galilee

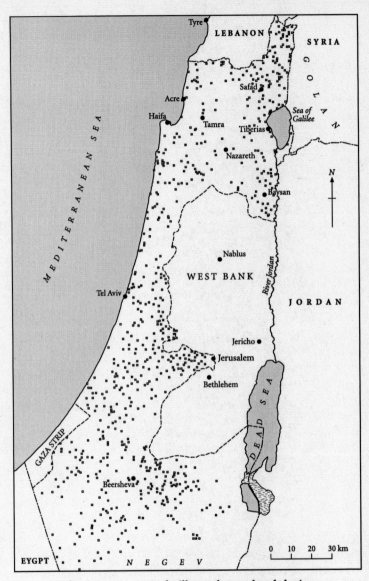

Palestinian towns and villages depopulated during
the foundation of Israel in 1948

xiii

Acknowledgements

It was a sweltering July night nearly two years ago when friends introduced me to Jonathan Cook, a British reporter based in the Israeli Arab city of Nazareth. The place of our meeting was the Beit al-Falastini (the Palestinian House), a renovated ancient stone building in the city's old market that during the day serves as a coffee house and at night is the nearest thing Nazareth has to a pub. We chatted in the dim surroundings of the cavernous interior, barely able to make each other out in the flickering candle-light. But it soon became clear from our conversation that we shared a common concern about the direction Israel is taking. For both of us, this was of more than academic interest: I have adopted this country as my new home, and Jonathan has adopted it through his marriage to Sally Azzam, a native Nazarene.

After our first meeting, Jonathan, ever the inquisitive journalist, arranged to come to Tamra to talk to me again. He published the interview in Britain's *Guardian* newspaper on 27 August 2003 under the headline 'A Jew Among 25,000 Muslims'. That article sparked worldwide interest in my story and brought me to the attention of HarperCollins, who have now encouraged me to publish a much fuller account of my journey from one side of the ethnic divide to the other. My deepest thanks go to Jonathan, who has been a companion on that journey, helping a novice author give expression to her thoughts, experiences and impressions. Without his guidance,

I have no doubt this would have been a poorer book. But most of all I want to thank Jonathan for his dedication to reporting the truth and his unwavering commitment to creating a more just and humane society in Israel.

My thanks also go to: Sally Azzam Cook for her patience, suggestions and help to Jonathan; Dr Asad Ghanem, head of politics at Haifa University, and his wife Ahlam for opening their home to me and helping to change the course of my life by teaching me about the reality of theirs; Dr Uri Davis for his steadfast friendship and sound advice on a wide variety of subjects, and his enormous contribution towards explaining the essence of the conflict; Rabbi Dr John D. Rayner for his support and enthusiasm regarding my move to Tamra; Dr Afif Safieh, the Palestinian delegate to the United Kingdom and the Holy See, for his support, guidance and encouragement; Dr Mahdi Abdul Hadi, head of the Palestinian Academic Society for the Study of International Affairs (Passia), East Jerusalem, for his friendship, support and the use of his wonderful library; Dr Daphna Golan, director of the Minerva Centre for Human Rights, Hebrew University of Jerusalem, for her friendship, shared concerns and time; Dr Adel Manna, of the Van Leer Institute, Jerusalem, whose phone call of support was deeply appreciated, and for his historical input; Dr Said Zidane, associate professor at Al-Quds University, East Jerusalem, for enlightening conversations held in his family's home in Tamra and for his continuing support of my endeavours; Amin Sahli, Tamra's city engineer, for teaching me the difficulties of planning in a town without land; Eitan Bronstein of Zochrot for his shared vision of what life could be in Israel and for his courage; Harry Finkbeiner of Kibbutz Harduf for help with research; the Gaza Community Mental Health Care Project for their guidance of and support for my work for Mahapach, and for their generous invitation to visit Gaza to learn from them; Wehbe Badarni of Sawt al-Amal (Voice of the Labourer) in Nazareth, for teaching me about employment discrimination and for his devotion to his work; Abdullah Barakat, assistant to the Governor of Jenin, for helping me meet the people of Jenin; Mayor Adel Abu Hayja and the Municipality of Tamra for welcoming me into their community; Richard Johnson, my editor, for his determination to see my story in print and for his continuous encouragement; Dr Carlos Lesmes, anaesthetist, for his ongoing help and support in pain control and his interest in the book, Dr Oded Schoenberg for his patience and compassion, and the rest of the team at the Herziliya Medical Centre who have been on my 'case' for the last five years: Arlette Calderon, Dr Nissim Ohana, Dr Daniel Kern, Avi Millstein; Professor Ya'acov Pe'er and the Department of Ophthalmology at the Hadassah hospital, Jerusalem, without whom I would never have got this far; Mahapach for their unique contribution to Israeli society; and my friends, too numerous to mention individually. Special thanks go to my 'family' in Tamra for their trust in me and for the remarkable way in which they absorbed me into their circle.

Finally, I have changed the names of some people who appear in the book, including my family in Tamra, for reasons of confidentiality and safety.

Susan Nathan
Tamra, Israel
December 2004

1

The Road to Tamra

The road to the other side of Israel is not signposted. It is a place you rarely read about in your newspapers or hear about from your television sets. It is all but invisible to most Israelis.

In the Galilee, Israel's most northerly region, the green signs dotted all over the highways point out the direction of Haifa, Acre and Karmiel, all large Jewish towns, and even much smaller Jewish communities like Shlomi and Misgav. But as my taxi driver Shaher and I look for Tamra we find no signs. Or none until we are heading downhill, racing the other traffic along a stretch of dual carriageway. By a turn-off next to a large metal shack selling fruit and vegetables is a white sign pointing rightwards to Tamra, forcing us to make a dangerous last-minute lane change to exit the main road. Before us stretching into the distance is a half-made road, and at the end of it a pale grey mass of concrete squats within a shallow hollow in the rugged Galilean hills. Shaher looks genuinely startled. 'My God, it's Tulkaram!' he exclaims, referring to a Palestinian town and refugee camp notorious among Israelis as a hotbed of terrorism.

A few weeks earlier, in November 2002, I had rung the removals company in Tel Aviv to warn them well in advance of my move to Tamra, a town of substantial size by Israeli standards, close to the Mediterranean coast between the modern industrial port of Haifa and the ancient Crusader port of Acre. Unlike the communities I had seen well signposted in the Galilee, Tamra is not Jewish; it is an

Arab town that is home to twenty-five thousand Muslims. A fact almost unknown outside Israel is that the Jewish state includes a large minority of one million Palestinians who have Israeli citizenship. Comprising a fifth of the population, they are popularly, and not a little disparagingly, known as 'Israeli Arabs'. For a Jew to choose to live among them is unheard of. In fact it is more than that: it is inconceivable.

When I told my left-wing friends in Tel Aviv of my decision all of them without exception were appalled. First they angrily dismissed my choice, assuming either that it was a sign of my perverse misunderstanding of Middle Eastern realities or that it was a childish attempt to gain attention. But as it became clear that my mind was made up, they resorted to more intimidatory tactics. 'You'll be killed,' more than one told me. 'You know, the Arabs are friendly to start with, but they'll turn on you,' advised another. 'You'll be raped by the men,' said one more. Finally, another friend took me aside and confided darkly: 'I have a telephone number for a special unit in the army. They can come in and get you out if you need help. Just let me know.'

The woman at the removals company was less perturbed. 'Will it be possible for you to move me from Tel Aviv to Tamra?' I asked, concerned that as far as I could discern no one was living as a Jew inside an Israeli Arab community. I told her that if they had a problem with the move, they should tell me now. 'Madam, we will deliver your belongings to anywhere in the state of Israel,' she reassured me.

I arranged for Shaher, who I had used often in Tel Aviv, to collect me from my apartment on the day of the move. On the two-hour journey north we would lead the way in his taxi, with the removal truck following behind. Shaher phoned the day before to reassure me. 'I have been looking carefully at the road map and I've devised a route to the Galilee which won't involve passing too many Arab villages,' he told me. 'But we are heading for an Arab town,' I reminded him. 'Why on earth would I be worried about the route?' Shaher did not seem to get my point.

We set off early the next day. Shaher was soon announcing, unbidden, his concern at my move to Tamra. What followed was a surreal exchange, the first of many such conversations I would have with taxi drivers and other Jews I met after I started living in Tamra. 'So why are you moving there?' he asked several times, apparently not persuaded by my reply each time, 'Because I want to.' Finally, he changed tack: 'You know it's an Arab area?' Yes, I said, I think I know that. 'So have you got an apartment there?' Yes. 'How did you get an apartment?' I rented it, I said, just as I had done in Tel Aviv. Under his breath I could hear him muttering, 'But it's an Arab area.' Then suddenly, as though it were a vital question he should have asked much earlier, he said: 'Do you have a gun?' Why would I need a gun, I asked. 'Because they might kill you.' I told him he was talking nonsense. Silence separated us until his face changed again. 'Ah,' he said, 'you must be working for the government and I didn't know it.' No, I said, I work just for myself. 'But it's an Arab area,' he said again.

It was a cold winter's day, but by the time we reached the road into Tamra I could see Shaher starting to break out into a sweat. In a final offer of help, he said: 'Susan, you have my telephone numbers. If you need to come back to Tel Aviv, just call me.'

We followed the only proper road in Tamra to the central mosque and then negotiated our way up a steeply sloping side-street till we reached my new home, hidden down a small alley. I was renting the top-floor apartment in a three-storey property belonging to a family I had already befriended, the Abu Hayjas. Several members of the family came out to greet me, including the matriarch of the house, Hajji, and one of her granddaughters, Omayma. I went into the ground-floor apartment and had been chatting for maybe twenty minutes when Omayma interrupted. 'Susan, why don't they get out and start moving your furniture?' I went to the door and looked over to the removal truck for the first time since we entered Tamra. The two young men sitting inside the cab looked as if they were afflicted with total paralysis. I turned to Omayma and replied, only half-jokingly: 'Because they think you are going to eat them.'

I went over to the truck and knocked on the closed window, telling them it was time to get to work. They didn't look too convinced, and could only be coaxed out when Hajji proved the natives' hospitality by bringing out a pot of coffee, two cups and some biscuits, and placing them on a table close to the truck. Once out in the street the removal men opened the back of the truck and did the job in no time, running up and down the stairs with the boxes. Finished, they hurried back into the truck and raced down the steep street back towards the mosque and onwards to freedom. I never saw them again. The reinforced cardboard packing boxes they were supposed to return for a week later remained in my spare room uncollected for weeks. Eventually I rang the company. 'I'm sorry, but they won't come back to an Arab area just for the boxes,' said the woman I spoke to.

It started to dawn on me that I had crossed an ethnic divide in Israel that, although not visible, was as tangible as the concrete walls and razor-wire fences that have been erected around the occupied Palestinian towns of the West Bank and Gaza to separate them from the rest of the country. Nothing was likely to be the same ever again.

I had no intention of hiding from Tamra's twenty-five thousand other inhabitants the fact that I was a Jew. But from the moment I arrived in the town to teach English I began redefining my identity, as a Jew, as an Israeli and as a human being. The first and most apparent change was that I was joining a new family, the Abu Hayjas, who immediately accepted me as one of their own, as integral to the family's life as any new daughter-in-law. In keeping with Arab tradition, I was soon renamed 'Umm Daniel' (Mother of Daniel), after my eldest son, a status conferred on older, and wiser, parents.

The immediate family I live with is small by Tamra's standards, consisting of only six other members. The eldest is the widowed Fatima, sixty-eight years of age and called Hajji by everyone because she has completed the hajj pilgrimage to Mecca, one of the duties incumbent on all Muslims during their lifetime. She married at seventeen, living with her husband for four years before he died. For a woman of her generation there was never any possibility that she could remarry, and so she has remained a widow all her adult life. Hajji had two children, a son and a daughter, but in Arab tradition only the son stays in the family home after marriage, while the daughter goes off to live with her new husband. So Hajji's son, Hassan, fifty, and his wife Samira, forty-seven, live with her in the same building, and the couple's two unmarried grown-up sons, Khalil and Waleed, each have their own apartments there in preparation for their marriages. Hassan and Samira's two eldest daughters, Heba and Omayma, are married, and so have left home to be with their new families, though they spend a large part of their time visiting their parents and helping in the house. That leaves only Suad, aged seventeen, the one daughter still at home.

Although that is the core of the family, it extends much further. Hajji's own father married twice, so we have a vast network of aunts, uncles and cousins, and half-aunts, half-uncles and half-cousins, who come to visit and drink coffee with us in Hajji's apartment. They are all related in complex patterns that I cannot even begin to unravel but that the rest of my family understand intimately. Unlike me, they are helped by a lifelong familiarity with their extensive family tree and by the Arabic language, which has adapted to accommodate these relationships in more sophisticated ways than English. Aunts, uncles and cousins have titles which denote the blood relationship to each parent's side of the family. So, for example, the word 'ami' tells any Arab child that one of his father's sisters is being referred to, while 'hali' reveals that one of his mother's sisters is being identified. The English equivalent for both words, 'aunt', is far less helpful.

And then beyond the extended family there is the bigger family structure, known as the 'hamula' or clan. There are four main hamulas in Tamra – the Abu Hayja, the Abu Romi, the Diab and the Hijazi – with each controlling a portion of the town, its quarter. My own family, as its name suggests, belongs to the Abu Hayja hamula, which dominates the southern side of Tamra. The hamula system means that everyone in our neighbourhood is related to us, even if it is in some very distant fashion. The importance of the hamula cannot be overstated: it is the ultimate body to which members of traditional Arab society owe their loyalty. In the West the hamula, or tribal system, is seen as backward and a block to progress, but I soon realised that this is a gross simplification. In Middle Eastern countries the tribe still fulfils a positive role (one usurped in the West by the welfare state), ensuring its members have access to land, housing, jobs, loans, and a pool of potential marriage partners. The hamula is the best protector of its members' rights, and it provides an impartial forum in arbitrating disputes. It is revealing that in Israel, where a strong welfare state has developed, at least for Jewish citizens, the hamula still plays an invaluable role in many Arab citizens' lives. Because the state continues to behave as though the Arab citizens are really not its responsibility, many choose to rely on the traditional tribal structure for support.

The hamula serves other functions. It is a crucial point of social reference, a guarantor, if you like, of an individual's good family name. For example, I soon noticed that when two Arabs met for the first time they would spend several minutes tied up in trying to establish a significant mutual acquaintance. Evidently it was important for both of them to identify each other's place in relation to the various hamulas. Sometimes there would be a series of 'Do you know so and so?' until both parties could relax at the discovery of a common bond; things could be tense if it took them some time to reach that point. Now, when people are introduced to me, they ask similar questions of me, and are reassured by my link to the good name of the Abu Hayja hamula and my immediate family.

For me, as for the rest of my family, the centre of gravity in our lives is to be found in a single figure: Hajji. Her ground-floor apartment is where we often congregate for food, and it is outside her front door that I like to sit with her on a stool first thing in the morning while she makes us strong black Arabic coffee over a stove. The ritual of coffee-making is taken very seriously in all Palestinian households, and Hajji is an expert practitioner. Over a gas flame she dissolves a home-made mixture of coffee and cardamom powder with water and sugar in a small open pot. Just before the liquid boils over she pulls it away from the heat, stirs it until it settles and then heats it again, repeating this process up to half a dozen times. Finally the pot is left standing for five minutes, a saucer over the top, as the sludge sinks to the bottom. When the coffee is ready, it is poured into tiny cups.

In the time I have been in Tamra, Hajji and I have forged a very deep bond, despite communication difficulties. Speaking in a mixture of broken English, Hebrew and Arabic, we laugh about our common ailments, and our love of flowers and nature. Hajji is an authority on traditional Arab remedies, and when I damaged my knee, for example, she suggested wrapping cabbage leaves around it to draw out the fluid.

Widowed at twenty-one, Hajji has known severe economic hardship, and raised her family in extreme poverty. She tells stories from her youth of going out into the fields to catch hedgehogs and, desperate for protein, stripping the animals of their prickly skin and roasting them on a spit. Hajji's skills in making the most of the little she has are phenomenal. She knits incredibly beautiful children's clothes without a pattern to follow; it's all there in her head. She also has a profound understanding of nature, which I marvel at whenever I watch her in the garden. She has large hands with delicate fingers that plant seeds at high speed and deftly pick out herbs. She selects the Arab mint, sorrel and chamomile plants for our tea, picks off the parts she doesn't want, and lays the rest out to dry in large round wooden sieves. Later she breaks them up into small pieces for storage in jars. There is a calm, rhythmic quality to her work that I find reassuring and meditative.

But she is getting weaker with age, and nowadays has trouble visiting the rest of the family, who live on the first and second floors of the building. So family occasions are invariably held in her flat. The family now jokes that the only time Hajji leaves her apartment is if someone in the extended family has a child, gets married or dies. It's more or less true. Recently, though, she has started going to an old people's centre, where she does embroidery and knitting. She is collected in the morning and arrives home early in the afternoon. But she generally prefers to be at home, and I don't like it when she is away too long. I never really knew either of my two sets of grandparents, and even though she is little more than ten years older than me, Hajji, I think, has become a surrogate grandmother.

Hajji and her daughter-in-law Samira together form the backbone of what in the West would surely have become a small business. For downstairs, next to Hajji's apartment, is a garden and covered area where they produce, manufacture and store the huge quantities of food the family needs. We are a restaurant, plant nursery, canning and pickling plant and bakery all in one. Every week there seems to be a different task, each one revolving around the particular growing season. It might be pickling cucumbers, cauliflowers and carrots for use during the rest of the year; or going to collect zatar (a herb akin to thyme and oregano) out in the wilds, then bringing it back to dry it, mix it with sesame seeds and grind it; or buying staples like rice, flour and bulgar wheat for storage in big containers. There are always piles of boxes, sacks and barrels waiting to be labelled and stored away.

A special occasion in the year is the olive harvest in late October, when we all disappear off to the edge of town, to a small patch of ground where the family has an olive grove. There for three or four days we crowd among the trees, up ladders picking off handfuls of the green and black fruit and throwing them onto tarpaulins below. At the end of the day the tarpaulins are gathered up and the olives bagged into sacks. Some we later pickle in glass bottles, while the rest goes to the press in town. After the harvest, the family gave me the first bottle of oil as a gift.

Much of our diet, however, grows next to us in the small garden. That is the traditional way in Arab communities, although it is a way of life slowly dying because of both the arrival of out-of-town supermarkets and the extensive confiscation of Arab communities' agricultural land by the Jewish state. Some Arab areas have lost all their farming lands, but at least Tamra has managed to hold onto some. The ever increasing territorial confinement of the town, however, means that few families can spare what little land they have left to grow subsistence crops for their own use. Instead they have tended to construct homes for other family members, building ever more tightly next to each other.

In my family's garden a huge number of herbs, some I do not know by any English name, grow amid the more common vegetables such as cabbages, peppers, courgettes, cucumbers and beans. We have our own orange and lemon trees, figs, pomegranates and vines. The leaves of the vines, like other vegetables, are cooked after being stuffed with a mixture of rice and meat. But first they must be stripped of their stalks, an art that both Hajji and Samira mastered decades ago but which, despite many attempts, I cannot perform without tearing the leaves.

Many of the dishes we eat here are uncommon to Western eyes, even though they are just as delicious and healthy as the cuisines of Mediterranean countries such as Italy and Spain. We serve up a huge array of stuffed vegetables, not just the more familiar vine leaves and peppers, but also artichokes, cabbage leaves, courgettes, aubergines and small marrows known as kari'a. Other familiar traditional dishes are okra in a rich tomato sauce (bamiye) or with beans (lubia); a dry lentil and onion stew (majedera); a tasty paste of green leaves known as mloukiye; and a seasonal thorny weed called akoub that is found in Galilean fields and has to be carefully prepared before eating. These dishes are made in large pots at lunchtime, the main meal, and then kept hot with a thick blanket wrapped around them so that family and visitors can eat at any time during the rest of the day.

But given the size of Arab families and the need to have something on the stove ready for guests, Hajji and Samira also make lots of healthy snack food. There are always large quantities of freshly made hummous available, far better than anything you can buy in a shop; a creamy sesame paste called tahina mixed with parsley; a puree of broad beans, tahina and garlic known as fool; a mash of aubergine and tahina called mutabal; and a bitter home-made yoghurt known as labaneh. All of these are served up with the local pitta bread, which we bake ourselves in a special oven. The equivalent of pizza here is something known as manakiesh, a bread topped with melted salty cheese or zatar. Hajji sits squat on the floor, as Africans do when preparing food, to roll out the dough. For special occasions the family will also make finger food: pastry parcels (ftir) stuffed with cheese, spinach or zatar; or mini-pizzas topped with meat and pine nuts (sfiha). The most prized dish of all is tabouli, a salad of minutely chopped parsley, bulgar wheat, tomato and spring onion, soaked in olive oil and lemon.

My apartment in Tamra was never meant as a temporary base, nor as a social experiment. It is as much my home as was Tel Aviv when I first arrived in Israel six years ago, or as was London before that. This is where, aged fifty-six, I am choosing to root myself for the foreseeable future. I have filled my apartment with all the most precious things I have collected over a lifetime: the mementoes of my childhood in Britain, of my many travels to South Africa, where much of my family still lives, and of my more recent life in the Middle East. I have original paintings by South African and Palestinian artists, Bedouin carpets on the floor, stacks of CDs of music from around the world, and a wide range of books on subjects that especially interest me: from psychology and politics to biographies. My father instilled in me a deep appreciation of Jewish culture and ethics, and many of my favourite books reflect that. Like me, it is an eclectic mix.

From my balcony the main view is of Tamra, its grey homes pressing upon their neighbours, offering no privacy at all. Electricity and telephone cables are slung haphazardly across the streets, attached chaotically to metal pylons or wooden poles, many of which are planted in the centre of roads, creating a major traffic hazard. The roads themselves drop precipitously in a network of lanes that no one appears ever to have planned, their surfaces only half-made or scarred by potholes. Every street is lined with rubble or rubbish, and piles of dust swirl in the wind. Children with no parks or even gardens to play in squat in the streets making games with stones, discarded bottles or sticks, dodging the passing traffic. In the winter, which is when I arrived, showers instantly overwhelm the drains, bringing torrents of water washing down the streets, a miserable stain of brown and grey.

But the story inside people's homes is very different. Amid all this public squalor, everyone maintains their private space in meticulous order. Homes are cleaned daily, with the surfaces so spotless that you could eat off them. Even the poorest families invest their energies in making their homes bright and attractive, bringing as much colour into their domestic lives as is possible within Tamra's dour surroundings.

Despite the oppressive atmosphere there are many compensations to living in Tamra, including the warmth and friendliness of the people and the town's location. Here in the Galilee the air is clean and the light pure. From my lofty position both on a hillside and on the building's top floor I overlook my neighbours to see far to the north, to the high hills of the Upper Galilee and almost to

Lebanon. The rocky slopes embracing Tamra change colour through the day, settling into wonderful hues of orange and purple at sunset. In the late afternoon the shadows of the tall cypress trees lengthen rapidly, like nature's timepieces. I love to look out at the clear sky at night, as the stars slowly emerge into life and a luminous moon rises over the horizon. Out on the nearby hills are to be found an amazing variety of wildflowers in the spring, including breathtaking displays of baby cyclamen and anemones. In the summer the air is filled with the perfume of the blossoms of jasmine, hibiscus, orange and oleander, which somehow manage to root themselves in spite of all the concrete. There are fig and pomegranate trees everywhere, affording another of the great joys of living here: being able to pluck the heavy fruit directly from the trees as one walks in the street.

Moving into an Arab community in Israel, however, means changing one's definition of privacy. There is no sense of the anonymity that is a major component of life in Tel Aviv, New York or London. Hajji's door is never closed, unless she is out. And it would never occur to anyone in the family to knock before entering her home, or to ask before opening her fridge. That doesn't just go for Hajji, it applies to everyone here. (Apart, I should add, from me. A special allowance is made in my case, and the family knocks before entering my apartment.) I find this lack of barriers both rewarding and a drawback. In my first few weeks I was invited to an art exhibition in Haifa by a well-known Palestinian artist, Salam Diab. We arrived back home late to find, unusually, the lights were still on. I went inside to say hello, only to discover Hassan and his two sons, Khalil and Waleed, sitting in a row on the sofa watching the television and nervously awaiting my return. When I saw their worried faces, I looked at Hassan, more than five years my junior, and announced, 'I'm back!' We both started laughing. Nowadays I always make sure that they can reach me on my mobile phone, because I know they worry about my safety. At first this seemed like an intrusion, but now I have come to see the advantages. Being absorbed into the family means that I enjoy its protection and its concern for my welfare.

Not all the loss of privacy is cultural, however. Someone I met in my first week in Tamra equated living here with being in a goldfish bowl. I already knew what she meant. On my first morning in my new apartment I opened the blinds of my bedroom window, at the back of the house, to find that I was staring directly across at my neighbours' house a few metres away – and at my neighbours, who were looking out from their own window. On all sides of the house, apart from my balcony at the front, neighbours' homes are pressing up against mine. If I have the blinds up, there is almost nowhere in the apartment where I can be free from prying eyes. Ghetto living is more than just a feeling of confinement; it is a sense of suffocation too.

During my first weeks the sense of being watched followed me into the streets. Walking around Tamra I felt like a specimen in the zoo, as if every article of clothing I wore, and every movement I made, was being observed from a thousand different angles. When I went to the shops everyone stared at me. Everyone. People would stop dead in their tracks, and on a few occasions there were nearly traffic accidents – the drivers couldn't quite believe what they were seeing. What, their eyes were asking, was a blonde-haired woman doing here alone? There was never any enmity in their looks; only surprise or bewilderment.

I cannot claim to be the only non-Arab woman ever to have lived here. There are a few others, though you'll find them concealed by the hijab, the Islamic headscarf. These women have found love with local men who studied or worked abroad, and returned home with them. There are even former Jews in the town, women who maybe met their husband-to-be at university or through work. But they have all converted – as they must do by law in Israel, where there is no civil marriage – and live here as Muslims. Many of these

13

newcomers struggle with the culture shock and the lack of amenities. A young doctor recently left Tamra with his new Romanian wife to live in the more cosmopolitan city of Haifa, perhaps the one place in Israel where Jews and Arabs can live in some sort of mutual accommodation, if not quite equality.

But for a woman to be living here without an Arab husband is unheard of. And for her to be a self-declared Jew is off the register. As I negotiated the town's streets during the first few weeks, learning Tamra's chaotic geography, I would see groups of people sitting outside their homes drinking coffee and chatting. The women's heads would move closer together as I went past. They never pointed – Arabs are far too polite for that – but it was clear I was the topic of conversation. After a few days, the odd person worked up the courage to stop me in the street and strike up a conversation. They always addressed me in Hebrew, a language Arabs in Israel must learn at school. This made me uncomfortable, especially after an early warning from one of my occasional neighbours, Dr Said Zidane, head of the Palestinian Independent Commission in Ramallah, in the Palestinian West Bank. His mother lives next to me, and on a visit to see her he advised me not to speak Hebrew as it might arouse the suspicion that I was working for the government or the security services, the Shin Bet, which is known to run spies in Arab communities. He suggested I exploit my lack of fluent Hebrew and speak English instead.

Always I would be asked where I had lived before moving to Tamra, and the questioners would be amazed by my reply. 'Why would you want to live here after living in Tel Aviv?' they would ask. Why not, I would say. 'But it's obvious: Tel Aviv has cinemas, theatres, coffee houses, proper shops, tree-lined streets, libraries, community centres, a transport system . . .' The list was always long. Their incomprehension at my choice revealed the difference between my life and theirs. Although I choose to live in Tamra, as a Jew I am always free to cross back over the ethnic divide. I think nothing of an hour's train ride from Haifa to Tel Aviv. But for them the trip involves crossing a boundary, one that is real as well as psychological. To be an Israeli Arab visiting a Jewish community is to be instantly a target, an alien identifiable through the give-aways of language, culture and often appearance. They must enter a space where they are not welcome and may be treated as an intruder. The danger, ever-present in their minds, is of encountering hostility or even violence. They know from surveys published in local newspapers that a majority of Israeli Jews want them expelled from the country. They also hear about frequent attacks on Arabs by Jewish youths and racist policemen. Many of my Arab friends have told me how uncomfortable they feel about going to Jewish areas. Khalil in my house, who is a film-maker, travels to Tel Aviv only when he has to, on business or to buy new equipment, and he leaves as soon as his work is done.

Unlike the cold, impersonal atmosphere of Tel Aviv, Muslim communities like Tamra take a pride in their hospitality to friends and strangers alike. But when you are living in – as opposed to visiting – an Arab community, the hospitality comes as a double-edged sword. One March morning I told Hassan I was going to the chemist, a couple of hundred metres down the hill. I was gone for an hour and a half: on the way, at least fifteen people stopped me for a chat or to invite me in for coffee. On my return Hassan asked with concern where I had been. When I told him, he laughed and suggested I start wearing the veil. 'At least that way you can go about your business without attracting so much attention,' he joked.

It's true that trying to get things done always seems to take longer in Arab society, and although being welcomed into people's homes is a wonderful thing, equally it can be inconvenient, time-consuming and stifling. The fear of insulting a neighbour or a friend by refusing an invitation for coffee or a meal can make a quick trip to the shops a dismaying prospect. There is a vague formula to invitations to people's homes, which in essence involves being offered a cold drink, possibly accompanied by nuts, fruit or biscuits. There may be tea later, or a meal depending on the time of day and the closeness of the relationship. The signal that the host needs to get on with something else – or that he or she is tired of your company – usually comes when they produce a pot of coffee.

Conversations in people's homes are wide-ranging, particularly with older Tamrans, who have experienced enough earth-shattering events to fill anyone's lifetime. One old man told me in detail about the different train routes that could be taken from the Galilee all over the Middle East before the creation of Israel, when the borders existed as no more than lines on maps produced by the area's British and French rulers. Here in the Galilee, he told me, we were at the very heart of the Middle East, with all the region's biggest cities – Beirut (Lebanon), Damascus (Syria), Amman (Jordan) and Jerusa-lem (Palestine) – a two-hour trip or less away. Today only Jerusalem is easily accessible: Beirut and Damascus are in enemy states and Amman lies across a heavily guarded international border. Personally I felt frustration at being barred from visiting most of these places, but for Arab citizens the borders represent something far more tragic. Many people in Tamra, like other Palestinians, have loved ones still living in refugee camps in Lebanon and Syria more than five decades after they were forced to flee during the war that founded the Jewish state. Israel refuses to let the refugees return, and neither Israel nor Lebanon or Syria want their populations crossing over the borders. So a meeting between separated relatives – even brothers and sisters, and in a few cases husbands and wives – remains all but impossible.

Few Israeli Arabs in the Galilee, apart from an educated elite, know much of the world outside their immediate region. Many venture no further than Haifa, less than twenty-five kilometres away. Few can afford to travel to Europe for a holiday, and most of the Arab states are off limits. They can at least go by bus to Jordan and Egypt, which have signed peace treaties with Israel, but even then the reception is not always warm. Egyptians in particular have difficulty with the idea that someone can be an Israeli and an Arab at the same time. The assumption – shared, to be honest, by most Westerners – is that if you are Israeli you must be Jewish. 'I get fed up hearing the Egyptian taxi drivers telling me that I speak good Arabic for a Jew,' Khalil once remarked to me.

Many conversations in Tamra concern the town's history. It had often occurred to me that Tamra looked much like a refugee camp. Like other Israelis, I had seen plenty of television images of the bleak camps of Gaza and the West Bank, the background to Palestinian children throwing stones at Israeli tanks. Those camps, some no more than an hour's drive from Tamra, and other Palestinian towns and villages are inhabited by more than three and a half million Palestinians who are not Israeli citizens but live under Israeli military occupation. What shocked me was that, as Shaher had observed, Tamra looked much the same as Gaza and the West Bank – only the tanks and the soldiers were missing. But Tamra's inhabitants, unlike those of the occupied territories, are not at war with Israel. They are citizens of a democratic state.

During a conversation one morning over coffee with Hajji, I learned that my observation about the town's appearance was far nearer the truth than I could have imagined. Much of Tamra was in fact a refugee camp. It was like a dark, ugly secret that no one in the town would dwell on for too long. But photographs from 1948, the year in which the Jewish state was declared, prompting a war with the indigenous Palestinian population, show not only a scattering of Tamra's stone houses but also a sea of Red Cross tents housing refugees from the fighting.

In 1947 Tamra had a population of no more than two thousand people, but a year later that figure had risen to three thousand. Today, according to Amin Sahli, a civil engineer and the local town planner, a third of Tamrans are classified as internal refugees, refused permission ever to return to their original homes. In the callous,

Orwellian language of Israeli bureaucracy they and another quarter of a million Israeli Arabs are known as 'present absentees': present in Israel in 1948, but absent from their homes when the authorities registered all property in the new Jewish state. Everything these refugees owned, from their land and homes to their possessions and bank accounts, has been confiscated and is now owned by the state. They and their descendants lost everything they had in 1948. The members of my own family are refugees too, having fled from neighbouring villages in the Galilee.

More than four hundred Palestinian villages were destroyed by the Israeli army during and after the war of 1948, to prevent the refugees from returning. There was even a special government department created to plan the destruction. So why did Tamra and another hundred or so Palestinian villages remain relatively untouched by the fighting fifty-seven years ago? Amin told me that the town survived for two reasons: first, it was located off the main routes used by the advancing Israeli army, and therefore its defeat was not considered a military necessity; and second, Tamra was a small community that had a history of, to phrase it generously, 'cooperating' with the pre-state Jewish authorities as well as with local Jewish businesses. It was, in other words, a useful pool of cheap labour in the area. Soon the farmers of Tamra were turning their skills to the advantage of Jewish farming cooperatives like the kibbutzim or were being 'reskilled' to work in building cheap modern estates of homes for the Jewish immigrants who flooded into the new state of Israel. Tamrans lost their traditional skills of building in stone and wood and learned to construct only in the bland, grey, concrete garb of modern Tamra.

According to Hajji, the first refugees into Tamra were sheltered in the homes of the existing inhabitants. But soon the town was being overwhelmed: hundreds of Palestinians arrived from the destroyed villages of Damun, Ein Hod, Balad al-Sheikh, Haditha and Mi'ar. The early warm welcome turned much colder. Most of the new arrivals fell under the responsibility of the Red Cross, who housed them in tents, but after a few years the international community passed responsibility for the internal refugees' fate back to Israel. It was some fifteen years before the last tents were gone, recalls Hajji, as many people were reluctant to give up the hope that one day they would be able to return to their original homes.

Stripped of all their possessions, the refugee families had to work and save money to buy land from the original inhabitants of Tamra, so that they could turn their fabric homes into concrete ones. That fact alone goes a long way to explaining the unplanned, chaotic geography of Tamra and other Israeli Arab communities. The roads, originally designed for the horse and cart, were simply diverted around the maze of 'concrete tents'.

During the subsequent decades Israel has re-zoned most of Tamra's outlying lands as green areas, doing yet more damage to the town's already unnatural development. Hemmed in on all sides by land that it cannot use, Tamra's rapidly growing population has been unable to expand territorially. Instead it has had to grow much denser. Today's twenty-five thousand inhabitants exist in a town that in reality barely has room for a quarter of that number. This is apparent in even the tiniest aspects of the town's infrastructure. Consider the toilets, for example. Nothing has been spent on improving the sewerage system since the days more than half a century ago when the few dozen houses here each had a basic hole in the ground. Now all families have a flushing toilet, but they all feed into an overstretched network of ancient pipes that catered to a different reality. In my first few days, the family tactfully explained to me why there was a bucket by the toilet. If I continued to flush toilet paper down the bowl, they warned me, I would block the pipes in no time.

The overcrowding isn't restricted to the humans of Tamra. Everywhere there are animals: not cats or dogs, but those more familiar from the farmyard. In the early evening it is common to see teenage boys riding horses bareback down the streets at high speed, jostling for space with the cars. When not being ridden, these horses are to be found tethered in families' tiny backyards or under their houses, along with pens of sheep and goats, and chicken sheds. In some parts of Tamra, particularly in the Abu Romi quarter, every home seems to be operating as a cramped small farm. Sheep and goats are often penned up in the space where you would expect to find the family car. I found this quite baffling until Hajji explained the reason. Before 1948 most of Tamra's families had either farmed commercially or owned land to subsist on, but in the intervening years Israel had either confiscated or re-zoned their fields. Families lost their crops, but they were at least able to hold onto their animals by bringing them to their homes. Samira's daughter Omayma, who lives with her husband's family in the middle of town on the main street, has a vast collection of animals. Until recently they included an impressive flock of geese, but their numbers were slowly whittled down by a pack of wild dogs.

Another striking feature of Tamra is the apparent absence of shops. None of the Israeli high street names are here, nor are the international chains. It is not for lack of local interest: Tamrans will drive long distances, to Haifa and elsewhere, to shop at the larger clothes stores, and they are as keen to eat an American burger as any Jew. Presumably, however, these chains are too nervous to set up shop in an Arab town. (McDonald's Israel claims to have a branch in Tamra, but in truth it is to be found well outside the town, on the opposite side of the dual carriageway, where it services the passing traffic.) The town's shops are all local businesses, though even their presence is largely concealed. Apart from a couple of dozen clothes, fruit and veg and electrical goods stores on the main street, it is impossible for a visitor to know where Tamrans do their shopping. The hairdressers, doctors and dentists, furniture shops, pharmacies and ice cream parlours are invariably in anonymous houses, hidden behind the same grey concrete and shutters as residential properties. The local inhabitants, of course, know precisely where to find these shops, but for quite some time the lack of clues made it a nightmare for me.

Such difficulties were exacerbated by the problem of orientating myself. Because of the unplanned streets and the lack of regulations on construction, the local council has never attempted to name roads or number houses. So if I asked directions the reply would always involve telling me to turn right or left at a building that obviously served as a landmark for the local population, but which to me looked indistinguishable from the rest of the concrete. After a year I started to recognise at least a few of these landmarks. One felafel shop might be used as a signpost rather than its neighbour simply because it had been around for decades, and the community felt its long-term usefulness had been established.

In the early days I would think, 'I will never find my way around this place, I will never understand how to get from A to B.' I started walking every day to learn the complex patchwork of alleys and side streets. I was immediately struck by the huge number of roads that were incomplete, unmade or scarred by endless potholes. Streets would come to an abrupt end or peter out. There were embarrassing moments when, having started to rely on a shortcut, using what I thought was a footpath or an empty piece of ground, I would find one day that it was now blocked by concrete walls. A family, it would be explained to me, was squeezing yet another house into one of the last remaining spaces open to them. Because it was me, no one ever showed offence at the fact that I had been tramping through their yard.

The sense of community in Tamra is reinforced by its festivals. Anyone who has been to the Middle East quickly learns that public space is treated differently in Arab countries. On their first night, foreign visitors usually wake in the early hours of the morning, startled by the loud wailing of the local imam over the mosque's loudspeakers calling the faithful to prayer. For the first week or so these calls to prayer – five times a day – disturbed me too, but they soon became part of the background of life, as reassuring as the sound of church bells echoing through an English village.

One of the things I soon noticed about Muslim festivals is how much they resemble those celebrated by religious Jews, including the Orthodox members of my own Jewish family. When Asad Ghanem, a political science lecturer at Haifa University and one of the country's outstanding Israeli Arab intellectuals, took me to Nazareth for a Muslim engagement party, he asked me on the way back: 'So, how was it at your first Arab party?' He laughed when I told him: 'It's just like being at an engagement party in North London. I feel like I'm living with my first cousins.' Israel, and more recently the West, spends a lot of time warning us about the dangers of 'the Arab mind', instilling in us a fear of Arab culture and of Islam by accentuating their differences from us and by removing the wider context. Even though intellectually I knew that Jews and Arabs were both Semitic races with their roots in the Middle East, I was still unprepared for the extent to which the traditions in Islam and Judaism and the two cultures were so closely related.

Take, for example, death. The rituals of the two faiths closely mirror each other. The most important thing is that the dead person must be buried on the same day, before sundown, or failing that as soon as possible. So when Samira's sister died early one morning, she was in the ground by 1 p.m. As in Orthodox Judaism, the family and close friends went to the home and gathered around the body to pray while it was washed and the orifices were stuffed with cotton. After the body had been buried, the family sat in the house for a three-day mourning period during which guests were welcomed to share in the sorrow (in Judaism this period lasts seven days). The purpose in both religions is the same: to expunge the grief from the mourners' souls in a communal setting, and thereby to allow them to move on. In both faiths the family continues to mark its grief for a longer period by abstaining from celebrations and parties, and not playing music. During the three days of mourning the family's house is open from early morning to late evening, with the men and women sitting apart. Another tradition both religions share is that neighbours bring food to the dead person's family during the grieving period. That is what happened when my mother died in London. In Tamra we laid out a large meal of meat, rice and pine nuts for the mourners. On the second day I brought coffee and milk to the women for breakfast.

The most joyous and lavish occasion is a wedding, which can last from three days to a week. If it is the marriage of the eldest son or an only son, the celebration is always huge. The basic schedule is three days: one for the bride's party, one for the groom's, and the third for the wedding itself. On each occasion the party starts at sunset and goes on till the early hours, with a guest list of a few hundred family and friends. Often the road where the family lives will be shut down to accommodate the party as it spills into the street. Music is played very loudly, with wild, throbbing, hypnotic beats that reverberate around the town. During the summer months there is rarely an evening when you cannot hear the thumping boom of wedding songs somewhere in Tamra. The noise is like an extended invitation, ensuring that everyone can join in – at a distance – even if they have not been officially invited.

On the bride's day the women come together to eat, dance and talk. I found it fascinating to see so many women, their heads covered by the hijab headscarf, dancing together. You might expect that their dancing would be modest, but there is something very sensuous and provocative about the way Arab women dance, slowly gyrating their hips and swaying as they twist their arms and hands in the air. The messages are very conflicting. At my first Arab wedding I felt overwhelmed by the noise, the dancing and the huge number of bodies packed together. Later in the evening a group from the groom's side was allowed to join the party. Arriving in a long chain, they danced into the centre of the celebrations, with everyone else standing to the side and clapping their hands in time.

As the noise grew louder, the clapping turned ever more excited until people were opening their arms wide and snapping them shut together, like huge crocodile jaws. Finally, a pot of henna was brought and the bride's fingers decorated with her and the groom's initials entwined. On her palm and the back of her hands were painted beautiful patterns to make her more attractive for the wedding.

The second party, for the groom, follows a similar pattern of eating and dancing. At the end of the night the groom is prepared for the wedding day with a ceremonial shaving. Carrying a tray bearing a bowl, shaving cream and a razor, his mother and sisters dance towards him. Just as with the henna, the tray is decorated with flowers. Then, as they sing, the closest male relatives put him on a chair raised up on a table and begin to shave him in a great flourish of excitement. Soon there is foam flying in all directions, with the raucous men smearing it over each other's faces. Everyone is having so much fun there is often a reluctance to finish the job. But once he is smooth, the groom is held aloft on the shoulders of a strong male relative who dances underneath him as he moves his arms rhythmically above. The symbolic significance of this moment of transition into manhood is immense: the close relatives often burst into uncontrollable tears.

On the final day, the groom's family must go to collect the bride from her parents' home and bring her to her new family. As in Judaism there is no equivalent of the church ceremony familiar in the West. Before they set off, the groom's family invites everyone for a great feast of meat and rice followed by sweet pastries. Then the groom's closest friends wash him while the women dance holding his wedding clothes. He is dressed, and the family is then ready to fetch the bride. In one of the family weddings I attended, we formed a long convoy of cars, taking a circuitous route through Tamra so that we could toot our horns across the town, letting everyone know we were coming. The lead car was decorated with a beautiful display of flowers and ribbons. The bride's family welcomed us with drinks and plates of delicate snacks while the bride stood by in her white dress. As the moment neared for her to leave, small goatskin drums were banged and the women ululated a traditional song, which to my ears sounded sad and tragic but which actually wishes her health and happiness in the future. It is an emotional moment for the bride, who often cries. She dances on her own, holding in each hand a lighted long white candle, surrounded by a circle of relatives. When she is finished she steps on the candles to extinguish them, and leaves.

The highlight of the year for me is Ramadan, the spiritual month of fasting that commemorates the first revelation of the Muslim holy book, the Koran, to the Prophet Mohammed by God. No food or drink may be consumed from the moment the sun rises till the moment it sets. Muslims are expected to reflect on their behaviour at this time of year, during which they should not lie, cheat or fight. Special TV programmes concentrate on the spiritual aspect of Ramadan, showing live footage from Mecca and talks by religious leaders. It is a very physically demanding time: we have to rise at 4 a.m. for breakfast and then endure the heat of the day without any sustenance. Some Middle Eastern countries effectively grind to a halt during Ramadan, with offices and shops closed during the day. But in Israel no allowances are made for non-Jewish religious festivals, so people have to carry on with their normal work.

A unique time of day during Ramadan is just before sunset, when the imams call out a special prayer on the mosques' loudspeakers. This is the signal to the community that they can start eating again. At the precise moment the imam begins his prayer, I like to think that the streets of every Muslim community in the world are like ours: deserted and profoundly quiet, in a way unimaginable at any other time. Nothing moves or makes a noise. Even the birds seem to know they should not stir. Inside the houses, families start with a watery soup to accustom their stomachs to food again, then tuck into a table filled with their favourite foods. By the end of Ramadan people have lost weight and look tired; it asks a lot of them.

Unlike Judaism, which has many festivals, there are only two major feasts in Islam: the three-day Eid al-Fitr, which marks the end of Ramadan, and the four-day Eid al-Adha. There is a huge celebration in Tamra at both times of year, with the centre of town grinding to a virtual halt as improvised stalls are set up along the edge of the main road, selling children's toys and sweets. Teenage boys show off their horse-riding skills, while the younger children are pulled along more sedately in a horse-drawn carriage painted in vivid colours. Tamra has no parks or public spaces where these festivities could be held more safely, so the stallholders, children, horses and cars simply jostle for priority.

Both of these eids entail endless visiting of relatives, especially for the younger children, who are dressed in smart new clothes for the occasion. They receive money as a gift from each relative they visit. Unfortunately the boys invariably choose to spend their windfalls on toy guns – convincing replicas of the weapons they see being used by Palestinian gunmen and Israeli soldiers on the television.

Homes are stuffed with sweets, chocolates, dried fruits and special shortbread biscuits filled with date paste. Extended families congregate in large circles, eating and drinking tea or coffee while they chat. But the main celebration at each of these festivals is the barbecue, when huge quantities of meat are consumed. The Eid al-Adha (Feast of the Sacrifice) is, as its name suggests, a celebration of meat consumption. The feast commemorates the familiar Biblical story in which Ibrahim – Abraham in Christianity and Avraham in Judaism – is asked by God to sacrifice his son Isaac as a sign of devotion. Ibrahim proves his devotion, but God substitutes a ram for his son at the last moment. For Muslims this story is quite literally re-enacted, with blood running in the streets as families slaughter a sheep, cutting its throat for the barbecue. I found it a shock to see an ancient story I had learned as a schoolchild coming to life before my eyes. Once butchered, the meat is cut into three equal parts: one portion for the immediate family, one for the extended family, and one for the poor. We then eat barbecued meat for four days.

At other times of the year, leisure time in most families revolves around a single object: the nargilleh, or what we in the West refer to as a hookah or water pipe. The popularity of the nargilleh in Tamra doubtless partly reflects the fact that there is no equivalent of the pub here. Although alcohol – mostly beer and whisky – is sold in a few grocery shops, people rarely drink outside the privacy of their home. But puffing on a nargilleh for an hour or so can be just as intoxicating as a few beers. The nargilleh plays a central role in my family's life: there is rarely an evening when I don't see Waleed or Khalil cleaning or carefully preparing the pipe before loading it with apple-flavoured tobacco. They own several nargillehs, large and small, each decorated in different colours. The family forms a circle of chairs around the pipe outside Hajji's house and begins smoking. Although I occasionally puff on the nargilleh, the other women in the house do not. It is generally considered unbecoming for a woman to smoke in public.

In the West, the most identifiable, and controversial, thing about Islam – after Osama bin Laden and al-Qaeda – has become the hijab, the headscarf widely seen as part of a system of oppression of Muslim women. The arguments against the hijab rarely touch on its significance in the lives of modern Muslims. I once asked seventeen-year-old Suad which tradition meant most to her, and was surprised when she replied: 'The wearing of the hijab.' Her head is uncovered and she is a very modern teenager, so I asked her why. 'Because it makes you proud of your femininity.' I asked what she meant. 'When you are covered by the hijab it is the opposite of being repressed; you feel free and proud to be a woman. It gives you your dignity.' Part of the problem in the debate in the West is that it focuses exclusively on the hijab, without seeing that the headscarf is only one – if the most visible – of the dress codes that apply to all Muslims, both men and women. The concept of personal and family dignity is deeply important to the society, and clothing is one of the overt ways a person demonstrates that they deserve respect.

Showing a lot of one's body to people outside the family suggests quite the opposite. How that rule is interpreted can appear quite arbitrary and eccentric to outsiders. So, for example, I quickly found that, whatever the heat, the men in Tamra would not dream of wearing open-toed sandals or shorts outside the immediate environment of the home. A code applied to them too: if they wanted to be accorded respect and earn it for their family, they had to dress in respectable ways. In the case of women, this policy of covering up can seem oppressive to Western eyes which have become used to the idea that women *should* show as much flesh as possible. Since living in Tamra, I find myself appalled every time I return to Europe or America to see the virtually pornographic images of women, and even children, crowding high street billboards. As they go unnoticed by everyone else, I can only assume that living in Arab society has fundamentally changed my perception.

This did not happen overnight. I arrived in Tamra with suitcases full of thin, almost see-through linen garments that I had relied on to cope with the Tel Aviv heat. I knew I had to be much more careful about the way I dressed in Tamra, but was unsure exactly where the boundaries lay. Certainly I was not about to wear the hijab, but that did not mean that I was going to refuse to accept any limitations. So during my first summer I would dress each morning and go down to Hajji's flat for a clothing inspection. She would extend her finger and turn it round to show that she wanted to see me from every angle. She would look at me in the light and out of the light, and then if she couldn't see anything she would give me the thumbs-up. T-shirts that showed my shoulders were out, as were skirts higher than the knee or tops that had plunging necklines. Some of my thinnest tops I realised I would have to wear with something underneath. Now this self-discipline has become automatic and unthinking. I have long ago thrown away all the tops that reveal too much. Visitors to Tamra are shown great tolerance when they break these unwritten rules, but living here I decided it was important that I earned people's respect by showing them similar respect.

Nowadays I find it shocking to return to Tel Aviv in the summer and see the women, including older women, wearing crop-tops that expose their stomachs, or blouses revealing their bras. It seems vulgar in the extreme. I see the Arab women around me as much more dignified; they even seem to move in a more upright, graceful manner. I now find the idea of being covered liberating in much the same way as Suad does: it frees me from confrontations with men, the kind of situations I had experienced all my life without fully realising it. With my body properly covered, men have to address what I am saying rather than my body. It was only after covering myself that I started realising I had been used to men having conversations with my body, rather than with me, most of my life.

Also, covering up gives me a sense of independence and self-containment that still surprises me. Like other Westerners I had always assumed that Muslim women were repressed, but I now know that's far too simplistic. Although there are places in the world where the hijab is misused as a way to limit women's possibilities, that is not by definition true. I have met plenty of professional Palestinian women, in Tamra and elsewhere, who wear the hijab but are strong-willed, assertive and creative. They expect men's respect and they are shown it.

Not that women's lives here are without problems. I find it difficult to accept the social limitations on young, unmarried women, including the fact that they can never venture out alone in the evenings. Teenage girls are definitely *not* allowed to date boyfriends, or in many cases even openly to have a boyfriend. When I asked

Suad how she coped, she admitted it was hard. She felt torn between two cultures: the Western way of life she sees on television and in many Jewish areas, where girls do what they please, and her own Arab traditions, of which she is proud and which she wants to obey. My own daughter did not hesitate as a teenager in London to tell me she was going to the pub or cinema with a boyfriend, but girls here simply are not allowed to do that. For a long time I wondered how anyone found a marriage partner, with all these restrictions. But in reality many girls have secret boyfriends whom they 'date' over the phone. The arrival of mobile phones has quietly revolutionised the dating game in Muslim communities. But even so, I still marvel how a girl ever finds a husband. In many cases she has few opportunities to meet men outside events like weddings, and so her choice of partners is pretty much limited to the men inside her hamula. But slowly, with more education about the problems of marrying a first cousin and the genetic legacy for the offspring, such marriages are being discouraged. The situation is far from static.

Although as Westerners we are encouraged to believe we have a right to sit in judgement of other cultures, what I heard from women in Tamra alerted me to the weaknesses in our own culture – flaws we are little prepared to acknowledge. For example, one evening a group of about a dozen local women visited me in my home so that we could learn more about each other. They were keen to know both why after my divorce I had left my children behind in Britain, and how I coped living alone in Tamra. In Arab society a woman would never separate herself from her family, even her grown-up children. Because I had left Britain they assumed I had abandoned Tanya and Daniel; they were astonished that I could turn my back on my children, even though they were in their late twenties and early thirties. I had to explain that in Britain grown-up children leave home, often moving long distances from their parents. Many mothers are lucky if they are visited by their children more than a couple of times a year. The group were appalled, and pointed out the huge advantages of having families that remain together for life. When I see how we all gather in Hajji's apartment, how she is never alone unless she wants to be, I can see their point. I have concluded that there are many benefits to having your family around you as you grow older.

The central place of the hamula in organising not only the lives of Tamra's individual families but also the political life of the whole community was revealed to me during the first municipal elections after my arrival. It was an uncomfortable lesson, revealing a side to Tamra that dismayed me. As one Israeli Arab academic, Marwan Dwairy, has observed: 'In politics we still have parties dressed up as families and families dressed up as parties.'

The aggressive and tribal nature of political campaigning in Arab areas is often cited by Israeli intellectuals as proof of the primitive character of Arab societies and their inability to cope with modern democratic principles. Apart from glossing over the tribal nature of Jewish politics inside Israel, that argument misses a larger point. The continuing feudal nature of Arab politics in Israel is neither accidental nor predetermined by the 'Arab mind'; it results from the failure of Israeli Jewish society to allow the country's Arab minority to join the national political consensus. Arab politicians are considered hostile to the state unless they join a Zionist party, and Arab parties have been excluded from every government coalition in Israel's history. These coalitions are a hotchpotch of diverse, often antagonistic and extremist, political parties, but the bottom line is that they must be Jewish. When Arabs are excluded from the Knesset table, it is not surprising that they fight for whatever municipal scraps they can get. Sensing that their voice is irrelevant to the process of their governance, they end up seeking solace in the kind of posturing and feudal politics familiar from the days of their grandfathers.

I experienced this in a very direct way myself: during Tamra's local elections I was quickly and easily sucked into the town's hamula-based politics. The fervour and excitement surrounding the elections were something I had never witnessed anywhere else, and contrasted strongly with the calm, slightly stultifying atmosphere of a British municipal election. In the final week of campaigning there were fireworks and street parties every night, with loud music and mountains of food on offer. The tribal divisions within the community were far more visible than usual, not least because the two candidates for mayor were the heads of the two largest hamulas. The campaign, it was clear, was less about competing political platforms than about rivalry between the family leaderships. On one side was Adel Abu Hayja, standing for the Communist Party, and on the other was Moussa Abu Romi, the incumbent mayor, representing the Islamic Movement. The victor would be in charge of the town's limited municipal budget for the next five years and so, in the great tradition of patronage systems, would be able to reward his followers. The stakes were therefore extraordinarily high, as each of the two biggest hamulas fought to secure the floating votes of the two smaller hamulas with promises. In the run-up to the election there were even incidents of young men from one hamula pulling guns or knives on those from another.

By election day the temperature in Tamra had rocketed. The whole town was alive with activity, with party buses roaming the town looking to transport supporters to the polling booth. Since I lived inside the Abu Hayja hamula, my support for Adel Abu Hayja's candidacy was taken for granted. There was never any question for whom I was expected to vote: I would vote for the family.

It was widely known in Tamra that I was making history: this was the first time that an openly Jewish woman had voted in a municipal election in an Arab area. When I arrived at the school on the hill above my home where I was due to vote I found complete pandemonium. Everyone was pushing and shoving and shouting. People who thought they had been waiting in line too long would start hitting those in front of them, and trying to push past to get to the room where the polling booth was located. Standing in their way was an old wooden door, holding back at least 150 people who were pushing each other up against it. One policeman was inside, desperately trying to keep the door closed as the crowd pressed forward, and another was doing his best, without success, to keep order. Finally one huge man lost control and started hitting the women in front of him before lunging for the door. Using all his might he managed to push it open and to get inside. The door closed behind him.

Hassan, the head of my family, who had come with me, was outside in the street but could see I was getting crushed. He is a big man, and he forced his way through the crowd to reach me so that he could hold me tightly around my shoulders, using his arms to protect me. I could tell how much he feared for my safety, because it is rare for Arab men and women, even husband and wife, to touch in public. But it was the only way to keep me upright and on my feet. When there was a brief gap in the crowd he pushed me forward and I was propelled through the door. The door slammed shut, but with all the hammering on it I feared it would come down. I found myself in a tiny room with a small window, and I remember thinking with a little relief that if I could not get out through the door, at least I could climb through the window.

I gave my ballot card to the Jewish official who was overseeing polling at the station. I also had to give him my ID card, and when he saw that I was a Jew and living in Tamra he gave me a strange look, as though there had been an administrative mistake he could not quite figure out how to correct.* But after a pause he pointed me towards the booth. Behind the curtain were two piles of official voting slips, with the names of Moussa Abu Romi and Adel Abu Hayja. Just before polling day, a rumour had been circulating in

---

* Until recently all Israeli ID cards divulged the ethnic group of the holder. New ID cards often have a row of stars in the place where nationality is identified (see glossary entry on citizenship, page 267). It is widely believed that the cardholder's ethnic group is revealed by the ID number.

Tamra that supporters of the incumbent mayor, Abu Romi, were planning to sabotage Abu Hayja's chances by printing his voting slips in an ink that would disappear over time, so that when it came to the count all his votes would be blank. My family had persuaded me that I must take with me another slip supplied by Abu Hayja's party, and I had hidden it in my purse. Standing in the booth, I hurriedly took it out and slipped it into the ballot box. The family's absolute belief in the truth of the story of the fading ink had led me to believe it myself. I had been so drawn in by the fervour of the elections, by the supreme importance attached to the outcome, that the normal rules of democratic participation could willingly be abandoned.

When I reached the exit door, I wondered how I would ever get out alive. The policeman opened it and I was confronted by a wall of agitated faces. And then everyone appeared to come to their senses. Most of these people I had never met before, but it appeared they knew who I was. In Arab communities the idea of a local newspaper almost seems redundant: by some kind of osmosis, everyone knows everyone else's news, good and bad. So, as if I were Moses facing the Red Sea, the waves parted. There was, for the first time that day, total silence. As I walked past, people reached out to shake my hand. But as soon as I had reached safety, the scrum resumed.

Apparently there was no truth to the tale of the fading ink, as in the event Abu Hayja was comfortably elected as mayor. The result was not accepted by all of Abu Romi's supporters: some took to the streets with firearms, and there were several days of fierce confrontations, including a gun battle after which one man was taken to hospital seriously wounded. My family warned me not to go out onto the streets. The violence ended only after the imam called out passages from the Koran over the mosque's loudspeaker, to calm everyone down.

Word of my presence in Tamra quickly spread further afield, to

Haifa and beyond, assisted by an interview I gave to the country's most famous Hebrew newspaper, *Ha'aretz*, in September 2003. A short time afterwards I received a phone call from Michael Mansfeld, a senior partner in a firm of architects in Haifa. He said he had been impressed by my critical comments about Israel not having invested in any new housing schemes for the Arab minority in the state's fifty-five years, despite the population having grown sevenfold. He told me his firm had been appointed by the Interior Ministry to draw up the masterplans for Tamra's development till 2020, and he wanted to explain what the government had in store. He said I'd be impressed by what I would see. I was sceptical but keen to see the plans, about which no one in Tamra seemed to have been consulted. I invited the newly elected mayor, Adel Abu Hayja, and Amin Sahli, the town planner, to come to my home to see Mansfeld's presentation.

But before the meeting I talked to Mansfeld privately. I told him about the severe land problems facing Tamra, and that I didn't see a future for Israel unless Jews and Arabs were able to become equal partners. When he agreed, I asked him: 'Why do so many Israeli Jews agree with me in private but refuse to speak out?' He replied that if he spoke publicly, things could be made difficult for him and his business, and that his family was his first priority. His words reminded me that it is not only the Arabs who live in fear of their own state, but Jews of conscience too. It was a depressing realisation. Mansfeld, whose father won Israel's most prestigious award, the Israel Prize,* is part of what might be termed the establishment Israeli left. If he does not feel he can stand up and be counted, who can? And without more people prepared to speak out and expose the crisis at the heart of the Jewish state, what kind of country will we leave to our children?

---

* Since 1953 it has been awarded each year to an Israeli citizen who has demonstrated excellence or broken new ground in a particular field.

The presentation which was supposed to impress us boiled down to the fact that Tamra's inhabitants would have to accept that there was a shortage of land in Israel. In Mansfeld's words, 'From now on we must all build upwards.' Afterwards, I took a copy of the plans to Professor Hubert Law-Yone, a Burmese academic who came to Israel after marrying a Jewish woman and who is an expert on town planning, based at the Technion in Haifa. He did a few quick calculations and concluded that the plan was bad news for Tamra: based on the population growing to forty-two thousand by 2020, it required very high-density living – eighty-eight people per acre. He suggested that the Interior Ministry brief probably had a hidden agenda, one familiar to the Arab population: the maximum number of Arabs on the minimum amount of land. Its reverse is of course the minimum number of Jews on the maximum amount of land. That is why the Jewish communities around Tamra – farming co-operatives and small luxury hilltop settlements like Mitzpe Aviv – have been allotted land for the benefit of their inhabitants that once belonged to Tamra. That's also why Tamra's Jewish neighbours have impressive villas with big gardens, often including swimming pools, and communal parks and playing areas for the children. The plan for Tamra, on the other hand, envisages ever more crowding in a community already stripped of all public space. In Professor Law-Yone's words: 'There is plenty of land in Israel. Building upwards is just code for cramming more Arabs in.'

Speaking to Amin later, I sensed that there was almost nothing that Tamra could do to change its bleak future. The government land bodies and the planning committees that set the guidelines for these masterplans are always Jewish-dominated, and often have no Arab members at all. Arab citizens have no voice in their own future, let alone the state's. Amin was deeply depressed. He had just returned from a meeting of the Knesset's economics commit-tee which, at the instigation of an Arab Knesset member, Issam Makhoul, had discussed the land and housing crisis in Tamra. Amin had compiled the figures, which showed that the town had little more than a thousand acres for building, all of which was developed. The rest of its six thousand acres were zoned either for farming or as Green Areas which could not be developed. The result, he told the committee, was that because the Interior Ministry refused to release any new land for development, young Arab couples had no choice but to build their homes illegally, often on their own land which was zoned for agriculture. Their parents could not build 'upwards' to provide them with an apartment – as Mansfeld had suggested – because they had already reached the building-regulation limit of four storeys for their homes. There were 150 buildings in Tamra under demolition orders, threatening hundreds of young couples and their children with homelessness and destitution.

I found there was nothing I could say to reassure Amin as he spoke in a tone of absolute despair about Tamra's future. He had exhausted all the official channels, commuting to Jerusalem regularly to try to persuade Jewish officials and politicians of Tamra's crisis, only to be met by a uniform lack of interest or by condescension. It seemed to me the height of irony, given our history, that the Jewish state has so little concern about the ghetto living it has forced on its Arab citizens. Amin said he felt humiliated and powerless every time a young couple came to him seeking help with their housing problems. All he could do was to turn them away empty-handed. It was not as though they had other choices available to them. Israel makes it virtually impossible for Arabs to live in Jewish communities, and other Arab communities are in the same dire straits. Couples would simply be moving from a ghetto they know to another they did not, to a place where they could not even rely on the support of their hamula.

'You know, Susan,' Amin said, 'even dying is a problem if you are an Arab in Israel. In Tamra we have run out of land to bury our dead.'

I asked him how he felt about living here. His head in his hands, he told me he was thinking about a way to leave Israel with his wife and three young children. If he did, he would be joining the rest of his three siblings, all of whom are doctors, in exile: his two brothers are in the United States, and his sister in France. 'It feels to me like a subtle way of ethnically cleansing me off my land,' he said. Today there are an equal number of Jews and Arabs living in the Galilee, he pointed out, but it is obvious from looking at the region's development plans that one ethnic group is benefiting at the expense of the other. 'These plans are about making life impossible for us, the Arabs, to remain here. Israel destroys the structure of our family life, making us weak and fragmented. If it continues like this, anyone who can leave will do so. I want to stay here, to raise my children in their homeland, but I have to be realistic. How can I stay when all the messages my state sends me are that I am not welcome?'

2

Death of a Love Affair

Inside the information pack from the Jewish Agency office in London was a badge and an accompanying letter: 'Wear this as you walk off the plane to begin your new life as an Israeli citizen,' the instructions stated. So on 10 October 1999, as I made my way down the flight of steps onto the tarmac of Tel Aviv's Ben-Gurion international airport, I had a badge pinned to my chest bearing the slogan: 'I've come home'.

The thought that I and the hundreds of other new immigrants arriving each week on El Al flights from all over the world were reclaiming a right that had lain dormant for two thousand years did not strike me as strange. For the fuel that brought me late in life to Israel as a new immigrant, with only a couple of suitcases of belongings with me, was a dream I had secretly harboured since my childhood. The object of my desire was to make aliya, the Hebrew word for 'ascent', an idea that in returning to Israel a Jew is fulfilling a divinely ordained mission.

At the age of fifty I was leaving behind my home in Wimbledon, South London, two grown-up children, Daniel and Tanya, a recently failed marriage and my work as an Aids/HIV counsellor. Other than these attachments, not much stood in my way: Israeli law entitles me and every other Jew in the world to instant citizenship if we choose to live in Israel. There are no visa applications, points systems or lengthy residency procedures. As a Jew I had a right to Israeli citizenship by virtue of my ethnicity alone. The Jewish Agency in London had been able to process my application for Israeli citizenship in just a week, and it made sure the immigration process was as pain-free as possible: my flight ticket was paid for, and accommodation was provided while I found my feet in the Promised Land. The only hesitation on my part was a reluctance, when confronted by an official issuing my Israeli identity card, to adopt a Hebrew name. My friends suggested I become either Shashana or Vered – the names of two flowers – but at the last minute I decided to stick with Susan.

I am not sure I can identify the exact moment I became a committed Zionist, but I do know that a single childhood incident changed the direction of my life, and my understanding of what it was to be a Jew. I was eleven years old and on an outing with some girls from my boarding school to nearby High Wycombe, one of the many commuter towns that ring London. Browsing through the shelves of a small bookshop in one of the backstreets, away from the other girls, I stumbled across the most horrifying picture book. As I leafed through its pages I found photo after photo of emaciated corpses piled high in pits, of men ripping out gold fillings from teeth, of mountains of hair and shoes. At such a young age I was not aware that these were pictures of the Holocaust, an event that was still fearsomely present in the imaginations of Jews around the world fifteen years after the end of the Second World War. But the awfulness of the images transfixed me.

I learned the story behind these photographs from my parents shortly afterwards, so beginning my compulsive interest in the Holocaust and Jewish history. The following year, 1961, after I had moved to a new boarding school in Buckinghamshire, the trial of the Gestapo leader Adolf Eichmann began in Jerusalem. I read the newspapers every day, appalled by the accounts of the Final Solution, Hitler's attempt to exterminate the Jewish people. I also recall weekends spent poring over copies of the *Jewish Chronicle* in my parents' home, reading in the personal columns the notices from individuals and families still searching for relatives in Europe they had been separated from for as much as two decades. These heart-rending messages were an uncomfortable reminder that the legacy of loss and destruction wrought by the concentration camps was continuing. My exposure to the Holocaust – and my new understanding that millions of Jews had died at the hands of the Nazis – launched me on an ever wider quest for knowledge: not only of what had happened to its victims, but also of what had led to such barbarity.

My own family, I was soon aware, had only narrowly escaped – by a quirk of destiny – the tragedy that had consumed so many others. My father's parents, before they met, were refugees from the pogroms in Lithuania in the 1880s, fleeing separately to Odessa where each hoped they might catch a ship to Hamburg and a new future in Germany. But when they arrived at the port they, and many other refugees, found the ship full and so were forced to travel on the only other vessel, bound for Cape Town in South Africa. As we now know, their fates and their children's were sealed by that missed boat: instead of finding themselves caught up in the rise of European fascism, they watched the horrific events unfold from the safe distance of Cape Town. My father was, however, in Europe at the outbreak of war. He had left South Africa in the late 1920s, travelling streerage class on a boat bound for Ireland, a penniless but brilliant medical student. He enrolled at Trinity College, Dublin, where he was mentored by Yitzhak HaLevi Herzog, the chief rabbi of Ireland and the father of Israel's sixth president, who helped him become a passionate Zionist. By the time Nazism was on the rise in Germany my father was a leading surgeon in London, where he met my mother, a nurse. They spent the war itself tending to the injured in Tilbury docks in Essex, one of the most heavily bombed places in Britain.

If my family had survived the war unscathed, the plight of the many who had not touched me deeply. As with many others, the story of the *Exodus* – as told by novelist Leon Uris – shaped my perception of the tragedy that had befallen my people. I read of the ship that left Europe in July 1947, its decks choked with Holocaust survivors in search of sanctuary in what was then Palestine; of the refugees who tried to jump ship and reach the shores of the Promised Land; of the decision of the British to send the 4,500 refugees to internment camps in Cyprus because they had agreed to limits on Jewish immigration to avoid further antagonising the local Palestinian population and neighbouring Arab countries; and of the horrifying eventual return of the ship and its Jewish refugees to Germany. I was outraged by the thought that British soldiers – ruling Palestine under a mandate from the League of Nations – could have acted with such callousness. My alienation from my country, Britain, began from that point on.

The middle classes exercised a subtle, sophisticated discrimination against Jews in post-war Britain which was apparent enough to make me increasingly aware of my difference. There were the comments about my 'funny name' – my maiden name is Levy. I heard tales that disturbed me about the clubs that excluded Jews as policy. Among my parents' friends there were worried conversations about the 'quotas' on Jewish children that might prevent their offspring from being admitted to a good school. And my mother, who was born a Protestant but converted to Judaism after marrying my father, would tell of how everyone in her family apart from her own mother disowned her for choosing to marry a Jew.

During my childhood, at the rural boarding schools outside London where most of my time was spent, I felt as if I were wearing a yellow star, as if my Jewishness was a visible stain to the teachers and other pupils. These were demonstratively Christian schools, with chapel services and morning prayers. I was aware of my vulnerability, too: out of hundreds of children, only four others were Jewish in the senior school I attended. I swung between contradictory emotions. On the one hand I feared appearing different, and on the other I wanted to proudly own that difference. Although I did not have the courage to refuse to attend morning prayers, I resolutely kept my mouth closed during the hymns. It was a very isolating experience: I felt outside the consensus, subtly but constantly reminded of my difference. This is, I think, a common experience for Diaspora Jews, but one little appreciated by Israeli Jews who were born and raised in a state where they comprise the majority.

My growing distance from British society was reflected in an ever greater attachment, if only emotionally, to Israel. I was raised on stirring stories of the great and glorious Jewish state. For non-Jews it is perhaps difficult to appreciate what an enormous impact the creation of the state of Israel had on us. It reinvented our self-image, anchoring our pride in a piece of territory that had been our shared homeland two thousand years before. It satisfied our sense of historic justice and showed we could forge our own place among the modern nation states. But more than that, many Jews, myself included, were excited by the triumphs of our army, particularly those of 1948 and 1967, when Israel took on its Arab neighbours and won substantial territory from them. Here we were, a persecuted, isolated people, freeing ourselves from the ghettos of Europe and rising phoenix-like from the ashes of the gas chambers to become warriors. No longer a helpless minority always at risk of persecution, we were a proud people reclaiming our homeland, and willing and able to fight to defend it on the battlefield. Young Jews need not imagine a future as either merchants or intellectuals, but rather as brave and courageous soldiers. We could call ourselves 'Sabra' – identifying with the prickly Middle Eastern cactus that flourishes in even the most hostile terrain.

I married my husband, Michael Nathan, a successful lawyer, in 1970 at the age of twenty-one. My early marriage, frowned upon by my parents, brought me into the embrace of a much more religious family than my own. Michael's mother and father were traditional and Orthodox, in sharp contrast to my own parents' secular, liberal background, and our differences in upbringing, culture and outlook would eventually push us apart. During the twenty-six years of our marriage, however, Michael and I only ever visited Israel together once, when we went to see his brother in Jerusalem. Michael never shared my attachment to the Jewish state, and on the seven other occasions I visited I was always alone. Our two children forged their own relationships with Israel, touring the country as part of youth groups or working on kibbutzim. But although this was officially my state I always left Israel as a tourist, an outsider, with a feeling that its inner substance had not been fully revealed to me.

So when I arrived to claim Israeli citizenship in 1999, my head was still full of romantic notions of Zionism and the Jewish state. The Jews had reclaimed an empty, barren land – 'a land without people for a people without land'. We had made the desert bloom, we had filled an uninhabited piece of the Middle East with kibbutzim, the collective farms that were the pioneering backbone of the state in its early years. At that stage, the thought that the country was full of strangers, people whom I and my countrymen lived alongside but entirely apart from, did not enter my head. The one million Arabs who share the state with Jews – Palestinians who remained on their land after the 1948 war that founded Israel, and so by accident rather than design became Israeli citizens – were invisible to me, as they are to almost all Israeli Jews. Their culture, their society and their story were a mystery.

The excitement of being in Israel did not quickly dissipate. My first months were filled with thrilling moments of feeling, for the first time in my life, that I belonged to the majority. I did not need to explain my family name, nor did I have to hide my pride in my Jewishness. I could have walked down the street with a Star of David emblazoned on my lapel if I wanted to; no one would have batted an eyelid. There was even a strange sense of liberation in calling a plumber and opening the door to a man wearing a kippa, the small cloth disc worn by religious Jewish men as a head covering. It made me think, I really am in the land of the Jews.

Even the stories that had inspired me as a child now came dramatically to life. Soon after my arrival I was hanging the laundry outside the kitchen window of my Tel Aviv flat when I noticed an old woman waving down to me from a neighbouring apartment block, a dilapidated building erected in the early 1950s. Noticing a new face in the area, she called out that her name was Leah, and asked who I was and where I was from. I told her, then asked whether she had been born in Israel. No, she replied, she had been born in Poland. During the Second World War she had been separated from her parents, who were later killed in a concentration camp. She went into hiding in the woods, staying with several Russian families, before envoys from the Jewish Agency tracked her down and put her on a ship to Palestine. That ship was the *Exodus*. She recounted the story of the trip in the packed boat that I had read about in my teenage years, and how they were turned back to Germany. She told me of the horrific overcrowding on the ship, of the bodies stuffed together, but also of the excitement as they neared the Promised Land. Here in Leah I had found a living, breathing piece of history, a woman who made flesh all the reasons why I felt attached and committed to Israel.

Most Jews are all too ready to tell you how much Israel means to them as a sanctuary. How safe they feel knowing that there is a country they can flee to should anti-Semitism raise its ugly head again. How reassuring it is to have a country that will protect them, having inherited the legacy of centuries of persecution and the horrors of the Holocaust. What they are much less ready to admit is that Israel is not just a safe haven and a homeland; it also embodies the value of naked Jewish power. What I felt arriving in Israel – as I suspect do many other Jews – was that through my new state I was defying a world that had persecuted my people. Being in the majority, and not needing to explain myself, was a condition I was unfamiliar with after five decades as a British Jew. The sense of being in charge, of putting the boot on the other foot, was more than a little intoxicating.

I did not come to Israel the easy way, though as a middle-class Londoner I could have strolled into any flat in Tel Aviv. I chose instead a path that I believed followed in the footsteps of the pioneering Jewish immigrants to Palestine. I arranged with the Jewish Agency in London to spend my first six months in an immigrant absorption centre in Rana'ana, close to Tel Aviv. I knew what I was letting myself in for: an apartment shared with strangers newly arrived from all over the world, separated by different languages, cultures and traditions. All we would have in common was the knowledge that we were Jews and that we wanted to become Israelis.

These first months were something of a culture shock that tested the resources of many of the inmates. I arrived with my British culture, but the absorption centre was also home to people from many other cultures, including Americans, Dutch, Russians, Swiss, French and South Americans. All of us had to adjust both to these other cultures and to the new Israeli culture. We also struggled with the abruptness of Israelis, which many took for rudeness. The Rana'ana centre has perhaps the most privileged intake of Jewish immigrants anywhere in Israel, with most coming from developed countries. It beats by a considerable margin the caravan transit camps reserved for Ethiopian Jews, the Jewish group most discriminated against inside Israel. Many of the one million Russian Jews who arrived in Israel during the 1990s following the collapse of the Soviet Union also stayed in far less salubrious surroundings.

Nonetheless, the absorption centre was a tough and uncomfortable introduction to Israel, which I remember left several people close to a nervous breakdown and ready to fly back home. I still have a cutting from a local newspaper, *Ha Sharon*, headlined 'Immigrants Complain of Poor Conditions'. A letter written by some of the

French and American inmates to the absorption centre's management is quoted: 'The apartments are old and full of mould and fungus. The kitchens are broken, the showers don't work properly, the walls are peeling and we have no air-conditioners.' And it is true that in many ways Rana'ana was as much a prison as a melting pot. Having spent my childhood from the age of seven onwards, however, in the harsh, disciplinarian atmosphere of British boarding schools, coping with these material hardships only slightly marred the wonderful experience of being absorbed into a new country and culture, and meeting so many like-minded Jews.

But in these early months I started to experience darker moments. A big disappointment was that the only family I had in Israel, religious cousins living in the southern city of Ashdod, who originally approved of my decision to make aliya, kept their distance from the moment I arrived. They did not even meet me at the airport. For a while their attitude baffled me, but eventually I came to understand how my migration challenged their sense of their own Israeliness. They belong to the right-wing religious camp, and still hold onto a vision of Israelis as pioneering frontiersmen, settlers implanting themselves in hostile terrain. I think they were convinced that, with my 'European softness', I would not be able to stay the course. And when I confounded them by securing almost immediately a well-paid position in Tel Aviv teaching English to business professionals, my easy assimilation served only to antagonise them yet further.

My job involved travelling from one office to the next, which meant that I quickly learned my way around Tel Aviv. I also met and got to know a range of Israelis with different political views and insights into the 'Israeli experience'. I heard from some of them about their own problems as immigrants being absorbed into Israeli society, about their concerns at their children serving in the army, and about the country's economy.

Four months after my arrival I suffered a devastating blow when

I was diagnosed with a rare form of eye cancer. I had to begin a crash-course in negotiating my way single-handedly around Israel's health care system, and eventually found myself in Jerusalem's Hadassah hospital, awaiting an operation on my eye. Hadassah occupies a striking position, set in a pine forest overlooking the old stone houses of Ein Kerem, a Palestinian village that was cleansed of its population in the 1948 war and is now a wealthy suburb of Jerusalem to which many rich Jews aspire to move. It has state-of-the-art medical equipment and is staffed by a mix of Israeli Jews and Arabs, and it was there that I got my first inkling that the country I had so longed to be a citizen of might not be quite what I imagined. I was lying in a ward surrounded by beds filled not just with other Jews but with many of the diverse, and confusing, ethnic and religious components of the Holy Land: Jews, Christians, Muslims and Druze. This was before the intifada of September 2000, but still it was surprising to see Israelis and Palestinians sharing the same ward. Even more confusingly, many of the Palestinians were Israeli citizens, members of a group I discovered were commonly referred to as the 'Israeli Arabs'. The Jewish state was clearly a lot less ethnically pure than I had been led to believe.

It was another experience on the ward that started me questioning what was really going on inside Israel. One day a young Orthodox woman arrived on the ward clutching her month-old baby, who had just undergone surgery on an eye. That evening her husband came to visit. He was wearing a knitted kippa, long sidelocks, and had a pistol on one hip and a rifle slung casually over his shoulder. This is the uniform of the nationalist religious right in Israel – better known abroad as 'the settlers'. The thought that a heavily armed civilian could wander freely around a hospital where women and children were ill appalled me. I engaged him in conversation as he was leaving. In a strong American accent he told me: 'I've just requisitioned an Arab home in East Jerusalem. I never leave home without a weapon.' I suggested to him that he would be better off living in the Jewish quarter in the Old City. No, he retorted. 'All of East Jerusalem belongs to the Jews.'

His words left a nasty taste in my mouth. Why was he stealing homes from Arabs in the Palestinian part of the city, the section captured by Israel in the 1967 war, when there were vast tracts of the country he could choose to live in? And why did I appear to be the only person on the ward who thought it strange for a visitor to arrive in a hospital wearing a gun?

I left the hospital confused by the signals Israel was sending me. Here was a state that prided itself on having one of the best medical systems in the world. And access to health care seemed not to be affected overtly by grounds of race or creed. But it was also clear that some Israelis had an unhealthy admiration for violence and an appetite for what did not belong to them. Israel did not appear to place many controls on their behaviour.

My strong humanist values derive from an understanding of both my family's history and my people's. My father raised me on stories about my great-grandfather, Zussman Hershovitz, who lived in one of the Jewish ghetto communities, the shtetls, in Lithuania. I was taught as a small child the consequences of being Jewish for men like my great-grandfather, how it was not possible for him to go to school as a boy, how he ended up as a peddler moving from place to place to avoid the pogroms. In addition my father, Samuel Levy, a respected Harley Street doctor, instilled in me a deep appreciation of Jewish ethics, culture and history. I cannot claim he was a good father. Much of my childhood was spent living in terror of his rages and under the shadow of his disappointment. But outside the immediate family circle he was never less than a fiercely loyal and dedicated healer. Although he was very successful, he believed he had wider social responsibilities than simply accumulating money from the wealthy clientele who visited his London practice. He continued to dedicate much of his time to a practice he started when he was younger in a deprived part of Essex. After he retired in 1973 he returned to the country of his birth, South Africa, during the apartheid years to be medical health officer and practise in a clinic for blacks only in Groote Schuur, Cape Town.

So even though I was soon earning good money as an English teacher in Tel Aviv, I could not simply accept the privileges that came with being a successful 'new Israeli'. A few months after I had recovered from the eye operation, I was approached by a student organisation called Mahapach, which had heard of my experience in community work and raising money for Aids charities in London. They asked if I could write a funding application in support of their work for disadvantaged communities inside Israel, particularly the indigenous Arab population and the community of Jews of Middle Eastern descent, known in Israel as the Mizrahim. Much of Mahapach's work involves encouraging students to go into deprived communities to teach such youngsters core subjects like Hebrew, Arabic, English and maths outside the often limiting arena of the formal classroom.

I sat down and read about these communities and their problems. I knew about the difficulties of the Mizrahim, who because of their Arab culture – they originally came from Morocco, Iraq, Syria and Egypt – have long been treated as inferior Jews by the European elite, the Ashkenazi Jews, who run Israel. But questions quickly began to surface in my mind about the indigenous Arab communities. Where did these Arabs I was writing about live? Why had they been so invisible, except briefly when I was in hospital, during my first two years in Israel? In those days I had little time for anything except my work as an English teacher. I would usually be up at 5 a.m., start work at six (before my clients' offices opened), and finish at 8 or 9 p.m. Still, I was not satisfied with simply regurgitating the dry statistics I found in newspaper articles which suggested that Israeli Arabs were discriminated against. They were as faceless and unconnected to my life as bacteria living at the bottom of the ocean. I wanted to meet these Arabs for myself. When the chance arose to visit an Arab town as part of the research, I leapt at it. The destination was Tamra in the western Galilee.

Within minutes of driving into Tamra I felt that I had entered another Israel, one I had never seen before. It was almost impossible to believe that I could turn off a main highway, close to the luxurious rural Jewish communities of the Galilee, and find myself somewhere that was so strikingly different from any Jewish area I had ever visited before, and not just culturally. It was immediately obvious that Tamra suffered from chronic overcrowding. The difference in municipal resources and investment was starkly evident too. And a pall of despair hung over the town, a sense of hopelessness in the face of so much official neglect. It was the first time I had been to an Arab area (apart from visits as a tourist to the Old City of Jerusalem), and I was profoundly shaken by it. A disturbing thought occurred to me, one that refused to shift even after I had driven back to Tel Aviv. Tamra looked far too familiar. I thought, where have I seen this before? I recognised the pattern of discrimination from my experience of apartheid South Africa, which I had visited regularly during my childhood. I could detect the same smell of oppression in Tamra that I had found in the black townships.

These initial impressions were reinforced by a meeting at the home of Dr Asad Ghanem, who lives in the neighbouring village of Sha'ab. One of the few prominent Arab academics in Israel, Dr Ghanem impressed me with his direct and unemotional explanations of the discrimination exercised in all spheres of Israeli life against the Arab population, from employment and education to land allocations and municipal budgets. But he found it difficult to remain detached about one topic he brought to my attention, an issue that would later become the theme of many conversations with my new Arab neighbours and friends. In Arab communities across Israel there are tens of thousands of homes judged illegal by the state, and under threat of demolition. In Tamra, Dr Ghanem told me, there were 150 homes facing destruction. Intermittently the police would target an Arab community, bringing in bulldozers at the crack of dawn and tearing down the illegal homes. The razing of these buildings, some of them up to four floors high, might mean dozens of extended families, comprising hundreds of people, were made homeless at a stroke.

I knew from my research that there was widespread illegal building in Arab communities, which was represented by the Israeli authorities as the act of law-breakers, people who were squatting on state land or who did not want to pay for a building licence. But as Dr Ghanem pointed out, no one chooses to invest their life savings and their dreams in a home that could be razed at any moment. Arab families have been forced to build illegally because in most cases the state refuses to issue them with building permits. And then he delivered the knockout blow: he told me his own beautiful home was illegal and threatened with demolition.

There can be little doubt that the land on which Dr Ghanem's home stands has belonged to his family for generations. From the salon, visitors can see the old stone foundations of his grandparents' house. A few years ago he had decided, with the arrival of his own children, that he and his wife Ahlam could no longer live in his parents' apartment; they would build a home on the only land the family had left. But the authorities refused him a building permit. Effectively branded criminals by the state – like tens of thousands of Arab families – he and Ahlam had been paying regular heavy fines ever since, as much as £15,000 sterling a time, to ward off demolition. Their lives have become a routine of paying the state to prevent the destruction of everything they hold dear.

The question that echoed in my mind as I heard Dr Ghanem's story was: where were he and his family supposed to live? What was the future envisaged for them by the state? I knew well that there were endless housing developments springing up all over Israel, and illegally in the occupied territories, for Jewish families. But where was the next generation of Arab citizens to live? Dr Ghanem and

Ahlam are the pillars not only of their own community in Shaab, but of the whole Arab community inside Israel. Nonetheless, the state is forcing them to live with a terrible threat hanging over their heads. They are raising their children in an environment of continual insecurity. Every day when they leave home they do not know whether they will return to find a pile of rubble. They have been made to live in an unstable world which I have no doubt is deeply damaging to them and their children.

My meeting with Dr Ghanem ended uncomfortably. In a matter-of-fact tone he asked me whether I had made aliya, whether I had claimed my right as a Jew to come to live in a country from which the overwhelming majority of his people had been expelled little more than half a century earlier. These Palestinians still live in refugee camps across the Middle East, refused the opportunity to return to their former homes in Israel. It was the first time I hesitated to answer this question. I understood that my privileges as a Jewish immigrant had come at the expense of his people. Sitting in his home, reality finally hit me. The intoxicating power trip had come to an abrupt halt.

As is my way, I could not live long in ignorance. So I began the long and difficult task of becoming informed. I read and absorbed anything I could find on the position of the Israeli Arabs, questioning the official narrative. My left-wing friends in Tel Aviv, mainly academics and people working in non-profit organisations whom I had met through a fellow inmate of the absorption centre, were quick to reassure me they had Arab friends. I asked who exactly were these friends? Where did they live? What did they talk about together? The reply was always more or less the same. They were on good terms with the owner of an Arab restaurant where the felafel was excellent. Or they got their car fixed in a garage in an Arab village where the prices were low. What did they talk to these 'friends' about? When did they meet outside these formal relationships? What intimacies did they exchange? The Tel Aviv crowd looked at me aghast, as if I were crazy. They did not have *those* sorts of relationships with Arabs.

In fact, it was clear they had no Arab friends at all. I was mortified. The revelation that I had stumbled across the same kind of master–servant relationship as exists in South Africa was something I was little prepared for. For a week I was racked by pains in my stomach and head. It was as if I was purging myself of all the lies I had been raised on.

When I was stronger, I returned to Tamra. Asad Ghanem's wife Ahlam invited me to spend the night with them. We ate dinner together, and then she and I sat on the terrace in the warm evening air and talked. We exchanged confidences and intimacies that people rarely share until they have known each other for a long time. I remember thinking as we sat close together that here were an Arab and a Jew getting to know each other at a very deep and personal level, and that this was the way it was supposed to be. Cut off briefly from a society that always privileges Jews, we could feel like equals. I went back to Tel Aviv firm in my resolution that something in my life would have to change. Israel, as it was presently constituted, required me to choose a side: would I carry on with my life in Tel Aviv, turning a blind eye like everyone else to the suffering of the Arab population; or would I do something to highlight the reality and work towards changing it?

As it happened, my mind was effectively made up for me. I started to see much more clearly the paternalistic and colonialist attitudes of my left-wing friends. Being around them became unbearably suffocating. Invited in the winter of 2001 by Asad to teach English to Arab professionals at his Ibn Khaldun Association in Tamra, I had little hesitation in agreeing to take up the position. The Abu Hayjas, whom I knew through my work for Mahapach, offered to rent me the empty top-floor flat in their home, on the hillside overlooking the town's central mosque.

I knew breaking away from the Jewish collective would be traumatic, but I could not know how profoundly I would alienate those I thought I was close to. Almost overnight I lost my Jewish friends. Individualism is highly prized in many societies, but not in Israel, where the instinct of the herd prevails. Doubtless the reasons can be found in Jewish history, in the centuries of persecution culminating in the Holocaust. There is an attitude of you're either with us or against us. No one should step outside the consensus, or question it, because this is seen as weakening the group. But human beings are immeasurably more important to me than labels or institutions. By choosing to live as a Jew in a town of Muslims I hoped I could show that the fear that divides us is unrealistic. It is based on ignorance, an ignorance that the state of Israel tries to encourage among its Jewish citizens to keep them apart from their Arab neighbours. I know Jews who have lived on a left-wing kibbutz near Tamra, yet have never ventured into the largest Arab community in their area.

I have pondered long and hard why I was able to break away from the Jewish collective when other Israelis and Jews feel so bound to it, prisoners of a belief that they must stand with their state and their people, right or wrong. At the core of modern Jewish identity is the idea of victimhood, shaped by our history of persecution and the singular outrage of the Holocaust. The sense among Jews in Israel and the Diaspora that they are uniquely victims, both as individuals and as an ethnic group, cannot be overstated. Victimhood has become something akin to a cult among Jews, even among the most successful in Europe and America. It is developed as part of the Jewish nationalist ideology of Zionism, creating an 'Alice Through the Looking Glass' world for most Jews: they sincerely and incontrovertibly believe that Israel, a nation with one of the strongest armies in the world, backed by the only nuclear arsenal in the Middle East, is in imminent danger of annihilation either from its Arab neighbours or from the remnants of the Palestinian people living in the occupied territories.

The improbability of this scenario, however, can safely be ignored by most Jews as long as suicide bombers wreak intermittent devastation on crowded buses in Tel Aviv and Jerusalem. No one can say I do not understand the suffering inflicted on families by these attacks. One day I was waiting at Ben-Gurion airport for a flight to the UK when a good friend called, her voice barely audible, to tell me that her son, a serving soldier, had been horrifically injured by a suicide bomber. I had introduced this young man to my daughter Tanya the previous summer, and the two had formed a deep bond. Since then he has undergone more than thirty-five operations to try to repair the damage done to his body. His father has suffered eight heart attacks. All their expectations about their life were destroyed in an instant. That suicide bombing has torn apart the lives of my friends as easily as a piece of paper can be ripped.

But while I understand that these attacks can be terribly destructive of Israelis' lives and their sense of their own security, they can easily become an excuse not to confront the reality of what is taking place, the wider picture. They can simply reinforce in a very negative fashion this sense of Jewish victimhood. I understand this well. Like most Jews, I was brought up to see myself as a victim too: in a collective sense, as a Jew raised in the shadow of the Holocaust, and in an individual sense, as a Jew growing up in a post-war Britain tinged with anti-Semitism.

I was born in January 1949 into the grey, tired world of Britain under rationing. My family in Grays, Essex, appeared to me even at a very young age to be unlike those around me: there were no grandparents, brothers, sisters, aunts or uncles. My father's family were thousands of miles away in South Africa, and my mother's immediate family were all dead, victims of the First World War, tuberculosis and bad luck. There were only me and my parents. But my isolation did not end there. My parents, preoccupied with the heavy duties of running a successful medical practice, abandoned me to the care of the cleaning lady. I was banned from playing with the local 'rough' children, who arrived with the building of a council estate near our home, and instead consoled myself with games with our Golden Retriever dog, Laddie, and my rubber doll, Pandora, in the back garden.

My only early recollection of true friendship is with a black servant called Inyoni who looked after me – effectively as a substitute mother – when I was two years old, when my father tried a brief experiment in returning to South Africa. It did not last long: after spending six months just outside Cape Town we headed back to Britain. But Inyoni is a vivid feature in all my memories of that period in South Africa, much more so than my grandparents, whom I can barely recall. In that half-year I formed a deep attachment to him. He would teach me to strap Pandora to my back and carry her the way the local black women carried their babies. (Back in Essex I would see other little girls in the street holding their dolls in their arms and tell them off, showing them how to do it properly.) I would also spend hours squatting with Inyoni on the floor in his servant quarters at the back of the house as he prepared the vegetables. At other times we would play tea-party games on the lawn with Pandora. After my family left South Africa in 1952 I felt the loss of Inyoni deeply.

I was a sickly child, suffering repeated bouts of severe sinusitis which served only to provoke anger and resentment in my father, whose repeated interventions with drugs and operations failed to improve my condition. In total contrast to the way he treated his patients, he had no sympathy for my suffering and would simply tell me to get a grip on myself. I suppose to a highly respected doctor my recurrent illnesses must have seemed like a reproof: in the very heart of his family was a sick child he was powerless to heal. This failure was compounded, in his eyes, by my lack of success at school by any of the yardsticks he held dear. The many days I missed from school, and his overbearing demands, took their toll on my academic performance. I was constantly being dragged off to teacher–parent meetings to discuss my poor results. Eventually, at the age of seven I was packed off to the first of my boarding schools, cut off from contact with my parents apart from one weekend out of every three. Even when I returned home my father was usually too busy with patients to spend time with me.

Before leaving for boarding school, during the long periods when I was sick at home my father would lock me in my room with what he considered educational material. He would give me a *National Geographic* magazine to read, or throw me a pile of postcards he had been sent from around the world and demand that I find the country or city they had been posted from in an atlas. Sometimes he would want me to draw the outline of the country too. I would be beaten if I could not answer his questions on his return. By the age of six I was an expert at finding foreign places.

There were compensations in this harsh regime, trapped in the small world of my bedroom, deprived of companions. The biggest was the *National Geographic* itself, which opened up another, far more exciting, world to me. In my head I had incredible adventures in places most British children had never heard of. Remote South American hill tribes became my friends, as did the pygmies of the Congo. They never seemed any stranger to me, maybe less so, than the children at school. My favourite place was the Himalayas, somewhere that looked awe-inspiring and magnificent; I would think that if only I could climb to the very top I would be able to see the whole world. I felt a huge desire to go to these places and experience them for myself.

One of the features in the *National Geographic* that fascinated me most was about India. I was attracted to the pictures of that country, as I was to those of Africa, because of the bright colours, the beauty of the landscapes, the different way of life and the great variety of groups living within one subcontinent. What fascinated me most about India was the caste system, and in particular the group classified as the lowest caste: the Untouchables. I would study the pictures that accompanied the article, and then read the copy that explained that the Untouchables were supposed to be the ugliest, dirtiest, most stupid Indians, and had to live on the outskirts of the towns. I would trace my fingers first around the faces of the Untouchables and then around those of the highest caste, the Brahmans, flicking backwards and forwards between the pictures. But however long I looked at them, I could not see where the difference lay. Why were the Untouchables supposed to be uglier? I could not understand how you could designate one group as dirtier or less worthy than another.

Although I have always rejected this fear of the Other, and the racism that it inevitably fuels, I have learned from experience that it is a deeply rooted need in the human psyche. At the slightest provocation we will put distance between ourselves and those we cannot or do not want to understand. At an early stage of the Aids crisis I trained to be a therapist at Great Ormond Street hospital in London. In the late 1980s, when without the slightest shred of scientific evidence there were stories all over the British media warning that Aids was highly contagious, I was working at the London Lighthouse Project with infected women and children, and with the partners of infected people. At the Project we tried to challenge people's prejudices by bringing Aids into the community: we even established a commercial restaurant, where the staff were all Aids- or HIV-infected, so people could see that they were not going to catch the disease simply by eating there.

Nonetheless, some evenings I would attend social functions with my husband Michael, and would wait for the moment when another guest would ask what I did. My reply – that I was an HIV/Aids counsellor – always elicited the same response: overwhelmed with revulsion, the other person would take a step back. There was a double disgust: the fear that I might be carrying that terrible disease, and also the incomprehension that a nice, presentable middle-class woman would be doing a 'dirty' job like mine. It was as though they thought they were shaking the hand of a Brahman only to discover that they had been tricked into making contact with an Untouchable.

Moving to Tamra seemed to cause equivalent offence to my former Jewish friends. While Israeli Jews looked at the Palestinian uprising and responded by choosing to disengage – either by building a wall to separate themselves from the occupied population their army rules over or, inside Israel, by boycotting Arab areas, refusing to buy felafel or get their cars fixed in Arab garages – I elected to put myself right in the middle of the problem. To join the Untouchables. The response of my friends, like that of the well-heeled party crowd in London, was to withdraw in revulsion. Now that I am outside the Jewish collective, outside the herd, I must be treated like the enemy, as if I have committed a crime of treason or incitement.

Although the decision to leave Tel Aviv and cross the ethnic divide seemed the natural reaction to my new understanding of what was happening inside Israel, it was never easy. There were days when I felt tearful and isolated. I cried not out of fear but out of a terrible sense of how much my country was failing not just its Arab citizens but also its Jewish ones, and how catastrophically fragmented it was growing. It dawned on me at an early stage that I had to be 100 per cent committed to my new course. My Jewish friends chose to dismiss my decision as a silly passing episode, and even some of my new friends in Tamra appeared to doubt whether I could withstand the pressures. Hassan's son Khalil said to me in the first few days: 'After three months you'll go back. You won't be able to stand it here without cinemas at the end of the road or elegant restaurants.'

Neither side could understand why anyone would choose a primitive life over a sophisticated one. There was a double error in this thinking. First, I never saw Tamra as more primitive. Life was simpler, certainly, but my view has always been that life's greatest pleasures are simple. Second, it ignored the fact that there are some values more important than being comfortable, such as developing a consciousness about the rights and wrongs of the society one lives in, and an awareness of what each of us can contribute to improving it. In this sense the sophistication of the West increasingly appears to me to be a veneer, concealing the fact that most of us have lost our understanding of where our communities are heading. We are encouraged to believe in the sanctity of the safe little bubbles we inhabit, to the point where we can imagine no other life, no other possibilities.

My rejection by my Jewish friends was matched by an early suspicion of my motives and my seriousness expressed by a few people in Tamra. An Israeli newspaper took pleasure in quoting a former Arab Knesset member and resident of Tamra, Mohammed Kaanan, when he was asked about me: 'I want to believe she is an innocent woman working in the interests of the inhabitants here, but if a suspicion arises that she is working for an organisation that is against the Arab population that may harm her. We won't stand for it.' I was saddened by Kaanan's comments, but understood where such distrust springs from: for the first two decades after the state of Israel was born the Arab minority lived under harsh military rule, and today their lives are still controlled by a special department of the Shin Bet security services, which runs a large network of informers inside Arab communities. In the circumstances good intentions from Jews are treated with caution.

Far more disorientating was the initial reaction of a Tamran woman who would later become one of my closest friends. I met Zeinab, an English teacher at the local high school, on my first trip to Tamra when I was doing research for Mahapach. In her home she greeted me warmly and invited me to sit with her and have coffee while we discussed the discrimination in education. She explained the smaller budgets for Arab schools, the bigger class sizes, the shorter learning days, the shoddy temporary buildings in which Arab children learn and which usually became permanent classrooms, the severe restrictions on what may be taught (restrictions that do not apply to Jewish children), and the rigid control exercised over the appointment of Arab teachers and principals by the security services, which weed out anyone with a known interest in politics or Palestinian history. She added that Jewish school-children receive hidden benefits not afforded Arab pupils, such as double the school allowance if their parents serve in the army. I learned that by law all classrooms must be built with air conditioners, a requirement strictly enforced in the construction of Jewish schools, but usually ignored in Arab ones. And she explained that in most cases heating equipment, computers and books have to be bought by Arab parents because Arab schools lack funds to pay for them.

Then, after calmly informing me of this discrimination, her eyes turned glittery with suppressed anger and she asked: 'Why all of a sudden are you so interested in the Arabs? Is it because of 9/11?' It had not occurred to me that there was a connection between my being here in Tamra and what had occurred in New York. But her accusing tone suggested otherwise: it was as though she was saying, 'We have been here all these years with the same problems and you Jews have always neglected us. Why the interest now?' As our meeting came to a close she showed me to the door and said, 'You are always welcome in an Arab home.' I had rarely felt less welcome in my life. Although I felt confused by her barely contained rage, I was also impressed by her and wanted to know her better.

On my subsequent visits to the Galilee I always called on Zeinab, and she was one of the first people I informed of my planned relocation to Tamra. As the day of the move neared I rang her from Tel Aviv. She answered, saying she had been cleaning the house and thinking about me. I asked her what she was thinking. 'I was wondering whether I will be able to trust you,' she replied.

It was at this moment I started to understand the roots of Zeinab's anger. I realised that she had always been let down by Jews, even those left-wingers who claimed to be on her side, and she had no reason to think I would be any different. The few co-existence groups in Israel operate mainly in the Galilee, often bringing together Jewish and Arab women, but they are almost always run by Jews, and the debate is always controlled and circumscribed by the group's Jewish members. Off-limits is usually 'politics', which in effect means any discussion that touches on the power relationship between Jews and Arabs. These groups almost universally failed to survive the outbreak of the second Palestinian intifada in September 2000, precisely because the central concerns of their Arab members had never been addressed. The Jewish participants had not been prepared to make any sacrifices to promote equality, believing that if they did so they would undermine the thing they hold most dear, the eternal validity of a Jewish state. Allowing their Arab neighbours an independent voice was seen as threatening the Jewishness of Israel. I felt Zeinab had set me a test in her own mind, convinced I would betray her like all the other well-intentioned Jews she had known. I began to persuade her otherwise by the very fact of moving to Tamra; she was soon at my door with a bowl of beautiful cacti.

In those early days in Tamra I also came to understand that my image as a Jew was problematic. Months before my move, in the spring of 2002, Israel had launched a massive invasion of the West Bank, known as Operation Defensive Shield, in which the army reoccupied the towns that had passed to the control of the Palestinian Authority under the 1993 Oslo Accords. All summer and winter, families including my own in Tamra sat each night watching disturbing images on Israeli television and the Arab satellite channels of Israeli soldiers ransacking Palestinian homes in Ramallah, Nablus and Jenin, or of tanks ploughing down the streets, crushing anything in their way, from cars to electricity pylons. For the people in Tamra, as in other Israeli Arab communities, these were even more dispiriting times than normal. Many had held out the hope that with the arrival of a Palestinian state next door maybe they would finally come to be accepted as equal citizens of the Jewish state, rather than as a potential fifth column. Now they saw that hope unravelling before their eyes.

There were several disturbing incidents at this time which brought home to me the fact that I had little control over how my image as a Jew was being shaped and distorted by my country, my government and my army. One came when I joined Suad, then aged fifteen, for a walk on the far side of Tamra. We reached a spot where a group of a dozen or so children aged between seven and eleven were playing outside the neighbourhood homes. It is a point of honour for most Arab families that they and their children are immaculately dressed, but these children were wearing ragged clothes. When they saw us, they rushed out shouting to Suad: 'Is she a Jew, is she a Jew?' and 'Jews are dirty, they kill people.' Looking upset, Suad refused to translate straight away, and called out to them: 'Stop it!' She wanted to run, but I told her to stay calm. As we walked away, the children picked up stones from the roadside and threw them in our direction, though not strongly enough to hit us. It was a symbolic demonstration. Shaken, I thought afterwards that I understood their message: 'We hate Jews, so stay away. They only ever bring trouble with them.'

On another occasion, when I was out with Samira, we took a shortcut through a school playground in front of a group of trans- fixed ten-year-olds. A few came running up behind me, shouting, 'Yehudiya, Yehudiya!' and throwing handfuls of leaves that I could feel caressing my back.

When I reflected on these incidents I understood that what most Arab children learn about Jews comes from the media, and what they see is violence, oppression and abuse. The image of the strong, aggressive Israel that had so enthralled me in my early Zionist days I now saw in a very different light. These children – lacking the sophistication to discriminate between the media image of the Jew as an ever-present, menacing soldier and the reality of many kinds of Jews living in different circumstances all around the world – related to me in the only way they knew how. They saw the children of Jenin or Ramallah throwing stones at the Jewish soldiers, and now they were mimicking them.

This problem of my image as a Jew was illuminated for me on another occasion when I visited the home of Asad Ghanem. As he introduced me to his two young children, they asked: 'Is your friend who doesn't speak like us a Jew?' Asad answered: 'Yes, but she's a good Jew.' I had been reclassified in a way that shocked me: I was not a human being, not an Israeli, and not even a Jew, but a 'good Jew'. I came to realise that for most Arab children living in Israel their first lesson – something they learn from watching what happens in Jenin, Nablus, Hebron or Gaza – is that Jews are bad. They have to be taught that not all Jews kill and destroy. This is something the older children understand: they have learned it as part of their survival training for later life, when they will have to venture into a society which will mostly treat them as an enemy. When they are old enough to leave the safety of Tamra, they must know when to conceal their Arabness and keep their mouths shut.

When I think of those children throwing stones at me, I don't get angry with them but with all those Jews who tell me that the Palestinians living inside Israel are unaffected by the occupation, that it has nothing to do with them. They forget or choose to ignore the fact that, although Palestinian citizens of Israel are separated from Palestinians in the West Bank and Gaza by the reality that one has citizenship and the other does not,* the bonds of their shared nationality – the fact that they are all Palestinians – are far stronger. Many Palestinian citizens, whether living in Tamra, Nazareth or Haifa, have family living under occupation in refugee camps in

---

* Citizenship offers protections to Israeli Arabs not afforded to Palestinians of the West Bank and Gaza. The rights and duties incumbent on Israeli citizens, Jews and Arabs, are set out in Israeli law, whereas Palestinians living under occupation are judged according to a complex mix of local laws that applied before the occupation, Israeli laws, Israeli military decisions and international humanitarian law. Israeli military judges have wide discretion in applying these laws, often in apparently arbitrary fashion. Nonetheless, Israeli Arabs still face considerable discrimination, mainly because Israel lacks a constitution codifying basic rights, such as equality, freedom of speech and religious freedom, and because important national group rights, which determine resource allocations, are only recognised for Jewish citizens.

the West Bank and Gaza, or in extreme poverty in Lebanon and Syria. When they see a child being shot in Jenin or Nablus, it could be a cousin or a nephew. Even progressive Jews appear deeply blocked in understanding this reality. When I explained the complex identity problems faced by Israeli Arabs to a left-wing friend from Tel Aviv who belongs to Rabbis for Human Rights, an organisation which vehemently opposes the occupation, he told me simply: 'But they live in the state of Israel. The occupation doesn't touch them.'

How wrong he is was proved one evening while I was still smarting from the stone-throwing incident. I was sitting in my home with a group of twelve Arab friends watching a video of Mohammed Bakri's controversial documentary film *Jenin Jenin*, originally banned in Israel and a powerful record of the traumatic effects on Jenin's inhabitants of the violent invasion by Israel of the West Bank city in the spring of 2002. It was a disturbing moment at many levels. Sitting there as the only Jew, I was aware that I had to choose where I stood in this battle between two peoples, and that I had to be committed to the cause of justice and humanity. I watched the film through my Arab friends' eyes, learning exactly how they see us Jews as occupiers and oppressors. It made me question very deeply how I had been able to identify with a country that could send its child soldiers to behave in this fashion.

The film prompted in me a recollection of a conversation I had had on one of my increasingly rare and strained visits to my religious cousins, Jeffrey and Doreen, in Ashdod shortly after Operation Defensive Shield. Their granddaughter's husband, a medic in the reserves, had been sent to the Jenin area, and Doreen was apoplectic at the media suggestions that there had been a massacre there. 'Good Jewish boys who serve in the Israel Defence Forces like our Ofer don't harm people,' she asserted confidently. And then, as if providing the proof, she told me that Ofer had even been asked by his commanders to give medical assistance to a Palestinian woman who was having a heart attack during the invasion. This level of naïvety and self-satisfaction I found profoundly unsettling. I told her: 'The reality is that no one can know what their children get up to in a war. Soldiers carry secrets they will never divulge to their families.'

Although I am sure there are soldiers who attempt to hold onto their humanist values while in uniform, I am also convinced that the inherent immorality of enforcing an occupation makes good intentions almost futile. Worse than this, there is plenty of evidence that many soldiers lose their judgement entirely under the pressure of the barbaric tasks they are ordered to carry out. One need only consider the reports in the Hebrew media of the high suicide rates in the army, of the number of soldiers who are receiving psychological help and counselling, or who are discharged from duty, to know the truth of this. But on this matter Israelis are in deep denial.

Later, after visiting Jenin, I was convinced that something terrible had happened there, and that atrocities had been carried out by the Israeli army. When I watched the film, before I had been there, I was unprepared for the horrifying details of what had taken place, and of the terrible destruction wrought on the inhabitants' lives as well as on the centre of Jenin camp. Watching the survivors, broken-hearted amid the rubble of their homes, hopeless and with an understanding that their voice would never be properly heard, I felt their rage. It dismayed me to realise that I too was seeing the Israeli army, full of those 'good Jewish boys', as a terrorist army, and that for the first time I was beginning to understand the emotions that can drive a suicide bomber to action. I could see how unfair it sounds to a Palestinian to hear a suicide bomber being labelled a terrorist when we refuse to do the same if an Israeli soldier bulldozes a house with a family inside.

As I attempted to cope with these images on the screen, I was also confronted by the unexpected reactions of my Arab friends watching alongside me. Afterwards we talked about the film, and though I felt near to tears, as they spoke about the horrifying events they were smiling. I vividly remember Heba from my family recalling one particularly unpleasant scene, when an old man tells of being shot in the leg at close range by a soldier, and all the while she maintained a fixed smile. I thought: 'Is this a mask, is this the only way she can contain her emotions, suppress the pain? And if it is, is the mask reserved for me, the Jew here, or is it one they maintain with each other too?' The answer possibly came when the group got up to leave. Zeinab turned to me at the door and said, with the same fixed smile and glittering angry eyes I had seen before: 'Sweet dreams.' It was as if I had been hit in the stomach. I desperately wanted to say, 'But that's not me, don't hold me responsible, I'm with you.' But anything I said would have been inadequate. Maybe that night was the ultimate test for me in Zeinab's eyes. Maybe she thought I would go running home to Tel Aviv the next day. But I didn't; I stayed. And afterwards my friendship with Zeinab deepened and strengthened.

Listening to and coming to understand the Palestinian narrative was an important part of unlearning my lifelong Zionist training, which had dismissed the Palestinians' history and culture as irrelevant or non-existent. One of the most poignant episodes occurred when I was reading the autobiography of the Jerusalem doctor Mufid Abdul Hadi, which had been given to me by his nephew, Dr Mahdi Abdul Hadi, the director of the Palestinian Academic Society for the Study of International Affairs (Passia), based in Jerusalem. There is a moving passage concerning his escape, along with many other refugees, from Palestine in 1948, after the Israeli state was declared. It concludes with a scene on a boat, *al-Malik Fuad*, which heads for Sweden packed with Palestinian refugees being taken away, most of them forever, from their homeland and their families. 'When *al-Malik Fuad* lifted its anchor and began its westward-bound journey, it met another ship going in the opposite direction. Its gunwale was occupied by hundreds of singing and rejoicing people, who were greeting "The Promised Land" for the first time. The happy people greeted our ship by waving the Jewish state's flag.'

Here was the flipside of the *Exodus* story that inspired my love affair with Israel. In all my time as a teenager learning my people's history I had never been encouraged to think in those terms, that our people's rejoicing came at the cost of another's bereavement. The Zionist story I had learned was that this country was 'a land without people'. But here was one of those supposedly non-existent Palestinians telling me his story of loss and betrayal. I thought how much we could change history if we could raise Jewish children with that simple understanding.

The obstacles to doing it are huge. The apparent inability of Jews in Israel and the Diaspora to address the true roots of the Middle East conflict and accept their role in the Palestinians' suffering is given an alibi by their fears, which are in turn stoked by stories in the media of the ever-present threat of anti-Semitism, a Jew-hatred in both Europe and the Arab world that we are warned has troubling echoes of the period before the Second World War. A disproportionate part of the media coverage of anti-Semitism concentrates on tarring critics of Israel with this unpleasant label. Anyone who has disturbing things to say about what Israel is doing to the Palestinians is, on this interpretation, an anti-Semite. I have little doubt that the motivation of Israel's defenders in many cases is to silence the critics, whether their criticisms are justified or not.

My own critique of Israel, that it is a state that promotes a profoundly racist view of Arabs and enforces a system of land apartheid between the two populations, risks being treated in the same manner. So how does one reach other Jews and avoid this charge of anti-Semitism?

Given the sensitivities of Jews after their history of persecution, I think it helps if we distinguish between making a comparison and drawing a parallel. What do I mean? A comparison is essentially a tool for making quantitative judgements: my suffering is greater or lesser than yours, or the same. Jews have a tendency to demand exclusive rights to certain comparisons, such as that nothing can be worse than the Holocaust, because it involved the attempt to kill a whole people on an unprecedented industrial scale. Anyone who challenges that exclusive right, for example by suggesting that Israel is trying to ethnically cleanse the Palestinians from their homeland, is therefore dismissed as an anti-Semite. The debate immediately gets sidetracked into the question of whether the argument is anti-Semitic rather than whether it is justified.

Drawing a parallel works slightly differently. It refuses, rightly, to make lazy comparisons: Israel is neither Nazi Germany nor apartheid South Africa. It is unique. Instead a parallel suggests that the circumstances people find themselves in can be similar, or that one set of events can echo another. Even more importantly, the emotions people feel in these circumstances may share something of the same quality. That common quality is what allows us to see their suffering as relevant and deserving of recognition, without dragging us into a debate about whose suffering is greater.

I will give an example from my first few weeks in Tamra. I had been visiting families and hearing stories of what had happened to them in the war of 1948, when 750,000 Palestinians were either deported or terrorised from their homes by the Israeli army to refugee camps across the Middle East. This is an event commemorated by Palestinians as the Nakba (the Catastrophe), the loss of their homeland to the Jewish state and the dissolution of the Palestinian people as a nation. 150,000 or so Palestinians managed to avoid this fate, remaining within the borders of the new state of Israel and becoming Israeli citizens. Nonetheless, many of them had experiences similar to the refugees: all the members of my own family in Tamra, for example, were internally displaced in the 1948 war. They lost their homes and most of their possessions when they were forced to flee from villages in the Galilee.

The family of Hassan's wife, Samira, were expelled from a small coastal village near Haifa called Ein Hod. She once tried to visit Ein Hod to see her parents' home, which still stands but for decades has been occupied by Jews. When she knocked on the door to ask whether she could look inside, the Jewish owners angrily told her to go away. She has not dared go back since. When I talk to Samira I see the pain she feels at being uprooted, at living only a short distance from her family's home, but having no access to it or right to reclaim it. In fact, she does not even have the right to a history: the state refuses to remember her story, commemorate it or teach it to new generations. Her past is denied her, which damages her sense of who she is. It is a feeling we Jews should know only too well. After all, Jews have campaigned for the right to reclaim their properties in Europe, seek restitution, win recognition of the wrongs done them, and build museums. In this battle they have been increasingly successful. Why is Samira's pain not equally worthy of acknowledgement?

This lesson was reinforced by Rasha, a bright eighteen-year-old girl to whom I taught English and who is hoping to go to Haifa University to study psychotherapy. During a tutorial I asked her how she felt about life in Tamra, and she replied that she always felt afraid. This was clearly a sensitive topic, and I proceeded carefully. I asked her what she knew of her family history, such as where her parents were born. She said they were born in Tamra. And what about your grandparents, I asked. She said she knew they weren't from Tamra. 'They came from a village,' she added, only revealing with hesitancy that they were among the hundreds of thousands of refugees forced out of some four hundred villages by Israeli soldiers in the 1948 war. I asked if her parents ever talked about this with her at home. 'No, because they are afraid too,' she said. 'I ask them questions, but they don't like to talk about it.'

Rasha, it struck me, was living in fear of connecting with her past and her roots. Her eyes filled with tears. I thought, this is the story of this country. How can we educate our Jewish children about the

Holocaust, the centuries of discrimination against Jews, and yet here sitting next to me is a Palestinian child who has been forced by the Jewish state to cut herself off emotionally and psychologically from both her personal and her people's narratives, who is truly afraid to learn about her past? I asked her how she felt about not knowing the truth, and not being able to talk about it in her home. She replied: 'I don't feel like I have a future.'

Other families told me of the massacres that took place in their villages and of the tactics used by soldiers to terrify them from their homes. These are not fanciful stories: they are supported by the research of respected Israeli Jewish historians who have spent years trawling Israel's state and military archives.

I heard one such disturbing account of his own family's history from Adel Manna, a history professor at Hebrew University and a fellow of the Van Leer Institute in Jerusalem, Israel's leading centre for intellectual thought. Dr Manna was born in late 1947, a few months before the creation of the state of Israel, in the Galilean village of Majd al-Krum, a few kilometres from Tamra. In November 1948, he told me, the advancing Israeli forces finally reached Majd al-Krum, causing the irregular Arab militia that was supposed to protect the village to flee. The local leaders surrendered to the Israeli army, promising to hand over all weapons in return for a pledge not to bulldoze their homes or kill the villagers, as had happened in other places. The next day both sides kept their part of the agreement.

However, a week later, Dr Manna explained, another unit of Israeli soldiers arrived at the village, and said they were giving the inhabitants twenty-four hours to hand over their weapons. The unit returned the following day to the central courtyard, but the village leaders pleaded that they had already surrendered their arms. Unpersuaded, the Israeli commander warned them that if no guns were produced within half an hour, he would begin executing the inhabitants. The mukhtar, the village head, repeated that he knew of no more weapons, and that if someone was hiding a gun he would be too afraid to admit it. 'But after half an hour the army took three men and shot them in front of the villagers,' said Dr Manna. The commander told the mukhtar that in half an hour three more villagers would die; and that is what happened.

Later that day, continued Dr Manna, a further three people – a woman and two men – were shot dead as they returned to Majd al-Krum from the nearby village of Shaab (the home of my friend Asad), taking the death toll to nine. They did not know of the soldiers' presence there, and according to Dr Manna they were killed in cold blood as they entered the village. 'The massacre was only stopped by accident,' he said. 'An Arab man married to a Jewish woman who was serving in the Israeli army came to visit relatives in Majd al-Krum. He was working for the intelligence services and knew that the village had already surrendered a week earlier. He persuaded the commander to stop the killings.'

The horror was not to end for the villagers, however. Many fled northwards after the massacre, hiding in the surrounding hills and among the trees. By the time they found the courage to return, the new Israeli government had adopted a policy of expelling as many Palestinians remaining in the Galilee as possible. The army came to Majd al-Krum twice more, deporting a total of 535 villagers – mostly young people and couples, including Dr Manna's family – to the West Bank, which by then was under Jordanian control. Dr Manna's family became refugees in Nablus, while others ended up in Jenin. But, determined that the family should not remain refugees, Dr Manna's father began plotting a route back to the village. They crossed over to the East Bank of the Jordan River, then moved up into Syria and finally came to Lebanon's Ein Helweh refugee camp, where they lived for the next two years. When Dr Manna's mother fell pregnant with their second child, her husband decided the dangerous return to Majd al-Krum must be undertaken quickly. 'He told my mother he would not allow a child of his to be born in a refugee camp,' said Dr Manna. Along with fourteen other refugee families they secretly took a boat from Lebanon to Acre in Israel, and walked through the night to Majd al-Krum. Eventually the family managed to get Israeli citizenship, claiming they had been missed in the registration drives during all the chaos following the war. 'My uncle was too frightened to make the journey, and his family are still there living as refugees in Ein Helweh.'

Most families have stories like these, if not as expertly researched as Dr Manna's. I remember one family telling me how the men were away working in the fields when the Israeli army arrived at their village. The soldiers burst into the homes and started to undress, making the terrified women run away. When the men returned later in the day, they were shot.

In the middle of the night, hours after hearing this story, I awoke in a panic. I sat bolt upright in bed, covered in sweat even though it was a cold winter night. I had been dreaming that I was running through the streets of Tamra in my nightgown while tanks and soldiers chased me and my neighbours from our homes. I remember the oppressive feeling that there was nowhere to flee to. It was then I realised I was experiencing the life of the Arab community as they live it. I became consumed by Rasha's fear. I began to have a sense of what it means to lose your home, to have your land confiscated, to live in a state which does not truly accept your right to be there, to have no sense of where you really belong. And that reminded me of the perennial suffering of the Jewish people: the discovery that the place where you thought you belonged rejects you.

Soon after that night I went to see Roman Polanski's film *The Pianist*, which documents the experience of Jews under Nazi rule in Warsaw. I watched the scenes of Polish Jews being herded from their homes into the ghetto, and then later their transportation in cattle trucks to the gas chambers. As I looked at the pictures of their belongings littering the empty streets of the ghetto, I could not help but see a parallel with what had happened to hundreds of thousands of Palestinians only three years after the Holocaust.

74

3

Second-Class Citizens

Soon after my move to Tamra, Samira's sister Nawal, who was in her early fifties, was diagnosed with an advanced brain tumour which her doctors said was inoperable. However, a surgeon in Frankfurt was found who was willing to perform the operation, and the people of the town rallied round to raise the money needed to send her to Germany. A few days before her journey, the family called Rambam hospital in Haifa, where Nawal was staying, to sort out arrangements for the flight. She would be transferred by ambulance to the airport, then carried by stretcher onto the plane. When Abed, the husband of Samira's eldest daughter Heba, called the Magen David ambulance service, the man on the other end of the line asked for the patient's name. His suspicions aroused by Abed's reply, he asked: 'Is she a Jew or an Arab?' Abed wanted to know what difference it made. The man from Magen David said: 'If she is a Jew, they can carry her straight onto the plane, but if she is an Arab she will have to undergo security checks first.' Nawal, close to death, would still need to be questioned and body searched by Israel's security services.

In the end she was spared the indignity and humiliation of the airport security procedures reserved for Arabs. A Jewish friend of the family was able to use his personal connections to persuade Ami Ayalon, a former director of the Shin Bet secret services who has grown a little left-wing in his old age, to intervene. The airport security staff agreed to drop the normal checks. Nonetheless, I was appalled that this terminally ill woman could so readily be stripped of her dignity simply because she was an Arab. It reminded me of an incident during a holiday in Durban, in the apartheid days of South Africa, when I was a teenager. I had opened the local newspaper to discover that a black man stabbed in a street fight had been rejected by the crew of a passing ambulance because it was reserved for whites only. The man bled to death while he waited for the ambulance for blacks to arrive. The blinkered and callous racism at the heart of the apartheid system seemed to have a disturbing echo in the airport procedures of Israel.

There cannot be an Arab citizen of Israel who has travelled abroad and does not have his or her own personal horror story of dealing with the security procedures at Israel's main Ben-Gurion airport, just outside Tel Aviv. An Arab's status as a citizen inside the Jewish state is immediately made clear the moment he enters the airport and produces his passport for inspection by one of the young Jewish officials who are charged with assessing the security threat posed by each passenger. The main criterion used by the security personnel is not whether the traveller is an Israeli or a non-Israeli, but a Jew or a non-Jew. Jewish passengers will almost always be allowed to pass without further checks. Foreigners will be asked questions about their activities, including whether they have had any dealings with 'Arabs', including Arab citizens, and their bags will be X-rayed and possibly inspected. Arab citizens are assumed by definition to pose a security danger, and are treated accordingly. They will be subjected to lengthy questioning about their activities and their acquaintances, and their reasons for travelling. If they pass these checks they will have their bags X-rayed, then intimately searched, and finally they may be body searched.

Where I stood in this hierarchy of security classifications after my move to Tamra was apparent whenever I passed through Ben-Gurion. The moment the airport officials realised I was living in an Arab area, the respectful initial interview would switch into a full-blown interrogation in which I was left in no doubt that I was considered a suspect. I would be asked endless questions about why I lived among Arabs, then a series of absurd enquiries about which Arabs I knew in Tamra, whether an Arab had brought me to the airport, what conversations I had had with Arabs, whether I spoke Arabic, and whether I knew any Arabs in the country I was travelling to. On the first few occasions this happened, I quickly tired of the interview and suggested that if they suspected I was a terrorist they should skip the questions and simply get on with X-raying my bags. 'Oh, don't worry, madam, we will be getting to that,' they would say. 'But you don't understand the way we work: we must ask you these questions first.'

This humiliating treatment is not reserved for those Arabs known to have been involved in subversive activities. It is not even reserved for those who fit a general security profile – male, young, not married, politically active – which suggests to the authorities that they ought to be treated with caution. All Arabs – whether Israeli citizens, Palestinians in the occupied territories, or from abroad – are assumed to be a danger, without exception. Thus hardly an eyebrow was raised when the Israeli media reported that one of the most respected Arab journalists in Israel, Lutfi Mashour, editor of the *Sinara* newspaper, was forced to abandon his trip as part of an official press delegation accompanying the Israeli President Moshe Katsav to France in February 2004. Mashour, the only Arab in the thirty-five-person party, was singled out for extra searches; when he refused, he was told he would not be allowed to board the flight. A few months later another senior Arab journalist, Ali Waked, who works for the website of the biggest-circulation Hebrew newspaper, *Yedioth Ahronoth*, was prevented from boarding a flight after he had been invited to join the Foreign Minister Silvan Shalom on a state visit to Egypt. On neither occasion did the Jewish journalists and officials in the delegations protest against the treatment of their Arab colleagues.

The damage that such wanton discrimination does to the identification of Israel's Palestinian citizens with their state was illuminated for me during a conversation with Dr Adel Manna at the Van Leer Institute. He told me: 'I often ask the security people at the airport, "What does an Arab have to do *not* to be a suspect?" I try to imagine what the profile of a suspect is. If I am in my fifties, a professor at Hebrew University, travelling with my wife and daughter, and they need to check us this thoroughly, what are they doing with everyone else? How can an Arab avoid being a suspect in this country? The officials never have an answer when confronted with this question. They tell me, "We do this to everyone." And I clarify for them, "You mean everyone who is not a Jew." Then they tell me to complain to their line manager. But the problem is with the system, not with the individuals in it. Often I find myself getting intentionally provocative. I say, "Do you sleep well at night?" and they ask why. "Don't you see that you are implementing a racist, discriminatory policy against Arabs?" I tell them. "No, sir," they reply. "We are only doing our jobs." And then I say: "Well, you know, the Nazis said they were only doing their jobs." That always outrages them. "Are you comparing what we are doing with the Nazis?" "Not exactly," I say, "but I want to make you uncomfortable, to get you to think a little about what you are doing. You know that if I was born to a Jewish woman you would not be doing this to me. You are doing it to me because I am an Arab." The reply is always the same: "Well, sir, those are the orders." But anyone can say they are following a policy; the problem is that the policy is a racist one.'

The blindness of Israeli society to the extent of this state-sanctioned racism, and the damage it does both to the Jewish officials who implement it and the Arab victims who have to endure it, cannot be overestimated. I innocently asked Dr Manna what, if any, effect his being Palestinian had on his non-professional life. Little did I realise the Pandora's Box I was opening. Momentarily he looked thrown by the question – I don't think anyone had ever asked him before – and then slowly he recalled one example of racism at the hands of officialdom, followed by a second, and a third, and a fourth. The catalogue of the abuse and humiliation he had endured came to an end only because we ran out of time for our meeting.

He told me that one incident was at the front of his mind: next week he was due in court to contest a heavy fine he had been issued by a policeman for supposedly having a worn tyre and faulty brakes on his car. He said that at first the policeman had been courteous when he stopped him for a spot check, but that he had soon grown suspicious, possibly because of Dr Manna's accent when speaking Hebrew, or because of some written material in Arabic he noticed on the back seat of the car. 'The policeman asked to see my driving licence. As soon as he saw my name, he dropped the "sir" and I became simply "Adel".' Although the car had only recently passed its annual test, and despite Dr Manna's protests, the policeman gave him a fine and told him to get the tyre and brakes fixed immediately.

Dr Manna took the car to a nearby Arab garage in East Jerusalem and asked the mechanic to check it. He could find nothing wrong with it. Dr Manna asked him to check again, especially the tyres and the brakes. Again the man gave the car the all-clear. 'I asked him to give me a certificate that my car had passed the test. He wanted to know why, because it was another ten months before the current certificate ran out. So I told him the story. When he heard what had happened, he shouted at me: "Are you crazy? You want me, an Arab, to give you a certificate against the police? They will come and close the garage tomorrow! Where do you think you are living?" He was very angry, cursing me and telling me to get lost. I asked him what I could do. He said: "Go to a Jewish garage. Are you a simpleton? They are the landlords of this country. Get out of here now." I followed his advice. When the Jewish garage also found that the car was fine, I told the owner the same story and asked for a certificate. He said, "No problem." I asked him, "Aren't you afraid of the police?" "Of course not," he replied.'

Dr Manna has his own airport horror stories, one of which will suffice. Two years previously his son Shadi went on holiday with his American Jewish girlfriend to the Greek island of Kos with the Israeli charter company Israir. When it was time for their return flight they took the shuttle bus from the hotel with the fifty other Israelis on their package tour. Shadi was near the front of the queue for the initial security check at the airport, but when the official saw the name on his passport he asked him to stand aside while he dealt with the other passengers. Shadi asked why. 'Because you will take more time, and I have lots of other passengers to do. I will come to you afterwards,' he was told. Shadi's girlfriend, who was next in line, said she was with him. The official was surprised. 'But aren't you Jewish?' he asked. 'Yes,' she replied, 'but I am his girlfriend.' She was told to stand aside too.

After the other passengers had been cleared, Shadi was told he and his girlfriend would not be able to catch the flight. He asked why. 'Because it will take us at least two hours to check your luggage, and the plane can't wait for you.' Shadi tried arguing that he and his girlfriend had been in a group, and that it was the official's fault for pulling them out of the line. The man said there was no discussion to be had; they would have to wait for the next flight. When would that be? 'Maybe tomorrow, maybe next week,' he was told. 'My son rang me and his girlfriend rang her parents in Chicago,' said Dr Manna. 'Then I got a call from her parents, very upset and asking whether our son had been in jail. Of course he had not, I said. "Then why won't they let him on the plane?" they asked. "This is Israel, not Chicago," I told them.'

Dr Manna called his other son, a lawyer. He rang the airport and threatened legal action against the security official, who started to sound nervous and said he would no longer speak to any of them. He told Shadi there would be another flight in eight hours, and that he could catch it if he signed a waiver form declaring that it was his fault he missed the earlier flight, because he arrived at the airport late. 'My son refused, and was told he would not be allowed on the next flight. In the end a law professor friend told me the form was of no legal significance, and that Shadi should sign it, adding the words "under the circumstances".' Later, after a precedent-setting legal battle, Dr Manna won damages from the Israeli government, Israir and the national carrier El Al, which is responsible for Israeli security at airports.

If this is what one of the most influential and well-connected Arab men in Israel suffers, what is the situation of most other Arab citizens, who are not friends of a battery of law professors? 'But even for me it's exhausting, humiliating and depressing,' Dr Manna said. 'You can't go fighting the system in court every other day, either for yourself, your son, your wife or your daughter. I don't have the energy or the time to do it. You just have to accept that this is your life. You fight sometimes, but in most cases you have to let it go.'

Many leading figures in Israeli life admit that there is rampant discrimination against the country's Arab citizens, but usually excuse it as an unattractive trait shared by most democratic countries where a distinctive minority population is to be found. For example, Amnon Rubinstein, a law professor and one of the founding members of the left-wing Meretz Party, has often observed in his newspaper columns that black citizens of Britain and America face the same discrimination as Arabs in Israel. But while racist attitudes undoubtedly pervade even the highest echelons of officialdom in Western countries, Rubinstein's comparison is pure sophistry. In Europe and America such racism exists only insofar as officials break the rules of state institutions and the country's legal codes; in Israel such racism is not only state-sanctioned, but actually encouraged by the institutions themselves – as is demonstrated by the security procedures at the airport. The only recourse an Arab citizen has is a lengthy, expensive, and often futile fight through the courts.

Some of the problem stems from the fact that Israel's legislators have refused to draft a constitution, partly because such a document would lack international legitimacy unless it enshrined principles of equality that would strengthen the Arab minority's hand in legally challenging acts of discrimination by state bodies. Instead, Israel has constructed a legal system that carefully veils its discrimination: although the Law of Return openly states that it offers special privileges to Jews only, other laws make the same distinction without being so explicit, often by stating simply that the benefit applies to anyone who 'qualifies under the Law of Return' – i.e. Jews. Other laws and government decisions apply only to those eligible for military service, again code for Jews.

After my move to Tamra, I quickly discovered for myself how the state had cultivated an atmosphere in which neglect and abuse of Arab citizens' rights were the norm. I also learned how wearying the struggle for equal recognition and treatment is, and how much it damages both one's sense of belonging to the state and one's sense of self-worth. On crossing the ethnic divide I noticed almost immediately that I had been redesignated by the state bureaucracy as a non-person. For example, I rang the state-owned airline El Al to check how many points I had accumulated on my frequent flyer card. The woman who answered asked for my personal details, including my address. I told her that I had moved from Tel Aviv and was now living in Tamra. 'Tamra?' she asked after a few moments. 'I can't find it on the computer.' I told her it was an Arab town close to Acre in the Galilee. 'Are you sure you don't live in Timrat?' she asked. The inhabitants of Timrat, a small rural community built on land that was confiscated long ago by the state from the expelled Arab villagers of Malul, near Nazareth, are exclusively Jewish. It was clear that Arab communities were not listed on El Al's system because no Arabs were expected to have frequent flyer cards. 'I live in Tamra,' I repeated. 'But you must live in Timrat,' the woman insisted. 'That's what I have on the computer.' I have subsequently learned that few Israeli computer systems include Arab communities, because for most Jews they simply don't exist.

On another occasion I stayed in the Sharon Hotel in Herziliya, by the coast a little north of Tel Aviv. On arrival I handed over my ID so that they could prepare my bill before my departure. As I was about to leave two days later, I noticed on the bill that I had been registered as 'Susan Nathan, from Tamara, Kfar Sava'. I called the manager over and pointed out that this was not my address. 'But you live there,' he insisted. I asked him to look again at the address on my ID card, and tell me what it said. 'Tamra,' he said sheepishly. When I asked why he had invented a fictitious address, he said he had been unable to find Tamra on the computer system. He began checking again. 'Don't bother,' I said, 'I'm sure it's not on there.'

The fact that I had become a non-person insofar as I was a resident of Tamra had many other troubling aspects. For example, the public utility companies clearly had little interest in servicing customers living in Arab areas. It is a scandal rarely mentioned inside Israel, or outside, that employment in the country's huge public sector is reserved almost exclusively for Jews. Nachman Tal, a former deputy head of the Shin Bet security services, found that only six of the thirteen thousand employees of the Israeli Electricity Corporation are Arabs. There are believed to be a similar number of Arabs among the ten thousand staff of Bezeq, the national telecoms company.

When I was living in Tel Aviv and I changed apartments there were several Bezeq offices I could visit or phone, and the next day an engineer would come to install a line. In Tamra there is no Bezeq office; one must travel to Acre or Haifa. After warnings from local families about the lack of telephone services in Tamra, I rang Bezeq three weeks before I moved there to book a time for an engineer to install a new line in my apartment. He never showed up. When I rang the company to protest, I was told: 'Well, you've got a cellphone, haven't you?' I badgered the Bezeq office every day, telling them how urgently I needed a phone line, but nothing ever happened. In the end I managed to get the number for the company's northern head office, and tracked down the direct line of the chief engineer. I told him I would go to the media and explain that Bezeq was discriminating against me for living in an Arab community if the line was not installed immediately. The next day he showed up at my home himself. Interestingly, the Bezeq office had blamed their inability to install a line on recent storms which, they said, had brought down many phone lines in the Galilee. I could not remember any such storms, and I received a very different explanation from the chief engineer. 'We don't like coming to Arab areas because when they see a Bezeq van they all come out of their houses saying they have a problem that needs fixing, and that they've have been calling for months.' From what I had seen, that seemed a more than plausible scenario.

Friends in Tamra told me that they believed the Jewish staff of the public utility companies were afraid to come to Arab areas because they feared they would be attacked. When I eventually managed to get a man from Tevel, the cable TV company, to connect up my television, he was so nervous he couldn't remember what he was supposed to do. In the end Khalil from the family, who is a film-maker, had to take over and do the work for him. Some friends in the nearby Arab city of Nazareth found they could not get IKEA to deliver a bedroom suite they had ordered from the store in Netanya. No one from the company would tell them what was causing the hold-up. However, a few weeks later the Israeli media revealed that another IKEA customer, the mayor's son in the Arab village of Kalansua, had been refused delivery of his furniture too. He was told it was company policy not to deliver to areas considered 'dangerous'.

I couldn't help thinking that such fears were preposterous. But if

Jewish staff really were too afraid to work in Arab areas, wasn't the obvious – not to say the fairest – solution to employ Arabs so that they could do the jobs their Jewish colleagues were too frightened to touch?

In one of those paradoxes that underpin life in Israel, many Jews have been boycotting Arab communities – refusing to eat in their restaurants or get cars fixed in their cheaper garages – following events shortly after the start of the intifada, in October 2000, when the Israeli police shot dead thirteen unarmed Arab demonstrators across the Galilee. At the time I was living in Tel Aviv, and these killings barely penetrated my consciousness. Like other Jews, all I heard from the Israeli media was that there had been what they termed 'Arab riots' in the north; the deaths were presented as the price that had to be paid for the defence of our state.

In fact, something rather different had taken place. The country's Arab citizens had staged official demonstrations and protests inside their communities against the killing of Palestinians in the occupied territories at the start of the intifada. In particular their anger had been inflamed by the television images of twelve-year-old Mohammed Durra being killed in a hail of bullets from an Israeli military position in Gaza as he shivered in terror, sheltering behind his father. The police in the Galilee either chose on their own initiative or were ordered from above – we are unlikely ever to know for sure – to strike pre-emptively to break up these protests. They stormed into towns and villages without riot gear but armed with rubber-coated steel bullets. Arab youths, outraged that their communities were under fire, and that other young men had been killed and injured, retaliated by throwing stones. When the police ran out of rubber bullets, as several policemen later testified to an official inquiry, they simply switched to live ammunition. A team of police snipers was also deployed in two towns, Nazareth and Umm al-Fahm, where several protesters were killed.

Those thirteen deaths, and the severe injuries inflicted on

hundreds more, have scarred the imagination of Israel's Palestinian citizens ever since, reminding them both that they have little reason to identify with their state, and that the country's security officials do not recognise them as citizens with rights comparable to those of Jews.

Several people in Tamra observed to me that a massacre of the country's Arab citizens has occurred once a generation, as if to remind Arabs that they should not forget the insecure nature of their citizenship. In 1956, when the Arab minority was living under martial law, forty-nine men, women and children were shot dead in cold blood by Israeli soldiers after the army placed a curfew on the village of Kafr Qasem at short notice. Villagers working out in their fields and unaware of the curfew were killed at a roadblock as they returned home in the evening. The commander who gave the order, Colonel Isachar Shadmi, was put on trial and fined one piaster – the lowest sum possible – by the judges.

In the second massacre, twenty years later in 1976, the police stormed the village of Sakhnin, close to Tamra, to prevent a demonstration against a wave of land confiscations that were stripping the community of its last land reserves. Six unarmed Arabs were killed.

'Now it is the turn of our generation to learn that Israel does not tolerate dissent when it comes from non-Jews,' said Wahid, one young man in Tamra. He and many others told me that after the thirteen deaths the police had stormed Arab communities in the Galilee, randomly rounding up men and boys, some as young as ten, and jailing them. Tamra was relatively quiet during the protests, but Wahid and his two brothers were arrested and spent several days in jail. 'We were lucky,' he said. 'Our father had connections with the local police commander and was able to get us released. But hundreds of other youngsters were detained for months by the police.'

An official judicial inquiry into the police shooting spree in the Galilee did not hold any of the police officers to account for the killings. But it did conclude that a common prejudice existed in the police force, shared across the ranks, that the country's Arab citizens were 'the enemy' and needed to be treated as such. During my conversation with Dr Manna I told him that it seemed to me this attitude to the Arab population had polluted every area of life in the country. For example, I had read that month in *Ha'aretz* about an official fraud that had been perpetrated for the past year by the Israeli Broadcasting Authority, the national body that regulates the television industry, in Arab areas. The IBA had set up illegal checkpoints at which officials demanded money with menaces from Arab motorists to cover TV licence fee debts, often sums invented on the spot. More than $5 million was taken in this fashion. Off-duty policemen hired to man the roadblocks were authorised to confiscate the driving licences or ID papers of drivers who couldn't or wouldn't pay. I said to Dr Manna that I could hardly believe such an illegal practice by an official body had continued for so long without any action being taken. If Jews had been targeted in this way by the IBA, the story would have been front-page news the next day.

'Actually, I was caught in one of those roadblocks myself,' he said. Why didn't human rights and legal groups challenge it earlier? 'There are so many cases of discrimination, you have to prioritise. There are Arab villages without water or schools or electricity. Are you going to try to help those people, or drivers being harassed for money in the street? The system is designed to exhaust not just the Arab public but the non-profit organisations and the public institutions designed to protect them. They are overwhelmed by the discrimination and harassment.'

Dr Manna's description of the problem is not exaggerated. My impression is that this panoply of discriminatory measures by official bodies is designed with one end in mind: to keep the Arab population ghettoised, afraid to leave the narrow confines of its towns and villages. An Arab citizen can avoid most dealings with the authorities – and therefore avoid getting into trouble – if he stays penned up in his community. The moment he steps outside, into Jewish public space, he faces physical, bureaucratic and legal challenges. From the state's point of view, as long as an Arab citizen is cooped up in his village, scared to leave, he is invisible, weak and silent. No wonder an exceptional, irrepressible man like Dr Manna, who spends much of his time moving between cities and countries, has such a difficult time with Israeli state officials.

I raise these examples of discrimination because they give a flavour of the different meaning of citizenship as experienced by Arabs and Jews inside Israel. Overt and state-sanctioned racism at the airport, from the police and by the public utility companies erodes the identification of Arab citizens with their state, and their identity as Israelis. They are made nationless. Quite how profoundly dislocating and damaging this experience is was revealed to me during a series of discussions with Arab friends and students about two topics that touch their lives most directly: education and employment.

My early conversations with Zeinab had opened my eyes to the injustices in the Israeli education system, but as our friendship grew deeper and I talked with other teachers I started to learn a great deal more about how the country's Arab schools operated. Israel has developed two separate school systems, one for its Jewish population and another for its Arab minority. The official justification is that the separate tracks allow the Arab population to preserve its culture, language and heritage. In practice, this is nonsense: having separate Arab schools has simply allowed Israel to maintain a weaker, underfunded Arab system to ensure lower educational standards prevail, to permit Jewish officials to interfere in the curriculum to remove any trace of Palestinian history or culture, and to intimidate Arab teachers and principals into silence on key issues concerning their schools.

The biggest crisis in the Arab school system is not a financial one, though that is severe enough, but results from the state's continuous undermining of the status of education among the Arab population. A former principal in Tamra, who has taught for more than twenty-five years, explained to me the damage being done to Arab education. 'I remember from my youth that teaching was always held in the highest regard, it was revered as a profession. This is the traditional Arab view of education: in the Arabic language we have a word, "ustaz", meaning teacher, which we use to address anyone who deserves to be emulated. But the problem in the Israeli educational system is that no Arab child respects or wants to emulate his teacher, because he knows that the Israeli security services vet all appointments in his school and control all promotions. Teachers themselves lose heart: they understand that their progress depends not on their skills in the classroom or their dedication to educating young minds, but on whether they are seen to be "reliable" by the Shin Bet. In fact, the better you do as a teacher in an Arab school, the more tainted you become in the eyes of the other teachers and the pupils. The system of surveillance and interference corrodes the values of education.'

I heard similar claims from other teachers, including Zeinab, and could not help wondering whether they simply reflected the mildly paranoid, if natural, suspicions of a minority group. But in the course of 2004 I learned from a very reliable source – Israel's most serious newspaper, *Ha'aretz* – that everything I had been told was true. In the spring a former senior Shin Bet official, Reuven Paz, admitted to the paper a long history of interference in the education system by the security services: 'The Shin Bet not only determined and intervened in the appointment of principals and teachers, but even decided who the custodians and janitors that clean the bathrooms in the Arab schools would be.' And later, in the autumn, *Ha'aretz* reported the director-general of the Education Ministry, Ronit Tirosh, admitting that the Shin Bet was still approving every appointment to Arab schools, and that it had no intention of discontinuing such practices. 'Due to the sensitivity of educational positions, all [Arab] teachers undergo security, personal and crimi-nal background investigations before being assigned to a position,' she said.

According to the newspaper, the vetting process is overseen by an official in the Ministry of Education, Alex Rosman. The reason for such intensive surveillance of the Arab education system is clear: to prevent any discussion of Palestinian history or culture in class-rooms. Teachers are effectively banned from teaching about the Nakba, the loss of the Palestinian homeland in 1948, or about their people's connection to Palestinians in the West Bank and Gaza and in refugee camps across the Middle East. If they break this rule, they are certain to be dismissed. As a result pupils grow up with little or no knowledge of their heritage and their people's history apart from confused and confusing titbits picked up from older family members – as I had found in conversations with pupils and adults in Tamra.

One woman, Manal, had spent three years training to be a teacher before abandoning her studies in the final year. 'I slowly realised I had no faith in the values taught in Arab schools. I started to look back on my own years at school and see them as empty years, years that were stolen from me. I think now of how I trusted my parents and teachers and feel like I was lied to.'

The system as crafted by the Shin Bet, I realised, was designed to strip Palestinian citizens from a young age of their political aware-ness, to make them a malleable, identity-less mass that could be better manipulated and exploited by the state.

Another teacher recalled her own experience of the Shin Bet's involvement in her school in Sakhnin. 'Parents and children know that teachers have to be approved by the Shin Bet; it is an open secret. But they also know – and this is much less spoken about – that the Shin Bet recruit spies among the pupils, usually via parents who are themselves in the pay of the Shin Bet. I will give you an example. A colleague of mine was teaching a class of sixteen-year-old boys who would not settle down. Instead of concentrating on the lesson, they kept asking him about the Palestine Liberation Organisation. This was before the Oslo agreements were signed. Maybe some of the boys had been having an argument about the subject in the playground before the class. Other teachers would simply have shut down the discussion, but he was a good teacher, committed to the values of his profession, so he gave them a brief history of the PLO. I knew this teacher, and he was not politically active by any stretch of the imagination. He simply told them what the PLO is and what it stands for according to its charter. The next day he was summoned to the local police station to "discuss" what had happened in class the day before. A few days later he lost his job. Now, who knew about that lesson? Only the boys in the class. So one of them must have given the information to the police. What kind of effect on the learning environment do you think that has?'

How teachers and children are supposed to develop an atmosphere of trust and respect under these circumstances defeats me. But, according to the former principal in Tamra, just as damaging as the Shin Bet's intrusive surveillance of schools are the efforts of Israeli politicians to further erode the status of Arab teachers and education by demanding that they promote Zionism and Jewish culture in the classroom. 'Imagine it: we are the remnants of the Palestinian people who lost almost all of our homeland in 1948, whose relatives were forced to flee into refugee camps, who have had our lands and homes confiscated by the state. Today we are sort of semi-citizens, not even included in the description of our country as a Jewish state. And how does the Ministry of Education want us to respond? It issues directives telling us to raise the Star of David flag above our schools when the children know the Palestinian flag is banned, to sing the national anthem even though its verses speak of the Jewish people returning to their homeland, and to teach a curriculum which highlights the great victories of Zionism in founding a Jewish state and extols the virtues of Jewish culture.

What do you think it feels like being a teacher when that is your job description? And what do you think the pupils make of the teachers who force-feed them this stuff every day? We are totally discredited in their eyes – and our own.'

Talking to my teenage students in Tamra I got a sense of how the school system was eroding their self-image, their relationship with the state and their future prospects. One day Suad showed me an English textbook that is used in Jewish and Arab schools. It was full of picture stories about Jewish kids with names like Gideon, Avner, Daphna and Anat wanting to be astronauts, actors and firemen. The book contained a single story of Arab life: two boys named Mahmoud and Yousef asking their uncle, Sheikh Salem, about how to become a good camel driver.

It was bad enough that images of Arabs were almost entirely absent from the curriculum, but that offence was then compounded by their brief appearance as an outdated and racist stereotype. Apart from a few tens of thousands of Bedouin in the country's southern Negev desert, Israel's Arab children have no more contact with camels than Jewish children do. I am still waiting to see my first camel in the verdant hills of the Galilee. And given Israel's determined policy of stripping all Arab communities of their farm lands, the idea that any of these children could – let alone would want to – aspire to be camel herders was almost comical.

But more harmful than the racist representations of Arab life in textbooks is the paucity of the wider curriculum. Despite claims that the separate Arab education system is designed to protect Arab culture and heritage, the Ministry of Education has ensured that these are the main elements excised from school courses. Almost all great Palestinian and Arab literature is off-limits to Arab pupils. The spotlight was briefly turned on this issue in 2000 when the former Education Minister, Yossi Sarid, from the left-wing Meretz Party, provoked a huge row by trying to include the most famous Palestinian poet, Mahmoud Darwish, on the country's literature courses for Jews. Although it is now technically possible for Jewish pupils to study Darwish, his writing is still banned from Arab schools. The curriculum used in Arab education is one agreed in 1981 by a committee whose sole Jewish member vetoed any works he thought might 'create an ill spirit', apparently code for literature that might connect Arab pupils to their heritage and culture.

'Studying Darwish, for me, is only a dream,' said Butheina, one female student I teach. 'In school I have much lower expectations than that: I would just like to be allowed to read a modern love poem in Arabic. Instead, all we can read are what are called the "jahiliya" poets, who lived hundreds of years ago and write in a language we can barely understand.' The experience of Butheina and her classmates was the equivalent of British students being forced to read only Chaucer. 'I know the classics are important, but they offer us a very limited understanding of our past, and it puts off the great majority of students. It makes our culture seem fossilised and irrelevant.' I feared that was probably the intention.

All my pupils told me about the lack of resources at their schools: many studied in crowded, temporary buildings that had long ago become permanent, they rarely had access to a computer, and the schools did not have the funds or teachers to offer the kind of after-school learning programmes that are common for Jewish children. One told me that when she took home her tattered Arabic textbook, her mother said she had used the same book twenty years earlier. 'Jews hardly ever learn Arabic, and so they don't bother updating the Arabic language textbooks,' she told me. In contrast to the colourful and illustrated Hebrew language textbooks, the pages of Arabic textbooks were a forbidding mass of endless text.

Comparative visits I made to schools in Tamra and in the deprived Jewish town of Kiryat Shemona as part of my work as a supervisor for Mahapach left me in no doubt about the rank discrimination in the funding of Arab education. Rather than accept my view, consider the school funding figures for 2001 published by the Central Bureau of Statistics in 2004. Each Arab student in Israel received resources – after teachers' salaries had been excluded – of £105 a year, less than a quarter of the sum, £485, spent on Jewish pupils in secular state schools. The state discriminated yet further in allocations to Jewish religious schools, where each pupil was getting resources worth £1,340, or twelve times as much as an Arab pupil. This has been achieved by a duplicitous system of double funding that allows religious Jewish schools to apply for money from both the Education Ministry and the Religious Affairs Ministry. (Almost no funds are available for the funding of non-Jewish religious schools.)

As a result many Jewish parents, including secular ones, choose to send their children to extremist religious schools so that they can benefit from the higher budgets. The dangers of this should have been apparent to the succession of Education Ministers who allowed the practice to continue: the religious schools take a less than en-lightened approach to subjects such as modern science and issues like women's rights. There has to be a serious question mark over why Israel should want to encourage this brand of Jewish fundamen-talism among the most impressionable members of its society.

The level of discrimination against Arab students is so great that in places where Jewish and Arab communities live close together there are increasing reports of Arab parents trying to get their children registered for Jewish schools. In Haifa, for example, the Arab Parents' Forum announced that the standards at the local Arab junior school were so dismal they wanted to register their children at Jewish schools for the 2004 academic year. Their efforts were blocked by the Education Ministry's regional chief, Aharon Zavida, who said such a transfer was impossible because Arab pupils were in 'a separate registration area'.

The best hope for most Arab parents, if they can afford it, is to send their children to one of the few private mixed Jewish and Arab schools in Israel. The Ministry of Education has tolerated a handful of these, categorising them as special interest schools, though it has been taking a much harder line of late. A government-appointed committee, the Dovrat Commission, recommended in early 2004 that no more special interest schools be allowed, arguing they are 'elitist'. As a result the opening of a bilingual school in the Arab town of Kafr Kara, the first mixed school in an Arab community, was blocked in June 2004, again by Mr Zavida.

Two other bilingual schools have been operating for a few years, one in Jerusalem and the other close to Tamra, in the Jewish community of Misgav. Asad Ghanem had decided he was going to send his young daughter Lina to the Misgav junior school, which teaches classes in Hebrew and Arabic. I asked him what advantages he saw in her meeting Jews at such a young age. Might she not get a misleading picture of Israeli life? Her equal treatment with the Jewish pupils at the school would not prepare her for the racism and discrimination she would face in later life. 'I know from the activities at the Misgav school that the Arab pupils there are much more open and have much more confidence than children in Arab schools,' Asad said. 'At least the teachers and the principal are appointed by a non-profit organisation that recruits them for their professional competence, and not by state officials working for the Shin Bet. As for the ideological effect of the school on her, I hope it will lead her to understand that our reality here is full of contradictions, that we must cope with a Jewish reality and a Palestinian reality. It's not that I am against sending her to an Arab school, it's just that I think she will be better prepared for the challenges she will face in later life if she masters these contradictions and the issues surrounding her complex identity from a young age. When you live inside Israel, I don't think you can really open your eyes to what it means to be Palestinian until you meet Jews. In this school, where she will get the chance to meet the Other, she will learn who she is and where she belongs. For me, I didn't mix properly with Jews until I went to university, and that is too late.'

I still wondered whether his daughter, aware of her Palestinian identity, culture and heritage from her private schooling, might not then find her move to university a damaging experience. Israeli universities, far from the beacons of academic freedom celebrated in the international media, are part of the same system of racist control. Despite pressure from the Arab community, the state has refused for more than five decades to create a single university teaching in Arabic. Less than 1 per cent of the country's university lecturers are Arabs, and many of the Jewish lecturers and researchers are 'sponsored' by national security bodies that require them to teach in military and police colleges as well. There are also severe restrictions on the forms of political protest open to Arabs, particularly at Haifa University, which has the largest Arab student body. Even for an Arab student to wave a Palestinian flag at a demonstration can get him or her arrested.

The entry requirements of Israeli universities are also skewed to favour Jewish over Arab applicants. For example, the matriculation exam on which the universities base their decision awards extra points to the best students of Hebrew, but not to students of Arabic. The psychometric tests are also weighted in favour of Jewish students because of their bias towards Western cultural norms. When the system was briefly reformed in 2003, in an attempt to help students from 'weaker' sections of society, the biggest beneficiaries were Arab candidates rather than Jewish candidates from deprived communities. When the Israeli Committee of University Heads realised the number of successful Arab candidates had risen significantly in the first year of implementation, it immediately abolished the new system and reintroduced the old tests. The committee's reason, in its own phrasing, was that 'the admission of one population [Arabs] comes at the expense of the other [Jews]'. The Arab student body is about 8 per cent of the total, even though they comprise 24 per cent of that age group.

Asad had no doubts about the advantages to his daughter of attending a mixed school. 'If you are telling me that the outcome of this choice is that my daughter will go to university with higher expectations, that she will be more mobilised and angered by the discrimination she encounters there, and that she will resist it more strongly, then that is one goal. I teach all my students [at Haifa University] that they have the right and the ability to achieve anything they want, so that when they go out into the wider world and find that they are denied their basic rights they will be more ready to fight for equality and to effect change. I see that as a positive thing.'

I knew from my own teaching in Tamra that the Arab children who got to university had to study far harder, were far brighter and far more committed than Jewish children. The reason so many adults in Tamra speak a language in addition to Arabic and Hebrew – such as English, German, Russian, Italian, or more obscure languages like Bulgarian, Romanian and Moldovan – is that their families have been forced to spend their life savings to send their children abroad, often to cheap East European states, to study because their own country makes it so difficult for them to enter higher education.

These difficulties were highlighted when seventeen-year-old Samiha, one of my cleverest students, applied for a place at university. She had worked tirelessly for her exams in the hope of winning a place at medical school, and achieved outstanding marks in her matriculation exam. However, when she started searching for courses she discovered that either she did not qualify for most of them because she had not served in the army, or that she would have to wait another three years before she could begin – the entry age for many courses is adjusted to take account of when Jewish youngsters finish their army service (three years for men, two years for women). She decided instead to apply for a place on one of the best law courses in the country, at the Netanya Academic Institute. When she told them of her high mark in the matriculation exam, they said they still had many places unfilled and she should send in her form immediately. She and her family were sure acceptance was a formality. But a few weeks later she received a letter saying she had been rejected, without even the offer of an interview. When the family called, the college refused to give a reason.

I was appalled that this talented young woman was being cast aside so casually. In other countries the outstanding children of disadvantaged communities are given every assistance to advance themselves; in Israel it looked to me as if obstacles were being thrust in her way to break her spirit. My fears that she would scale down her ambitions and that her family would resign themselves to this rejection were soon confirmed: Samiha started applying to poorly regarded colleges for courses as a physiotherapist.

While living in Tamra I have been trying to help reverse some of the damage done to these pupils by the Israeli education system, through both my work as a supervisor for Mahapach and my involvement with the only Arab music conservatoire in Israel, Beit al-Musica. Mahapach, founded by Jewish and Arab university students in 1997 as a way to bridge the vast educational gaps in Israel by helping disadvantaged children, has built seven 'learning communities' in Jewish and Arab towns. The students work privately with a young pupil once a week to help build their confidence. Mahapach widens the meaning of education to include the environment in which pupils learn, acknowledging that economic and cultural factors play a role in students' ability to develop and prosper. In each town, children are encouraged to take a more active part in their communities by improving their educational achievements, honing leadership skills and promoting community projects that relate to educational, environmental and housing issues. Children from the different ethnic communities are also given the chance to step across the divisions designed to separate them and meet the Other.

The need for these kinds of programmes is particularly strong in Arab communities, because they lack even the most tenuous bond of belonging to the state. Denied the chance to serve their country – neither they nor their state want them fighting in the army – and deprived of an Israeli identity, Arab youngsters are not able to establish a connection to their country at the national level. But by volunteering, whether by helping old people, establishing groups to empower women or campaigning for improved services, they can contribute to a better life for themselves and their town. It is a long, hard battle to develop that connection, but given time Mahapach can help them to create their own meaning of citizenship.

A good example is a Mahapach project currently being developed by a group of sixteen-year-old schoolchildren in Tamra to give names to the town's streets and numbers to the houses. Most of the Arab towns and villages in Israel do not have official street names, largely because the state has taken away all formal planning controls from the minority. Instead Tamra, like other Arab communities, has developed in higgledy-piggledy fashion, like a refugee camp. Overcrowding and the consequent illegal building by families, often in the form of extensions, mean that numbering systems break down. The only way people from the outside world can send mail to us in Tamra is through a post-office box number. The priority the children have given to assigning names to their streets and numbers to their homes reflects their recognition that it is vital to their sense of belonging: 'Here we are on the map,' they are saying, 'this is our town, this is where we live.' For them it means they can be identified – and just as importantly they cannot be ignored.

Through Mahapach I am also attempting to encourage a pride in their culture and history among the youngsters. In Tamra we have been organising after-school classes where they can discuss the aspects of their past that are withheld from them in school, and we have created an atmosphere in which they feel confident to speak their own language, Arabic. Although Arabic is an official state language of Israel, many children and adults are reluctant to talk their mother tongue outside the confines of Tamra because they are afraid of being overheard by Israeli Jews. They fear the aggressive reactions that using their language may provoke.

The state, as might be expected, is trying to undermine the work of Mahapach, an organisation with few resources on which to draw. For example, the thirty or so student workers developing projects in Mahapach's seven learning communities should each be entitled to a government scholarship. These funds are one of the main sources of revenue supporting the organisation's work. But despite its legal obligations and in a clear example of racist policy-making, the Ministry of Education is honouring the scholarships only of the Jewish students who participate; Arab students cannot receive a scholarship unless they agree to work in a Jewish community. Faced with this outrageous condition, Mahapach has faced two stark choices: the unacceptable one of pulling most of the students out of Arab areas and concentrating on the Jewish communities; or footing the bill for its Arab student staff. The large burden of this extra cost is threatening the long-term survival of Mahapach. The organisation could challenge the government policy in court, but is afraid that if it does so it may lose the scholarships of the Jewish students too. To an extent this divisive government policy, intended to empower Jewish students while disenfranchising Arab students, is working.

Another important way of countering the damaging effects of Arab education is through encouraging a greater awareness in local children of their rich Arab and Palestinian heritages. There are few opportunities to do this, especially after decades in which Israel has sought to strip both its Palestinian citizens and the Palestinians of the occupied territories of much of their cultural heritage – mainly as a way to deprive them of a sense of their own shared Palestinian identity.

This destruction of Palestinian culture has been well described by Omar Barghouti, a writer who is also the choreographer of the award-winning El-Fanoun folk dance troupe in Ramallah, which has been hounded by the Israeli authorities over much of the past twenty years. Some of its leaders have even been arrested. He observes that bemused visitors often ask why the dancers are so committed to their art when tanks and soldiers are wrecking buildings and lives all around. 'I never asked myself that question. Do we have to stop creating dance, music, art and literature to join the battle of "reconstruction"? Is reconstruction only applicable to devastated buildings, roads, water pipes and electricity poles? How about shattered dreams and shaken identities, don't they need reconstruction as well?'

Barghouti believes the need to reassert and reinvigorate a Palestinian identity derives from a collective sense among Palestinians of the failure in 1948 to prevent the destruction of the Palestinian nation. Palestinians in the occupied territories have come to realise that only though establishing a strong sense of who they are can they hope to withstand the ever greater erosion of their rights at the hands of Israel. 'Our very humanity has been restricted, hampered, battered by the relentless dehumanising efforts of our tormentors. As a reaction, the process of decolonising our minds assumes crucial precedence. Restoring our humanity, our dreams, our hopes and our will to resist and to be free, therefore, becomes even more important than mending our infrastructure. Thus, we dance.'

This is an eloquent statement of the need for all Palestinians to connect to their past and their future. It is a process well underway in the West Bank and Gaza but only in its infancy inside Israel, where Palestinian citizens have been severed from their culture and history for nearly six decades. One institution that is beginning to repair that damage is the Beit al-Musica (Music House), based in the Arab town of Shefaram, near Tamra, and run by the inspirational figure of Amer Nakleh. A distinguished oud player, Amer has worked tirelessly since the 1990s to bring his love of traditional Palestinian music first to the youth of Shefaram and now to the whole Arab community inside Israel. Beit al-Musica teaches a vast array of classical Arab instruments unfamiliar in the West such as the oud, the Middle East's lute, the derbeki, a goatskin drum in the shape of an hourglass, and the qanun, an Arab zither played on the lap of the musician.

Confronted by the unstintingly high standards of musicianship at the Beit al-Musica, the Israeli Ministry of Education finally agreed to recognise it as the country's first Arab music conservatoire in 2004. This achievement will have impressive cultural benefits for the Arab population. As well as classical Arabic music, Beit al-Musica also promotes a rich tradition of modern songs and poetry set to music, a knowledge of which is essential for Palestinians to revitalise their culture. Many of these songs deal with the community's longing for the land that has been lost to them and with their sense that they are now strangers in their own country.

Hopefully, with official recognition of Beit al-Musica, its activities can grow. Already its programme ranges from introducing children of kindergarten age to musical games to the training of some of the finest professional musicians in the country. It had plans to organise a major concert with leading black South African jazz musicians to forge ties between the two countries' musicians. But, in a sign of how short South Africa's memory is, the country's authorities have repeatedly turned down funding.

I have been raising money for Beit al-Musica by launching a programme for local and international donors to sponsor gifted children who have little hope of developing their talent without financial help. Jewish children of course can rely on many scholarships and grants paid for by the Israeli government or Jewish overseas organisations. Little of this money is available to Arab children. As a first step, I have myself sponsored a ten-year-old boy named Fadi who is an exceptional oud player but whose musical career was in jeopardy after his mother fell ill with cancer and his father lost his job.

Another inspirational figure in the Arab community whose work deserves mention is Said Abu Shakra, a talented artist and the founder of the Umm al-Fahm art gallery. Umm al-Fahm, a deprived part of Israel in an area known as the Triangle, in the centre of the country next to the West Bank, is not an obvious place to find one of the nation's most important exhibition spaces. The gallery's success can be attributed to Said's vision, his single-mindedness and his refusal to be intimidated. His own art, however, reveals his fraught relationship with the state.

I remember him once taking me round the school run by his wife Siham and finding myself stunned as he showed me a small walled-off square of tarmac, measuring a mere twenty-five metres square, that served as both the staff car park and a playground for eight hundred pupils. I found the idea that eight hundred children could even squeeze into this space, let alone play there, almost inconceivable.

Said, a former police officer who worked with Arab juvenile delinquents, is putting his art gallery to very worthwhile communal use, as a place not only where the community's imaginative horizons are extended, but also where mentally and physically disabled local children and those from deprived families can express themselves through art and drama workshops. The proportion of children suffering disabilities is far higher in the Arab minority than the Jewish population, largely as a result of the traditional practice of first cousins marrying each other. Nonetheless, there is almost no investment by the state in special needs schools for Arabs, though of course they exist for Jews. Said has been doing his best to fill the gap.

The discrimination that destroys most Arab children's hopes of ever realising their full potential, or of understanding who they are and where they belong, follows them throughout their lives. Just as they are made fully aware that they are second-class citizens in the classroom, they equally understand that their parents are second-class citizens both in and out of the workplace. When periods of high unemployment arrive, Arab citizens are always the first to lose their jobs; and even the highly educated often find themselves forced to work in construction, quarrying or factories because there is little work available in what is effectively the 'Jewish economy' of Israel.

By the Jewish economy I mean the significant areas of the economy that are off-limits to Arab citizens, usually on the pretext that the work is security-related. These include not only the vast array of military industries, such as the Rafael Armaments Authority, the nuclear reactor at Dimona, and the country's secret nuclear weapons factory, but the prisons, the Israeli Aircrafts Industry, the national carrier El Al and the country's airports. Also falling under the security rubric are the giant government corporations, such as the telecoms firm Bezeq, the Mekorot water company, the Electricity Corporation, the state textile industry and even the Bank of Israel.

In addition, Arab citizens are excluded from most of the vast civil service, the country's biggest employer, except for the health, religious affairs and education ministries, where they are needed to provide services to Arab communities. Areas such as engineering, surveying and architecture are also difficult for Arabs to enter because the work is treated as security-related – possibly because these professions are intimately involved in planning the infrastructure of the illegal Jewish settlements in the occupied West Bank and Gaza, and the roads that connect them to Israel proper. State employers therefore make it abundantly clear that they regard Arab citizens as 'the enemy' in precisely the same way as do the airport security staff and the police force.

Before 1948 most Palestinian families outside the cities relied chiefly for their living on agriculture. Today that course is no longer available to them: the state has confiscated most of their lands and passed them to Jewish farming communities such as the kibbutzim and moshavim, which receive big subsidies on water and are able to farm intensively on a large scale. Even those Arabs who still have small private landholdings cannot possibly compete. Most of the Arab workforce has been transformed into what might be termed a 'village proletariat', casual labourers who must commute each day to Jewish areas to work on construction sites, in factories or as hired farm hands. In Tamra large numbers of these day labourers can be seen in the dawn hours waiting in groups on the streets for a minibus to take them to their work. When hard times arrive in Israel they are always the first to lose their jobs.

A report in 2004 by Adva, a research centre based in Tel Aviv which monitors inequality inside Israel, found that the thirty-six worst black spots for unemployment were all Arab areas. But rather than try to help Arab towns and villages out of their desperate plight, the state has been pumping money to Jewish communities instead. Some of this comes via a system of 'national priority zones' whose residents and businesses are entitled to extra benefits and grants. At the time of writing, four very small Arab villages had priority 'A' status, compared with 492 Jewish communities.

I only started to understand the systematic nature of the state's racist employment practices after meeting Wehbe Badarni, an out-standing individual who is waging a lonely battle on behalf of Arab workers through his small Nazareth-based organisation, the Voice of the Labourer. Scraping for funds and facing the determined oppo-sition of the authorities, Wehbe's Voice – like that of the country's Palestinian minority – has all but been drowned out.

'Let's take the jobless figures,' he told me. 'Arab towns and villages are always at the very bottom of the pile by a large margin, even according to the official statistics. When unemployment is high in the whole economy – say about 10 per cent, as it has been through much of the second intifada – the figures show that the average is about twice as high in the Arab sector. But this doesn't even begin to tell the real story. In reality the jobless total is far higher in Arab communities, but it doesn't look that way because the figures are massaged by the state, which only includes in its head count those receiving benefits – and many Arab citizens are made ineligible for benefits. There is a story of terrible unemployment and dire poverty in Arab communities which is hidden by these figures.

105

'There are two main ways the state strips Arabs of their entitlement to benefits, both of which are cleverly cloaked so as to make it appear that they are not discriminatory. First, benefits are not available to unemployed youngsters up to the age of twenty. This does not affect many Jews: they are being provided for by the state, either as wage-earning conscripted soldiers in the army, or as religious students entitled to special grants from the government. But Arabs in this age group are excluded from military service, and most cannot study at university. There are almost no jobs for them at this age, so the great majority are unemployed. The problem continues in a modified form as they get older: between the ages of twenty and twenty-five claimants are not entitled to any benefits until they can prove they have worked for at least one and a half years. Many Jews in this age bracket are not yet in the workforce: they are at university after having completed their army service, or they are still studying Torah at religious colleges. But just about all Arabs are searching for work, most of them unsuccessfully. Were Arab youngsters between the ages of eighteen and twenty-five included in the jobless totals, it would push up the unemployment rates in Arab areas significantly.

'Second, there are severe restrictions on unemployment benefits for people who own land and property. In theory this rule appears to be non-discriminatory, but in practice it ensures that Arab claimants are treated entirely differently from Jewish claimants. That is because the overwhelming majority of Jews do not own land: they are given long-term leases on some of the 93 per cent of the land owned by the state. Most Arabs, on the other hand, are excluded from living on state land and so must build their homes on plots of overcrowded private land – the 3 per cent of land inside Israel owned by Arabs. But their ownership of land puts them in the same category as the tiny minority of Jewish private landowners, usually wealthy businessmen, who use their large landholdings for income-generating housing, farming or business projects. The effect of this rule is simple: while almost all unemployed Jews are eligible for benefits, a large number of unemployed Arabs are ineligible.'

Wehbe digs out a confidential government document from the 1980s which sets out the rules for dealing with claimants who own land and property. Its cover features a cartoon of a man in Sherlock Holmes costume peering intently through a huge magnifying glass at a house. The illustration neatly sums up the purpose of the dossier: it is a web of legal regulations designed to make most unemployed Arab citizens ineligible for benefits. A special form issued to unemployment offices in rural areas in 2002 also lists a series of questions that should make it clear to a jobless Arab citizen that he is wasting his time seeking help from the state. If a claimant owns land, has any animals, has more than one apartment in his name, or lives with relatives, his application is likely to be rejected.

'These rules are designed to be a Catch-22 for Arab claimants. One has to remember that there are different living patterns in Arab and Jewish society. Traditionally Arab families live in close proximity. And nowadays, given the chronic shortage of land, most sons usually build their apartments directly above their father's ground-floor home. But because the land is registered in the father's name, he immediately becomes ineligible for benefits if he loses his job. That is because he is effectively treated by the state as a landlord, charging rent from his sons. Even if he registers the land in the name of his sons, he is assumed to have sold the land and he cannot claim benefits for five years. Jews on the other hand are unaffected by these rules, because they can rely on the state making its land freely available to them.'

Wehbe says there are even cases of Arab claimants losing their benefits after they have had their lands confiscated by the state. 'One unemployed man from Kafr Kara lost all his benefits after officials found he still had land registered in his name. It was a surprise to him: the land they were referring to had been taken from him years ago by the state, and now has a Jewish settlement built on it. But apparently the authorities never cancelled his tabu [title deeds] to the land, and so he cannot get benefits.'

Other Arab citizens who still own a small plot of the land they held before the creation of Israel are also caught in this kind of bureaucratic trap. 'The owner cannot build on the land or develop it because the state will always refuse him the necessary permits, and he cannot leave it fallow because the state would then have a legal pretext for confiscating it. So what usually happens is he plants an olive grove on it. It would be an exaggeration to say he is farming the land, because he cannot hope to compete with the state-subsidised intensive Jewish farms; he simply harvests the olives on his plot for family use. Nonetheless, the state can treat the land as income-generating and withhold benefits if he loses his job. It is a measure designed to increase the pressure on him to sell his land to the state.'

About the time I first met Wehbe, two stories broke in the media that keenly illustrated the problems of discrimination also faced by those Arab citizens who do work. In the first, in March 2004, the *Maariv* newspaper reported that Arab construction workers building a new wing of the Knesset in Jerusalem were being required to wear a white hard hat with a large red cross painted on the top. The story was accompanied by a picture of the branded workers at the site. According to officials, the crosses were being used by snipers stationed on the Knesset's roof to track the Arab workers' movements while months-long security checks were completed by the Shin Bet. Amazingly, the hats of other workers at the site, mainly from China and Thailand, who are not citizens, were left unmarked. Apparently the authorities trusted their own citizens less than they did imported workers.

In the second story, a twenty-year-old Arab woman, Abeer Zinaty, was sacked by the manager of her local McDonald's, even though she had recently won an award from the company for being their 'Excellent Worker 2003'. Zinaty's claim that she had been dismissed for speaking Arabic to a colleague was at first denied by McDonald's. However, a media investigation confirmed her story. In correspondence over the dismissal Talila Yodfat, the human resources director for the Israeli branch of the chain, wrote that there was a well-known company directive instructing employees not to speak Arabic 'in order to prevent discomfort felt by clients and staff, who mostly speak Hebrew'. She was of course forgetting that for 20 per cent of Israel's population – and a similar number of McDonald's potential customers – Arabic is their first language.

Zinaty's case was unusual only because she chose to speak out about the discrimination. Most Arabs are far too afraid to raise their voices against this common practice. For example, Omayma in my family in Tamra, a nurse in one of the biggest hospitals in Israel, told me that she and the other Arab staff had been repeatedly instructed not to speak Arabic while on duty. She was not prepared to take on her employer.

Wehbe knew of similar cases to Zinaty's. 'This informal ban on Arabic has always been a problem, but it has become much more severe since the intifada broke out in September 2000. There are many examples of workers being sacked for speaking Arabic even though it contravenes Israel's equal opportunities laws. Getting that law enforced, however, is pretty difficult. For example, I have been dealing for many, many months with the case of the sacking of an Arab catering manager and thirteen Arab staff at a hotel on the shores of the Dead Sea. He was sacked after he refused to fire the Arab staff under him. The hotel bosses told him guests had been complaining about the presence of Arabs in the hotel. They were afraid of bad publicity if they sacked the workers themselves, so they tried to make him do it. They thought that because he is an Arab it would not look so bad. I have not been able to get any of them reinstated.'

Such overt discrimination against Arabs can be traced back to the days well before Israel was founded, says Wehbe, when Jewish immigrants arrived in the country hoping to establish their own state in Palestine. With stiff competition for control of the land and resources, the immigrants developed the concept of 'Hebrew labour': favouring Jews over Arabs both in access to jobs and in levels of pay. Whenever possible, Jewish-owned companies, small businesses and farms would try to employ Jews only.

What is shocking is that this Zionist concept of Hebrew labour has survived to this day in the state of Israel, even though such discrimination should be illegal. Although it is never admitted publicly, racist employment practices and the exclusion of Arabs from wealth-generating sectors of the economy are the bedrock of state planning policies. 'There are almost no economic development zones in Arab areas or industrial zones,' said Wehbe. 'If a factory is built, it is always in a Jewish area. Even if an Arab can get work in the factory, the business rates and development grants it generates go to the Jewish municipalities and not the Arab ones.' Wehbe points out that for several years there was even a website called 'Hebrew work', which promoted businesses that refused to employ Arabs. He and other Arab organisations had to press the authorities repeatedly before they finally agreed to take action against the site in January 2005.

Historically, the main actor in promoting the concept of Hebrew labour has been the Histadrut, a Jewish trade union federation founded in Palestine in 1920. Although the Histadrut promotes itself as a trade union, early on in its development it became a strange hybrid beast, acquiring control of large sections of the local economy. Both before and after the establishment of the state of Israel, it merged the roles of trade union and major corporation in a confusing manner. For example, it established the country's biggest national health-care system, Kupat Holim; the Workers' Bank, Bank HaPoalim, which went on to become Israel's largest bank; a giant industrial concern, Koor Industries; a major construction firm, Solel Boneh; a dairy production company, Tnuva; the national bus company, Egged; a national daily newspaper, *Davar*; and most of the cooperatives responsible for the country's agricultural output.

Arabs were excluded from any association with the Histadrut until 1943, when they were allowed to join a special Arab section. They had to wait until 1959 – eleven years after the creation of Israel – before they could nominally become members. However, the Histadrut's Hebrew labour ideology was never abolished. 'In the early 1990s, when hundreds of thousands of Russian Jews poured into Israel following the collapse of the Soviet Union, Arab workers – even well-qualified doctors – were sacked to make way for the new immigrants,' said Wehbe. 'The Histadrut never protested those job losses nor the discriminatory policies behind them.'

This marginalisation of Arab workers by the Histadrut has severely limited their employment opportunities. In 1971 the state made the Histadrut the sole legal representative of organised labour in Israel, and by the late 1980s Histadrut-related companies were reported to be generating a fifth of national income and employing more than a quarter of a million workers. But Arab membership of the federation, which at its peak reached about a hundred thousand workers, today stands at only a few thousand. Why the dramatic fall?

'The reason the Histadrut opened itself up to Arabs was because it wanted to destroy the Palestinian trade unions,' said Wehbe. 'It was determined to grow stronger, both numerically and financially, and it didn't want competition. It attracted Arab members because it offered welfare services, particularly health insurance, which Arabs couldn't afford otherwise. The Histadrut severed its ties to these services in the mid-1990s and the Arab membership quickly fell away. Today, Arab workers realise the Histadrut has nothing to offer them. Its primary function is to protect the privileges of the tens of thousands of highly-paid, *Jewish* employees of state firms like Bezeq and the Electricity Corporation. The income earned by the Histadrut is invested in the Jewish sector, in clubs, education centres and health centres. There is no investment in Arab areas, in training

Arab workers or in creating industrial zones in Arab communities. The Histadrut simply became irrelevant to Arab workers.'

As things stand, it is unclear to me how Arab citizens can hope to end their exclusion from the Jewish economy. There are, however, a few self-made figures in the Arab community who have shown that it is possible to succeed even when the system is designed to defeat you. One of the most inspiring is Sobhi Nakleh, whom I know through my work for his son Amer's Beit al-Musica. Struggling to provide for his wife and children as a taxi driver in the early 1970s, Sobhi sold his cab and opened a grocery shop in Shefaram. He had a passion for Arabic coffee, and experimented endlessly with blends until he found one formula that proved a particular hit with customers. Although his business became very successful in Shefaram, he held onto a bigger vision: to make his coffee famous throughout the Galilee and Israel. In the late 1970s he began selling out of the back of a van, and today Nakleh Coffee is the biggest-selling brand of Arabic coffee in the country. He even has a steadily growing export business.

This rags-to-riches story reminded me of examples I knew from my childhood of Jewish entrepreneurs who had succeeded against overwhelming odds. I thought of Michael Marks, who started Marks & Spencer's, and Sir Isaac Wolfson, the chairman of Great Universal Stores, who was a close friend of my parents. One winter in my youth my family made a sea crossing on the mail boat from Tilbury to Cape Town with Sir Isaac and his wife Edith. I remember him sitting with me on the deck, telling me about his youth in the Glasgow tenements. When soon afterwards he met Edith, he told her that one day he would buy her the biggest diamond she had ever seen. And on that boat she showed it to me.

Sir Isaac Wolfson had fought to earn every penny, and so it is with Arab citizens like Sobhi Nakleh. There are no handouts or leg-ups for them; they are truly self-made. Although Jews like to celebrate their own success stories, most fail to recognise the same spirit of creativity, imagination and daring in the Arab population. Whenever I heard Israeli Jews talking about Arabs, they almost always referred to them as primitive and lazy, or as welfare scroungers. Most Jews have no idea about the Palestinian entrepreneurs and professionals who had to battle to educate themselves or build a business in spite of huge obstacles placed in their way. They fail to understand that Jews and Arabs have known the same sort of institutional racism, and that ultimately they share the same dreams. This lack of empathy serves only to make Jews fear their fellow citizens, to encourage them to see their Arab neighbours as alien and menacing.

The need to change Israeli Jews' assumptions about the Arab minority is pressing indeed. I had asked Dr Manna during our long conversation why he believed Israeli Jews found the idea of an Arab citizen identifying himself as 'Palestinian' so disturbing. 'As long as we are called and call ourselves "Israeli Arabs", then Jews are not reminded of the history of the country. If we are Israeli Arabs, then Jews can feel reassured that we have forgotten our roots and our history before 1948. And if Jews and Arabs are persuaded that the country's history only started in 1948, then Israeli Arabs are really just guests in the country who can either be integrated into the Zionist project or expelled. But at the same time – in a sort of contradiction – the majority of Israeli Jews believe Arabs must not regard themselves as full Israelis but as second-class citizens, with no identity or equality. The Arab population disagrees: "Sorry, but we will define our own identity and we will struggle for equality. You tried to make us forget we are Palestinians, but after a time we have rediscovered our identity – not least because Israel does not give us an alternative identity." Any Jew in Britain, France or the US is a full citizen of that country, but in Israel we are not equal even according to the law. On the best view we are second-class – if not worse than that. We are the Other.'

Listening to Dr Manna, I realised how far Israel has to travel before it can confront its past and atone for its sins. It will need much help in making that transition. South Africa is an obvious example to which it can look for guidance, from the work of Desmond Tutu's Truth and Reconciliation Commission to the small-scale initiatives of organisations and individuals whose work is far less trumpeted. One such person is my friend Mike Abrams, a South African who was active in ending white rule. In 1999 Mike established a non-profit organisation called Change Moves which tries to heal the deep institutional and personal scars left by apartheid as blacks and whites find themselves in a society where they must learn to integrate. One of the most impressive programmes he runs helps South African businesses overcome failures of management caused by the lingering trauma of apartheid.

A big problem he has identified is that white managerial staff are finding it difficult to adjust to a new reality, where they must work alongside or even under black managers. His team finds that new black middle managers often complain of being unable to work effectively because they do not feel they have all the information they need. When he sets up counselling groups for managers to discuss these issues, it emerges that white managers are withholding the information. Why? 'Often it's because there is a deep-seated resentment among the white managers caused by their lack of confidence in the new political arrangement or because they still cling to the racist ideology of apartheid and don't want black managers succeeding,' he says. 'Under the new political system white, black and coloured workers are suddenly thrust together, but they have not had time to address what the issues are that are still separating them, why they still don't trust each other. You can't really move forward until you address those issues.'

Mike, who is Jewish and who lived for several years in Israel, says he can see the similarities with South Africa every time he visits. What he tries to do is give people a safe place from which to confront and overcome their fears and prejudices. Just as white South Africans were happy to see a black man cleaning their swimming pool, but not sitting across from them on the other side of a desk, so Jews hold irrational fears about coming to Arab areas or working alongside Arabs as equals.

'The state wants our loyalty, but it is not loyal to us; it wants our lands and our resources without also wanting to develop us,' Dr Manna told me. 'The state keeps us in our underdeveloped villages because it fears that if one day we are strong enough we will take revenge for the years of discrimination – just like the white settlers in South Africa were afraid that if power passed to the blacks, they would be decimated. In Israel what you see is the mentality of the settler who is afraid of what he has done. We remind Israelis that we are the natives.'

4

Echoes of Apartheid

For some time I had resolved to visit Ein Hod, the village from which Samira's parents had been forced to flee in 1948, before they found refuge in Tamra. Unlike most of the more than four hundred villages that were depopulated in that war, Ein Hod still stands largely intact, its homes saved from destruction by a group of Jewish artists who were given permission by the new state of Israel to colonise them. Today the community of Ein Hod is an important centre for both art and tourism inside Israel, the artists drawing inspiration for their work from the dramatic setting of the village and its old stone structures, and the tourists attracted by the sculptures, statues and installation art that litter the village's gardens, balconies and narrow lanes.

Samira had described to me the traumatic experience of visiting Ein Hod for the first time a few years earlier to see her parents' home. It had taken much courage to make the journey, knowing as she did what had happened to the village subsequently. She was accompanied by a young friend visiting from Sweden, who perhaps gave her both the resolution and the excuse to venture there. Samira told me that she eventually located the family home and knocked on the front door to be confronted by the Jewish owner, a woman artist. Samira explained who she was, that this house had once belonged to her family, and that if possible she would like to look inside. Angry and uncomfortable, the woman refused and told her to leave. She was about to close the door in their faces when the Swedish girl stepped forward and pleaded with her: 'Please, my friend has brought me all this way to see her family's home. Let us just come inside for a minute.' Embarrassed, the woman stood aside and let them briefly look around before ushering them out. Samira told me she had not returned since.

Samira's experience stood in stark contrast to a story told me by Rabbi Dr John D. Rayner, the retired head of the Liberal Jewish Synagogue in London and a long-standing family friend. Some years ago he decided to return with his daughter to Berlin, the city in which he was raised until the rise of Nazism tragically tore apart his family. As a boy, John was one of several thousand Jewish children transported from Europe to Britain on trains and boats that were known as the Kindertransport, leaving his parents behind; they were eventually caught by the Gestapo and transported to Auschwitz, where they both died. The most emotional part of the trip for John was visiting the family's home in Berlin with his daughter. The new owners received the two of them warmly, showing them around the house and inviting them to sit in the garden, drinking coffee and listening to the rabbi's memories of the house and Berlin in his childhood. John was assured he was always welcome to return.

It occurred to me that the difference in the treatment of John and Samira spoke volumes about the difference in the readiness of these two nations – Germany and Israel – to acknowledge their respective pasts and to make amends. Whereas Germany had accepted its responsibility and atoned for the Holocaust, Israel was still pretending to itself and the world that the Nakba had never taken place. Whereas Germany had for decades been paying large sums of compensation to individual Holocaust survivors and to Israel, Israel had yet to apologise for the expulsion of the Palestinian population, let alone pay money to the victims of its aggression, mostly peasant farmers trying to hold onto their lands.

I hoped to persuade Samira to take me to Ein Hod along with

her youngest daughter Suad. But despite regular assurances to both of us that she would soon make the journey, Samira always found a reason to put off a second visit. Eventually I concluded she could not face seeing Ein Hod again, so Suad and I arranged to travel there without her.

The old Arab village is in a stunning location: sitting on the lower slopes of the great Carmel Ridge, which extends southwards from the city of Haifa, Ein Hod overlooks the Mediterranean sea. The backdrop is the luxurious foliage of the Carmel Forest, a national park of pine and cypress trees that extends over much of the Carmel Mountain. Official guidebooks and tourist information describe the village in glowing terms, as one of the most picturesque sites in Israel, but carefully avoid referring to its Arab history. The Ein Hod artists' website, which also happily eulogises the village's scenic qualities, makes no mention of its past apart from euphemistic and misleading references to earlier occupants – the generations of Palestinians documented as having inhabited the village since the twelfth century – who, it says, belonged to 'the Turkish Empire':

> *Ein Hod is characterised by the special setting of a village sitting on a hillside, surrounded by olive groves, with a view of the Mediterranean Sea where baroque sunsets end each day. Despite lack of funds and development resources, the village has managed to preserve its original, historic nature and the romantic and simple charm of Israel in its first years of independence. Very few places in Israel have managed to retain the authentic quality of the Mediterranean. One can still discern in the old structures the many textures and architectural forms of earlier occupants from the Christian Crusades to the Turkish Empire.*

As soon as Suad and I walked from the car park into the artists' colony – as Ein Hod officially describes itself – I could see why Samira was reluctant to make the return journey again. The artists had managed both to preserve and to transform the village at the same time. They had saved the buildings simply to reinvent them in a way designed to conceal their original identity as Arab homes. The old mosque in the centre of the village is now the Dona Rosa restaurant, selling alcohol to its patrons, its front wall adorned with a sculpture of a naked woman stretching up her arms provocatively to reveal her breasts. The giant grinding stones that once belonged to the olive press have been propped up against old stone walls to transform them into works of rustic art, deflecting attention from the fact that they once served as practical objects of a vibrant Arab farming community. Doorways, balconies and gardens are stuffed with sculptures and artworks which obscure the Arab origins of the village.

Despite the claims of the website, I struggled to see what remained authentic in this 'Mediterranean village'. Rather than an exercise in honesty, Ein Hod is a case study in deception: the landscape has been reinvented to create what appears to be an entirely Jewish space. Clearly impressed at seeing an old village like this – Israel has made sure there are very few such examples left in the country – Suad pointed out the Arabic writing over some of the doorways. But the artworks and sculptures disturbed her. 'They make me feel like a stranger here,' she said. At one spot we found a decrepit wooden gate, and pushed it open to reveal an overgrown garden and behind it a neglected stone building. Finally we had found somewhere untouched by the artistic mayhem all around us, and Suad, I saw, could at last connect to the village her grandparents once inhabited, to the generations of ancestors who called this place home, and to the earth from which her family had been so violently uprooted.

When we returned to Tamra, Suad and I sat with Samira to tell her of our day in Ein Hod. I could see it made for painful listening. At the end, Samira could find no words, except, 'Tamra is nothing compared to Ein Hod. It is nothing.' For the first time I realised quite how bitterly she felt about her family's displacement and the destruction of her heritage.

The story of Israel – and the policies that led to the ethnic cleansing of Arab communities like Ein Hod – has two intimately entwined themes: land and people. These are the twin Zionist obsessions, nowadays spoon-fed to almost every Jew on the planet. It is no coincidence that the mantra of the early Zionist leadership was that in settling Palestine they had found 'a land without people for a people without land'. That was the slogan I was raised on and accepted throughout my adult life until I came to Israel. The terrible tragedy for the Palestinian people is that Israel has succeeded in convincing not only Jews to accept this myth as an article of faith, but the rest of the world too.

According to the most reliable figures, more than 1.3 million Arabs were living in Palestine on the eve of the Jewish state's birth. Zionist writers and organisations have tried to rewrite this historical fact, but one need not even trawl the usual Palestinian sources to demonstrate that there had been a long-standing Palestinian presence in the Holy Land.

In 2003, on one of my trips back to South Africa, I was carrying out research in the library of Cape Town University, where my father completed his first medical degree, when I stumbled across a record of a little-known speech made by former South African Prime Minister Jan Smuts, an ardent Zionist and one of the country's venerable statesmen. He had visited Palestine in February 1918 on behalf of the British government, which was soon to rule Palestine under a mandate from the League of Nations and which had recently issued the Balfour Declaration, promising to use its influence to create a Jewish homeland in the Holy Land, ignoring the fact that there was a well-established Palestinian population already living there. On his return to South Africa, Smuts addressed representatives of the Jewish community in Johannesburg to tell them about the difficulties of implementing the Balfour plan:

The problem there is one of great delicacy because a large Arab population is still living in Palestine. You have a minority of Jews there, and the policy that will have to be promoted and fostered in future will be the introduction of larger and ever larger numbers of Jews into Palestine. [Cheers.] It is easy to see that there are possibilities of conflict, of misunderstanding, in a situation like that, between the old Arab population and the new Jewish population. The whole situation will have to be handled with great great delicacy, with great tact.

Smuts's predictions were right about the numbers of Jewish immigrants needed to realise the Balfour Declaration's intention, if optimistic about the 'delicacy and tact' with which that policy would be pursued. During the British Mandate period,* more and more Jews found refuge in Palestine, until by the late spring of 1948 David Ben-Gurion, the leader of the Jewish people in Palestine, felt confident enough to declare the establishment of the state of Israel on the territory known to a majority of its inhabitants as Palestine. A war between the Palestinians and the Jews was the inevitable outcome.

Dating the first shots in the war of 1948 – what was to be known in Israel as the War of Independence – is not easy: tensions had been simmering between the native Palestinians and the more recent Jewish arrivals for many years under British rule. But by late 1947, as the two communities sensed events were coming to a head with the end of the British Mandate, tit-for-tat attacks became a regular occurrence, with dozens of civilians killed on both sides. In December 1947 and January 1948 the Haganah, the pre-state Jewish army, raised the stakes, calling up young Jews for military service and ordering large shipments of arms from abroad. Jewish fighters launched a series of harsh retaliatory strikes against Arab villages

* See Glossary, pages 266–7.

suspected of firing on or attacking Jews. In several cases massacres were committed at Arab villages in the western Galilee and in the Tel Aviv area. According to Israeli historian Benny Morris the first Arab village was entirely abandoned as early as December 1947.

As in all wars, terrible deeds were committed by both sides. But trying to cast blame for who started the war or who committed the most atrocities serves only as a useful way to distract us from the central issues. The first is that the traditional Zionist account of the 1948 war – the one I was brought up on – is entirely mythical. According to the Zionists, a small Jewish community faced almost impossible odds in defending itself against a sea of hostile Arabs. Its triumph was little short of a miracle. That account hardly seems to square with the historical facts. The Jewish community, though only half the size of the Palestinian one, was far better organised, armed and prepared for war than were the Palestinians. The Jewish immigrants were mostly staunch Zionists with a high degree of commitment to the project of creating a Jewish national home in Palestine. Many Palestinians, on the other hand, were poor, isolated rural farmers who felt little personal involvement in the preparations for war. Although the first soldiers with the Arab Liberation Army (ALA) started arriving from neighbouring countries in January 1948, most historians seem agreed that they were disorganised, poorly equipped and often not highly motivated. Almost all the early retaliatory attacks launched by the ALA on Jewish communities were repulsed, often with heavy losses to the Arab side.

The second is the tendency among Zionists to overlook the context in which the war occurred. The Palestinians were defending themselves and their homeland from the aggressive colonising of their land by Jewish immigrants. Zionists counter that argument by claiming that the Jews were entitled to their state: its birthright was based, they say, both on the Balfour Declaration and the rejection by the Palestinians of a United Nations Partition Plan in 1947: the plan gave the Jewish population 55 per cent of the territory, and the indigenous Arab population 44 per cent, with Jerusalem coming under international control. Although most modern commentators blame the Palestinian leadership for making a historic error in rejecting this deal, they choose to overlook several simple facts: the Palestinians at that time still had a large numerical majority in Palestine (they were estimated to comprise two-thirds of the total population); most of the 650,000 Jews in their midst were recent and unwelcome colonisers; and, despite a well-funded campaign of land purchases run by an international Zionist organisation called the Jewish National Fund, local Jews had managed to buy only 7 per cent of Palestine. In the circumstances the offer of 44 per cent of their own homeland by the UN may not have seemed overly generous to Palestinians of the day.

Thirdly, Zionists seek to deflect attention from the outcome of the war. Whatever atrocities were committed by both sides, the result of the fighting was that 750,000 Palestinians – not Jews – were either terrorised or expelled from their homes and beyond the borders of the new state. The majority of them were not fighters but civilians, mostly poor rural farming families. Plenty of evidence has emerged, including documents concerning a military operation known as Plan Dalet, to suggest that it was probably always the intention of the Jewish leadership to cleanse the Jewish state of its Arab inhabitants. Even if that was not their intention at the start of the fighting, it quickly became their goal when they sensed their military superiority. Further proof is provided by the fact that the Israeli army demolished in wholesale fashion all the villages from which the refugees were forced to flee, to ensure that they could never return.

Over the course of the ensuing war, Israel won some 78 per cent of Mandatory Palestine, losing only the West Bank and Gaza. With its territorial windfall, the Jewish state had a free hand to rewrite the history of Palestine, in terms of both the people and the land. Having forced out 80 per cent of the 900,000 Palestinians whose homes were located inside the new state of Israel – either directly, by expelling them across the borders to neighbouring Arab states, or by terrorising them away through a policy of well-publicised massacres such as the one described by Dr Adel Manna in his own village of Majd al-Krum. The army then organised the razing of the homes. The refugees, in exile in camps across the Middle East, had their homes, lands and bank accounts in Israel appropriated by a new official of the Jewish state called the Custodian of Absentee Property.

It was not only the refugees in exile who found their homes and lands taken by the Custodian; so did a sizeable number of the 150,000 Palestinians who had become Israeli citizens. Israeli bureaucrats – adept at abusing language in Orwellian ways – created a classification of citizen called the 'present absentee' (present in Israel but absent from their homes). To be so classified, a family needed only to have been away from its home for one day during the war. But the consequence was irreversible and permanent: the present absentees were barred from ever returning to their villages. Like my own family in Tamra they became internal refugees, with no choice but to begin their lives again from scratch. Although there are no precise figures, the number of internal refugees is today believed to be a quarter of a million Israeli Arab citizens, or one in four of the Arab population.

The material and emotional losses sustained by the Palestinians in 1948 are the true root of the Middle East conflict, although no one – not diplomats, journalists or politicians – dares to say so. Instead we are told that the conflict began with the 1967 war, when Israel occupied the West Bank and Gaza. On this view, a solution requires only that the occupation be reversed and a Palestinian state created in the occupied territories, on 22 per cent of the Palestinians' historic homeland. No one, it seems, wants to remember that such a solution would entirely ignore the losses inflicted on hundreds of thousands of Palestinian refugees – and millions of their descendants.

The dispossession of the Palestinians, it is often assumed, is a historical event which may be unfortunate, but little can now be done to correct it. Left-wing Jewish friends to whom I talked would often tell me not to reflect on this too much. But Israel's dispossession of the Palestinians continues in unremitting fashion. This was brought home to me in an encounter with a man whose family originally came from Ein Hod. While most of the village's refugees ended up either in camps in the West Bank and Jordan or in Galilean communities like Tamra, one expelled family lives only a short distance from the artists of Ein Hod, in another village that goes by almost the same name: Ayn Hawd.

I first heard about Mohammed Abu Hayja through an organisation he founded in the late 1980s called the Association of Forty. His own family, like that of Suad, was forced out of Ein Hod in 1948, but unlike Suad's family his battle with the state is not over the right to become an equal citizen but over the right to exist at all. His story – and that of tens of thousands of Arab villagers in the same situation – is one of the most dishonourable episodes in Israeli history.

To meet Abu Hayja, Suad and I needed to drive through the grounds of a religious moshav, Nir Etzion, that occupies and cultivates the lands once farmed by the expelled Arab villagers of Ein Hod. We passed through the metal gates of the moshav, past its communal swimming pool and the manicured lawns and neat detached homes that belong to the Jewish inhabitants, through a field containing an enormous milking factory, before we reached a winding path that led into the Carmel Forest and onwards over the ridge to Mohammed Abu Hayja's village.

As we drove down into the huddle of houses, Abu Hayja was there to greet us, standing on the terrace of his home. His deeply lined face suggested many years spent in the sun – and possibly too many worries for one man easily to bear. I introduced Suad and, in a routine I had grown familiar with, Abu Hayja asked a series of questions to identify which branch of the family she belonged to. When he was certain of who she was, he launched into a short reminiscence. 'My father often used to recall your grandfather,' he said. 'Once, a short time after the war had ended, when it became clear that the state had no intention of honouring its obligations to allow us to return to the village, your grandfather decided to take matters into his own hands and return without permission. The village was empty then, because it was before the artists arrived in 1954. Under cover of dark, your grandfather left Tamra, stole back into the village and reoccupied his brother's home. Of course, the police soon found out and arrived to evict him.'

Abu Hayja's own branch of the family have been living next door to their former homes since they were expelled in 1948. Rather than fleeing the region, Mohammed's grandfather, Abu Hilmi, took his family a short distance further up the slopes of the Carmel to live in hiding by the village's cattle sheds. There he waited for the fighting to subside and to be allowed back to Ein Hod. But when the war was over, Israel did not restore Ein Hod to its former owners; instead it sealed off the area as a closed military zone in preparation for the destruction of the homes. For several years it was impossible to access the village – until the mid-1950s, when a group of artists led by Marcel Janco, a Romanian painter and one of the founders of the Dada movement, was given permission to settle it.

Aware that he would never be able to return, Abu Hayja told us, his grandfather decided to create a new village where his family was encamped, and to call it Ayn Hawd, the Arabic name of his old village before the artist colonisers Hebraicised it to Ein Hod. Ever since, the villagers of the new Ayn Hawd have had to fight to hold onto their corner of the Carmel, a tiny sliver of the land that originally belonged to them, against the unremitting pressure of Israeli officialdom's attempts to dislodge them.

'It is a long and complex story, but I will try to make it as easy as I can,' said Abu Hayja. 'It began in 1958 when officials from the

Me aged about eighteen
months, with my father.

My parents on the beach at Blouberg
Strand near Cape Town, April 1976.

A view of the street from my terrace in Tamra. The people are gathering for a wedding.

View of Tamra from my apartment.

My street in Tamra. Note the telephone and electrical cables strung from pole to pole.

Election poster for the Hadash party – for which I voted – in Tamra, 2004. The successful mayoral candidate, Adel Abu Hayja, is in the centre.

A home with a farmyard of sheep, goats and chickens in the garden. Such houses are common in Arab communities inside Israel, which have been stripped of most of their farming land since the creation of the Israeli state.

My neighbours in
Tamra during an
engagement party.

A Tamra neighbour
making traditional pitta.

Engagement party in Tamra.

Street scene in Tamra during the festival of Eid al-Adha

Surrounded by all that is left of their furniture, a Palestinian family stand on the site of their former home in the Galilean village of Beaneh, where five houses were demolished by the Israeli authorities in February 2004. Five hundred Arab homes inside Israel were destroyed in 2003, usually without warning.

The Dona Rosa restaurant in the Ein Hod artists' colony, which before Israel's creation in 1948 was a mosque in the Palestinian village of Ayn Hawd. The mother of my family in Tamra was expelled from the village in 1948.

At an event held to mark the Palestinian 'nakba' (catastrophe) on 27 April 2004 – Israel's Independence Day – an Israeli Arab boy distributes signs naming some of the four hundred Palestinian villages destroyed by the Israeli army in the 1948 war that founded the Jewish state.

Eitan Bronstein (in baseball cap) of the Israeli Jewish lobby group Zochrot (Remembering) helps erect a signpost in Hebrew and Arabic alerting local residents in the city of Haifa to the fact that Arab neighbourhoods existed there before they were cleared during the war to found Israel. Such signs are invariably removed shortly after they have been put up.

government arrived at the village to tell my grandfather that they had confiscated not only the buildings of Ein Hod, which we knew, but also all its farmlands, including the spot where we now live. All of it was declared state land. At the time it did not mean much to us, but a few years later, in 1964, more officials arrived, this time to erect a fence tightly around our homes, forcing us into a ghetto. There were a few concrete homes in the village by then, including a two-room school. I can prove it because I still have an Israeli newspaper cutting from 1965 showing the teacher and me and my friends standing outside the school with the fence visible just in front of us.

'The fence was a major problem for our parents because they needed to graze the village's herds of goats, sheep and cattle – that was our livelihood. I remember my father telling me and the other children to pull down the fence so that he couldn't be blamed or punished by the authorities. We pulled it down three times and they re-erected it three times. It was like a game to us.

'Though we didn't know it, our situation grew much worse the following year, in 1965, when the government passed the Planning and Building Law. Under this law the state decided that there were to be 123 Arab communities. That was it. It didn't matter where you lived or how long you had lived there: if you weren't on that list you didn't exist. The way they did it was to create a masterplan for the whole of Israel. In the case of every community they listed, Jewish and Arab, they set down a border for its development: what they called the blue lines. In the case of Arab communities these were tightly drawn around the houses, so that there was no room left for development. In the case of Jewish communities they were drawn loosely, so that there was plenty of space for them to expand and develop.'

This has led to shameful anomalies, as had been explained to me before by Asad Ghanem. The Arab population of Israel today stands at a little over one million – seven times the number it was more than half a century ago – but the state has refused to create a single new Arab community. The result is chronic overcrowding of the sort I know only too well from Tamra. The land lost to these Arab towns and villages has simply been passed to Jewish settlements for their benefit. Thus, for example, the Arab town of Sakhnin has a population of twenty-four thousand and jurisdiction over 2,500 acres of land, while the neighbouring Misgav bloc of Jewish settlements has a smaller population, eighteen thousand, and control over an area twenty times larger – fifty thousand acres. Or take the Arab city of Nazareth, from which land was taken by the state in the late 1950s to build a Jewish city virtually on top of it. Today the Jewish city, Upper Nazareth, with fifty thousand residents, has three times as much land as Nazareth but only two-thirds of its population.

'Everything outside the blue lines created by the Planning Law was deemed agricultural land, on which it was illegal to build,' continued Abu Hayja. 'Our village was not listed among the 123 Arab communities, no blue lines were drawn around us, and therefore we were living on agricultural land. Our homes were retroactively deemed illegal and faced demolition. We were not alone: there were dozens of other Arab villages in the same situation, most of which had been standing on their lands for centuries. In many cases the villagers had the tabu [land titles] from the Ottomans and the British to prove they owned the land. None of that made any difference to the state. Of course in those days none of us understood the game that was being played with our lives, and no one from the state came to explain it to us either. It took nearly two decades before we realised the extent of the policy we were facing.'

More than a hundred thousand Arab citizens – or one in ten of the Arab population – are classified under the Planning and Building Law as living in what the state considers 'unrecognised villages'. The majority of them, about seventy thousand Bedouin, live in appalling conditions in the Negev desert region in the country's south, where they are forced to live in tents or tin shacks because anything more permanent would be demolished by the authorities.

Very few Jews know about the abuses heaped on the unrecognised villages, and in particular the Bedouin population. I can recall journeys I took to Beersheva, the capital of the Negev, during my stays in Israel before my immigration, when I would see dishevelled encampments comprising dozens of huts and tents dotted along the landscape. They registered in my mind then – as I am sure they do for other Jews – as the primitive way of life chosen by the Bedouin, who I assumed were resisting the best efforts of Israel to bring them into the twentieth century. Little did I appreciate that my own government had pushed them back into a dark age that might have astonished even their forebears.

At least many of the inhabitants of Ayn Hawd have managed to build concrete homes without having them destroyed. Nonetheless, says Abu Hayja, there has been relentless pressure on them to evacuate the village since the passing of the Planning and Building Law. 'No one ever put a gun to our heads: the authorities were far too clever for that. Instead they made a series of masterplans that none of us understood. The first was the National Carmel Park Law in 1971, which makes it illegal to build a house inside the park. And where does the park exist? It begins south of Haifa and follows the contours of the mountain till it reaches the last house in our village. We are entirely encased in the park. But in the case of our immediate neighbours, Ein Hod and Nir Etzion, the boundaries loop carefully around them.'

It was at this point that Abu Hayja said something that surprised and shocked me. He pointed to the slopes of the Carmel Mountain and told me that all the pine and cypress trees I could see spreading in every direction through the national park were planted by Israel after 1948. The state uprooted the natural vegetation of olive, carob and fruit trees the area was renowned for and which the villagers had cultivated for generations, and surrounded them instead with the useless pines. 'I am sure the point was to prevent us from making a living from our old trees,' Abu Hayja said.

I interrupted him to say that many years before I had stayed at the Carmel Forest Spa Resort, which is just visible from the road leading to Ayn Hawd. In those days I had wondered at the glory of the forest and national park; it had never occurred to me that the whole landscape was artificial. Learning that a modern pine forest had been imposed on these mountains at the expense of its ancient and fruitful flora had unsettling parallels. Again I could feel the solid ground on which another of my Zionist assumptions had been built give way. The sensation, however common it was by now becoming, was no less easy for that.

According to its own figures, the Jewish National Fund (JNF) has planted more than 240 million trees – mainly fast-growing pines – across the country. They have been paid for by Jews from around the world who were encouraged to 'buy a tree' for Israel. Such schemes exist to this day. On many Israeli and Jewish websites the JNF has prominent advertisements asking readers to 'show you care' by donating a tree. 'Give the gift that grows: A gift that lasts for generations!' it says. Jews around the world are asked to donate $18 to plant a tree in Israel for a special occasion, including births, bar mitzvahs, graduations, birthdays, weddings, or as a way to commemorate someone's life.

The true purpose of these mass planting programmes, however, is rarely discussed. In the early years of the state, the government claimed that the trees were needed to ensure supplies of wood for fuel and construction. But in fact much of the greenery paid for by the Jewish Diaspora has been planted either directly over the ruins of the Arab villages destroyed in 1948, or on land that Arab communities were once able to farm. It has been used as another weapon in their continuing dispossession.

This point was driven home during several trips I made to destroyed villages in the Galilee. For example, the razed Palestinian village of Lubia, between Nazareth and Tiberias, is now covered with the lush pine trees of 'South Africa Forest', paid for by Zionist organisations in South Africa. For Israeli Jews it is simply a pleasant spot to enjoy a picnic or barbecue at the weekends, or to go on organised hiking trips as I had done there in my Zionist days. They are entirely unaware – as I once was unaware – that in 1948 about 2,500 Palestinians were expelled from this same site.

In April 2004, during the national celebrations for Independence Day, when Israeli Jews enjoy a day of rejoicing over the founding of their state, I joined a family from Nazareth who quietly commemorated the Palestinians' mirror event, Nakba Day, which marks the Palestinians' loss of their homeland. We visited a Jewish moshav called Tzipori, close to Nazareth, which has been built over the ruins of their parents' village, Saffuriya. I cannot even say that we managed to see their former home: the site of the Arab village is now hidden behind barbed wire and covered by the thick growth of yet another forest planted by the JNF. The only visible clues that Palestinians once lived there are the great mounds of cacti that Arab communities traditionally used as the boundaries to separate properties. Despite the best efforts of the JNF to poison and burn these indigenous Middle Eastern plants, the cacti have refused to die or disappear.

The Jewish National Fund website tells visitors nothing of this. Instead it claims in its title to be 'the caretaker of the land of Israel, on behalf of its owners – Jewish People everywhere'. In July 2004 the organisation announced in a press release that it had been given the distinction of United Nations status: 'Our acceptance by other countries into the United Nations legitimizes our award-winning efforts in water, environment and sustainable development.' UN status, according to the press release, will allow the JNF to sit on the world body's environment committees and give its advice on sustainability and afforestation programmes.

Abu Hayja told me that more officials arrived throughout the 1970s to warn the villagers that they were sinking ever deeper into illegality. The army created a firing range alongside the village which extends from the first house to the last. At another point Ayn Hawd was declared an archaeological site. And in 1975 the Black Goat Law was passed, declaring that it was illegal to keep goats in a national park because they posed a threat to the young pine trees. To make sure we understood the plight of his village, he recapped: 'By the end of the 1970s we knew our homes were standing on land that was state-owned and for agricultural use only – although we were not allowed to graze our herds. It was also an archaeological site. It had been declared a military firing range, and it was designated a national park. So by that stage we had lost everything: the land, the goats and cattle, our trees. All we were left with was our homes, and they were all facing demolition.'

The worst was not over, however. 'In 1981 the government passed the Services Law, which stated that no house without a licence could be connected to any public service: to the water and sewerage network, to the electricity grid and to the telephone lines. We were not allowed roads, or to have our garbage collected, or to have mail delivered to our village. And the state had no obligation to provide us with educational or medical services. If we wanted a doctor or to educate our children we would have to send them long distances to recognised communities.'

The state was actually just formalising practices that had been used by the authorities against all the unrecognised villages since the establishment of Israel. 'We were never provided with water or electricity by the state. Our parents used generators and had to carry water from the river in the valley below. There was no road to Ayn Hawd apart from a winding dirt track through the forest that often collapsed during the winter rains. We had to collect our mail from Nir Etzion. We had a kindergarten, but it was illegal: we covered the building with metal sheets so that the spy planes that circle over us and the officials who arrived unannounced would think it was a shack and wouldn't demolish it.'

I found it difficult to make sense of the way Israel treats the inhabitants of the unrecognised villages. Despite all the discrimination, the rights to education and health care they enjoy by virtue of their citizenship are honoured. But because they are effectively invisible to the authorities as the inhabitants of the places they actually live in, the state is not responsible for providing them with services in their communities – as it would be if they were living in a recognised village or town. They are like 'free-floating' citizens. Their children can turn up at a school in a recognised locality and will have a place, but the state does not have to take account of how they get there. In the Negev I had heard that the children of a village called Abda had to make a round trip of seventy kilometres each day to go to school.

'As a boy I had to go to high school in Haifa, without help from the state,' Abu Hayja told me. 'I would wake at 5 a.m., walk three kilometres through the woods to Nir Etzion and try to catch a lift from the moshav down to the main road. If there was no one around I would have to walk to the main road myself. Then I would catch a public bus to the central station in Haifa and change onto a local bus to the school. It took three hours there and another three hours back. Sometimes I would get back so late I would have to walk through the forest in the dark. I still remember one night when I hid up a tree, frightened by the darkness and the sounds of animals. My parents found me hours later, past midnight. Such difficulties continue to this day. We still have no water from the state. We built a pipeline from the moshav, which agreed to let us siphon off water in return for voting for their party's candidate to the Knesset. We still use generators for electricity. A few years ago, when my daughter was at school, she made the same journey as me.'

Abu Hayja finished his education studying engineering at the Technion in Haifa, and later landed a job with the Interior Ministry in the neighbouring Druze council of Daliyat-Isfiya. Only then did he start to realise that what was happening to Ayn Hawd was being replicated across the country. 'Our parents had been farmers. We had no connection to anything outside the village. The limits of my world as a child were the mountain and the forest. The only Jews I knew were policemen and soldiers. None of us realised what all these separate pieces of legislation amounted to. It had been going on so long that we had grown to accept it as normal, as the way our lives would always be.'

Recognising the qualities of his young grandson, Abu Hilmi appointed him the leader of the village's committee in 1978. After the passage of the Services Law three years later, Mohammed Abu Hayja decided the villagers should take the government on directly. 'People of my generation in the village said we cannot live like this any longer. "How can it be that the cows of the moshav are entitled to electricity and water, and we are denied them?" they asked. "Do we have less rights than the cows?" We decided to open our problem to the world, even if by doing so we risked retaliation from the government and the destruction of our homes. We organised a demonstration of Arabs and Jews on the mountainside. We managed to recruit one Jew from Nir Etzion and another two from Ein Hod. In those days I believed in the support of these left-wing Jews, but after twenty years of dealing with them I no longer believe in their good faith.'

I asked him why these Jews had come to the demonstration if they did not really support him. 'Maybe the three of them were embarrassed we didn't have water or electricity. Who knows? But over time it became clear these left-wingers did not want us to have the same rights as they enjoyed in their own communities.'

Two weeks later a demolition order was served on each home in Ayn Hawd. 'The authorities were amazed by our cheek. "You want services! Forget it: you're illegal," they said. So we had to begin fighting in the courts, not for the services we wanted, but so that our homes would not be destroyed.' By this time Abu Hayja knew that many other villages were in the same position as his, and he decided in 1988 to form an umbrella organisation, the Association of Forty,* to campaign inside and outside Israel for their rights.

Sitting across the table from Abu Hayja, I marvelled at the quiet, gentle defiance in his eyes. He had been battling for three decades against the emissaries of his own state – soldiers, policemen, planners and politicians – each one determined to deprive him of everything he had ever owned, and yet they had utterly failed to strip him of his most powerful weapon: his incontrovertible belief that no one had the right to violate the dignity of his family and his village. Abu Hayja's refusal to compromise on his rights, and his ingenuity and passion have so far saved his village from the wrecking crews; many other unrecognised villages have been far less lucky. Most weeks there are reports of the police entering an Arab community to destroy a handful of homes. In 2003 a total of five hundred Arab houses were demolished inside Israel.

After six years of vigorous lobbying in Israel and abroad, Abu Hayja's association won a symbolic victory in 1994. The government of Yitzhak Rabin agreed to recognise a handful of the villages in the Galilee, though the majority of unrecognised villages in the south, in the Negev, were ignored. However, Ayn Hawd's recognition changed nothing on the ground. 'Recognition in itself means nothing. You need recognition and a masterplan from the regional council before you can get services. For ten years the regional council did nothing about the masterplan, and our situation stayed the same.'

In the summer of 2004, after decades of struggling and campaigning, Ayn Hawd finally won a masterplan from Hof HaCarmel regional council. There have been a few fringe benefits for the 250 inhabitants. The village now has an elected representative – Mohammed Abu Hayja – on the council, sitting among fifty or so Jewish representatives. The council has agreed to collect the rubbish, and to do so it has had to build a primitive concrete road over the

---

* So named to commemorate the fortieth anniversary of the 1948 Universal Declaration of Human Rights.

dirt track so that its trucks can reach the village. A school bus also now collects the children to take them to Haifa. And there is a road sign to Ayn Hawd located far from the main road, at the entrance to Nir Etzion moshav.

Abu Hayja is far from satisfied by these successes, which have taken more than fifty years to achieve. 'Hof HaCarmel agreed to provide these minimum services on condition we paid taxes to them. That is the deal. But on the big issues we are no nearer a solution. The masterplan the council has approved for us is entirely unacceptable. It simply draws a tight blue line around what is already here, a bit like the fence the state erected all those years ago, leaving us with no room to expand or develop. Where are our children supposed to live? Where can they establish businesses, schools and medical clinics? Where is the room for them to make their quality of life better than ours?'

But worse than that, the masterplan has not even lifted the threat of demolition from their homes. 'I have been telling the other villagers for three decades that our homes will be made legal next year, that we will get services next year. And I am still telling them that today. And maybe theoretically one day we can get licences for our homes and make them legal. And then maybe we can get water and electricity. But before we can do that we need to own the land on which our homes stand. We have to persuade the government to redesignate this land as ours, rather than as state land. At the moment they don't seem even close to agreeing. So we remain a community of criminals living illegally in Ayn Hawd.'

Back at the founding of the Jewish state, the land on which Ayn Hawd now stands was transferred – along with the lands of hundreds of thousands of other Palestinian refugees – to the Custodian of Absentee Property. There is not a single case of the Custodian returning property to its former Arab owners. It is hard to imagine how Israel could ever sanction such a move: it would be too concerned that returning land, even to the villagers of Ayn Hawd, would be the first step in conceding the right of return for millions of other Palestinian refugees. That, as all Jews around the world have been told endlessly by their leaders, would make the Jews a minority in Israel, and so destroy the Jewish state.

Abu Hayja is no dreamer. As he waved us off, he had a parting word for Suad. 'Forget the old Ayn Hawd. You will never be allowed back.' I asked whether he did not want to return to the old village himself. 'No, I never think about going back,' he said. 'Ein Hod belonged to my parents, not to me. I was born in the new village, and I will keep on building here.'

Even this small demand – the return of a tiny fraction of the lands that once belonged to the Abu Hayja hamula – will require a concession from the state that is inconceivable. Despite the fact that his family never left this hillside, Abu Hayja is as likely to get the title deeds to the new Ayn Hawd as the refugees in Lebanon and Syria are to regain the destroyed villages of Majedal (now covered by a Jewish town called Migdal Haemek), al-Bassa (now covered by the industrial estate of the Jewish town of Shlomi) or Tantura (now a Jewish coastal resort called Dor).

The historical flipside to the Palestinian story of dispossession is the Israeli story of rebirth, of the 'ingathering of the exiles' in a Jewish state. The Zionist movement had been arguing since the end of the nineteenth century that the Jews needed a state of their own, a safe haven from the persecution they had experienced in Europe throughout their history. The three main Zionist organisations – the World Zionist Organisation, the Jewish National Fund and the Jewish Agency – worked tirelessly to encourage Jews to come to Palestine, both by buying land for them and by easing their passage there. In 1948, with the creation of Israel, these organisations finally achieved everything they had longed for. Filling the new state with Jews was not difficult: immigrants flooded into the country, fleeing their experiences and memories of the Holocaust. In the process the myth of the 'land without people for the people without land' was confirmed. Vast empty spaces, where once Palestinian villages had stood, greeted these immigrants, who had little idea about their new homeland's past. Recruited to land-hungry farming communities like the kibbutzim and moshavim, these pioneers truly believed they were 'making the desert bloom'.

Now, after more than five decades of aggressive land confiscation policies towards the country's Palestinian citizens, 93 per cent of Israeli land is owned either by the state or the Jewish National Fund. This figure, in itself unremarkable, is significant because the land is held by the state not for the benefit of its citizens, all Israelis, but in trust for the Jewish people around the world. Almost all of it is being used for the exclusive settlement of Jews. The rest of Israeli territory, 7 per cent, is split between private Jewish and Arab owners. Even so, much of the 3 per cent of the land held by the country's Arab population has been put under the jurisdiction of Jewish regional councils which refuse to give permits to Arab citizens to develop it.

Today there are hundreds of settlements exclusively for Jews across Israel, part of what the state terms its 'Judaisation' programmes: moving Jews into traditionally Arab areas so that Arab communities can be brought under Jewish dominion. The first such communities to be built – some in pre-state days, but the majority in the 1950s and 1960s – were the collective communities known as the kibbutzim and moshavim, promoted internationally as experiments in communal living. The glorified image of the kibbutz continues to this day: one liberal and widely respected British newspaper columnist, Will Hutton, recently praised the kibbutz as 'a noble' idea. 'The kibbutz movement was a living example of how to build a new society based on genuine equality of opportunity and mutuality of respect in collective democratic communes that actually worked,' he wrote in Britain's *Observer*. In reality the kibbutzim, which were usually established on the land of destroyed Palestinian villages, have always barred Arabs from living in them. So much for equality of opportunity and mutuality of respect!

More recently, the state has been creating a new model of the exclusive Jewish community known as the mitzpe, or 'lookout' settlement. Developed in the 1980s and 1990s, the mitzpim are self-consciously rural communities designed to attract Israel's wealthier Jews, those tired of living in the crowded and congested centre of the country. In contrast to the kibbutzim and moshavim, the mitzpim are usually established next to, and on, land confiscated from existing Arab towns and villages. They are always built on hilltops, and their function is essentially no different from that of the settlements established on the hills of the West Bank: to locate Jews in commanding positions overlooking their Arab neighbours. These mitzpim are designed to observe the Arab communities they watch over, to ensure the Arab inhabitants do not attempt to claim back their confiscated lands by building on them. In Tamra we have our own mitzpe sitting close by us and on land confiscated from us: Mitzpe Aviv.

For anyone who cares to visit a town like Tamra, the land policies of Israel are immediately clear – if only because of the overcrowding and squalor that is visible everywhere. But understanding the complex legal edifice on which such policies have been constructed, and the veiling of the racism at the heart of the country's land management system, is no easy task. I talked to dozens of Arab families who tried to explain how they had suffered at the hands of Israeli bureaucrats, but I – and I suspected even they – found it almost impossible to unravel the tissue of regulations that were ruining their lives.

My guide in this difficult education was a man I was introduced to soon after my move to Tamra. On my return to Britain in early 2002 I had visited Rabbi John Rayner to tell him about the dramatic new twist in my life. John, ever supportive, suggested I get in contact with Dr Uri Davis, who had been based in the neighbouring Arab town of Sakhnin for several years. Until that point I had believed I was the only Jew to be openly living in an Arab community, so I was keen to meet him, hoping that he shared the same vision as me of an Israel that encouraged Jewish–Arab solidarity rather than fostering ethnic division, and that advocated equality between all citizens. I was not to be disappointed.

Uri Davis is one of the most remarkable individuals I have met. Born in Israel, he spent most of his life here until his political views found disfavour with the government in the 1980s and he was forced into exile in Britain. A lifelong pacifist and defender of human rights, he absolutely rejects the Zionist conception of Israel as an ethnic state. Allowed to return to Israel in 1994 following the signing of the Oslo Accords, he soon chose to move to Sakhnin to highlight the fact that the state is enforcing policies of ethnic segregation. He has suffered for taking this humanitarian stance: he is shunned by much of Israel's Jewish society, and has found it hard to work as an academic in Israel in his chosen field, anthropology. I now consider it an honour to be counted among his close friends.

Uri's offence in the eyes of Israeli society is his conclusion that the Jewish state is really an apartheid state. These are not the musings of an ivory-tower intellectual. He has reached his views after years of detailed examination of the racist laws that underpin life in Israel, and much time spent dedicated to fighting human rights abuses through his non-profit organisation Al-Beit, which he runs jointly with a successful Arab lawyer named Tawfik Jabareen.

'Let me make a first point, which is that in reaching this assessment [that Israel is an apartheid state] I make a clear distinction between apartheid and popular racism or xenophobia,' he told me. 'I use the term apartheid in a specific sense to mean the regulation and enforcement of racism and xenophobia in law. Apartheid is a system where the parliament, the judicial system and the law enforcement bodies impose racist and xenophobic choices on the population. To the best of my knowledge, following the dismantlement of the legal structures of apartheid in South Africa, Israel remains the only member of the United Nations that is an apartheid state.'

Uri acknowledges that Israel has been careful not to replicate the worst excesses of the apartheid system notorious from South Africa. Israel has avoided what he calls the 'petty elements' of apartheid, and has concentrated instead on the core elements of its apartheid project, which concern the control of land. 'When a visitor arrives at the airport in Israel, apartheid does not hit him or her in the face in the way it did visitors to apartheid South Africa. You go to the toilets in the airport and there are not separate toilets for Jews and non-Jews; you go to a public park and there are not separate benches for Jews and non-Jews; you use public transport and there are not separate buses for Jews and non-Jews. And it is this veil over Israel's apartheid that has made it possible to project Israel in the West as an enlightened liberal democracy.'

The core element of all apartheid states, according to Uri, is a structure of laws that allows the colonising population to exploit the resources of the state – mainly land – to the disadvantage of the native population. In South Africa the white population derived grossly disproportionate benefits from the country's land and mineral wealth, particularly diamonds; in Israel the Jewish population derives grossly disproportionate benefits from the region's land and water resources.

'Looked at in that way, Zionist apartheid is definitely comparable to South African apartheid, and is in fact more radical and devastating. In South Africa 87 per cent of the territory under the sovereignty of the apartheid government was designated in law for the exclusive settlement, cultivation and development of whites, while 13 per cent was designated in law for non-whites. In Israel 93 per cent of the land is designated in law as state land for the settlement, cultivation and development of Jews only, and less than 7 per cent is private land and so theoretically accessible to non-Jews. So if we accept that the core of the conflict is the battle between the indigenous people and the colonial settler society for control over the land and the subsoil, then Israeli-Zionist apartheid is in fact more radical than its South African cousin.'

The 93 per cent of land owned by the state and the JNF is leased to communities like the kibbutzim, moshavim and mitzpim – the backbone of the apartheid system identified by Uri. He has been closely involved in a long-running fight to open up just one of these communities, a mitzpe called Katzir, so that Arab citizens can live there too. The vehement resistance of the authorities to this campaign reveals everything about the true purpose of these communities.

'In the early 1990s, plots of land were being marketed in Katzir by the Jewish Agency to Jewish applicants who wanted to build their own villas,' Uri said. 'Katzir's location is attractive for anyone who needs to commute to the major employment centres on the coast, either Haifa or Tel Aviv, and it quickly took off among well-established, middle-class families. Today it is an attractive leafy suburb. Like the hundreds of other mitzpim, moshavim and kibbutzim, Katzir is known in Israel as a cooperative association. The advantage of these settlements is that by law they can only be accessed by applicants who are prepared to submit to an interview process. Each community's selection committee has the legal authority to authorise or deny membership. So joining these communities is rather like joining a club. It is true that not all Jewish applicants are admitted. Cooperative associations have developed the features of a closed society: single mothers, people with a physical disability, unmarried couples, elderly people and homosexuals are not usually welcomed. So Jewish applicants are rejected as well as Arab applicants. But at least if you are a Jew you have the right to apply; Arabs don't even qualify for application. If a Jew arrives at the doorstep of a cooperative association, he will be given the application papers. If an Arab applicant arrives, he will be refused them.'

I had visited Katzir earlier to hear the story of Adel and Iman Qaadan, a couple living in the nearby Arab town of Western Baqa, who have been fighting for ten years to move there with their three daughters – so far without tangible success. Katzir was created in the early 1990s by the then Housing Minister, Ariel Sharon, as part of his scheme to 'Judaise' a small region of central Israel known as the Triangle, which is heavily populated by Arab families and lies close to the West Bank. Perched on a hilltop overlooking Palestinian villages around Jenin, Katzir has been built on a large swathe of land confiscated from the neighbouring Arab communities of Umm al-Fahm, Arara, Bartaa and Ein Sahia. The inhabitants of those towns and villages are barred from living in Katzir, as they are from all other cooperative settlements. The Qaadans, however, hoped to challenge their exclusion from tranquil, spacious Katzir and its luxury villas in the courts, and so leave behind the overcrowding of Baqa.

The Supreme Court sat on the case for five years, apparently hoping to delay reaching a decision indefinitely. In 2000, however, after embarrassing international scrutiny, Chief Justice Aharon Barak issued a ruling. Describing it as one of the most difficult decisions he had ever faced, Barak ordered Katzir's selection committee to consider the Qaadans' application. The ruling was hailed by many observers as a revolution in Israel's land laws. But it was never enforced, and for the next four years the Qaadans' application was ignored by Katzir. In May 2004, the day before the Qaadans' appeal was due to be heard, the Israel Lands Authority, a government body responsible for managing state land, announced that it would sell the family a plot of land, apparently concerned that if it lost a second court case a dangerous legal precedent on Arab land rights might be established. However, at the time of writing the Qaadans were still waiting to be allowed into Katzir.

Uri has been actively involved in the Katzir case too. Out of the view of the media, he has been helping in a very direct way another Arab couple, Fathi and Nawal Mahameed, to build a home in Katzir. 'Fathi started his career as a manual labourer in a small company run by his father that went on to build many of the homes in Katzir,' he told me. 'But he harboured a dream to build his own home there if he ever made it in the building business. By 1995 he was the proprietor of a successful construction and investment company called the Fathi Brothers, so he presented himself at the door of the Katzir cooperative. Many people there know him – he has built many of their homes – and he is well-liked. He presented his ID card and said he wished to buy a plot in Katzir. The person at the desk said something to the effect of: "Sir, you must know that Katzir is only meant for Jews and you are an Arab." He replied: "Well, I may be an Arab but I am also a citizen of the state of Israel and I would like to build my home in Katzir." The official repeated: "I am sorry, but Katzir is only for Jews."'

Fathi Mahameed turned for help to Al-Beit. They were aware that the Qaadan case was stuck in the courts, and suggested a different tack. 'We took as our model the "tester" system used in the United States. There, for example, if a black family wants to buy a home but suspects that reluctance on the part of the vendor to sell is motivated by racism, they can check their suspicions by using a white tester. If the property is offered to the tester, the black family can begin legal proceedings for racism and violation of US law. When Mahameed approached us, Jabareen immediately said: "Let's send in a tester." He suggested I act on Mahameed's behalf to buy the plot of land he needed.'

Under Israel's Agency Law, Uri was under no obligation to declare to the Katzir committee that he was acting on behalf of Mahameed. 'I was aware that one factor in my dealings with Katzir would assist me: racism makes people blinkered and stupid. The committee would see an elderly, white-haired, middle-class gentleman, an academic and fluent speaker of Hebrew, and would therefore assume that my decision to move into Katzir was driven by Zionist and settler-colonial motivations. My assumption proved to be correct. I put on the table my ID card, which registered me as a Jew with a home in the Jewish community of Kafr Shemarayhu – at that stage I was not yet living in Sakhnin. Where Mahameed encountered outright rejection because he was an Arab, I was offered to sign the initial paperwork on the day I showed up.

'In order to build a home in Katzir you have to pass through four contractual stages. The first is an interview with the cooperative association, at which they decide whether to accept you as a member. I sailed through the interview. With a letter endorsing my membership of the association, I went to the next stage. I signed a contract with the Katzir Economic Development Corporation, the body that develops Katzir's infrastructure: the sewerage, road and pavement system, the public gardening and so on. Having signed these two papers, I was then entitled to go to the Jewish Agency and sign a contract with them, a contract which is available only to Jews. And with these three documents I was able to go to the final stage: signing a contract with the Israel Lands Authority, which unlike the Jewish Agency is a state body.

'In the contract with the Jewish Agency there is an explicit reference to Jews and non-Jews, but the text of the Israel Lands Authority contract makes no such distinction. However, you can't sign the Israel Lands Authority contract unless you bring the previous three pieces of paper. So representatives of the Lands Authority can stand up in public and truthfully say: "I challenge you to show me one Israel Lands Authority contract which makes a distinction between Jew and non-Jew." That is true, but they don't also tell you that you cannot sign a contract with the Lands Authority to join a cooperative settlement like Katzir, or a kibbutz or a moshav, unless you bring these three documents first, which do make such a distinction.

'The hundreds of communities classified as cooperative settlements and governed by these rules are also the settlements that control almost all of the 93 per cent of the territory of Israel. Together their populations represent much less than 10 per cent of the Israeli population. In other words, less than a tenth of the population is sitting on legal communities that control 93 per cent of the territory of Israel. And the primary purpose of these communities is to make sure that Arabs don't get property rights in them, that they can't join them.'

Armed with all the legal forms, Uri pretended he was employing Mahameed to build his dream home in Katzir. 'Mahameed put all his heart and professional skill into building that house and its garden, and it took time. I had applied for a plot in 1995, but it was 1999 before the finishing touches were being put to the house. Shortly before I was officially due to move in, I needed to sort out a technical problem over the boundary between Mahameed's plot and the adjacent one. I attended a meeting at the Katzir Economic Development Corporation with my neighbour. The matter was easily sorted out, but as we were about to leave the director asked me to stay a moment longer. He said: "Uri, there are rumours that you are not going to enter the house, and an Arab family is going to enter in your place. Is that true?" I tried to fob off the question, saying it was only a rumour. He persevered: "Can you give me an assurance that you will enter the house?" I said: "Yes, not only can I assure you that I will enter the house, but I can give you a date." I didn't lie. It was correct that I would enter the house on the date specified, but I didn't owe him an explanation about what would happen after that. I entered the house, and a few days later we had a house-warming celebration. We invited lots of friends and activists, and at the end of my speech I handed over the keys to Fathi Mahameed.'

Uri and the Mahameeds had broken no laws in failing to reveal their true intentions to the Katzir selection committee. Nonetheless, they had achieved a result that the land management system in Israel was designed to render impossible. 'Katzir went straight to the courts, and the case has been stuck there ever since. We are demanding that the Israel Lands Authority transfers the property rights registered in my name to Fathi Mahameed. The Israel Lands Authority refuses to do so.'

Not only have the Mahameeds yet to get their property rights registered, they have also been evicted by Katzir. Uri is now living in the house a few days a week to prevent it being repossessed. 'The bylaws of cooperative associations are such that Katzir can claim the Mahameeds' home is abandoned property if it is not occupied for any length of time. It is quite possible that Katzir hoped that by evicting Fathi Mahameed they would have an excuse to repossess his home. In a cooperative association one cannot rent a home to someone who has not passed the same interview process faced by prospective buyers. So Katzir can bar Mahameed from renting his property, as well as from living there. However, there is one person who can legally occupy the house without going through the interview, and that is me. So I now divide my residence between Sakhnin and Katzir – and make sure the garden looks nice.'

I was shocked that the Mahameeds were now only allowed to enter their own home as guests. It was difficult to believe that Katzir could act in such a racist manner with the courts' backing, or at least their complicit silence, and that the other inhabitants of Katzir appeared to be allowing all this to happen without an outcry.

Uri is convinced that eventually both the Qaadans and the Mahameeds will win their legal fights to live in Katzir. But both face a long struggle ahead to achieve it. 'There are two possible ways of looking at this story,' said Uri. 'The first says: "This proves that Israel is a democracy. The Mahameeds are succeeding; the Qaadans are succeeding. If you adhere to Israel's democratic procedures, you can win your case." That's not my view. My view is that it stinks that a citizen of the state of Israel should have to resort to such procedures, to use a tester, to go to the courts, to battle for a decade to get his rights. The Mahameed and Qaadan stories do not highlight Israeli democracy; they highlight the depth of apartheid inside Israel. It should not be necessary for these families to lose years of their lives, their energies and resources to establish their rights, whereas someone registered as a Jew is exempt from all these delays, insults and sufferings. What took me, Dr Uri Davis, a few weeks to achieve

– namely to get the papers signed and sealed – will take a Palestinian citizen of Israel a decade or more. This discrepancy cannot be recovered. The time that has elapsed cannot be retrieved. The Qaadans and Mahameeds have been tied up in legal battles for a decade, and still do not have their property rights registered.'

Both Uri and I have tried to show by our own example that Jews and Arabs can live together in peace and understanding. What Katzir and the hundreds of other cooperative communities in Israel have been designed to do is persuade Jews and the world that precisely the opposite holds true.

Perceptions can only be changed once Israel's apartheid system is ended and Jews and Arabs are offered the possibility of choosing where and how to live, including living together inside open communities. But how can this be achieved? The first step must involve the dismantlement of Zionist organisations like the Jewish National Fund and the Jewish Agency which determine and shape land policies inside Israel in the interests of Jews rather than in the interests of all Israeli citizens. Both these organisations long predate the founding of Israel. In fact, they were established precisely to bring about the creation of a Jewish state in Palestine through the buying of land for the settlement of Jews. Once statehood was declared – and their purpose achieved – they should have withered on the vine. The new sovereign state of Israel should have concentrated its efforts on creating a new 'Israeli' identity open to Jews and Arabs; it should have developed a notion of citizenship premised on equality for all; and it should have provided fair access to its resources.

Instead, as Uri observes, Israel chose the path of apartheid, incorporating the Jewish Agency and the Jewish National Fund into the framework of the state. One of the early acts of the government, for example, was to transfer huge tracts of land to the JNF. By 1953 the organisation had been given nearly 500,000 acres of confiscated land, and that figure continues to grow. Today the JNF owns 13 per cent of the land in Israel – in the main habitable regions, on which more than two-thirds of Israeli Jews have a home – none of which, according to the organisation's own charter, can be leased or rented to Arab citizens. Most of the rest of the country's lands are managed by the Israel Lands Authority, but even here the JNF is really pulling the strings. The Jewish National Fund nominates half the members of the ILA's governing council, thereby determining the policies of the ILA too. Such gross discrimination is almost impossible to challenge in the courts or elsewhere because the JNF and the Jewish Agency are not state agencies. They exist in parallel to the state, as shadow bodies that have the power to exercise great control over the management of resources but cannot be held to account through any of the normal channels.

In practice, this means that the JNF can act without penalty as a kind of bullying overlord towards the country's Arab citizens, constantly seeking to confiscate private land on the flimsiest pretext and transfer it to its own or state ownership for the sole benefit of Jews. There are few restraints on the JNF's behaviour, and even fewer recourses to law open to Arab citizens when it behaves in an arbitrary fashion.

I was aware of all this in theory, but it did not lessen the impact when I saw for myself the JNF in action against a neighbour of mine in Tamra. I knew Ali Diab from the pharmacy he owns at the bottom of my road. Belonging to one of Tamra's elite families, Ali is visibly a wealthy man. The reason is to be found in the story of his family's lands. Unlike Samira, Ali can trace his lineage back many generations in Tamra, and he has the tabu (title deeds) to extensive private lands surrounding the town. Samira and all her descendants, on the other hand, lost their property rights in 1948 when the Custodian of Absentee Property confiscated their home and lands in Ein Hod. Whereas my family in Tamra has only the small patch of land it was able to buy to build a home, Ali is still by Arab standards a substantial landowner. 'On the south side of the town I have twelve dunums [three acres] planted with olive groves,' he explained to me as I waited for a prescription one day. But precisely because Ali is one of the last remaining major Arab landowners, he has been attracting the less than benign attention of the JNF. He told me that he and many other members of the Diab family had been losing their landholdings to the aggressive tactics of the JNF. I said I would like to see his fields, and we arranged to drive out to them later that day.

The southern road out of Tamra ends abruptly as one enters the last neighbourhoods, becoming a rocky track descending into the valley. Here, in Tamra's most fertile soil, cucumbers are grown – and reputed by many in the Galilee to be the tastiest and most succulent in Israel. I could make out on the far side of the valley, halfway up a gentle hillside, an isolated small concrete building painted a distinctive pale blue-green. We reached it via a more recently created stone and dirt track. 'This is my agricultural store,' said Ali, pointing to his glorified shed. It stood in a spectacular location, overlooking Tamra to the north and a forest of pine trees to the west. Less than half a kilometre to the east were visible the nearest detached homes of Mitzpe Aviv, Tamra's Jewish neighbours. Next to the shed were carefully tended olive trees.

The JNF had banned Ali from using his land for business, trade or housing, but nonetheless he is obliged to put it to some use: fallow land can be confiscated by the state or the JNF. That is the reason he planted the olive groves. By law, anyone who owns and cultivates more than ten dunums is entitled to build an agricultural shed to help him store his tools and machinery. For Ali the building is also a useful place for him and the family to rest, out of the midday heat in the summer and away from the chill winds of a Galilean winter, and to prepare meals while working all day in the fields. Although the JNF could not stop him building the store, he was sure they did not really want him to be able to use it. 'They have tried to get me off this land in every way they can think,' he told me.

I asked him what evidence he had. 'Where do I begin?' he said wearily. 'My latest problem is that they won't connect the shed up to public services, and particularly to the electricity supply, which I need for my agricultural work. The electricity company has come out here and approved the route of the cables, and I have shown I can afford the connection charges, but the JNF refuses to give the go-ahead.' When I wondered why out loud, Ali thrust a letter into my hands from the JNF which stated that his store was 'too isolated for any infrastructure'. It seemed a strange reason, given that we were standing only a stone's throw from the houses of Mitzpe Aviv. But then again, Mitzpe Aviv is a cooperative association just like Katzir, and serves only Jews. Maybe there was a law too that electricity cables from a mitzpim could not be redirected to help an Arab like Ali.

Lack of electricity, it soon became clear, was the least of Ali's worries. He pointed to the thick forest of pine trees to the west, and told me they had been planted thirty years ago, on the land of a relative of his. 'The JNF accused him of failing to cultivate his fields regularly enough, so they established the forest on them,' Ali said. 'I am determined not to make the same mistake.' Nonetheless, the JNF had made it clear that it covets his fields too: on several occasions a representative had come offering him money to buy them. 'The sums were always far below the market price,' he said. 'The first time they came they offered me $2,000 per dunum. On the last occasion I had already planted the olives you can see, so he doubled the price. I refused. There is no price he can offer me for this land that I will accept.'

The JNF, however, appears unwilling to accept Ali's no. Recently they confiscated part of his lands, arguing that he had not been cultivating them. 'They produced aerial photographs which they said showed that the soil was rocky, and that therefore I was not tending the ground. Other pictures they said they took a few years earlier showed the same. This was proof, they said, that I wasn't working the land. So they took that part of my fields.' The JNF lost no time in transforming Ali's land in the way it knows best: it planted young pine saplings all over the recently confiscated land, rendering it unusable. Looking back down into the valley from Ali's shed, a swathe of young pine trees are visible, taking root in his most fertile soil.

The loss of fields that had been in his family for generations spurred Ali to stake an even stronger claim to his remaining fields: he planted olive trees on every available bit of land. The increased workload of tending to these groves had required the building of his store. 'The JNF understood my predicament very well, so they have been trying to prevent me from getting to both the store and my fields,' he said. The only way to reach Ali's land is via an access route whose coordinates are plotted on a local survey map of the area. Checking it closely with a surveyor, Ali found that the land confiscated by the JNF also deprived him of his access track: the JNF had planted trees over the only route by which he could reach his fields. If he could not get to the olive groves, he could not tend them. In a few years the JNF would have the pretext to confiscate them too. Ali consulted lawyers, and found that he was entitled to restore the access road and to destroy any trees planted over it – as long as they were still saplings. So a few months earlier he had taken a bulldozer and carved a path back up the hillside to his shed.

Ali's problems are far from unique even in this small valley. His cousin faces exactly the same problem on his neighbouring fields. 'The JNF planted trees over a two-metre strip of land they have confiscated from him that cuts across the only access path he has to his olive groves. Then they put up a barbed wire fence. When he argued that they were blocking the only access to his land, the officials offered a compromise: they would give him back his two metres on condition that in return he gave them two dunums [two thousand square metres] of fields, including the olive trees. So far he has refused, but he is too frightened to tear down the fence and pine trees. He sits at home wondering what to do next. I keep telling him that if he doesn't act soon the JNF will be able to say he hasn't cultivated his fields, and they will take them.'

These have been the tactics used by the JNF against the country's Arab population for more than fifty years. Every dunum of land coveted by the JNF, every hillside needed for a new Jewish settlement, every fertile valley needed for a kibbutz, has been won in a struggle in which the JNF has a free hand to write and rewrite the rules. No Arab citizens can cry foul, because the JNF is not subject to the normal procedures by which government and public bodies are held to account. Ali had managed to keep hold of some of his land by sheer force of will, by his quick-wittedness and by his refusal to be intimidated or worn down. But my guess is that eventually either his stamina will be exhausted, or he will find he cannot match the resources of the JNF, with its battery of well-trained officials and legal advisers.

I had one more question for him. 'How does the JNF keep track of what you and your relatives are doing in this valley?' I asked. 'Look over there,' he said, pointing to the largest house on the edge of Mitzpe Aviv, the building closest to Tamra. 'That house is owned by a representative of the JNF. He is the one who used to come to me offering me money for my land. Nothing happens here that he doesn't know about.'

I knew several Jews living in Mitzpe Aviv from meetings I had attended which were arranged by co-existence groups promoting dialogue between Jews and Arabs. Mitzpe Aviv is considered one of the more left-wing communities in the Galilee. Ali's story was a disturbing reminder that the true purpose of these mitzpim, however well-meaning many of the inhabitants are, is to spy on their Arab neighbours. And, as Uri had explained to me, the mitzpim are designed to sit on as much land as possible, to occupy it on behalf of Jews while denying access to Arab citizens. It does not matter that some of the residents of Mitzpe Aviv see themselves as enlightened and liberal: the purpose of their community, and of the Jewish state, is to enforce an apartheid system of land tenure.

Mitzpe Aviv was founded many years ago on land confiscated

from Tamra and from the Diab hamula by officials of the JNF using tactics like those being used against Ali now. Today, five hundred Jews live in Mitzpe Aviv, occupying a thousand dunums of land, while the twenty-five thousand Arabs of Tamra are squeezed into 4,600 dunums. Each Jew in Mitzpe Aviv has access to more than ten times the land that is available to a Tamran. That explains why they have large detached homes and private gardens, while we in Tamra are trapped in suffocated apartment blocks, without gardens, parks or public spaces.

'Each time the man from the JNF came to me,' said Ali, 'he pleaded with me to sell my land. He said Mitzpe Aviv desperately needed more space so that it could grow and so its children would have room to build their homes. He told me: "Without the land, what kind of future will the next generation have in Mitzpe Aviv?"'

5

The Missing Left

After I had been living in Tamra for slightly less than a year, my presence here finally registered on the radar of the Israeli media. A reporter, Sara Liebovitch-Dar, rang me from Israel's most famous newspaper, *Ha'aretz*, saying she had seen an article about me in Britain's *Guardian*, and wanted to interview me and learn more about my views. It seemed like a breakthrough: maybe now I would get the chance to tell ordinary Israeli Jews about what life is really like for the country's Arab population.

Ha'aretz is by far the most progressive of Israel's dailies, and during the intifada has even dared to give a flavour of life as it is experienced by Palestinians in the occupied territories. It employs two highly distinguished – if unpopular – journalists, Amira Hass and Gideon Levy, who have made it their job tenaciously and bravely to uncover abuses by Israeli soldiers enforcing the occupation of Palestinian land. Hass, living in Ramallah in the West Bank, experiences the army's atrocities first-hand, while Levy regularly ventures into dangerous areas to give a voice to ordinary Palestinians and expose their daily suffering and misery at the hands of soldiers. In doing so, both are breaking the law, which bans Israeli journalists from entering Palestinian-controlled areas.

Nonetheless, *Ha'aretz* scarcely even attempts to report as fairly on the Palestinian minority living inside the country. While Amira Hass and Gideon Levy have recounted in heartbreaking words the disaster that befalls Palestinian families when, for example, an army bull-dozer razes their homes, neither is apparently allowed to write about the same actions when they are carried out by the Israeli police against the country's Arab citizens. The irony is that the abuses inflicted on Palestinians under occupation are far better-reported than the same abuses inflicted on Israeli citizens who are also Palestinian. This failure is compounded by the Hebrew media's almost total exclusion of Arabs from their ranks of journalists. At the time of writing, *Ha'aretz* employs only one Arab on its staff – a sports correspondent. In effect this policy is given legal sanction by the Israeli Broadcasting Law, which defines the media's role as representing Jewish society, reinforcing Jewish, Hebrew-speaking culture and establishing a bond between Jews living in Israel and the Diaspora.

So when I received the phone call from *Ha'aretz* I knew there was little point in asking them to send an Arab reporter to interview me. But I recognised the name Sara Liebovitch-Dar from the paper's Friday features supplement section, where she writes sympathetically about social issues, including discrimination against women and many of the marginal Jewish communities inside Israel, such as the Jews originally from Arab countries, the Mizrahim, and the Ethiopians. She was one of the more socially aware correspondents, and I assumed she would give me about the best hearing I could hope for from the newspaper.

From our initial contact, however, there were clues that I should be on my guard. When Sara called, her first words, uttered in irritated exasperation, were: 'Is that Susan Nathan? I've been looking for you everywhere!' I immediately felt reduced to the status of a wayward toddler. After I reassured her that she had indeed found me, she followed the first enquiry with an accusing question: 'So, where are you living?' As she had read the *Guardian* article, I had no doubt she knew exactly where I lived. 'I live in Tamra, Sara. It's near Acre.' She was not placated. 'But where *is* that?' I told her to get a map of Israel and look for it. 'So, Tamra's an Arab village, is it?' she said, in what appeared to be an attempt at clarification but was in reality the expression of a common Israeli prejudice: that Arabs do not live in towns, but only in villages, the assumption being that these are primitive places, out of touch with the times. The idea of a modern town of twenty-five thousand Arabs inside the state of Israel is possibly too threatening for most Israeli Jews to contemplate. 'No,' I said firmly. 'We are a town, and we are twenty minutes from Acre.'

Despite her air of bravado, she sounded nervous and uncomfortable. I asked if she had ever been to an Arab town before. 'Well, I've been to Ramallah,' she said, referring to the Palestinian city in the West Bank close to Jerusalem where the late Palestinian leader Yasser Arafat was effectively imprisoned for much of the intifada by Israeli military hardware. A few Israeli journalists had made the pilgrimage there to interview him, but I think it more likely that Sara ventured there in more conciliatory times, before the outbreak of fighting, as part of one of the regular delegations of Israeli journalists who met with the Palestinian leadership. Her reply suggested that she was familiar neither with the nature of the occupation of the Palestinians nor, more importantly, with the issues facing her fellow citizens in the country's dozens of Arab communities. I ended the conversation by giving her directions to the mosque in the town centre, and suggesting she call me when she reached it.

No one had ever before got lost following my directions, but Sara managed it. In the morning I waited for her call; when it finally came she was in a near-hysterical panic. 'I can't find you! I can't find you!' she shrieked. 'I'm at the top of the hill and they are all looking at me!' Although I knew she could be in no danger, her voice sounded so strained that I found myself starting to panic too. I rushed down the hill from my house, but she was nowhere to be seen. The phone rang again and, finally realising that she had driven past the mosque and on up the hill to the far end of the town, I told her to turn back and follow the main road downhill. But she wasn't listening. Instead, all I could hear was her wailing: 'I've gone up! I've gone up!' I tried again to calm her down: 'Turn back, Sara, and come down. You can't miss me: I'm blonde. I'm the only one who doesn't look like an Arab.' Then at last I saw her in the distance, at the steering wheel of a rental car coming down the hill. (It occurred to me that a *Ha'aretz* feature writer would need to own a car for her line of work, but maybe Sara felt it would be unwise to bring her own car to an Arab area.)

She pulled up outside the mosque, trying to look as unflustered as possible. I climbed into the car and we exchanged brief greetings. In her late thirties, she was clearly ignorant of or insensitive to local Muslim culture: she was wearing a crop top that showed her navel, something no Muslim woman in Tamra would ever do. She seemed suitably unnerved by the steep ascent along the potholed road to my neighbourhood, but as we turned left into the narrow street where I live she tried to lighten the mood: 'Oh, it's very pretty.' The comment made me smile. Did she really imagine that this was pretty? Maybe she was simply making small talk, or desperately trying to ignore the visible poverty, overcrowding and filth, and convince herself she was driving down a narrow village lane in Tuscany or Provence. Or was she hoping to conceal from me any trace of her true thoughts: 'Why on earth would any sane person choose to live here if they didn't have to? Why would someone move from Tel Aviv to *here*?'

She came up to my apartment and surveyed it with some interest. I could see she was surprised. Though my home is not the best in Tamra, it is a nice, clean, airy space with a fine view from the balcony. She asked if it was like this when I rented it. I told her that structurally it was the same, but I had furnished it with my belongings. It was obviously not quite the mud hut she was expecting.

I had assumed that a journalist from a paper like *Ha'aretz* would arrive with some sense of what avenues she hoped to explore in the interview, or some idea of the framework she wanted to impose on our encounter. But once seated, Sara simply leaned forward with her huge notepad on her lap and said: 'Well . . . begin.' It was at this point that I realised that the woman before me had failed utterly to internalise any of the things she had read about me. She didn't know where to start, or what issues to raise. As far as she was concerned, I was the star of a freak show, and she was intrigued to see my act. I was expected to perform for her, to horrify and appall her.

A more experienced interviewee, I suspect, would have bailed out at this point. That was what my instincts were telling me to do, but I suppressed them and began telling her my life story. I told her about my difficult childhood, my obsession with the Holocaust, and my Zionist upbringing. But her interest was spiked only when I mentioned an incident in South Africa when I was sixteen. My family was dining at my wealthy aunt's home when she rounded on a coloured servant in his early twenties and severely rebuked him for serving us without wearing white gloves. The meaning of her comment registered with me as: 'We don't want to see your black skin. You're good enough to serve us, but you aren't good enough to touch our food.' I had already secretly befriended this young man, and felt his pain and humiliation as she addressed him. I literally couldn't swallow my food. I excused myself from the table and followed him to the kitchen. There we talked and, feeling a strong mutual attraction, put our arms around each other and ended up having sex on the kitchen table.

Sex between a white woman and black man in apartheid South Africa was not just a physical act, it was also an act of the most powerful political dissent. In breaking the ultimate racial taboo, we were also breaking the law. Both of us, but most especially he, were taking a huge risk. At the age of sixteen I felt both exhilarated and empowered: I was sticking two fingers up to apartheid and to members of my racist family in South Africa. I was separating myself in every way I could from what was going on on the other side of the door.

Sara, it was clear, was far more interested in the act itself than she was in the political circumstances in which it took place, or for that matter the motives that lay behind my decision, forty years later, to move to Tamra. I suggested to her that Zionism was a colonial ideology that might have made sense when it was first developed in the nineteenth century, but now stood in opposition to the spirit of the times. I argued for the abolition of the Law of Return, which gives all Jews the right to Israeli citizenship while denying it to millions of the expelled indigenous population, the Palestinian refugees. I questioned the viability of a Jewish state, especially when Palestinians would soon form a majority of the population.* None of these arguments surfaced cogently in her report, published in September 2003 under the title 'Living with Them'. The 'them' presumably referred to the country's Arab citizens. The racist headline reflected the tone of the article, which opened with a sensationalised account of my having sex with the black servant in South Africa.

I should have expected no less. Sara had spent all day in my apartment, but her questions were always punctuated with the same despairing assessment: 'I don't understand you, I just don't understand your life.' The interview descended into a series of confrontations where she tried to question my credentials – as a Jew and as an Israeli citizen – and my right to criticise my newly adopted state. She asked, for example, if I had other passports. Like many Israeli Jews, I do: I have a British and a South African one. She then said: 'If you don't like it here, why don't you use those passports and go home and leave it to us Israelis?' I wondered which 'us Israelis' she was referring to: presumably not Israelis who are Arabs. But I was more astounded by her nerve. After all, she was not the one protesting about the Law of Return, which uniquely privileges Jews from

---

* Israeli demographers believe that within ten years the Palestinian population will outnumber Jews inside Israel and in the territories it occupies.

anywhere in the world to come to Israel and receive automatic citizenship. 'Sara,' I snapped back at her, 'don't tell me one minute that you want Jews like me to come from the Diaspora, the ones who have money and are well qualified, so that we can increase your demographic strength against the Arabs, and then tell me to take my passports and bugger off out of here when I start criticising the way you run the country.' There was an uncomfortable silence.

Next she began delving into my background, concentrating her questions on the fact that my mother was not born a Jew, but converted from Protestantism after marrying my father. I knew where she was leading the interview. 'Listen, Sara,' I said impatiently, 'this is not an inquisition into my parents. You came to Tamra to interview *me*.' In halakhic law – the theological edicts of the Orthodox rabbinate – only the children of a Jewish mother are considered Jews. This is still the official position in Israel, where the state gives official standing only to the Orthodox stream of Judaism, to the exclusion of the other two main streams, Reform and Conservative. It does not have to be this way. In the United States, for example, the majority of Jews belong to the more enlightened Reform stream, which makes conversion much easier.

In Orthodox Judaism, being a Jew is a little like belonging to a closed society, membership of which is highly restricted. The Orthodox rabbinate's long-standing stranglehold on the bureaucracy of the Israeli Interior Ministry means that there is no civil marriage allowed in Israel, and it is impossible to identify oneself as an atheist or agnostic. By law all Israeli citizens must be classified along confessional lines – be it Judaism, Islam or Christianity – and can only marry members of the same sect. (Couples from different confessions are forced to marry abroad, usually in Cyprus.)

The inconsistency Sara Liebovitch-Dar was trying to tease out was that, in the official Israeli view, the Jewishness of a Jew like me is suspect – even if according to the Law of Return I am considered Jewish enough to make aliya to Israel. Under that law, a Jew is defined as anyone who has one Jewish grandparent. The reason for the generous terms of the Law of Return is that the state has taken the pragmatic view that it cannot prevent large numbers of people who identify themselves as Jews, and are classified as such by Reform and Conservative rabbis, from claiming citizenship of a country that defines itself as the state of the Jews. In any case, Israeli governments decided long ago that they needed to recruit all the Jews they could find in their demographic battle to keep a majority of Jews ruling over the Palestinians. Thus, despite my non-halakhic status, the Jewish Agency approved my application to immigrate to Israel in just a week. Nonetheless, as far as the religious authorities inside Israel are concerned, I am a sort of 'pseudo-Jew', or second-class Jew. Hundreds of thousands of Israeli Jews are stuck in this identity-limbo, especially since one million Russian Jews arrived following the collapse of the Soviet Union in the early 1990s. Many were the children or grandchildren of a marriage between a Jew and a non-Jew. Today, they are unable to marry 'proper' Jews inside Israel. They and I cannot be buried in Jewish cemeteries. And their children will inherit this official 'flaw' in their Jewishness.

Sara was truly baffled by how I could fill my time in Tamra. 'But what does your life here consist of?' she kept asking. The facts that I supervise the local branch of a welfare organisation, Mahapach, that I am involved in women's empowerment projects, that I help promote a local music conservatoire and that I teach English were apparently not enough. 'But what else? What about your personal life?' she asked. I said that in the evenings I visited friends and neighbours. She was genuinely astonished: 'You mean you have friends here? You walk on the streets at night and go into people's homes?' She looked perturbed. 'Maybe I will understand all this better after I have read my notes,' she said, as if she were a doctor trying to piece together a particularly problematic case study.

Finally she suggested that maybe I should move to the West Bank, and live with the Palestinians there. I had an inkling of what she was really saying: 'Go live with Amira Hass, then we can pigeonhole you as a Palestinian-lover.' That way my criticisms would be less dangerous. I could be dismissed as a 'self-hating Jew' by right-wingers, and recruited by left-wingers as another Jew who advocated the creation of a Palestinian state to solve all our problems. But as long as my attention was focused on the discrimination against Arab citizens inside Israel, my criticisms threatened the self-identity of Jews like Sara Liebovitch-Dar who believe they are the only and eternal victims of this story.

Sara drank half a cup of tea all day, and managed a couple of mouthfuls of the salad I had prepared for lunch. At the end of the interview, as she got up to leave, I pointed out to her that she had not been to the toilet once in all the time she had been here, and it might be sensible to go before she set off on the long journey back to Tel Aviv. 'Oh, yes,' she said, as if jolted back into reality.

Sara's interview was published in Hebrew but was never translated for the paper's English edition, even though its subject matter concerned a British citizen, concentrated on my schooling in England and, in touching on matters of discrimination against Arabs, should have been of interest to an international audience. I suspected, however, that the piece was meant only for a domestic audience, and to place me outside any consensus Israeli Jews could understand. I wrote a right of reply which the paper's editors refused to publish. But despite the distortion of what I had said, a number of Jews understood the point of my criticisms. What was most gratifying was to receive supportive calls from Holocaust survivors. One eighty-year-old man called, saying: 'You know what we do to the Palestinians was what was done to us in Europe. We Jews have to realise that we do not have a monopoly on suffering, we don't have to be special in everything.' He added that despite his failing health he was considering going to live in the West Bank. He and other survivors said they felt the memory of the Holocaust was being cheapened.

This episode was a wake-up call to me in many ways, but perhaps most importantly it accelerated my rapidly growing disenchantment with what is known in Israel as 'the left'. This vague term is used by many Israelis as a withering criticism of anyone who doesn't uphold the exclusive claim of Jews to the Holy Land, or who is committed to the idea that Arabs should be entitled either to some level of rights or to a state. Politically, however, the label is almost meaningless. The Labour Party, which has ruled the country for most of its five decades, is usually considered left-wing, but has overseen the most aggressive periods of settlement activity in the occupied territories. One disillusioned Israeli journalist, Daphna Baram, summed up the party's sham philosophy: 'Labour tradition is mostly about pragmatism, which translates into pragmatic expansionism or pragmatic moderation, according to changing circumstances. Its goal is to grab the most land with the fewest Arabs on it, while maintaining a measure of international acceptability for Israel. The means: building a large number of settlements in the occupied territories, not too near Palestinian centres of population – thus asserting facts on the ground while maintaining a constant soundtrack of peacemaking.'

The left encompasses a broad swathe of opinion that is equally pragmatic: from Israel's mainstream left-wing parties, Labour and Meretz/Yahad, and their peace campaigning offshoot, Peace Now, to a handful of what are considered by most Israelis as extremist, if not possibly subversive, organisations such as Gush Shalom. In truth, the position of Gush Shalom, led by the veteran peace campaigner Uri Avnery, is moderate in the extreme: it supports the end of the occupation and the creation of a Palestinian state on less than a quarter of historic Palestine. It is prepared to recognise in theory the rights of the Palestinians expelled in 1948, the refugees, but in practice it rejects any Palestinian return that might threaten the demographic superiority of Jews or compromise the state's Zionist mission. It also, of course, has little to say about the injustices perpetrated on the country's Palestinian citizens.

The number of Israelis who adopt positions more 'left-wing' than Gush Shalom's can be counted on the fingers of a few hands. And if I had any doubts of that, a series of encounters with people who considered themselves left-wingers, even radical left-wingers, soon settled the matter for me. My first taste of the racism at the heart of the left-wing and intellectual establishment came in my first days in Israel, after I arrived as a new immigrant. I had befriended a leading Israeli academic during his regular visits to Britain, and after my arrival in Israel I spent much time at his home. I vividly recall one day watching a programme about the intifada on Israeli TV with him. We saw footage of a young soldier in Ramallah shooting an old man in the leg who had approached him with his hands in the air. I was appalled. 'What is going on?' I said. My friend replied with the air of a man who could find endless excuses for such behaviour when it is perpetrated by Jews: 'Susan, he is young and he is under pressure. That is why he shot him.' On another occasion, while crossing the campus of his university we walked past a flight of steps where Arab students like to congregate. 'Can't you smell them?' he said as we passed. I wondered what kind of ideas a man like this was inculcating in the young minds he was responsible for.

Many middle-class Israelis introduce themselves as left-wing, but their conversations soon give them away. In the days when I taught English to professionals, I remember talking with an official of a well-known Israeli bank who often boasted of his left-wing credentials. Because he deals with finance issues, I made the observation that wherever I went I could see wonderful housing developments for Jews and advertisements for government-approved mortgage schemes to encourage Jews to buy their dream home. 'That tells me very publicly how much my state values me as a citizen,' I said. 'But if I am an Arab citizen I don't see such developments open to me, and I don't qualify for the mortgage schemes, or even in the rare case that I do, I will get a much lower discount. What does that tell me about how much my country values me?' His reply was disdainful. 'So what? They can look after themselves. I want this country for me and my children.' He might also have admitted while he was at it that his bank refuses to employ Arabs in the most senior positions. (Worse still, the Central Bank of Israel, which has more than eight hundred staff, employs no Arabs at all.) 'Why is there no Arab on your board of directors?' I asked him. 'Well, it's not just down to me,' he replied feebly. I found his answer morally repugnant. If someone in his position cannot begin the process of change, who can?

There have been innumerable such disheartening moments. Another that I find hard to dislodge from my memory occurred in the wake of my move to Tamra. About the only Israeli friend who supported my decision to live in an Arab town was a middle-aged archaeologist at one of the Israeli universities who is in charge of major digs in northern Israel, where she supervises Jewish and Arab students. She would tell me constantly about her interaction and friendships with Arabs, and how it made her heart sing to drive all over the West Bank in the days before the intifada because of her love of wild open spaces. Just before I moved to the Galilee, when I invited her to visit me, she replied: 'Try keeping me away.' She always talked about visiting Arab areas as though it was some adventure, like going on safari.

After I had settled into Tamra and started understanding much better the trauma inflicted on Arab society by the war of 1948 and the ongoing suffering of the internal refugees, I explained my new thinking to her during a phone call. I told her I now realised that there could not be peace until Israel recognised the right of the Palestinian refugees to return. 'You are an extremely intelligent but naïve woman!' she exploded. 'If we let them back they will be everywhere!' Suddenly the Arabs she had spoken so fondly of were a contagion, an outbreak of smallpox that threatened to wipe out the Jews. She continued an angry rant which I finally interrupted by saying: 'I'm sorry I raised the subject.' 'Yes, I'm sure you are,' she said, closing the matter. A few days later, I opened my email to discover she had sent me a link to an offensive Zionist website that monitors the rantings of obscure Muslim clerics against Israel. She never made contact again.

I soon came to understand that these so-called left-wingers were hypocrites of the worst kind. The fact that they are to be found everywhere in Israeli society, in the government, in academic institutions, in charge of major companies and even responsible for Jewish and Arab co-existence groups, makes this realisation all the more depressing. Is it any wonder that Jews in the Diaspora have almost no understanding of what really goes on Israeli society when these people, the country's brightest and best, are responsible for projecting its image abroad?

The most disturbing moment came during an encounter I had expected a great deal from. I was introduced to a former businessman who is a leading figure in more than one of the most prominent Jewish–Arab co-existence groups in Israel. This man has a sizeable influence on the establishment left in the country, and several people suggested that there might be ways we could work together. When we met in his office in Tamra he opened the conversation by saying: 'I think you are a brave woman.' I couldn't help thinking that if he shared my views he would not find my behaviour so brave, but I let it pass. He asked me what had prompted me to take my decision to move to Tamra. I told him I was disturbed by the direction I saw Israel taking, and that I was pessimistic about the chances for peace unless we started to be more honest with ourselves. I could see he was barely able to control his anger. When I described the lack of equality, the failure to invest in Arab areas and the sense that Arab citizens had no future, he leapt in to interrupt me: 'Well, you in Britain can't speak. Look at the way the British government treats asylum seekers. Look at the way you put them in holding centres. You can't speak, you don't treat them so well.'

As he spoke, the obvious flaws in his argument struck me. Since when had I become a representative of the British government? I was speaking to him as a concerned Israeli citizen about official Israeli policies, yet he wanted only to categorise me as a Briton and restrict my criticisms to British policies. And, although I hold no brief for the British government on its treatment of asylum seekers, how was the analogy fair? The Israeli Arabs are not immigrants trying to gain entry to a foreign country on humanitarian grounds, they are citizens whose rights are supposedly enshrined in law. But faced with his rising ill temper, I kept my mouth shut on these points. Instead I asked him how as someone who was so active in Jewish–Arab educational activities he could justify the fact that Israeli educational institutions had such an appalling record of employing Arab academics: according to reports, less than 1 per cent of the country's university lecturers are Arabs. 'Oh, that was an oversight,' he said dismissively. I raised the subject of my experience in South Africa, but he swatted that away too: 'I am familiar with South Africa.' I mentioned the problems I had at the airport. 'You remind me of my daughter,' he mocked. 'You have principles.'

I had assumed that he had principles too. 'Are not principles what underpin civilised life?' I asked. Exasperated by my interjections, he launched into a speech about how a Zionist state required as its core principle that it be a Jewish state. One could play nice games about helping the Arabs, he said, but at the end of the day Israel had to be a Jewish Zionist state. He concluded: 'I know what I have just said is elitist and Ashkenazi.' There was a silence which seemed to last an eternity. He sat on the other side of the desk looking at the wall because he could not bear to look at me directly, while I sat staring at him. Eventually I stood up and said, 'Yes, it is.' I offered him my hand; it was a long time before he took it.

The lesson I learned from this meeting was that many prominent left-wing Jews are not really interested in justice or the suffering of the Arab population. They engage in left-wing activity, I suspect, either because they feel it gives them and their country a more presentable face, or because it helps them sleep a little easier at night. When I told Asad Ghanem, who has worked closely with this man, about our conversation, he could hardly believe it. 'But he's the left,' he said. 'I've known him for some time, and he's the left.'

'Exactly,' I replied.

The problems faced by Arab academics who want to promote equality at Israeli universities were revealed to me in a conversation with the head of the Jewish–Arab Centre, Faisal Azaiza. At the beginning of the academic year, he told me, he had printed a banner to hang above the entrance to the centre's office. On each side it said innocuously in Hebrew and Arabic: 'Welcome to the students of Haifa University. Feel free to use the Jewish–Arab Centre.' When the university's management heard about the sign there was indignation, and they demanded that it be removed. They wanted it printed only in Hebrew, as are other official signs at the university. Dr Azaiza had to appeal to the dean of the university to get special dispensation to print the sign in the two languages.

His story left me speechless. Arabic is one of Israel's two official languages, and a fifth of the students at Haifa University are Arabic-speakers. What could possibly be the objection to including both languages on a sign for a Jewish–Arab Centre? But what astounded me even more was that there were no protests from the university's lecturers' association or from the Jewish students' union. What message does that send to the Arab students from what is supposed to be one of the more enlightened educational institutions in Israel?

Despite these incidents, I hoped to find in my area Jews who thought a little more like me. The Galilee, because its population is almost equally divided between Jews and Arabs, has more co-existence projects than anywhere else in the country. My experience with most, however, was far from reassuring. I attended a couple of meetings with one of the most left-wing, the Alternative Voice in the Galilee, whose Jewish and Arab members are active in the area around Tamra. My friend Dr Uri Davis introduced me to the group, feeling that it would be helpful for me to meet other left-wing Jews who wanted to alleviate the discrimination faced by their Arab neighbours.

The first meeting I attended was in Mitzpe Aviv, the luxury Jewish 'outlook' settlement right next to Tamra, built on land that was confiscated from our town. When I was introduced to the group as 'Susan from Tamra', the Jewish chairman stared at me in bewilderment and asked, 'From *where*?' I repeated that I lived in Tamra. He was not satisfied: 'But where were you from before that?' I told him Tel Aviv. He had an uncomfortable smirk on his face that I had seen many times before from left-wingers. It said: You have gone too far. You are embarrassing us. You are making us look bad.

The next meeting was a short distance away in the Arab town of Sakhnin, where I struck up a conversation with a regular Arab participant. I asked him what he thought of these gatherings. He replied with an air of resignation: 'Any contact with the Jews is better than none.'

I soon realised I had little to offer these groups, which pay mere lip-service to the notion of co-existence. They concentrate on coffee mornings and 'getting to know each other' sessions, but the Jewish participants generally refuse to allow any talk of what they term 'politics'. That approach can never work, because the problems faced by Arabs in the Galilee are profoundly political: the discriminatory policies promoted by the state are designed to benefit the region's Jewish citizens at the expense of the Arab citizens. The Jews who belong to the Alternative Voice enjoy their privileges in land, housing and economic allocations because of government policies that disadvantage their Arab neighbours. If Jews in these co-existence groups refuse to face that simple fact, how can they help the Galilee's Arabs?

This was illustrated in very stark fashion by the case of friends of mine who live in Sakhnin. Ali Zbeidat is married to a Dutch woman, Terese, and the couple have two delightful teenage daughters, Dina and Awda. For the past six years they have been living in a Kafkaesque world where their beautiful home overlooking the olive trees Ali's ancestors have farmed for generations is under constant threat of demolition. Their house is built on land owned by Ali's family, it lies inside Sakhnin's municipal boundaries, and the Sakhnin municipality believes Ali and his family should be allowed to live there in peace. But neither Ali nor the Sakhnin municipality has any say over what happens to his home. A Jewish regional council called Misgav has been given jurisdiction over the land by the government – and it wants the house demolished. Thousands of Arab families have been caught in this kind of administrative trap created by the state to prevent Arab families from building homes and expanding the spaces they live in.

Ali and Terese are victims of the 'Judaisation' of the Galilee. For decades the state has been pursuing this goal by taking land from Arab communities and passing it to the control of Jewish communities. The figures tell it all: Sakhnin has twenty-four thousand inhabitants and slightly less than 2,500 acres of land, while Misgav has eighteen thousand inhabitants in a few dozen scattered luxury communities that have control over fifty thousand acres. Those fifty thousand acres have been taken from Arab towns like Sakhnin.

Terese and Ali have been paying endless fines to the Misgav council to try to fend off the demolition order, but Misgav is determined to enforce the destruction of their home through the courts. Ali was even arrested in a late-night police raid on his home and jailed for not paying a fine on time. Sakhnin has suggested to Misgav that the Jewish council return the small area on which Terese and Ali's home is built to Sakhnin's jurisdiction. Ali produces the response from Misgav, which reveals everything about its policies. 'We refuse to give even one centimetre of our land,' it says. 'In fact we want the opposite: we need more land and we want to take more of it into our jurisdiction.'

Terese is scathing about the support she has received from the Alternative Voice, many of whose members belong to Jewish communities inside Misgav. 'At a personal level most of them are lovely people, but they really don't begin to understand what the problem here is. They don't want to get involved in what they call the politics of it. One told me, "Don't worry, if the bulldozers come we will be there." But by then it will be too late. We don't need solidarity visits, we need them to be lobbying their councillors, picketing Misgav's council offices, producing banners saying "Stop demolishing homes" or "Give Sakhnin its land back". They must put pressure on their own leaders – that is the only thing I want from them.'

I could not agree more with Terese. The Jewish members of the Alternative Voice have to be ready to take on the government and the Jewish regional councils in a public showdown, but there is not the faintest sign that they are prepared to do it. Why? Because it would make their own lives too uncomfortable. Do I hear any of them saying: 'Tamra is desperately overcrowded. The government has been promising for three years to return land to Tamra, but has done nothing to make it happen. We in Mitzpe Aviv are on the land of Tamra, and if our government won't act we will give the land back to Tamra ourselves.' Not a chance!

I did make one lasting friendship through the Alternative Voice. Harry Finkbeiner, a German non-Jew who moved to Israel after marrying his Israeli wife Hannah many years ago, lives on one of the most left-wing kibbutzim in the country, a short distance from me. Harduf is situated a kilometre or two from another Arab town, Shefaram, in a superb location high on a Galilean hilltop where it enjoys commanding views towards the coast and Haifa. Unlike most kibbutzim, Harduf was not built on the ruins of an Arab village. It was allocated the lands from the state in the early 1980s. Harduf, like other kibbutzim, benefited from the generosity of the state because its members are Jewish.

Today Harduf is a wealthy community, with each family owning a lovely detached house with a neat garden. It has a flourishing farming business, including a deal with the dairy company Tnuva to produce organic food, and hi-tech dairy sheds. The kibbutz has a large communal swimming pool, two playgrounds, a hostel, a kindergarten and one of only five Waldorf schools in Israel.* It is a truly wonderful, peaceful place to live. And it is committed to the principle of living in harmony with its Arab neighbours.

But even at Harduf the practice of co-existence, as opposed to the principle, seems more than a little hollow. I was invited to see the kibbutz's Jewish–Arab meetings at first hand by the group's organ-iser, Yaakov. At a planted forest on its eastern side, the kibbutz has created what in less politically correct times would have been called a Red Indian camp, with a large, billowing awning tied between the trees and a campfire at its centre. There we congregated, but as is typical at such meetings the Jewish members sat on one side and the Arabs on the other. I sat with the Arabs. The two sides got together only when photographs were needed of them holding hands – apparently these pictures are sent to left-wing Jewish organisations overseas as part of fund-raising drives.

By the campfire each participant spoke in turn about the need for love, understanding and mutual respect. When it came to my turn, I talked of my reasons for moving to Tamra: to show Jews that most of the views they have of Arabs are based on emotion rather than fact. I asked the Jewish participants: 'Why do you find it so difficult to come to Tamra, when we in Tamra have no problem coming to you?' The Jews looked stunned. (The question had been

---

* Waldorf schools educate children according to the principles established by the German social philosopher Rudolf Steiner: that they should be given as much opportunity and creativity as possible in order to develop their personalities fully.

prompted by an earlier, private comment from Yaakov. Despite having lived in Harduf for twenty years, he admitted to me that he had never visited Tamra.) I also suggested to the group that co-existence could not work unless Jews and Arabs first had equality of citizenship. As the meeting broke up, the Jewish members either ignored me or said goodbye looking at the ground. It was as if I was holding up a mirror to them, and they were too embarrassed or too appalled to look at the reflection. The Arabs, from Tamra, Shefaram and Sakhnin, came up and offered warm support. I decided these campfire photo-opportunities were not for me. They were intended to make Jews feel better, to let them believe they were doing their bit. I could not see how they were helping to end discrimination against Israel's Arab citizens.

The message of love and brotherhood promoted by the Jews of the Alternative Voice and Harduf – to the exclusion of all political discussion – echoed an interesting analysis I had read by a British Jew, Paul Eisen, who is director of Deir Yassin Remembered, an organisation committed to commemorating one of the worst massacres perpetrated by Jews on Palestinians in 1948. He argues that as the immorality of the Palestinian dispossession has become clearer to Jews in Israel and the Diaspora, they have fallen back on ever more convoluted moral justifications for their behaviour. One that appeals particularly to left-wingers is what he calls the 'sin of moral equivalence', which claims that the core of the problem between Israelis and Palestinians is not the brutal dispossession of the Palestinian people, but a tragic clash between two conflicting and equal rights:

> In this new narrative Israel is not guilty, because no one is guilty, and Israel is not the oppressor, because there is no oppressor. Everyone is an innocent victim. Variations on the theme include the 'I've suffered, you've suffered, let's talk' approach, and what has been called the psychotherapy approach to conflict resolution,

174

'You feel my pain and I'll feel yours.' Proponents of this theory say that the two sides are not listening to each other. If only each side would hear the other's story a solution would surely be found. But it is not true that neither has heard the other's story. Palestinians have heard the Zionist story ad nauseam, and they have certainly heard enough about Jewish suffering. It is not, then, both sides that need to listen: it is Israelis, and Jews, who need to listen.

I regularly visited Harry Finkbeiner at his chiropractor's clinic in Harduf, where he was treating a problem with my back. He told me his wife Hannah was curious to meet me and see how I lived in Tamra, so we arranged a date. Arriving with a bunch of flowers she had picked from her garden, she was at pains to point out to me that she was left-wing despite coming from a well-known military family. She asked me about my views of Israel, and I expressed my well-worn criticisms about the rampant discrimination and the lack of equality for its Arab citizens. She sat there silently and listened. Then she said with concern: 'Susan, do you hate Jews?'

I could not quite believe what I had heard, and it took me a few moments to recover. I had to tell myself: Susan, the problem is hers, not yours. I assume Hannah had never heard her society examined in this way, apart possibly by Arab or foreign critics whom she could easily dismiss as anti-Semitic. In a less direct way, that was how she was trying to label me, too. Her comment revealed to me very clearly the inability of most Jews to see what kind of society Israel has become. We expect Arabs to be self-critical, but we do not require the same of ourselves. Hannah's reaction was ludicrous – as ridiculous as those Jews who accuse other Jews who criticise Israel of being self-hating – but unfortunately it is all too common. What she could not understand is that it is precisely because I take human rights so seriously, and want to treat others the way I expect to be treated myself, that I speak out.

Harry also introduced me to David Lisbona from Harduf, a Londoner who came to Israel twenty years ago. He is the coordinator of Middleway, a group of Arabs and Jews from inside Israel who visit Palestinians in the occupied territories in an attempt to promote peace. David came to have coffee at my home, and we had a difficult if amicable conversation. His assumption – one I come across all the time – was that my decision to move to Tamra was related in some strange way to the peace process. It is not just Jews who think like this: plenty of people in Tamra made the same assumption when I first arrived. It disturbed me that they found it so hard to understand why a Jew would want to protest against the discrimination they, rather than the Palestinians in the occupied territories, experience.

I suggested to David that he would do better to deal with problems on his own doorstep before charging off to the West Bank at the drop of a hat to give support to the Palestinians. 'We are Israeli citizens, we pay our taxes to Israel, not the Palestinian Authority, so should we not see it as our first duty to take responsibility for the injustices that happen here? How can we cure injustices over there when we are blind to them here?'

David's answer was evasive. In Umm al-Fahm, he told me, an Arab town which has earned a reputation for Islamic radicalism, no one was talking any longer of injustice. All the shopkeepers wanted now was for the Jews to come back on Shabbat and eat hummous again. I could not dispute the fact that the Arab population has been crushed in the last four years: since the start of the intifada the community's most important political and religious leaders have been put on trial or jailed. There was little mood at the moment for confrontation. But even so, I warned him that the teenagers in Tamra were not going to accept what their parents and grandparents had accepted. They want equality, they demand the same rights from the state as those given to Jews. 'David, you want them to accept second best, to accept that they don't need to be equal

citizens.' I told him Arab citizens would not remain resigned indefinitely to having their rights ignored and trampled on by the state.
'The issues you are raising are not even in the Israeli consciousness,'
he said. Well, I thought, they are not there because supposedly
left-wing people like you are not putting them there. At the end of
the meeting David suggested I see Middleway in action and come
on their next trip, a peace walk in the West Bank. Intrigued, I agreed.

I am not the sort of person who easily dons a white sash and a
badge bearing the emblem of a tree and the slogan 'The Middle
Way'. On the day of our peace walk I kept wondering: the middle
way between what? It is no clearer to me still. Maybe it was meant
to convey only a sense of the participants' reasonableness and
moderation.

As a group we drove to an army checkpoint – a gated section of
the wall Israel is building in the West Bank, and the official crossing
point into occupied territory – close to the Arab town of Bartaa.
On the other side we were to meet a Palestinian delegation. As we
passed through Bartaa itself we had a chance to see for ourselves
the insane folly of Israel's 'security barrier'. Until the completion
of the wall in this area in the summer of 2004, Bartaa had been a
thriving town straddling the Green Line, the border between Israel
and the West Bank that was erased with Israel's conquest of the
latter in 1967. Technically, Bartaa has existed in two halves: on one
side of the line is the Palestinian town of Eastern Bartaa, and on the
other the Israeli town of Western Bartaa. In practice, however, for
nearly forty years the two sides have been indistinguishable from
each other, and most residents have only a vague idea of where the
official dividing line lies.

The inhabitants of both towns are ethnically Palestinian – though
on the western side they hold Israeli IDs and on the eastern side
Palestinian IDs – and are drawn from the same network of families
and hamulas. Until the wall was built through the town, brothers
and sisters, aunts and uncles lived on either side of what was just a

theoretical border. They mingled freely in Bartaa's well-known market and could visit each other's homes without hindrance. That was still the situation when we visited in April 2004. But shortly afterwards the market – and with it the centre of life in Bartaa – was demolished to make way for the wall. Now the same families are effectively living in different countries, separated by razor wire, military guntowers and 'sterile approach zones' protecting the wall from infiltrators.

At the crossing point I could feel the tension in the air. It was rather like approaching a high-security prison: there was razor wire everywhere, soldiers with machine guns, and camouflaged watchtowers. These checkpoints have been built in deserted locations, surrounded by open ground to ensure a good line of vision for the soldiers. On the nearby hills, the scrub has been burned to improve visibility still further. On the Israeli side, some distance from the gate, was what I can only describe as a Third World bus stop. A small patch of corrugated iron sat atop four metal posts: this was the sole shelter from the sun provided by Israel for those waiting to cross. There were no seats – not even upturned crates – toilets or refreshments. Nothing.

And because only Arabs are usually waiting to cross at these checkpoints, the wait can be long indeed. You are allowed to cross only when a soldier decides it is your time. It can take half an hour, or two hours, or most of the day, for him to crook his finger in your direction. You have to watch silently while he drinks from a can or chews on a sandwich, or chats with a friend. However urgent your business, you must wait till he is ready to deal with you. At one point we saw an old man bent over nearly double, who could walk only with the help of a stick, hobbling futilely towards a soldier who shouted at him: 'I didn't say you could approach yet.' A young man, propped up on crutches as he stood under the corrugated iron shelter, told me he had been waiting three hours to cross. He had not been told why there was a delay. Uncertainty like this hangs in the air all the time. A feeling pervades that control over your life, your fate, has passed to a stranger, a teenager dressed in an army uniform. It is not a pleasant feeling.

I could see across to the other side of the checkpoint, where the queue of cars and pedestrians waiting in the late-morning heat was much longer. Getting permission to enter Israel is always much harder than leaving it. Nearly all of the people I could see on the other side were probably Israelis, as Palestinians are rarely allowed entry to Israel. But of course they were not Jews; they were Arab citizens returning from visits to see relatives, from the weddings of cousins or the funerals of uncles, or from business trips.

Israel has made arrangements in the West Bank a maze of bureaucratic complications. Strictly speaking Israeli citizens – whether Arabs or Jews – are not allowed to enter Palestinian territory. But one of the few surviving legacies of the Oslo agreements is the carving up of the West Bank into different security zones, called Zones A, B and C. Zone A, which covers the main Palestinian population centres, falls entirely under the control of the Palestinian Authority, while Zone C, the largest area of the West Bank, falls entirely under Israeli military control. Zone B is a grey area of supposed cooperation. Although Israeli citizens are banned from entering Zone A, it is possible for them to receive permits to enter Zones B and C.

Our group had permission to enter a Palestinian village called Yabad, not far from Jenin, which is in Zone C and so under Israeli military authority. David Lisbona had received written permission from the army for us to cross over that day, and the soldiers at the checkpoint already knew our details. I could see that our peace walk had taken a fearsome amount of organising. If we had been Jewish settlers we could have passed effortlessly over to the other side of this wall on special bypass roads that connect Israel with illegal settlements deep inside Palestinian territory. But Israel appears to have little interest in making life easy for peace campaigners – even if the soldiers were not heaping the humiliation on us reserved for Arabs. Whether it is the army's intention or not, the menacing atmosphere at the checkpoint would be enough to put off all but the most committed peace activists.

After we had crossed over we were greeted by a Palestinian delegation that included Abdullah Barakat, the assistant of the governor of Jenin. They escorted us to an olive grove close to the checkpoint, where we stood in a big circle and introduced ourselves. Several of the Jews made short speeches about how much they wanted to come to Palestine, and that they brought with them love and understanding. I felt an impulse to shout out that the situation had long since passed the point where what was needed was love and understanding.

The Palestinians, on the other hand, spoke about their desperate situation. They described how they did not have enough water or food, and how for long periods when they were under curfew they had no access to hospitals or to schools for their children. The dissonance – between the Palestinians telling us how they were being stripped of their basic rights, and the Jews' reply that their hearts were full of love – was jarring. David's group appeared to have brought with it exactly the same flawed thinking that had been so visible by the campfire at Harduf. They were telling the Palestinians to keep politics out of this encounter, and to concentrate on the belief that we were all one big happy family.

When it was my turn to speak, I told the group that I had come to witness the Palestinians' lives at first hand, and that I did not believe there could be peace or co-existence until there was a full recognition of rights for the Palestinians. 'When you are equals in every sense of that word, then we can live together,' I concluded. Again I saw the hushed disapproval from the Jews that had been so obvious at the Harduf meeting. Afterwards the Palestinians came up to me and thanked me for what I had said. Abdullah Barakat told me: 'You are welcome with us any time. Any time we can help you, or you want to learn about our lives, or just visit us, you are welcome.'

Among the Israeli group was a Sufi sheikh from Nazareth, Abdul Salam Menasre, who warned me to be careful of the other Jews on the walk. 'My dear, they will hate you for what you have said.' I asked him why. 'Because you have come to the crucial issue – and that is of rights. They have not even begun to reach that point.'

It was noticeable how desperate the Palestinians, like Israel's Arab citizens, were for any contact they could have with Israeli Jews, whatever the terms. And just how unequal these meetings were. The Palestinians and Israel's Arab citizens kept their mouths shut because they knew that the Jews would withdraw their contact and their support were they to express their true feelings.

From that moment I felt an outsider, an observer of the day's proceedings. The Jewish members' hostility to me was apparent. It was made clear to me that most of the group did not agree with me when I said the Palestinians were entitled to equal rights by virtue of their being human. I was told in no uncertain terms that the Palestinians would get their rights when they had quietened down and started to behave themselves. In a subsequent email from Maya, one of the participants, forwarded to me by David Lisbona, she said she had gone as an 'emissary of love', and commented about the day's peace walk: 'I heard words of political agendas and requests to help promote statehood . . . This is not my understanding of our purpose in visiting. Some of us found ways to express that we are here for a social spiritual foundation.'

I am not sure what 'a social spiritual foundation' is, but whatever the group's intentions it was yet more proof of the faultiness in the thinking of the left: rights were being treated as though they were to be earned for good behaviour, like gold stars to be added to a child's name on the class register. There appeared to be no concept among these left-wing Jews that rights are basic and universal.

One exception was an ultra-Orthodox rabbi from Jerusalem, a

young American named Eliyahu, who sought me out. 'What you are doing is the most extreme form of Judaism,' he said. 'It encapsulates the very essence of what Judaism is about.' Also in the group was a Swiss woman, Dominique Caillat, a non-Jew whose father had been active in the Swiss diplomatic corps. She had been commissioned by the German government to write a play about the conflict. Later in the day she came over and said: 'I don't understand the Israeli left. Is this really it?' I told her it was, and about as far left as she would find. 'It's appalling, they are so out of touch with the real issues,' she said.

Jeeps arrived to drive us to Yabad, a village in poor shape after it had been damaged by a series of army incursions. We were taken to a courtyard where a wonderful lunch of barbecued meats, with salads and fruits, had been prepared. The villagers were poor but desperate to welcome us and show us that normal contact with Palestinians was possible. I found it heartbreaking and humbling to sit there and have them supply us with this feast, and I ate some distance from the other Jewish members of the party, sitting among the local children who wanted to practise their English. An Arab man in his mid-thirties came over and told me he knew me from having seen me on Al-Jazeera TV, which had interviewed me in Tamra some months earlier. He said: 'I know why you are here. But tell me, why are *they* here? Have they come just to make their consciences feel better?' My impression is that privately many Arabs feel like that. There is huge resentment, anger and bitterness.

Israelis often criticise the Palestinians for lacking a proper peace camp, saying there is 'no partner for peace' on the other side. But this is a grossly unfair interpretation. Many Palestinians are desperate to work for peace, and want to join like-minded Israeli activists. The welcome given to the peace walk group alone is confirmation of that. But when Palestinians meet Jewish peace activists they find they are talking an entirely different language. There is rarely discussion of strategies of non-violent protest or campaigns of civil

disobedience from the Israelis; they talk only of love and understanding. Israelis also forget that the risks in taking part in peace
activities are far greater for the Palestinian population than they
are for Jews. Israeli soldiers have shown little compunction in shooting unarmed Palestinians who violate military orders, even if their
actions pose no threat to the army. Palestinians also risk being
arrested and held in Israeli jails for months or years, often without
a trial or being charged. All of this is well documented but is largely
forgotten by Israeli peace activists, who take none of these risks
when they stage officially approved peace walks.

After lunch we were driven back to the checkpoint. I noticed that
two petrol pumps close to the olive grove where we had met, the
only source of fuel for many kilometres around, had been crushed
by a tank in the few hours we had been away. Why? Apparently the
army had decided that Palestinian vehicles should not be allowed to
refuel at the site any more. It was an illustration of how quickly and
unpredictably things change here, from day to day, from hour to
hour, without warning or explanation. The result if not the purpose
of such constant 'reorganising' of Palestinian life is to make any
attempt at establishing a daily routine unbearably stressful and
difficult.

In Yabad I had gone walking in the old alleyways, and had caused
quite a stir. Women peering out of their windows had shouted out
'Al-Jazeera, Al-Jazeera!' as I passed underneath. For the population
of Yabad, as in other Palestinian towns and villages, much of the
time in the last months and years has been spent under curfew,
locked inside their homes. The only available entertainment is
the television, the best explanation I could offer for why everyone
seemed to have seen me on the channel.

I asked many of the people I met: 'If next time we could bring
just one thing to help you, what would it be?' The answer was always
the same: 'We need more water.' This was not surprising. The West
Bank sits atop the most prolific acquifers in the Holy Land, one

reason given by some observers for why Israel is so reluctant to end the occupation and return the territory to Palestinian control. Most Palestinian water is taken by the Israeli water company, Mekorot, and sold to Israelis. While Palestinians in the West Bank have their water cut off at frequent intervals (and, I noticed, didn't even have enough water for flushing toilets), the Jewish settlers who live nearby splash around in private swimming pools and have sprinklers to keep their lawns looking green.

At the checkpoint while we were waiting to cross back into Israel I told David of the conversations I had had with the Palestinians, and added: 'If you really want to help the people of Yabad, then arrange for tankers to deliver water to them.' Looking uptight, he replied: 'I will have to look into what the real problems are here.' I thought, it's not as if it's a secret that there are huge water shortages in the West Bank. And if he doesn't know what the main problems are, why has he not asked the local inhabitants? His reply seemed too much like an evasion.

At the checkpoint I was spotted by a friend, Tamar, from Kibbutz Hazorea. She volunteers for Machsom Watch, one of the few left-wing groups that is doing something practical and positive to mitigate the worst effects of the occupation. The women of Machsom Watch stand at the checkpoints observing and noting down the behaviour of the Israeli soldiers. Their very presence there, they hope, deters some of the young soldiers from committing the worst human rights violations, but sometimes they also try to intervene if a soldier is behaving in a particularly unreasonable manner. Tamar came over and threw her arms around me, causing great annoyance to the soldiers, one of whom shouted: 'Move, move, I want this area sterile.'

I asked Tamar what she had seen while she had been on duty that day, and she said it had been relatively quiet. However, just before we had arrived, she said, a soldier had lost control and started shouting wildly at the queuing Palestinians: 'We have to teach you bastards a lesson! You need to be taught a lesson!' She had gone over to the soldier to ask him precisely what lessons he intended to teach the Palestinians. A commander quickly intervened, separating them and telling the soldier he would not tolerate that kind of behaviour. I told Harry about Tamar's account, and he said: 'You know, Susan, I see it from all sides.' I asked what exactly he saw from the occupying soldiers' side. 'You have to understand the terrible compulsion in Israeli society to conform. These soldiers feel the pressure of the peer group.'

His answer reminded me of a question I often asked my parents about the Holocaust, to which I never received a satisfactory reply. 'Why did so many German soldiers say they were only following orders?' Harry's response served only to confirm my fears that we have become a nation of soldiers simply following orders. That is what our young people are being trained to do.

At the checkpoint there were two queues trying to cross back into Israel. One was a long tailback of cars, each of which was being searched and its driver questioned. The other was a line of pedestrians, often the passengers of the cars, who had to pass down a narrow alleyway separated from the drivers by razor wire and a fence. There were both male and female soldiers on duty, but the women were noticeably more aggressive than the men. One blonde-haired soldier with a gun slung over her shoulder was screaming obscenities and abuse at the Palestinians trying to cross over from the other side. I could see no reason for her behaviour apart from the fact that she wanted to demonstrate to them, and her male comrades, her absolute power. I was reminded of an account by a prisoner in Dachau I had read when I was younger, in which he described the particular brutality of the women guards.

Then the girl turned round to deal with the human traffic going in the other direction, and her gaze fell on me. 'Where are *you* from?' she demanded. It was as if she was saying: 'What the hell do you think you're doing over there with the Palestinians, wasting my time?' I took out my ID card and handed it to her. 'So, you are an Israeli.' Yes, I said. She made me pass through the metal detector, and the alarm sounded. I went through again, and set it off again. She was getting angrier and angrier, shouting at me. Finally, a young male soldier told her he would take over. He asked me to remove my earrings and watch, but I still set off the alarm. Then it occurred to me that I was wearing a special belt for my back which included metal rods for support. I lifted up my top to show it, in a farcical mimicry of the Palestinian men made to take off their shirts to show that they are not wearing suicide belts. In the only moment of humour, the two of us laughed as I said: 'If you don't mind, I prefer not to have to get totally undressed here.' He searched my bag and I was let through. The female soldier was glowering at me the whole time. The next member of our party to be searched was shown even less respect. A woman from Fureidis, an Arab town close to Haifa, was taken off to a room for a strip search.

Although I had been deeply unimpressed by the peace walk, I continued my friendly contacts with the members of Kibbutz Harduf. Only later did I discover, almost by chance, that the criticism I had levelled at David Lisbona and his group during our first encounter – that he should take more notice of what was going on in his own backyard before chasing off to the West Bank – was even closer to the truth than I could ever have imagined.

I was being treated at Harry's chiropractic clinic when I heard the familiar wail of the muezzin as he called Muslims to prayer. I knew there was no mosque in Harduf, so where was the sound coming from? Harry told me a Bedouin tribe lived right next to the kibbutz, in a village called Sawaed Chamera. The residents of Harduf and Sawaed, he said, were on excellent terms, and several of the Bedouin were employed on the kibbutz. The two communities loved each other like brothers, he remarked, in a phrase I would hear several times more when the people of Harduf and Sawaed spoke of each other.

Later Harry took me to Sawaed to meet the inhabitants for myself. I was surprised by the village's proximity to Harduf: just a small olive grove separated them, and from the last houses on Harduf's western flank you could make out the top of the mosque's minaret. Harry appeared right about the good relations between Harduf and Sawaed, especially compared to the usual dismal standards of dealings between Jewish and Arab communities. The kibbutz had even refused a special grant from the government to build a fence to 'protect' itself from Sawaed. In contrast, another neighbouring Jewish community, a moshav called Adi, had taken the money and built a fence to separate itself from its Bedouin neighbours. Although it is never reported outside Israel, there are countless such fences and walls separating Jewish and Arab communities. They go entirely ignored while the world concentrates on the much larger wall being built across the West Bank.

In Sawaed I met Taha, the village's sixty-four-year-old mukhtar, or leader, and one of his sons, Amin. Taha told me the history of his tribe, which had originally arrived in Palestine many generations ago from Syria. They had not owned land but had moved around the area grazing their herds of cattle, camels, goats and sheep. In the summer they would move to an encampment on the 'sand area', the shoreline by Haifa, while in winter they would move up into the Carmel hills in search of food for their animals. Taha said that Haifa had grown much busier following the First World War, as Jewish immigrants arrived from Europe. The sand area became increasingly developed, leading to tensions between what he called the 'animal people', the Bedouin, and the 'land people', the Jews.

The village of Sawaed was founded close to the town of Shefaram because of the vision of Taha's grandfather, Faizal Hussein Mohammed Sawaed, who foresaw a time when the Bedouin way of life would no longer be possible. He spotted the piece of land on which the village now stands one day in 1920 when he was out riding his horse. It was owned by a Moroccan tribe known as the Mjirbin, and he negotiated its sale from them. Taha said his grandfather chose this piece of land because of its beautiful location, overlooking the coastal plain towards Haifa, and its rich pastureland. The village also had easy access to the waters of the River Tzipori.

In 1942 Faizal died, and his son Faiz was recognised by the British Mandatory authorities as the new mukhtar. During the war that founded Israel in 1948 Faiz decided the tribe would not flee to Lebanon or Syria, as did the populations of many other villages, but would remain close to its lands. The tribe therefore relocated to a site a little north of Karmiel, which Faiz thought would be safer. They encamped there for a few weeks waiting for the fighting to subside. When they returned they found their village untouched; it was too far from the main highways to be considered a threat by the advancing Israeli army.

Taha inherited the mantle of mukhtar from his father in 1965, at the age of twenty-four. That year was to prove fateful for his village. The Israeli government passed the Planning and Building Law, which, as Mohammed Abu Hayja of Ayn Hawd had explained to me, zoned all the land inside Israel, listing only 123 Arab communities as recognised by the state. That list sealed Sawaed's fate just as it did Ayn Hawd's. Sawaed was not included, and it has been fighting ever since for proper recognition. Taha still has the tabu, the land deeds, for his village dating from 1941, before the founding of Israel. The Jewish state implicitly recognised the legality of the document when it offered him money to sell the land, but he refused, and his village has been under threat of demolition ever since. On several occasions, he said, the authorities came to Sawaed and destroyed houses to try to intimidate the 250 villagers into selling. They have, however, refused to budge. 'I am going to keep the land that my grandfather bought, and no one will force me off it,' he said.

Taha's son Amin told me that Jewish land officials used to come after the demolitions, hoping the villagers had been 'softened up'.

On one occasion, he said, his uncle, Taha's brother, agreed to sell his share of the land to the state representatives. 'He told the official to bring some scales and they would close the deal. The official asked why he wanted the scales. My uncle replied: "We will put each lump of earth on one side of the scales and a similar weight of gold on the other, and then you will know how much this land costs." We have not seen another official since that day.'

But Amin says the villagers have to be on their guard at all times. 'Once an old [Arab] man from Shefaram came to my father, telling him he had no land left to build a home for his sons and asking if he could buy a plot of land from us. My father took pity on him and gave him the land at a low price. Only later did he find out that the man was really working for the state as a land buyer. This is the way the state hopes it can slowly take our land and homes from us.' It made me wonder whether the members of Harduf really knew how the land that had been given to the kibbutz was originally acquired by the state. In all my conversations with them, no one had ever told me. My impression was that none of them ever asked such questions. Maybe they were afraid to hear the answer.

As with other unrecognised villages, Sawaed receives no public services. It is not connected to the electricity or water grids, it has no sewerage services, it does not have proper roads. All the houses are illegal and under constant threat of demolition. Sawaed is invisible as far as the planning authorities are concerned, so they make no allowances for the villagers in terms of the provision of schools or doctors. The village's one recent success is a kindergarten building funded by the German government, which the state has promised not to demolish.

I asked Taha what he felt he had achieved for his village. 'In reality I have nothing except the words of some of my Jewish friends that things will get better.' When he told me that, it reverberated in my mind as a shameful indictment of Harduf. I could not live in the kibbutz and know that my neighbours were enduring these kinds of conditions. Why was Harduf not challenging the authorities to do something? Why were they not picketing the government until the state agreed to give Sawaed the same privileges it gave Harduf? I strongly suspect that if Harduf publicly refused electricity or water from the state until it was also given to Sawaed, the ensuing media storm would win the Bedouin village the rights for which it has been pleading for the past forty years overnight.

Instead, the main debate inside Harduf about its relations with Sawaed concerns the kibbutz's newly built swimming pool. After much discussion, Harduf has decided that it wants the pool to be open to its Arab neighbours, but nonetheless there is much agonising about what that will entail in practice. Almost all of the men in Harduf I spoke to expressed their concerns about the local Bedouin boys being able to watch the kibbutz's young girls at the swimming pool. 'I am not sure I want my daughter being looked at by the boys of Sawaed when their own sisters are covered up,' said one. This seemed to me a sort of soft – or liberal – racism. So what if the boys want to ogle their daughters? That is what boys do. Are Jewish boys also not ogling these girls when they wander around the kibbutz wearing their crop tops and skin-tight jeans?

My conversations in Harduf, I think, reflect in microcosm the problem of the Israeli left. The feeling that dominates in the kibbutz is: the Bedouin must adopt our values and beliefs before we can allow them access to our community and our standards of living. We are superior to them because their lives are primitive. That approach can never lead to co-existence. One has to accept that differences exist. In mixing together as equals, Harduf and Sawaed will find their own common ground. If the members of Harduf are right and the kibbutz's ways are superior to those of Sawaed's, then the Bedouin youngsters will be influenced and changed by being exposed to them. Maybe what really frightens the members of Harduf is the thought that actually they have as much to learn from Sawaed as Sawaed has to learn from them.

I do not want to sound overly critical of the members of Harduf. They have been trying to alleviate the worst injustices experienced by Sawaed's residents. They paid, for example, for one of Sawaed's brightest children, Taha's son Amin, to go to Britain to complete his higher education as a sports teacher, and they now employ him at the kibbutz's prestigious Waldorf school. Harduf has also supplied a single pipe of water to the village, though many members of the kibbutz complain bitterly about the fact that a large number of the villagers in Sawaed do not pay them for the water. When I spoke to people in Harduf there seemed to be no understanding of the economic pressures on their neighbours. Running your own private generator for electricity is not cheap. And each villager has to pay regular and heavy fines to the authorities to prevent their homes from being demolished. Fines can be as high as a thousand shekels (£120) per square metre. As a result the people of Sawaed are constantly in debt to the state. Surely a wealthy and successful kibbutz like Harduf could afford to be a little more magnanimous in sparing the piped water.

Many of the inhabitants of Sawaed do not conform to the stereotype of the Bedouin Israel likes to present to its Jewish citizens. One, for example, is a sociologist who has been forced to work far away, in the Negev, because there is no work in Sawaed. Another of Taha's sons, Amel, is a doctor who qualified in Italy. But Amin's achievements stand out. In his early forties, he is a bright, articulate, handsome man who speaks fluent Arabic, Hebrew, English and German. His early schooling was in Germany, paid for by his parents because of the difficulties of educating him properly in the Israeli system. The question of identity must be far more complicated for Amin than it is either for me or for the kibbutzniks of Harduf. When I asked him how he saw himself, he replied: 'I am Bedouin, Muslim, Palestinian and Israeli – in that order.' He added: 'Part of me feels proud to say "I am Israeli," but in a way this identity is imposed on me by the Jewish state.' His behaviour as an Arab and as a Bedouin, he said, was always under scrutiny from Jews: he felt he had to be perfect, to prove himself, to be better than the Jews, to refrain from dissenting or being argumentative.

I had the strong sense that Amin did not really feel free to speak his mind or demand his rights – despite being better informed and more educated than most of the other villagers. I asked him if he felt a pressure, given that Harduf had paid for his education, to be the model Arab. He skirted the issue: 'You have to understand that we need to look in our own backyard before we blame others.' He said some in Sawaed were even afraid of the village being recognised, fearing that they would have to pay taxes for street lighting and garbage collection when they didn't have the money. 'We don't serve in the army, so many of the villagers can't get proper work. They worry about how they can ever pay for services if the state provides them.' The villagers appeared to be stuck in a circle of despair.

I felt that in some sense Amin's compliance had been bought, as he depended on Harduf for his education and his employment. When I heard the members of Harduf and the villagers of Sawaed refer to each other as brothers, it sounded like an evasion of the real issues that needed addressing between them. The people of Sawaed know that the members of Harduf are the only allies they have in a system that abuses them at every turn; they know they cannot afford to upset the left-wingers who call them brothers. And I could understand how tempting it would be if you lived in Harduf to persuade yourself that there was a real brotherly love between you and the Bedouin. But the truth is that it is a romantic illusion, and neither side has the courage to admit it.

6

A Traumatised Society

The first time I met Bar she was wearing army fatigues and had a rifle slung casually over her shoulder. Sitting with me overlooking the golden beaches of Herziliya, a little north of Tel Aviv, she was at pains to point out that she was not allowed to let the gun out of her sight. I had made contact with twenty-year-old Bar through her parents, who live on a moshav close to Tamra. This Ashkenazi family and thousands of similar ones across the country were once the backbone of the Jewish state. They belonged to the pioneering rural cooperative communities, the moshavim and the kibbutzim, whose members toiled the land in the belief that they were making the desert bloom and who unquestioningly sent their children to fight a series of wars against the Arabs. These families produced the earliest leaders of Israeli society: the generals, the diplomats and the politicians. Their ethos was one of service and unwavering loyalty to the state.

But those days of Zionist certainty are coming to an end for privileged families like Bar's. Her mother is a left-wing extremist, or at least an extremist by Israeli standards, who wants an end to the occupation and the right of return for the Palestinian refugees. Her father, a former high-ranking officer in the army and now in the security services, once took the establishment's view of Israel's conflict with the Palestinians: that they needed to be crushed and contained. Today, he is a reluctant reader of *Ha'aretz* and in particular the columns of Gideon Levy. Most Israelis despise Levy and regard him as little more than a traitor for his reports of Palestinian suffering at the hands of Israeli soldiers. But Bar's father affirms that everything Levy writes about the occupied territories is true. 'This is what the army does,' he says despairingly to her. She describes her father as an increasingly irascible man living in a bewildering world, torn between his need to be a patriotic, loyal citizen and his understanding that Israel is committing grave war crimes. Unlike her parents, however, Bar is not opposed to the occupation. She believes both that it is needed to ensure Israel's survival in a hostile Middle East, and that she has the same obligation as her friends from school to defend, and possibly die for, her country. Every state needs an army to protect it, she says, and Israel should be no different.

When we first met, Bar was coming to the end of her six months' intensive training for a combat unit. She had yet to see any action in the occupied territories; indeed, she had never visited either the West Bank or Gaza in her life. She had barely met a Palestinian, even one from inside Israel. Bar knew from her parents and from newspaper articles that the army does terrible things in ruling over the Palestinians. She also knew about the refusal movement, hundreds of soldiers who have refused to serve in the occupied territories, but she said that path was not for her. 'Why should I not serve when all my friends are in the army?' she said, before adding: 'Anyway, it is too easy to refuse.'

But there she was wrong. The refuseniks' numbers have remained low in part because it is so difficult for teenagers barely out of school, especially for boys, to refuse to serve in their country's army. All Israeli male Jews are drafted at the age of seventeen or eighteen for three years of military service, except for religious Jews studying in special schools called yeshivas. (The country's Arabs are also excluded from military service, apart from the small and vulnerable Druze community and a tiny number of Bedouin – Israel's most deprived group – who are encouraged to volunteer, normally as desert trackers.) The state will usually do a quiet deal with the families of youngsters who simply want to avoid fighting, agreeing to give them a desk job well away from the occupied territories. But true conscientious objectors – either pacifists or non-pacifists who selectively refuse to join an army that is occupying another people – are hounded mercilessly by the state. They face spells in military jail not just for refusing their initial conscription, but also every time they refuse the call-up for their reserve duties, which they must continue to perform intermittently well into their forties. The refuseniks are effectively criminalised for much of their adult life.

Worse than the prison terms are the social pressures. Objectors are shunned by Israeli society, including their school friends and in some cases their parents and wider families. Their treatment is little different from that of those non-combatants in Britain during the First World War who received a white feather: the assumption is that they are cowards, and happy to leave their country open to invasion. That is a heavy burden to endure when you are a teenager.

Economic pressures exist too. The refuseniks are excluded from a sort of secret society the Israeli military represents. Soldiers form powerful friendships with the other men and women in their battalions, and later in life these connections can help them win jobs, particularly in politics and the security services, as well as admittance to the more prestigious communities inside Israel. In practice, refuseniks find themselves in much the same position as the Arab minority: because they have not served, they do not qualify for a whole basket of financial privileges such as mortgages and government grants, as well as for many jobs for which military service is stipulated as a precondition.

For Bar at least the pressures were less strong. A determined young woman can usually find excuses for forgoing military service: the family doctor can be asked for a certificate exempting her on medical grounds without too many questions being asked. As a last resort she can even get pregnant. The ideological conflict is usually less acute too: women are not sent into combat units in the occupied territories unless they volunteer, so it is easy to keep away from the fighting. More than 1,300 men had refused to serve in the army by the time the first female objector, Laura Milo, was jailed in the summer of 2004 for refusing on grounds of conscience. She was not a pacifist, but opposed serving in what she called an occupation army.

Bar saw things very differently from Laura. She said the stories she had heard of the atrocities and regular abuses by soldiers made her all the more determined to serve. And not just in a cushy job behind a desk well away from the frontline; she wanted to be in a combat unit enforcing the checkpoints, the system of blockades placed all over the roads of the West Bank and Gaza designed to allow or prevent Palestinian movement at Israel's unchallenged discretion. 'If I am at the machsom [the checkpoint] I can show the Palestinians that there is a human side to Israelis, and not just the inhuman side they are used to.' As well as hoping to prove to Palestinians that not all Jews are bad, she said she would show other soldiers by example that it is possible to be polite and civil at the checkpoint. She believed she could change the army from within.

I was concerned about how a young woman, still unsure of what she should be doing, of where her true moral responsibilities lay, would cope with the demands of enforcing an occupation that is illegal under international law and that daily forces soldiers to make immoral choices. I asked her whether she knew that while thirty Israeli soldiers were killed in combat in 2003, another forty-three killed themselves, mostly using their own guns. That was a 30 per cent increase in the army's suicide rate on the previous year. Although it is not widely discussed, reports show that mental health problems are rife in the army, especially among young conscripts doing their early military service. According to Brigadier General Eitan Levy, head of the army's personnel division, between 30 and

40 per cent of conscripts seek referrals to a mental health officer during their first year of service.

I asked Bar about her training for checkpoint duty. She told me that she and her fellow conscripts spent most of their time with a senior officer who had served in a combat unit in the territories, and who provided them with a series of scenarios they might have to face. One she recalled was the following: 'What if you have been on guard duty for eight hours in hot and dusty conditions, and you are tired and irritable and want to sleep? There is a long queue of Palestinian pedestrians and vehicles that need searching. Then an ambulance arrives with the driver telling you that someone is critically ill on the other side of the machsom. You want to tell the driver to go straight through, to reach the ill person on the other side, both because you are tired and because the person needing help is very ill, but you also know you should search the ambulance in case there is a suicide bomber inside. What do you do?' Bar looked at me in bewilderment: 'What *do* I do?' I wish I could have offered her an easy answer, but there was none. 'Look, Bar,' I said, 'you have chosen to go into the army. You will face these kinds of situations every day, several times a day.'

I could see that this young woman was filled with doubts and questions. She said towards the end of our meeting that she was not sleeping well because such questions were tormenting her. The army, I thought, would not be able to help her resolve these issues. I asked her how she was getting along with the other soldiers in her unit. Usually soldiers form intense friendships during their service, bonds that last a lifetime. They become blood brothers and sisters. But Bar said she felt a distance. 'Many of them just talk about how much they hate Arabs. They are filled with hatred. They say they can't wait to get behind a gun and show who is boss.'

I wondered where such hatred sprang from at the age of eighteen. The only answer I could imagine – one confirmed by the accounts of left-wing Jews of their upbringing inside Israel – was that these young people had been fed a diet of stories by their teachers and the media suggesting that the Palestinians only wanted to kill Jews, to drive them into the sea; that the Arabs were Nazis trying to replicate the Holocaust. Such ideas were reinforced by the TV images of the aftermath of suicide bombings in Jerusalem and Tel Aviv. Of course, these youngsters had never been to Jenin or Nablus to test whether such stories were true. And when they did have the chance to visit these Palestinian cities, they would not be there to talk with Palestinians but to enforce the occupation at the barrel of a gun.

Most Israeli youngsters have been brainwashed into fearing an amorphous enemy that wants to exterminate the Jews, and its only identifying feature – or so they are told – is that it is Arab. Such fears last beyond childhood, dominating reasoned argument among Israeli adults. So what checks are placed on the behaviour of an eighteen-year-old armed with a gun and licensed to behave as he thinks best? Soldiers are rarely punished when Palestinian civilians are killed because of their actions. Israel could, of course, wait till its youth had finished university and gained a little maturity and insight before recruiting them to the army. But the state wants them young, impressionable and angry. I admired Bar for thinking she could change this culture from within, but as we parted I could not help thinking the attempt would prove futile.

It was a month before I saw Bar again, when she was on leave from her unit. She had just completed her first tour of duty, ten days manning a checkpoint in the volatile Palestinian city of Hebron. Postings don't get much worse than Hebron. Here some 150,000 Palestinians live besieged by a few hundred fanatical armed Jewish settlers who have taken over the city centre. Hundreds of soldiers are there in order to protect the settlers, effectively bringing life in much of the city to a permanent halt. There are regular stories in the Hebrew media of the settlers, many of them Jewish fundamentalists from America, being guarded by soldiers as they attack local Palestinians, either with stones or with their own weapons. The settlers' children are taught to spit at Palestinians, and to curse them as animals.

Bar arrived at my home in Tamra in the evening, telling me that her mother had been worried about her coming to an Arab town after dark. I did not know whether to laugh or cry at this misplaced concern. She sat in my living room in a floral summer dress, her dark hair tied up in a Bavarian-style bunch at the back of her head, wearing clumpy schoolgirl shoes and short white socks. Her innocent appearance, combined with her pretty young face, somehow made what she had to tell me even more disturbing than it would have been if she were in uniform and armed. She was pale and nervous. I asked her how she felt about being in Hebron. Defensively, she replied: 'I want to start by saying that there are some good people in my unit.' She looked close to tears, so I didn't press her on what she meant by 'good'. She continued: 'But when we start to talk about "The Problem", the situation with the Arabs, they become totally different people. I feel totally alone in my unit, because they all hate Arabs. If we don't talk about that subject, I get on with them like the best of friends. But as soon as that subject is raised, it's me versus them.'

She said it was a real test of her principles to be on the checkpoint. The week before, on the day of a suicide bombing inside Israel, her unit had been given orders to shut down the checkpoint so that no one could pass. 'We were told it was being closed for twenty-four hours, and no one could cross for any reason: not to reach hospital, because a relative had died, nothing.' But this was also the first day of the Palestinian school year, and in the morning hundreds of parents arrived with their children to cross the checkpoint to register them for classes. When their way was blocked, the parents grew increasingly angry and began shouting at the soldiers that the people of Hebron had nothing to do with the suicide bombing, and that they should be let through. 'It was terrible to see the little children standing there with their new school bags waiting to go through, and us refusing to let them cross,' Bar said. Then some of her friends in the unit approached the crowd with their guns levelled at them, shouting: 'Fuck you! Get back!'

Bar said she had tried to be polite, telling the parents that she was sorry but that they were not allowed to pass today because those were the orders. 'And because I was nice to them, they just laughed at me and pushed past.' I thought, what the hell did she expect? She was enforcing an occupation illegal under the Geneva and Hague Conventions, and carrying out immoral orders to collectively punish the local Palestinian population, including small children. But I was more interested in how she had coped with their response. 'I think this was like a test. I must learn to be firmer,' she said.

Another incident troubled her. A few days earlier her unit had been sent on an operation to enter the homes of four Palestinian families to find if they had any materials that might be useful in making explosives. After the soldiers had forced their way into the homes, they were instructed to divide the men from the women and children, and to keep them in different rooms. They were ordered to separate the group of Palestinians by pushing them apart at gunpoint. The message they were supposed to give to the Palestinians, Bar said, was simple: 'Our guns are "watching" you at all times.' The soldiers did not ransack the homes themselves, as happens in some units, but in each one they ordered a Palestinian captive to empty the drawers and wardrobes while a soldier stood close by with a gun pointed at him. Bar said she could not level her gun at the Palestinians, and held it down at her side while she directed them using her hand, rather like a traffic policewoman. I asked her why she couldn't raise the gun. 'I felt too uncomfortable,' she said.

I suggested to her that maybe the reason she felt so uncomfortable was that she knew deep down that what she was being asked to do was immoral, that she knew it was wrong to invade these people's homes. I said: 'Bar, has it not occurred to you that the whole occupation is illegal, and is putting you in a position in which you are forced to make illegal and immoral choices?' She agreed, but said that was all the more reason why she had to be there. 'I am there to show that there is a human face to Israel, that there are decent human beings here.'

It appeared that she did not understand that she was already not behaving decently, that just by participating in the occupation she was compromised. She had been at the checkpoint for less than a fortnight, but the tension implicit in being a 'good soldier of the occupation' was already almost too much for her to bear. As she continued her service, I suspected, she would come to appreciate that she had only two choices: to join the refuseniks, or to slip into the same hardened behaviour she so criticised in the other soldiers. It would be a traumatic experience whichever way she went.

Bar told me that her unit found nothing in the Palestinians' homes, and on their return to base they were called in by the commander for a debriefing. He asked if they had any questions. Bar asked: 'Did you have prior information that there would be bomb-making equipment in these homes? What was the point of the operation?' The commander hummed and hah-ed for a while before saying to her: 'You have to remember that it is important that we show them who is in control.' His answer seemed to trouble her as much as it did me. I asked her how she felt about the operation. 'I saw these terrified children clutching at their parents and saw how we create hatred. If the children grow up seeing their parents being humiliated and abused at our hands, won't they just want vengeance?' I said she could always leave. 'I hate the army and hate what it does, but I have to be part of it,' she replied. I could only think: 'God forbid she kills someone, or is killed herself.'

Bar had only been a serving soldier in the occupied territories for ten days, but already the moral dilemmas of trying to be good when one is ordered to do something essentially bad were tearing her apart. She looked close to a breakdown. The idea repeated as a mantra by Israeli society – that its army is the most moral in the world – had vanished into thin air for Bar. I hoped she would soon have the courage to refuse to serve. She was only beginning to see what serving in an occupation army entailed. If she carried on much longer, she would see far worse things.

For too long a wall of silence has shielded many Israelis and the rest of the world from knowing about the abuses committed against Palestinian civilians in enforcing the occupation. Glimpses into this reality have occasionally been provided by the women of Machsom Watch, who issue monthly reports into the soldiers' behaviour at the few checkpoints they are able to observe. But almost no one apart from a few hardened activists reads those reports. Very occasionally, the Israeli army itself has admitted that things are not quite as wholesome as they would wish to convey. A handful of soldiers have been put on trial – a drop in the ocean compared to the hundreds of Palestinian civilians the army agrees have been killed by its forces – revealing yet more clues as to what really takes place. One such trial began in September 2004. The accused was the commanding officer at the notorious Huwara checkpoint near Nablus, and the trial came about after he was accidentally filmed by the Israeli army's education division beating a handcuffed Palestinian and assaulting another man as he stood at the checkpoint with his wife and children. A subsequent investigation revealed that this officer had imposed a reign of terror at the checkpoint, his actions including smashing the windscreens of cars waiting to cross. No fewer than seventy-two paratroopers, however, came to his defence, signing an affidavit presented to the court that the use of force at the checkpoints was standard behaviour, and was necessary if they were to carry out their assignments. The soldier's battalion commander, Lieutenant Colonel Guy Hazut, said in his testimony to the court that he had often seen similar behaviour from ordinary soldiers, but was disturbed to see an officer commit such abuses. Nevertheless, he called the defendant 'an impressive officer in the battalion. He is cut from the same cloth from which we wish our officers to be made.'

The self-enforced silence of ordinary soldiers, however, is finally coming to an end. For the first time combat soldiers are talking publicly about what they are doing – and not just in Hebrew for a local audience. A series of officers in elite combat units have submitted letters criticising the Israeli army for its immoral activities in the occupied territories. In the autumn of 2003, for example, twenty-eight reservist pilots issued a letter warning that they would no longer carry out attacks on Palestinian residential areas from the air. They were all suspended from duty, and two active pilots were dismissed. A year later, in 2004, the *Maariv* newspaper revealed that four team commanders from the air force's undercover commando unit 'Kingfisher' had written a letter to the chief of staff, Moshe Yaalon, saying that the bulldozing of houses was 'immoral', and that the army 'harms innocent civilians'. None of the commanders, however, said they would refuse to carry out such immoral orders.

The personal accounts of less senior soldiers have created more impact. The first group of soldiers to put on an exhibition of photographs and personal videotaped accounts of life in the army were members of a unit which had recently finished a tour of duty in the Palestinian city where Bar was serving: Hebron. Called 'Breaking the Silence', the show was staged for a month in Tel Aviv, and caused a storm of outrage in the Hebrew media. Military police raided the exhibition, claiming they were searching for evidence that might later be used in the prosecution of soldiers. Then, shortly afterwards, four of the soldiers who organised the event were interrogated on suspicion of having taken part in illegal actions. One of them, Micha Kurtz, observed of the police operation: 'They're not going to shut us up, because we have a lot to say, and they're not going to scare us off.'

Much of the sensation concerned the photographs, many of which focus on the hatred felt by the Jewish settlers for Arabs. One shows a wall inside the Palestinian city spraypainted with the words: 'Arabs to the gas chambers'. In another, settler children tear down the wall of a Palestinian shop brick by brick. Sixty sets of car keys were also on display, evidence of the common army practice of confiscating the keys of Palestinians caught driving in a forbidden area. They are supposed to be returned later to the driver, but often aren't, as the exhibit proved.

Just as powerful as these visual exhibits are the video accounts recorded by the soldiers. They vividly describe the hypocrisy of the occupation:

> Our job was to stop the Palestinians at the checkpoint and tell them they can't pass this way any more. Maybe a month ago they could, but now they can't. On the other hand there were all these old ladies who had to pass to get to their homes, so we'd point in the direction of the opening through which they could go without us noticing. It was an absurd situation. Our officers also knew about this opening. They told us about it. Nobody really cared about it. It made us wonder what we were doing at the checkpoint. Why was it forbidden to pass? It was really a form of collective punishment. You're not allowed to pass because you're not allowed to pass. If you want to commit a terrorist attack, turn right there and then left.

One soldier, a teacher in civilian life, explains how easy it is to slip from the good intentions of someone like Bar into the barbarity of an occupation soldier:

> I was ashamed of myself the day I realised that I simply enjoy the feeling of power. Not merely enjoy it, I need it. And then, when someone [an Arab] suddenly says no to you, you say: what do you mean no? Where do you get the chutzpah from to say no to me? Forget for a moment that I think that all those Jews [the

Jewish settlers in Hebron] are mad, and I actually want peace and believe we should leave the Territories, how dare you say no to me? I am the Law! I am the Law here! Once I was at a checkpoint, a temporary one, a so-called strangulation checkpoint blocking the entrance to a village. On one side a line of cars wanting to get out, and on the other side a line of cars wanting to get in, a huge line, and suddenly you have a mighty force at the tip of your fingers. I stand there, pointing at someone, gesturing to you to do this or that, and you do this or that, the car starts, moves towards me, halts beside me. The next car follows, you signal, it stops. You start playing with them, like a computer game. You come here, you go there, like this. You barely move, you make them obey the tip of your finger. It's a mighty feeling.

Another soldier imagines how he would feel if the tables were turned, if it were Palestinian soldiers coming to search his parents' home:

If I try to imagine the reverse situation: if they had entered my home, not a police force with a warrant, but a unit of soldiers, if they had burst into my home, shoved my mother and little sister into my bedroom, and forced my father and my younger brother and me into the living-room, pointing their guns at us, laughing, smiling, and we didn't always understand what the soldiers were saying while they emptied the drawers and searched through the things. Oops it fell, broken – all kinds of photos, of my grandmother and grandfather, all kinds of sentimental things that you wouldn't want anyone else to see. There is no justification for this. If there is a suspicion that a terrorist has entered a house, so be it. But just to enter a home, any home: here, I've chosen one, look, what fun. We go in, we check it out, we cause a bit of injustice, we've asserted our military presence and then we move on.

Many of these accounts question what exactly the point of having the soldiers in Hebron is. One soldier relates a day when he was ordered to protect a group of fundamentalist Jews visiting Hebron:

> That morning, a fairly big group arrived in Hebron, around fifteen Jews from France. They were all religious Jews. They were in a good mood, really having a great time, and I spent my entire shift following this gang of Jews around and trying to keep them from destroying the town. They just wandered around, picked up every stone they saw, and started throwing them in Arabs' windows, and overturning whatever they came across. There's no horror story here: they didn't catch some Arab and kill him or anything like that, but what bothered me is that maybe someone told them that there's a place in the world where a Jew can take all of his rage out on Arab people, and simply do anything. Come to a Palestinian town, and do whatever he wants, and the soldiers will always be there to back him up. Because that was my job, to protect them and make sure that nothing happened to them.

These testimonies are now being supported by the accounts of soldiers from other units. The refuseniks are seeking out disillusioned or troubled soldiers who are ready to speak out. One of the bloodiest places where Israelis are enforcing the occupation is in Nablus, where much of the Palestinian population has been under curfew for dozens of days at a time, only allowed out of their homes for a few hours once a week to stock up on food. One soldier interviewed by the refuseniks explained how his combat unit, which he described as having an exemplary discipline record, operated in the city. Stationed in Nablus between December 2003 and May 2004, the unit scored sixteen 'X's – meaning Palestinian deaths. Eleven of those killed were armed, and four were children, he said. 'At some point they told us that, since we took down only four kids, they [would] give our company tasks because we are known as a company that doesn't hit innocent civilians.' Some soldiers take killing a child very hard, he added, but others just laugh: 'Yes, now I can draw a balloon on my weapon. A balloon instead of an X. Or a smiley.'

Anyone who doubts the ease with which some Israeli soldiers shoot Palestinian children should consider the case of Iman al-Hams, a thirteen-year-old schoolgirl who was shot dead in cold blood in Gaza in late 2004 by an officer identified by the Israeli army as Captain R. The incident came to light only after soldiers under his command went to the Hebrew media on discovering that the army was trying to hush up the killing. On a taped radio conversation of the incident, Iman was identified as a 'girl of about ten' and 'scared to death' when she was shot in the leg from an army position. According to the statements of other soldiers, as she lay bleeding on the ground, Captain R approached her to 'confirm the kill', and shot her twice in the head. He walked away, then returned to empty his magazine into her body. Doctors found she had been shot at least seventeen times. Shortly after the incident, Captain R is recorded saying: 'Anything that's mobile, that moves in the zone, even if it's a three-year-old, needs to be killed. Over.'

The Nablus soldier's unit was often allowed to go on shooting sprees in Nablus, he said, using live ammunition indiscriminately: 'No one would ask why, no one would ask anything.' If a child was killed, there would be no investigation or trial; the unit's commander would be fined a hundred shekels (£12). Out of his unit of nine soldiers, only three didn't behave 'like retarded kids'; the rest enjoyed hurling stun grenades at the children throwing stones at their armoured vehicles, even though the soldiers were in no danger. 'There's no need to throw stun grenades at them, making them deaf for a month,' he said.

The soldier confirmed suspicions aroused by widely seen TV footage of Israeli army tanks driving over parked Palestinian cars and electricity pylons; these were attempts to cause as much damage as possible, he explained. In some cases, during curfews, his unit's armoured vehicles would chase 'live cars' – cars being driven by Palestinians – and crash into them. The driver would be beaten when he was caught. In other operations, if soldiers suspected they were closing in on a terrorist, they would take a neighbour as a human shield to knock on his door. That way, if the suspected man decided to resist arrest, the neighbour was more likely to be hit in the crossfire than a soldier. 'It's obvious to me that this is wrong, but not strange,' he said. 'This is something that happens all the time. A well-known procedure.'

After a kill, the soldier said, his friends would prop up the corpse and take photographs with it. The pictures are 'of people with a V sign over his [the corpse's] head. They don't touch the corpse ... There was no mutilation ... but they took photos like twenty-year-olds in a normal world do.' His account appeared to be substantiated a few months later, in November 2004, when the Israeli army began investigating reports of such incidents.

The soldier said that at the time they had no sense that they were doing something wrong. 'I mean, you don't have the awareness. I don't know. It sounds stupid, but you don't know how what you're doing is bad. Only later, maybe after two years, maybe after you become a commander and you become more balanced, grown up. You start realising what you did there.'

I met precisely one such reformed soldier by accident. I was returning from Herziliya by taxi when the driver, a Jewish man in his thirties named Eitan, asked me why I was heading for Tamra. When I told him I lived there, he asked: 'Are you married to an Arab?' I said no, I had chosen to live there to challenge the way Jews see Arabs. 'Then maybe I can talk to you,' he said. He told me that he had just completed a two-month jail term in military prison for refusing to do his reserve duty in a tank unit in Gaza. 'I realised over a period of time that we are crushing other human beings, and one day I just decided I couldn't do it any more,' he said. 'I could no longer justify it to myself.'

I had never been to the tiny Gaza Strip: it is almost impossible for Israelis other than soldiers and a few thousand Jewish settlers to enter the area, which is home to 1.2 million Palestinians. From the land the Strip is entirely sealed off by an electrified fence, and its short coast is constantly patrolled by Israeli gunboats. It is the nearest thing imaginable to an open-air prison. To enter the Strip, even diplomats and journalists must sign a waiver form that, in the event of their being shot, they will not hold the army responsible. For this reason, the horrors that occur in Gaza are reported far less widely than they should be. The Israeli army has been carrying out some of its harshest operations in Gaza, particularly around Rafah. It has demolished hundreds of Palestinian homes in the usually fruitless search for tunnels built to smuggle cigarettes and weapons under the Strip's southern border, shared with Egypt. During the course of the intifada hundreds of Gazan children under the age of fifteen have been shot dead.

When Eitan told me that he had served in Gaza, I was interested to hear his version of what was happening there. It is one thing to read about these things, quite another to meet a man who has seen them with his own eyes. What was it like, I asked. 'You are in the tank and all you can see around you are hundreds of children aged between eight and fourteen throwing stones at you,' he said. 'But to be honest, you don't feel threatened. You know you are in the tank and they can't hurt you.' What happens while you are sitting in the tank, I asked. 'You receive orders.' What kind of orders? There was an uncomfortable pause before he replied: 'Sometimes, orders to fire.' I said: 'Let us be clear, so there is no mistake. You are telling me that you receive orders to shoot at children who are unable to protect themselves and who don't pose any threat to you.' There was a long silence before I heard an almost inaudible whisper from the front seat: 'Yes.'

As we drove on in silence, I felt as if the whole weight of the country was falling on my shoulders, just as it had on Eitan's. I could no longer doubt that Israel was committing massive war crimes. I asked whether it had taken a long time for him to reach the point where he could refuse to serve in the army. 'Yes, it was gradual,' he said. 'First of all I refused to serve in the tank, and so they put me on guard duty at the gate to Kfar Darom [an illegal Jewish settlement in Gaza]. But eventually I realised I could not carry on serving.' Why had it taken so long? 'I suppose peer pressure and the general pressure in Israeli society to conform. One is expected to be part of the herd, to stick together in times of trouble.' He said that carrying out orders had pushed some of the people he served with over the edge, and that they were having psychiatric treatment or taking strong medication. Use of illegal drugs, particularly marijuana, was rife, just as it had been among American soldiers in Vietnam. 'Is it safe to have soldiers on drugs behind guns?' I asked. 'Probably not,' he replied.

The psychological trauma inflicted on these soldiers does not only affect their behaviour when they are in uniform and serving in the occupied territories. As a notice at the entrance to the 'Breaking the Silence' exhibition observed: 'Hebron isn't in outer space. It's one hour from Jerusalem.' These soldiers bring their dysfunctional behaviour back with them to Israel when they are on weekend leave and when they finish their tours of duty. They return to parents, partners and children living anything from a few minutes to a couple of hours from where they are enforcing the occupation. This may in part explain the reports of rocketing levels of domestic violence in Israel, as well as the high death toll on the roads.

But even more importantly, these soldiers return from their service with all their racist attitudes towards Arabs reinforced. Many pursue careers as policemen or security officers, where they work within a professional culture that treats all Arabs, including Arab citizens of Israel, as the enemy. This was the verdict of a Supreme Court judge, Justice Theodor Or, in his commission of inquiry report into the security forces' killing of thirteen unarmed Arab citizens in the Galilee in October 2000, at the start of the intifada. One of his central recommendations was: 'It is important to act in order to uproot phenomena of negative prejudices that have been found regarding the Arab sector, even among veteran and esteemed police officers. The police must inculcate among its personnel the understanding that the Arab public as a whole is not their enemy, and that it is not to be treated as the enemy.'

Israel feels and behaves like a traumatised society. How could it be any other way? Three Israelis whose paths have crossed mine during my time in Israel, however, have given me some hope for the future. They have demonstrated, in their different ways, that the traumatised society can be healed, slowly and patiently, from within. All three emerged from their military service deeply scarred, but subsequently rebuilt their lives in ways that offer a vision of how Israel may begin to reform itself. Unlike most Israelis, they have understood and come to terms with the fact that the army corrupted them morally. They have also realised that it is within their power to seek in the mistakes of their respective pasts some of the solutions for the future. Each is trying to breathe life into another Israel.

I met Irit one evening in Kibbutz Harduf, where she is the principal of the community's prestigious Waldorf school. A small, delicate, softly-spoken woman in her mid-thirties, it was hard to picture her ever serving on the frontlines of the army. But that was exactly what she was doing during the first Palestinian intifada, which erupted in the dying days of 1987 and stretched on for another five years. Like Bar, Irit is from one of the established left-wing kibbutz families, the sort of families that once supplied the army with its leaders and best fighters. But by the time she received her call-up papers the star of the kibbutz children was already waning, their place usurped by the sons and daughters of the more fanatical national-religious communities, many of them settlers in the occupied territories. 'As a teenager,' she told me, 'I remember our teachers asking us: "What's going on? Why aren't we producing the outstanding soldiers any more?" There was a real sense of crisis. It was as though we weren't fulfilling our duty to take care of the country.'

Irit had doubts about serving in the territories from the outset, but given her upbringing and the sense of national responsibility she was raised with, she never questioned that she would put on the uniform of the Israeli army and serve in one of its elite units. Almost immediately, however, she found herself being sent to the West Bank. 'I have an uncle who was very senior in the army and could pull strings. He helped me to get out of the West Bank, but that didn't really solve the problem. I was still uncomfortable serving the occupation. I found myself facing a crisis: either I could refuse to serve and go to jail, or I could put off the problem a little longer by opting for the officers' course. I chose the officers' course. When I finished it, I got my new posting: I was being sent back to the West Bank. I cried for about forty-eight hours, and then packed my things and went. I was an officer, and could no longer get out of my responsibilities.'

Irit was sent to Jenin, where she spent fourteen months as an operations officer, responsible for planning the military missions inside the town and its neighbouring refugee camp. As she recalled those days, her voice faded to barely a whisper. She alluded to the terrible things she had seen, without often managing to bring herself to describe them in words. 'For the first four months I tried to escape the reality by planning all kinds of things in my mind, like destroying the whole of the [Jenin] camp. I was suffering terribly. I couldn't sleep from what I was seeing and what I was doing. It wasn't even as though I was out on the battlefield. I was in the war room. But I saw enough . . .'

She was given a month's leave to visit her mother who lived in Ireland, and she seriously considered never returning to Israel. But then, she says, she decided to go back and try her best to be a good officer and to be as humane as possible. 'It was an important stage in my life: no one can come to me and say, "You don't know what is going on there." That is a common put-down from men in Israel. "You have never been there, so you can't speak." That is how they try to silence you. Nobody can tell me that I don't know what is going on there. I know very, very well.'

Irit says she saw outrages committed by both sides. 'There was a Palestinian woman with a broken bottle in her stomach because she was believed to have collaborated with the Israeli army. I saw the Palestinians' poverty, and I saw the Israeli soldiers destroying houses, taking women and children out of their homes and onto the streets so that they could bomb their homes ... After fourteen months I felt like I had lost all my skin, that there was no skin around me any more.'

By the time Irit left the army, she said, she felt as if she needed twenty years to recover. That was twelve years ago, and it was clear that she had not entirely laid to rest the ghosts of those brief years in the army. Her military service had left her, she said, with a question she had been trying to answer ever since: what are the moral principles that should guide the relationships between individuals? Perhaps unsurprisingly, she has ended up in education, and is now teaching citizenship classes in the kibbutz's high school. One of five Waldorf schools in Israel, Harduf is driven by a philosophy that children's learning abilities can best be developed by encouraging their natural talents to feel, create and think for themselves. The school is full of art and craftwork, which is how the children first explore the world around them, and only later and slowly do they come to think about the meaning of things and to make judgements.

'We try to be as free as possible, free from government interference and from economic constraints,' says Irit. 'We decided to let the state fund us because otherwise only the rich could afford to send their children – which is the case with Waldorf schools in most other countries. Nonetheless, the parents have to contribute something because the government never gives us enough. There is a constant fight for more money and more freedom. The freedom bit is key: in other Israeli schools, teachers can't really teach what they want to. Sometimes it's because the Ministry of Education interferes, and sometimes it's just because teachers don't realise that they are allowed to teach a much wider range of things. Too many are given the textbooks and simply assume they must teach what is written in them.'

Israel's citizenship curriculum, which is taught only to older children, those in the last years before their matriculation exams and their military service, is less dishonest than other subjects such as history, she says. 'In history it's pretty easy to manipulate the facts, but in citizenship classes it's a little harder. The citizenship textbook we use is the same in both Arab and Jewish schools, which is very unusual. Equality is at the core of the concept of citizenship, so it has to be the same book. When they wrote the curriculum, the officials knew both Jews and Arabs would be using it, so it's a little bit more balanced than normal, but still ... it's a Jewish country. That's even the title of the textbook: *Being a Citizen in Israel: A Jewish Democratic Country*.

'I have to teach what is in the book, and they need that to pass their bagrut [matriculation] exam. However, most Israeli teachers understand that there is a contradiction at the heart of what we teach: something is clearly not right with the concept of a state that is both Jewish and democratic. But that is the basis of the whole subject; it's the theme of the whole course of study. I know most other teachers don't ask questions in class about how it can be both a Jewish and a democratic country. OK, they will admit to the children that there are differences of opinion: some Israelis, for example, think we should live in a religious state, and others think the settlers should leave the occupied territories. It's widely agreed that the Jewish holidays should be the formal holidays. You can tell lots of nice stories about these things. But as to it being a Jewish and a democratic country – that can't be questioned.'

In her classes Irit tries to expand the subject beyond the strict bounds of the curriculum, encompassing topics rarely touched on in Israeli schools, either Jewish or Arab. She takes her students on a journey through Israeli society, beginning with the Ashkenazis, the WASPs of Israel, the white, mainly European pioneers like her own family who founded the state. Socialists and nationalists, they built the country and still hold most of the key positions in the army, academia, the media, the judiciary, business and politics. Then she discusses the rise of the national-religious, the first group in Israel to challenge the pre-eminence of the secular Ashkenazis. Drawing their strength from a literalist reading of the scriptures, their moment arrived with the capture of the Palestinian territories in 1967 and the vision of a Greater Israel. Ever since, they have been working to take the West Bank and Gaza from the Palestinians through an inexorable process of settlement building, backed by government funds.

Next, she examines the difficulties posed by the swelling ranks of the Mizrahim, the Jews who were encouraged or forced to leave neighbouring Arab countries and move to Israel after the establishment of the Jewish state. Their arrival posed a difficult question for the state's Ashkenazi founders: was Israel to try to remain a cohesive society of one colour, or to open itself to becoming a more fractured but pluralistic society? The same tensions have been exacerbated by the arrival of other, later, Jewish immigrant groups, such as the Russians and the Ethiopians.

Irit also discusses the failure to integrate into Israeli society the Haredim, the ultra-Orthodox Jews who place their allegiance to God well before their loyalty to a Jewish state and its secular laws. In fact, Israeli leaders have done their best to avoid confronting the contradictory impulses of the secular and religious communities inside the state. They even abandoned the attempt at drafting a constitution, as promised in the Declaration of Independence of May 1948, after recognising that it would break the fragile

Jewish consensus holding together the new state. Instead Israel has failed to incorporate important legislation on human rights that would upset the ultra-Orthodox and has given wide-ranging jurisdiction to Orthodox rabbis to determine personal status issues governing births, marriages and deaths, and to decide who is a Jew. Secular and religious laws therefore exist in uncomfortable parallel.

The hardest part of the course comes when Irit's lessons cut through the country's founding myths to discuss its real history, and the situation of the Arab minority. 'I teach them about the country before 1948, and about the war in 1948. I tell them: "Most of the people here used to be Arabs, do you know that?" I tell them the numbers and I show them the maps. They can see that before 1948 there were hundreds of villages that are no longer here, and that after 1949 the maps show fifty or sixty Jewish villages in the same place. There is no mention of the Arab villages having ever existed. They can see it with their own eyes for the first time. For many of them it's like jumping into deep, deep water, and they are very afraid. They go home, they sleep and they come back the next day and say, "Was it the same in the Holocaust? Did we suffer the same in the Holocaust?"

'As a teacher I find these thoughts troubling. There is no need to equate the Holocaust with the Nakba, but that doesn't make what happened in 1948 all right. The Holocaust was bad enough, and what the Arabs suffered was bad enough. To lose your village and lose your land is bad enough. It creates an ideal atmosphere for breeding hate and violence and war. And the combination between their hate and fear and our hate and fear is lethal. To heal this problem we have to notice and understand the Other, and to stop thinking about our own suffering all the time. My grandmother's family died in Auschwitz, but if you are stuck in your suffering all the time you can do nothing positive with it. Better to look into the mirror and tell yourself: "I am afraid of them, I am afraid of losing

my country and my land. I am afraid they are going to kill me."
Even inside me I know there is a layer of this fear which warns me
that one day there will not be a Jewish majority here, and maybe
there won't be democracy either. There is a fear, and it's all right to
admit that I'm afraid, because then I can do something with that
fear. I can educate other people, I can meet and share my fears with
other people. To ignore it and say it is not there is a lie. But if I can
work with it, at least there is hope.'

If Irit still struggles with her own fears after years of confronting
them, her students find it far harder. 'During these classes I see fear,
resistance, shock. And great shame. They tell me they don't want to
belong to this society. They say, "It's not mine. I'll go to India, or
live in Europe." I feel the same sometimes. My husband and I start
asking ourselves why we don't move to Switzerland, where my sister
lives and where it's green and quiet. Or New Zealand.'

Compared to Irit, who is quietly trying to change the way young
Jews passing through her school view their citizenship, Daphna
Golan has enjoyed a much higher profile and more notoriety. A
law lecturer at Hebrew University in Jerusalem, where she teaches
human rights, she is also one of the founders of Btselem, possibly
Israel's most famous human rights organisation. Btselem has been
working tirelessly since the first intifada to document abuses by
Israelis in the occupied territories and to educate the Jewish public
and the international community about the human rights violations
that are common there. Its reports regularly embarrass the Israeli
government and the army. Daphna is also a former director of
Bat Shalom, an Israeli women's peace group opposed to both the
occupation and to the militarisation of Israeli society.

Daphna and I have become good friends through another aspect
of her work. Like me, she is heavily involved in Mahapach, helping
advance social rights and create local leadership in deprived communities, Jewish and Arab. Both of us are committed to a greater
role for civil society inside Israel, and to trying to strengthen it

against the encroachment of the militarism we see all around us. I admire Daphna for her determination to fight on all fronts against prejudice, racism and discrimination.

At her home in West Jerusalem she told me that it had only dawned on her slowly that much of what she had been told since her childhood about Israel and its history was untrue. 'All through my life I had heard things on the radio or been taught things at school that seemed hard to believe. But the turning point came for me during the war in Lebanon,' she said.

Israel's invasion of Lebanon in 1982 was a turning point for many Israelis. Until the early 1970s only about a hundred Jews had resisted the national draft. Although the numbers crept up after the occupation of the West Bank and Gaza in 1967, refusal remained a minor phenomenon. But the invasion of Lebanon severely tested the patriotism of Jews raised on the doctrine of Israel's 'purity of arms'. Personally directed by Ariel Sharon, the march into Lebanon included an attempt to install a puppet regime in Beirut that would be sympathetic to Israel, the horrors of Sabra and Chatilla, two Palestinian refugee camps where many of the inhabitants were butchered by Lebanese Christian militias under the watch of the Israeli army, and eighteen years of Israeli occupation of south Lebanon. The death toll from the invasion is estimated at nearly sixteen thousand Arab dead, most of them civilians, and 650 Israeli soldiers.

For the first time the principle of limited refusal gained legitimacy among sections of the Jewish public. A senior brigade commander, Colonel Eli Geva, refused to lead his troops into Beirut and later resigned his post in protest. A letter signed by eighty-six reservists, including fifteen officers, stated their opposition to the war and requested military service only within Israel. And a new refusers' organisation, Yesh Gvul (There is a Limit), argued that a border must exist beyond which Israeli soldiers should not serve. By June 1983 some 1,700 soldiers had joined. Fifteen months after the invasion, in September 1983, a total of eighty-six Israelis had been jailed for refusing to serve. Probably there were many more who were dealt with quietly by the army to avoid publicity.

Daphna recalls a formative moment in her own decision to oppose the invasion. 'It was a rainy winter's day, and I heard the radio presenter announce that our planes had bombed south Lebanon and returned home safely. It was a line I had heard hundreds of times before, but that day – maybe because of the rain and the cold – it sounded like too much of a lie. I thought, "What do they mean, the planes 'bombed'?" All sorts of questions flooded into my mind. Where did those bombs fall, whose homes did they destroy, where are those families now, how are they coping without a home on this cold and wet night? I had images of Lebanese families standing amid the rubble of their bombed homes, and I asked myself, "Why are we never told what happens to the people we bomb?" Afterwards I became very active in Yesh Gvul, which defined a border that soldiers should not cross.

'Another moment came with the birth of my daughter. I thought, "What am I going to tell her when she grows up? That I did nothing?"' The geographical proximity of Palestinians to Israel also made their plight difficult to ignore. 'I think there is no way we can say we are a democracy without taking account of what happens to the Palestinians. That feeling is even more pressing when you live in Jerusalem, which is so close and yet so far from the Palestinians. During the first intifada we could hear the helicopters and the bombing going on, so it was very difficult not to get involved.'

Today, however, with the system of checkpoints and the erection of the wall, Daphna fears that it is harder for Israelis to connect with and to understand what is happening in their name in the occupied territories. 'I want my students to see what is going on, but the university won't let me take them into occupied territory. In fact it is now usually illegal for Israelis to enter the West Bank or Gaza except as settlers or soldiers. But I do take them to the checkpoints between Israel and the West Bank, particularly those in East Jerusalem.'

She says few parents know what their soldier children are up to in the occupied territories. 'I talked with some of the mothers of the soldiers who organised the "Breaking the Silence" exhibition, and they all said they had no idea that their sons were behaving that way. "We were sure that our boys were not like that," they said. But I thought, no way. The moment you send them there, that is what is going to happen. Some soldiers behave worse than others, but you are forcing them into an impossible situation, one they will never be able to cope with.'

Daphna fears that the minds of both Israelis and Jews in the Diaspora are profoundly closed to the idea of acknowledging Palestinian suffering. 'We are a people who, because of our history, have attached so much importance to memory and the act of remembering, and yet we refuse to allow another people, the Palestinians, their own memory and their own feelings about the past.' She gives an example of that kind of psychological and emotional blockage: 'We had a visit from a delegation of the Canadian Friends of Hebrew University, and several of my law students spoke to them. All my students are working for human rights organisations, and the stories they were telling truly confused the Canadian visitors. One student, a Palestinian who works with Rabbis for Human Rights, explained that she was involved in interviewing families whose homes had been demolished in East Jerusalem. The delegates came up to me afterwards, saying, "What does she mean? Israel isn't demolishing houses in Jerusalem." I tried to explain that masterplans were never approved for East Jerusalem, so the Palestinian inhabitants could not get building permits. They had no choice but to build illegally, and the authorities responded by demolishing their homes. The Canadians were shocked, but not in a positive way. My impression was that they still went away with closed minds. It was information they were not ready to hear. One said, "Do you teach them about human rights in Arab countries?" Another said, "How can you teach them about rights when we are facing suicide bombers?" They could not begin to see that the Israeli army was terrorising Palestinians.'

There are glimmers of hope, however. 'There has been some progress. For fifteen years I have been saying the same things about the occupation, but it sounds much more legitimate now than it did then. When we tried to talk about the occupied territories in the late 1980s, people would deny that the West Bank and Gaza were even occupied. They would get really abusive. I think a big change has come about because the information is so much more accessible now. In many ways, the big issue inside Israel has shifted away from questions about the occupation to questions about the nature of Israel as a Jewish state. Nowadays that is a much more contentious issue than the idea of a Palestinian state. The majority of Israelis understand that the occupation cannot go on. But if a Palestinian state is created, it will throw the question back to us about what kind of country we want Israel to be: should it be a Jewish state, or a state of all its citizens? That is a debate most Israelis are not ready to have, because it would signal the beginning of the end of Israel being a Jewish state, and it would open the door to the Palestinian refugees' right to return. It is a given for 99 per cent of Israeli Jews that the country must be a Jewish state. To an outsider it probably sounds bizarre to object to the idea of a state of all its citizens. But I teach at a law school, and everyone there thinks I'm nuts even to consider the idea. You'd think that university students and lecturers would be all in favour of a state of all its citizens, but my guess is I'm alone in supporting it.'

Daphna believes we will see the establishment of a Palestinian state in the coming years, and that we must wait till that day before beginning a discussion about the status of Israel's Palestinian citizens. 'Most Jews realise that there should be some kind of political negotiation of a Palestinian state – not by this government, but maybe by the next one. Eventually there will be a Palestinian state, and then the real discussion will start about what happens here in Israel. We can't begin discussing our future as citizens here unless there is a solution in the occupied territories. Once there is a serious negotiation about two states, then the position of the Arabs in Israel will have to be raised. This internal discussion can only be seriously confronted when there is a Palestinian state. Until then the Arabs will always be seen as the enemy. That is the only way I can understand the racism towards Arabs. Why do we have it? Because in the imagination of Jews, Tamra, Jenin, Nazareth, Ramallah – they are all enemy territory.'

I was not convinced by the final part of Daphna's argument. Why was she so sure that Israel would be ready to make the sacrifices necessary to create a Palestinian state in the occupied territories, when it could not bring itself to do something that should have been far easier: recognising the rights of its Arab minority and the equality of their citizenship? My feeling is that all the elements of the equation will have to be dealt with together: a just solution for the Palestinians in the occupied territories will require a similar just settlement for Palestinians who are citizens of Israel and the Palestinians living in exile as refugees. The reason Israel appears so reluctant to create a viable Palestinian state is precisely because it will open up the question of what constitutes justice for these other two long-overlooked groups. It will reopen the debate about what really happened in 1948, a history that has long been overshadowed by what has happened following Israel's conquest of the West Bank and Gaza in 1967. It will bring the war crimes of 1948 back into the spotlight, and that is what really frightens ordinary Israelis.

Irit and Daphna are trying to effect change by educating Jews about the issues of citizenship and human rights. But however important these issues are, they are not in themselves enough. Israelis also have to face the tough moral questions raised by the way Israel was founded in 1948, the wholesale destruction of hundreds of Palestinian villages and the expulsion of 750,000 Palestinians from their homes. They have to be reconciled to their past, and be prepared to apologise for it. Only once they have recognised the historic injustices done to the Palestinian people as a whole in 1948 can they begin to make amends today.

I was under the impression that no organised attempt was being made to address such difficult questions inside Israel until friends of mine in Tamra told me about Eitan Bronstein, the founder of a small pioneering organisation called Zochrot (Remembering). Later I heard that he was one of the organisers of a right of return conference in Haifa which I was due to attend in the spring of 2004. At the conference I sought him out, only to discover that he had been trying to meet me too. He had read about me in *Ha'aretz*, and was pleased to see we held the same views about the need to educate Jews about the Nakba.

His participation in the conference, which addressed the rights of some five million Palestinian refugees to return to Israel, revealed everything about the bravery of this man. The right of return is the ultimate taboo for Israelis, because it threatens to end the demographic superiority of Jews inside Israel, and thus the state's pretensions to being both Jewish and democratic. Simply put, the existence of a Law of Return, which encourages Jewish migration to Israel, and the ban on a right of return, which would enable Palestinian refugees to reclaim the homes stolen from them in 1948, constitute together a sophisticated way in which to skew the numbers inside the state to ensure Jewish dominance. Israel is a democracy-made-to-measure: the majority will decide, but only after we have first made sure that Jews are the majority. The conference was the first time a major debate on the right of Palestinian return had ever been held inside Israel. Zochrot's participation, alongside several Arab groups, was the key to ensuring the event took place.

Zochrot, which counts a few hundred Israeli Jews among its membership, was founded in 2002 and has since been developing a programme to educate Jews that the war they celebrate as their

Independence is also the Palestinians' Nakba. A website database called 'Remembering the Nakba in Hebrew' offers historical information about what took place in 1948, including maps showing the destroyed villages and personal accounts from those who lost their homes. Zochrot stages study days on the Nakba and the plight of the refugees. But most importantly it arranges tours of the villages that were destroyed, including regular ceremonies at which a signpost in both Hebrew and Arabic is erected at the site, giving the village's name and basic details about its inhabitants. Such signposts provoke extremely hostile reactions from any Jews who see them. Eitan says they rarely survive more than a few minutes or hours before being torn down.

I have huge admiration for Eitan and his brave stance in the face of so much hostility. The extent to which he is brushing against the grain of his society was revealed in the summer of 2004 when a commentary piece in *Maariv*, the second-biggest Hebrew mass-circulation newspaper in Israel, denounced him and his organisation in libellous terms under the headline 'Hamas Among Us'. The paper equated Zochrot's objectives with what it described as the goal of the Islamic fundamentalist group Hamas to drive the Jews into the sea.

Sitting in a café in Kafr Shemaryahu, outside Herziliya, Eitan told me that the transition from being a loyal Israeli to a dissenter had not been easy. 'I was raised on a kibbutz near Tulkaram to be both a good citizen and a good soldier. In those days there existed between the various kibbutzim a sort of competition for which would produce more combat soldiers and pilots, and which would have more soldiers in the elite units. I joined an artillery unit in November 1979 and finished my service in November 1982. I think it would be true to say that by the yardsticks of my society I was an excellent soldier.'

But Eitan reached a moment of personal crisis when the government decided to invade Lebanon five months before his military service finished. 'From the very start I was against it. All of us in the army knew that the real plan was to reach Beirut, despite the lies [Prime Minister Menachem] Begin told about us not going within forty kilometres of the city. The others in my unit were very excited about going, but I was at the end of my three years and I did not want to get involved. At the outbreak of the war I was away on a course for tank commanders. On Saturday night our commanders started calling each of us by phone to order us to return to base. I was at home on the kibbutz, and managed to avoid the calls. So the next day, on Sunday, I went to the place where the course was being held, to find it completely empty. I had no choice but to go back to the base, south of Beersheva. When I arrived, my friends were very angry. "Where have you been?" they said. I played dumb, as though I didn't know what was going on. It was before the arrival of cellular phones.

'In fact we weren't called up to the fighting, which disappointed everyone else. However, by October, when the main battles were over, we were sent to Lebanon for one week. I had never disobeyed an order in my life, so I went for the week. A month later I was released from the army, but I had only postponed the problem. I knew that within six months I would get my reserve call-up. I talked to other reservists on my kibbutz, but while they didn't support the war, there was no way they were going to question an order. By then Yesh Gvul had started, and I decided to join them and refuse to report for duty. I was jailed for one month. It was a moment of profound personal crisis: I had crossed the red line from being a good citizen-soldier to a refuser. Later, when the first intifada came, I already knew that I was going to refuse to go. I was jailed twice. But by then it had become something routine and was not a dilemma.'

Eitan began a new career, at the margins of Israeli society. For the past ten years he has worked as a teacher at the School for Peace at Neve Shalom/Wahat al-Salam, a unique community north of Jerusalem where Jews and Arabs live in a cooperative environment on an equal footing. Built on private land that belongs to the Catholic Church, the village is, according to its website, regarded by the state as a threat to the status quo: 'The government tolerates the existence of the village and gives the minimum of support required by its municipal status'. As a director of the school's youth programme, Eitan has facilitated hundreds of encounters between Jews and Palestinians.

'What I found out was that a huge gulf of understanding about the past, about 1948, existed between the two peoples. If you compare their respective positions concerning the 1967 occupation of the West Bank and Gaza you won't find this gap. Even Jews who are in favour of the occupation understand that the Palestinians don't like it, that it harms them in some way. And many Israelis oppose the occupation and want to find a way to end it. Even [Prime Minister Ariel] Sharon says the occupation is not OK. So there is some sort of consensus on this issue. But I started to understand that 1948 was the key period rather than 1967, and that it was determining relations between the two peoples in this land.

'I also realised that there was a huge gap in terms of the understanding of the two sides about what had happened. One side, the Palestinians, was completely defeated, exiled and dispossessed – and that is how they see it. The other side, the Jews, won an incredible victory, but they don't therefore concede that the other side were the losers. Instead they say things like, "It was the Palestinians' fault that they chose to fight us," or "We didn't start anything," or "We just wanted to be free and have a state." When they do admit that their victory came at the expense of the Palestinians, such as in the case of terrible massacres like the one at Deir Yassin, a village where more than a hundred Palestinian civilians were butchered by Jewish militias, these are seen as exceptional incidents. "That was carried out by a few bad apples," or "That stuff happens in any war," they say.

'So there is this huge gap in the understanding of both sides about what took place. To be honest, neither side has much idea about what really did happen. Even the Palestinians mostly rely on their own families' personal experiences of 1948 for their understanding of these events, largely because they are not taught about them in school. They don't have a wider view of what happened. It seemed that it was an important task to deal with this lack of understanding on both sides; that until we deal with it there is no chance of a reconciliation.'

The personal turning point came for Eitan while he was taking groups of Jews on an 'alternative tour' around an area close to Neve Shalom called Canada Park, an Israeli tourist attraction just inside the occupied territories. It has been built over three Palestinian villages destroyed after 1967: Yalu, Imwas and Beit Nuba. Before the development of my own understanding of Israeli history I, like thousands of other Jews, had enjoyed hiking through Canada Park, enjoying its forests and views.

'Canada Park was established in the 1970s by the Jewish National Fund using $15 million in tax deductible donations from all over Canada,' Eitan told me. 'The JNF created a very beautiful and different sort of park. There are many parks in Israel built over destroyed villages. South Africa Park is built over the village of Lubia in the Galilee, for example. There you have wooden tables and a space to have a barbecue at the weekends or on holidays. But Canada Park is more like a museum or an educational space. The money has been invested in recreating the traditional ways of agriculture. Through a series of signs and notices visitors learn about the old methods of farming and about the area's Jewish, Roman, Byzantine and Ottoman history. All its history is there, apart from any reference to its Palestinian history. Despite the destruction of the Palestinian houses, two of the cemeteries remain, as do the water wells, but there is no information about who built them. It's as though the Palestinian heritage has been made not to exist. It is invisible.

'I was working for the School of Peace guiding tour groups, mostly

Jews, through the park and giving them a critical appreciation of the landscape the JNF refuses to tell them about. I would show them the destroyed villages and explain that I thought they revealed something about the poor state of relations between the two peoples. These were intelligent and curious people, but what I said was entirely new to them. They would be shocked, and would say, "All my childhood I came here, but I never knew that there were three villages with five thousand people here." I would show them pictures of the villages, including photos of the destruction and expulsion as it took place. By accident there was a kibbutz photographer working in the area during the 1967 war, and he captured it all on film. After one of the tours I said to myself, "Although it's important to tell these groups about the villages, we can do more. We can post signs indicating where to find Imwas cemetery and Yalu mosque. And if they are removed, we can post them again." Other people I told liked the idea.'

Zochrot performed the first signposting in March 2002, at the remote site of the destroyed village of Miska near Kafr Sava on behalf of the Shbeta family, refugees now living some distance away in the Israeli Arab town of Tira. The sign was promptly removed, probably by the inhabitants of a kibbutz which now sits on Miska's land. Then in 2003 Zochrot and Neve Shalom commemorated thirty-six years of the occupation in Canada Park. About two thousand people attended, including ten refugees from the original three villages. Zochrot posted a big sign, one side in Hebrew and the other in Arabic, at the centre of what was once Yalu village, saying 'Welcome to the village centre' and giving details about the size of the village, how many mosques and schools it had, the number of people who lived there and where they were now.

'Afterwards we posted two signs at Yalu and Imwas cemeteries, and intentionally I left some Zochrot brochures lying near the signs which included my telephone number. After two days I got a call from someone called Mr Cohen, the maintenance manager of

Canada Park. He asked why we had posted the signs. I said so that people would know what had been there. He replied, "But it's not legal." I laughed and said there were hundreds of thousands of illegal signs all over the country, and no one cared. "Yes," he said, "but your signs are political." So I retorted: "Are your signs which tell the Jewish and Roman history of the site but exclude its Palestinian history not also political?" "Ah," he said decisively, "but they are legal."

'Mr Cohen said he would remove our signs, but that we could write to the JNF to ask for permission to post new ones. So that's what we did. We wrote a letter to the JNF, and after a month I got a one-line letter from the head of the organisation: "The JNF does not deal with political issues so please address the relevant body." Our lawyer found out that because the park is in the occupied territories we had to write to the military authorities in Beit El, to the Higher Planning Commission. So we wrote asking to post the signs. Under the law anyone can post a sign with permission, but they have to promise to maintain it and pay the relevant taxes and so on. We told them we were ready to do all that. We sent several letters over a six-month period, but they never replied. Eventually we threatened action, which frightened them a little as they understood that to mean we would go to the Supreme Court. By law they have to tell us something, so they sent a letter apologising and saying they were working on a reply. But their lawyer admitted to ours that his commanders could not decide what answer to give us. They knew that they would be setting some sort of legal precedent. If they allowed us to post a sign in the park, we could start doing it everywhere. So far we have still not heard anything, so we are challenging them in the Supreme Court.

'It was a strategic decision to start posting the signs before we had permission. We could be held up writing letters to the authorities for years before we got any response. Our strategy is to post signs and start a debate. For us it doesn't matter that people remove the signs.

If they tear them down it means we are touching something in them. Maybe it would be worse if they just left them there and ignored them. These signs are not provocative in any obvious way. They simply state that people once lived here; they don't say those people were expelled or terrorised, just that there was once a village there. In one place, Ijlil, where Cinema City now stands, a great mall of cinema complexes near Herzliya, we brought a Palestinian family who once lived there and posted a large sign on a raised hillock overlooking the car park. If you parked there you could see the sign telling you that an Arab village once existed there. It stood for three weeks before someone removed it. They had to scramble through a wire fence and up over rubble to reach it.'

Eitan says he sees his responsibility as educating Jews, not Arabs, who must deal with their own history. 'We are not a co-existence group: we are dealing only with raising Jewish consciousness. Teachers often come to our meetings, and I hear them saying: "We teach the children lies for the bagrut [matriculation], and we know they are lies." It's remarkable to me that these teachers know they are teaching lies. That is positive in a way. We want to start taking a special Nakba curriculum package to schools.'

Although Zochrot is a young organisation, its message is already striking a chord. 'At our first events we had to call our friends and persuade them to come. Maybe there were twenty people there. Now I don't call anyone. We have an evening and people come of their own accord. Always there are new faces. And if they keep coming, something will change in them: if you keep hearing the other side's story, you have to think and feel differently. I think if Israelis said tomorrow that they had a large responsibility for the Nakba and they apologised for it, 90 per cent of the problem would be solved. When you acknowledge your responsibility in front of a Palestinian, something in the air changes – I've seen it. The relations between the people change. From my point of view I think I can do things to change my society from within, to prepare it for the future. If the change comes tomorrow, if there are suddenly different international circumstances, it's important that organisations like Zochrot have prepared people for the shock, that the change doesn't come out of nowhere.'

Most of Zochrot's members, Eitan says, are not drawn from the traditional left-wing. 'Some of us come from very mainstream families and backgrounds. One of my colleagues is the son of a general who is head of the army's Central Command and a close friend of [former Prime Minister Ehud] Barak. Another is the daughter of a combat pilot, and she was raised in pilots' bases and married to a pilot.

'We deal with the Nakba, the memory of the other side, and our responsibility for what happened. We are not a political movement in the narrow sense: we don't prescribe a particular course of action or a solution to the conflict. Our initiative is something much wider. If, for example, there were ever to be an agreement on a one-state solution and the right of Palestinian return, Zochrot's purpose would not come to an end. We are dealing with the suffering of the other side, and we are trying to understand our responsibility for that suffering – that is a role that will continue to be needed for a very long time. There has been change in South Africa, but the reconciliation between the black and white populations and their acknowledgement of the past is a process, a process that is eternal.'

Eitan understands how difficult it is for Israeli Jews to alter their understanding of the past, because it is something he had to face up to himself. 'I was raised on Kibbutz Bahan, near Tulkaram. Close by the kibbutz was a place called Qaqun I was always visiting as a child. It was a barren hill, and one of the places most dear to me as a boy. I and my friends would ride our bikes there, and later we would drive the kibbutz's tractor to it. On the top of the hill were still standing the remains of several big buildings which we had always been told were part of a Crusader fortress. This is what I knew all through my childhood and my adult life. Then, about four years ago, when I started my personal adventure of looking for other histories, I was surfing the internet looking for sites on the Nakba. I found a website which listed among the destroyed villages in the Tulkaram district a place called Qaqun. I was shocked, and to be honest I was even a little offended. I thought, "What does it have to do with you? This is my childhood, why are you putting it on your website?" I clicked the mouse on the link to Qaqun, and I was amazed to find that there had been a village of two thousand people living there. It was really a great shock.

'But this click on the mouse is what Zochrot is all about. This process of clicking and opening our minds to another history. I feel like a child moving inside the space of the Israel I think I know, and discovering that there is also another landscape I have never seen before. For me Zochrot is like reliving my childhood.'

7

Where Next?

The walled Old City of Jerusalem was conquered, along with the rest of East Jerusalem and the West Bank and Gaza, by Israeli soldiers in the 1967 war. For Jews around the world it was Israel's most glorious moment since its founding two decades earlier. What excited them was the thought that for the first time in two thousand years the heart of Jerusalem had been brought back under Jewish control: Israel was now master of the Old City and its prized Jewish religious sites, including the Temple Mount, a raised section of land where the Second Temple, built by Herod, once stood. The temple had been destroyed in AD70, but ever since small numbers of devoted Jews had been coming to the Old City to pray at the only remaining part of it, a retaining wall known as the Western Wall, or the Wailing Wall, which it is believed was constructed using stones from the First Temple, built by Solomon.

Since the seventh century, when Jerusalem fell under Muslim rule, an accommodation between Jews, Muslims and Christians was maintained in the Old City: each of the three religions lived in their own quarters, close to their holiest sites. The Jewish district was near the Western Wall, the only place at the destroyed temple site where the rabbinical authorities allow Jews to pray; the Christian quarter encircled the Church of the Holy Sepulchre, built over the site where Jesus is believed to have been crucified and resurrec-ted; and the Muslim quarter, the largest, was a jumble of crowded buildings around the eastern and southern sides of the Temple Mount, which for centuries has belonged to Islam and is known to Muslims as the Noble Sanctuary (the Haram al-Sharif). This compound includes the Aqsa and Dome of the Rock mosques, the latter a building whose golden dome is the centrepiece of most pictures taken of the Old City. The Dome of the Rock is built on the spot where Muslims believe the Prophet Mohammed ascended to heaven on a winged animal.

However, the centuries-long status quo started to break down during the British Mandate as the local Arab population grew increasingly unhappy at what they rightly saw as British attempts to transfer a large part of their homeland to the Zionist immigrants, Jews who had arrived in Palestine not because of their devotion to Judaism but because of their commitment to creating a secular Jewish state there. Jerusalem was at the very centre of these clashes. For the Palestinians it was the traditional confessional, commercial and geographic hub of their lives, with a profound religious significance to the wider Arab and Muslim worlds; for the Zionists, the city and its possession represented a chance to underpin the foundations of their new state with a powerful symbol that united both religious and secular groups.

The war of 1948, however, had an inconclusive outcome from the point of view of the Zionists. Jerusalem was divided rather than falling under Israeli sovereignty: the western half was captured by Israel, and its Palestinian inhabitants were mostly expelled, while the eastern half, including the Old City, was occupied by Jordan, and the small Jewish community forced out. Only in the 1967 war did Israel manage to occupy East Jerusalem and so begin to realise its dream of 'unifying' the city. It annexed the Palestinian half of Jerusalem to the Jewish state, in violation of international law, and began consolidating its hold by building a ring of Jewish settlements around the eastern neighbourhoods. Jerusalem's municipal boundaries were expanded to include these settlers to bolster Israeli claims that the city truly had been unified as the capital of the Jewish state.

But while Israel waged a demographic battle for political control of the whole of Jerusalem, it also wanted to stake a claim to the city's main Jewish holy site, the Temple Mount, which was located deep in the Muslim quarter of the Old City. It had to proceed more carefully here, as it feared provoking international opposition to its plans, as well as worldwide Muslim anger. Nonetheless, it had soon demolished dozens of Palestinian homes near the Western Wall and evicted their owners in order to build an impressively large plaza that hosts the many visitors to the wall.

The waqf, the Islamic religious trust that is the guardian of the Noble Sanctuary mosques, was left in charge of the compound, but Israel made repeated symbolic attempts to encroach on the site. The most notable were Binyamin Netanyahu's decision to build a tunnel under the compound of mosques in the late 1990s, and Ariel Sharon's now notorious visit to the Temple Mount in September 2000 to assert Jewish sovereignty there, igniting Palestinian rage. The next day a violent crackdown by Israeli police against the protests, which left several Palestinian youths dead, triggered the second intifada.

Israel's symbolic assaults on Islamic sovereignty over the Noble Sanctuary have been overshadowed by an uglier, creeping physical annexation of the Muslim quarter around the holy site. Messianic Jews have replicated the tactics of fanatical settlers in the West Bank and Gaza by occupying Palestinian homes around the Noble Sanctuary. According to their leaders, they hope soon to be in a position to blow up the mosques and build the Third Temple, heralding the coming of the Messiah. They have derived some of their inspiration from Ariel Sharon, who on 15 December 1987 provocatively bought a house in the Muslim quarter of the Old City. He was quickly followed by dozens of young religious extremists. Today, Sharon's house – although he has never lived there – stands incongruously in the midst of Palestinian homes, with an elongated Israeli flag draped from an upper window.

This illegal physical annexation of the Muslim quarter by Jewish extremists has been continuing for nearly twenty years, and its extent was revealed to me in striking fashion one day as I wandered the normally busy streets of the Old City. Most visitors probably pass through the Muslim quarter without noticing what is happening, but if you look closely the signs are there for all to see. For example, at a junction between three narrow alleyways close to the Noble Sanctuary I found half a dozen armed Israeli soldiers standing below protective wire mesh fixed across the width of the alleyway. The mesh was littered with objects, from lumps of concrete to bottles and rubbish.

From my conversations with Bar, the young soldier I had befriended, I had an idea of why the protection was needed. In the centre of Hebron the extremist religious settlers had taken over the upper apartments of buildings in the city centre and been terrorising the local Palestinian traders by hurling objects at them. The army had erected the same type of mesh as in Jerusalem to protect the Palestinian stallholders below. However, the settlers had simply switched tactics, pouring boiling oil on the shop owners instead. Even before the intifada, when a supposed peace reigned under the Oslo accords, large sections of Hebron's market had been closed by the army, supposedly to safeguard the Palestinians. No one had suggested that the Jewish settlers perpetrating these vicious attacks be arrested or removed.

As I ventured down one of the Old City's narrow alleys close to the Noble Sanctuary I saw stall owners hurriedly closing up their shops. One of them told me that a party of Jewish extremists was visiting the area, and he thought it better to shut down. Near the entrance to the compound of mosques, I found the group. They were waiting at a barrier guarded by well-armed Israeli policemen; behind the barrier, yet more Palestinian stallholders selling trinkets were packing up. It was clear that the Jewish group was entirely comprised of the religious-nationalist camp of the settlers: the men wore knitted skullcaps, while the women were dressed in long skirts and had their heads covered. Most were trailing young children and pushing prams; many of the settlers view their mission to displace the Palestinians largely in terms of a battle of numbers, so they have huge families, the women seeing themselves as little more than Zionist incubators.

I spoke to one of the policemen, who told me the group were holidaymakers who had come to visit the house of a long-dead rabbi overlooking the Temple Mount. Anyone was welcome to join them, he said. So I followed the group inside, into the long covered alley that leads Muslim worshippers to the gate by which they reach the compound of mosques. A little before that entrance we turned left into a side alley and up a twisting flight of stone steps. Near the top we entered a narrow stone passageway where I was hit by the nauseating smell of urine and faeces. Around me was rubbish and decaying food. No one else in the group seemed to notice.

The true shock came, however, as we stepped out of the passage-way and into a small courtyard beyond. There standing impassively watching us were several hijabbed women and an old man; at their feet a group of young children were playing with dolls and a battered old tricycle. We had burst uninvited into the homes and lives of these Palestinian families, though their faces showed that they knew they were powerless to prevent our entry. The Jewish group pushed past the children, who seemed hardly aware of their presence, and carried on up another short flight of steps.

At the top was an incredible sight. The floor above the Palestinian families had been taken over by armed Jewish settlers, who had built a watchtower from which they could train their guns on the families below. The 'holidaymakers', I now realised, were there to show their support for this militarised outpost in the middle of the Muslim quarter. I was reminded of the incident a few years earlier when I was in hospital, before the outbreak of the intifada. Then I had seen a settler brandishing his gun in the ward who had told me that he had 'requisitioned' an Arab home in Jerusalem. Now I knew precisely what he meant.

I left the settlers on their tour of this outpost and went back down the steps to talk to the families below. They told me that the settlers had taken over the top-floor home several years ago, and become their unwelcome neighbours. The settlers' purpose was to make these families' lives so unbearable that they would choose to leave and the settlers' control could be extended. The old man said there were no horror stories of the settlers shooting at them. Instead these Jewish extremists were using methods that apparently neither the police nor the Israeli courts objected to. The passageway was being used by them as a toilet, both so that the Palestinian families would find their homes pervaded by the revolting smell, and so that they would be frightened that their children playing outside might pick up a disease. The messianic Jews lived in the outpost in shifts, so that they could make noise all night to keep their Palestinian neighbours awake.

'They think they can break us and make us leave,' said one woman. She told me that the settlers had occupied another apartment near them two years ago after the owner, an old Palestinian woman, died; the settlers claimed it was also part of the rabbi's home. The families were currently trying to challenge the illegal occupation in the courts. 'We will not be forced out,' said the old man defiantly. 'It is our home and we have nowhere else to go to.'

I turned away from this demonstration of naked Jewish power feeling a mix of anger and revulsion. For me it encapsulated everything that the modern state of Israel has come to represent: a compulsive, racist and colonial hunger for land and the control of resources in the face of opposition from a largely powerless but implacable Palestinian population. Although the methods vary in Tamra, Jerusalem and Hebron, the goal is always the same: the accumulation of land by whatever means possible for the exclusive use of Jews.

I remember once being asked by the Christian Peacemaker Teams – an organisation founded by American Churches in the mid-1980s to promote inter-faith non-violent resistance – to come to Hebron, where one of their main tasks is escorting young Palestinian children to school because they are afraid to walk alone past the armed Jewish settlers who threaten them. The Peacemaker Teams wanted me to visit because the children had never before met an unarmed Jew. They wanted me to show these children that not all Jews hate them and want to harm them. Bar, whose jobs included accompanying the Hebron settlers to the synagogue, had told me of the brutal treatment by the settlers, particularly the children, of the local Palestinian population. She would watch helplessly as Jewish youths cursed and spat at old Palestinian men, or threw tomatoes at pregnant Palestinian women. She said it made her physically ill to see the way these Jewish children were being raised.

Today there is an almost universal commitment among world Jewry to the Zionist project. It is worth noting that it was not always thus. Many prominent Jews rejected the idea of a Jewish state in Palestine, both before and shortly after its creation. Sigmund Freud, for example, foresaw with uncanny prescience the danger that in settling Palestine the Zionists would unleash a new form of Jewish fanaticism. In a letter in early 1930 to his friend Dr Chaim Koffler, the head of the Jewish Agency, who was asking for Freud's signature on a petition condemning riots among the Palestinian population against the waves of Jewish immigrants, he wrote:

> It would have seemed more sensible to me to establish a Jewish homeland on a less historically burdened land. But I know that such a rational viewpoint would never have gained the enthusiasm of the masses and the financial support of the wealthy. I concede with sorrow that the baseless fanaticism of our people is in part to be blamed for the awakening of Arab distrust. I can raise no sympathy at all for the misdirected piety which

*transforms a piece of a Herodian wall into a national relic,
thereby offending the feelings of the natives.*

Unlike Freud, we do not have the luxury of wishing away the existing
bitter conflict. In this intifada alone, hundreds of innocent people
have died on both sides as the two national groups battle over the
same piece of land. But everyone – apart, apparently, from our
current leaders in Washington and Jerusalem, and a few Islamic
extremists – is agreed that armed conflict can offer neither side a
meaningful 'victory'. At some level ordinary Israelis understand that
the Palestinian nation's desire for independence and freedom cannot
be defeated with weapons; and most Palestinians accept that they
cannot vanquish one of the most powerful armies in the world with
their light arms and suicide bombers.

A Palestinian friend of mine, Dr Said Zidani, a professor at
al-Quds University in East Jerusalem, has observed of both sides'
original hopes: 'Neither the Israeli Jews were drowned in the sea, as
the Palestinians wished, nor did the Palestinians disappear into the
distance, as Israeli Jews wished.' Rather than holding onto one of
these absolutist positions, Dr Zidani has been trying to devise a
workable solution to settling the conflict, one he believes that in the
right circumstances can be accepted by both sides. He is in an ideal
position to make such an attempt. Born in Tamra (his mother is
my next-door neighbour) and educated in a mixed Jewish and Arab
school in Haifa, he understands the fears of Jews intimately. But
also, as a resident of the West Bank for the past twenty years,
teaching at Bir Zeit University, near Ramallah, as well as at al-Quds
University, he knows first hand how soul-destroying it is to live
under occupation.

Said dismisses the oft-expressed idea that the conflict between
Israel and the Palestinians is over either religious or moral rights. It
is not, he says, a clash of civilisations or cultures, as popular opinion
now casts it. Although religious and moral sentiments have polluted

the debate about the need for a Jewish state, and Palestinian counter-claims, he rightly points out that the essence of the conflict is rival political demands from two national groups for sovereignty over the same territory. 'As soon as you start using religious or moral justifications for a Jewish state you are in a logical minefield,' he told me. 'The idea that Jews have a moral or religious right to return to this land after the passage of more than two thousand years is plain crazy. Are these historic rights? And if so, what about the historic rights of Palestinians uprooted nearly forty and sixty years ago? Don't they have rights? Or are the Jews' superior rights based on the length of absence? Surely, it should work the other way round.' A viable solution, he says, must forgo such nonsensical debates and concentrate instead on the political realities.

Since Israel's occupation of East Jerusalem, the West Bank and Gaza in 1967, the debate about ending the conflict has swung between two incompatible positions: what have come to be known as the one-state and two-state solutions. The two-state solution is usually premised on the idea of two secular, democratic states living alongside each other, one Palestinian based on 22 per cent of historic Palestine (East Jerusalem, the West Bank and Gaza), the other a Jewish state based on the remaining 78 per cent that is Israel. The problem for the Palestinians is that in practice their mini-state would be weak and overcrowded, and it would be living in the shadow of a very powerful neighbour. In any case, Israeli governments, whatever their declared intention, have never appeared even close to conceding such a state. Its creation would require the uprooting of more than 400,000 Jewish settlers, many of them armed and some of them holding fanatical messianic beliefs. It would also transfer to Palestinian control the large acquifers under the hills of the West Bank, Israel's main source of drinking water.

The one-state solution, in contrast, is usually based on the idea of a binational democratic secular state, in which Jews and Palestinians live as equal citizens. Although it should appeal to both sides'

241

notions of equality and justice, in practice it has very few takers. For the Palestinians it would mean abandoning their cherished dream of independent statehood, and trying to merge their own fledgling national institutions with those of the long-established Jewish state. For Israelis it would effectively mean the end of the Jewish state, both in the sense of a state controlled by Jews and in the sense of a state which ensures a strong Jewish majority. Within a few years, the Palestinians would be a demographic majority in any binational state, provoking Jewish fears both that such a state would not be democratic and that its Jewish citizens would have to surrender their privileges.

Said, however, believes it is a mistake to assume that the possible solutions exist only at these two poles. 'There are in fact a range of solutions between these two extremes. We should think not in terms of a just solution, by which I mean giving to everyone what is due to them, but rather a solution that is reasonable and accommodative, one which people feel they have a stake in and which they can live with.' He proposes a modified two-state solution, which involves elements of separation along the lines of the two-state solution, and elements of sharing along the lines of the one-state solution. There would be one secular, democratic country, but it would be divided into two confederated states, one Palestinian and the other Jewish, each with its own political institutions. This plan would allow most of the two populations, Jewish and Palestinian, to remain in their present homes, including the 'problematic' cases of the settlers in the West Bank and East Jerusalem, and the Palestinian citizens who live inside Israel. In the new country each citizen could choose the place they want to live: the Arab citizens could move to Palestine or remain inside Israel, and the settlers could live under Palestinian rule or return to Israel. The security of each minority would be guaranteed by legal codes that banned discrimination and ensured equality of citizenship. Resources would have to be divided equitably between the two states and within each state. The Palestinian refugees would be able either to return to the Palestinian state or to be compensated.

One of the advantages of Said's idea is that it makes the damaging ideology of Zionism redundant. It offers a way out of the mutual recriminations and the pervasive atmosphere of fear, allowing for confidence-building between Jews and Palestinians, and it could lead slowly to the sort of reconciliation achieved between whites and blacks in the new South Africa. As Said says, his solution is dynamic and does not preclude the possibility that the new joint country of Israel and Palestine could evolve eventually into a binational state.

However, neither he nor I is naïve enough to believe that his proposal is likely to be adopted by either side in the near future. The two-state solution is the one currently fashionable in Europe, America and increasingly among Israelis, even if the Israeli government's policies are fatally undermining the chance of its realisation by entrenching most of the settlers inside the West Bank and East Jerusalem. The problem, says Said, is that the world is still blindly committed to the Zionist enterprise, and believes that a simplistic two-state model is the only way to ensure a Jewish state in the long term.

'But what does everyone mean by a "Jewish state"? There are many possible meanings, the least problematic of which is a state in which Jews are the numerical majority. But in fact the world is using the term "Jewish state" in its most problematic sense: a state owned by Jews and which privileges Jews both inside the country and outside it in the Diaspora, through the Law of Return. A state designed to exclude Arabs from its resources and benefits.

'I remember a discussion with [left-wing law professor] Ruth Gavison at a panel at Tel Aviv University. I said, "OK, I am a liberal democrat and you proclaim yourself a liberal democrat. All I want is that both of us should be equal citizens within one state." She agreed at the theoretical level, but then told me I had to appreciate the improvement in my situation over the past twenty or thirty years, and that the steps to end discrimination would have to be gradual. She and other Israelis are not ready for anything more than this, because it would mean the end of Zionism. If we had liberal democracy in Israel that would mean the end of Jewish nationalism. Israel doesn't even want to change the personal status laws [on marriage and conversion] because it worries that it would lead to the assimilation of Jews.'

The main obstacle to reaching a peaceful solution to this conflict is not, as most commentators observe, age-old hatreds or religious wars. It is not even incompatible nationalisms. It is a psychological condition demonstrated by Israelis – and mirrored by Palestinians – that sociologists have termed 'learned helplessness'. In societies where people feel events are outside their control, either because they see themselves as effectively disenfranchised or because they believe powerful and uncontrollable forces are at work, they give up, refusing to take responsibility for their lives or their choices. Their response ranges from 'Nothing will make any difference, so I won't bother trying,' to uncritical support for strong, even fascistic, leaders.

Mamphela Ramphele, a founder member of the Black Consciousness Movement and a former Vice-Chancellor of Cape Town University, describes the phenomenon in her book *Steering by the Stars* (2002), about growing up in South Africa: 'How else can one explain why it took so long for the voting white public to realise that apartheid was not only bankrupt politically, socially and economically but also unsustainable in a modern world? The authoritarian culture that enveloped much of apartheid South Africa encouraged learned helplessness and an over-reliance on authority to make all the important political and social decisions.'

But it is not just the whites who suffer from this legacy in South Africa. Following the fall of apartheid, after years of living in the shadow of white assumptions about their inferiority, Ramphele says, many of the country's blacks have lost the sense of themselves as equals. Their lack of self-belief is compounded by a despair resulting from exhausting, long years of struggle for liberation and the devastating impact of economic apartheid on their lives.

The parallels with the present psychological condition of Israelis and Palestinians hardly need pointing out. For Palestinians in Israel and in the occupied territories, Israeli rule has truly ghettoised them, making it difficult for their intellectuals and leaders to organise and develop a vision of the future. There is no doubt in my mind that it is Israeli state policy to fragment Palestinian society, making it weak and ineffective – something I know well from my work with Mahapach. The tragedy is that because of this too many Palestinians have started to believe the Israeli narrative which tells them that they are inferior and incapable of challenging Israeli domination. Once persuaded of this, they are more likely to abandon dialogue and moderate strategies of resistance, such as civil disobedience, and turn instead either to the path of fatalism or to radical strategies such as suicide bombings, the ultimate weapon of the weak.

Too often I hear both Jews and Palestinians, even their leaders, asking me, 'Ma la'assot?' ('What to do?'), as though they have no stake in their future or power to change events. For example, when a judicial panel, the Or Commission, investigating the shooting of the thirteen unarmed Arab citizens in the Galilee at the start of the intifada, refused to identify the policemen and commanders who were responsible for ordering and carrying out the killings, I heard just such a comment from Arab Knesset member Issam Makhoul. Justice Or had refused to allow the Arab families to participate in the proceedings or to cross-examine the witnesses. I told Makhoul that the inquiry had chosen to make the political voice of the Arab minority irrelevant. Makhoul tried to put a gloss on it: 'This is the best we have had so far.' He was presumably referring to the fact that the commission's report did at least admit that there had been decades of discrimination against the Arab population. But his kind of attitude – which always resigns itself to second-best – is not good enough.

Makhoul's comment reminded me of another statement I had heard – this time by the architect Michael Mansfeld, a Jew – that he could not speak out about the discrimination against Arabs because it might result in life being made very difficult for him and his business. 'My responsibility is to my family,' he told me. But do we not also have a responsibility to the health of our society, including the values we raise our children with?

Although my friend Asad Ghanem does not use the term 'learned helplessness', he has strong views about how living in a Jewish state has damaged the Arab minority. It has, he says, made it impossible for them to identify with their state and so learn the true meaning of citizenship; it has eroded their sense of their own Palestinian identity and the collective rights that flow from that fact; and these two factors together have fragmented the Arab political leadership, which has singularly failed to articulate a vision for the Arab minority, as citizens of either a future Palestinian state or of a reformed Israeli state.

'The one area of our lives where we have equality is our right to participate in elections,' he told me. 'But even that is not as it appears. As citizens we expect to be able to influence the election result, but that is not what happens. Our electoral participation is completely symbolic; our parties are never allowed to join the government. Instead the state is mobilised entirely to its Jewishness, to its identification with the Jewish people and with its Jewish character. In this sense the key to the allocation of resources is not derived from citizenship, as it is in a normal democracy, but from ethnic belonging. Israel is what I call an ethnocracy, a state that depends on ethnic support, rather than a democracy, a state that needs the support of the demos [the body of citizens]. As Arabs we can have no meaningful place or role inside such a state.'

I knew what Asad meant. Israel has plenty of Jewish political parties in the Knesset, many of them small religious or extreme nationalist parties which sit in government coalitions making outrageous demands, such as passing more powers to the rabbis or expelling Palestinians and the Arab minority from the country. Such language is considered entirely acceptable, and nowadays is echoed even by senior members of the country's biggest party, the Likud. By contrast, no Arab party has ever been allowed to sit in the government; instead, Arab Members of Knesset (MKs) are allowed only to shout from the sidelines of the parliamentary and public debate. The two small Arab parties, and the equally tiny joint Arab–Jewish Communist Party, are effectively outside the national consensus. Even the main platform of the Arab parties – that Israel should be transformed from a Jewish state into a 'state of all its citizens' – contravenes basic legislation which requires all candidates to the Knesset to swear allegiance to a 'Jewish and democratic state'. In the 2003 general election, three senior Arab MKs were disqualified by the Central Election Committee from standing on just such grounds, although the decision was overturned by the courts.

Televised parliamentary debates on controversial issues in which Arab MKs speak invariably make for dismal viewing. As soon as the MK stands up to speak, he finds himself being howled down by the Jewish Members around him. If he shouts back, as unfortunately Arab MKs too often do, the Speaker ejects him from the chamber. There are regular instances of Arab MKs being punished by the Knesset's ethics committee, or being investigated for incitement by the attorney-general, after delivering speeches in the Knesset; Jewish MKs never seem to face these sanctions. In the Israeli media widespread animosity is expressed for the Arab political parties, a hostility only too readily accepted by the public and the security officials. A report by the Arab Association for Human Rights in Nazareth in 2002 revealed that during the parliament eight of the nine Arab MKs had been assaulted by the police or army at demonstrations, several on more than one occasion. In most cases the officers were fully aware of whom they were attacking.

According to Asad, however, the symbolic nature of citizenship for the Arab population has played a significant role in damaging their understanding of their wider rights to a collective Palestinian identity. As members of the Palestinian nation they should be entitled to cultural, language and social rights – just as Jews enjoy these rights – inside Israel. Recognition of these rights is vital in protecting Palestinian heritage and traditions, and therefore also the Palestinian minority's national identity.

'Although the courts safeguard some of our individual rights, which derive from our Israeli citizenship, they ignore other types of rights, most notably our collective or national rights. It is historically true that in countries founded on colonial occupation, such as the United States, Canada and Australia, the offer of full citizenship to the indigenous people – however magnanimous it sounded – was really another form of colonialism. The same is true in Israel. Here, for example, the authorities tell us we have to be "fully Israeli", that is to make our heritage and our past subsidiary to our citizenship, before we can have the right to belong. As happened in the US and Australia, we are expected to renounce our traditions and identity before we can become proper citizens. We must stop being Palestinian before we can be allowed to be Israeli. But I don't accept this in our case. So far Zionism has not succeeded like the white settlers of America and Australia. We still have the strength to believe we are a national group and that we deserve our rights both as a national group and as citizens.'

I was reminded of the comments of a Palestinian political activist in Nazareth, Ziad, who had once believed strongly in co-existence but who told me that since the start of the intifada he had grown profoundly disillusioned. 'Before we can co-exist, we must first exist,' he said. 'The problem is that we don't exist for the Jews. It's about time we woke up to that fact.' Asad fears that the Palestinian minority's national identity is being increasingly undermined by the Arab leadership in Israel, a subject on which he is outspoken. He says that traditionally the minority's leaders fell into two camps: either they collaborated with the system, accepting that the Jews were a privileged group, or they rejected the system entirely, refusing to deal with it. Now he says the Israeli policy of divide and rule has found its ultimate partners among the Arab minority.

'A third political group has emerged in the last fifteen years, from a generation which is more educated and more aware of the different aspects of our lives, but which is also far more opportunistic. The sole mission of these politicians is to keep their seat; they say whatever it takes to remain popular. One day they will criticise the Palestinian leadership in the occupied territories, and the next day meet with it. This group of leaders is disconnected from the real needs of their electorate. They are what I call a TV phenomenon: they give soundbites, speak of the hardships they have endured, but only ever visit Arab areas like Tamra just before an election. Maybe they have adopted this strategy partly because they have seen that in the past true leaders were usually jailed or deported by the Israelis. But because they are so opportunistic, there is no real coordination between them. They are not a collective leadership, they are not taking decisions together, they are not sitting down to formulate a common strategy. In fact they don't meet or speak at all. But the precondition for success, however limited, in our struggle as a minority must be a collective vision.

'Undoubtedly, our leaders' political failure reflects a wider failure in our society. We, the public, have changed too: after the collapse of communism and Arab nationalism, individualism has become the dominant ideology. Most people see their duty on election day as putting a mark on the ballot paper rather than as being part of a collective body. In the end people will follow their politicians just because they have no one else to follow. But really this is a dangerous illusion. When you are a majority, such as the Jews here, you have the privilege of an institutionalised collective leadership called the government. But Arab citizens cannot allow themselves to behave like the Jewish majority when they are really a minority. Instead of our opportunistic and competing leaders, we need a single inspirational figure like Nelson Mandela or Mahatma Gandhi.'

Asad has been campaigning to abolish the main political institution in the Arab sector, a body known as the Higher Follow-Up Committee, which comprises dozens of Arab leaders, from the Knesset representatives to the local mayors. With all the leaders pulling in different directions, each championing their own causes, the committee has become little more than a talking shop, which few in the Arab community bother to listen to any more. Asad, on the other hand, has suggested creating a new supreme Arab political body, a sort of mini-parliament, which would be elected by direct national elections among the Arab citizens.

'Discrimination, and Jewish dominance, are at the heart of the system. As a community we long ago reached the conclusion that the system is incapable of offering us equality. And yet we keep struggling for equality. Instead we have to alter the debate, to talk about the real change that must happen both in our society and in the Jewish society to achieve some sort of equality. We must recognise that we are stuck in a dead-end in the fight for equality, that the system will never allow us to be equals. Our new institutions must be ready to enter into a confrontation with the authorities. Only in this way can we move forward.'

Asad understands how difficult and frightening such an option is. In the spring of 2003 Israel jailed the leader of the Islamic Movement, Sheikh Raed Salah, the nearest thing the Arab community has to a spiritual leader. Salah is a widely respected and uncompromising figure behind whom much of the community – religious and secular alike – had united. After his arrest, leaks in the Hebrew media suggested he would be charged with having links to terrorists in the occupied territories, but when the charges finally came they referred only to financial irregularities regarding fund-raising activities and to the channelling of a small amount of funds to humanitarian causes in the West Bank and Gaza. Even though the police have admitted that Salah is being held on charges of technical breaches of Israeli law, at the time of writing he had been refused bail and had spent more than eighteen months in jail during a lengthy trial.

'Of course people are afraid,' says Asad. 'We are a fragmented and disorganised community. If you enter into confrontation like Raed Salah you are alone. Nowadays hardly anyone speaks of him – and he has a party and town behind him. If I speak out, no one at all will notice. I will simply disappear. But if we are more organised, a person who is arrested can be sure that a lawyer will be sent to the jail, that a demonstration will be organised, that members of the community will be ready to make sacrifices. I need to know someone will take care of my wife and children if I am in prison. We have to start organising the society from the bottom upwards.'

Today the same charge of disunity can be levelled, to a lesser degree, at the Palestinians in the West Bank and Gaza, where poverty and lengthy army-enforced curfews are undermining a strong tradition of solidarity. The 'What to do?' philosophy is beginning to take hold there too. But it is important to keep these failings in perspective. They derive from the damaging experience of discrimination and occupation enforced by Israel. The Palestinian population is not in a position to help itself without winning allies inside Jewish society, particularly from the left. Without Jewish partners and the support of the international community, the Palestinians can achieve little against the might of the Israeli army. But apart from some of the people who have been mentioned in this book – Uri Davis, Eitan Bronstein, Daphna Golan – and a few hundred others who support their work, Israeli Jews are in deep denial. They are even more the victims of learned helplessness than the Palestinians.

Said Zidani accurately describes the intellectual complacency of

Israeli left-wingers: 'They know that they came from Europe, took a country that was not theirs and displaced and dispossessed hundreds of thousands of Palestinians and their descendants. And then they tell you, "But we had no other choice. We had to rescue our people." This is an argument that might convince the Americans, the French or the British, but do they really think that they can convince the Palestinians that they had no choice but to displace us, to disinherit us, to kill us? It is just an absolute evasion of responsibility.'

His comments echo a similar discussion I had with historian Dr Adel Manna of the Van Leer Institute in Jerusalem. Dr Manna's work includes lecturing Jewish audiences, often comprising senior academics, about an alternative, Palestinian narrative of the war of 1948. We discussed the reactions he typically gets.

'Usually they respond either by simply refusing to hear the other narrative or by trying to tell me their narrative instead. As a historian, I can say this is natural when two peoples are in a bloody and continuous conflict: each side has its own story and portrays its camp as the victim and the other camp as the aggressor. But I think in the case of Jews the response is complicated by the fact that, because of their long history as victims all over the world, they are unusually convinced that they are the ultimate and eternal victim of everybody else. This makes them closed to the idea that a victim could be transformed into the victimiser or aggressor. They cannot accept it. So whatever I tell them, they always have an excuse for why their side has to behave in this way. If Palestinian civilians are killed, how else can Israeli soldiers respond to terrorism? If children are killed, it's the Palestinians' fault for sending their children to the street.

'Even outside the terms of the conflict they refuse to think of the Palestinians as victims. I ask them to see it from a humanitarian point of view. I say, imagine you have a home that has been in your family for generations and a stranger comes along and says, "I am

252

poor and need refuge. Can you let me stay in one of your rooms?"
Would you not tell this man, "This is my house, I am the owner
and you are a guest." And they reply, "But we cannot think of it in
this way, this is Eretz Israel, this is our homeland." And I say, "Yes,
but think about it from the other side, from the viewpoint of the
Palestinians who lived here." "No, no, there were no Palestinian
people," they say. "They are not a nation."

'OK, I say, let's assume that they are not a nation; they are just a
collectivity of people living in their homes. They still have rights in
their homes. How would you feel if someone came along and said,
"Now we are the landlords, this is our house. Maybe we will keep
you here as tenants, or maybe not"? What would your response be?
But they refuse to discuss it. I talk in front of groups of doctoral
students and professors, and almost none of them is able to think
in this way. Even if they can understand what I am saying at a
human level, they refuse to take responsibility for it. They admit it
is tragic, that it is just cause against just cause, but still it's the
Palestinian leadership to blame, or the Arab world – anyone but
their people. In other words, they cannot take responsibility for
what their people did to the Palestinians even after they have understood the Palestinian tragedy of 1948. That makes me very pessimistic. If that is the response of the stronger side, where are we
to go?'

I witnessed this absolute refusal to accept responsibility in a
packed auditorium at the Van Leer Institute in the autumn of 2004,
filled with left-wing Israelis who had come to hear a presentation
by Arun Gandhi, the grandson of Mahatma Gandhi, on the philosophy of non-violence. Most of the audience had been invited by the
peace activist networks and were keen to hear about non-violent
strategies. Gandhi spoke of his childhood in South Africa with his
grandfather, of the evils of apartheid and of the lessons the Mahatma
had taught him about the power of non-violent resistance. He had
learned from his grandfather, he said, that non-violent resistance

was only possible once one had let go of anger and found peace within oneself. He spoke calmly and gently, but I was struck by his failure to understand the depth of the anger and fear on both sides that stands in the way of non-violence in Israel. I know of that fear myself, because I was raised with it: I once thought of Arabs as marauding savages and that their only goal was to drive us Jews into the sea.

Gandhi was joined by a panel of academics and activists who spoke about their practical experiences of trying to encourage the participants in this conflict to adopt non-violent strategies. The best speakers were Lucy Nusseibeh, a British Palestinian, and Shai Carmeli, an Israeli film-maker. Lucy works for Middle East Non-violence and Democracy (Mend), a project which specialises in teaching Palestinian children how to react non-violently to the occupation. She said much of the organisation's time was spent explaining to youngsters that they should not throw stones, even when taunted by Israeli soldiers, and that she always found widespread support for non-violent strategies inside Palestinian communities.

Shai, who is in his late twenties and is studying at Tel Aviv University, showed us a documentary he had just completed on the ways Palestinian villagers have been non-violently resisting Israel's building of its 'security barrier' on their land. It was a remarkable diary of the kind of protests that are never given coverage by the Western media. We saw villagers chanting against the soldiers, and children standing in line holding banners. And we saw the army's response too: soldiers firing teargas and rubber bullets, and individuals entirely losing control as they beat children and old people. Shai had taken the film to the Israeli Broadcasting Authority and to international broadcasters, but none of them wanted to touch it. The reaction was always the same: 'This didn't happen in Israel,' they told him. His experience shows the level of denial adopted by Israeli society and the world.

When the talks came to an end, the floor was thrown open to the audience. After a brief hushed pause, a sixty-year-old rabbi stood up and told us that he had been in the 'business of peace' for a long time, and that the speakers had entirely misrepresented the situation. 'You have failed to understand the effects of the suicide bombings on Israelis,' he said. Then someone else stood up, and said the same thing. Another asked indignantly: 'Is this a court of law? Are we Israelis being judged?' His comment reminded me of Harry's wife who had asked me if I 'hated Jews'; it was another example of the same persecuted psychology. Another member of the audience said: 'We have the right to be afraid.'

Lucy Nusseibeh bravely tried to respond to the barrage of comments, and began by saying that the issue of suicide bombings had been sensationalised. I had a pretty good idea of the point she was trying to make: that the issue of someone strapping on a suicide belt has become *the* issue, overshadowing everything else, including the occupation. But we never heard the rest of her reply, because at that point most of the audience became hysterical. The evening came to an abrupt halt.

Emerging from the hall, I bumped into Adel Manna's wife, who looked as disgusted as I felt by what had just taken place. I had raised my hand in the auditorium, but had not had a chance to speak. I told her I had wanted to say that not once had I heard a Jew saying that we ought to be asking ourselves what makes people so desperate that they believe they need to blow themselves up. Even on the rare occasion the question is raised outside Israel, it is immediately made clear that such a line of thought is totally unacceptable. British Prime Minister Tony Blair's wife Cherie, for example, found herself forced to apologise for the innocuous comment that Palestinian suicide bombers felt 'no hope'.

The Jewish refusal to listen to the Palestinian narrative, to understand the Other's feelings and to take responsibility for our role in his misfortune, was again demonstrated to me one summer afternoon when I was by the sea in Herziliya. The beaches were packed with French Jews on their vacations making solidarity visits to Israel. I was talking to one group that was keen for me to know that they were first-generation French, their families having survived the Holocaust. Each had relatives who had been gassed in the concentration camps. They were fascinated by the idea of my living in an Arab town. 'But the Arabs are primitive,' one said. 'They have a primitive mentality.' How did they know that, I asked. 'Because they want to push us into the sea,' they said, parroting the Zionist propaganda I knew only too well myself.

They asked me about life in an Arab community, so I explained to them the ways in which we as Jews oppress Arabs in Israel, that we discriminate against them and steal their land. They were interested in a dispassionate way that suggested they did not really see it as their problem. Then one of the men interrupted: 'I want to ask you a question which I am sure you will know the answer to. Tell me: we hear stories that in 1948 we ethnically cleansed the Arabs from their villages. Is it really true?' I told him yes. He looked at me blankly, then raised up his hands helplessly, lost for a response and unable to come to terms with the gravity of my answer. Finally he said: 'But after all we have been through, all the persecution, the Holocaust, why could they not just have opened their arms and let us in?'

From his condition of learned helplessness, his statement probably sounded perfectly reasonable. But to me it made about as much sense as asking: 'Why did the Palestinians force us to kill and ethnically cleanse them?' It was a refusal to take responsibility for our past and for our crimes. It was like saying, 'We are so persecuted, our history is so much worse than anyone else's, we don't have to take responsibility for what we do.' That was the Zionist ideology I was raised with. I tried a different tack: 'Can't you see the similarity between what happened to us in Europe and what we are doing here? Can you not see that the persecution is the same?'

What they could not accept was that the Palestinian story is essentially a Jewish story. That is what I have learned from living in Tamra, listening to my new family and my Palestinian friends. The tale of Adel Manna's parents taking a boat journey under cover of night to return to their village is a Jewish story. So why do most Jews close their minds when faced with the Palestinian narrative?

'I understand why the majority of Jews are afraid to open their eyes,' Dr Manna had told me. 'Psychologically speaking, if you see the reality and acknowledge the narrative of the other side as your victim, you have a problem. If you take responsibility for what your side did, you endanger your relations with your family, friends, colleagues, the whole society – with everything you have, in fact. You find yourself in a tiny, marginalised minority facing a majority that sees you as a traitor. If you are strong enough you can face it and fight against it, but most people are not strong enough. Most are not able to do it, and so they either get depressed, emigrate, or suppress what they know. I understand that. It is a big sacrifice to make.

'Against the background of Jewish history, and each individual's fear of opening his mind and accepting responsibility, Jews in Israel are in addition educated to believe that if they give something to the Palestinians, the Palestinians will want more and the Jews will lose everything. The fear is that if you are not strong in the way the Zionists tell you to be, you will weaken the collectivity, and then you may find yourself with nothing. You may end up the victim again. And that is the complexity of this case.'

I do not think I truly appreciated those words until I made a trip to the town of Umm al-Fahm to visit Palestinians torn from their families by a combination of Israel's increasingly dismal human rights record and the wall that is being built to separate the Palestinian populations under Israeli rule. Umm al-Fahm lies in the Triangle region, close to the Green Line which officially separates Israel from the West Bank. From the hill at the far end of the town, Jenin and its surrounding villages are visible.

Jihad, a portly, middle-aged Palestinian, took me to meet several families whose lives can only be described as horror stories. Like many others now living in Israel, these families have been forced into hiding because of an outrageous piece of legislation passed by the Knesset in the summer of 2003. An amendment to the Citizenship Law has made it all but impossible for an Arab citizen of Israel to live legally inside Israel with a Palestinian spouse from the occupied territories. The measure, universally condemned by international human rights organisations, has created a whole new class of 'underground families' in Israel, living in fear of being discovered by the authorities. The Palestinian partner, often the husband, cannot work or claim benefits for fear of being discovered and then forcibly deported to the West Bank; the wives must hide their marriages even from friends; and the children have to live with the ever-present fear of suddenly 'losing' their father if they say a wrong word. The fact that this law passed in the Knesset with barely a murmur from anyone inside Israel, including most of the left, is a sign of the society's complete loss of moral direction. It is the ultimate proof of the extent to which learned helplessness syndrome has gripped Israeli Jewish society.

Afterwards, Jihad took me back to his home for lunch with his family. I had first met him during my peace walk in the West Bank with David Lisbona's organisation Middleway. I had not been impressed by the peace walk, or by the motives of the Jewish participants, and had ended the trip wondering what Arabs like Jihad gained from these encounters. I knew from Harry that Jihad was the most active of the Arab members, even sitting on the Middleway steering committee. Did Jihad have a vision of a fair and equal future for the Palestinian people? And if he did, did he really believe the Jews on the peace walks shared the same vision? Or was there a more cynical motive behind his involvement?

On the peace walk Jihad had seemed pushy and arrogant, and I had viewed him suspiciously. But as I sat in his home I started to reconsider. Although he was inarticulate about what exactly he thought Middleway stood for, he did seem genuinely and passionately loyal to it as an organisation. 'I believe in peace,' he said repeatedly, 'but I know I cannot get equality. So I concentrate on peace instead.' He spoke of David in more than glowing terms, as though he was some sort of guru.

I was curious to know more about Jihad. I asked him about his family's history, and he told me that before the creation of Israel in 1948 his father had been a wealthy resident of Umm al-Fahm, with a large house and forty dunums (ten acres) of land. During the war, however, his parents had been forced from Umm al-Fahm and into the Jenin refugee camp a few kilometres away, on the other side of the Green Line. Born shortly afterwards, in 1951, Jihad never knew Umm al-Fahm: he grew up as a resident of the West Bank, then under Jordanian control, first in a tent and later in a small apartment provided for his family by the United Nations refugee agency. But Jihad was determined to get out of the refugee camp: he lived and worked abroad for many years, slowly making a small fortune as an English translator in Saudi Arabia and later as the manager of a water and sewerage company in Jordan.

After 1967, when Israel captured the West Bank and effectively erased the Green Line that until then had separated Palestinian families living in Israel and the occupied territories, Jihad met and married a woman from his parents' town of Umm al-Fahm. Unlike the other families he had introduced me to that day, he had managed to get himself Israeli citizenship after a few years. With an Israeli ID card he had the choice of raising his family on the Israeli side of the Green Line, in the squalor and overcrowding of Umm al-Fahm, or of staying on the West Bank side. He chose the latter option, building a large home in the village of Taibe, not far from Jenin. There he could afford not only a good home but also three dunums of land, on which he planted an olive grove. Through hard work he had earned back a little of the quality of life and the self-respect stolen from his family in their massive dispossession in 1948.

Taibe was home to Jihad, his wife and their five children when the intifada erupted in late 2000. Then, in 2002, Israel began building the first sections of its 'security barrier', on the pretext that it needed to protect itself from suicide bombers. (That argument rings a little hollow, as Israel did not choose the Green Line for the route of the wall, but instead let it cut into large swathes of the West Bank, thereby justifying the effective mass annexation of Palestinian land, particularly land over the West Bank acquifers that supply Israel with most of its water.) The first sections of the hundreds of kilometres of wall went up in the area between Umm al-Fahm and Jenin, effectively re-establishing a border between the neighbouring Palestinian populations that had been erased nearly forty years earlier.

Jihad at least had a choice about where to live, unlike many others who have been trapped on one side of the wall or the other, cut off from family and friends because they had the wrong ID card. But the choice facing Jihad's family was still a stark and terrible one. They could remain in Taibe, keeping everything they had built up over many years, but then watch their life slowly crumble under the weight of the Israeli army occupation of the West Bank and the collapse of an economy starving behind a wall of razor wire and concrete. Or they could pack up the things they could carry, take them to Umm al-Fahm and begin again from scratch.

Jihad chose the second course, returning to Umm al-Fahm more than five decades after his family was expelled. But he did not come back in some glorious right of Palestinian return, compensated with land or money by Israel for the years of his family's dispossession. No, he returned to Umm al-Fahm with his wife and five children as a penniless itinerant. He had been made a refugee by Israel yet again.

Today, Jihad and his family live in a run-down rented apartment, the seven of them squashed into a few small rooms with almost no furniture. Jihad, who damaged his back several years ago, has no savings left, cannot find someone to rent his home in Taibe, and has paid no contributions to the Israeli welfare system. He has had to leave everything behind on the other side of the wall.

I asked Jihad where he felt he was from. 'From Jenin refugee camp,' he said. But where do you want to be, I asked. 'Back in my house in Taibe.' And if there was a just peace tomorrow, where would you want to be? 'Back in Umm al-Fahm with my forty dunums,' he said decisively. 'But only if I can return as an equal citizen with equal rights.'

'But that's not the kind of peace Middleway wants,' I pointed out. 'The peace they want is not the same as the peace you want. They want an end to the shooting and killing, but they also want the Jews to stay in control.'

He nodded, shrugged his shoulders and said: 'What to do?'

There it was again: the cry of learned helplessness. Jihad, it was now clear to me, had no conception of himself as an equal citizen. He was happy to be with Middleway because all he had come to expect after years of dispossession and mistreatment was any scraps he could get from the Jews' table. His words confirmed my view that Jihad was being exploited by Middleway, which needs Arabs like him to give it an air of inclusivity and legitimacy. But they were using him as little more than a guide dog to the West Bank. It reminded me of a moment on our trip to Yabad when Harry had pulled out from his wallet a photograph of himself shaking Yasser Arafat's hand. 'That's my protection if I ever get in trouble,' he said proudly. Was that not also Jihad's role for the peace walkers?

What was really distressing was to see how Jihad was so dislocated from everything: his past, his nation, his natural surroundings, even his family. Middleway had become everything for him, like some sort of peace cult which promised nothing but allowed him the slim hope that one far-off day a little of what was owed to him might be returned. After everything else had been taken from him, Middleway gave him back his sense of belonging, of being part of a community.

Jihad and the other families I had met that day had each been made refugees several times over. The Palestinian people is overwhelmingly a refugee nation, and like many others Jihad had been uprooted from the place he called home more than once. The fate of Palestinians like him so closely mirrors the fate of the Jewish people through the centuries that it strikes me as amazing that it is so rarely remarked upon. What makes Jihad's story so terribly tragic is that those responsible for turning him and his people into eternal refugees are the Jews themselves. Israel was created precisely to stop the Jewish people being a nation forever wandering, forever homeless. The price of creating such a homeland has been to inflict the Jewish story on another people, the Palestinians. It does not matter where in Israel or the occupied territories you go – Tamra, Jenin, Umm al-Fahm, Hebron, Rafah – you will find a Jewish story of dispossession and wandering; but the victims this time are the Palestinians.

Hearing Jihad's words about not knowing where he really belonged, I thought this must have been how the Jews felt after the Holocaust. I was also struck by another, frightening thought. Jihad's story sounded so like mine. Like Jihad I too had never known my roots, or where I belonged. My grandparents had been hounded from Lithuania to South Africa; my father had left South Africa, where he could not get the education he needed, to go to Europe; I had left Britain, where I felt few emotional attachments, to live in Israel; and finally, and most ironically, I had felt compelled to uproot myself from the 'Jewish' side of Israel through my new understanding that my state was built on a lie. Just as Jihad was destined to be the wandering Palestinian, I was destined to be the wandering Jew.

Jihad's story made it clear to me that Zionism has forced upon Israeli Jews a terrible choice: they feel they must continue rooting themselves in someone else's soil, the Palestinians', because otherwise they would have to uproot themselves yet again. This, I was becoming aware, was why we Jews find the idea of facing up to the truth about Israel, about our past, so impossibly difficult. To live honestly inside Israel as a Jew is to plunge oneself once again into a state of rootlessness.

I remember attending a co-existence meeting in the Galilee at which Jews and Arabs discussed planning issues in the region. One Jewish woman, a recent Russian immigrant, asked in exasperation: 'Why are the Arabs so attached to the land?' In Hebrew she used a word for 'attached' that conveys also the sense of being glued to it. But the Palestinians are no more glued to the land than are the Jews. The prospect for both peoples, if they are not deeply rooted to the land, is just too terrifying to contemplate. The cycle that has to be broken is not a cycle of violence, but a cycle of lies we Jews tell ourselves to persuade us that we have a two-thousand-year-old title deed to this land.

Whereas Jihad had been forced by Israel to become an eternal refugee, I have chosen my fate of wandering, of being rootless, by questioning the very basis of the Jewish state. I cannot pretend it was an easy choice. I have had to develop a new sense of belonging: to the struggle to help a new country emerge here to which one day we all, Jews and Palestinians, will belong. I hope others will take the same path as me because a true peace, a just reconciliation with the Palestinians, can never happen until Israelis and Jews accept that this was not their land, that they are, in Dr Manna's words, living uninvited in someone else's house. But I do not want to disguise from anyone the fact that being honest with oneself, seeing the truth beneath the layers of lies and misinformation, is not deeply disturbing.

After I had been living in Tamra for some time my thirty-two-year-old son Daniel, who at the time was working in Germany for a sportswear firm and planning his marriage to a Swedish woman, came to visit me in Israel. In one intensive day I took him on a similar journey to the one you have taken in this book. I showed him around Tamra and introduced him to my friends and neighbours. I explained the discrimination and the way the state steals land from Palestinians. I took him to the machsom, the checkpoints where Jewish youngsters humiliate Palestinians and control their lives. I showed him the wall as it cuts through the very centre of Bartaa, chopping a Palestinian community and its families in half. I must have explained it ten times to him, and still he could not make sense of the lunacy of it.

My son had a Zionist upbringing and spent much of his youth in Israel, working on summer camps or volunteering on kibbutzim. He is a very typical Diaspora Jew, and he found it a profoundly troubling day. 'How do you think the Jews in the Diaspora will cope with this?' he asked me. 'I can see that what you are showing me is not what I was brought up to believe. That there is a whole other story I never knew about. In one day you are trying to change my whole perspective. You are showing me that everything I believe is a falsehood.'

I realise as I finish writing this book that my journey was not really about crossing a divide, but about a far harder journey: one in which I have learned that the divide is really an illusion. It is an artefact we have created in our imaginations – just as we have built a concrete wall in the West Bank – to protect us from the truth. It is not about living in Tamra or Tel Aviv, or for that matter Umm al-Fahm or Jenin. It is not about *where* we live, but about *how* we live. It is about learning to look honestly at the places we inhabit and want to call ours, to understand the past, and to face up to the crimes committed in our names. Then we Jews will be ready to apologise and to reach out a welcoming hand across that divide. To embrace the Other, who is really ourselves.

Glossary

By JONATHAN COOK

Terms in italic are explained in greater detail elsewhere in the glossary.

Aliya – The Hebrew word – literally 'ascent' – used to describe the immigration of Jews in the *Diaspora* to Israel. It has Biblical connotations, suggesting that Jews were ordained by God to return to the Promised Land. Nearly three million Jews have made aliya, brought to Israel by the *Jewish Agency* under the *Law of Return*, since the founding of Israel in 1948.

Ashkenazim – The Hebrew word, originally meaning 'German', for Jews of north and east European origin, distinguishing them from the *Sephardim*, Jews of Mediterranean/Arab origin. The Ashkenazi experience of persecution led many European Jews to become early and enthusiastic supporters of *Zionism*. Almost all leaders of the pre-state Jewish organisations in Palestine were Ashkenazi, and that political, cultural and religious dominance continues to this day in Israel.

Balfour Declaration – A letter written in November 1917 by the British foreign minister, Arthur Balfour, to the banking magnate Lord Rothschild, in which Britain officially declared its support for the goals of the Zionist movement, namely to create a Jewish national homeland in Palestine: 'His Majesty's Government views with favour the establishment in Palestine of a national home for the Jewish people and will use their best endeavours to facilitate the achievement of this object, it being clearly understood that nothing shall be done which may prejudice the civil and religious rights of the existing non-Jewish [i.e. Palestinian] communities in Palestine or the rights and political status enjoyed by Jews in any other country.'

Bedouin – Israel's 200,000 Bedouin are comprised of two separate populations: the majority, living in the *Negev*, originate from the Sinai peninsula; while a much smaller group, living in the *Galilee*, are descended from tribes that arrived from Syria and Lebanon. Most of the Bedouin, the poorest social group in Israel, live either in *unrecognised villages* or in state-planned urban reservations, although more privileged communities exist in the north, where the men volunteer to serve in the army, usually as trackers. The Bedouin are also well represented in the Arab neighbourhoods of the '*mixed cities*' of Ramle and Lod, in the centre of the country, where they were forcibly relocated by the state after 1948 to provide a pool of cheap labour serving the construction industry in Tel Aviv.

Blue lines – The Planning and Building Law (1965) established 'blue lines' around every community in Israel. Development can occur only within these blue lines; all land outside the blue lines is considered agricultural. Many tens of thousands of Arab homes, particularly in the *unrecognised villages*, are located outside the blue lines and are therefore illegal and face demolition.

British Mandate – British and French officials carved up much of the Middle East empire of the defeated Ottomans according to the Sykes–Picot Agreement of 1916. Britain occupied Palestine in September 1918, two years later securing a Mandate for the region from the San Remo Peace Conference. The Mandate for Palestine, an area defined as running from the Mediterranean Sea to the River Jordan, was confirmed by the Council of the League of Nations in 1922. Under the *Balfour Declaration* of 1917, the British government promised the Zionist movement that it would assist in the creation of a Jewish national homeland in Palestine. The first British census in Palestine in 1922 recorded 670,000 Palestinians and eighty thousand Jews in Palestine. By 1946, on the eve of the establishment of the state of Israel, an Anglo-American commission estimated the population at nearly 1.3 million Palestinians and 600,000 Jews. The Mandate ended in May 1948.

Citizenship – Two pieces of legislation, the *Law of Return* of 1950 and the Nationality Law of 1952, define the ways in which Israeli citizenship can be acquired: by birth to Israeli parents; by residence; by naturalisation; and, in the case of Jews, by return. These laws did not automatically apply to the country's Arab population: some thirty thousand *present absentees* received citizenship belatedly when the Nationality Law was amended in 1980. Government officials have wide-ranging powers to prevent non-Jews from gaining Israeli citizenship, and in some cases even residency rights. A harshly critical report by the Association of Civil Rights in Israel (ACRI) in December 2004 observed that the Interior Ministry's rules for assigning citizenship to non-Jews are 'shrouded in mist', and that the ministry has demonstrated 'an endemic, systematic and pervasive bias against non-Jews'. Often the children of marriages between an Israeli and a non-Jew are also denied citizenship. Since 2002 it has been impossible for Palestinians from the occupied territories to acquire citizenship on marrying an Israeli, effectively forcing the couple to live apart. Conversion to Judaism – another possible route to citizenship – is exclusively controlled in Israel by the *Orthodox rabbinate*, which approves a tiny number of converts each year and demands they become strictly observant. The relationship between citizenship and nationality is far more problematic in Israel than in other countries. Although the 6.5 million inhabitants of Israel all enjoy Israeli citizenship, none – Jew or Arab – is considered an 'Israeli national'. The Interior Ministry has assigned 137 other nationalities to the country's citizens so that it can perpetuate the idea that Israel is a nation identical with the Jewish nation. Registered nationalities include Jew, Georgian, Russian and Hebrew through to Arab, *Druze*, Abkhazi, Assyrian and Samaritan. The courts have rejected the claims of individuals seeking to be registered as Israeli.

Custodian of Absentee Property – An Israeli state official responsible for the confiscation of the homes, lands and bank accounts of all Palestinians made refugees in the *War of 1948* and their descendants, both four million Palestinians registered today as living in refugee camps across the Middle East and 250,000 internal refugees who live as Israeli citizens. Estimates put the value of confiscated moveable property alone (bank accounts, shares, jewellery, farm equipment, etc.) at many tens of billions of dollars at today's prices. These assets were used to finance the immigration of Jews to Israel. Palestinian confiscated lands – worth far more – were used to settle Jewish immigrants. No compensation has been paid to the Palestinians by Israel.

Declaration of Independence – A document published on 14 May 1948, at the expiry of the *British Mandate*, proclaiming 'the establishment of a Jewish state in Palestine' and promising to 'uphold the full social and political equality of all its citizens, without distinction of religion, race or sex'. The declaration also promised to draw up a constitution 'not later than the 1st October 1948'. That obligation has never been honoured because of two major obstacles faced by Israeli legislators: first, a constitution would provide a set of legal principles by which Arab citizens could challenge the many state policies which discriminate in favour of Jews; second, the privileging of secular law over *halakha* (rabbinical) law would break the fragile

Jewish consensus with the *ultra-Orthodox* community. Instead Israel has relied on eleven Basic Laws, which include elements of a constitution. Two Basic Laws passed in 1992 – Human Dignity and Freedom, and Freedom of Occupation – for the first time codified in law some key human rights. However, the right to equality, freedom of expression and freedom from religious coercion, as well as social rights such as the right to education, health care, work and welfare, are still not guaranteed in law.

Declaration of Principles – See entry on *Oslo Accords*.

Destroyed villages – Some 750,000 Palestinians were forced from their lands during the *War of 1948* that created Israel. The four-hundred-plus villages they lived in – some estimates suggest more than five hundred, but are based on a looser definition of what constituted a village – were demolished by the Jewish state in the aftermath of the war to prevent the refugees' return. The *Jewish National Fund* was responsible for planting forests over many of the destroyed villages. The farm lands of the destroyed villages are usually leased by the state or the JNF to exclusive Jewish communities such as the *kibbutzim* or *moshavim*.

Diaspora Jews – The world's total Jewish population is estimated at a little over thirteen million, with roughly five million living in Israel. A larger number, about 6.5 million, live in North America. About 1.5 million Jews live in Europe, the majority in Western Europe (particularly France and Britain), and a shrinking number in Eastern Europe and the Balkans. Zionist demographers are particularly concerned at the high rate of assimilation, mainly through intermarriage with non-Jews, among Diaspora Jews.

Druze – A secretive sect, originally from Egypt, that broke away from Islam in the eleventh century. Today more than half a million

Druze live in the mountainous regions of Lebanon, Syria, Israel and Jordan. Inside Israel there are 100,000 Druze, the majority living in the *Galilee* who became Israeli citizens in 1948, and a smaller number who were captured along with the *Golan Heights* from Syria in the *War of 1967*. Before the creation of Israel the Galilee Druze were an integral, if distinct, part of the Arab Palestinian population, and many still live in mixed communities alongside Muslims and Christians. However, during the *War of 1948* the Druze leadership reached a deal with the new Jewish state to fight on the Israeli side. The 1956 Compulsory Conscription Law formalised that relationship by obliging Druze youngsters – unlike those of the other Arab communities – to do military service. Today, Israel treats the Druze as a separate nation, identifying them as Druze on their identity cards and educating them according to a separate school syllabus overseen by a Druze department in the Education Ministry. Despite their inhabitants' military service, many Druze villages are among the poorest in Israel. After conscription Druze youngsters have few employment opportunities apart from joining the security services, often as low-paid policemen or prison wardens. The Druze have earned a reputation among Palestinians in the occupied territories and inside Israel for holding virulently anti-Arab attitudes and being quick to use violence. In recent years a fledgling anti-conscription movement has emerged among them.

dunum – One thousand square metres, or a quarter of an acre. Traditional land measurement used in the Middle East.

Galilee – The most northerly region of Israel, which is home to the country's largest number of Arabs, at about 600,000. After decades of government *Judaisation* programmes, the region's population is now evenly split between Jews and Arabs.

Golan Heights – An area of land belonging to Syria east of the *Galilee* occupied by Israel in the *War of 1967*. The Golan population of 250,000 was reduced to just eight thousand, mainly *Druze*, by the fighting. Most of the Golan Druze remain loyal to Syria (and do not serve in the army), although a minority took *citizenship* when the region was annexed by Israel in violation of international law in 1981. Jewish settlement of the Golan has been limited: about eighteen thousand Jews live among a similar number of Druze.

Green Line – The armistice line agreed between Israel and Jordan in 1949, following the *War of 1948* that founded Israel. Until 1967 the Green Line separated Israel from the West Bank, which was under Jordanian occupation. After the *War of 1967*, when Israel occupied the West Bank, the Jewish state's leaders considered the Green Line effectively erased and even removed it from official maps. In violation of international law, Israel has moved large numbers of Jewish settlers into the West Bank and smaller numbers into Gaza. Outside Israel, the Green Line is widely considered to be the only feasible future border between Israel and a Palestinian state in the West Bank. The wall and fence Israel is building to separate itself from the Palestinians deviates substantially from the Green Line, effectively annexing large parts of the West Bank.

halakha – The legal system of Judaism based on the Torah and developed by later rabbinical interpretations. *Orthodox* and *ultra-Orthodox Jews*, unlike the Conservative and Reform streams, subscribe to a literalist reading of halakha. At the founding of the state, Israel's leaders reached a deal with the *Orthodox rabbinate* giving it exclusive regulation of *personal status laws*, and the right to define who is a Jew for the purpose of public records. The rabbinate insists on official bodies observing the Sabbath and kosher (kashrut) laws governing food preparation and consumption. Halakhic law exists in uncomfortable parallel with secular laws passed by the *Knesset*.

Hamula – Arab clan or extended family.

Intifada – Arabic word meaning 'shaking off', as in the shaking off of the Israeli occupation. The word is used to refer to two popular uprisings by Palestinians in the occupied territories, the first between 1987 and 1993 and the second which began in September 2000, following a visit by Ariel Sharon to the sacred compound in the Old City of *Jerusalem* known to Muslims as the Noble Sanctuary and to Jews as the Temple Mount. Palestinians often refer to the second intifada as the Aqsa intifada, after the biggest mosque in the Noble Sanctuary compound.

Israel Defence Forces (IDF) – The Israeli army. Muslim and Christian citizens are excluded from serving in the army, and as a result lose the right to many benefits – grants, loans, mortgages, scholarships, jobs – which depend on military service (although most of these benefits are still available to *ultra-Orthodox Jews*, who are exempted from military service). Conscription was made compulsory for the small *Druze* community in 1956. The *Bedouin* can volunteer to serve in the IDF, usually as desert trackers. In practice, only a small minority do so.

Israel Lands Authority (ILA) – A government body which manages all land owned by the state and the *Jewish National Fund*, today some 93 per cent of all the territory inside the borders of Israel. Such land is generally used for the settlement of Jews only. Half the members of the ILA Council, which determines land policy in Israel, are nominated by the JNF.

Israeli Arabs – The term originally used by the government, state bodies, Israeli media and most Israeli Jews to describe those Palestinians who were not expelled from Israel during the *War of 1948*. However, since 1967 Israel has included the 230,000 Palestinians of East *Jerusalem* in its figures on Israeli Arabs (even though few East

Jerusalemites have accepted Israeli *citizenship*). According to the Central Bureau of Statistics, there are nearly 1.3 million Israeli Arabs, comprising 19 per cent of the Israeli population. The main Israeli Arab communities are Sunni Muslim (81 per cent), Christian (10 per cent) and *Druze* (9 per cent). Israel also often chooses to distinguish between its Muslim and *Bedouin* populations. Israeli Arabs live in 116 Arab-only communities and what are known as seven '*mixed cities*'. Israeli Arabs may also refer to themselves – or be referred to – as Palestinian citizens of Israel, Israel's Palestinian minority, Palestinians of '48.

Jerusalem – East Jerusalem was occupied by Israel in the *War of 1967*, along with the Palestinian territories of the West Bank and Gaza, in what Israel hailed as the unification of the city's two halves. East Jerusalem was officially annexed, in violation of international law, a few weeks later. Israel has repeatedly expanded Jerusalem's municipal boundaries to increase the number of Jews considered resident in the city. There are now some 680,000 residents, roughly a third Palestinian, a third Jewish settlers in East Jerusalem, and a third Jews living in West Jerusalem. Israel has declared Jerusalem its 'eternal capital', a change of status rejected by the UN. Most countries continue to regard Tel Aviv as the capital of Israel.

Jewish Agency (JA) – A Zionist organisation established in 1929 to act as the political representative of the Jews in Palestine and to help in the creation of a Jewish national home through the 'ingathering of the exiles': i.e. the encouragement of mass immigration by Jews in an attempt to change Palestine's demographic balance. Today, the JA encourages Jews in the *Diaspora* to make *aliya*. The JA is regarded as a charity by most countries and donations are tax-exempt.

Jewish National Fund (JNF) – Known in Hebrew as the Keren Kayemet LeIsrael (Perpetual Fund for Israel), the JNF was established in

1901 as an organ of the *World Zionist Organisation*. Its main task before the founding of Israel was to buy land on behalf of the Jewish people in Palestine. Although there is some dispute about how much land the JNF actually bought, it is known that before 1948 Jews owned no more than 7 per cent of what was to become Israel, much of that privately bought by wealthy Jews. Today, following a policy of land confiscations from the Arab population, the state and the JNF together own 93 per cent of the land (13 per cent is held by the JNF and 80 per cent by the state). According to its charter, the JNF can lease land only to Jews. It also oversees tree-planting operations and manages some forests, particularly on *destroyed villages* and land confiscated from Arab owners. The JNF is regarded as a charity by most countries and donations are tax-exempt.

Judaisation – A long-standing government policy in the regions of the *Galilee*, *Negev* and *Triangle* to change the traditional demographic balance so that Jews outnumber Arabs. The purpose is to strengthen Jewish control and dominance of land in these traditional Arab heartlands. Jews are encouraged to move to these peripheral regions by offering them incentives, usually cheap land and housing.

Kibbutz (pl. kibbutzim) – Collective rural Jewish communities originally intended as socialist communes. Inhabitants usually depend on farming to generate income. Traditionally, all property is communally owned. Today, with the kibbutzim generally unprofitable, much of their land is being sold off to private developers.

Knesset – The Israeli parliament, with 120 members. Each party selects its Knesset members from its candidate list in strict proportion to its share of the national vote. The leader of the single largest party in the Knesset usually forms the government. For much of Israel's history, power has resided in the hands of the Labour Party, but since the late 1970s the more hawkish Likud Party has become dominant. To form a government, the biggest party needs a coalition of smaller parties to give it a majority of seats in the Knesset (i.e. more than sixty). The choice is usually between *ultra-Orthodox* parties demanding a more openly theocratic state, and extremist right-wing parties demanding a harsher policy towards Palestinians in the occupied territories, and in some cases espousing the expulsion of *Israeli Arabs*. Currently there are two small Arab parties, one the nationalist Tajamu party (known as Balad in Hebrew) and the other the United Arab List, an ad hoc alliance between an Islamic faction and a Bedouin leader. There is also a small joint Arab–Jewish Communist party, known as Jebha in Arabic and Hadash in Hebrew. In most elections the Labour and Likud parties each puts forward one or two Arab candidates, with Likud usually choosing former senior-ranking *Druze* soldiers. No Arab party has ever been allowed to sit in the government. Arab parties are regularly threatened with disqualification at election time through legislation which bans parties whose platforms 'negate the existence of the state of Israel as the state of the Jewish people' or 'the democratic character of the state'. The demand for 'a state of all its citizens', the platform of most Arab parliamentary candidates, is regarded as contravening the legislation because it opposes the idea of Israel as both 'Jewish and democratic'.

Law of Return – A piece of legislation passed by the Knesset in 1950 which guarantees every Jew in the world the right to come to Israel as an immigrant and receive citizenship. The law defines a Jew as anyone with one Jewish grandparent, as opposed to the stricter definition of *halakha* – rabbinical law – that a Jew must be born to a Jewish mother. Exceptions to the rights conferred by the Law of Return are made only for political dissidents and certain convicted criminals.

Military government – Israel established a military government to restrict the movement and rights of the 150,000 Palestinians it inherited after the *War of 1948*. No Arab citizen was allowed to leave his town or village without a permit from the local military governor. The regime was abolished in 1966.

Mitzpe (pl. mitzpim) – Literally a 'lookout' settlement. Exclusive Jewish rural settlements developed in the 1980s and 1990s as a way to attract middle-class Jews to live in Israel's rural Arab heartlands. The name 'mitzpe' derives from the idea that the inhabitants should watch over their Arab neighbours to ensure they do not build and thereby try to reclaim land the state has confiscated from them.

Mixed cities – There are seven 'mixed cities' inside Israel, although officials often include an eighth: annexed East *Jerusalem*. They are Tel Aviv-Jaffa, Ramle, Lod, Haifa, Acre, Upper Nazareth and Maalot-Tarshiha. The label 'mixed city' is misleading, as in all these cases *Israeli Arabs* live in distinct, separate communities, usually poor ghetto neighbourhoods, attached to what is effectively a Jewish city. By the design of state planners, Arabs are never supposed to comprise more than 20 per cent of the population of a mixed city.

Mizrahim – See entry on *Sephardim*.

Moshav (pl. moshavim) – A rural community similar to the *kibbutz*, but each family privately leases its own farmland and home and makes its own decisions. Only buying and selling is organised cooperatively.

Nakba – Arabic word meaning 'catastrophe' used by Palestinians to describe the defeat and mass dispossession of the Palestinians that occurred during and after the *War of 1948*.

The Negev – The large southern desert region of Israel which has been inhabited by semi-nomadic *Bedouin* tribes for many generations. After mass expulsions during and after the *War of 1948*, the number of Bedouin dropped precipitously. Today, after state-sponsored *Judaisation* programmes, the 145,000 Bedouin in the Negev comprise a quarter of the population there, with half living in urban reservations created by the government and the other half living illegally in *unrecognised villages*. The Negev's Bedouin have one of the highest fertility rates in the world, and are regarded as a 'demographic time bomb' by most Israeli officials.

Orthodox Jews – The name for Jews who observe *halakha*. Although there are several streams of Judaism, Orthodoxy is the only one with official standing in Israel. Since the creation of Israel, particularly following the *War of 1967*, a significant proportion of Orthodox Jews have adopted nationalist and Messianic views, which encourage them to regard the settling of the *Palestinian occupied territories* as a religious duty.

Orthodox rabbinate – The rabbinical authorities in Israel are drawn exclusively from the Orthodox stream of Judaism, ignoring the other major, and more liberal, streams of Conservative and Reform Judaism. Since the founding of the state the Orthodox rabbinate has been given control over *personal status laws* for Jews and over deciding who is a Jew for public records. Traditionally there have been two chief rabbis, one representing *Ashkenazi* Jews and the other representing *Sephardi* Jews. Nonetheless, Sephardi Jews often complain that Ashkenazi rabbis have greater powers, particularly in controlling religious education. Splits have developed in the rabbinate between those supporting the settlement project in the *Palestinian occupied territories* and those opposed to it.

Oslo Accords – After secret talks in the summer of 1993 in Oslo, Israel and the *Palestine Liberation Organisation* signed an accord at the White House on 13 September 1993. Called the Declaration of

Principles, the accord provided for Palestinian self-rule in much of Gaza and in the small West Bank town of Jericho, followed by promises of Israeli troop withdrawals from the main Palestinian population centres. By 1999 the Palestinians had control of about 40 per cent of the West Bank and 70 per cent of Gaza. However, any chance of effective Palestinian sovereignty was severely eroded by the doubling of the Jewish settler population to 200,000 in the West Bank during the Oslo period. Progress made under the Oslo Accords was reversed following the failure of talks at Camp David in July 2000 and at Taba in February 2001 to reach a final-status agreement. A Palestinian *intifada* erupted in September 2000, and Israel subsequently reoccupied much of the West Bank.

Palestine Liberation Organisation (PLO) – An umbrella organisation, created in 1964 to represent the Palestinian people, which called for the establishment of a single democratic and secular state in the area of Mandatory Palestine (what is today Israel, the West Bank and Gaza). After Israel's occupation of the West Bank and Gaza in 1967, the PLO declared armed struggle as the only way to liberate Palestine, and two years later Yasser Arafat, leader of the biggest Palestinian faction, Fatah, became chairman. In 1988 the PLO renounced violence and recognised the state of Israel. When Israel officially lifted its ban on contacts with the PLO in 1993, the path was laid for the signing of the *Oslo Accord*, in which Israel for the first time recognised the PLO as the representative of the Palestinian people. The creation of a Palestinian Authority, led by Arafat in the West Bank and Gaza in 1994, effectively marginalised the signifi-cance of the PLO.

Palestinian occupied territories – The West Bank, Gaza and East *Jerusalem*, occupied by Israel in the *War of 1967*. The West Bank has a population of 2.3 million Palestinians as well as 200,000 Jewish settlers living in communities illegal under international law. Israeli

Jews often refer to the West Bank by its Biblical names of Judea and Samaria. The tiny Gaza Strip has 1.2 million Palestinians and a Jewish population of seven thousand settlers who were due to be withdrawn by the Israeli government in 2005. The Palestinian areas of the Gaza Strip are some of the most densely populated places on earth. Unlike the *Israeli Arabs* and the Jewish settlers, both of whose rights and duties derive solely from Israeli law, the Palestinians in the occupied territories are affected by a web of overlapping legal systems, including local laws (based in the West Bank on Jordanian law that applied till 1967), Israeli laws, Israeli military decisions and international humanitarian law. Israeli military judges have wide-ranging powers to approve the detention of those arrested by the army and to sentence them, often on secret evidence. Adjudication in disputes over the application of laws in the occupied territories is overseen by the Israeli Supreme Court, which according to leading Israeli jurist David Kretzmer has served to clothe 'acts of military authorities in a cloak of legality'.

Personal status laws – Under Israeli law, issues relating to births, marriages and deaths are the exclusive preserve of the religious authorities of each religious community. Separate religious courts exist for Jews, Muslims, *Druze* and the Christian denominations, each having sole authority within their community to rule, for example, in cases of divorce. The only marriages permitted in Israel are religious ones, thus making it impossible for members of different faiths, say a Muslim and a Jew, to marry unless one converts (although Israel does recognise inter-faith marriages performed in civil courts outside Israel). Jewish personal status laws are particularly problematic in relation to defining who is a Jew. Since the founding of the state, exclusive control of personal status laws has been invested in the *Orthodox rabbinate*. The world's two other major, more liberal Jewish streams – Conservative and Reform – have no official standing in Israel. This has led to the anomaly that

Jews eligible for citizenship under the *Law of Return* (which defines a Jew as having one Jewish grandparent) are not considered Jews by the Israeli religious authorities (who use the *halakhic* definition of a Jew as someone born to a Jewish mother). Such Jews are effectively invisible in terms of their personal status: they cannot marry in Israel, they cannot be buried in Jewish cemeteries, they cannot be ascribed a 'Jewish nationality' on their identity cards. A large number of such Jews arrived following the collapse of the Soviet Union: some estimates suggest half of these one million 'Russians', as they are called, are not Jewish according to halakha.

Present absentee – The Israeli state's term for an internally displaced Palestinian citizen (expelled refugees are known simply as 'absentees'). The present absentees were present in Israel after its founding (and therefore gained *citizenship*, although in many cases belatedly), but are considered by the state to have been absent, even if briefly, from their property during the *War of 1948*. Present absentees lost all rights to their homes, lands and bank accounts. These were passed to an official known as the *Custodian of Absentee Property*. Today, a quarter of *Israeli Arabs* – 250,000 – live as 'present absentees'.

Sephardim – The descendants of Spanish and Portuguese Jews. After the Jews' expulsion from Spain and Portugal in the fifteenth century they settled mainly in North Africa, Turkey and Greece. The label Sephardi is often also applied to Oriental Jews, known in Israel as the Mizrahim, who have no ancestral ties to Spain. Descended from Jews who remained in the Middle East, their main population centres were in Yemen, Iraq and Iran. Many of the Sephardim and Mizrahim were late or unwilling converts to *Zionism*: those living in Arab countries were often forced to leave after the creation of Israel strained relations with neighbouring Arab states.

Shin Bet – Officially known as the General Security Services, the Shin Bet is Israel's domestic security service and has various subdivisions monitoring *Israeli Arabs*, Jewish extremist organisations and foreign diplomats, as well as protecting senior military and political figures. After 1967 the Shin Bet moved its intelligence-gathering operations into the *Palestinian occupied territories*, where it runs an extensive network of spies and collaborators. It sometimes cooperates overseas with Mossad, the foreign intelligence service.

Six-Day War – See entry on *War of 1967*.

The Triangle – A thin, triangular-shaped strip of land in central Israel close to the northern West Bank which is populated by 150,000 Arabs. Government *Judaisation* programmes have largely failed to bring Jews into the area. In many places the wall being built by Israel runs directly through mixed *Israeli Arab* and Palestinian communities (e.g. Baqa and Bartaa) astride the *Green Line*, thereby splitting families in half. Several Israeli leaders, including Ariel Sharon, have raised the idea of a land swap with the Palestinians which would transfer the Triangle into a future Palestinian state in the West Bank.

Ultra-Orthodox Jews – Fundamentalist Jews, numbering about 700,000 in Israel, who refuse all modern innovations and subscribe to a literalist reading of the Scriptures. The ultra-Orthodox are strongly opposed to *Zionism*, mainly because the Talmud enjoins Jews not to emigrate en masse to the Promised Land until the coming of the Messiah. The ultra-Orthodox are exempted from serving in the army and enjoy special state subsidies to study in seminaries. After the *Bedouin*, they have the highest birth rate in Israel. Also known as the Haredim (the 'God-fearing').

Unrecognised villages – Several dozen Arab communities that Israel has refused to recognise since its creation in 1948. Some 100,000

Arab citizens live in these villages – one in ten of the Arab population. By law, the unrecognised villages cannot be supplied with services from the water, electricity, sewerage and telephone utility companies. The homes in unrecognised villages are all without licences and therefore subject to demolition. In the *Negev* unrecognised villages usually comprise tin shacks and tents because anything more permanent would be demolished.

War of 1948 – Known by Israel as the War of Independence. A year-long war, following the end of the *British Mandate*, between the Israeli army and Jewish militias on one side, and a combination of Palestinian militias and armies from neighbouring Arab states on the other. For many months before May 1948, when the Jewish leadership in Palestine issued the *Declaration of Independence* establishing Israel, there had been tit-for-tat killings, mainly of civilians, culminating in several well-planned and large-scale massacres by Jewish militias, including the most famous, Deir Yassin, on 9 April 1948. During the war Israel captured 78 per cent of Palestine (excluding the West Bank and Gaza) and expelled 750,000 Palestinians (or 80 per cent of the 900,000 Palestinians under its control). The refugees, most now in Lebanon, Syria, Jordan, the West Bank and Gaza, have never been allowed to return. During the war Israel declared a state of emergency, adopting emergency regulations drafted by the British during the Mandate, which has never been revoked. The emergency laws give the government draconian powers.

War of 1967 – Known by Israelis as the Six-Day War, when Israel captured the Palestinian areas of the West Bank and East *Jerusalem* from Jordan and the Gaza Strip from Egypt. Israel also occupied the Sinai peninsula, which was returned to Egypt in a peace deal in 1982, and the *Golan Heights*, which Israel has yet to return to Syria.

War of Independence – See entry on *War of 1948*.

World Zionist Organisation (WZO) – A body established by the First Zionist Congress in Switzerland in 1897 to work towards the creation of a Jewish national home. It continued in existence after the founding of Israel in 1948 and today is active in financing settlement projects in the *Palestinian occupied territories*.

Zionism – An ideology, which became a popular political movement, usually ascribed to Theodor Herzl, who articulated the idea of a state for the Jews in his book *Der Judenstaat* (1896). Critics of Zionism have observed that not only did it emerge in the context of growing nationalism in Europe, but it also shared the assumption of many anti-Semitic Europeans that the Jews were a separate nation who could not be integrated into the European nations and should therefore be forced to live apart. Zionism spawned a set of key institutions: the *World Zionist Organisation*, the *Jewish Agency* and the *Jewish National Fund*. Conceived of as a secular nationalist movement by Herzl, Zionism has developed several offshoots, including a strong religious movement inside Israel. Today, secular Zionists often blur these distinctions by using Biblical justifications for the establishment of Israel in the 'Promised Land'.

Sources

INTERVIEWS

Dr Asad Ghanem, Tamra, 24 May 2004

Dr Adel Manna, at the Van Leer Institute, Jerusalem, 13 June 2004

Dr Daphna Golan, West Jerusalem, 13 June 2004

Eitan Bronstein, Kfar Shemaryahu, 5 July 2004

Dr Uri Davis, Sharon Hotel, Herziliya, 13 August 2004

Dr Said Zidani, American Colony Hotel, Jerusalem, 3 October 2004

REFERENCES

Chapter 1: The Road to Tamra

Marwan Dwairy, lecture at the First Annual Conference of the Palestinian Arab Minority in Israel, Nazareth, 10 June 2004

Chapter 2: Death of a Love Affair

Sara Liebovitch-Dar, 'Living with Them', *Ha'aretz*, 26 September 2003 (only in Hebrew)

Mufid Abdul Hadi, *The Other Side of the Coin*, Passia, 1998, p.138

Chapter 3: Second-Class Citizens

Yair Ettinger, 'Arab Editor Opts out of Katsav Trip after Airport Flap', *Ha'aretz*, 17 February 2004

Michal Aharoni, 'Either Racism or Journalism', *Maariv online*, 13 June 2004

Yossi Melman, 'Even the Shin Bet is Against Discrimination', *Ha'aretz* supplement 'Arab Snapshots', 25 May 2004

Anat Balint, 'IBA Illegally Confiscated Papers of Arabs', *Ha'aretz*, 1 June 2004

Sigal Shambiro, 'IKEA Refuses to Deliver to Israeli Arab Town, Citing "Danger" ', *Ha'aretz*, 23 July 2004

'The Official Summation of the Or Commission Report', *Ha'aretz*, 2 September 2003, www.haaretz.com/hasen/pages/ShArt.jhtml? itemNo=335594

Aryeh Dayan, 'Teachers' Pests', *Ha'aretz*, 1 October 2004

Shahar Ilan, 'Report: Haredi School Spending Twice as Much per Pupil as State Schools', *Ha'aretz*, 6 August 2004

David Ratner, 'MK Urges Debate on Arab Schools After *Ha'aretz* Exposé', *Ha'aretz*, 16 July 2004

Yuli Khromchenko, 'Ministry of Education Scuttles Plan to Open Jewish-Arab School in Kafr Kara', *Ha'aretz*, 2 July 2004

Aviad Kleinberg, 'Numerus Clausus', *Ha'aretz*, 16 December 2003

Omar Barghouti, 'On Dance, Identity and War', *Al-Ahram Weekly*, 13–19 June 2002

Yair Ettinger, 'Survey Finds Few Arabs in Top Echelons of Civil Service', *Ha'aretz*, 11 November 2004

Shlomo Swirski and Etty Konor-Attias, 'Israel: A Social Report 2003', Adva Centre, February 2004, http://www.adva.org/ISRAEL_2003_ENG.pdf

Moshe Gorali, 'Second-Class Status and a Fear of a Fifth Column', *Ha'aretz*, 24 May 2004

Ramit Plushnik-Masti, 'Israel Marked Helmets of Arab Workers', Associated Press, 9 March 2004

Jonathan Cook, 'McDonald's Manager Admits Arabic Led to Firing', *Electronic Intifada*, 10 March 2004, http://electronicIntifada.net/v2/article2492.shtml

Chapter 4: Echoes of Apartheid

'Ein Hod artists' village' homepage, http://ein-hod.israel.net/aboutus. htm

Jan C. Smuts, 'Address to the Jewish Community of South Africa', 3 November 1919, Johannesburg Town Hall

Jewish National Fund website, http://www.jnf.org/site/PageServer? pagename=Trees

Jewish National Fund website, http://www.jnf.org/site/PageServer? pagename=PR_UN_NGO_Status

Uri Davis, *Apartheid Israel*, Zed Books, 2003

Will Hutton, 'How the Zealots are Killing a Dream', *Observer*, 25 July 2004

Chapter 5: The Missing Left

Jonathan Cook, 'A Jew Among 25,000 Muslims', *Guardian*, 27 August 2003

Sara Liebovitch-Dar, 'Living with Them', *Ha'aretz*, 26 September 2003 (only in Hebrew)

Daphna Baram, 'A Sham at the Heart of Israel', *Guardian*, 1 September 2004

Motti Bassok, 'Klein: Central Bank Favors Hiring Arabs', *Ha'aretz*, 31 May 2004

Vered Levy-Barzilai, 'Know Thy Neighbour – But Don't Hire Him', *Ha'aretz*, 12 July 2001

Paul Eisen, 'Speaking the Truth to Jews', in *Speaking the Truth about Zionism and Israel*, ed. Michael Prior, Melisende (London), 2004

Chapter 6: A Traumatised Society

Amir Rapoport, 'Suicide No. 1 Cause of Death in IDF', *Maariv online*, 15 July 2004

Gideon Alon, '30–40 per cent of Conscripts Request Psychological Help', *Ha'aretz*, 18 August 2004

Rabbi Jon-Jay Tilsen, 'Conscientious Objection to Military Service in Israel', Beth El-Keser Israel website, undated, http://www. beki.org/conscientious.html

Zvi Harel, 'The Defendant was an "Impressive Officer"', *Ha'aretz*, 9 September 2004

Jonathan Lis, 'IDF Questions Reservists who Organised Hebron Photo Exhibit', *Ha'aretz*, 23 June 2004

Molly Moore, 'Breaking the Silence on West Bank Abuse', *Washington Post*, 24 June 2004

Yitzhak Laor, 'In Hebron', *London Review of Books*, 22 July 2004

Anonymous, 'A Soldier in Nablus', Znet, 5 September 2004, http://www.zmag.org/content/showarticle.cfm?SectionID=22%20&ItemID=6172

Chris McGreal, 'Israeli Officer: I was Right to Shoot 13-Year-Old Child', *Guardian*, 24 November 2004

Amir Buhbut, 'Elite Soldiers Contend Razing Palestinian Houses is "Immoral"', *Maariv online*, 27 September 2004

'The Official Summation of the Or Commission Report', *Ha'aretz*, 2 September 2003, www.haaretz.com/hasen/pages/ShArt.jhtml?itemNo=335594

Neve Shalom/Wahat al-Salam website, Frequently asked questions, http://nswas.com/article278.html

Yoav Keren, 'Hamas Among Us', *Maariv*, 11 July 2004 (only in Hebrew)

Chapter 7: Where Next?

Sigmund Freud, 'Letter to Dr Chaim Koffler', 26 February 1930, http://www.freud.org.uk/arab-israeli.html

Said Zidani, 'Palestinians and Israeli Jews: Divide and Share the Land', personal position paper, August 2003 (unpublished)

Mamphela Ramphele, *Steering by the Stars*, Tafelberg, 2002, p.109

Jonathan Cook and Alexander Key, *Silencing Dissent*, Arab Association for Human Rights, 22 October 2002

The following reliable websites have English pages dealing with issues related to the Arab citizens of Israel:

ARAB

Adalah

http://www.adalah.org/eng/index.php

Established in 1996, Adalah ('Justice' in Arabic) is a legal organisation dedicated to protecting the human rights of Israel's Arab minority, mainly through legal challenges in the courts. It publishes an informative monthly newsletter on its website, as well as its annual *Review* in Arabic, Hebrew and English which carries articles by leading lawyers and academics on key issues facing the minority.

Arab Association of Human Rights (HRA)

http://www.arabhra.org/

The HRA was founded in 1988 to promote the political, social, economic and cultural rights of the Arab minority inside Israel by lobbying major international bodies such as the United Nations. It also runs programmes in schools to educate Arab children in their rights. It has published a series of six comprehensive factsheets on its website, and regularly issues reports on aspects of Israeli discrimination against the Arab minority. Each week it publishes a digest of reports from the local Arab media.

Arab Centre for Alternative Planning

http://www.ac-ap.org/indexeng1.asp?levelid=1&showid=1&itemid=15

The centre was created in 2000 in response to the huge pressures on the Arab minority in terms of land, planning, housing and development. In 2004 ACAP became the first independent Arab organisation ever to win the right to file objections on local and national planning procedures. The website includes a newsletter and articles on planning and land matters.

Association of Forty

http://www.assoc40.org/

The website of the lobby group begun by Mohammed Abu Hayja (see Chapter 4) to win recognition for those Arab communities the Israeli state refuses to recognise, commonly known as the 'unrecognised villages'. There are some hundred thousand Arab citizens living in such communities, including seventy-five thousand Bedouin in the Negev. The website includes historical and statistical information on the unrecognised villages.

Galilee Society

http://www.gal-soc.org/

Established by health-care professionals in 1981, the Galilee Society campaigns for equality for Arab citizens in their health, environmental and socio-economic conditions. Much of its work concentrates on training programmes and compiling data and surveys. Its Rikaz database, which includes much demographic information on the minority, can be found at http://www.rikaz.org/en/index.php

I'lam

http://www.ilamcenter.org/

I'lam was founded in 2000 as the minority's first media centre to try to open up the Israeli media to little-heard Arab perspectives, combat bias in the Hebrew media, and improve standards in the local Arab media. It was one of the key organisations documenting police violence towards the minority during the October 2000 events. The website includes useful information about discriminatory policies in the Israeli media.

Ittijah

http://www.ittijah.org/about/about01.html

Ittijah is the umbrella organisation for all the non-profit groups working for the Arab minority, helping to coordinate their activities.

The website includes several factsheets and a regular newsletter providing details of forthcoming activities by its members.

Mada
http://www.mada-research.org/
Established in 2000, Mada is an Arab-run research institute developing public policy proposals advancing the national rights of Arab citizens. It also organises conferences and seminars exploring issues of citizenship, national identity and democracy models in multi-ethnic states. It has published a detailed book on the situation of Arab citizens in Israel called *Citizens Without Citizenship*. In 2005 it was due to publish the first edition of a new journal called the *Palestinian Review*.

Mossawa
http://www.mossawacenter.org/en/about/about.html
Mossawa, an advocacy centre for Arab citizens founded in 1997, works both locally and internationally to raise the profile of the minority. It specialises in compiling comparative data on social and economic discrimination against the Arab minority. The website includes some short reports in English and press releases.

JOINT ARAB AND JEWISH
Alternative Information Centre
http://www.alternativenews.org/
A well-established anti-Zionist website run from Jerusalem and Bethlehem by Israelis and Palestinians. Although its main focus is on the occupied territories, it does also publish informed factsheets and articles on the Arab minority. The AIC publishes a monthly magazine, *News from Within*; some of the articles are available from its separate website: http://www.newsfromwithin.org/

Sikkuy

http://www.sikkuy.org.il/english/about.html

Founded in 1991, Sikkuy is jointly managed by an Arab and a Jewish director. The Jewish branch has established three civil action groups in Jewish areas to lobby for equal rights for their Arab neighbours. Sikkuy is also behind an initiative to encourage Jewish and Arab municipalities to increase levels of cooperation. The website publishes an important annual report monitoring equality in government programmes, budgets and resources.

JEWISH

Adva

http://www.adva.org/indexe.html

An organisation dedicated to analysis of Israeli policy towards marginalised communities, including women, Mizrahi Jews and Arab citizens. The website includes comparative data in the 'Social Gaps' section, as well as analysis reports.

Association for Civil Rights in Israel

http://www.acri.org.il/english-acri/engine/index.asp

Founded in 1972, ACRI is dedicated to protecting human rights inside Israel and the occupied territories, mainly through legal challenges in the courts. The website has useful information on discrimination inside Israel, particularly against the Bedouin.

Zochrot

http://www.nakbainhebrew.org/index.php?id=49&searchword= english

Most of the Nakba in Hebrew website, as its name suggests, is in Hebrew, but there are a few articles and reports on Zochrot events on the above page.

Palestine Remembered

http://www.palestineremembered.com/

An invaluable website with much relevant material about the hundreds of Arab villages destroyed in 1948. The best feature is a geographically listed guide to each of the villages, with information on the date of its ethnic cleansing, the Israeli army operation in which it was attacked, the amount of land owned by the village and its population, where the survivors are now, and which Israeli settlements have been built over the village. Refugees also have a noticeboard on which they can leave stories, messages and photographs.

Index

P.S.

Ideas,
interviews
& features ...

About the author

About the book

Read on

Writing *The Other Side of Israel*

Sarah O'Reilly talks to Susan Nathan

SINCE ITS FIRST publication in 2005, *The Other Side of Israel* has courted controversy. 'It has evoked a wide range of reactions,' Susan Nathan acknowledges. 'I've seen people become very aggressive; others are dismissive; I've had the expected hate mail, and even a few death threats.' Is she perturbed by the backlash? 'I've learnt how to handle it,' she says philosophically. 'Once you understand where the criticism is emanating from, and the deep emotions that drive it, it becomes easier to take a step back and deal with it.'

Indeed, Nathan has been pleasantly surprised by the amount of support she's received in some quarters: 'I was a guest at two major book fairs in 2005, one in Edinburgh, the other in Antwerp, and the interest that I received at both was quite overwhelming.' And she takes pleasure in the fact that her book has also found its way into academic circles, cropping up on a number of university reading lists around the world. She likens its reception to 'watching a gathering storm – especially in the United States, which is now beginning to focus on the book.'

It may be causing ripples in the West, but she is still waiting for it to appear in Hebrew in her adopted country. 'No publisher has been brave enough to take it on, even though worldwide it has been taken up by highly respected publishing houses. The reason they give is that it is of no commercial value in Israel,' she complains. But Nathan has another theory as to why it hasn't yet found a publisher: 'This country has become adept over the years at deflecting censure and using a wide range of excuses not to be self-critical. The irony of this, of course, is that it expects from others the very kind of soul-searching that it eschews.'

What about Nathan's day-to-day life – has it been affected by the book's publication? 'Well, I've received a number of unsolicited visits from people from all over the world who have literally turned up on my doorstep in Tamra!' she laughs. 'But my daily life continues more or less as normal. Amongst the Arab community everybody knows me, but this doesn't greatly impact upon my life – Arabic people are not intrusive and there is a lot of respect shown for my privacy.'

With a documentary about her life and work in the pipeline, this may soon change. But Nathan has resolved not be diverted by the attention: 'I strongly believe in staying focused on my work. Early on I promised myself that I would never read the interviews I gave or watch myself on television in case it distracted me from the task in hand. And I have to say, one unexpected benefit of publishing my story is that the book has placed me firmly outside the grey area of the debate, which has made my life infinitely easier!'

It may have made her life easier, but being outside the grey area of the debate has also ▶

❝ One unexpected benefit of publishing my story is that the book has placed me firmly outside the grey area of the debate, which has made my life infinitely easier. ❞

LIFE
at a Glance

BORN

1949, Greenwich, London

EDUCATED

Godstowe School, High Wycombe

Hampden House, Great Missenden

Queen's College, Harley Street

Froebel College, Roehampton Institute

Westminster Pastoral Foundation

Great Ormond Street Hospital

FAMILY

Susan Nathan is divorced. She has two grown-up children who live in Europe

CAREER

Teacher

Community support worker for people with HIV/AIDS for the Terrence Higgins Trust ▶

Writing *The Other Side . . . (continued)*

◀ left Nathan open to a volley of criticism from those within Israel whose views differ from her own. 'I've faced a variety of criticisms within the country, the most prevalent of which is that because I wasn't born in Israel it's easy for me to be outspoken about what's happening here,' she admits. But despite these difficulties, she cannot see herself ever leaving her adopted country: 'I am firmly rooted in the struggle for a more just and equitable society and I simply cannot imagine myself living anywhere else.'

Nathan's childhood was spent in postwar England, punctuated by frequent trips to her relatives in South Africa. Witnessing apartheid at first hand left an indelible impression. It was, she recalls, 'the sheer enormity of the inequality' that was so shocking: 'I recognized very early on in my life that there was a link between the politics of apartheid and full-scale poverty. I was appalled by the conditions under which migrants were forced to work in the East Rand Proprietary gold mines, and I remember talking to servants in my friends' homes and learning that black South Africans were required to carry a permit to enter white areas. These things contributed to my sense that this inequality couldn't, and shouldn't, last.'

But it was attacking the inequality within the state of Israel, which Nathan witnessed when she took up the Right of Return in the late 1990s, that was to become her life's work, and the subject of her first book. The realization that Israel, 'a land without people for a people without land', had a rather different history from that promulgated by the authorities precipitated a kind of personal crisis. 'There were days when I felt that my life was crumbling away as my ideological beliefs were slowly eroded by what I saw,' she recalls. 'Living in an Arab community and researching the "other" forced me to confront the disparity between my ideological support for Israel and the reality of life for its Arab citizens.' But the trauma of this experience was followed by a sense of relief when she was able to put pen to paper: 'Now my vision of what is happening here is clear and uncluttered by government propaganda, and that is a powerful feeling.'

Does she have any role models – people that inspire her to take a stand against the injustice she perceives? 'I can remember when I was young being impressed with Mahatma Gandhi's teaching of non-violent resistance,' she says. 'And of course Nelson Mandela and the whole anti-apartheid movement was enormously inspiring. As were the ordinary black South Africans I know who endured such deprivation under the old regime.'

She cites Mamphela Ramphele, one of the founders of the black consciousness movement and the first black woman to be offered the post of Vice-Chancellor at the University of Cape Town, as another role model, and Aung San Suu Kyi, leader of the National League for Democracy in Myanmar and Nobel Peace Prize winner: 'Her resilience in the face of long-standing detention is extraordinary.'

Nonetheless, for Nathan, 'it's the ordinary citizens that I see around me who are ▶

LIFE *at a Glance*
(continued)

◀ Counsellor and group facilitator for people with HIV/AIDS at the London Lighthouse

Since moving to Israel in 1999, Susan Nathan has worked as a supervisor for the N.G.O. Mahapach and been actively involved in a number of community projects

5

Writing *The Other Side . . .* *(continued)*

◀ struggling against poverty and discrimination that really fuel me, and have made me see that political ideologies must always come second to our common humanity.' And the fact that she is a woman has been a boon to her struggle to establish greater equality between all of Israel's citizens. 'I believe that women have a great deal to offer in conflicted societies. They tend to begin their dialogue from different starting positions to their male counterparts. They immediately sense that resolution is not necessarily a question of win/lose, but rather a question of win/win, with the emphasis upon understanding the "other" and drawing parallels between the two sides, rather than emphasizing difference,' she argues. For Nathan this observation offers hope: 'I think that this broadens the range of possibilities for resolution.'

Nathan is insistent that Jews within Israel and throughout the world must acknowledge the reality behind the founding of the state of Israel. But does she think that the international community could be doing more to support this aim? Or must the process, if it is to truly revolutionize the terms of the conflict, be instigated by Jewish people inside Israel themselves? 'There's no doubt in my mind that the largely one-dimensional history of the founding of the state of Israel that's taught to Jews both here and in the Diaspora has had a catastrophic influence upon the way in which this country is viewed by the majority of its citizens and the international community,' she argues, 'but it's also true that many European and American

❝ Political ideologies must always come second to our common humanity. ❞

6

politicians know the reality of the situation. Unfortunately there is a lack of moral courage and a lot of political cowardice that has contributed to a kind of silence around the issue, and in reality it is us, the Jews, who have to lead the fight.'

So how does she view recent developments in the region – the new Palestinian leadership, for example, and the recent Israeli disengagement from Gaza? 'Personally I never considered Arafat an obstacle to the search for a resolution,' Nathan says of the recently deceased Palestinian leader. 'He made some grave mistakes, for which the Palestinian people are still paying today, but his greatest achievement was preventing the conflict from becoming a religious one. Not to mention the fact that he succeeded in placing the struggle of the Palestinian people at the top of the international community's agenda.'

With regard to Mahmoud Abbas's leadership, she is less complimentary: 'I'm afraid that this government is too weak to be effective in negotiations. Israel has done absolutely nothing in real, concrete terms to empower the Palestinians. The disengagement has attracted international attention, but in reality it's simply given rise to profoundly misleading hopes. Gaza remains occupied as a result of continued Israeli control. The situation is volatile and will remain so for as long as Israel continues to demolish homes, expand its settlements, uproot the Arabs' olive groves and build its wall in the West Bank.'

During the period in which *The Other* ▶

> ❛The disengagement has attracted international attention, but in reality it's simply given rise to profoundly misleading hopes.❜

7

Writing *The Other Side . . .* (continued)

◄ *Side of Israel* was written it can't have escaped Nathan's attention that the politics of our post 9/11 world have radically altered: today fear has replaced hope; instead of building a brave new world we are focusing on protecting our existing one from terrorism. Is Nathan afraid that this will have ramifications for the work that she and others in Israel are doing to bring about greater understanding between the different ethnic groups? 'No,' she replies. 'It merely serves to make me realize that we have a tougher fight on our hands. I hope that my book, and indeed my life, illustrate how empowering it is not to live in fear of another ethnic group.' But she is critical of the way in which Western powers have intervened in the region, and have failed to address the real source of terrorism. 'There has been terrible hypocrisy when it comes to the attitude of the US and the UK towards the Middle East. Both have supported oppressive regimes in this part of the world to serve their own purposes. That's why it's so important that ordinary citizens are able to confront the political status quo.'

And it is ultimately with the people that Susan Nathan's hopes for the future lie: 'Politicians themselves should remember that in the long run it's their citizens who have the power to change the societies in which they live. We can see from examples all over the world, from nations as diverse as South Africa and India, that it can happen.' ■

⟨ I hope that my book, and indeed my life, illustrate how empowering it is not to live in fear of another ethnic group. ⟩

Identity Revisited

by Susan Nathan

IT WASN'T UNTIL I completed this book, after three years of living in Tamra, that I finally came to understand that the issue of my identity had started to trouble me deeply during my teenage years.

Identity, of course, means different things to different people, and the way in which it is formed is a matter of debate. Does it come from being a citizen in a nation state, where one can relate to a flag and a national anthem, developing a sense of pride in one's citizenship, a feeling that one belongs in, and is valued by, one's country? Or does it derive from something else? From the feeling of 'being different', being on the 'outside' – an identity which is predicated on being in opposition to, rather than in harmony with, the values of the country in which one lives?

As a child I carried within me the knowledge of my grandparents' suffering in the pogroms in Russia, and my great grandparents' suffering before them, and I was conscious of being part of a tiny minority with a strange name and strange religious observances that, at that time, I wasn't able to fully understand. In grey, postwar Britain, my sense of being different was compounded by being the only Jew in a school of some 300 students. I felt alienated: included yet excluded, both a member of my society, and an alien in its midst. To this day the question of my identity, which was prompted by the feeling of never being quite at home in the country in which I lived, has remained a matter of internal conflict. ▶

Identity Revisited *(continued)*

◄ I now know that the experiences of my Jewish forebears were responsible for instigating my quest to discover where I belonged. As a Jew I have always felt that my very existence is a political statement: this may in part explain why an allegiance to the state of Israel was formed inside me at an early age. My loyalty to this state – a feeling that is hard to articulate but which I felt very powerfully – derived from the sense of security that it offered me: it was a country where I had no need to explain my needs or myself; a place that might be a refuge for me should my life become intolerable in Europe.

Throughout my childhood and much of my adult life, the feeling of always being on the edge of disaster was part of my environment, and I internalized it at a very deep level. But little did I realize that I was committing myself emotionally to a state that was perpetuating the same sort of discrimination that my own family had suffered from.

My parents' devotion to their work in medicine – one was a surgeon, the other a nurse – and their humanitarianism were guiding factors in my decision to live in Tamra. As a family we were less concerned with the rituals of Judaism, although we certainly observed them, than with the essence of the religion, its teachings and its ethics. Our deep involvement with the Jewish community meant that our home was always open to guests, and my favourite memories from childhood are of being allowed to participate in the large, stimulating and

> ❝ Throughout my childhood and much of my adult life, the feeling of always being on the edge of disaster was part of my environment, and I internalized it at a very deep level. ❞

10

lively dinner parties that my parents gave frequently. They offered a platform for ferocious debates on politics, medical ethics, poverty, education and culture, and, although too shy to contribute anything, I would absorb it all avidly.

My belief that being Jewish entails certain responsibilities arose from this childhood. It is precisely because of my personal history that I find myself in conflict with my Jewish/Israeli identity and the politics of my country's government. The irony of the Palestinian dispossession inside the state of Israel, its 'internal refugees', has not been lost on me, the child of refugees, always unsettled, always insecure.

As this book testifies, the act of making 'aliyah' brought me to the point where I had to question my ideology and the nationalism that fired it. For me, being a Jew through the accident of one's birth is not enough. Embracing Judaism must signify one's belief in the essential equality of human beings; the equal right to complete citizenship and all that it entails; the sanctity of human life and the protection of the individual's dignity. For me, Judaism is about what I can contribute to my society, and not about what my society can do for me.

Currently, I find myself outside the consensus of my country, but not alone in these thoughts. The discontinuity between the state's politics and my vision of Judaism is being noticed by a growing number of the Jewish Israeli population who seek a different, realistic and viable alternative to the current situation. ▶

Susan Nathan's
Recommended
Reading

Crossing the Border
Uri Davis

Women and the Politics of Military Confrontation
Nahla Abdo and Ronit Lentin

Sharon and My Mother-in-Law
Suad Amiry

The Politics of Denial
Nur Masalha

Middle East Illusions
Noam Chomsky

Apartheid Israel
Uri Davis

A Jewish Understanding of the World
John D. Rayner

The Other Israel – Voices of Refusal and Dissent
Roane Carey and Jonathan Shainin

Drinking the Sea at Gaza
Amira Hass

The Palestinian-Arab Minority in Israel, 1948–2000
As'ad Ghanem

11

Identity Revisited *(continued)*

◄ Progress in my region of the world will depend on freedom, justice and compassion. These are the concepts that a civilization is built on. Identifying one's Judaism with one's nationality, as occurs here in Israel, means little if it is devoid of these guiding principles.

Throughout history there have always been individual citizens whose identity has been forged by their opposition to their society's behaviour or beliefs. I feel an obligation to record what is happening in my country because to do so is an integral part of what it means to me to be a Jew, no matter how difficult or politically incorrect it may be, and no matter how unpopular I may become or how much I may be viewed as an outsider. ■

❝Progress in my region of the world will depend on freedom, justice and compassion.❞

If You Loved This,
You Might Like ...

Strangers in the House: Coming of Age in Occupied Palestine
Raja Shehadeh
Human rights activist Raja Shehadeh's memoir of growing up in Ramallah after the seizure of his family's property in nearby Jaffa in 1948. After attending law school in London, Shehadeh became the first Western-educated lawyer to return to practise on the West Bank. In this book he recounts both his family's struggle to come to terms with their loss and reveals the systematic cruelty of the territory's Israeli occupiers that led him to found Al-Haq, the first organization to document human rights violations and report on Israeli-implemented legal changes in the West Bank.

Seeking Mandela: Peacemaking Between Israelis and Palestinians
Heribert Adam and Kogila Moodley
A speculation on what might have happened in the Middle East had there been 'a Palestinian Mandela' to provide a unifying moral and strategic leadership in the Palestinian-Israeli conflict. Drawing upon examples from 1980s South Africa, the authors highlight how comparisons between the two nations shed light on current debates about the actions and future of Israel. ▶

If You Loved This . . . *(continued)*

◄ *Drinking the Sea at Gaza: Days and Nights in a Land Under Siege*
Amira Hass

In 1993, *Ha'aretz* reporter Amira Hass became the first Israeli journalist to take up residence in Gaza, the grim Palestinian enclave that she described as 'terra incognita for Israelis'. There she found an embodiment of the entire saga of the Israeli-Palestinian conflict, arguing that the region, a mere 147 square miles of land, represented 'the central contradiction of the state of Israel – democracy for some, dispossession for others; it is Israel's exposed nerve'. *Drinking the Sea at Gaza* is Hass's account of her time living in occupied territory: a first-hand description of what daily life is like for its population, and an account of a turbulent few years in the region's history, from the initial euphoria at the Oslo peace accords to the start of the intifada.

The Other Israel: Voices of Refusal and Dissent
edited by Roane Carey and Jonathan Shainin

A collection of essays written by thirty prominent Israelis condemning their country's occupation of Palestinian territory. Concerned for Israel's diminishing moral stature and sensitive to the corrupting tendencies of the occupation, their voices provide a comprehensive overview of the conflict. Other issues covered include dissent in Israel; reports from the ground of the escalating war, and the increasing brutality of Israeli actions in the territories;